Motivation for Learning and Performance

*Sometimes it takes 56 years to find your MO.
Perhaps, by reading this book, you will find yours sooner!*

Motivation for Learning and Performance

Bobby Hoffman
University of Central Florida
Orlando, Florida

AMSTERDAM • BOSTON • HEIDELBERG • LONDON • NEW YORK
OXFORD • PARIS • SAN DIEGO • SAN FRANCISCO • SINGAPORE
SYDNEY • TOKYO
Academic Press is an imprint of Elsevier

Academic Press is an imprint of Elsevier
525 B Street, Suite 1800, San Diego, CA 92101-4495, USA
The Boulevard, Langford Lane, Kidlington, Oxford OX5 1GB, UK

Copyright © 2015 Elsevier Inc. All rights reserved.

No part of this publication may be reproduced or transmitted in any form or by any means, electronic or mechanical, including photocopying, recording, or any information storage and retrieval system, without permission in writing from the publisher. Details on how to seek permission, further information about the Publisher's permissions policies and our arrangements with organizations such as the Copyright Clearance Center and the Copyright Licensing Agency, can be found at our website: www.elsevier.com/permissions.

This book and the individual contributions contained in it are protected under copyright by the Publisher (other than as may be noted herein).

Notices

Knowledge and best practice in this field are constantly changing. As new research and experience broaden our understanding, changes in research methods, professional practices, or medical treatment may become necessary.

Practitioners and researchers must always rely on their own experience and knowledge in evaluating and using any information, methods, compounds, or experiments described herein. In using such information or methods they should be mindful of their own safety and the safety of others, including parties for whom they have a professional responsibility.

To the fullest extent of the law, neither the Publisher nor the authors, contributors, or editors, assume any liability for any injury and/or damage to persons or property as a matter of products liability, negligence or otherwise, or from any use or operation of any methods, products, instructions, or ideas contained in the material herein.

Except for individuals specifically noted as "Motivational Leaders", all characters appearing in this work are fictitious. Any resemblance to real persons, living or dead, is purely coincidental.

ISBN: 978-0-12-800779-2

British Library Cataloguing-in-Publication Data
A catalogue record for this book is available from the British Library.

Library of Congress Cataloging-in-Publication Data
A catalog record for this book is available from the Library of Congress.

For Information on all Academic Press publications
visit our website at http://store.elsevier.com/

Typeset by MPS Limited, Chennai, India
www.adi-mps.com

Printed and bound in the United States

Publisher: *Nikki Levy*
Editorial Project Manager: *Barbara Makinster*
Production Project Manager: *Lisa Jones*
Designer: *Matthew Limbert*

Contents

Preface	xi
Acknowledgments	xv

Part I The framework of human motivation — 1

1 Underpinnings: Five foundational doctrines of motivational science — 3
- Introduction — 3
- Principle #1—Motivational inequality is a measurable reality — 6
- Principle #2—Motivation can be defined, but not universally — 8
- Principle #3—There is no such thing as being unmotivated — 9
- Principle #4—Behavior ≠ motivation, and there are no "motivational" types — 11
- Principle #5—Individuals may not recognize or understand their own motives — 12
    - Chapter summary/conclusions — 14
    - Assess your basic knowledge — 15
    - Next steps — 16
    - End of chapter motivational minute — 16
- References — 17

2 Contentious issues: How evidence refutes motivational misconceptions — 21
- Principle #6—Motivational beliefs differ from motivational knowledge — 22
- Motivational Leader—*Bernard Madoff* — 25
- Principle #7—Motivational evidence can only answer certain questions — 26
- Principle #8—Motivation is related to learning and performance, but causality is an uncertainty — 29
- Principle #9—Motivation is subordinate to character and personality — 31
- Principle #10—Motivation is the responsibility of leaders and can be taught — 34
- Principle #11—Theoretically, motivated behavior operates on a continuum — 35
- Principle #12—Optimal motivation is obtainable — 37
    - Chapter summary/conclusions — 41
    - Next steps — 42
    - End of chapter motivational minute — 42
- References — 43

3	**The biopsychology of motivation: Using evidence from neurology and endocrinology to understand motivated behavior**	**47**
	Principle #13—Neurological/endocrinological evidence informs or refutes behavioral evidence	48
	Principle #14—Neurological/endocrinological inferences are multi-dimensional	50
	Motivational Leader—*Alexis Dixon*	53
	Principle #15—The brain is a perceptual filter influencing subjective reality	54
	Principle #16—Neurological system organization facilitates or inhibits action	56
	Principle #17—Power and social dominance displays mimic sympathetic nervous system activation	57
	Principle #18—Displays of affiliation mimic parasympathetic nervous system activation	59
	Principle #19—Achievement and incentive reward share similar neural response patterns	62
	Principle #20—Humanity is motivated to seek pleasure and avoid pain	64
	Principle #21—Motivated behavior is heritable and evolutionary	68
	Chapter summary/conclusions	71
	Next steps	72
	End of chapter motivational minute	72
	References	73
4	**Ch, ch, changes: The developmental trajectory of motivation**	**79**
	Principle #22—Biological change is predictable, motivational change is not	81
	Motivational Leaders—*Rebecca and Cheryl Hines*	84
	Principle #23—Academic and competency motives have developmental trajectories	86
	Principle #24—Excellence judgments influence effort direction and intensity	90
	Principle #25—Evolution of values and morality mediate moral motivation	93
	Principle #26—Gender congruity evaluations substantially influence perceptions of "fit"	95
	Chapter summary/conclusions	99
	Next steps	100
	End of chapter motivational minute	100
	References	101
5	**A rose by any other name: The influence of culture on motivated behavior**	**107**
	Principle #27—Culture transcends demographics	112
	Principle #28—Ethnic identity shapes self-concept and self-relevant motivations	113

Motivational Leader—*LaSonya Moore* 117
Principle #29—Motivational differences exist between individualistic and collectivistic cultures 118
Principle #30—Communication and language patterns are revealing cultural markers 121
Principle #31—Leadership is subjectively interpreted according to culture 126
    Chapter summary/conclusions 130
    Next steps 131
    End of chapter motivational minute 131
References 132

Part II   The powerful role of individual differences and self-beliefs   137

6   You say to-may-toe, I say to-mah-toe: Individual differences in motives guide focus and effort   139

Principle #32—The source of motives determines goal emphasis and strategy choice 144
Motivational Leader—*Nick Holes* 148
Principle #33—Individual reaction to incentives is variable, and predictable 149
Principle #34—Goal type and orientation are reliable and accurate predictors of behavior 154
    Achievement goals: Mastery, normative, or multiple? 157
    Organizational promotion or prevention? 161
Principle #35—Interest is a multi-faceted contributor to motivational intensity 164
    Chapter summary/conclusions 167
    Next steps 168
    End of chapter motivational minute 168
References 169

7   Mount Rushmore: Bedrock theories of applied motivation   179

Principle #36—Past performance guides future motivation 182
Motivational Leader—*Nick Lowery* 188
Principle #37—Certain motives are extraordinarily difficult to suppress 189
Principle #38—After ability, self-efficacy explains more performance variation than any other motivational self-belief 192
Principle #39—Motivational theory is applied temporally and situationally 197
    Chapter summary/conclusions 201
    Next steps 201
    End of chapter motivational minute 202
References 203

8	**Can I see the real me?: The powerful influence of self-beliefs on motivated behavior**	**207**
	Principle #40—The psychological or physical presence of others may alter normative behavior	212
	Principle #41—Pro-social behaviors are compliant, adaptive, and predictable	216
	Principle #42—Pro-social motives are egoistic and altruistic	220
	Motivational Leader—*Jessi Colter*	221
	Principle #43—Performance inhibiting strategies augment self-worth	225
	Chapter summary/conclusions	229
	Next steps	229
	End of chapter motivational minute	230
	References	231
9	**No place to hide: Motivation and emotion**	**237**
	Principle #44—Emotional reactions are localized, subjective, and learned	240
	Principle #45—Anxiety and boredom are performance-restricting culprits	245
	Anxiety	245
	Boredom	247
	Principle #46—Positive affect is a powerful performance determinant	250
	Motivational Leader—*Alec Torelli*	251
	Principle #47—Individuals restructure affect to regulate their emotions	253
	Chapter summary/conclusions	259
	Next steps	260
	End of chapter motivational minute	260
	References	261

Part III Mediation and implementation strategies to promote optimal learning and performance 267

10	**Ready, aim, fire…repeat?: Self-regulation strategies to improve adaptive motivation**	**269**
	Principle #48—Self-regulation is personalized, transitory, and marginally predictable	274
	Principle #49—Self-regulatory ability is depletable; accurate calibration is essential	281
	Motivational Leader—*Darren Soto*	288
	Principle #50—Optimal motivation demands monitoring, metacognition, and metamotivation	290

	Chapter summary/conclusions	294
	Next steps	295
	End of chapter motivational minute	296
	References	297

11 Location, location, location: Creating and implementing context-specific interventions   305

	Promoting adaptive academic motivation	307
	Strategies to motivate work performance	312
	Motivational Leader—*Robert Knowling, Jr.*	317
	Optimizing motivation for athletic and public performances	325
	Motivational strategies to enhance online learning and instructional design	329
	Chapter summary/conclusions	334
	Next steps	335
	End of chapter motivational minute	335
	References	336

12 The transformers: Overcoming resistance to motivational change   345

	Why do people resist change?	346
	Which strategies will individuals use to refute change?	355
	Motivational Leader—*Amanda Boxtel*	358
	Overcoming change resistance in others	360
	Instructional strategies supporting conceptual change	362
	Promote strategy awareness	362
	Identify plausible alternatives	363
	Provide refutational evidence	364
	Create personal relevance	364
	Scaffold strategy change	365
	Learning from leaders	367
	Epilogue	369
	References	370

Appendix   375
Index   399

See: www.booksite.elsevier.com/9780128007792 for supplementary materials.

Preface

Did you make any important decisions today? You may have contemplated what clothes to wear, which foods you will eat, or what time to leave your house, if at all. You may have pondered the challenges in your life and considered which tasks you were ready to tackle. Outcomes from these daily decisions will likely influence what you accomplish, your mood and feelings, your physical well-being, and possibly how others perceive you and your abilities. Conceivably, you may have also thought about some more significant decisions today, such as what school to attend, where to work, or who is worthy of your time and affection. Perhaps you are carefree and resist making concrete plans. Instead, you take each day as it comes and rarely worry about what happens next. Friends may describe you as "having a clear head" or "being a free spirit." Regardless of your approach, the focus of your thoughts and energy is directed toward reaching specific goals that may range from not getting off the couch to developing a cure for Ebola. But, if you are like most people, you often set attainable targets through conscious planning, deep thinking, and sustained effort as a means to reach those goals.

The design of the book

Three overarching objectives guided the design of this book, starting with clarifying the reasons for individual variation in our own thought and subsequent behaviors. Have you ever wondered *why* you are interested in some topics but not others, *how* you decided upon a job or career, or even *what* contributes to your choice of friends or a partner in life? Answers to these types of questions can explain the intensity and direction of your effort, otherwise known as understanding *motivations* and *motivated action*. For example, why might *you* decline an invitation to attend a wedding, while others in your family attend enthusiastically? Why do *you* perform better on some tasks than on others? Why is it that some people dominate meetings or classroom discussions while *you* rarely respond when a question is asked? Do you think you know the motives behind your behavior? Maybe you do, but more likely you do NOT, according to motivational science! As you read this book, you will become increasingly aware about who you are and *why* you do the things you do. Greater awareness will help you set realistic goals, enhance the probability of reaching your targets, and allow you to consider alternative and efficient strategies to reach your desired objectives.

A second goal of the text is to help you understand the intentions, thoughts, behaviors, and motivation of *others*. Many of us are responsible for the leadership and guidance of students, co-workers, peers, or family members. As an educator, manager, coach, or parent, you are likely highly influential in teaching others new skills, modeling behaviors or setting performance targets, and helping others achieve their goals. For instance, do you know why some students willingly spend many hours on homework, yet others devote only a few minutes? Why do some employees work better in groups, while others barely pull their weight? Why do some athletes choke under pressure, while others with lesser skills excel? Your understanding of the personal motivation of others is one key to designing customized and optimal instruction, creating exciting learning environments, and cultivating performance excellence.

The third, and potentially the most important purpose of this book, is to deconstruct and describe the latest motivational research and empirically verified motivational strategies to improve learning and performance. Initially, you will learn the foundational principles of motivational science, including how to decipher different types of evidence. Next, you will develop a deep understanding of motivation by exposure to key motivational principles, empowering you to interact with teachers, psychologists, business leaders, athletes, and classmates, or most anyone interested in motivation. By the time you finish the book, you will know how to identify important motivational clues, how to interpret the evidence you discover, and which strategies and solutions work best to enhance performance motivation across a variety of diverse populations, cultures, and settings. Ultimately, you will learn how to apply motivational knowledge to influence change and achieve the academic, business, or personal goals of yourself and others.

The style of the book

Unlike some traditional textbooks, you will not dwell on memorizing theories or interpreting fabricated case studies to understand motivation because, in practice, you assess and mediate motivational challenges by talking with people! You will read candid and revealing stories about how others (including some celebrities) navigated motivational hurdles while attempting to reach their goals. In addition to the latest research and evidence-based findings, you will learn the scientific reasons behind the motivational strategies advocated in this book. You will be exposed to ways of accurately measuring and evaluating motivation, and you will master a host of well-supported diagnostic and interpretative tools to assist you in becoming a motivational expert, what I like to call an "MD," or a Motivational Detective. Finally, unlike some texts that exclusively address improving academic, business, or sports performance, I examine motivation using a multi-disciplinary lens, including relevant research-based findings from psychology, education, business, and athletics. Additionally, the book includes the latest evidence from neurology and cognitive psychology as a means to boost your motivational intelligence, regardless of your current discipline, job, or existing knowledge of motivation.

The structure of the book

In addition to scientific evidence, this book profiles 12 diverse and unique individuals. Each person was personally interviewed by me and through that exchange, each shared his or her most intimate feelings, passions, and thoughts. Some of the interviewees are the type of people you encounter every day at work or school. Others are celebrities or public figures whom you may recognize. First, you will read their stories and gain insight to their values, challenges, triumphs, and defeats as they share the thinking behind their decisions. Next, you will learn how their thoughts were converted to behaviors and actions, including which strategies they chose to address obstacles and overcome adversity. You will learn how and why each person shifted gears, changed goals, or ultimately gave up. Each person profiled in the book is examined using the exact methods you would likely use if you met the person face-to-face—asking them questions and engaging in conversation. You will learn how to evaluate motivational clues and recognize how backgrounds, experiences, cultures, beliefs, and preferences contribute to motivated action.

Key components of the book

Chapters include the following components to support your motivational mastery:

- **Principles** *(What are the defining concepts you will master?)* You will learn 50 key, evidence-based motivational concepts. This foundational knowledge will serve as a baseline of information to help you craft solutions to motivational challenges.
- **Terminology** *(Do you speak the language?)* You will learn the language of motivational professionals. Your knowledge of terminology will help you deconstruct and decipher scientific jargon and apply it to your personal and professional practice.
- **Evidence** *(Are your interpretations correct?)* You will learn how to interpret and analyze complex scientific data. Your knowledge of evidence will help you avoid common sense errors resulting from media sensationalism and anecdotal conclusions that are often wrong.
- **Measurement** *(How do we know?)* You will learn how motivation is measured, including key performance indicators that define adaptive motivation, such as confidence, effort, and optimal thinking. You will have access to a list of measurement instruments that are compiled in Appendix A and described throughout the book.
- **Analysis** *(What's the issue?)* You will know how to analyze the information you accumulate. This approach will provide a "big picture" view enabling you to differentiate the extraneous from the sublime, the fallacies from the reality, and the important from the irrelevant.
- **Application** *(Which solutions are most appropriate?)* You will learn which strategies work best, in which circumstances, and when to use each solution. You will avoid haphazard and trial-and-error approaches by amassing a repertoire of justified, evidence-based strategies to solve motivational challenges.

In summary, this book will provide you with a wealth of diagnostic and analytical knowledge, partially revealed through the eyes of motivational leaders, to help you determine and modify the learning and performance concerns you encounter. When you master the content, you will become more aware of your own motivations, understand the thoughts and behaviors of others, and be fortified with a wealth of strategies to qualify you as a bona fide MD.

Bobby Hoffman

April 26, 2015

Acknowledgments

Scanning the convoluted recesses of my mind to publically acknowledge the contributions of *others* to my work is a formidable task, particularly for someone afflicted with a dominant internal locus and entrenched control beliefs. However, this time, recognizing the immeasurable influence and gratuitous assistance of others who made this book possible is indeed automatic and effortless. The single-author narrative you are about to read was by no means created through the solo efforts of one person. Realistically, this work would be incomplete and rendered irrelevant without the pervasive inspiration, encouragement, and guidance of those individuals mentioned below.

First, the idea for this book was conceived by my students. I thank them for convincing me to write the book, and unbeknownst to them (or me), these same students subtly became my teacher. Their encouragement provided an exceptional opportunity for me to vastly enhance my own knowledge of motivational research. I am forever grateful to my academic parents, Gregory Schraw and Gale Sinatra, for their tutelage and wise advice that continues to influence me daily. Of course, without the motivational leaders profiled in the book, this effort might be considered mundane. The leaders' contributions were extraordinary, not only for their stories, experience, and wisdom, but because of their inspiration. Each leader in their own unique way taught me that despite enormous physical or psychological obstacles, motivated action is within the grasp of anyone, at anytime.

Second, I am indebted to those individuals who provided constructive feedback to refine the book. Those named endured two years of incessant questions, proofreading, and editing.Sean O'Dell, Lisa Sabino,and Morgan McAfee should be immortalized for their informed suggestions, language mastery, and exceptional copy editing and grammatical skills, which clearly I lacked. I thank Neil Schatz, Glenn Hoffman, and Richard Feenstra for their unwavering support by indulging me and listening to my excessive ramblings, while trying to decide on the tone and content of the book. I applaud Gene Dooley and Denise Kay for knowing one-half of the world's population and introducing me to several of the motivational leaders featured in the book. And of course, I appreciate the commendable Elsevier team of Nikki Levy, Barbara Makinster, Lisa Jones, and Cindy Minor, who were geographically distant, but highly efficient and effective in helping to polish, produce, and market the book.

Despite intrinsic motives, personal achievements are functionally meaningless without the support and recognition from friends and family. I was quite fortunate to have the unconditional love and encouragement of my entire family, most notably Eugene, Nancy, Rebecca, Robert, Glenn, Patti, and Caroline. I thank my University of Central Florida colleagues for providing me the unencumbered time to conceptualize the book. Finally, every day, I thank Karen Heller. She is a woman of keen wit, profound patience, and unvarying temperament. As my co-pilot in life, Karen is someone who makes the darkest moments bright by providing a voice of reason with thoughtful suggestions, despite enduring my daily lunch-time diatribes. If given a nickel for every comment, suggestion, and countless chapter she reviewed Karen could retire a very wealthy woman. Her gift to me as a motivational model is immense and her unwavering love has, and will continue to be, why I consider myself to be a very affluent man.

Part I

The Framework of Human Motivation

Underpinnings: Five foundational doctrines of motivational science

Chapter outline

Introduction 3
Principle #1—Motivational inequality is a measurable reality 6
Principle #2—Motivation can be defined, but not universally 8
Principle #3—There is no such thing as being unmotivated 9
Principle #4—Behavior ≠ motivation, and there are no "motivational" types 11
Principle #5—Individuals may not recognize or understand their own motives 12
    Chapter summary/conclusions 14
    Assess your basic knowledge 15
    Next steps 16
    End of chapter motivational minute 16
References 17

Introduction

The morning of September 1, 2012, was a typical weekend day, for *me*. I had little interest in doing work, few deadlines approaching, and some time to kill. I quickly realized the timing was perfect to reach one of my personal goals, completing a 50-mile bicycle ride. This goal would be a major milestone for me, something I had never attempted, and an accomplishment I could brag about to my family, friends, and co-workers. After all, at least judging by social media standards, many people like to broadcast their accomplishments, right?

I was committed to reaching my goal. Without reservation, I loaded my backpack with food, energy drinks, and a second shirt to deal with the searing 90-degree heat and humidity of the Florida noon-day sun. Although I had been biking regularly for 8 months, I had a good deal of skepticism, considering my declining 56-year-old body. Did I have the stamina and endurance to complete 50 miles? Could I finish early enough to avoid the inevitable afternoon thundershowers? What streets should I take, and how could I avoid as much traffic as possible? I consciously planned my route, well aware of when I would need to rest and how long it would take me to finish. Most importantly, I thought about how I would motivate myself to continue cycling when swarms of insects flew in my face and mouth, or when my legs started to burn from the heat and exhaustion.

I never found out if I could pedal the entire 50 miles. While waiting for the incessant traffic to abate at mile 34, my motivation changed. The traffic light signaled green, and I pushed off the curb into the crosswalk. According to police records, four seconds later, I was thrown onto the road, screaming in agony, when a reckless driver plowed into my bicycle at 40 miles per hour. First, I was hurled onto the hood of the car, and then my helmet-protected head slammed into the windshield, causing the glass to shatter. I was then propelled into the air and plummeted to the hot asphalt. At that moment, I was only motivated to survive.

In what seemed like seconds, the ambulance arrived. I was immobilized and rushed to the trauma center, blood dripping down my face from the deep lacerations on my forehead. Upon arrival at the hospital, radiology determined I had nine broken bones: left clavicle, six ribs, right hip, and left scapula. Immediate surgery was necessary to repair and plate my shattered clavicle, the most frequently broken bone in bicycle accidents. That was when the really bad news arrived: doctors informed me that I would be in the hospital for several weeks and confined to a wheelchair for at least 3 months. The assurance of a full recovery was doubtful. The intravenous morphine was insufficient to ease the pain from my massive injuries or to keep me from obsessing about how horrible my life had suddenly become.

The passing weeks were filled with mental anguish, erratic rest, night fevers, and abdominal shots to thwart the blood clots that might kill me. I was immobilized for over a week. The only seemingly normal aspect of my existence was my mind, groggy but still working like before. As a professor of educational psychology at a major university, I was scheduled to teach three online courses that semester. I also decided that studying Italian was a brilliant idea in preparation for an eventual trip abroad. How could I continue under the circumstances of my injuries? How would my potential absence affect my students? I thought deeply about my circumstances and decided to continue teaching and elected not to use my accident as an excuse to drop my Italian class. I was committed to living up to my responsibilities despite the constant reminders of pain and agony that still linger to this very day. I never did miss a day of work and earned an "A" in my Italian class.

The story you just read is true and illustrates many points that will be covered in this book. You may not have noticed, but my story was about setting goals, picking strategies, contemplating alternatives, and reflecting on accomplishment. This book is not about me, though; this book is about you. It will take you on a journey of self-exploration, revealing what motivates both you and others. You will gain a deep understanding of the principles of motivation, all substantiated by empirical scientific evidence. Through a series of candid interviews and stories like the one you just read, you will learn about the motives, reasoning, and behaviors of driven, motivated individuals. Some will be recognized, others just names without a face. You will read about how these leaders determined their goals, executed strategies, and achieved results. You will learn why some individuals prosper and some fail. You will understand why some people persevere through obstacles, while others simply give up. Decision making and choice will be analyzed to explain why the rest of the world may think and act differently from the way you do. Most importantly, by studying the principles in this book, you will become a motivational detective (MD), motivationally wise and strategically gifted with the ability to diagnose, analyze, and influence the motivational challenges that you will invariably encounter during your daily journey through life.

First, you should read the story of Ginny and Jerry, two fraternal twins raised together in the same 1980s suburban New York home by the same nurturing parents. As children, the twins were inseparable: They attended the same schools, went to the same summer camps, and always shared the same circle of friends. Their father, Mel, provided well for his family, commuting 50 miles a day while working long hours as a licensed NYC accountant. Rose, a stay-at-home mom, ruled the house with an iron hand. Rose made sure that Ginny and Jerry had a predictable routine. The twins always made their beds immediately upon waking, and if they were not at the table precisely by 7:00 AM, there would be no breakfast for them that day. Homework had to be completed before meeting friends or playing board games with each other, the twins' favorite childhood pastime. Both children had obligatory chores: Ginny walked the family dog Leary, while Jerry was always taking out the trash or bundling old newspapers for the local paper drive. Both worked before they were teens. Ginny was a babysitter because she loved children, and aspiring entrepreneur Jerry ran a paper route, delivering newspapers, before he was barely 12 years old. Now adults, Ginny and Jerry are barely recognizable as siblings and are radically different individuals. Each twin possesses a unique approach to life that belies genetic similarities. Many people who know the twins don't even realize the familial connection because they look, act, and navigate life so differently. The explicit differences between these adult fraternal twins serve as an ideal depiction of one of the first principles you will learn to unravel the mysteries of motivation: motivational inequality.

Ginny's story

As a teen, Ginny was carefree, perpetually focused on having fun, often at the expense of her schoolwork. She frequently skipped school to go the beach or just hang out with her friends, usually as the center of everyone's attention. Her mother was often found nervously pacing the kitchen floor whenever teenage "Gin-Gin" went out for the night. Over the years, Mrs. T had her fair share of phone calls from neighbors and visits to the principal's office to coax her adventurous daughter out of trouble. Ginny was always considered bright, but she had a proclivity for finding trouble and was suspended from high school at least three times. Her beauty was magnetic and few adolescent boys could resist her charismatic charm. Married three times before she turned 30, Ginny was unpredictable and impulsive, jumping at any opportunity to travel or to show off her sensitive, but mischievous side. Eventually, Ginny became a devoted mother but had few close friends, avoiding contact with many of those from her past.

Ginny was a resounding success professionally despite lacking a college degree. Once she put her mind to something, Ginny was unstoppable. Supporting herself for many years, Ginny parlayed her love of music into a career in the recording industry. She managed her own studio, producing recordings for some of the top names in rock and roll, such as Robert Plant of Led Zeppelin fame and Sting from the Police. Her spontaneous and robust attitude allowed her to meet new people from all occupations, something she really enjoyed. Now retired, Ginny spends her days reading and enjoying her New England estate during the summer, while spending winters in the Caribbean on the yacht she was awarded from her second divorce.

> **Jerry's story**
>
> Jerry's idea of a good time was radically different from that of his sister. As a child he was always outside. The season or the reason didn't matter; energetic and gregarious, Jerry was always found carrying a football or basketball, even when he went to bed. A straight "A" student, Jerry loved science and math and dreamed of becoming an astronaut. He insisted his room have posters of the planets on the ceiling and a table of the elements on his wall. A record-setting athlete, Jerry was a high school track star holding records that remained for 30 years. A qualifier for the US Olympic team in swimming, Jerry's athletic career was cut short by a knee injury sustained in an auto accident when he was 17. He rarely dated, instead preferring to associate with a small group of close friends. Thirty-five years later, he is still married to his high-school sweetheart, Patti.
>
> Jerry's professional accomplishments are a model of thoughtful planning and stability. In college, he earned two degrees as a double major, one in science and another in engineering. He worked for the same company for over 20 years, being promoted three times and twice winning the coveted "Manager of the Year" award for mentoring junior employees. In his spare time, he volunteered to coach Little League and was frequently team leader, raising funds for the Boy Scouts or his local church. Jerry spent most of his free time entertaining old friends or doing yard work. He recently added a new deck to his house and has remodeled three bathrooms, all on his own. When Jerry was asked to describe his greatest accomplishment, he quickly replied "raising my three boys." Jerry has no plans to retire and is currently contemplating a return to school to study theology. Jerry hopes to be a minister one day because making a difference for the people in his community is one of his highest priorities.

Principle #1—Motivational inequality is a measurable reality

What are we able to conclude about motives from the stories of Ginny and Jerry? First, we can deduce that significant motivational differences exist between individuals in the direction and intensity of organized effort. Ginny thrives on socialization, whereas Jerry is studious. Ginny takes every day as it comes, and Jerry is a serious planner. Ginny loves people, and Jerry wants to get things done. It would be speculative to comment upon the reasons and sources of the motivational differences between the twins based upon the limited information provided; however, motivational inequality is a verifiable cultural universal (Adams, 1965; Alderman, 2004; Nicholls, 1979). *Cultural universals* are "domains of human experience that have existed in all cultures past and present" (Brophy & Alleman, 2006, p. 5). For now, we will operate under the assumption that regardless of age, gender, race, ethnicity, or any other innate individual differences, all individuals are NOT created equal, *motivationally*. This inequality manifests in a wide degree of preferences as to what tasks individuals will attempt, how and why they set goals, and what behaviors or strategies they use to obtain and evaluate objectives.

The embodiment of motivational inequality in practice can be observed through a careful examination of learning and performance contexts. In the classroom, learners exhibit a broad spectrum of topical interest and academic engagement ranging from intense focus measured by active involvement in learning, to academic passivity whereby the learner is physically present but cognitively disengaged. The most egregious forms of disengagement result in deliberate apathy and conscious withdrawal from the learning process (Hoffman, Badgett, & Parker, 2008; Maeroff, 1988; Skinner, Furrer, Marchand, & Kindermann, 2008). A 2009 survey of 42,754 high school students indicated that over 66% of students admitted to being bored or disinterested while in school, and sporadic engagement was linked to accelerated dropout rates (Yazzie-Mintz, 2009). Student engagement is highly relevant to achievement, as it is positively correlated with adaptive academic motivation (Reeve, Jang, Carrell, Jeon, & Barch, 2004) and the quality of learning outcomes (Fredericks, Blumenfeld, & Paris, 2004).

At work, motivational inequality may develop as employees assess and value their roles within an organization. By design, organizations create a hierarchy of labor and entitlements based upon the purported market value of the skills and abilities that employees possess. When employees perceive their pay equity, organizational stature, or work role as compromised or incommensurate with organizational norms, work performance may suffer. Rooted in equity theory (Adams, 1965; Morand & Merriman, 2012), employees have a sense of entitlement based upon the expectation that their contributions (e.g., skills, talent, abilities) should be appropriately rewarded and recognized. The perception of imbalance between what employees believe should happen and organizational realities can result in performance issues, deviant workplace behavior, and lower levels of job satisfaction, which ultimately influence performance motivation.

Recognizing motivational inequality has important implications for both educators and leaders. First, for teachers, the motivational disparities of students may prompt unconscious and even deliberate alteration of teaching strategies, such as assigning easier work to students who are perceived as having lower academic motivation. Personal bias toward certain learners can lead to self-fulfilling prophecies, where less is expected of the motivationally inferior learner, resulting in adverse changes as to how teachers interact and communicate with students (Martin & Dowson, 2009). Although recent evidence suggests that only 5% to 10% of students are typically affected by self-fulfilling prophecies, the impact on the quality of learning outcomes is extraordinary (Jussim, 2012). In addition, the consequences of interacting differently with students demonstrating low academic motivation disproportionally affects at-risk learners, thereby exacerbating the obstacles for those learners that need the most support (Dolan & McCaslin, 2008; Tulis, 2013).

Organizational consequences of not recognizing motivational differences are equally troubling. Although the utility of equity theory has been questioned in recent years due to an emphasis on collectivist values and evolution of the labor market

(Skiba & Rosenberg, 2011), individual workers may still consciously withhold effort in situations where an injustice is perceived. A prerequisite for organizational prosperity is the emphasis by leaders on instilling a coalesced corporate culture, but not at the expense of ignoring personal motivation and individual values. The dualistic emphasis provides employees with a sense of organizational justice, while maintaining the delicate equilibrium between worker individuality and organizational focus (Kleiner & von Post, 2011).

Principle #2—Motivation can be defined, but not universally

Before we proceed, we should clarify exactly how researchers and scientists operationally define motivation. *Operational definitions* avoid scholarly debates about the meaning of words but, instead, describe concepts in terms of measurable observations that can be tested through scientific methods (Stanovich, 2013). Operational definitions exclude personal feelings, opinions, and experiences because these proprietary interpretations of phenomena defy scientific scrutiny and cannot be directly replicated with or by other individuals. For example, if I told you that before I complete a boring obligatory task, such as doing laundry, I motivate myself by thinking of little green men with guns shooting sunbeams at me, then you would infer my personal definition of motivation is "extraterrestrials that encourage me to complete boring tasks." Hopefully, my definition of motivation isn't the same as yours, and surely we conclude that the definition cannot be tested; thus, my experience serves no purpose in operationally defining the concept of motivation.

So, what exactly is motivation? Textbook and conventional definitions vary, but all interpretations of motivation etymologically originate from the Latin verb *movere* "to move." Motivation has been defined as "the condition of being eager to act or work" (Merriam-Webster, 2015), "the process whereby goal-directed activity is instigated and sustained" (Schunk, Pintrich, & Meece, 2008, p. 4), and as the internal processes that give behavior energy and direction (Reeve, 2009). These related interpretations of motivation all evolve around the core concept of explaining the internal causes that trigger and sustain the course of human behavior. For our purposes, motivation is defined as *the degree of effort and intensity directed toward a goal related to learning or performance*. The use of motivation terminology is such a formidable and debatable challenge that Murphy and Alexander (2000) devoted over 50 pages attempting to convince the scientific community that a shared lexicon of terminology is essential for motivational research findings to be of value to practitioners. Semantically, *motivation* will be used as a term to describe the process of directing and applying effort *and* to describe the outcomes of behavior, such as in the example "Ginny was motivated to find a great job (an *outcome*) despite her lack of academic motivation (a *process*)."

The study of motivation is wrought with seemingly accurate and logical individual interpretations of motivated behavior, described as "folk wisdom" (Stanovich, 2013,

p. 13). These conceptions comprise apparently indisputable personal truths and beliefs about the nature of human behavior, although these beliefs are frequently unsubstantiated or are direct distortions of scientific evidence, such as the conventional wisdom that worker productivity is increased by higher wages. The study of motivation is particularly susceptible to this conventional wisdom, sometimes referred to as "common sense" because individuals across Western cultures are bombarded by motivational symbolism, hackneyed clichés, and incessant commercialism suggesting reasons to initiate and sustain behavior. After all, isn't it common knowledge that "you can't teach an old dog new tricks," that "practice makes perfect," and that merely by wearing Nike apparel with an embroidered "swoosh," you will be energized to achieve athletic prowess never before thought possible?

Motivational metaphors and subliminal messages abound throughout popular culture and media, suggesting reasons why we should use certain strategies to achieve our goals and ensure predictable consequences of our effort. The Beatles contended "all we need is love," Frank Sinatra crooned he did it "his" way, Bon Jovi is "living on a prayer," and the "Boss" (Bruce Springsteen) espouses his theory of biological influences on motivation by proclaiming, "Baby, we were BORN to run!" Less metaphorically, when reading the stories of Ginny and Jerry, did you come to the potentially erroneous conclusion that Jerry was less adventurous than Ginny and wouldn't possibly do anything to risk his physical safety or the security of his job and family? Deliberately excluded from Jerry's parable was mention that he is a competitive skier, who frequently competes in extreme black diamond skiing events, leaving his wife and family at home to go skiing with the "guys." The problem with folk beliefs and common sense is these conceptions are frequently wrong, as supported by Principles #3 and #4.

Principle #3—There is no such thing as being unmotivated

Have you ever uttered the words "he is unmotivated" or "she has no initiative," when describing a spouse, partner, child, student, or co-worker? Most likely, if you haven't spoken those words, you have probably heard them! My interactions with teachers and business leaders frequently suggest that academic apathy or lack of engagement in the classroom signifies the absence of motivation. Lay descriptions of motivated behavior repeatedly suggest that motivation is a quantifiable resource, akin to a glass of fine wine, which if not sipped slowly and judiciously conserved, will quickly disappear. Although, strong evidence supports qualifying both academic motivation (Pintrich & Zusho, 2002) and personal motivation (e.g., self-control) as a depletable resource (Muraven & Baumeister, 2000), "having NO motivation" is a convenient misnomer commonly used by parents, teachers, and managers to describe the recalcitrant or indifferent individual who does not meet his or her personal performance expectations. Consequently, one of the most prevalent ways that we evaluate the performance of others is by comparing them to ourselves (Darnon, Dompnier, Gilliéron, & Butera, 2010; Festinger, 1954; Swift, Abrams, & Marques, 2013), which often leads to flawed conclusions concerning a person's motivation.

Ascribing NO motivation to a *living* individual suggests a potential discrepancy between the beliefs of the individual making the assessment and the beliefs of those being assessed. Sometimes labeled as "individualism" in Western cultures, displaying personal attributes implies that each person is a "unique entity that is bounded and fundamentally separate from its social surrounding" (Kim & Chu, 2011, p. 58). Perhaps the best illustration of individualism is the highway dilemma. Everyone knows that the person driving faster than you is reckless and irresponsible, whereas the person driving slower than you is obviously deficient in both driving ability and intelligence. Such biased reasoning likely leads to the erroneous conclusion that your driving behavior is entirely appropriate and justified, but the other person is wrong.

The apparent absence of a particular behavior signifying no motivation is a common misconception refuted by the multiplicity of factors that undermine motivation. Scholars in motivational science have identified at least 24 different ways to interpret motivated behavior (Reeve, 2009), many of which have obvious inconsistencies with the understandings and expectations of teachers, parents, or business leaders at any one time. Table 1.1 lists several of the most popular perspectives that researchers have used to categorize *applied* motivation, many of which are examined throughout this text.

The previous paragraph and Table 1.1 suggest that understanding motivated behavior is a complex process that can be accomplished in a wide variety of ways and viewed through a vast number of theoretical lenses. We can also surmise that at any one time, different individuals consider an assortment of goals when assessing the direction and intensity of their intended efforts. For example, we might suspect that an individual is *academically* unmotivated (Hidi & Harackiewicz, 2000) but conclude that the person is more inclined to satisfy other raging priorities or needs. The discrepancy between expected behavior and observed behavior in a particular context does not signify the absence of motivation. Instead, the inconsistency suggests that individuals undergo a perpetual internal dogfight, evaluating and prioritizing their cognitions as a conduit to determine when, where, why, and how they will direct their effort and attention.

Table 1.1 Popular perspectives used to categorize motivated behavior

Motivation category	Reference citation
Academic	Schunk et al. (2008)
Achievement	Elliot (1997)
Biological/Evolutionary	Pinker (2002)
Choice	Tversky and Kahneman (1992)
Optimal	Csikszentmihalyi (1997)
Performance	Privette (1981)
Personal	Ryan and Deci (2000)
Social	Dunning (2011)

Principle #4—Behavior ≠ motivation, and there are no "motivational" types

Some of us may believe that by simply observing an individual's behavior, we can reasonably conclude what caused the behavior. For example, if we watch a young woman with height proportional to weight consume a voluminous amount of food at the school cafeteria, we would likely believe this individual was famished. Similarly, we might make predictions about the nature of collective behavior. Imagine that a group of normally productive hourly workers are not meeting production targets. A potential solution to boost output could be giving an across-the-board wage increase. We might expect that productivity would immediately spike following the raise because most workers are motivated, at least in part, by earning more money. Unfortunately, both the cafeteria and production suppositions would be wrong. Research indicates that only 33% of college females eat for reasons based upon hunger alone (Mintz & Betz, 1988), and the relationship between worker pay and productivity has been on a gradual, but steady, decline since 1987 (Long, Dziczek, Luria, & Wiarda, 2008). These examples suggest that behavior is a poor indicator to predict what motivates an individual because of a phenomenon called *equifinality* (McDougall, 1923) that develops when similar behaviors represent entirely different motives (Dunning, 2011).

Diagnosing the cause of behaviors is further complicated by the dynamic, multidimensional nature of motivations, which vary situationally both within and between individuals. Motives are generally guided by some combination of biological, psychological, social, and emotional forces that will be discussed in detail throughout the text. However, simplistic singular explanations of motivation discount the proclivity of individuals to concurrently have multiple motives, some subordinate to others. Although researchers debate whether individuals prioritize motives in a well-defined hierarchy (Maslow, 1958), constancy of change in motives is inevitable. Motives are sometimes described as "ultimate" when a desired outcome is reached or as "instrumental" when subordinate goals are attained that sustain momentum toward the individual's desired end state (Batson, Ahmad, & Stocks, 2011, p. 104). For example, one may ultimately desire to earn a medical degree and demonstrate accomplishment, perseverance, and determination in the process (ultimate motive) but to avoid embarrassment, may drop an elective course if failure is imminent (instrumental motive).

Understanding the meaning of observed behaviors is further complicated by the dispositional nature of motivation (Spence, 1944) when intervening variables, such as context, affect, or mood, can change both the direction and intensity of individual effort. Consider when you learned about the "9/11" tragedies that resulted in the deaths of over 3,000 people. You may have experienced feelings of fear, anger, and sadness that day, which subsequently inhibited your ability to effectively complete any work. Your inability to focus on work did not represent either a questionable work ethic or laziness, but instead your efforts were redirected by an emotionally charged event. Thus, accurately deciphering observed behavior requires an understanding of the specific reasons *why* motives and goals are redirected, which cannot be confirmed by behavioral observation alone.

The presumption that motives frequently change is contrary to some popular press conceptions that infer that motivation is a stable, predictable characteristic that often defines the individual (Lowe, 2009; Pink, 2011). Pop descriptions of motivation may lead the uninformed practitioner to believe that completing "diagnostic tools" that offer dichotomous choices between behaviors will lead to an instant detailed description of monistic motivation. In contrast, the confluence of evidence suggests that motivation is a fluid, malleable, and variable combination of needs, drives, interests, attributions, and intentions (Reeve, 2009; Ryan, 2012). Individuals invariably set and approach tasks by using a repertoire of strategies that frequently change based upon their experiences, situational goals, emotions, and the context of their efforts. Although some individuals possess deeply entrenched beliefs with strong cultural or secular values that manifest in predictable and resistant patterns of behavior, constancy of human motives is a conceptual fantasy propagated by those seeking simple unitary solutions to human behavior. It is the variability *within* individuals that discounts the veracity of having a predictable motivational type.

Withstanding the fallacy of labeling individuals, researchers have identified multiple *types of motivation* (e.g., intrinsic versus extrinsic; Ryan & Deci, 2000) suggesting that individuals may have habitual or preferred motivational tendencies. Researchers also frequently classify individuals into homogeneous subgroups by using empirically supported analysis techniques, such as latent profile analysis that cluster similarities between individuals together as a method to study motivation (Marsh, Lüdtke, Trautwein, & Morin, 2009; Pastor, Barron, Miller, & Davis, 2007; Schwinger, Steinmayr, & Spinath, 2012). However, these person-centered approaches are primarily predicated upon evaluating individuals in experimental and simulated contexts that inhibit generalization to other populations, tasks, or settings. Thus, although intuitively we may believe that individuals have dominant motives, motives will fluctuate within individuals, and motives should be expected to change, *frequently*.

Principle #5—Individuals may not recognize or understand their own motives

As you likely realize by now, objectively deciphering the meaning of motivated behavior, even when using sound scientific practice, is a formidable challenge for both researchers and practitioners. Unlike the pronounced physical attributes that distinguish human beings, psychological markers, such as beliefs, preferences, and personal expectancies, defy direct observation and are even more difficult to interpret precisely. Self-report is often chosen as the preferred methodology to collect information about individuals and ascertain the meanings of behaviors. The enigma of analysis is complicated by the reality that individuals may not recognize the sources of their own subjective behaviors, resulting in the frequent misinterpretation of motives (Feldon, 2007). In other cases, people will deliberately distort the meanings of their own behaviors (Hyman & Sierra, 2011). Many individuals feel a perceived obligation to present positive or expected self-images to researchers (Greene, 2015), resulting in response inaccuracies based on the contrived perceptions of social desirability

(Johnson & Fendrich, 2002). Reporting and interpretative errors are so rampant that in a study investigating which personal beliefs influenced problem solving, Feldon (2010) concluded that "participants' self-explanations are largely inaccurate" (p. 395).

The origination and the evolutionary nature of motives compound inaccurate reporting and interpretation. Motivations are frequently categorized into two types: (1) as self-determined and conscious intentions, which are deemed *explicit*, and (2) as spontaneous automatic actions that operate with limited or no active awareness by the individual, which is termed *implicit* (Kehr, 2004; Ryan & Deci, 2000; Thrash, Maruskin, & Martin, 2012). Motives described as *explicit* are relatively easier to evaluate because they are readily identifiable by an individual and typically are associated with the pursuit of a specific measurable goal. When a person feels thirsty, he or she takes a drink. When a person expects to attend a birthday party, he or she consciously decides to bring a celebratory gift. Explicit motives are typically primed by contextual or social factors (Aarts & Custers, 2012) and evolve from routine experience-related memories that are exemplified by conscious intentional behavior (Kehr, 2004). When describing explicit motives, individuals can *potentially* articulate the linkages between their planned actions and exhibited behaviors with accuracy due to conscious processing. However, these descriptions are susceptible to errors of bias, such as the common practice of telling researchers exactly what they want to hear in an attempt to appear compliant and support scientific inquiry.

Although intentional behaviors may begin explicitly, a variety of cognitive and affective factors may influence the direction and intensity of subsequent actions. Implicit motives develop as an individual executes goal-directed behavior outside of conscious awareness. A long history of research suggests that "any skill—perceptual, motor, or cognitive—requires less and less conscious attention, the more frequently and consistently it is engaged" (Bargh & Barndollar, 1996, p. 458). Classified as *habits*, these deeply engrained actions are acquired through practice and are perhaps the best examples of unconsciously motivated behaviors. The implicit nature of habits is illustrated by my imaginary friend Peter Parker, who actively seeks to park his car at work in the same parking space every day. Peter, we might say, is a creature of habit. One day, while arriving late for work, the habitual parker is forced to find a spot on the opposite side of the parking lot because an ambitious early arriver had taken his regular spot. After a grueling day at the office, the practiced parker in a zombie-like post-work state walks directly to his usual parking spot, only to find that he has walked in the opposite direction of where his car is parked.

This rather simplistic explanation of habitual behavior, although quite common, fails to take into account a multitude of other factors that can implicitly redirect an individual's cognitions and effort. When faced with situations requiring regulation of their behaviors, individuals are confronted with numerous analytical and judgmental propositions that are directly influenced by implicit cognitions and motives (Greenwald, 1992). Dispositions, such as those related to prejudice, stereotyping, overconfidence, and the selective recall and inconsistent scrutiny of information, are frequently influenced by implicit motivations. Regardless of the types of these implicit motives, many of which will be discussed throughout the text, the real problem for the practitioner is trying to interpret motivated behavior.

Almost universally, the source of misinformation for *practitioners* originates from rather naive, limited-capacity, emotionally charged individuals who have only marginal access to understanding their own behaviors! Schultheiss and Brunstein (2010) in their voluminous work on the derivatives and impact of implicit motives suggested "people cannot validly report on their motivational needs" (p. 4), and Fiedler (2012) lamented that even when people are shown data representing their implicit motives they "miss the story behind it" (p. 4). This rather despondent description of an individual's inability to accurately report why one engages in certain behaviors is a reality of interpreting motivated behavior. However, the analytical challenge becomes even more difficult when taking into account a host of measurement and statistical inference liabilities, which are discussed throughout the text. As for now, we should merely conclude that measuring and understanding motivational difference goes far beyond observing behavior or examining self-reported evidence. Avoiding interpretive pitfalls are an important first step to assessing and evaluating one's self-awareness as well as the motives of others.

Chapter summary/conclusions

Based upon the dubious implications of the first five principles, you might be thinking that the process of identification, diagnosis, and resolution of issues related to enhancing motivation for learning and performance is more of a fairy tale designed to sell books than an obtainable scientific reality. However, a wealth of confluent scientific evidence suggests that motivated behavior can be objectively evaluated and that evidence-supported strategies can be applied to influence how individuals approach, persist in, and complete the tasks they choose to pursue. Research evidence provides the substance for the solutions that are gradually revealed as the defining motivational principles unfold.

Although the diagnosis of motivational issues is a challenge, the mediation process starts with the acknowledgment that the motivational profile of each individual is, indeed, unique. Like a fingerprint, each individual exhibits a diverse set of behaviors that are instigated by a variety of motives, some more prominent and obvious than others. The natural diversity of motives between and within individuals is subject to constant revision as the individual navigates his or her own proprietary perceptual, contextual, and social environment. The inequality of motivation means that the behaviors exhibited by one individual may mean something radically different from similar behaviors displayed by another person, leading to the MD's dilemma of how to best understand and mediate motivational challenges. Unfortunately, reliance upon individuals to disclose the nature of their motivations may not be the best repository of information. However, individual representations combined with systematic analysis, based upon scientific knowledge grounded in methodological rigor, supply a wealth of information to assist the practitioner.

Through a process of gathering information from a variety of parables and descriptions, the reader will likely experience a catharsis of self-exploration and self-awareness. The profiles in the text allow the aspiring diagnostician to use real-life examples to practice the science of finding and promoting motivation in the self and others. An ancient proverb succinctly illustrates the ongoing approach of enhancing our own knowledge through the experiences of others: "A wise man will hear and increase in learning, and a man of understanding will acquire wise counsel" (New American Standard Bible, 1995, Proverbs 1:5). Thus, we shall frequently turn to our wise counsel for advice because theories alone are insufficient to answer all questions.

Assess your basic knowledge

One goal of this chapter was to dispel some of the common misconceptions concerning motivation. Unfortunately, many of the descriptions of motivation by the popular press are not scientifically sound or validated by empirical evidence. Thus, there are many misconceptions concerning motivational science. Many of these familiar fallacies will be refuted and dispelled in the upcoming chapters. Before we embark on our continuing journey of finding motivation and discovering the strategies than can enhance motivation for learning and performance, let's put your knowledge to the test: Proceed cautiously, and take the motivation quiz....

The following statements can be considered either true or false. The number in the right column signifies in which chapter(s) the principle relating to the question is discussed.

Question	Answer	Discussed in chapter
1. There is no such thing as optimal motivation.	True or False?	2
2. A reliable strategy to enhance performance is to provide extrinsic rewards, such as grades or money.	True or False?	6
3. Your personal knowledge of motivation and use of motivational strategies can help foster behavior changes in just about anyone.	True or False?	12
4. The amount of effort dedicated toward a task can be hindered by emotions, such as happiness, excitement, or enthusiasm.	True or False?	9
5. If a task is too difficult, motivation to complete the task will decrease.	True or False?	6
6. Learners rarely care about both grades and gaining expertise. It is either one or the other.	True or False?	6
7. Research indicates you can be an effective instructor even if you believe some students are better learners than others.	True or False?	5
8. Effort is more important than expertise when it comes to academic excellence.	True or False?	10
9. It is usually a good idea to offer help to a learner when you suspect the learner is struggling.	True or False?	8
10. A motivational strategy effective in one domain may fail in another.	True or False?	11

(*Continued*)

Question	Answer	Discussed in chapter
11. Thinking patterns and motivational tendencies are closely related.	True or False?	2
12. If you think you will fail at a task, you will likely underperform on the task regardless of your abilities.	True or False?	7
13. There is no such thing as being in the "zone."	True or False?	9
14. The most successful learners are those who rely minimally on the teacher and take responsibility for their own learning.	True or False?	10
15. Cultural factors can be strong determinants of motivated behaviors and can supersede ability.	True or False?	5
16. Research indicates that motivation and motivational strategies vary according to age.	True or False?	4
17. Learners with test anxiety need to accept the fact that being nervous is just part of the process of learning and assessment.	True or False?	9
18. Most workers report job satisfaction when they are well paid.	True or False?	6
19. There is a genetic basis for motivational tendencies.	True or False?	3
20. Motivation toward a task varies according to your level of expertise.	True or False?	7

Next steps

Thinking back, you may have wondered about the stories of Ginny and Jerry, the fraternal twins. The twins will be referenced later as we navigate the course of understanding motivation. We will also return to my own story later as a means to show how planning, evaluation, and reflection impact ensuing behavior. However, before we transition into a discussion of some of the individuals profiled in the book, we should realize that not all questions about motivation can be answered through scientific methods. Further, despite the advantage of empirical evidence to explain behavior, many areas of motivational science are subject to ambiguity and debate. Sometimes, studies reveal inconsistent patterns of evidence or provide data that can be interpreted in multiple ways. We next turn our discussion to some of the enigmatic and contentious issues complicating the life of the MD and virtually meet **Bernard L. Madoff**, who some might contend exhibited the pinnacle of performance motivation.

End of chapter motivational minute

Principles covered in this chapter:

1. **Motivational inequality is a measurable reality**—the expectation that individuals from different backgrounds and cultures are equally advantaged in the type and quantity of motivation they demonstrate is a regrettable fallacy.
2. **Motivation can be defined, but not universally**—although consensus indicates that motivation for learning and performance is "the degree of effort and intensity directed toward a

goal," researchers continually debate the precise meaning and representation of a myriad of motivational constructs.
3. **There is no such thing as being unmotivated**—the apparent "absence of motivation" is a common description used when individuals appear not to be focused in the same direction of the person evaluating their motivation. Everyone is motivated, but motivational diversity within and between individuals is dramatic.
4. **Behavior ≠ motivation, and there are no "motivational" types**—many popular press conceptions of motivation are not supported by scientific evidence, primarily due to the notion that any particular behavior can represent a multitude of motives.
5. **Individuals may not recognize or understand their own motives**—unfortunately, most individuals cannot accurately report the causes of their own behaviors due to the implicit nature of many motivations. Additionally, individuals are susceptible to personal bias and the perceived need to demonstrate socially desirable behaviors.

Key terminology (in order of chapter presentation):

- **Cultural universals**—domains of human experience that have existed in all cultures past and present.
- **Operational definitions**—describing concepts in terms of measurable observations that can be tested through scientific methods.
- **Applied motivation**—the use of scientific evidence and empirical knowledge to mediate issues of motivation in practical settings, such as the classroom or workplace.
- **Equifinality**—behaviors between individuals that represent entirely different motives.
- **Self-report**—the reliance upon individuals to provide personal interpretation of their motives, typically gathered through surveys or interviews.
- **Explicit**—motives within the stream of consciousness accurately recognized and interpreted by the individual.
- **Implicit**—automatic motives not readily recognized within the direct stream of consciousness of an individual.
- **Habits**—deeply engrained motives, behaviors, and actions acquired through experience or practice.

References

Aarts, H., & Custers, R. (2012). Unconscious goal pursuit: Nonconscious goal regulation and motivation. In R. M. Ryan (Ed.), *The Oxford handbook of human motivation* (pp. 232–247). New York, NY: Oxford University Press.

Adams, J. S. (1965). Inequity in social exchange. *Advanced Experimental Social Psychology, 62*, 335–343. http://dx.doi.org/10.1016/S0065-2601(08)60108-2.

Alderman, M. K. (2004). *Motivation for achievement: Possibilities for teaching and learning* (2nd ed.). Mahwah, NJ: Lawrence Erlbaum Associates.

Bargh, J. A., & Barndollar, K. (1996). Automaticity in action: The unconscious as repository of chronic goals and motives. In P. M. Gollwitzer & J. A. Bargh (Eds.), *The psychology of action* (pp. 457–481). New York, NY: Guilford Press.

Batson, C., Ahmad, N., & Stocks, E. L. (2011). Four forms of prosocial motivation: Egoism, altruism, collectivism, and principlism. In D. Dunning (Ed.), *Social motivation* (pp. 103–126). New York, NY: Psychology Press.

Brophy, J. E., & Alleman, J. (2006). *Children's thinking about cultural universals*. Mahwah, NJ: Lawrence Erlbaum Associates.

Csikszentmihalyi, M. (1997). *Finding flow: The psychology of engagement with everyday life*. New York, NY: Basic Books.

Darnon, C., Dompnier, B., Gilliéron, O., & Butera, F. (2010). The interplay of mastery and performance goals in social comparison: A multiple-goal perspective. *Journal of Educational Psychology, 102*(1), 212–222. http://dx.doi.org/10.1037/a0018161.

Dolan, A. L., & McCaslin, M. (2008). Student perceptions of teacher support. *Teachers College Record, 110*(11), 2423–2437.

Dunning, D. (2011). *Social motivation*. New York, NY: Psychology Press.

Elliot, A. J. (1997). Integrating the "classic" and "contemporary" approaches to intrinsic motivation: A hierarchical model of approach and avoidance achievement motivation. *Advances in Motivation and Achievement, 10*, 303–337.

Feldon, D. F. (2007). The implications of research on expertise for curriculum and pedagogy. *Educational Psychology Review, 19*(2), 91–110. http://dx.doi.org/10.1007/s10648-006-9009-0.

Feldon, D. F. (2010). Do psychology researchers tell it like it is? A microgenetic analysis of research strategies and self-report accuracy along a continuum of expertise. *Instructional Science, 38*(4), 395–415.

Festinger, L. (1954). A theory of social comparison processes. *Human Relations, 7*, 117–140. http://dx.doi.org/10.1177/001872675400700202.

Fiedler, K. (2012). Meta-cognitive myopia and the dilemmas of inductive-statistical inference. In B. H. (2012). Ross (Ed.), *The psychology of learning and motivation* (vol. 57, pp. 1–55). San Diego, CA: Academic Press.

Fredericks, J. A., Blumenfeld, P. C., & Paris, A. H. (2004). School engagement: Potential of the concept, state of the evidence. *Review of Educational Research, 74*, 59–109. http://dx.doi.org/10.3102/00346543074001059.

Greene, B. A. (2015). Measuring cognitive engagement with self-report scales: Reflections from over 20 years of research. *Educational Psychologist, 50*(1), 14–30. http://dx.doi.org/10.1080/00461520.2014.989230.

Greenwald, A. G. (1992). New Look 3: Reclaiming unconscious cognition. *American Psychologist, 47*, 766–779. http://dx.doi.org/10.1037//0003-066X.47.6.766.

Hidi, S., & Harackiewicz, J. M. (2000). Motivating the academically unmotivated: A critical issue for the 21st century. *Review of Educational Research, 70*(2), 151–179. http://dx.doi.org/10.3102/00346543070002151.

Hoffman, B., Badgett, B., & Parker, R. P. (2008). The effect of single-sex instruction in a large, urban at-risk high school. *Journal of Educational Research, 102*(1), 15–35. http://dx.doi.org/10.3200/JOER.102.1.15-36.

Hyman, M. R., & Sierra, J. J. (2011). Adjusting self-reported attitudinal data for mischievous respondents. *International Journal of Market Research, 54*(1), 129–145. http://dx.doi.org/10.2501/IJMR-54-1-129-145.

Johnson, T., & Fendrich, M. (2002). A validation of the Crowne-Marlowe Social Desirability Scale. Retrieved on April 2, 2015 from: <http://www.srl.uic.edu/publist/Conference/crownemarlowe.pdf>.

Jussim, L. (2012). *Social perception and social reality: Why accuracy dominates bias and self-fulfilling prophecy*. New York, NY: Oxford University Press.

Kehr, H. M. (2004). Implicit/explicit motive discrepancies and volitional depletion among managers. *Personality and Social Psychology Bulletin, 30*(3), 315–327. http://dx.doi.org/10.1177/0146167203256967.

Kim, H. S., & Chu, T. Q. (2011). Cultural variation in the motivation of self-expression. In D. Dunning (Ed.), *Social motivation* (pp. 57–77). New York, NY: Psychology Press.

Kleiner, A., & von Post, R. (2011, January 19). A corporate climate of mutual help. *Strategy & Business*. Retrieved on January 6, 2015 from: <http://www.strategy-business.com/article/11102?gko=34ff9>.

Long, M. C., Dziczek, K. M., Luria, D. D., & Wiarda, E. A. (2008). Wage and productivity stability in U.S. manufacturing plants. *Monthly Labor Review*, *131*(5), 24–36.

Lowe, T. (2009). *Get motivated!: Overcome any obstacle, achieve any goal, and accelerate your success with motivational DNA* (1st ed.). New York, NY: Doubleday.

Maeroff, G. I. (1988). Withered hopes, stillborn dreams: The dismal panorama of urban schools. *Phi Delta Kappan*, *69*(9), 632–638.

Marsh, H. W., Lüdtke, O., Trautwein, U., & Morin, A. J. S. (2009). Classical latent profile analysis of academic self-concept dimensions: Synergy of person- and variable-centered approaches to theoretical models of self-concept. *Structural Equation Modeling: A Multidisciplinary Journal*, *16*(2), 191–225. http://dx.doi.org/10.1080/10705510902751010.

Martin, A. J., & Dowson, M. (2009). Interpersonal relationships, motivation, engagement, and achievement: Yields for theory, current issues, and educational practice. *Review of Educational Research*, *79*(1), 327–365. http://dx.doi.org/10.3102/0034654308325583.

Maslow, A. H. (1958). A dynamic theory of human motivation. In C. L. Stacey & M. DeMartino (Eds.), *Understanding human motivation* (pp. 26–47). Cleveland, OH: Howard Allen Publishers. http://dx.doi.org/10.1037/11305-004.

McDougall, W. (1923). *An outline of psychology*. New York, NY: Scribner.

Merriam-Webster.com. (2015). Motivation. Retrieved on January 6, 2015 from: <http://www.merriam-webster.com/dictionary/motivation>.

Mintz, L. B., & Betz, N. E. (1988). Prevalence and correlates of eating disordered behaviors among undergraduate women. *Journal of Counseling Psychology*, *35*(4), 463–471. http://dx.doi.org/10.1037//0022-0167.35.4.463.

Morand, D. A., & Merriman, K. K. (2012). "Equality theory" as a counterbalance to equity theory in human resource management. *Journal of Business Ethics*, *111*(1), 133–144. http://dx.doi.org/10.1007/s10551-012-1435-y.

Muraven, M., & Baumeister, R. F. (2000). Self-regulation and depletion of limited resources: Does self-control resemble a muscle? *Psychological Bulletin*, *126*, 247–259. http://dx.doi.org/10.1037//0033-2909.126.2.247.

Murphy, P., & Alexander, P. (2000). A motivated exploration of motivation terminology. *Contemporary Educational Psychology*, *25*, 3–53. http://dx.doi.org/10.1006/ceps.1999.1019.

New American Standard Bible (1995). *Proverbs 1:5*. La Habra, CA: The Lockman Foundation.

Nicholls, J. G. (1979). Quality and equality in intellectual development: The role of motivation in education. *American Psychologist*, *34*(11), 1071. http://dx.doi.org/10.1037//0003-066X.34.11.1071.

Pastor, D. A., Barron, K. E., Miller, B. J., & Davis, S. L. (2007). A latent profile analysis of college students' achievement goal orientation. *Contemporary Educational Psychology*, *32*(1), 8–47. http://dx.doi.org/10.1016/j.cedpsych.2006.10.003.

Pink, D. H. (2011). *Drive: The surprising truth about what motivates us*. New York, NY: Riverhead Books.

Pinker, S. (2002). *The blank slate: The modern denial of human nature*. New York, NY: Penguin.

Pintrich, P. R., & Zusho, A. (2002). The development of academic self-regulation: The role of cognitive and motivational factors. In A. Wigfield & J. S. Eccles (Eds.), *Development of achievement motivation* (pp. 249–284). San Diego, CA: Academic Press.

Privette, G. (1981). Dynamics of peak performance. *Journal of Humanistic Psychology*, *21*(1), 57–67. http://dx.doi.org/10.1177/002216788102100106.

Reeve, J. (2009). *Understanding motivation and emotion* (5th ed.). Hoboken, NJ: John Wiley & Sons.

Reeve, J., Jang, H., Carrell, D., Jeon, S., & Barch, J. (2004). Enhancing students' engagement by increasing teachers' autonomy support. *Motivation and Emotion, 28*(2), 147–169. http://dx.doi.org/10.1023/B:MOEM.0000032312.95499.6f.

Ryan, R., & Deci, E. (2000). Self-determination theory and the facilitation of intrinsic motivation, social development and well-being. *American Psychologist, 55,* 68–78. http://dx.doi.org/10.1037//0003-066X.55.1.68.

Ryan, R. M. (2012). Motivation and the organization of human behavior: Three reasons for the reemergence of a field. In R. M. Ryan (Ed.), *The Oxford handbook of human motivation* (pp. 3–10). Oxford, England: Oxford University Press.

Schultheiss, O., & Brunstein, J. (2010). *Implicit motives*. Oxford, England: Oxford University Press.

Schunk, D. H., Pintrich, R., & Meece, J. L. (2008). *Motivation in education: Theory, research, and applications* (3rd ed.). Upper Saddle River, NJ: Pearson/Merrill Prentice Hall.

Schwinger, M., Steinmayr, R., & Spinath, B. (2012). Not all roads lead to Rome—comparing different types of motivational regulation profiles. *Learning and Individual Differences, 22*(3), 269–279. http://dx.doi.org/10.1016/j.lindif.2011.12.006.

Skiba, M., & Rosenberg, S. (2011). The disutility of equity theory in contemporary management practice. *Journal of Business & Economic Studies, 17*(2), 1–19.

Skinner, E., Furrer, C., Marchand, G., & Kindermann, T. (2008). Engagement and disaffection in the classroom: Part of a larger motivational dynamic? *Journal of Educational Psychology, 100*(4), 765–781.

Spence, K. W. (1944). The nature of theory construction in contemporary psychology. *Psychological Review, 51*(1), 47–68. http://dx.doi.org/10.1037/h0060940.

Stanovich, K. E. (2013). *How to think straight about psychology* (10th ed.). Boston, MA: Pearson.

Swift, H. J., Abrams, D., & Marques, S. (2013). Threat or boost? Social comparison affects older people's performance differently depending on task domain. *Journal of Gerontology, 68*(1), 23–30. http://dx.doi.org/10.1093/geronb/gbs044.

Thrash, T. M., Maruskin, L. A., & Martin, C. C. (2012). Implicit–explicit motive congruence. In R. M. Ryan (Ed.), *The Oxford handbook of human motivation* (pp. 141–156). Oxford, England: Oxford University Press.

Tulis, M. (2013). Error management behavior in classrooms: Teachers' responses to student mistakes. *Teaching and Teacher Education, 33,* 56–68. http://dx.doi.org/10.1016/j.tate.2013.02.003.

Tversky, A., & Kahneman, D. (1992). Advances in prospect theory: Cumulative representation of uncertainty. *Journal of Risk and Uncertainty, 5*(4), 297–323. http://dx.doi.org/10.1007/BF00122574.

Yazzie-Mintz, E. (2009). *Charting the path from engagement to achievement: A report on the 2009 high school survey of student engagement*. Bloomington, IL: Center for Evaluation and Education Policy, Indiana University. Retrieved on January 6, 2015 from: <http://ceep.indiana.edu/hssse/images/HSSSE_2010_Report.pdf>.

Contentious issues: How evidence refutes motivational misconceptions

2

Chapter outline

Principle #6—Motivational beliefs differ from motivational knowledge 22
Motivational Leader—*Bernard Madoff* 25
Principle #7—Motivational evidence can only answer certain questions 26
Principle #8—Motivation is related to learning and performance but causality is an uncertainty 29
Principle #9—Motivation is subordinate to character and personality 31
Principle #10—Motivation is the responsibility of leaders and can be taught 34
Principle #11—Theoretically, motivated behavior operates on a continuum 35
Principle #12—Optimal motivation is obtainable 37
    Chapter summary/conclusions 41
    Next steps 42
    End of chapter motivational minute 42
References 43

As an impressionable child reared in New York City during the 1960s, I was affectionately known in the neighborhood as "BM." Scatological connotations aside, my childhood moniker "big mouth" developed from a penchant to share my naive worldly views with anyone who would listen. For years, I truly believed, and regularly tried to convince my friends, that deliberately crossing your eyes would result in a permanent facial deformity. I held strong convictions about my esotropic belief, based upon repeatedly hearing this same proclamation almost daily from my stern-eyed mother. Little did I realize at the time that her fabricated science was merely a maternal manipulation, designed to quell my cross-eyed reactions to her repetitive requests. Like most children, I made little, if any, distinction between what was true and what I believed.

    The influence of individual belief convictions is not endemic to loquacious toddlers. Many seemingly well-balanced, educated, and productive adults embrace beliefs supported only by conjecture and speculation. According to a 2005 poll of Americans, 61% believed in the existence of a physical hell, 24% reported that extraterrestrials have visited Earth, and 37% believed that houses can be haunted (www.gallup.com, Gallup, 2005). In a similar survey, participants reported experiencing at least one of the following: personally communicating with the dead (29%), visiting a fortuneteller or psychic (15%), and endorsing reincarnation (24%) (Pew Forum on

Religion and Public Life, 2009). If you doubt these statistics represent the views of highly intelligent and educated people, think again. The frequency of future educators possessing pseudo-scientific beliefs in such topics as the Loch Ness Monster and Big Foot closely parallels that found in the general adult population. These proportions apply even to those individuals indicating an interest in teaching science, including a majority who reported that teaching evolution without discussing divine intervention was patently "false" (Losh & Nzekwe, 2010).

Principle #6—Motivational beliefs differ from motivational knowledge

The probability of ghosts or extraterrestrials appearing in your living room, classroom, or office is slim (except in Area 51, of course). However, it is highly likely you will encounter individuals with a variety of esoteric beliefs about learning and performance (tastefully referred to as "misconceptions" by psychologists). Motivational beliefs are defined as a set of propositions that are accepted as true by an individual, regardless of evidentiary support, and that influence the direction and intensity of effort toward a target. Examples of motivational beliefs include, but are not limited to, the assessment of your own intelligence; challenge you perceive in a specific task; degree of interest you have toward a topic; personal estimates of task value, utility, and importance; and presumed likelihood of successfully completing a task. Individual belief frameworks also consider how we are perceived by others and what criteria others use to assess and value our accomplishments.

The influence of beliefs on motivated behavior is pervasive, especially for teachers. Research affirms that teacher beliefs filter what information is taught to students, how knowledge is framed during a classroom discussion, and which teaching strategies are used by the instructor (Fives & Buehl, 2012). Pragmatically, teacher beliefs determine the goals teachers set for their learners, the effort and perseverance they invest in teaching, and the extent of cognitive engagement with subject matter (Bandura, 1997). Perhaps the most salient aspect of personal beliefs is the resistance to belief change (Vosniadou, 2001), even in the face of disconfirming scientific evidence (Dole & Sinatra, 1998).

Misconceptions develop as a result of learned experiences or observations, when few negative consequences are associated with holding a specific belief (Hynd & Guzzetti, 1993). Misconceptions about motivation become especially murky when the influence of personal emotion supersedes objectivity and individuals embrace ideas despite the availability of clear disconfirming evidence, resulting in what Shermer (2012) called *false beliefs*. Susceptible individuals fall into the emotional trap of wanting to advance convictions based on fact but, instead, rely on strong emotional connections to their championed cause. In the most egregious of circumstances, false beliefs turn into *false enlightenment* (Phillips & Burbules, 2000). In these situations, individuals become so fervently entwined with their skewed interpretations of reality that they begin to consciously and deliberately assert to others the apparent veracity of their contentions.

The annals of history are replete with examples of self-righteous beliefs. Consider Erik the Red sailing 1600 miles from Norway to a barren wasteland and naming it Greenland, or the miscalculating King George III of England who thought taxing the tea of American colonists would imbue loyalty to the mother country. Support of highly partisan beliefs continue to the present day, as evidenced by the unwavering patronage or utter contempt held by some Americans concerning the Affordable Care Act that overhauled the US health care system. Depending upon whom you ask, the law provided needed health coverage to over 7,000,000 previously uninsured Americans or raised the health insurance premiums by 18% to 81%, depending upon the age demographic (www.forbes.com, Forbes, 2013).

Misconceptions are a realistic source of contention for the motivational detective (MD) because the false enlightenment can be so pervasive that it results in accepted paradigms within the seemingly unbiased scientific community. French psychologists and early twentieth century thought-leaders Alfred Binet and Theodore Simon, creators of the first intelligence tests, were vocal proponents of scientific inquiry and gathering empirical evidence to make informed decisions. In their seminal work "Mentally Defective Children" they asserted, "Psychologists are studying the value of evidence, and are thinking out better methods of arriving at truth, in order to discover reforms which may be introduced into the organization of justice" (Binet & Simon, 1914, p. 2). The same pair proceeded to reach the preposterous conclusion that developmentally delayed children could be categorized into two main classes: "feeble-minded" and "ill balanced." Their categorization scheme was based primarily upon behavioral observations, which led them to the appalling conclusion that "the more likeable the child is represented to be, the greater the amount of retardation one may safely attribute to him" (p. 20). Considering the longstanding influence of renowned scientists, such as Binet and Simon (for a marvelous exposition of belief misconceptions and their influence on human history see the classic work "Mismeasure of Man" by Steven J. Gould), it becomes prudent for MDs to distinguish between their own self-serving, socially constructed subjective views and the primary goal of science, which is to objectively pursue knowledge verification through scientific evidence (Shermer, 2002).

The distinction between truth and beliefs is, indeed, a slippery slope. Four frequently encountered scenarios will illustrate my point. Scenario one dictates that you have a belief and hypothesize it to be true. For example, if you stand outside in the rain, you would predict that you would get wet. Soggy evidence will likely confirm your prediction. Let's call this scenario the "sure thing" because the physical evidence of wetness indisputably supports your rain hypothesis. Scenario two asserts that sometimes you embrace a personal truth that is, indeed, false. By example, the absurd theory advanced by Simon and Binet that likeability and retardation were related was based on a conclusion supported by belief, not evidence. Scenario three asserts that truth exists, but we are either preoccupied with alternative ideas or lack the necessary skills or understanding to recognize the truth. Scenario three develops primarily because our personal beliefs act as cognitive and emotional filters obscuring the truth, or secondarily when we are unable or unwilling to interpret available evidence (Chinn & Brewer, 1993). A great example of scenario three is the "discovery" of gravity by Galileo in the early seventeenth century. Galileo asserted that gravity accelerates all objects at the same rate and that differently weighted objects travel at the same speed when falling to the ground. This phenomenon was aptly named the "acceleration hypothesis"; however, gravity was an unrecognized truth before Galileo's experimentation. Most of the medieval populace, like many current learners, possessed misconceptions about weight and inertia similar to the hackneyed debate about what falls to the ground faster, a pound of feathers or a pound of bricks (Chi, 2005; Lair & Cook, 2011). The delay in embracing the acceleration hypothesis clearly did not mean that the physical properties of matter were nonexistent; they were merely *unrecognized*. Finally, we will encounter scenario four, illustrated by early human attempts to emulate avian flight. There was no truth to affirm the belief that human flight was possible, and fortunately, most of the populace recognized that humans could not fly. Unfortunately, many would-be aviators needed *hard* evidence to modify their false beliefs. Going forward, I highlight the differences between our own motivational beliefs and scientific knowledge, as illustrated by scenario three, keeping in mind that many individuals will harbor profound beliefs despite available evidence to the contrary.

Pragmatically, untangling the impact of beliefs on the motivated action of a particular person can be a daunting task, even for the most seasoned scholars of motivational science. The dilemma of ardently embracing biased conceptions and harboring unwavering beliefs despite verified evidence is perhaps best illustrated by the ubiquitous media portrayal of the enigmatic financier Bernard "Bernie" Madoff. Arguably, no other person's story in the annals of financial history is more contentious than that of Madoff. In 2008, confronted by voluminous amounts of indisputable incriminating evidence, Madoff confessed to masterminding the largest financial scheme in the history of mankind, which at the time federal prosecutors estimated defrauded investors out of $65 billion (Bandler & Varchaver, 2009). On June 9, 2009, he was sentenced to 150 years in a federal prison. However, are the predominantly villainous conceptions of Madoff based upon beliefs or sound, justified evidence? At face value, the story of Bernie Madoff seems like one of greed and corruption, with newspaper accounts of his sordid behavior resulting in the financial ruin of thousands of investors (Smith, 2010). However, there is more to know about Bernie that has not been accurately depicted in the popular media.

In reality, the federal investigation that produced objective and verified evidence revealed the surprising discovery that Madoff actually returned most, if not all, of the investment principal entrusted to him. Although the case details are inconsequential to the study of motivated behavior, fear of criminal implication convinced certain wealthy investors to return $9 billion to the case trustee that had been prematurely withdrawn in violation of trust agreements with Madoff. In total, $14 billion was recovered by the case trustee. Despite the inflated value of $65 billion of investor losses still reported in the press and on the Internet to this day, the official and allowed client losses were valued at $7 billion, as determined by the US Government Accountability Office, discounting the popular misconceived belief concerning the financial impact of Madoff's transgressions (United States Government Accountability Office, 2012).

Ironically, the knowledge-or-belief dilemma was a motivating force in Madoff's fateful decision to circumvent security laws and engage in risky economic transactions.

Motivational Leader—*Bernard Madoff*

Bernard (Bernie) Lawrence Madoff grew up in Laurelton, Queens, and like many of his peers aspired to the American dream of success and financial security. The only son of first-generation American parents, Bernie's father managed a sporting goods business, while his mother tended to the home. After graduating from Far Rockaway High School in 1956, Bernie attended the University of Alabama for a year, before transferring to Hofstra University, where he graduated with a BA in Political Science. At the behest of his father, Bernie reluctantly attended Brooklyn Law School for a year, before taking the $500 he saved from his summer job as a life guard to start his own brokerage firm. Suddenly, the life of Bernie Madoff became far from ordinary.

Starting his own investment firm required meeting statutory and legal requirements, including approval from the US Securities and Exchange Commission (SEC). Bernie explained "at the time the SEC was so amazed that I had the nerve to start with so little capital that they required I undergo an interview with their staff" (B. Madoff, personal communication, August 14, 2014). Bernie agreed to the SEC interview and eventually grew his initial $500 investment into $900 million by 2008, all through legitimate investments and securities trading, completely separate and unrelated to his vilified arbitrage and investment advisory business reported by the press.

Bernie went from an obscure law school dropout to begin an illustrious 45-year march toward the pinnacle of professional and financial success, building massive wealth for himself, his family, and his celebrity clients. Along the way, the brilliant Bernie Madoff assumed leadership positions in the world's largest and most respected organizations, serving in many senior executive roles and corporate advisory positions, including as Chairman of the NASDAQ stock exchange and member of the board of directors of the National Association of Security Dealers. Bernie was internationally recognized as an innovative financial genius, as evidenced by his appointments to regulatory and industry positions, including as the Chairman of the National Securities Clearing Corporation, Chairman of the Depository Trust Company, Vice Chairman of the Securities Industry Association, and member of the SEC advisory committee, with most appointments lasting for up to 10 years.

Although receiving minimal publicity, Bernie was highly philanthropic, donating time and millions of dollars to multiple organizations. He served on the boards of the NYC Ballet, Hofstra University, and the Yeshiva University, where he also served as Chairman of the Board for the Yeshiva School of Business. In addition, he was the founder of the Long Island and North Shore Hospital in New Hyde Park, NY, and, along with his wife Ruth, managed the Madoff Family Foundation, a charity organization recently valued at $19 million.

In Madoff's case, the false enlightenment that often accompanies entrenchment of unwarranted beliefs was instrumental in his professional demise. Madoff mistakenly harbored the false belief that demonstrating exceptional ability was more important than moral integrity or fiduciary responsibility. In Madoff's case, generating massive returns on investments for clients and earning the perception of financial wizardry superseded rational decision making. Madoff indicated, "I allowed the greed of a few clients to head me down a path that while I knew was dangerous and wrong, my inherent insecurity and wish to always please overcame my realization of the risk I took to please others." Commenting on his personal motivation, he added that his behaviors were "to both please my clients and demonstrate my financial ability" (B. Madoff, personal communication, September 25, 2014).

Although clearly Madoff was highly motivated for success, he was obviously influenced by deeply entrenched self-beliefs that manifested in questionable business practices. He followed misguided ethics according to the normative values and beliefs of most cultures. In retrospect, Madoff realized how his flawed thinking based upon faulty beliefs resulted in his pattern of corruption. His contrition continues to this day, as he told me, "Please understand that I am in no way suggesting the recovery of my client's principal excuses the pain and suffering I have caused, nor does it eliminate the remorse that I suffer daily" (B. Madoff, personal communication, August 14, 2014). The intimate glimpse into Madoff's motives is one stellar example of the power of self-beliefs (discussed throughout the text), conceptions which may or may not be based on sound and verifiable evidence.

Principle #7—Motivational evidence can only answer certain questions

Although the famous philosopher Karl Popper (1963) proclaimed that "there are no ultimate sources of knowledge" (p. 54), some sources of knowledge are, indeed, more reliable than others. First, knowledge can originate through individual experience; nevertheless, this type of knowledge is usually biased and limited in scope. Personal knowledge is filtered through the mind of the beholder, is frequently subjective, and cannot be duplicated by others under similar circumstances. Second, knowledge can be based upon cultural tradition; however, traditional knowledge is potentially flawed, as it is largely based upon collective experience and, in essence, resembles personal knowledge in that it lacks veracity of origin or replication. Third, knowledge can be authority based and predicated upon the power of the knowledge originator. Dictated knowledge is typically transient and self-serving to meet the needs of the entity initiating the knowledge, as evidenced by the goal of race annihilation at the whims of ruthless dictators throughout history. Fourth, the source of knowledge most relevant for the scientific study of motivation is described as "justified" knowledge. Justification implies that the knowledge will survive empirical scrutiny, it can be replicated under controlled conditions, and, if true, the knowledge can be analyzed and applied without bias or subjectivity.

Most definitions of knowledge include three important components: truth, belief, and evidence (Southerland, Sinatra, & Matthews, 2001). A prerequisite to verify truth is the ability to evaluate a belief rationally against an external and objective evidentiary standard. A personal belief, sometimes called a *proposition*, is the conviction that a set of rules, evaluations, or circumstances are assumed to be true (Southerland et al., 2001). Evidence is information gathered and evaluated objectively and systematically. The evidence can be replicated and verified while ruling out other plausible interpretations. If the evidence is subjective or cannot be externally verified, we describe the belief as *unjustified* (Sinatra & Seyranian, in press), lacking sufficient substance to classify the evidence as knowledge. If sufficient evidence is gathered, and other plausible explanations can be ruled out, we warrant the evidence as knowledge with explanatory power, otherwise known as a *justified true belief* (Gettier, 1963).

Sometimes providing learners with concrete evidence helps clarify the distinction between knowledge and beliefs. One important principle of cognition is the realization that humans have information processing limitations. Students usually acknowledge that there are restrictions to the amount of information they can hold in their heads at any one time; this restriction is known as *working memory capacity*. If you have ever tried to remember someone's phone number while also being asked directions, you will quickly realize the limitations of your working memory. When I teach, I ask students to turn off their cell phones and refrain from texting during class. Invariably, some learners do not heed my warning and text anyway. Fortunately, my warning has sinister intentions and results in a fantastic teaching opportunity when someone texts in class. Typically, when caught texting, learners quickly affirm, contrary to most scientific evidence, that they have the unique ability to multi-task and usually swear they can text and pay attention simultaneously. The first question I ask after students make this resounding proclamation about multi-tasking is, "How do you know?" Typically, learners proceed to recount various examples of personal experience, indicating how they believe they can complete multiple tasks simultaneously. Multi-tasking, however, is one of many "urban legends" in education (Kirschner & van Merrienboer, 2013, p. 169) that is quickly dispelled by evidence. To make my point, I merely ask the student to recite the alphabet using a normal speaking pace and write the letters of the alphabet *simultaneously*. The outcome is usually unintelligible writing, or an alphabet recital that resembles a geriatric moose signaling its mate. This strategy usually does the trick and changes their beliefs about multi-tasking because learners fail at the task (go ahead, try it yourself, and then see if you can lick your elbow). Typically, the results from these amusing scenarios show that working memory is limited and that personal experience has limited explanatory power. This teaching scenario easily launches a discussion of what questions can be answered by scientific inquiry, while driving home the distinction between justified knowledge and beliefs.

Once future MDs realize the power of belief-bias, they are then able to successfully address the need for scientific inquiry as the source of knowledge. Although there is little consensus on the perfect process to conduct scientific inquiry (Shermer, 2002), most experimental regimens include making predictions, gathering evidence, analyzing data, and reaching plausible inferences about what the data means, while ruling out plausible rival hypotheses. By using systematic data collection and interpretation, knowledge is warranted, or certified, and defensible on methodological grounds, avoiding conclusions based upon perception, opinion, or conjecture. In other words, how knowledge is attained and disseminated will, in part, determine the validity of the knowledge.

The premise of fallibility dictates that knowledge is transient and always subject to revision (Phillips & Burbules, 2000). Justified knowledge must have the ability to be falsified by disconfirming evidence. Knowledge without contradiction has little explanatory power because it is stagnant. A stagnant theory cannot evolve by experimentation, nor can it be debunked. The pink elephant dilemma may convince you of the necessity of my fallibility contention. Most justified knowledge about elephants universally describes the animals as large, gray, sometimes tusked mammals with big floppy ears, equipped with a long proboscis designed to extract peanuts from small children, tourists, and the palms of zoologists. My elephant hypothesis suggests that pink polka dot elephants may exist but have yet to be discovered. My hypothesis is contrary to the justified knowledge that elephants only come in 50 shades of gray. *Today*, my outlandish idea is only an unjustified belief because no pink polka dot elephants have ever been observed. But is my hypothesis false? Does this mean no polka dot elephants exist? Surely, it is *possible* that one day we will discover pink polka dot elephants. Perhaps, our visually acuity is insufficient for us to see the polka dots that are already there. Thus, the theory of gray elephants can potentially be falsified and subsequently evolve. Today, we can rule out other plausible interpretations of the elephant data and reasonably infer that all elephants are, indeed, shades of gray, until an alternative hue of pachyderm is unearthed. Knowing that my theory is viable and testable, all the knowledge from the theory is warranted with explanatory power.

Now, we have illuminated the three foundational premises necessary to evaluate scientific inferences. Recapping, we should first verify the source of the knowledge; next, we must determine if the knowledge is justified or not; and finally, we should closely examine whether or not our inquiry can meet the falsification test. If these three criteria are met, we can confidently proceed and determine what questions can or cannot be answered by motivational science. Table 2.1 describes actual inquiries meeting the three principles of inquiry, along with some provocative situations that we shall encounter as we elaborate on the scientific evidence that explains motivation for learning and performance throughout the remainder of the book.

The answer to every question in the left-hand column of Table 2.1 is "yes." Although you may debate the veracity of these findings based upon your own personal beliefs, each finding is supported by objective evidence warranting a justified knowledge conclusion. The studies cited all used rigorous scientific methods to rule out alternative explanations before reaching conclusions. Although the answers to all of the questions are affirmative, we should be cautious not to generalize these findings beyond the scope of the research question. The answers are warranted only for the specific situation described. The questions in the right-hand column of the table represent questions that cannot be answered through scientific inquiry. Answers to these questions are largely subjective (cake or fruit), unethical to investigate (anger and suicide), or impossible to measure using existing research methods (ancestry). Cognizant of the unique evaluation criteria needed to evaluate motivational research, we turn to the evidence and see precisely what practical inferences can be confidently made.

Table 2.1 Examples of what questions motivational science can and cannot answer

Inquiries motivational science CAN answer	Source	Inquiries motivational science CANNOT answer
Can we predict if mentally preoccupied people prefer cake or fruit?	Shiv and Fedorikhin (2002)	Does cake taste better than fruit?
Do monetary rewards lead to less effective work performance?	Ariely, Gneezy, Loewenstein, and Mazar (2005)	Do professional athletes prefer higher earnings or fame?
Can biological evidence substantiate evolution?	Geary (2008)	Were our distant relatives apes?
Do future teachers believe in zombies and ghosts?	Losh and Nzekwe (2010)	Are zombies and ghosts real?
Do people make better decisions when angry or calm?	Moons and Mackie (2007)	Are angry people more likely to commit suicide?
Can certain written words promote happiness in others?	Kloumann, Danforth, Harris, Bliss, and Dodds (2012)	Is this the best book about motivation ever written?

Principle #8—Motivation is related to learning and performance but causality is an uncertainty

Terrell Howard Bell, former Secretary of Education in the Ronald Reagan administration, had a clear vision about education. Bell claimed that there were only three things necessary to ensure effective education. The first was motivation, the second was motivation, and the third was motivation! However, can we reliably conclude that motivation is the cure for everything that ails education? Probably not (this is a research question methodologically impossible to answer), although thousands of studies have investigated the relationship between motivation and a variety of learning and performance variables.

Ideally, when investigating motivation, the MD seeks to determine the causality of behavior. Armed with knowledge of what factors result in specific behaviors, the investigator can determine appropriate strategies to mediate the undesirable behavior or sustain that which is desired. Although the ultimate goal is behavioral change, sometimes only behavioral consequences, not motives, are addressed. For example, one of the most frequent issues with which teachers wrestle in the classroom is academic procrastination (Katz, Eilot, & Nevo, 2013), where a resounding 75–90% of undergraduate college students are estimated to delay completing academic tasks, such as homework (Steel, 2007). Typical solutions used to address the homework problem include giving extra credit for timely completion of work, granting special privileges to homework completers, or perhaps overemphasizing the role of homework when determining course grades. However, none of these "solutions" actually addresses the reasons underlying academic procrastination, including questionable beliefs about learner competency, lack of interest in the subject, or the perception of a controlling teaching environment and loss of autonomy. Teachers addressing academic procrastination with incentives may successfully change behavior, but rewards do little to address *why* students fail to complete homework in the first place.

The homework dilemma brings to the forefront one of the most salient issues when interpreting scientific evidence: establishing a clear interpretive distinction between correlation and causality. The homework example suggested that certain factors cause procrastination, while teacher incentives, such as grades, are associated with reducing academic procrastination. My favorite example of the difference between causality and correlation is a variation on Stanovich's claim that appliance ownership can influence birth control (Stanovich, 2013). As many people know, most single people only need a two-slice toaster because they live alone and must regulate their carbohydrate intake to maintain positive self-esteem. Four or six slice toasters are reserved for people with families, restaurants, and school cafeteria lunch ladies. Thus, there is a positive association between family size and type of toaster. However, I sincerely hope you don't believe that smaller toasters reduce fertility! In fact, there are more plausible explanations for a large family size than the girth of your toaster. The proclivity for snap judgments creates vulnerability to accept potentially *spurious* interpretations of data, which happens when you falsely assume the influence of one factor on another. Wrongly attributing causality to a correlational relationship masks the true causal factor underlying the behavior of interest and creates a situation ripe for misinterpretation. Now upgrade your toaster, or at least read Stanovich's exceptional book *How to Think Straight about Psychology*.

Due to a variety of methodological issues, the bulk of motivational research is correlational. This doesn't mean that certain motivational variables cannot be identified as casual factors; instead, it means that the nature of motivational research is not conducive to experimental research that seeks to investigate causality. Motivation has been linked to literally dozens of variables, including some highly influential in learning and performance. Maehr and Meyer (1997) in their assessment of the state of motivational research at the time listed over two dozen factors related to adaptive motivation, including persistence, learning, achievement, creativity, effort invested in learning, positive emotions, school interest, and, of course, the quality of student knowledge. Not surprisingly, classrooms that comprise learners with high academic motivation have fewer classroom management issues, promote a stronger sense of learning community, and support a context of focused learner engagement (Ames, 1990; Perry, Turner, & Meyer, 2006).

More recent research broadly examines individual motivation and strategy differences among individuals. Studies frequently investigate the role of socioeconomic factors, culture, and other contextual and social influences on learning and performance outcomes. The common thread throughout these studies is understanding how interactivity among motivational variables influences optimal motivation for learning and performance. Perhaps, the most significant revelation is the idea of reciprocity between learning outcomes and sustaining personal beliefs about motivation (Schunk, Pintrich, & Meece, 2008). As students encounter success in learning, motivation to learn is enhanced. Students begin to believe in their own success and gain confidence that the strategies they use are influential in the learning process. When the learning strategies lead to success, students are motivated to continue using the effective strategy. Reciprocally, learner perception of content mastery leads to reaching academic goals, further improving motivation. The reciprocal relationship becomes a powerful cycle for the success of the student. Reciprocity can be equally devastating when students develop counterproductive beliefs and exhibit maladaptive motivation patterns when learning obstacles or failures are encountered. Although these findings imply causality, only under rare circumstances should we confidently conclude that one factor actually *causes* the other to happen.

Principle #9—Motivation is subordinate to character and personality

What's so different about character, personality, and motivation? Speaking about character, the irreverent author Mark Twain believed that every person is like a moon, with a dark side shown to no one. As explained in Principle #5 (p. 12), Twain's comments echo the introspective and sometimes opaque nature of how *Homo sapiens* portray themselves to the external world. Each of the above elements contribute to how we think, feel, and express ourselves, but distinct differences exist among the three constructs. "Character" and "personality" are frequently conflated, with the terms sometimes used interchangeably throughout the social psychology and personality literature. The primary distinction between character and personality revolves around qualitative judgments of the patterns of behaviors that define an individual. "Character" implies arbitrary standards and culturally specific evaluations indicating that some attributes are morally or socially preferred to others (Doris, 2002). Character is frequently studied by examining how people rationalize behavioral choices. For example, you see a parent smack a misbehaving child at the mall. As a bystander, should you intercede and admonish the outraged parent and say that his or her behavior is unacceptable? Does the parent have a reprehensible character because of how the child was disciplined? The parent's decision and the evaluator's moral code would provide insight into the person's character. Unfortunately, the "theory" of character is problematic and easily falsified when individuals with seemingly "good" character display culturally unorthodox behavior. Examples of character gone haywire include the 2013 sexting fiasco of former democratic Congressman Anthony Weiner, who repeatedly sent lewd photos of himself to random women online, even after resigning from US Congress, or the outlandish conduct of beleaguered Toronto mayor Rob Ford, who openly glorified crack cocaine use to his constituents and the highly interested media.

Personality, a more frequently researched construct than character, was defined by Cattell (1950) as "that which permits a prediction of what a person will do in a given situation" (p. 2). However, the prediction business is quite risky because of the lack of constancy in behaviors both within and between individuals. The same people react differently in similar situations, different people respond similarly in similar situations, and different people react differently to same event. The question then becomes what accounts for the differences within and between individuals, and why is behavior so inconsistent? Corr, DeYoung, and McNaughton (2013) appeased this contentious reality by suggesting that "in order to answer this *why* question, we must discover what drives people's actions and reactions" (p. 158), leading us back on the seemingly circular path to motivation as an explanation of behavior.

The most widely accepted and empirically supported personality framework is the five-factor model, aptly named the "Big Five" (John, Naumann, & Soto, 2008). The model distinguishes five expansive dimensions of personality, primarily measured through observation and self-report inventories: Openness (O), Conscientiousness (C), Extraversion (E), Agreeableness (A), and Neuroticism (N). Each factor represents a series of *traits*, some of which are correlated with academic motivation, most notably social interaction among learners (Zeidner, 2009). The classroom and the boardroom provide robust environments to observe the expression of personality traits, as individuals frequently work in teams, necessitating regular interpersonal communication. Logically, individuals high in (A) and (C) typically demonstrate attributes necessary for project success, including willingness to agree, control of personal impulses, more regulated and predictable affect, and a pronounced helping orientation toward others (John et al., 2008). Table 2.2 lists definitions and behaviors associated with the "Big Five" personality dimensions.

Perhaps the most relevant contribution of personality theory to the study of motivation is the enacted bias of individuals high in (E) who consistently display behaviors indicative of active engagement. The (E) personality exemplifies energy, enthusiasm, and sociability, all qualities found to predict academic and vocational success. However, important developmental trajectories (see Chapter 4) are noted in the evolution of (E), suggesting an inverse relationship between age and extraversion—that is, as people age they become more introverted. The decrease in extraversion is largely a function of the highly competitive environment students encounter in middle school and beyond (Zeidner, 2009), conditions that are frequently perpetuated in the workplace through performance incentive systems. The expressive inclinations described above are important because of their relation to achievement but minimally explain the nature of individual motives and provide little causal explanation for demonstrated behaviors (Corr et al., 2013).

Personality and motivation are both exemplified by a series of behavioral patterns. Motivation is subordinate to personality, more situational, transient, and just one of many influences on personality. The description of the "Big Five" dimensions as traits suggests a generalized tendency for individuals to exhibit behaviors that are consistent and predictable. However traits, like motives, can either be enduring or transient depending on the person (see Principle #4, p. 11). For example, students typically confident in their mathematics ability and accustomed to solving problems accurately without restrictions may develop temporary performance anxiety when forced to solve problems under time constraints (Hoffman, 2010). Conversely, mathematics anxiety can be a static and stable trait of the individual, experienced across a broad variety of environments (Miller & Bischel, 2004) and less amenable to intervention (Chen, Gully, Whiteman, & Kilcullen, 2006). Regardless, even the most anxious individual will exude an aura of contentment and confidence under optimal conditions. Stability suggests a personality connotation, whereas transience implies motive. In either case, we must acknowledge that traits, like motives, will vary according to the context of observation (Cloninger, 2009) and that neither can be predicted with complete accuracy.

Table 2.2 Definition and explication of the "Big Five"

Factor	Extraversion	Agreeableness	Conscientiousness	Neuroticism	Openness
Verbal labels	Energy Enthusiasm	Altruism Affection	Constraint Control of impulse	Negative Emotionality Nervousness	Originality Open-mindedness
Conceptual definition	Implies an energetic approach toward the social and material world and includes such traits as sociability, activity, assertiveness, and positive emotionality.	Contrasts a prosocial and communal orientation toward others with antagonism and includes such traits as altruism, tender-mindedness, trust, and modesty.	Describes socially prescribed impulse control that facilitates task- and goal-directed behaviors, such as thinking before acting; delaying gratification; following norms and rules; and planning, organizing, and prioritizing tasks.	Contrasts emotional stability and even-temperedness with negative emotionality, such as feeling anxious, nervous, sad, and tense.	Describes the breadth, depth, originality, and complexity of an individual's mental and experiential life.
Positive behavioral examples	Approach strangers at a party and introduce myself; take the lead in organizing a project; keep quiet when I disagree with others.	Emphasize the good qualities of other people when I talk about them; lend things to people I know; console a friend who is upset.	Arrive early or on time for appointments. Study hard in order to get the highest grade in class; double-check a term paper for typing and spelling errors.	Accept the good and the bad in my life without complaining or bragging. Get upset when somebody is angry with me. Take it easy and relax.	Take the time to learn something for the joy of learning; watch documentaries on TV; come up with novel setups for my living space; look for stimulating activities that break up the routine.

Reprinted with permission of John, Naumann, & Soto from Paradigm shift to the integrative Big Five trait taxonomy: History, measurement, and conceptual issue. In O. P. John, R. W. Robins & L. A. Pervin (Eds.), *Handbook of Personality: Theory and Research*, (pp. 114–158). © 2008 Guilford Press. Reprinted with permission of The Guilford Press.

Principle #10—Motivation is the responsibility of leaders and can be taught

Considering the conundrum in deciphering the difference between beliefs and knowledge, combined with the uncertainty as to what causes motivation and personality, you might be a wee bit skeptical that "motivation" can actually be taught. The prevalence of university motivation courses, combined with a walk down the self-help aisle of any bookstore minimally attests to at least a broad interest in the topic of motivation. A random search of the world's largest marketplace, Amazon.com, during January 2015 using the keyword "motivation" revealed an astounding 191,490 books or products in the motivation category! Perhaps the more relevant question, with a potentially more elusive answer, is how to teach motivation. Is it realistic for us to believe that we can change the deeply entrenched beliefs that guide behavioral decisions? The answer to the question is a resounding "yes," as responsibility for explicitly teaching motivation falls to the classroom teacher (Alderman, 2004), the aspiring business leader (Cummings, 2014), and the athletic coach (Berinato, 2013).

The first step in the process of teaching motivation is modeling interest and enthusiasm toward the topic you teach. Sadly, I have seen dozens of training professionals and teachers lacking even basic enthusiasm during instruction. Hallmark behaviors of negative models are those exerting obligatory effort or taking a compliant approach to instruction. Comments, such as, "We need to discuss evolutionary science today because it's required curriculum, but I don't really believe in evolution," or "I don't agree with this new policy, but we have to follow it anyway" will quickly alienate learners and cultivate passive engagement and behavioral apathy due to the learners' perception of the educator's lack of interest in or low evaluation of the content.

Brophy (2004), specifically addressing classroom learning, suggested that the starting place for stimulating motivation for learning is to capitalize on the existing motivational dispositions of learners. The term *dispositions* refers to the insights, skills, and values that influence behavior. Brophy advocated that through modeling and clear communication of expectations, along with specific and detailed content feedback, academic motivation can be accelerated because the teacher can make personal connections with the learner. Brophy also made an important distinction concerning how motivation is taught. One can teach specific conceptual skills and strategies directly, but values and learner insights should be consciously addressed as well.

Borrowing strategies from the literature on conceptual change, discussed in detail in Chapter 12 (p. 345), we know that changing beliefs is challenging and potentially frustrating for the person promoting change. Even when learners express openness to change and espouse a willingness to modify beliefs, change may be fleeting and shallow (Dole & Sinatra, 1998). Realistically, we should operate under the primary premise that students and scientists alike will blatantly reject data inconsistent with their current ideologies (Chinn & Brewer, 1993) and expect that old conceptions will not easily die but, instead, gradually fade away. Mere presentation of anomalous evidence that challenges existing beliefs is insufficient because data may be challenged on the grounds of inaccuracy (bad measurement or interpretive practices), the source of origination (some sources are more credible that others), or applicability (e.g., you are correct, but your belief doesn't apply to me in "this" situation). Although customized strategies to teach specific aspects of motivated behavior are outlined in Chapter 12, changing beliefs can and should first be addressed in a more general way. The road to belief enlightenment starts with an explicit focus on understanding how learners view the creation and application of their own knowledge. But first, are you conscious of your own beliefs? Do you recognize the origin and pattern of knowledge building? What models do you use to evaluate and subsequently certify your own knowledge? Polonius, the mythical counselor in Shakespeare's Hamlet, sternly warned Laertes (Hamlet's nemesis and eventual killer), "To thine own self be true," stressing the importance of self-awareness of motives. Being true begins with the informed and objective approach of analyzing our own beliefs before we can ever expect to understand and potentially influence the beliefs of others.

Principle #11—Theoretically, motivated behavior operates on a continuum

Analyzing our own beliefs starts with having a theory. The purpose of a theory is to serve as a baseline or benchmark of established knowledge providing researchers and MDs with a platform to test the validity of new knowledge. As new evidence is amassed and empirically tested, the theory will either be supported or refuted by the data. Theories that are most useful to consumers of motivation research are those that offer viable explanations of motivated behavior that can be applied across contexts, cultures, and people. Since personal motivation is a fluid, situational, and malleable collection of actions and strategies, a theory should offer a comprehensive lens that explains both the antecedents and the consequences of actions across a wide spectrum of exhibited behavior. Two theories highly useful to explain motivated behavior are the Theory of Knowledge Acquisition proposed by Reynolds, Sinatra, and Jetton (1996) and Organismic Integration Theory conceived by Ryan and Deci (2000). Both views examine the breadth of motivated behavior and describe observations along a continuum, emphasizing that behavior progressively evolves based upon contextual influences and the degree of individual self-regulation and reflection.

The continuum crafted by Reynolds et al. (1996) was not intended to explain learner motivation but, instead, explains how knowledge and beliefs are acquired and represented in the mind. Although we are not interested in learning theory per se, the reciprocal linkages between learning and motivation described earlier can be symptomatic of underlying motivations as to why and how learners seek knowledge; this will contribute to a clearer understanding of observed performance. The continuum posited by Reynolds et al. (1996) serves as an adaptive model to explain potential links between motivation and the process of knowledge acquisition. Five orientations are described, classified along the dichotomy of "centeredness" suggesting that ultimately knowledge can be either "experienced" or "created." On one end of the spectrum, individuals are highly polarized in their views of the world, believing that knowledge is absolute in the way it is constructed. In the simplest form, knowledge is merely a series of stimulus–response bonds that result in uniform behavior. In other words, one thing consistently leads to another. Individuals that display this learning orientation are merely a function of what they have encountered in life, demonstrating little ability to consider divergent views or accept alternate conceptions of knowledge. This polarized experience-centered perspective discounts the influence of social motives and the ability of individuals to creatively problem-solve and reason when encountering unorthodox or unfamiliar situations. From a motivational perspective, embracing the experience-centered perspective can often mean limited interest, or even potential contempt, for diversity of thought.

The opposing end of the Reynolds et al. (1996) knowledge continuum is described as mind centered, with individuals applying meaning to the world through active integration of purposeful cognitive representations formed through social experience. Individuals with a mind-centered orientation also represent knowledge acquisition as a function of environmental interaction, but unlike the experience-centered individual, the mind-centered individual adapts and changes conceptions situationally. Those with a mind-centered orientation are strongly influenced by the culture of their existence, showing less rigidity in thought and action. Mind-centered individuals exercise more volition in their worldly endeavors, demonstrate less passivity, and do not readily accepting the *status quo*. Like the experience-centered person, beliefs are equally as prominent; however, the caliber of beliefs of the mind-centered individual shows a greater openness and willingness to influence the world, as opposed to the acceptance orientation of the experience-centered individual.

The second continuum, proposed by Ryan and Deci (2000), is rooted in one of the most prominent orientations to explain motivated behavior, Self-Determination Theory (SDT). The theory, discussed in detail in Chapter 6 (p. 139), emphasizes that individuals have three prominent needs that must be satisfied for optimal motivation: competence, autonomy, and relatedness. Competence implies that individuals are energized through self-assessments and self-reflections of their personal capabilities and are confident in their own knowledge and abilities. In order to meet the need of competence, individuals must also perceive the ability to exercise free will, or autonomy, in order to demonstrate their competence. Demonstrating autonomy allows free expression of behaviors as a means for the individual to feel self-determined and not controlled by the context of their efforts. Relatedness is the tendency to seek external validation or recognition from others as the person exhibits competence by exercising autonomy. Feeling self-determined and successful in executing actions is, in part, influenced by the ability to gather social support for personal effort. Ryan and Deci caution, as outlined in Principle #7 (p. 26), that SDT is not causal but, instead, describes the conditions and circumstances necessary to develop and sustain self-determination.

The continuum proposed by Ryan and Deci is designed to illustrate the incremental and regulatory nature of motivated behavior, which outlines the distinction between individuals who are self-motivated in comparison to those who rely on external influences as the reason for their actions. The crux of a long line of confirming research suggests that individuals judiciously expend energy toward a goal because of two reasons: (1) the internal value of the goal or (2) external coercion and incentives. The regulatory nature of motivation indicates that contingent upon the underlying reason for selecting and approaching a task, individuals will demonstrate varying levels of commitment, intensity, interest, and strategies in pursuit of a goal. Ideally, individuals who pursue tasks based totally upon personal choice will be highly committed to reaching their goal and persistent in overcoming obstacles. Conversely, those individuals who select and value a task only because it is required, expected, or rewarded will display behaviors ranging from apathy to drudgery. Task completion has marginal meaning and is generally perceived as unavoidable to accomplish other more satisfying objectives.

The paradigms introduced above illustrate the range of motives and the spectrum of beliefs that can undermine motivated behavior. The explanations provided by each perspective are well supported by warranted evidence with explanatory power. However, these views are by no means universal, exclusive, or as simplistic as described. We can infer from these primary principles that individuals use specific frameworks or mental orientations that determine how they approach tasks and navigate the world. Each framework will be accompanied by a repertoire of complementary behavioral strategies designed to meet specific objectives. The motives described and the strategies deemed effective will change based upon numerous social and contextual factors. The variability suggests, at least idealistically, that for each task, there is an ideal set of motivations and corresponding strategies. If true, then perhaps the goal of all teachers, leaders, and coaches should be to orchestrate social and contextual conditions that promote optimal motivation. But is there such a thing?

Principle #12—Optimal motivation is obtainable

I have a proposition for you. I am going to *hypothetically* give you $300,000,000, provided you complete one simple task; all you have to do is spend $30,000,000 in 30 days. There is a caveat, however: You may tell no one that you inherited your fortune, and you cannot waste any money or show any assets from your spending spree. This formidable challenge, which appears easy at first glance, is actually the premise of a 1985 movie called *Brewster's Millions*, starring John Candy and Richard Pryor. Brewster is totally absorbed in his quest to diligently spend the money and will stop at nothing to reach his goal despite the many humorous obstacles he encounters on his lavish spending spree.

From a motivational perspective, Brewster exemplified the type of drive, focus, and determination that we yearn for in school and at work. Brewster demonstrated "optimal performance," a state in which an individual blocks out external distractions and dedicates all available attentional, cognitive, and motivational resources to the task at hand. Distractions can be a huge obstacle, shifting our attention from a task, even when we are highly motivated to complete the task. Distractions that interfere with optimal performance may include environmental factors, such audience noise or uncomfortable temperatures; physical factors, such as poor health or lack of sleep; and emotional and cognitive instigators, such as anxiety, worry, doubt, and other feelings of inferiority. All of these might interfere with an unwavering focus on the task. In the face of cognitive and affective intrusions, performance can suffer dramatically, unless the individual deliberately and consciously recognizes the source of the disruption and uses a series of strategies to offset the interference.

Sometimes known as being "in the zone," the phenomenon of peak performance has been scrupulously investigated across disciplines to identify under which conditions individuals are able to achieve results that demonstrate "the superior use of human potential" (Privette, 1981, p. 51). Perhaps there is no better example of being in the zone than the 38-point game-winning performance of Michael Jordan in the 1997 NBA finals. Jordan was battling food poisoning, nearing collapse, and had been confined to bed rest during the 48 hours before the game. Doctors insisted it was impossible for Jordan to play due to severe dehydration and weight loss. Despite their warnings, Jordan emerged from his bed with a high fever, just 2 hours before start time. Playing 44 out of 48 possible minutes, he led his team to a last-minute victory on a miraculous fade away three-point jump shot. After making the game-winning score, he collapsed from physical and mental exhaustion into the arms of teammate Scottie Pippin. Jordan enhanced his legendary status and, in turn, provided us with a great benchmark of determination, demonstrating the influence of motivation on performance.

Substantial debate prevails across disciplines as to the definition, components, and contextual conditions necessary for optimal performance, especially when identifying which motivational components, if any, drive episodes of superior functioning (Hallett, 2011). The Jordan example illustrates the phenomenon known as "peak performance" that occurs when an individual accesses, selects, and flawlessly executes skills needed to complete a task on demand and while under high-stakes pressure to deliver results (Hallett & Hoffman, 2014). Performance tasks in the workplace, such as consulting, selling, and presenting, are tasks that might require peak performance to ensure success, while high-stakes classroom testing best represents the type of condition that necessitates optimization in the classroom. Fictitious and athletic performances are intriguing examples but provide little substance as to the precise skills or environment needed to cultivate optimal motivation.

Research in psychology and education focuses on a variety of contextual, affective, and cognitive factors that contribute to "optimal experience," "flow" (Csikszentmihalyi, 1997), or "cognitive and motivational efficiency" (Hoffman & Schraw, 2010). Collectively, the terms represent a series of prerequisite attributes, goals, emotions, and conditions needed if individuals wish to maximize performance while regulating their cognitive and motivational resources in a quest to achieve desired results. Flow theory maintains that during the course of everyday living, individuals will encounter a variety of tasks and events conducive to achieving "optimal experience." The quality of the experience is measured by factors that include the degree of motivation, concentration, creativity, satisfaction, and relaxation that individuals report when completing a task (Csikszentmihalyi & LeFevre, 1989). One criterion necessary to achieve optimal experience is to have suitable opportunities to act upon and use one's abilities. The experience includes an intentional focus of cognitive energy toward a task that has sufficient challenge for the individual, based upon his or her existing skill set. Tasks that are too difficult will impede "flow" because overly challenging tasks have the potential to induce anxiety, worry, or doubt concerning the ability to complete the task. Overly easy tasks will hinder flow because individuals may become bored or apathetic toward a task that has no perceived potential for challenge or excitement. Task feedback is an important component in the quest to maintain flow; that is, the individual must have a perception of success in order to maintain flow. Feedback includes the internal generation of positive feelings while performing the task but can also include external markers, such as making progress in completing a puzzle or realizing you have answered a test question correctly. In all cases, the flow experience requires the ability to set clear task goals, approach a task with skills commensurate to the challenge, and an inherent task mechanism that enables the participant to calibrate his or her task effectiveness.

If the conditional aspects of flow are met, the individual becomes fully engaged in task completion, blocking out any motivational or cognitive intrusions. Individuals experiencing flow report a loss of time sensation. The flow experience is exemplified by a sense of deliberate and focused consciousness, thereby insulating the individual from negative ruminations and distractions. The flow experience only occurs during absolute focus, a state so intense that the individual does not recognize typical emotions, such as feeling happy or content. If the individual recognizes and evaluates her own emotions during a task, flow has been interrupted because the individual has shifted from a task focus to a personal and evaluative focus. Flow experiences are often reported by individuals engrossed in video games or competitive events because individuals target and regulate their thoughts and efforts only toward completing successive steps that result in progress toward the ultimate goal. However, it is not what we do that influences the ability to achieve flow, but, rather, it depends on how we approach and complete the intended target of our attention (Csikszentmihalyi, 1997).

By employing a method called "experience sampling" Csikszentmihalyi and LeFevre (1989), used beepers and asked individuals at random times during the day to indicate exactly what activity they were doing and to numerically rate how they felt about the activity at the exact moment of sampling. Individuals more frequently reported experiencing the factors associated with flow when they were working (54%), in comparison with those participating in leisure activities (17%), with similar results observed across individuals in managerial, clerical, and blue-collar jobs. Motivation, measured by responses to the question, "Do you wish you had been doing something else?" (p. 817) was more closely related to leisure activities than work. However, in contrast to expectations, individuals reported a diminished role for motivation during flow experiences. Surprisingly, the most uniformly positive experiences were reported when individuals were driving. Csikszentmihalyi suggested that leisure activities (but not driving) provide less challenge, and thus, individuals are not afforded the ability to invest serious mental effort in leisure, which results in a lower probability of performance optimization. Although individuals are highly motivated to participate in leisure, work is often perceived as more challenging and potentially satisfying and, thus, more conducive to episodes of optimal experience.

Efficiency theory uses a similar conceptual scheme as flow to suggest that there are certain conditions needed to maximize cognition and motivation. Unlike flow theory, efficiency theory places a greater emphasis on the quantitative input of effort and what factors may potentially impede optimal performance. Efficiency is described as "increases in the rate, amount, or conceptual clarity of knowledge, versus costs, such as cognitive effort, needed to attain knowledge" (Hoffman, 2012, p. 133). Although most efficiency research targets learning outcomes, several contributory variables have motivational implications, such as the amount of mental effort an individual invests in completing a task, beliefs concerning the probability of achieving certain task outcomes, and an evaluation of the task concerning which strategies learners are willing and able to use to achieve desired outcomes.

Efficiency theory suggests that optimization of motivation is crucial to cognitive efficiency, overall learning, and problem solving because each task has a unique set of parameters that warrant a complementary and ideal skill set to complete the task efficiently (Hoffman & Schraw, 2010). For example, individuals overly confident in task success may deliberately withhold effort toward completing a task based upon their perception that the task is easy. The poor calibration of the skills and the associated strategies needed for task success may inadvertently result in diminished task success or ultimate task failure (Vancouver & Kendall, 2006). A common, yet unfortunate, representation of this phenomenon is texting while driving. Many individuals believe that they can efficiently drive and text without consequence and, as such, consciously divert their attention away from the road to their devices. In 2009, there were 5,870 reported incidences of deaths due to distracted driving (Wilson & Stimpson, 2010), perhaps suggesting that for certain tasks, the drivers were fatally wrong, and there is, indeed, an ideal set of skills, beliefs, and motivations that result in optimal task performance.

Although we can debate whether humans are realistically capable of achieving optimal motivation or performance for a given task or learning goal, we can easily subscribe to the premise that minimally optimal motivation and subsequent performance can serve as a benchmark by which we can compare actual behavior. In fact, some disciplines, such as economics (Sanfey, Loewenstien, McClure, & Cohen, 2006) and health care (Jacobs, Smith, & Street, 2006), determine performance optimization by calculating efficiency as the deviation between an expected standard and observed results. The deviation method allows individuals to calibrate how closely their observed performance compares with their performance potential. James (1890) was likely the first scholar to consider calculating personal efficiency, although he did not label the behavior according to the current terminology. James postulated that the maintenance and development of self-esteem were determined, in part, by how individuals assess and evaluate themselves according to their own expectations or standards. James used an equation to determine the ratio of self-esteem to expectation. A higher observed ratio was indicative of higher self-esteem and feelings of task accomplishment, thought to contribute to setting more aggressive future goals. Low ratios had the opposite effect. When individuals believed that accomplishments fell short of expectations, feelings of shame and doubt could potentially develop based upon perceptions of personal failure.

Although James' insight did not consider the role of social comparison or cultural factors on goal setting and motivation (see Chapter 6, p. 139), his approach was an important first step in understanding how learners purposely regulate and evaluate their own performances based on upon past results. Appropriate evaluation of outcomes and an understanding of how to regulate effort are critical factors required to realize optimal performance. Improperly timed assessments are intrusive and usurp precious cognitive resources that otherwise might be dedicated toward task completion. During evaluation, motivation can be affected and potentially redirected. Sometimes, the reflection positively promotes added persistence through an examination of the strategies used to reach learning or performance goals. Alternatively, if unfavorable or untimely assessments prevail, the evaluation can derail a learner's goal progress. In the short term, negative perceptions of task success may quickly lead to reductions in effort or enhanced task anxiety, leading further to frustration and the impossibility of achieving flow while minimizing efficiency. Even worse, in the long term, learners who are unwilling or unable to effectively evaluate and regulate their own motivation can make emotionally charged academic decisions, negatively influencing future task choices, effort, and strategies used (Wolters, 2003). The beliefs learners harbor about learning and performance may change, sometimes for the better but potentially for the worse. Ultimately, like many aspects of motivation, beliefs about the self may determine when or if an individual can ever reach the "high-water mark" (Shepherd, 1966 p. 28) and experience the bacchanalia of flow and optimal motivation.

Chapter summary/conclusions

The ability to achieve and cultivate instances of optimal motivation begins with the MD possessing a clear understanding of the distinction between knowledge and beliefs. Conscious effort must be devoted toward untangling those beliefs that are supported by evidence as opposed to those that are personal representations of individual reality. Relying upon motivational science for answers requires that the MD acknowledge the difference between evidence that reliably leads to causal conclusions and that which only illustrates the relationship between two or more factors. Once individuals have a clear conception of how to interpret evidence, they can strive toward meeting the more meaningful goal of situationally determining what factors influence motivation, with the understanding that not all inquiries can be resolved through motivational science.

Acknowledging the distinctions among character, personality, and motivation provides the MD with a way to understand which aspects of the individual are amenable to intervention. Changing belief conceptions is, indeed, a formidable challenge that starts by understanding where individuals stand on the conceptual continuum of motivation. Such factors as the degree of individual mind-centeredness and an understanding of the source of motives provide promise to leverage the resistant, but fluid and malleable, nature of motivation beliefs. Although debates persist concerning the effectiveness of actually teaching motivation, through modeling and the judicious introduction of goal and strategy choices, MDs can actively influence how learners view themselves, as well as when and how they can influence the motivation of others. The nirvana of determining optimal motivation according to task has yet to be empirically confirmed, but we do know that peak performance is realistically obtained, as illustrated by the story of Michael Jordon and from the Experience Sampling Method used to determine flow.

Next steps

Thinking back, you may have wondered about the stories of Ginny and Jerry, the fraternal twins. Based upon the description of their behaviors, you may have thought it was quite odd that they seemed and acted so differently despite being raised in the same home and despite their biological and genetic similarities. You may have surmised that the influence of genetics and biology as a tool to understanding motivation was minimal, or possibly non-existent. In reality, a robust field of well-designed programmatic research supports the view that motivation, like most other human qualities, is heritable. Chapter 3 takes a closer look at biopsychological evidence, which shows a surprisingly strong link between motivated behavior and individual physiology. You will also be introduced to our next motivational leader, **Alexis Paige Dixon**, a remarkable young lady who exemplifies how motivation exerts a resounding influence on physical performance and growth.

End of chapter motivational minute

Principles covered in this chapter:

6. **Motivational beliefs differ from motivational knowledge**—knowledge originates from many sources. Beliefs can easily be misconstrued as knowledge. In order to verify knowledge as justified, it must be supported by objective evidence validated against an external standard.
7. **Motivational evidence can only answer certain questions**—objective science cannot answer all questions, especially those based upon personal convictions. Care should be taken to avoid making causal conclusions from the bulk of motivation evidence, which is correlational.
8. **Motivation is related to learning and performance but causality is an uncertainty**—the methodological distinction between correlation and causality is crucial to understanding motivational evidence. Correlation implies a relationship between two or more variables, while causality suggests the underlying reason explaining observed behavior.
9. **Motivation is subordinate to character and personality**—distinct differences exist among the constructs of character, personality, and motivation. Personality is more trait based and stable, character is socially derived, and motivation is transient and a function of situational factors.
10. **Motivation is the responsibility of leaders and can be taught**—teachers and leaders serve as appropriate models to teach learners about motivation. An education in motivation is not all-inclusive because strategy use may be a function of beliefs.
11. **Theoretically, motivated behavior operates on a continuum**—understanding motivation requires consideration that motivation is fluid and malleable. Two primary continuums are the Knowledge Perspective of Reynolds et al. (1996) and Organismic Integration Theory of Ryan and Deci (2000).
12. **Optimal motivation is obtainable**—flow and motivational efficiency perspectives suggest that an optimal set of beliefs, conditions and behaviors exist and can promote efficient, robust, and predictable learning and performance outcomes.

Key terminology (in order of chapter presentation):

- **False beliefs**—the tendency of individuals to adopt beliefs about motivational processes contrary to established scientific evidence.
- **False enlightenment**—a strong belief conviction contrary to existing objective evidence that is extremely change resistant despite evidence.

- **Knowledge**—knowledge includes three important components: truth, belief, and evidence. Verifiable evidence supports the contention that knowledge is justified.
- **Unjustified belief**—a conception that is not supported by objective evidence and cannot be consistently verified or replicated by others not holding the belief.
- **Justified belief**—a belief substantiated by evidence objectively gathered and interpreted.
- **Spurious**—an erroneous interpretation attributing causality to an unwarranted cause when examining the relationship between two or more variables.
- **Traits**—a generalized tendency to exhibit behaviors that are consistent and predictable.

References

Alderman, M. K. (2004). *Motivation for achievement: Possibilities for teaching and learning* (2nd ed.). Mahwah, NJ: Lawrence Erlbaum Associates.

Ames, C. (1990). Motivation: What teachers need to know. *The Teachers College Record, 91*(3), 409–421.

Ariely, D., Gneezy, U., Loewenstein, G., & Mazar, N. (2005). Large stakes and big mistakes. *Research Review, 4*, 11–13.

Bandler, J., & Varchaver, N. (2009). How Bernie did it. Retrieved on January 7, 2015 from: <http://archive.fortune.com/2009/04/24/news/newsmakers/madoff.fortune/index.htm>.

Bandura, A. (1997). *Self-efficacy: The exercise of control*. New York, NY: Freeman.

Berinato, S. (2013). If you want to motivate someone, shut up already. *Harvard Business Review, 91*(7), 24–25.

Binet, A., & Simon, T. (1914). *Mentally defective children*. New York, NY: Longmans, Green & Company.

Brophy, J. (2004). *Motivating students to learn*. Mahwah, NJ: Lawrence Erlbaum Associates.

Cattell, R. B. (1950). *Personality: A systematic theoretical and factual study*. New York, NY: McGraw-Hill.

Chen, G., Gully, S. M., Whiteman, J., & Kilcullen, R. N. (2006). Examination of relationships among trait-like individual differences, state-like individual differences, and learning performance. *Journal of Applied Psychology, 85*, 835–847.

Chi, M. T. H. (2005). Commonsense conceptions of emergent processes: Why some misconceptions are robust. *Journal of the Learning Sciences, 14*(2), 161–199. http://dx.doi.org/10.1207/s15327809jls1402_1.

Chinn, C. A., & Brewer, W. F. (1993). The role of anomalous data in knowledge acquisition: A theoretical framework and implications for science instruction. *Review of Educational Research, 63*, 1–49.

Cloninger, S. (2009). Conceptual issues in personality theory. In G. Matthews & P. J. Corr (Eds.), *The Cambridge handbook of personality psychology* (pp. 2–27). Cambridge, England: Cambridge University Press.

Corr, P. J., DeYoung, C. G., & McNaughton, N. (2013). Motivation and personality: A neuropsychological perspective. *Social and Personality Psychology Compass, 7*(3), 158–175. http://dx.doi.org/10.1111/spc3.12016.

Csikszentmihalyi, M. (1997). *Finding flow: The psychology of engagement with everyday life*. New York, NY: Basic Books.

Csikszentmihalyi, M., & LeFevre, J. (1989). Optimal experience in work and leisure. *Journal of Personality and Social Psychology, 56*, 815–822.

Cummings, T. G. (2014). *Organization development and change* (10th ed.). Mason, OH: Cengage.

Dole, J. A., & Sinatra, G. M. (1998). Reconceptualizing change in the cognitive construction of knowledge. *Educational Psychologist, 33*(2–3), 109–128.

Doris, J. M. (2002). *Lack of character: Personality and moral behavior*. Cambridge, MA: Cambridge University Press.

Fives, H., & Buehl, M. (2012). Spring cleaning for the "messy" construct of teachers' beliefs: What are they? Which have been examined? What can they tell us? In K. R. Harris, S. Graham, & T. Urdan (Eds.), *APA educational psychology handbook: Volume 2 individual differences and cultural and contextual factors* (pp. 471–499). Washington, DC: American Psychological Association.

Forbes (2013). Obamacare raises healthcare premiums especially for the young. Retrieved on January 7, 2015 from: <http://www.forbes.com/sites/matthewherper/2013/12/05/obamacare-raises-health-insurance-costs-especially-for-the-young/>.

Gallup (2005). Paranormal beliefs come (super) naturally to some. Retrieved on May 14, 2015 from: <http://www.gallup.com/poll/19558/paranormal-beliefs-come-supernaturally-some.aspx>.

Geary, D. C. (2008). An evolutionarily informed education science. *Educational Psychologist, 43*, 179–195.

Gettier, E. (1963). Is justified true belief knowledge? *Analysis, 23*, 121–123.

Hallett, M. (2011). Peak performance training. Retrieved on April 6, 2015 from: <http://etd.fcla.edu.ezproxy.net.ucf.edu/CF/CFE0004116/Thesis.pdf>.

Hallett, M., & Hoffman, B. (2014). Peak performance training in the workplace. *Consulting Psychology Journal: Practice and Research, 66*, 212–230. http://dx.doi.org/10.1037/cpb0000009.

Hoffman, B. (2010). I think I can, but I'm afraid to try: The influence of self-efficacy and anxiety on problem-solving efficiency. *Learning & Individual Differences, 20*, 276–283.

Hoffman, B. (2012). Cognitive efficiency: A conceptual and measurement comparison. *Learning and Instruction, 22*, 133–144.

Hoffman, B., & Schraw, G. (2010). Conceptions of efficiency: Applications in learning and problem-solving. *Educational Psychologist, 45*, 1–14. http://dx.doi.org/10.1080/00461520903213618.

Hynd, C. R., & Guzzetti, B. J. (1993). Exploring issues in conceptual change. In D. J. Leu & C. K. Kinzer (Eds.), *Examining central issues in literacy research, theory and practice* (pp. 374–381). Chicago, IL: The National Reading Conference.

Jacobs, R., Smith, P. C., & Street, A. (2006). *Measuring efficiency in health care: Analytic techniques and health policy*. Cambridge, England: Cambridge University Press.

James, W. (1890). *The principles of psychology*. New York, NY: Henry Holt.

John, O. P., Naumann, L. P., & Soto, C. J. (2008). Paradigm shift to the integrative Big Five trait taxonomy: History, measurement, and conceptual issues. In O. P. John, R. W. Robins, & L. A. Pervin (Eds.), *Handbook of personality: Theory and research* (pp. 114–158). New York, NY: Guilford Press.

Katz, I., Eilot, K., & Nevo, N. (2013). "I'll do it later": Type of motivation, self-efficacy and homework procrastination. *Motivation and Emotion*, 1–9. http://dx.doi.org/10.1007/s11031-013-9366-1.

Kirschner, P., & van Merrienboer, J. (2013). Do learners really know best? Urban legends in education. *Educational Psychologist, 48*(3), 169–183. http://dx.doi.org/10.1080/00461520.2013.804395.

Kloumann, I. M., Danforth, C. M., Harris, K. D., Bliss, C. A., & Dodds, P. S. (2012). Positivity of the English language. *PLoS One, 7*(1), 1–7. http://dx.doi.org/10.1371/journal.pone.0029484.

Lair, J. C., & Cook, J. D. (2011). A study of a common misconception in Appalachian Kentucky seventh and eighth grade science students: Free fall and inertia. *Journal of the Kentucky Academy of Science, 72*(2), 73–83. http://dx.doi.org/10.3101/1098-7096-72.2.73.

Losh, S. C., & Nzekwe, B. (2010). Creatures in the classroom: Preservice teacher beliefs about fantastic beasts, magic, extraterrestrials, evolution and creationism. *Science & Education, 20*(5-6), 473–489. http://dx.doi.org/10.1007/s11191-010-9268-5.

Maehr, M. L., & Meyer, H. A. (1997). Understanding motivation and schooling: Where we've been, where we are, and where we need to go. *Educational Psychology Review, 9*(4), 371–409. http://dx.doi.org/10.1023/A:1024750807365.

Miller, H., & Bichsel, J. (2004). Anxiety, working memory, gender, and math performance. *Personality and Individual Differences, 37*, 591–606.

Moons, W. G., & Mackie, D. M. (2007). Thinking straight while seeing red: The influence of anger on information processing. *Personality and Social Psychology Bulletin, 33*(5), 706–720. http://dx.doi.org/10.1177/0146167206298566.

Perry, N. E., Turner, J. C., & Meyer, D. K. (2006). Classrooms as contexts for motivated learning. In P. A. Alexander & P. Winne (Eds.), *Handbook of educational psychology* (pp. 327–348) (2nd ed.). Mahwah, NJ: Lawrence Erlbaum.

Pew Forum on Religion and Public Life, (2009). *Many Americans mix multiple faiths: Eastern, new age beliefs widespread.* Washington, DC: Pew Research Center. <http://pewforum.org/docs/?DocID=490#1>.

Phillips, D. C., & Burbules, N. C. (2000). *Postpositivism and educational research.* New York, NY: Rowman & Littlefield.

Popper, K. R. (1963). *Conjectures and refutations.* London: Routledge & Kegan Paul.

Privette, G. (1981). Dynamics of peak performance. *Journal of Humanistic Psychology, 21*(1), 57–67.

Reynolds, R. E., Sinatra, G. M., & Jetton, T. L. (1996). Views of knowledge acquisition and representation: A continuum from experience to mind centered. *Educational Psychologist, 31*(2), 93–104.

Ryan, R., & Deci, E. (2000). Self-determination theory and the facilitation of intrinsic motivation, social development and well-being. *American Psychologist, 55*, 68–78. http://dx.doi.org/10.1037//0003-066X.55.1.68.

Sanfey, A. G., Loewenstein, G., McClure, S. M., & Cohen, J. D. (2006). Neuroeconomics: Cross-currents in research on decision-making. *Trends in Cognitive Science, 10*(3), 108–116.

Schunk, D. H., Pintrich, R., & Meece, J. L. (2008). *Motivation in education: Theory, research, and applications* (3rd ed.). Upper Saddle River, NJ: Pearson/Merrill Prentice Hall.

Shepherd, J. (1966). *In God we trust: All others pay cash.* New York, NY: Broadway Books.

Shermer, M. (2002). *Why people believe weird things.* New York, NY: W. H. Freeman.

Shermer, M. (2012). *The believing brain: From ghosts and gods to politics and conspiracies—how we construct beliefs and reinforce them as truths.* New York, NY: St. Martin's Griffin.

Shiv, B., & Fedorikhin, A. (2002). Spontaneous versus controlled influences of stimulus-based affect on choice behavior. *Organizational Behavior and Human Decision Processes, 87*(2), 342–370. http://dx.doi.org/10.1006/obhd.2001.2977.

Sinatra, G.M. & Seyranian, V. (in press). Warm change about hot topics: The role of motivation and emotion in attitude and conceptual change about controversial science topics. To appear in L. Corno & E. Anderman (Eds.). *APA Handbook of Educational Psychology.*

Smith, A. (2010). Madoff ruined thousands including his son. Retrieved on January 7, 2015 from: <http://money.cnn.com/2010/12/11/news/companies/mark_madoff_victims_lawsuits/>.

Southerland, S. A., Sinatra, G. M., & Matthews, M. R. (2001). Belief, knowledge, and science education. *Educational Psychology Review, 13*(4), 325–351.

Stanovich, K. E. (2013). *How to think straight about psychology* (10th ed.). Boston, MA: Pearson.

Steel, P. (2007). The nature of procrastination: A meta-analytic and theoretical review of quintessential self-regulatory failure. *Psychological Bulletin, 133*, 65–94. http://dx.doi.org/10.1037/0033-2909.133.1.65.

United States Government Accountability Office. (2012). Customer outcomes in the Madoff liquidation proceeding. Retrieved on January 7, 2015 from: <http://www.gao.gov/assets/650/648237.pdf>.

Vancouver, F. B., & Kendall, L. N. (2006). When self-efficacy negatively relates to motivation and performance in a learning context. *Journal of Applied Psychology, 91*, 1146–1153. http://dx.doi.org/10.1037/0021-9010.91.5.1146.

Vosniadou, S. (2001). What can persuasion research tell us about conceptual change that we did not already know? *International Journal of Educational Research, 35*(7–8), 731–737. http://dx.doi.org/10.1016/S0883-0355(02)00012-5.

Wilson, F. A., & Stimpson, J. P. (2010). Trends in fatalities from distracted driving in the United States, 1999 to 2008. *American Journal of Public Health, 100*(11), 2213–2219.

Wolters, C. (2003). Regulation of motivation: Evaluating an underemphasized aspect of self-regulated learning. *Educational Psychologist, 38*(4), 189–205. http://dx.doi.org/10.1207/S15326985EP3804_1.

Zeidner, M. (2009). Personality in educational psychology. In P. J. Corr & G. Matthews (Eds.), *The Cambridge handbook of personality psychology* (pp. 733–747). New York, NY: Cambridge University Press.

The biopsychology of motivation: Using evidence from neurology and endocrinology to understand motivated behavior

Chapter outline

Principle #13—Neurological/endocrinological evidence informs or refutes behavioral evidence 48
Principle #14—Neurological/endocrinological inferences are multi-dimensional 50
Motivational Leader—*Alexis Dixon* 53
Principle #15—The brain is a perceptual filter influencing subjective reality 54
Principle #16—Neurological system organization facilitates or inhibits action 56
Principle #17—Power and social dominance displays mimic sympathetic nervous system activation 57
Principle #18—Displays of affiliation mimic parasympathetic nervous system activation 59
Principle #19—Achievement and incentive reward share similar neural response patterns 62
Principle #20—Humanity is motivated to seek pleasure and avoid pain 64
Principle #21—Motivated behavior is heritable and evolutionary 68
    Chapter summary/conclusions 71
    Next steps 72
    End of chapter motivational minute 72
References 73

Did you look in the mirror today? What did you see? Perhaps your attention was drawn to a blemish on your face or to your disheveled hair upon arising. Instead, maybe you embraced a more holistic view of your physical being and were beaming with confidence as you assessed the results of a recently implemented dieting or exercise regime. Most likely, the subjective appraisal of your body did *not* include an evaluation of the 180 billion cells that comprise a complex network of neurotransmitters, synapses, and hormones that collectively encompass your neuroanatomy (Kolb & Whishaw, 2009). However, the precise composition of your brain, with an emphasis on your nervous and endocrine systems, is arguably one of the most reliable predictors of ensuing behavior, more consistent than many self-reported descriptions of motivation (Falk, Berkman, Mann, Harrison, & Lieberman, 2010). Perceptions and self-reflections about how the mind and the body interact are the essence of over 2,000 years of ardent philosophical and scholarly ruminations concerning the etiology of human behavior.

Historically, classical thinkers, such as Socrates, his student Plato, and Plato's student Aristotle, contended that the conceptual framework of human behavior was guided by three separate and distinct forces: the body, the mind, and the soul. Socrates held the unpopular belief that human "will" mediated and controlled bodily actions. Lacking any hard evidence to support his beliefs, Socrates was eventually shunned by the majority of the secular ancient Greek populace and suffered the fate of death by poison hemlock for his seemingly radical views. Protégé Plato had similar contentions as his mentor, but he differed in the exact descriptions and terminology that he used to describe motivated behavior. Unlike Socrates, who took a conciliatory approach to the influences of reason and spirit as mediating the carnal urges of the body, Plato believed that a divisive and eternal conflict vexed the human psyche (Singpurwalla, 2010). Aristotle advanced the views of Plato, placing a greater emphasis on logical interpretations while still believing that the mind was guided by a combination of competing urges. Aristotle's views on motivated action led to the revelation that behavior was attributable to seven causes: chance, nature, compulsion, habit, reason, passion, and desire (Aristotle, 2004). Collectively, the deterministic views of the ancient scholars all sought to answer the same pressing question: Which metaphysical aspects of human existence accounted for motivated behavior?

The tripartite view of the mind perpetuated until the seventeenth century when Descartes, the noble laureate and inventor of Euclidian mathematics, declared, "Cogito ergo sum" ("I think, therefore I am"). The metaphysical argument advanced by Descartes led to the enduring concept of *dualism*. This interpretation of human existence hypothesized that the body and the mind (centered in the brain) were physically distinct, qualitatively different, and yet, somehow, worked together (Kolb & Whishaw, 2009). Descartes never effectively explained how the body and mind interacted and mistakenly thought that the pineal gland, which regulates the hormone melatonin, was the moderator of thought and action. Despite the biological imprecision advanced by Descartes, his dualistic philosophy launched the study of biopsychology and influenced the origins and explanations of motivated behavior for well over 300 years. Today, the discipline of biopsychology extends the views of Descartes and focuses on substantiating how the brain and the neurological system intertwine, determining which areas of the brain activate motivations, and clarifying the meaning of the behavioral expressions triggered by physiological events.

Principle #13—Neurological/endocrinological evidence informs or refutes behavioral evidence

First, let's consider how biobehavioral evidence helps the motivational detective (MD) understand motivated behavior. Can evidence garnered through biopsychological sources have any utility for a teacher or leader? For example, does it really matter

The biopsychology of motivation

		Behavioral evidence	
		Supports	Refutes
Biological evidence	Supports	Explains the motivation underlying behavior	Suggests individual differences in motivation
	Refutes	Suggests diverse motivations are likely	Provides no explanation of motivated behavior

Figure 3.1 Four possible interpretations of neurological/behavioral evidence.

what part of your brain is activated when you are anxious about an upcoming interview or test? Although your initial reaction may be a resounding "NO," from an applied perspective, biopsychological evidence helps either support or refute the contentions advanced by observation or individual self-report alone. However, the interpretation of biopsychological evidence is complex due to the hierarchical and interactive nature of the neurological system and because behaviors rarely align exactly with specific anatomical changes.

Biopsychological evidence can be interpreted in at least four ways. Figure 3.1 depicts the nexus of four possible outcomes when interpreting the relationship between behavioral and biological evidence. In cases when *homogeneous* behaviors result in predictable physiological reactions, the confluence of evidence suggests that the observed behaviors are a consistent and accurate reflection of individual motives. When *heterogeneous* behaviors result in predictable physiological reactions, we might conclude that individual differences or contextual variables (e.g., social factors) have a prevailing influence on determining underlying motivations. Conversely, if behavioral *heterogeneity* is observed in association with unpredictable or novel physiological changes, the likely interpretation would be that the exhibited behaviors are related to a diverse set of motivations. Finally, inconsistent behaviors that show little correlation to physiological changes would represent no specific relations between behavior and motivation. The ongoing scrutiny of behavioral triggers and associated biological patterns becomes instrumental in accurately interpreting what the diverse behaviors encountered in the classroom or workplace actually represent. Thus, attention to physiological markers, such as facial expressions, speech tones, or breathing patterns, can prove valuable, falsifying otherwise sound behaviorally determined explanations of motivated behavior.

A practical example demonstrating the functional utility of physiological evidence is the largely involuntary and innate physiological response to conscious fear. Using brain imaging technology, such as functional magnetic resonance imaging (fMRI) or electroencephalography, fear manifests neurologically by accelerating activation patterns in different areas of the brain, including the amygdala, insula, thalamus, and the occipital cortex, concurrent with the release of the neurotransmitter serotonin (Klucken et al., 2013). Typical human behavioral reactions to fear include freezing, pupillary dilation, facial constriction, decreased salivation, and not surprisingly, as any frightened individual will attest, increased urination and a rapid heart rate (Davis, 1992).

Gunner on one of his happy days.

I regularly encounter a potential fear-inducing stimulus on my street: His name is Gunner, a handsome, yet unpredictable white German Shepherd. Since I have been bitten by dogs at least three times, I approach Gunner with cautious apprehension. I never know if my tail-wagging buddy will afford me affection or growl in disdain when he is having a bad day. For argument's sake, assume that I never leave my house unencumbered, always hooked up to my portable fMRI machine that monitors my brain functioning and fear responses. Immediately upon seeing Gunner my heart rate increases, my pupils dilate, and serotonin production increases (yet my pants remain dry). The fMRI flashes to show blood rushing to the fear receptor in my amygdala. Likely, one would conclude that Gunner is the cause of my fear-induced motivation, as both my physiological symptoms and my cautious and self-protective behavior are aligned. In order to further test my hypothesis of Gunner-induced fear, I lend my fMRI to 20 other monitored friends and ask them to approach Gunner. To my surprise, none of my friends shows brain-based fear localization or increased serotonin production. However, when approaching Gunner, some of them exhibit changes in facial expression and pupil dilation. Interpreting these results, we would likely conclude that the physiological reactions of my friends to Gunner are, indeed, different from my own, not involving the motive of fear. Curious about the observed results, I would feel compelled to ask my friends why they were not afraid of my nemesis, Gunner. As you might expect, many of them have dogs of their own, and the observed physical reactions were biological markers of affection. In this example, we can conclude that the nexus of neurological and behavioral evidence was significantly more helpful in understanding the nature of motivations than behavioral evidence alone.

Principle #14—Neurological/endocrinological inferences are multi-dimensional

Despite the logic advanced in the prior paragraph, neurological evidence should be interpreted cautiously for at least three reasons (Cacioppo & Berntson, 2009). First, as aspiring diagnosticians of motivated behavior, whenever possible, our aim is to decipher the causes of observed behavior. Regrettably, humans have a strong tendency to seek out remedies that require minimal investment of cognitive effort (Stanovich, 2009). In other words, given a choice, we prefer simple and quick explanations. The proclivity for simple solutions creates vulnerability to accept potentially *spurious* interpretations of data. This happens when causality is wrongly inferred to a particular variable based upon a correlational relationship, masking the true causal factor underlying the behavior of interest. For example, a confluence of neurological evidence indicates that males have elevated levels of testosterone when winning sporting events, playing chess games, and having success during games of chance, compared with when they experience defeat (Mazur & Booth, 1998). Women also show testosterone increases when participating in identical events, albeit to a far lesser extent than men. Analyzing these findings might lead to the widely accepted inference that biological sex causes testosterone production. However, this conclusion would, indeed, be spurious. In reality, contextual differences, such as the type of task performed and a number of social variables, including group dynamics, exerts a greater influence on testosterone production in both men and women, than sex alone (Hines, 2011).

Second, there may be a tendency to underestimate the immense complexity of neurological networks and associated hierarchies in the nervous system and to falsely attribute behavioral observations to a unitary neurological source. Interpretive errors may develop because unlike behavioral evidence, which is usually interpreted at the individual or group level, physiological observations can be interpreted at six different levels of specificity (Berntson & Cacioppo, 2008; Cacioppo & Berntson, 2009). Table 3.1 illustrates the perfect storm of potentially skewed interpretations of multi-level hierarchical neurological evidence. Each level can have an independent influence on behavior or multiplicative levels can have singular influences. Thus, looking at level alone is insufficient to evaluate the relationship between biopsychological evidence and behavior.

Third, compounding accurate analysis of evidence is the potential interactivity of behavioral stimuli and neurological responses. Since the neurological system is structured in a complex hierarchy, at any given time, behavioral stimuli can activate one or more dimensions of the neurological hierarchy. McNaughton and Corr (2009) used the example of nine possible emotional responses to perceived threat,

Table 3.1 Neuropsychology studies at different levels of neural activation

Level of activation	Type of evidence	Source
Genetic	Genetic code of neurons	McConnell et al. (2013)
Synaptic	Visual attention	Lakatos, Karmos, Mehta, Ulbert, and Schroeder (2008)
Autonomic	Sensory perceptions, smiling behavior	Schilbach, Eickhoff, Mojzisch, and Vogeley (2008)
Skeletal	Reflexive actions, pain withdrawal	Rainville (2013)
Cognitive	Language syntax	Petersson, Folia, and Hagoort (2012)
Systems	Information processing	Rypma et al. (2006)

including increased respiration (autonomic), freezing (skeletal), and muscle energy in the form of adrenaline and glucose production (synaptic). The neuronal reactivity can be activated either independently or dependently of other neuronal pathways or more likely in a combined fashion, suggesting interactivity of responses. For example, we know from an environmental perspective that heat induces perspiration in humans; however, the degree of perspiration is moderated by humidity. Given a particular temperature, an individual may not perspire to the same extent, unless the humidity is above a certain threshold. Although both heat and humidity influence perspiration separately, interactive analysis provides much more important information to understand how heat and humidity together influence perspiration. Additional interpretive concerns arise when determining the sequences of neurological responses to activating stimuli. Any one neuronal reaction could be prompted at a particular time, one triggering the next; alternatively, the neurological responses can all fire simultaneously. McNaughton and Corr (2009) cautioned against assuming that "all stimuli activate a single neural representation of threat and this, in turn, activates the separate response systems" (p. 714).

Additionally, we must expect that neurological responses to motivation-provoking stimuli will generalize inconsistently across contexts. Although I periodically fear Gunner, I can assure you that I often show no fear response to other canines, but I *always* fear a charging rhinoceroses. Finally, due to the high incidence of correlational studies in neurological research, combined with our quest to determine causality of behavior, we should be consciously concerned about *ambiguous temporal precedence* (Shadish, Cook, & Campbell, 2002), a fancy term that illustrates the classic chicken versus egg dilemma. It may be unknown whether neurological reactions precede motivation, or vice versa, if the motivation precedes the reaction. Thus, I cannot tell if my heart beats faster because I fear my canine culprit Gunner, or if the faster beat of my traumatized ticker is responsible for my fear response (see Chapter 9 (p. 237) for a detailed discussion of motivation and emotion).

In total, these interpretive cautions suggest that biopsychological analysis of motivation can be an effective source of data for the MD. However, analysis of behavior should be undertaken not only in a generalized fashion (i.e., do animals evoke fear in humans?) but also at the individual level of specificity (i.e., does heart rate change based upon the size of the animal?) to accurately infer meaning from acquired data. Causal conclusions without this degree of scrutiny may, indeed, be unwarranted, resulting in the cardinal error of believing that factors are related when, indeed, they are not. As McNaughton and Corr declared, "the definition of a psychological construct should map to a specific aspect of a coherent neural and functional system" (p. 711). Cognizant of the interpretive liabilities when analyzing neurological data, we now turn to specific inferences from neurological studies that help understand motivation in applied settings, such as the classroom and the workplace, and many other aspects of our daily lives.

However, before moving forward, read the incredible story of a courageous and determined young lady, Alexis Paige Dixon, who, as a result of massive and unpredictable biological change, has transformed herself into a medical miracle and model of adolescent motivation.

Motivational Leader—*Alexis Dixon*

Alexis (Alex) Paige Dixon contracted pneumonia halfway through fourth grade. Prior to that, she was a bright, kind, and sometimes socially awkward child. Academics came easily to her. She loved animals, playing the piano, art, and being outside. The pneumonia triggered a glitch in her central nervous system (CNS), and she would never fully recover from her illness. The glitch caused her body to contort, and she experienced considerable pain.  She missed a great deal of school and spent many of her days in hospitals seeking a cure for her illness. By the time she began sixth grade, she was painfully confined to a wheelchair.

Despite her illness, Alex began sixth grade in the gifted program. She continued to excel academically as well as in art and piano. However, her condition worsened halfway through sixth grade, 2 years after the initial onset. Her body began contorting in terrible ways, causing hundreds of dislocations daily. It seemed that she would not survive. She was flown to a hospital in the Midwest and placed in a coma in an attempt to buy time as new medications were introduced, but to no avail. On February 23, 2010, Alex underwent brain surgery as a last effort to save her life. It was her sister's 10th birthday and Alex was just 12 years old. The surgery did not go as planned, although it did resolve her original problems. A mishap caused a massive stroke to the left hemisphere of Alex's brain. She was placed in a coma for weeks in order to increase her likelihood of survival. Her classmates were behind her and folded a thousand paper cranes so that she might get her wish and find motivation to live.

Alex survived. She emerged from the coma and slowly recovered the memories of her life experiences, but not of her academics. She knew her family, but not their names. When I spoke with Alex, she told me, "I only really have half a brain, my left hemisphere was destroyed. My motor skills were intact, but everything else was gone" (A. Dixon, personal communication, March 23, 2014). She did not even know her own name. She came home from the hospital in June, 4 months after the surgery, and was determined to enter seventh grade with her peers in August. More motivated to succeed than ever before, Alex met her goal.

Now, 5 years after her stroke, Alex struggles to be "normal like everyone else" (A. Dixon, personal communication, March 23, 2014). She devotes her time to relearning how to eat, walk, care for herself, speak, read, write, and do math. She has more determination than can be imagined. She is in regular classes with a one-on-one aide. She works nonstop. Although her right hand is no longer very useful, she has learned to write better than many with her left hand. She has not given up on her right hand and spends countless hours in therapy trying to regain use. During her recovery, she discarded first the wheelchair and, eventually, her cane, and now she is walking unassisted (and playing a mean game of tennis as well)!

At the end of ninth grade, Alex passed both her state algebra and reading tests, achieving a five-out-of-five score in algebra. She is liked by her peers and adored by her teachers. She has a "Yes I Can" attitude that is nothing less than contagious. Alex has certainly encountered roadblocks and hardship resulting in significant disabilities over the past 5 years. However, her resilience, strength, and determination are unmatched, and her future is wide open. When asked why she did not give up, Alex replied, "Obstacles make me want to work harder. I am going to do something great, it's easier to give up than to keep on going" (A. Dixon, personal communication, March 23, 2014).

Alex has decided to take her experiences and put them to good use by providing motivational presentations to teachers, parents, and medical professionals. At the tender age of 17, she has given keynote speeches at several educational and psychology research conferences. A marvel of perseverance and energy, Alex has found her "MO," albeit in the most unorthodox way, through the massive biological upheaval brought about by her stroke. Alex feels that by sharing her story and how she overcame such immense hardships, she can motivate others to do the same. Every day, she gets one step closer toward her intended career as a rehabilitation specialist, specializing in motivating others to reach personal goals, regardless of the obstacles.

Principle #15—The brain is a perceptual filter influencing subjective reality

I would like to encourage you to try a simple experiment. You do not need any fancy materials or equipment, just paper and pencil and a family member or friend. Turn on the television, or watch any YouTube video for 5 min. Pretend that you and your partner are crime scene investigators, and individually write down the most important details you noticed about what you viewed. Upon conclusion, compare your notes with your investigative partner. Likely, there were some things on your list that were not on your partner's list, and vice versa. Perceptual interpretations are at the root of your discrepancies. Where you focused attention, the details you deemed important, and what words were used to describe observations can all be attributed to subjective reality imposed upon you by your brain.

What occurred in the experiment described above is the phenomenon of individualized representations of external perceptions. Philosophically, subjective reality implies that no two individuals have the identical perceptual lens. This notion is termed *qualia*, and the proponents of this notion of reality contend that virtually all visual, auditory, and essentially every other sensory input is imbued by the properties of conscious experience, creating individualized perceptions of external reality (Dennett, 1988). This esoteric approach to examining physical evidence accounts for how we explain the world around us. Physiological evidence supports the notion that reality is, indeed, subjective. If you have ever used a dog whistle you will know what I mean and quickly understand how the same stimulus can be interpreted differently based upon perceptual capability. The average human is able to detect sound between the approximate ranges of 16 hertz (Hz) (low pitch sounds) and 16,400 Hz (high pitch sounds). A canine's hearing range is more expansive, approximated between 60 and 60,000 Hz. Dog whistles are crafted to produce pitches between 20,000 and 48,000 Hz, which exceeds the ability of human detection, so for us, the whistle is silent. Lack of auditory perception, of course, does not indicate an absence of sound, but it does mean that perceptual abilities across species are inconsistent due to brain differences.

Consequently, we acknowledge that perceptual realities will vary between individuals because "no two brains are identical" (Kolb & Whishaw, 2009, p. 149): ample neurological evidence supports this hypothesis. Differences in sensory acuity transcend hearing and influence the brain's filtering process whenever sensory input is detected. Sensory stimuli are processed through a complicated regimen of neuronal gate-keeping, centered in the thalamus region of the brain. First, stimuli are evaluated, and then specific neurons are fired, modulated, and transferred to other brain areas for higher-order processing, if necessary. The degree of attention devoted to incoming stimuli, whether or not we acknowledge information to be worthy of our attention beyond initial perception, and even how we process information cognitively are all a function of perceptual filtering done through the thalamus area of the brain (Lee & Sherman, 2008).

More importantly, for our purposes, the brain's perceptual filter has many applied implications. For decades, Elizabeth Loftus has examined the radical and real-life consequences associated with how the brain selectively filters, recalls, and interprets information. The brain can be tricked into believing propositions that have never occurred, such as during "suggestibility" studies, where false information is provided to participants in the hope that the messages will be so persuasive that individuals will believe the information to be true. Evidence reveals that the type and timing of investigative questions about an auto accident can affect the accuracy of witness's recall, leading to memory alternations and potential wrongful convictions of perpetrators (Loftus, 1975). Other studies have induced humans to vehemently attest to remembering events that never happened, such as being lost in a mall (Loftus, 1997) and even recalling false, yet more traumatic events, such as being abused as a child (Laney & Loftus, 2013).

Suggestibility may also prompt positive motivations. Laney, Morris, Bernstein, Wakefield, and Loftus (2010) falsely led some adults to believing that they loved to eat asparagus when they were children. Subsequently, the same individuals completed surveys indicating that they would be more likely to eat asparagus (a healthy motivation) and pay more to purchase asparagus, compared with a control group that was not exposed to the false beliefs. Findings of this nature reveal the real-life consequences associated with how the brain processes and filters information. Findings also show how these memorial representations might possibly influence future behaviors based upon differences in how individuals process and respond to perceptual information. The message here is to exercise extreme caution when evaluating individual interpretations of seemingly straightforward events. What appears true for one may, indeed, be flagrantly false for another.

Principle #16—Neurological system organization facilitates or inhibits action

Evaluating the structure and organization of our neurological system is a study in contrasts. You may recall from high school biology that the nervous system includes the central nervous system (CNS), which comprises the brain and the spinal cord, and the peripheral nervous system (PNS), which encompasses a neural network throughout the body and organs that communicate with the brain. The PNS is further divided into the somatic nerve system, which is responsible for sensory reception in the nerves, organs, and skeleton, and the autonomic nerve system (ANS), which regulates involuntary bodily functions, such as heart rate and breathing. The ANS is further divided into the "antagonistic" (Beck, 2004, p. 44), yet symbiotic, parasympathetic nervous system and sympathetic nervous system (SNS), which are most relevant to understanding the range of behaviors and corresponding emotions that influence motivation.

The divisions of the ANS are largely responsible for the regulation of bodily energy. The SNS deploys energy in response to threatening stimuli, such as when you are anxious about taking a test or running away from the charging rhinoceros I described earlier. The perception of stress induces the body to release of a series of nonmonolithic, but correlated, hormonal and neural metabolites, such as testosterone, epinephrine, and cortisol. The hormonal changes during stress dilate pupils, trigger decrements in saliva production, elevate blood pressure, and accelerate heart rate. Concurrently, energy is redirected from the digestive and urinary systems in response to the "fight or flight" mechanisms needed to resolve whatever the brain perceives as stressful.

Assuming that you successfully outsmart or outrun the charging rhino, the parasympathetic system returns your body to a state of homeostasis through a gradual process of relaxation and hormonal stability evidenced by pupil constriction, increased production of saliva, and a slowdown in the circulatory and respiratory systems. The digestive and urinary systems would return to prestress states as the body offsets the physiological actions activated by the SNS. The primary neurotransmitter associated with the regulating activities of the parasympathetic system is acetylcholine. However, the neuropeptides progesterone and oxytocin (OT), which are related to some forms of social behavior, also accompany parasympathetic regulation (Gamer & Büchel, 2012). The competing nervous systems clearly show recognizable symptoms of motivated behavior that ebb and flow based upon how our brains perceive and evaluate environmental stimuli.

Lessons in neuroanatomy may seem unimportant to the MD, but surprisingly, the divisions of our neurological system in many ways parallel how we navigate the world around us. Although it is unlikely you will actually have a charging rhino in your classroom or boardroom, it is probable you will be exposed to a series of stressful events and disturbing people, metaphorically acting like charging rhinos or hissing snakes. A primary human motive is avoiding or minimizing stimuli perceived as aversive and stressful and to gravitate toward those circumstances or people deemed desirable. This dichotomous framework of rival motivations is described using a variety of polarized terminology, including "approach versus avoidance" (Berntson & Cacioppo, 2008, p. 193), "initiation versus prevention" (Kolb & Whishaw, 2009, p. 146), or "arousal versus inhibition" (Schultheiss & Burnstein, 2010). Collectively, these labels represent humans' perpetual quest to take courses of action that provide pleasure and reward and avoid circumstances that interfere with our personal definitions of satisfaction. Which labels you use is secondary to the realization that behaviors routinely exhibited in the classroom and workplace surprisingly mirror hormonal and neurological triggers in the sympathetic or parasympathetic nervous systems. We next examine biological correlates of common motives related to learning and performance, including the needs for power, affiliation, achievement, and the dispositions of seeking pleasure and attaining overall well-being.

Principle #17—Power and social dominance displays mimic sympathetic nervous system activation

You don't know the power of the Dark Side, I must obey my master.
Darth Vader, Star Wars

Universally, displays of power motivation abound. Teachers insist students complete homework, bosses demand increased productivity from their workers, and coaches dictate who will be in the starting lineup. As a teenager, I asked my mother (Mrs. Darth Vader), "Why do I have to go to college?" She firmly removed any doubt in my mind by calmly saying, "Because I say so, that should be good enough for you!" The display of power is a prominent theory of motivation that helps explain why some individuals defer to autocratic and controlling leadership and teaching styles as a means to influence performance (McClelland, 1975; Winter, 1973). Power motivation occurs when individuals assume that they have the ability to make decisions, control, or take actions to determine the behaviors of others (Magee & Langner, 2008). Reeve (2009) identified three criteria representative of a controlling motivational style: prioritizing your own perspective over the desires of others, deliberately attempting to convince others that your way is the best way, and the persistent application of pressure to induce behavioral change in subordinates. Individuals with a high power motivation are more aggressive and assertive and less willing to negotiate disagreements (Winter, 2000). Most importantly, self-proclaimed high-powered individuals, when exposed to experimental manipulations where power motivation can be readily displayed and measured, exhibit biological response patterns similar to those of people facing abject fear or a threat of harm.

The biological markers of the SNS, primed during displays of power and dominance, include increased production of the hormones epinephrine, norepinephrine, testosterone, and cortisol (Schultheiss & Brunstein, 2010). "Dominance" refers to the motivation of an individual to nonaggressively achieve or maintain a high social status (Mazur & Booth, 1998). The omnipresent effect of testosterone is usually associated with power and dominance, with diverse studies revealing that testosterone increases occur in both men and women when playing sporting events (Mazur & Booth, 1998; Schultheiss & Brunstein, 2010), during video game contests (Carré, Campbell, Lozoya, Goetz, & Welker, 2013), when chopping down trees (Trumble et al., 2013), and even vicariously among spectators watching sporting events (Bernhardt, Dabbs, Fielden, & Lutter, 1998). Testosterone increases are implicated in these types of studies because the competitive nature of the tasks provides an opportunity for individuals to display socially acceptable dominance as ancillary to completion of the task. Like the peacock spreading his plumage or the warbling canary, competition serves as the stage for humans to "strut their stuff" and show off their abilities. However, there is one caveat: Baseline testosterone routinely decreases when *men* lose competitions, but the same outcome is only sporadically observed in *women*. Although researchers provide many different explanations for this gender discrepancy, the most likely reason for differences may be the general passivity associated with female gender roles across cultures (Carré et al., 2013; Schultheiss et al., 2005).

Regardless of gender, increased levels of testosterone have repercussions for organized and motivated behavior. Foremost, testosterone lowers the threshold for aggressive behaviors (Schultheiss et al., 2005) and is related to greater social control, persistence, and combativeness (Dabbs, Alford, & Fielden, 1998). Besides the very obvious ramifications for more aggressive behavior while participating in sporting events, students or workers involved in competitions may display overzealous status seeking, or exhibit manic behaviors as part of their competitive spirit. Kohn (1999) outlined the detrimental consequences of classroom contests, including increased learner anxiety, a diminished sense of empowerment, and less individual accountability. Similarly, workplace competitions instill a weakened team focus in employees, creating animosity and alienation between those succeeding and those individuals that fail. Fortunately, increased testosterone is not all bad, as individuals showing elevated levels who achieve successful outcomes are prime candidates for focused engagement in future tasks and are more likely to achieve learning gains (Stanton & Schultheiss, 2009).

Cortisol is also related to the perception of stress, but with a special emphasis on perceived stress due to social factors. For example, some individuals under observation while performing mental arithmetic and giving speeches are more inclined to exhibit anxiety, freezing, or wanting to completely withdraw from a task compared to performing in isolation (Roelofs et al., 2009). In response to social stress, the adrenal gland releases the hormone cortisol; however, unlike testosterone, high basal cortisol levels are linked to anxiety and social avoidance. Conversely, low basal cortisol levels are linked to decreased stress and behaviors related to embracing social situations (Mehta & Josephs, 2010). Individuals with high cortisol levels have been found to be more inclined to exhibit dominance behaviors, such as repeatedly trying to beat the same opponent on a task. As for power motivation and cortisol, few studies exist, but Wirth, Welsh, and Schultheiss (2006) observed increases in cortisol after "high-power motivated" individuals lost a contest, but the same individuals did not have increased cortisol after winning. These results suggest that people high in power motivation will likely be stressed when they lose a contest or when they cannot complete a task, more so than individuals with other dominant motivations.

Although these laboratory studies provide useful insight into the relationship between hormonal releases and power motivation, these studies have been exclusively conducted in synthetic settings and leave unexplored the relation between *different* motivation styles and cortisol production. Experimental manipulation of motivation style while measuring hormonal production allows the researcher to determine what specific teaching and leadership approaches are perceived as stressful and which instructional strategies facilitate performance and engagement. In one of the few studies of its kind, Reeve and Tseng (2011) had educational psychology students solve puzzles while being exposed to either a controlling style of teaching, where a voice recorded instructor barked out solution strategies, provided pressured feedback, and reminded participants of time limits, or an autonomous style, where participants were encouraged to complete the puzzle logically and given supportive and nurturing feedback. No surprise, results interpretation revealed that motivation style affected cortisol production, with heightened cortisol being associated with the more stressful classroom situation. Thus, we can surmise that methodologies incorporating both behavioral outcomes and online physiological measures, such as hormonal secretions, provide a gateway to understand how biological markers of the SNS can indeed be useful predictors of future performance.

Principle #18—Displays of affiliation mimic parasympathetic nervous system activation

The quixotic power of love and kinship has engendered cultures and debilitated empires for over 4,000 years. Ranging from the 20-year quest of Menelaus in 1190 BCE avenging the abduction of his tempestuous wife Helen of Troy (which led to the Trojan Wars and the death of at least 150,000 people), to the promiscuous Cleopatra, who aided the collapse of the Roman Empire, to the abdication of King Edward VIII of England in 1948 to marry a commoner, the desire to be loved has immutably altered the course of history. The contentious view that love and platonic bonding conquers all is supported by some scholars of motivational science, who suggest that a primary motive of human existence is predicated upon fulfilling the need to feel connected to others (Gordon, Martin, Feldman, & Leckman, 2011; Ryan & Deci, 2000).

The motive of affiliation presumes that humans desire intimate physical and emotional connections to others that are selective, enduring, and consensual (Feldman, 2012). Historically, affiliative bonds with other individuals, groups, or communities were necessary for genetic propagation and human survival. Unified societies thrived, in part, *because* the constellation of affiliative group behaviors enhanced the probability of protection from threat and harm. Today, strong affiliative bonds are unnecessary for foraging food, fending off attacking animals, or appeasing disenchanted members of competing tribes (staff meetings excluded). However, the actualization of social attachment and the demonstration of pro-social behaviors are instrumental for overall psychological health. Confluent evidence from the disciplines of biology, psychology, and sociology reveal that the formation of early and enduring affiliative bonds is related to longevity, enhanced immunity to disease, and a lower incidence of psychological disorders (Puig, Englund, Simpson, & Collins, 2013). For our purposes, knowledge of the connection between biological and psychological indications of love and affiliation are useful to understand the purpose, process, and outcomes of performance behavior.

Recall that the parasympathetic nervous system is associated with regulating the body to a state of homeostasis, partially achieved through stress reduction. Physiologically, when the parasympathetic nervous system is activated, heart rate drops, blood pressure decreases, and erratic breathing is modulated. Behaviorally, stereotypic anxiety subsides as you relax and are overcome by an aura of contentment, relief, and satisfaction. A variety of recursive hormonal and autonomic neurological changes restore your body to pre-stress conditions. Now, evaluate the types of feelings you have when you are with a likeable partner, sibling, or friend, someone whose company you especially enjoy. Most people asked to describe bonding behaviors mention affectionate touch, interpersonal focus, and matched dyadic states related to feelings of calm, gratification, and safety (Schneiderman, Zagoory-Sharon, Leckman, & Feldman, 2012). You may have even experienced the phenomenon of temporary relief of cold or headache symptoms when you are with a certain special person. Logically, you may deduce similarities between behaviors associated with forming and maintaining platonic and romantic attachments, and parasympathetic nervous system activation. Feldman (2012) described this process of reciprocal integrated engagement and regulation of psychological and neurohormonal systems as "biobehavioral synchrony" (p. 381). The concordant biological and behavioral evidence concerning the need for affiliation reveals that changes in the parasympathetic nervous system and associated affiliative behavior are, indeed, coordinated and positively correlated (Schultheiss & Brunstein, 2010): Amorous feelings calm the brain.

The majority of studies that examine affiliative synchronicity investigate pair bonding, where attachments are formed between two individuals. Research most frequently examines mother–infant relations, although biopsychological evidence has now emerged revealing parallels to the formation of adult romantic and platonic bonds. The hormone Oxytocin OT is most frequently implicated as coinciding with affiliative behavior. Neurologically, OT transmission is part of the hypothalamic–pituitary–adrenal axis and related to dopaminergic neurons. When contextual conditions warrant the acceleration of bonding, such as when feeling safe and secure, parasympathetic efference increases prefrontal cortex activity, which concurrently accelerates OT–dopamine interactions, facilitating the motivation to bond (Feldman, 2012). Psychologically, individuals feel a sense of warmth, interpersonal trust, and security synchronized with corresponding increases in requited affection. Unique to OT transmission is the stability and reciprocity in hormonal activity between partners and even among triads (parental, romantic or filial, Feldman, 2012) whereby parallel transmissions result in mutually rewarding coordinated social behavior, such as reciprocated eye gaze, perception of closeness, feelings of mutual trust, and accurate detection of emotional states (Ross & Young, 2009). The effect of OT is so alluring that some researchers refer to OT as the "love drug" or the "cuddly chemical" (Dreu, Greer, Kleef, Shalvi, & Handgraaf, 2011).

Despite the purported benefits of OT, evidence for the universality of affiliative benefits is inconsistent. Specifically, certain populations (e.g., older women, Taylor, 2006) and those who experience loneliness or lack of social support (Bartz, Zaki, Bolger, & Ochsner, 2011) indicate *decreased* basal levels of OT despite affiliative behavior. These discrepancies suggest that OT levels may be stress indicators as well biological markers that orchestrate affiliation-seeking behavior in the quest to raise basal OT levels. In other words, the expectation of affiliation, not the affiliate bond per se, may be the underlying cause of OT transmissions.

Although elevated OT production is not the "love potion" described in some supplement advertisements and in the popular media (http://oxytocinspray.org), knowledge of the connection between affiliation motives and OT production is of practical value for at least three reasons. First, the results from dozens of studies suggest that OT production moderates social behavior (Ross & Young, 2009). I do not recommend offering learners or workers OT-laced brownies or advocate workplace socialization that interferes with policy or productivity; however, highly-functioning work teams and classrooms, as well as topics appropriate for constructivist learning, are naturalistic settings that can leverage the power of OT-affiliative synchronic bonds. Creating performance opportunities where collegial participants work together will likely jumpstart the OT pump, enhancing the probability of a coordinated work effort. Considering that group work requires the exchange of ideas and debating the relative merits of individual suggestions, we can presume that individuals will be more cooperative and open to suggestions when OT levels are elevated than when not. Empirical evidence in OT studies supports the hypothesis that individuals with strong affiliative motives exhibit measurable receptivity and foster group cohesiveness (Baumgartner, Heinrichs, Vonlanthen, Fischbacher & Fehr 2008; Gordon et al., 2011).

Second, although results from some studies are ambiguous (Theodoridou, Penton-Voak, & Rowe, 2013), frequently, individuals with higher basal OT levels are more perceptive of social and emotional cues (Domes, Heinrichs, Michel, Berger, & Herpertz, 2007; Guastella, Mitchell, & Dadds, 2008). These cues can range from understanding the meaning of nonverbal behavior to having more accurate perceptions of emotions of an individual when evaluating facial expression. The ability to detect feelings and emotions is critical considering nonverbal communication may frequently conflict with verbalizations, resulting in discrepant interpretation of messages (Argyle, 1988). Domes et al. (2007) used the phrase "affective mind reading" (p. 732) to describe the process of inferring dispositions and affect from physical cues emanating from the eye region alone, leading to the conclusion that high OT can predict more accurate inferences about affective states. These findings are especially useful to those individuals who may have difficulties interpreting socially relevant cues or who have sensory deficits, including children diagnosed with autism spectrum disorder (Bartz et al., 2010).

Third, higher basal OT levels are related to attachment and trust (Campbell, 2010). OT production, in many ways, mirrors the neurological pathways reminiscent of dopamine release in anticipation of monetary reward. The anticipation paradigm suggests that the expectation of reward is a powerful motivator correlated with positive mood and affect. This line of thought also hypothetically implies that high-OT individuals should be more receptive to creative problem solutions and more likely to take academic risks (e.g., answering questions in spite of the probability of being wrong) because of the higher degree of trust and comfort among constituent group members. Although many studies on the subject of reward anticipation use financial incentives (Foti & Hajcak, 2012), for others, social motivation alone is an equally powerful incentive to cultivate group performance. Regardless, the research on OT production leads the MD to understand that organizational trust is an integral factor in cultivating high performance in individuals and teams (Kramer & Lewicki, 2010).

In summary, cultivating OT production is not a panacea, nor is it a performance proxy suggesting that students or employees with high affiliation motive are stellar performers. Study results are ambiguous, and OT production is clearly mediated by a variety of contextual and biological factors, such as circadian rhythm, menstrual cycle, and interaction with the complex integrative human neural network (Campbell, 2010). In addition, some studies suggest that gaps in social relationships or anticipation of social harmony also catalyze OT production. However, any strategy that can replicate the contextual conditions associated with OT production will likely be organizationally advantageous and leverage the physiological corollaries of affiliation motives.

Principle #19—Achievement and incentive reward share similar neural response patterns

Most of us have personal strivings for success. We envision being the best at something, For example, you might strive to be the best parent, have the lowest golf score, or bake the best brownies. My friends Ron and Becky want to be known as the people who have the most nutcrackers on display in their home at holiday time! Whatever your preference, determining the target of our personal optimism involves a complex series of implicit and explicit estimations grounded in the process of setting goals. Sometimes the goals we set are motivated in comparison with others performing a similar task, such as selling more Girl Scout cookies than your neighbor does. Alternatively, we may strive to meet criteria of excellence, such as scoring above passing grade on a certification examination. Other times, we may focus on bettering our performance in comparison with our own prior results. Regardless of how goals are determined, individuals who are motivated by striving for excellence show a high need for achievement.

The need for achievement is well documented in the annals of motivation history. Pioneered by work in the mid-twentieth century, early views concerning achievement motivation were predicated upon a dichotomous philosophy espousing that individuals operated under two broad assumptions: they either approached tasks with the anticipation of success or avoided tasks when failure was expected (McClelland, Atkinson, Clark, & Lowell, 1976). This view suggested that positive emotions, such as excitement and pride, were associated with success, whereas negative consequences, including feelings of anxiety and shame, were related to failure. According to this polarized view, accomplished individuals would feel personally rewarded when reaching goals, whereas those unsuccessful would suffer frustration and potential humiliation because of the perception of failure. The behavioral cycle of success and failure closely aligns with how our neurological system responds to financial reward and incentive seeking, suggesting the interesting hypothesis that knowledge is actually a reward.

Empirical evidence for the biopsychological correlates of achievement is considerably more elusive than for other motives (Schultheiss & Brunstein, 2010). Studies generally reveal three systematic corollaries: increased dopamine levels in the brain, specific brain areas targeted, and hormonal release. Biologically, incentive seeking and reward activate the mesocorticolimbic system, focused in the ventral striatum, which comprises the nucleus accumbens, ventral caudate, and putamen (Knapp & Kornetsky, 2009). Collectively, these areas of the brain are one of the primary receptors of the neurotransmitter dopamine. The brain responds to the release of dopamine with feelings of confidence, serenity, and euphoric mood elevation. Although knowing the exact location of brain activation (referred to as *localization*) is important for neurologists, understanding motivation dictates that we also examine the behaviors that trigger the neuronal responses.

Most studies investigating achievement motivation control for motivational style or test for brain localization differences contingent upon completing certain tasks. McClelland (1995), in the first study of its kind, asked participants to complete mental math problems and found that high achievement motivation predicted better memory recall and decreased urination compared with a control group with low achievement motivation. McClelland speculated that since the hormone arginine vasopressin is an antidiuretic (substance that causes water retention), it was somehow linked to achievement motivation; however, this line of research surprisingly has remained relatively dormant since McClelland's pioneering efforts to link physiology and a motivation for achievement.

Mizuno et al. (2008) used fMRI measures to compare the neural substrates activated by academic reward in comparison with those linked to monetary reward. Bilateral putamen activation was observed with strong localization similarities between those academically and financial motivated. Similarly, Lee, Reeve, Xue, and Xiong (2009) found unique, but overlapping, brain activations in the ventral striatum (where the putamen is located) for both financially motivated and inherently achievement-motivated individuals, leading to the conclusion that neural pathways of reward processing and episodic memory were shared. When varying incentives were offered during a pattern identification task, Taylor et al. (2004) observed similarities in neuronal activity between occasions when participants were offered a higher incentive compared with a lower one, and when participants activated executive control mechanisms of their working memory (highly related to achievement motivation). Finally, Kang et al. (2009) used a trivia task to investigate the relationships among intellectual curiosity, recall, and brain localization. Results analysis revealed that heightened curiosity (a proxy for achievement needs) predicted neuronal patterns similar to those in individuals anticipating reward. Answering trivia questions incorrectly was linked to higher putamen activation (the dopamine receptor), suggesting that the desire to learn new material may have a specific biological marker in comparison with the recollection of existing knowledge.

We can infer from these studies constancy in biological response patterns that align achievement motivation and reward paradigms in human laboratory subjects. Converting this knowledge to practice, we can confidently confirm the hypothesis that for many people, knowledge is rewarding. Thus, consideration of any activities that enhance knowledge would likely boost the engagement and productivity of individuals with achievement motivation, even if that motivation is not directly related to a particular task. We might also conclude that in well-defined conditions, extrinsic monetary reward may be a catalyst, inducing feelings of satisfaction and contentment based upon the biological corollary of dopamine release in the brain associated with reward anticipation. Of course, the extrinsic reward inference does not mean that focused attention or more efficient information processing can be artificially induced because not all individuals will have strong achievement motivation, and at times financial incentives can actually decrease interest and motivation (Lepper, Greene, & Nisbett, 1973). We should also remember that there is a general lack of consensus as to the exact neural mechanisms involved in regulating reward experience, and the information above shows that neural pathways of reward can be stimulated in multiple ways. The effects of reward will change within individuals over time and between tasks, thus cautious implementation of reward systems is essential.

Principle #20—Humanity is motivated to seek pleasure and avoid pain

A man hath no better thing under the sun than to eat, and to drink, and to be merry.
The Bible, Ecclesiastes 8:15

For there was never yet a philosopher that could endure the toothache patiently.
Shakespeare, Much Ado about Nothing

Under the guise of Shakespeare's quill and God's voice, much of life is dichotomized by a series of extremes: good versus evil, conservative versus liberal, controlled versus automatic, involved versus apathetic, hedonistic versus altruistic, Wilma versus Betty. These dualistic conceptions of human existence suggest that absolutes exemplify our beliefs and behaviors. In 1798, long before scholars scientifically investigated the nature of motivation, Jeremy Bentham espoused his utilitarian philosophy grounded in the dictum that all mankind seeks to maximize pleasure and minimize pain (Sober & Wilson, 1998). Bentham's ideas illustrate psychological hedonism, a theory that closely resembles Principle #14 (p. 50), which indicates that humans are motivated to attain certain targets while avoiding others. Specifically, hedonistic theories of motivation contend that behaviorally and psychologically, all individuals are ultimately preordained to have an aversion to pain and a desire to actively pursue sensory pleasures. This explanation of motivation suggests that humans set goals and regulate behavior solely to satisfy hedonic needs: All else is subservient to hedonic pleasure, the singular focus of our daily efforts (Sober & Wilson, 1998).

Philosophically, few would debate that the prevailing goal of human existence, at least in part, is survival and a desire for all things subjectively satisfying. However, at least three conundrums discount the plausibility of hedonic behavior as the single force regulating the direction and intensity of our efforts. First, we pursue both *ultimate* goals, which are desired end-states, and *instrumental* goals that serve as incremental milestones to achieve our ultimate objectives (see pp. 155–157 for a detailed explanation of goal types). If we examine the chain of events that occurs between setting ultimate goals and enhancing the probability of reaching the goal, a personal willingness to endure pain (or at least discomfort and delay of gratification) is usually part of the formula. Examples abound, such as the "no pain, no gain" maxim associated with exercise; tolerating intellectually painful, but required, courses in order to earn a degree; or enduring the potential of conflicting motives associated with the seasonal visit to one's in-laws as the sacrifice for a strong spousal relationship. Culturally desirable practices further illustrate that humans are willing to endure pain to enhance social standing and gain aesthetic pleasure. By example, 40% of the adult US population between the ages of 26 and 40 years pays someone to inject them with iron oxide and disazodiarylide, risking possible infection to flaunt permanently emblazoned body art, otherwise known as a tattoo (Pew Research Center, 2009). These examples suggest that although subjective pleasure or well-being are primary goals, considerable debate and entire books from eminent scholars argue that sensory pleasure alone does not dominate human behavior (Higgins, 2012).

Second, we must consider the subjective nature of pleasure and pain. By most accounts, pleasure is a conscious affective reaction to a stimulus that is perceived as biologically or psychologically rewarding for the organism (Kringelbach & Berridge, 2010). However, in order to be considered pleasurable, the stimulus must also be both liked and wanted. Although I *like* meatballs, I avoid meatballs when I wear my freshly starched white tuxedo shirt. For me, meatballs are a typically pleasing stimulus that becomes situationally aversive due to my cosmopolitan demeanor. I differ from my colleague Dr. Alex, who loves to eat sardines and wear t-shirts. For Alex, nothing beats the culinary delight of a hearty sardine and mustard sandwich on chewy Dreikernebrot bread while lounging in his favorite tattered Billy Bob's Hideaway t-shirt. If your salivary reflex (which is an unconscious pleasure reaction) remains dormant, then you are likely nauseated by the taste or distinctive aroma of a freshly opened can of Norwegian sardines, suggesting that pleasure motivation varies according to individual. Hopefully, the scenario I just described is not so revolting that you begin to have feelings of pain, which according to some descriptions is defined as an unpleasant sensory experience. Pain, like pleasure, has motivational, affective, and neurological characteristics that are selectively interpreted by individuals

(Guindon & Hohmann, 2009). Evaluation of pain usually coincides with conscious avoidance of the pain target, as the source of pain minimally has the potential for neural sensitivity or soft tissue damage. Most examples of environmentally induced pain are readily addressed by MDs (e.g., patching up injuries, regulating room temperature, and eliminating rancid odors, to name a few) and are not an interpretive concern here. However, subjective perceptions of interpersonal dynamics, organizational culture, or even responses to current events may become realistic interpretive nightmares due to the possibility of prompting a wide range of unpredictable cognitive and affective reactions associated with pain perception.

Third, we should ponder whether hedonic motivation is prompted by reaching the goal or by the process of goal pursuit. As Higgins (2012) suggested, we should avoid arbitrary conclusions that satisfaction of hedonic motivation is the *cause* of observed behavior. An obvious illustration is the satisfaction of hunger. Some of us indulge ourselves by ordering dessert after a large meal. Clearly, satisfying a specific bodily deficit is not the impetus for ordering a pie, with ice cream on the pie and syrup on the ice cream. Devoid of the physiological necessity for homeostatic restoration, we might surmise that ingestion is also a function of habit, social protocol, or perhaps the subjective positive valence associated with the process of consumption. Consider my neighbor Eugene, who spends hours casting his fishing line into our well-stocked bass pond but throws the fish back every time, apparently unconcerned about memorializing the goal! Those with amorous inclinations may also begrudgingly admit that the thrill of the romantic chase is more important than catching the fish (i.e., marrying your partner). Hopefully, these examples illustrate that hedonic motives are not exclusively satisfied by target attainment or successful avoidance. Instead, we should consider that irrespective of the target, behavioral–psychological reactions to the process of achieving goals are, at times, a sufficient motivating force to engage in the targeted behaviors. Fortunately, the culinary, haberdashery, and romantic dilemmas described, like many behavioral reactions to pleasurable or innocuous stimuli, have distinguishable neurobiological mechanisms both within and between individuals that assist motive identification (Berridge & Kringelbach, 2008).

Pleasure and pain can be measured in a variety of stereotypical ways, including facial expressions, pupil dilation, and orgasms (Kringelbach and Berridge, 2010). These obvious external indicators are a primary means of assessing the apparent affective state of an individual. The focal point is the façade, or what seems "apparent," which may lead to inaccurate motivational inferences. Many times, superficial physiological indicators are unreliable indications of an individual's underlying affect or cognitions. The unreliability of superficial measures dictates examination of a variety of "hedonic hotspots," or nerve receptive centers in the brain to help enhance inference ability when evaluating hedonic behavior. Figure 3.2 illustrates the major hotspots and neural pathways in the brain that are activated when exposed to external stimuli that the individual perceives as potentially rewarding or debilitating. Similar to the biopsychological process of reward described earlier, neural receptors in the brain, such as the ventral palladium and nucleus accumbens, receive the neurotransmitter dopamine when stimulated during activities, such as eating, drinking, or sex.

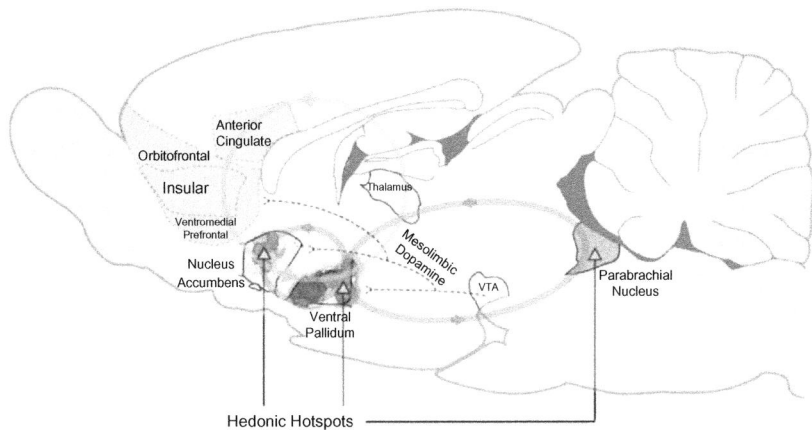

Figure 3.2 Hedonic hotspots and associated neural pathways.
Reprinted with permission of Oxford University Press, USA from Smith, Mahler, Pecina, & Berridge (2008) in M. Kringelbach & K. C. Berridge (Eds.), Pleasures of the brain.

Dopamine release triggers a positive affective valence and the individual perceives these activities as pleasurable. Although these reactions are important, further elaboration on these pedestrian and carnal topics should not be of interest to the MD for a variety of ethical and statutory reasons.

Examination of neurological research conducted in a number of common social settings reveals startling similarities to neural activation patterns observed when individuals are rewarded or punished. When studying the effects of deliberate exclusion from a cyber ball-tossing game, Eisenberger, Lieberman, and Williams (2003) used fMRI readings and observed greater activation of the anterior cingulate cortex (ACC, a pain hot spot) during game exclusion than during inclusion, which led to the conclusion that "social pain is analogous in its neurocognitive function to physical pain" (p. 292). Likewise, using fMRI measures, ACC activation was noted in bereaved women presented with familial grief-related stimuli picturing a mother or a sister, but activation in the nucleus accumbens (an affiliation *reward* center) was observed in women with self-reported stronger attachment to the departed individual (O'Connor et al., 2008). Individuals referring to themselves with negative self-referential cognitions, such as "I'm unlovable" or "no one desires me" activate biological consequences quite similar to those found in clinically depressed individuals (Slavich, O'Donovan, Epel, & Kemeny, 2010).

Conversely, activation of the striatum, which is usually observed during reward-related studies of satiety and thirst (see Principle #17, p. 57), was observed by Izuma, Saito, and Sadato (2008), who paired an individual's positive personality feedback with an individual's picture. Similarly, striatum neural activity is commonly observed when individuals believe they are treated fairly (Tabibnia, Satpute, & Lieberman, 2008), as well as when they are afforded the opportunity to give money to charitable causes (Izuma, Saito, & Sadato, 2010). Striatum activity is found during games of chance, usually when participants win. Curiously, similar striatum activity is found when some players lose, provided another's loss is greater (Dvash, Gilam, Ben-Ze'ev, Hendler, & Shamay-Tsoory, 2010), perhaps suggesting that individuals take pleasure and are more motivated in defeat, but only when someone else suffers more!

A number of practical conclusions can be advanced when examining the positive and negative evidence associated with hedonic research. First, the subjective affective valence associated with external stimuli varies within and between individuals. People interpret similar stimuli through their own unique lens. What may be perceived as rewarding to one individual may be disdained by another. Further, individuals strive for a sense of optimal homeostatic balance (Leknes & Tracey, 2008), endeavoring to regulate emotional highs and lows. Although MDs will prosper by devoting substantial effort to determining what constituents perceive as pleasurable or noxious, generalization among individuals would likely be foolhardy. Awarding a turkey to a vegetarian or a box of chocolates to a fitness enthusiast may have null or unanticipated negative performance consequences.

Second, many organizations have deeply entrenched hierarchical structures that undermine who gets included and who does not. Appropriate inclusion criteria should be a concerted effort on the part of leadership, fostered by soliciting participants to volunteer when motivated to participate in a project. Excluding individuals without concrete justification based upon level or status alone may be perceived as the conscious infliction of emotional pain.

Third, neurological studies reveal dopamine production in anticipation of reward or a positive event. It seems prudent to avoid communicating unrealistic promises or false expectations to employees, who will easily become frustrated if expectations are not fulfilled.

Fourth, it seems that some individuals can be motivated by the expectation of pain as an instrumental goal. Individuals, such as athletes and dancers, who persevere through pain, intentionally orchestrate a positive posthedonic experience akin to a self-imposed and self-regulated reward. As Leknes and Tracey (2010) indicated, "let us not forget that enduring some discomfort is an efficient way of increasing pleasure and returning to homeostasis. Who has not tried fasting before a feast, or stayed in the sun until almost unbearably hot before jumping in the pool?" (p. 326). Consequently, it appears that for some, pain perceived as within one's control may be judiciously used as a powerful motivator.

Principle #21—Motivated behavior is heritable and evolutionary

Are you feeling lazy? Tired of reading? Wishing this chapter was done? You can probably blame your parents, at least to a certain extent. Motivation, like hair color, height, and intelligence, has a specific heritable component. By heritable, I mean that behaviors, such as task orientation, the degree of conservatism you espouse, and even your spiritual commitment, are all determined, in part, by your unique genetic code. Of course, behaviors are also influenced by the environment, but to what extent?

The field of behavior genetics reveals exactly what proportion of your disposition and behavior can be explained by the integrative role of genetics *and* environment. Mathematical heritability estimates measure the probable contribution of genetic factors as the source of a particular trait or behavior. These estimates are derived primarily from studies of monozygotic twins (identical) or from adopted children raised in similar or different environments. By comparing groups of identical twins raised in separate environments with genetically dissimilar groups of adopted siblings raised in the same environment, correlations are calculated that determine what percentage of a particular factor is estimated to be influenced by heredity. Although a host of methodological concerns are implicated in heritability calculations, statistical inferences from these types of studies provide valid data that suggest motivation has a heritable component. Table 3.2 shows selective heritability estimates, which, in general, indicate that 40–50% of the behavioral differences between individuals are explained by heredity (Plomin, 1990).

Once estimates of heritability are calculated, we then must consider the proportion of variability between individuals that is *unexplained* by genetics, in hopes of determining how environmental factors influence motivated behavior. The interpretation of heritable estimates should be guided by the concept of *niche picking* (Scarr & McCartney, 1983), which suggests that we are inclined to choose environments that leverage our inborn tendencies. Thus, if you are genetically predisposed with strong verbal ability, it is more likely that your parents will take you to the library than to a basketball court. Niche picking is empirically supported by the well-known phenomenon affecting reading motivation called the *Matthew Effect* (Stanovich, 1986). This effect suggests that skilled readers are deliberately afforded participation in more activities that promote reading comprehension, while their less advantaged peers tend to be relegated to learning contexts that do not support reading growth. Stanovich used the popular phrase "the rich get richer" to describe advantaged individuals who have the economic and social means to readily improve their existing talent and capitalize on existing strengths. In the absence of supportive contextual conditions, motivation to read is impeded, and the obstacles of

Table 3.2 Heritable estimates of selected motivational constructs

Behavior	Heritable estimate (%)
Anxiety	70
Sociability	64
Dominance	60
Emotionality	54
Task orientation	50
Control	44
Aggression	40

Source: McCartney, Harris, and Bernieri (1990).

the impoverished are intensified. Fortunately, the vicious cycle can be broken, and unfavorable genetic–environmental correlations can be "uncoupled" (Berk, 2008, p. 88). Uncoupling involves a concerted effort by caregivers to actively address and provide needed support. Several motivation variables are shown to be malleable to uncoupling interventions, including resilience (Kim-Cohen, Moffitt, Caspi, & Taylor, 2004), prosocial behavior (Knafo & Plomin, 2006), altruism (Krueger, Hicks, & McGue, 2001), and aggression (Moffitt, 2005). In aggregate, these studies confirm that despite genetic predisposition, proactive and intentional strategies can overcome the negative influence of latent genetic–environmental risks (Moffitt, 2005).

The conclusion that innate predispositions can be mediated through defined actions provides interesting fodder to contemplate the evolutionary nature of motivated behavior. Although the empirical evidence supporting the heritability of motivation is strong, due to the current methodological restriction for time travel, little, if any, empirical data can inscrutably verify that motivated behavior has historical variation. However, a variety of evidence at the cellular and behavioral levels suggests that humans functionally change when a particular strategy is determined to be useful and beneficial. A premise of evolutionary theory is that human characteristics evolve as a means to help the organism survive and reproduce and variants in efficacious behavior are passed along to future generations at a greater frequency than those strategies shown to be less beneficial (Sober & Wilson, 1998). Scholars debate the source and type of psychological adaptation (Confer et al., 2010), but clearly at minimum, survival and mating strategies have an evolutionary trajectory (Buss, 2005). Nairne, Thompson, and Pandeirada (2007) used variations in memory priming tasks and found that participants had a higher probability of recalling words related to survival mechanisms (e.g., remembering landmarks, constellations, weather patterns, and food words) than words with no survival connotation. Additionally, a host of other strategy-based interventions have concluded that evolutionary-based preferences exist for some behaviors, such as how females choose a mating partner, how groups deal with performance laggards, and how female superiority with regard to spatial skills has evolved (Confer et al., 2010). Collectively, these studies suggest that domain-specific adaptation in behaviors is influenced by survival motivation.

Additionally, albeit likely of far less interest to the MD, developmental neuroscience provides conclusive evidence to support neuronal *plasticity* (i.e., molecular changes to existing mechanisms at the cellular level); that is, as organisms, both animals and humans adapt to changes in their respective living environments. Behaviors as fundamental as a baby crying because of separation anxiety, as seen in experiments where rat pups are involuntarily removed from the mother, are routinely studied at both the cellular and behavioral levels. Rat mothers show measurable changes in neurotransmitter receptors in the brain when involuntarily separated from their pups. Corresponding behavioral reactions of heightened anxiety ensue (Hofer, 2009). In other words, evolved changes in the detection system of the rat mother can be observed at both genetic and behavioral levels, with each mechanism showing graded responses over time. Parallel regulatory mechanisms exist in humans, suggesting that as successive generations undergo behavior adaptations, measurable genetic changes should also be expected.

Although conclusive evidence supporting the evolutionary nature of behavior continues to emerge at the human level, we can reliably conclude that at the very least, motivated behavior is determined in multiple ways (Cacioppo & Berntson, 2009). As MDs, acute awareness of the behavioral manifestations of human motives found in the classroom or workplace can be positively or negatively associated with biological markers. Research in humans that use techniques, such as event-related potentials, that measure brain voltage have been shown to discriminate changes undetectable by behavioral observation alone (Mills et al., 2013). Multiple diagnostic approaches enhance the ability to decipher relevant evidence from what Confer et al. (2010) referred to as "noise" (p. 110), which happens when unique combinations of biological and contextual factors result in random unpredictable behaviors, potentially leading to false inferences. Clearly, the consideration and realization that unitary behavioral evidence is insufficient, yet necessary, to advance conclusions will serve the aspiring student of motivational science well.

Chapter summary/conclusions

Faced with a myriad of evidence that requires constant vigilance to determine situational relevance, the MD is bombarded with seemingly isomorphic behaviors. The challenge of deciphering the exact integrative nature of the behaviors and to what extent the behaviors can reliably yield conclusions about an individual is quite puzzling. The first step in the process of mediation is the realization that individual perceptions are most likely selective and arbitrary interpretations of stimuli that may significantly vary both within and between individuals.

Although behavioral observation alone can be misleading and potentially lead to spurious interpretations, individuals will be hard pressed to control or disguise the representations of their biological markers. Accurate detection of biophysical evidence, in many cases, will provide the gateway to affirmation for the practitioner. Nervous system and corresponding hormonal activity are predictable, albeit challenging to observe. Pacing the hallways with fMRI equipment or thermodynamic instruments is impractical for most; however, the concomitant physiological accompaniments of behavior can be readily observed, as individuals routinely display repetitive response patterns to people and events. Evidence of neurological activity, such as pupil dilation, breathing patterns, and facial expressions, can be easily detected and should be a routine part of the MD's diagnostic process when contemplating the source of motivations.

The current state of biopsychology research presents two main challenges. First, new findings occur regularly and require active practitioner diligence to remain current. Second, biopsychological findings are frequently ambivalent, creating interpretive difficulties. In spite of these concerns, the evidence presented in the current chapter should clearly add to the toolbox of the MD. Regardless, identification of confluent patterns of behavior and biology together will provide more robust and reliable interpretive data than either source in isolation.

Next steps

The current chapter has illuminated a number of findings that generate a foundation of knowledge concerning how human neuronal and hormonal mechanisms interact with certain behaviors. Clear links between biology and motivation are supported by empirical evidence, but how does motivation change over time? As individuals grow and mature, biological change is inevitable. Additionally, as individuals interact with their environments, they undergo a series of psychological changes based upon reactions to their collective experience. The experience, in turn, influences motives, which, like many aspects of human existence, have a defined developmental trajectory that shapes the goals we set, the strategies we use, and the outcomes we attain. As an example to help understand the trajectory of motivation, we will examine the maturation of two siblings **Cheryl and Rebecca Hines**, who, at face value, appear to be drastically different: One is a famous actress and the other a prominent college professor. We next turn to how motivation changes over the course of the lifespan and discuss critical periods of change that influence how we choose to navigate our lifelong motivational journey.

End of chapter motivational minute

Principles covered in this chapter:

13. **Neurological/endocrinological evidence informs or refutes behavioral evidence**—many behaviors have predictable physiological corollaries. Analysis of behavior and biological markers together typically yields more accurate inferences than analysis of behaviors alone.
14. **Neurological/endocrinological inferences are multi-dimensional**—a complex interaction exists between observed behavior and human physiology. Evidence can be interpreted at the genetic, synaptic, autonomic, skeletal, cognitive, or systems levels, unitarily or in combination.
15. **The brain is a perceptual filter that influences subjective reality**—humans process information through the limitations of their perceptual and belief networks. Similar stimuli can evoke multiple responses depending upon context and interpretive variables.
16. **Neurological system organization facilitates or inhibits action**—the body strives to maintain a comfortable state of homeostasis. Reactions to behaviors, routinely exhibited in practice, mirror biological triggers found in the CNS.
17. **Power and social dominance displays mimic sympathetic nervous system activation**—when individuals make decisions, control, or take actions that determine the behaviors of others the biological response patterns resemble an organism that is primed for flight or fight.
18. **Displays of affiliation mimic parasympathetic nervous system activation**—when individuals exhibit bonding behavior, the physiological corollaries resemble an organism in a state of homeostasis, marked by stress reduction and OT production.
19. **Achievement and incentive reward share similar neural response patterns**—the biological responses associated with achievement motivation closely align with how our neurological system responds to financial reward. Contextual conditions that promote inclusion and involvement can positively motivate individuals.
20. **Humanity is motivated to seek pleasure and avoid pain**—humans pursue ultimate and instrumental goals. Hedonistic theories of motivation contend that, ultimately, all human motivations are based upon attaining pleasure and avoiding pain.

21. **Motivated behavior is heritable and evolutionary**—substantial evidence supports the view that motivation has a heritable component. Emerging evidence in the field of evolutionary psychology confirms that motives undergo change at the genetic level.

Key terminology (in order of chapter presentation):

- **Neuroanatomy**—the study of human neurological and hormonal systems.
- **Dualism**—a philosophical orientation which asserts that human behavior is explained by two distinct and ontologically separate governing entities.
- **Spurious**—the process of attributing causality to an unwarranted cause when examining the relationship between two or more variables.
- **Ambiguous temporal precedence**—the uncertainty related to determining the casual path of variables. By example, it is unknown if physiological reactions precede a behavior, or if initiation of a behavior precedes the physiological response.
- **Localization**—the process of pinpointing specific areas of the human anatomy responsible for particular hormonal or neurological functioning.
- **Plasticity**—the ability of human physiological architecture to undergo changes in neuronal and cellular composition based upon experience.

References

Argyle, M. (1988). *Bodily communication*. New York, NY: Methuen & Co. Ltd.
Aristotle (2004). *Rhetoric* (Dover Thrift, ed., W. R. Roberts, Trans.). Mineola, NY: Dover Publications.
Bartz, J. A., Zaki, J., Bolger, N., Hollander, E., Ludwig, N. N., Kolevzon, A., et al. (2010). Oxytocin selectively improves empathic accuracy. *Psychological Science, 21*(10), 1426–1428. http://dx.doi.org/10.1177/0956797610383439.
Bartz, J. A., Zaki, J., Bolger, N., & Ochsner, K. N. (2011). Social effects of oxytocin in humans: Context and person matter. *Trends in Cognitive Science, 15*(7), 301–309.
Baumgartner, T., Heinrichs, M., Vonlanthen, A., Fischbacher, U., & Fehr, E. (2008). Oxytocin shapes the neural circuitry of trust and trust adaptation in humans. *Neuron, 58*(4), 639–650.
Beck, R. C. (2004). *Motivation: Theories and principles* (5th ed.). Upper Saddle River, NJ: Pearson/Prentice Hall.
Berk, L. E. (2008). *Infants, children, and adolescents* (6th ed.). Boston, MA: Allyn and Bacon.
Bernhardt, P. C., Dabbs, J. M., Fielden, J. A., & Lutter, C. D. (1998). Testosterone changes during vicarious experiences of winning and losing among fans at sporting events. *Physiology and Behavior, 65*(1), 59–62.
Berntson, G. G., & Cacioppo, J. T. (2008). The neuroevolution of motivation. In J. Y. Shah & W. L. Gardner (Eds.), *Handbook of motivation science* (pp. 188–200). New York, NY: Guilford Press.
Berridge, K. C., & Kringelbach, M. L. (2008). Affective neuroscience of pleasure: Reward in humans and animals. *Psychopharmacology, 199*(3), 457–480. http://dx.doi.org/10.1007/s00213-008-1099-6.
Buss, D. M. (2005). *Handbook of evolutionary psychology*. Hoboken, NJ: Wiley.
Cacioppo, J. T., & Berntson, G. G. (2009). Integrative neuroscience for the behavior Sciences: Implications for inductive inference. In G. G. Berntson & J. T. Cacioppo (Eds.), *Handbook of neuroscience for the behavioral sciences* (pp. 3–11). Hoboken, N.J: J. Wiley.

Campbell, A. (2010). Oxytocin and human social behavior. *Personality and Social Psychology Review, 14*(3), 281–295. http://dx.doi.org/10.1177/1088868310363594.

Carré, J. M., Campbell, J. A., Lozoya, E., Goetz, S. M. M., & Welker, K. M. (2013). Changes in testosterone mediate the effect of winning on subsequent aggressive behaviour. *Psychoneuroendocrinology, 38*(10), 2034–2041. http://dx.doi.org/10.1016/j.psyneuen.2013.03.008.

Confer, J. C., Easton, J. A., Fleischman, D. S., Goetz, C. D., Lewis, D. M. G., Perilloux, C., et al. (2010). Evolutionary psychology: Controversies, questions, prospects, and limitations. *American Psychologist, 65*(2), 110–126. http://dx.doi.org/10.1037/a0018413.

Dabbs, J. M., Alford, E. C., & Fielden, J. A. (1998). Trial lawyers and testosterone: Blue-collar talent in a white-collar world. *Journal of Applied Social Psychology, 28*, 84–94.

Davis, M. (1992). The role of the amygdala in fear and anxiety. *Annual Review of Neuroscience, 15*(1), 353–375. http://dx.doi.org/10.1146/annurev.ne.15.030192.002033.

Dennett, D. (1988). Quining qualia. In A. Marcel & E. Bisiach (Eds.), *Consciousness in Modern Science* (pp. 42–77). Oxford, U.K.: Oxford University Press.

Domes, G., Heinrichs, M., Michel, A., Berger, C., & Herpertz, S. (2007). Oxytocin improves "mind-reading" in humans. *Biological Psychiatry, 61*(6), 731–733.

Dreu, C. K. W. D., Greer, L. L., Kleef, G. A. V., Shalvi, S., & Handgraaf, M. J. J. (2011). Oxytocin promotes human ethnocentrism. *Proceedings of the National Academy of Sciences, 108*(4), 1262–1266. http://dx.doi.org/10.1073/pnas.1015316108.

Dvash, J., Gilam, G., Ben-Ze'ev, A., Hendler, T., & Shamay-Tsoory, S. G. (2010). The envious brain: The neural basis of social comparison. *Human Brain Mapping, NA–NA*. http://dx.doi.org/10.1002/hbm.20972.

Eisenberger, N. I., Lieberman, M. D., & Williams, K. D. (2003). Does rejection hurt? An fMRI study of social exclusion. *Science, 302*(5643), 290–292. http://dx.doi.org/10.1126/science.1089134.

Falk, E. B., Berkman, E. T., Mann, T., Harrison, B., & Lieberman, M. D. (2010). Predicting persuasion-induced behavior change from the brain. *Journal of Neuroscience, 30*(25), 8421–8424.

Feldman, R. (2012). Oxytocin and social affiliation in humans. *Hormones and Behavior, 61*(3), 380–391. http://dx.doi.org/10.1016/j.yhbeh.2012.01.008.

Foti, D., & Hajcak, G. (2012). Genetic variation in dopamine moderates neural response during reward anticipation and delivery: Evidence from event-related potentials. *Psychophysiology, 49*(5), 617–626. http://dx.doi.org/10.1111/j.1469-8986.2011.01343.x.

Gamer, M., & Büchel, C. (2012). Oxytocin specifically enhances valence-dependent parasympathetic responses. *Psychoneuroendocrinology, 37*(1), 87–93. http://dx.doi.org/10.1016/j.psyneuen.2011.05.007.

Gordon, I., Martin, C., Feldman, R., & Leckman, J. F. (2011). Oxytocin and social motivation. *Developmental Cognitive Neuroscience, 1*(4), 471–493. http://dx.doi.org/10.1016/j.dcn.2011.07.007.

Guastella, A. J., Mitchell, P. B., & Dadds, M. R. (2008). Oxytocin increases gaze to the eye region of human faces. *Biological Psychiatry, 63*(1), 3–5.

Guindon, J., & Hohmann, A. G. (2009). The endocannabinoid system and pain. *CNS & Neurological Disorders Drug Targets, 8*(6), 403–421.

Higgins, E. T. (2012). *Beyond pleasure and pain: How motivation works*. New York, NY: Oxford University Press.

Hines, M. (2011). Gender development and the human brain. *Annual Review of Neuroscience, 34*, 69–88.

Hofer, M. A. (2009). Developmental neuroscience. In G. G. Berntson & J. T. Cacioppo (Eds.), *Handbook of neuroscience for the behavioral sciences* (pp. 12–31). Hoboken, NJ: John Wiley & Sons, Inc.

Izuma, K., Saito, D. N., & Sadato, N. (2008). Processing of social and monetary rewards in the human striatum. *Neuron*, *58*(2), 284–294. http://dx.doi.org/10.1016/j.neuron.2008.03.020.

Izuma, K., Saito, D. N., & Sadato, N. (2010). Processing of the incentive for social approval in the ventral striatum during charitable donation. *Journal of Cognitive Neuroscience*, *22*(4), 621–631.

Kang, M. J., Hsu, M., Krajbich, I. M., Loewenstein, G., McClure, S. M., Wang, J. T. Y., et al. (2009). The wick in the candle of learning epistemic curiosity activates reward circuitry and enhances memory. *Psychological Science*, *20*(8), 963–973.

Kim-Cohen, J., Moffitt, T. E., Caspi, A., & Taylor, A. (2004). Genetic and environmental processes in young children's resilience and vulnerability to socioeconomic deprivation. *Child Development*, *75*(3), 651–668.

Klucken, T., Alexander, N., Schweckendiek, J., Merz, C. J., Kagerer, S., Osinsky, R., et al. (2013). Individual differences in neural correlates of fear conditioning as a function of 5-HTTLPR and stressful life events. *Social Cognitive and Affective Neuroscience*, *8*(3), 318–325. http://dx.doi.org/10.1093/scan/nss005.

Knafo, A., & Plomin, R. (2006). Prosocial behavior from early to middle childhood: Genetic and environmental influences on stability and change. *Developmental Psychology*, *42*(5), 771–786.

Knapp, C. M., & Kornetsky, C. (2009). Neural basis of pleasure and reward. In G. G. Berntson & J. T. Cacioppo (Eds.), *Handbook of neuroscience for the behavioral sciences* (pp. 781–806). Hoboken, NJ: John Wiley & Sons, Inc.

Kohn, A. (1999). *Punished by rewards*. New York, NY: Houghton Mifflin.

Kolb, B. E., & Whishaw, I. Q. (2009). Neuroanatomy/neuropsychology. In G. G. Berntson & J. T. Cacioppo (Eds.), *Handbook of neuroscience for the behavioral sciences* (pp. 136–151). Hoboken, NJ: John Wiley & Sons, Inc.

Kramer, R. M., & Lewicki, R. J. (2010). Repairing and enhancing trust: Approaches to reducing organizational trust deficits. *The Academy of Management Annals*, *4*(1), 245–277.

Kringelbach, M. L., & Berridge, K. C. (Eds.). (2010). *Pleasures of the brain*. Oxford, England: Oxford University Press.

Krueger, R. F., Hicks, B. M., & McGue, M. (2001). Altruism and antisocial behavior: Independent tendencies, unique personality correlates, distinct etiologies. *Psychological Science*, *12*(5), 397–402.

Lakatos, P., Karmos, G., Mehta, A. D., Ulbert, I., & Schroeder, C. E. (2008). Entrainment of neuronal oscillations as a mechanism of attentional selection. *Science*, *5872*, 110–113. http://dx.doi.org/10.2307/20054942.

Laney, C., & Loftus, E. F. (2013). Recent advances in false memory research. *South African Journal of Psychology*. Scholarly Paper No. ID 2310679. Rochester, NY: Social Science Research Network.

Laney, C., Morris, E. K., Bernstein, D. M., Wakefield, B. M., & Loftus, E. F. (2010). Asparagus, a love story: Healthier eating could be just a false memory away. *Experimental Psychology*, *55*(5), 291–300.

Lee, C., & Sherman, S. (2008). Synaptic properties of thalamic and intracortical inputs to layer 4 of the first- and higher-order cortical areas in the auditory and somatosensory systems. *Journal of Neurophysiology*, *100*(1), 317–326.

Lee, W., Reeve, J., Xue, Y., & Xiong, J. (2009). Similarities and differences in the neural activities of intrinsic motivation and incentive motivation. *NeuroImage*, *47*(Suppl. 1), S137. http://dx.doi.org/10.1016/S1053-8119(09)71357-6.

Leknes, S., & Tracey, I. (2008). A common neurobiology for pain and pleasure. *Nature Reviews Neuroscience*, *9*(4), 314–320.

Leknes, S., & Tracey, I. (2010). Pain and pleasure: Masters of mankind. In M. Kringelbach & K. C. Berridge (Eds.), *Pleasures of the brain* (pp. 320–336). Oxford, UK: Oxford University Press.

Lepper, M. R., Greene, D., & Nisbett, R. E. (1973). Undermining children's intrinsic interest with extrinsic reward: A test of the "overjustification" hypothesis. *Journal of Personality and Social Psychology, 28*, 129–137.

Loftus, E. F. (1975). Leading questions and the eyewitness report. *Cognitive Psychology, 7*(4), 560–572.

Loftus, E. F. (1997). Creating childhood memories. *Applied Cognitive Psychology, 11*, S75–S86.

Magee, J. C., & Langner, C. A. (2008). How personalized and socialized power motivation facilitate antisocial and prosocial decision-making. *Journal of Research in Personality, 42*(6), 1547–1559.

Mazur, A., & Booth, A. (1998). Testosterone and dominance in men. *Behavioral and Brain Sciences, 21*, 353–397.

McCartney, K., Harris, M. J., & Bernieri, F. (1990). Growing up and growing apart: A developmental meta-analysis of twin studies. *Psychological Bulletin, 107*(2), 226–237. http://dx.doi.org/10.1037/0033-2909.107.2.226.

McClelland, D. C. (1975). *Power: The inner experience*. New York, NY: Irvington.

McClelland, D. C. (1995). Achievement motivation in relation to achievement related recall, performance, and urine flow, a marker associated with release of vasopressin. *Motivation and Emotion, 19*, 59–76.

McClelland, D. C., Atkinson, J. W., Clark, R. A., & Lowell, E. L. (1976). *The achievement motive*. Oxford, England: Irvington.

McConnell, M. J., Lindberg, M. R., Brennand, K. J., Piper, J. C., Voet, T., Cowing-Zitron, C., et al. (2013). Mosaic copy number variation in human neurons. *Science, 342*(6158), 632–637. http://dx.doi.org/10.1126/science.1243472.

McNaughton, N., & Corr, P. J. (2009). Central theories of motivation and emotion. In G. G. Berntson & J. T. Cacioppo (Eds.), *Handbook of neuroscience for the behavioral sciences* (pp. 710–730). Hoboken, NJ: John Wiley & Sons, Inc.

Mehta, P. H., & Josephs, R. A. (2010). Testosterone and cortisol jointly regulate dominance: Evidence for a dual-hormone hypothesis. *Hormones and Behavior, 58*(5), 898–906. http://dx.doi.org/10.1016/j.yhbeh.2010.08.020.

Mills, D. L., Dai, L., Fishman, I., Yam, A., Appelbaum, L. G., St. George, M., et al. (2013). Genetic mapping of brain plasticity across development in Williams Syndrome: ERP markers of face and language processing. *Developmental Neuropsychology, 38*(8), 613–642. http://dx.doi.org/10.1080/87565641.2013.825617.

Mizuno, K., Tanaka, M., Ishii, A., Tanabe, H. C., Onoe, H., Sadato, N., et al. (2008). The neural basis of academic achievement motivation. *NeuroImage, 42*(1), 369–378. http://dx.doi.org/10.1016/j.neuroimage.2008.04.253.

Moffitt, T. E. (2005). The new look of behavioral genetics in developmental psychopathology: Gene-environment interplay in antisocial behaviors. *Psychological Bulletin, 131*(4), 533–554. http://dx.doi.org/10.1037/0033-2909.131.4.533.

Nairne, J. S., Thompson, S. R., & Pandeirada, J. N. (2007). Adaptive memory: Survival processing enhances retention. *Journal of Experimental Psychology: Learning, Memory, and Cognition, 33*(2), 263–273.

O'Connor, M. F., Wellisch, D. K., Stanton, A. L., Eisenberger, N. I., Irwin, M. R., & Lieberman, M. D. (2008). Craving love? Enduring grief activates brain's reward center. *NeuroImage, 42*(2), 969–972. http://dx.doi.org/10.1016/j.neuroimage.2008.04.256.

Petersson, K. M., Folia, V., & Hagoort, P. (2012). What artificial grammar learning reveals about the neurobiology of syntax. *Brain and Language*, *120*(2), 83–95.

Pew Research Center, (2009). Retrieved on August 16, 2014 from: <http://www.pewresearch.org/daily-number/the-tattoo-divide/>

Plomin, R. (1990). *Nature and nurture: An introduction to behavior genetics*. Pacific Grove, CA: Brooks/Cole.

Puig, J., Englund, M. M., Simpson, J. A., & Collins, W. A. (2013). Predicting adult physical illness from infant attachment: A prospective longitudinal study. *Health Psychology*, *32*(4), 409–417. http://dx.doi.org/10.1037/a0028889.

Rainville, P. (2013). Pain and the emotional responses to noxious stimuli. In J. Armony & P. Vuilleumier (Eds.), *The Cambridge handbook of human affective neuroscience* (pp. 223–240). New York, NY: Cambridge University Press.

Reeve, J. (2009). *Understanding motivation and emotion* (5th ed.). Hoboken, NJ: John Wiley & Sons.

Reeve, J., & Tseng, C.-M. (2011). Cortisol reactivity to a teacher's motivating style: The biology of being controlled versus supporting autonomy. *Motivation and Emotion*, *35*(1), 63–74. http://dx.doi.org/10.1007/s11031-011-9204-2.

Roelofs, K., Van Peer, J., Berretty, E., De Jong, P., Spinhoven, P., & Elzinga, B. M. (2009). Hypothalamus-pituitary-adrenal axis hyperresponsiveness is associated with increased social avoidance behavior in social phobia. *Biological Psychiatry*, *65*(4), 336–343.

Ross, H. E., & Young, L. J. (2009). Oxytocin and the neural mechanisms regulating social cognition and affiliative behavior. *Frontiers in Neuroendocrinology*, *30*(4), 534–547. http://dx.doi.org/10.1016/j.yfrne.2009.05.004.

Ryan, R., & Deci, E. (2000). Self-determination theory and the facilitation of intrinsic motivation, social development and well-being. *American Psychologist*, *55*, 68–78. http://dx.doi.org/10.1037//0003-066X.55.1.68.

Rypma, B., Berger, J. S., Prabhakaran, V., Bly, B. M., Kimberg, D. Y., Biswal, B. B., et al. (2006). Neural correlates of cognitive efficiency. *NeuroImage*, *33*, 969–979.

Scarr, S., & McCartney, K. (1983). How people make their own environments: A theory of genotype→environment effects. *Child Development*, 424–435. http://dx.doi.org/10.1111/1467-8624.ep8877295.

Schilbach, L., Eickhoff, S. B., Mojzisch, A., & Vogeley, K. (2008). What's in a smile? Neural correlates of facial embodiment during social interaction. *Social Neuroscience*, *3*(1), 37–50.

Schneiderman, I., Zagoory-Sharon, O., Leckman, J. F., & Feldman, R. (2012). Oxytocin during the initial stages of romantic attachment: Relations to couples' interactive reciprocity. *Psychoneuroendocrinology*, *37*(8), 1277–1285. http://dx.doi.org/10.1016/j.psyneuen.2011.12.021.

Schultheiss, O. C., & Brunstein, J. C. (2010). Introduction. In O. C. Schultheiss & J. C. Brunstein (Eds.), *Implicit motives* (pp. ix–xxvii). New York, NY: Oxford University Press.

Schultheiss, O. C., Wirth, M. M., Torges, C. M., Pang, J. S., Villacorta, M. A., & Welsh, K. M. (2005). Effects of implicit power motivation on men's and women's implicit learning and testosterone changes after social victory or defeat. *Journal of Personality and Social Psychology*, *88*(1), 174–188.

Shadish, W. R., Cook, T. D., & Campbell, D. T. (2002). *Experimental and quasi-experimental designs*. Boston, MA: Houghton Mifflin.

Singpurwalla, R. (2010). The tripartite theory of motivation in Plato's republic: Plato's tripartite theory of motivation. *Philosophy Compass*, *5*(11), 880–892. http://dx.doi.org/10.1111/j.1747-9991.2010.00343.x.

Slavich, G. M., O'Donovan, A., Epel, E. S., & Kemeny, M. E. (2010). Black sheep get the blues: A psychobiological model of social rejection and depression. *Neuroscience & Biobehavioral Reviews*, *35*(1), 39–45.

Smith, K. S., Mahler, S. V., Pecina, S., & Berridge, K. C. (2008). Hedonic hotspots: Generating sensory pleasure in the brain. In M. Kringelbach & K. C. Berridge (Eds.), *Pleasures of the brain* (pp. 27–49). Oxford, UK: Oxford University Press.

Sober, E., & Wilson, D. S. (1998). *Unto others: The evolution and psychology of unselfish behavior*. Cambridge, MA: Harvard University Press.

Stanovich, K. (2009). *What intelligence tests miss: The psychology of the rational mind*. New Haven, CT: University Press.

Stanovich, K. E. (1986). Matthew effects in reading: Some consequences of individual differences in the acquisition of literacy. *Reading Research Quarterly*, *21*, 360–407.

Stanton, S. J., & Schultheiss, O. C. (2009). The hormonal correlates of implicit power motivation. *Journal of Research in Personality*, *43*(5), 942–949. http://dx.doi.org/10.1016/j.jrp.2009.04.001.

Tabibnia, G., Satpute, A. B., & Lieberman, M. D. (2008). The sunny side of fairness: Preference for fairness activates reward circuitry (and disregarding unfairness activates self-control circuitry). *Psychological Science*, *19*(4), 339–347. http://dx.doi.org/10.1111/j.1467-9280.2008.02091.x.

Taylor, S. E. (2006). Tend and befriend: Biobehavioral bases of affiliation under stress. *Current Directions in Psychological Science*, *15*(6), 273–277. http://dx.doi.org/10.1111/j.1467-8721.2006.00451.x.

Taylor, S. F., Welsh, R. C., Wager, T. D., Luan Phan, K., Fitzgerald, K. D., & Gehring, W. J. (2004). A functional neuroimaging study of motivation and executive function. *NeuroImage*, *21*(3), 1045–1054. http://dx.doi.org/10.1016/j.neuroimage.2003.10.032.

Theodoridou, A., Penton-Voak, I. S., & Rowe, A. C. (2013). A direct examination of the effect of intranasal administration of oxytocin on approach-avoidance motor responses to emotional stimuli. *PLoS One*, *8*(2) e58113–e58113. http://dx.doi.org/10.1371/journal.pone.0058113.

Trumble, B., Cummings, D., O'Connor, K., Holman, D., Smith, E., Kaplan, H., et al. (2013). Age-independent increases in male salivary testosterone during among Tsimane forager-farmers. *Evolution and Human Behavior*, *34*(5), 350–357.

Winter, D. G. (1973). *The power motive*. New York, NY: The Free Press.

Winter, D. G. (2000). Power, sex, and violence: A psychological reconstruction of the 20th century and an intellectual agenda for political psychology. *Political Psychology*, *21*, 383–404.

Wirth, M. M., Welsh, K. M., & Schultheiss, O. C. (2006). Salivary cortisol changes in humans after winning or losing a dominance contest depend on implicit power motivation. *Hormones and Behavior*, *49*(3), 346–352.

Ch, ch, changes: The developmental trajectory of motivation

I watch the ripples change their size, but never leave the stream of warm impermanence and, so the days float through my eyes. But still the days seem the same, and these children that you spit on as they try to change their worlds, are immune to your consultations. They're quite aware of what they're going through.

—*David Bowie*

Chapter outline

Principle #22—Biological change is predictable, motivational change is not   81
Motivational Leaders—*Rebecca and Cheryl Hines*   84
Principle #23—Academic and competency motives have developmental trajectories   86
Principle #24—Excellence judgments influence effort direction and intensity   90
Principle #25—Evolution of values and morality mediate moral motivation   93
Principle #26—Gender congruity evaluations substantially influence perceptions of "fit"   95
    Chapter summary/conclusions   99
    Next steps   100
    End of chapter motivational minute   100
References   101

The prophetic lyrics extracted from the song "Changes" are ironically in stark contrast to the optimism implied by the title of Bowie's 1971 hit album "Hunky Dory." Philosophers and scholars since ancient times have lamented about the enduring nature of change. Heraclitus of Ephesus (c. 500 BCE) proclaimed "the only thing constant is change itself," espousing the strongly entrenched belief held by many that our world is a compendium of unpredictable contradictory propositions that are often voraciously resisted. Explaining and understanding the nature of change, and helping individuals and groups overcome resistance to change, has subsidized the careers of many psychologists and spawned the cottage industry of change management consulting. A 2014 Google search using the words "change management training" returned a whopping 378,000,000 results! Apparently, change is here to stay.

As you may remember from Principle #5 (p. 12), contrary to Bowie's proclamation, when it comes to motivation, we likely are unaware of what we are going through.

The tacit nature of motivation creates interpretive dilemmas for both researchers and practitioners, specifically understanding if, when, and how motivations change over the course of the lifespan. Researchers seek to identify the underlying causes of changing motives and hope to discover evidence-based patterns that can predict behavior. Practitioners can use the chronology of change to serve as an interpretive framework to address motivational challenges. Unlike Bowie, motivational scientists instill greater optimism to the process of change by describing change as "development." From the perspective of the motivational detective (MD), development means adaptation to the environment as reflected by changes in values, morals, thinking, socialization, emotion, and personal self-regulation over the lifespan. Development implies changes at the structural level, including what aspect of the individual changes (e.g., neurological, hormonal, or cognitive change), or at the functional level, which shows the impact of structural changes on behaviors and actions (Bjorklund, 2012). As MDs, we are more focused on "function," because motivations have a greater applied impact on functions than on structures.

In psychology and education scholars debate (1) the way individuals change (is change consistent or abrupt?), (2) the stability and direction of change (does experience permanently alter individuals or is change merely temporary or recursive?), and (3) the source of the change (what is more important, nature or nurture?). The continuity debate suggests that individuals change in one of two ways: either gradually with a smooth progression or incrementally in a series of easily identifiable steps or stages. The stability debate focuses upon the consistency of behaviors and whether or not individuals resort back to qualitatively more immature states of thinking and reasoning (a social–cognitive perspective), or if the biological make-up of the individual changes based experience (known as "plasticity"). The nature–nurture debate is a contentious one: which aspect has a greater influence on overall behavior? Although the three debates mentioned above are of keen interest to researchers, ultimately the debates are of marginal value to the MD because changes in motivation may or may not be related to chronological and biological development and are more likely a function of the integrative nature of beliefs and values associated with adaptations to specific environments.

You now know from Principle #1 (p. 6) that motivational inequality exists both within and between individuals. Operating under the theoretical assumption of inequality, our view of development focuses specifically on identifying the most important motivational factors that distinguish differences among individuals as they grow and mature. Knowledge of individual development will assist the MD in determining which strategies are optimal to mediate behavior at a particular point in the individual's lifespan. In other words, as our personal knowledge of motivation evolves we will gain precision about which tools or strategies work best for a particular challenge in a particular situation. Selecting the best strategy will avoid the consequences of trying to kill the proverbial fly with a hammer, or the miscalibration of rewarding the recalcitrant and temperamental child at the mall with the promise of a Victoria's Secret gift card. Unlike Bowie's artistic affirmation, motivation science reveals justified evidence that a series of beliefs and contextual influences (e.g., adaptations to gender and cultural expectations, beliefs about our own competency, and an understanding of what drives our moral compass) are highly predictive indicators of changing motivational patterns across the lifespan. Ultimately, knowledge of individual developmental differences will arm the aspiring MD with a set of specific strategies to clearly influence behavior and dispute Bowie's lyrical assertion that changes are "immune to your consultations."

Principle #22—Biological change is predictable, motivational change is not

Biological change is an inevitable and orderly process easily verified through the observation of an organism as it grows, matures, and eventually dies. In all likelihood, the Smurf mobile in your crib gripped your attention before you or your mischievous sibling mustered the skills or nerve to tear it down. You crawled before you walked, and you babbled before you spoke intelligibly. Unless you had disruptions in typical biological functioning due to congenital disease or illness, your physical development was predictable and fixed, with little or no variability in the *sequence* of change between you and your peers. The latency or timing of your physical development may have been noticeably more erratic and less predictable, and perhaps you were a "late bloomer." The timing of your biological changes were influenced, in part, by a variety of environmental factors, such as the prevalence of opportunities for development, the amount of attention received from your caregiver, and various socioeconomic factors, including nutritional quality and the availability of medical care. Variance in environmental influences may have accelerated or delayed your development, but the sequence of your physical changes compared with others was identical.

Unlike the programmatic and progressive nature of physical development, the evolution of cognitive and psychosocial change is far less predictable or consistent. Cognitive development consists of how we acquire and process information, including the functions of attention, memory, decision making, and reasoning. The sophistication of cognitive development is illustrated by how we learn and demonstrate acquired skills, including language, reading, or complex problem solving. Socioemotional development is typically assessed by the nature and degree of culturally determined success we reach while attracting and interacting with others. Typical examples of psychosocial development include the strength of bonds with significant others, such as our parents, the appropriate demonstration of social behaviors consistent with our chronological age, including the suitability of emotional expression, and how we evaluate ourselves in relation to cultural expectations. Psychosocial development also includes a morality component, with evaluations based upon what facts or beliefs are considered during decision making and how the beliefs change over time. Conspicuously absent from these developmental perspectives is any direct focus on the role of motivation or how motivation might influence cognitive and psychosocial growth, if at all.

Bjorklund (2012) identified three critical cognitively oriented dimensions indicative of developmental change. First, he proposed that we must account for how individuals mentally represent the external world; that is, there are distinct age-related differences between individuals in the way we categorize and organize our thoughts. For example, given the opportunity to analyze a literary passage for comprehension, we would deduce that an individual who detects literary symbolism in the passage has a more complex and sophisticated network of mental representations than a student who merely summarizes the story plot (Perfetti, 1992). Developmental influences in mental representations are also observed when individuals complete complex reasoning and spatial tasks (Flavell, 1988), but performance differences are often attributed to environmental factors, such as practice and the available opportunity to perform (Demetriou, Spanoudis, & Mouyi, 2011; Stanovich, 1986). Surprisingly, motivation is rarely mentioned explicitly as an intervening variable related to mental representation.

Second, Bjorklund (2012) maintained that the strategies we select during problem solving have a developmental trajectory. Individuals use a wide variety of strategies to solve problems, depending on their goals and the task, with certain strategies "selected" and employed frequently, while others may be suppressed by the individual as ineffective, or situationally, inappropriate. Young children often respond to the absolute physical properties of a problem, whereas older children and adults respond to relational properties of a task or challenge (Harnishfeger & Bjorklund, 1990). For example, the very young child might believe that $10 + 1 = 101$, while the cognitively mature person would realize that sequential additive strategies result in a wrong solution. In other words, learners, depending upon their age, employ a mediational approach to problem solving. Individuals determine which solutions to extract from their strategic repertoires, depending upon their perception of the problem state coupled with their developmental level. Bjorklund implies that strategy selection relates to available capacity to use strategy knowledge and indicated individuals may have the "mental ability to use strategies but for *some reason* (emphasis added) do not produce them unless prompted" (p. 153). Thus, we may surmise that some individuals may not know how or when to use a strategy, while others may actually know the strategy but are consciously unwilling to deploy what they know, possibly due to motivational influences concerning their problem perception (Schraw & Moshman, 1995).

Third, Bjorklund (2012) cautioned we must accurately identify the underlying mechanisms of developmental change and the structure of development. The structural view suggests an increased focus on understanding root causes of development, frequently assessed by comparing individuals who demonstrate a skill or ability with those who do not. The plurality of variability in performance between and among individuals across tasks is influenced by depth of knowledge gained through experience (Ericsson & Lehmann, 1996) and by available processing capacity (Passolunghi & Siegel, 2001). Regardless of the performance antecedents, as task complexity escalates, more effort is needed to be successful, suggesting that individuals employ different amounts of effort based upon their perception of the challenge (Smith & DeCoster, 2000; Stanovich, 2004). Individuals unwilling or unable to exert greater effort toward task completion will likely experience performance deficits, while those with both the skill and initiative will accelerate or sustain effort, when needed (Csikszentmihalyi, 1997; McCombs & Marzano, 1990).

Consequently, as individuals develop skills and expertise, performance targets and associated effort change (Heckhausen, Wrosch, & Schulz, 2010). Individuals with increased knowledge and experience become more efficient in cognition, reaching comprehension or problem-solving goals faster and with fewer errors (Kirschner, Sweller, & Clark, 2006). To be efficient, cognitive processing shifts from a slow, deliberate, conscious, and effortful process to one that is fast and automatic, far less effortful and demanding of cognitive resources for the expert than for the novice (Hoffman, 2013; Kalyuga, Ayres, Chandler, & Sweller, 2003). The direction and intensity of effort shifts because the individual directs effort toward targets seen as realistic and obtainable. When an individual no longer believes time or cognitive resources are available to reach task goals, goal striving abates. Effort is directed toward a more probable goal to avoid the self-perception of incompetence or dysfunctional strivings inappropriate with chronological age (Heckhausen et al., 2010). Research across diverse domains indicates that individuals must have requisite knowledge to meet learning and performance goals, combined with the desire to effectively solve problems and reflect on their progress and capabilities (Mayer, 1998; Walczyk & Griffith-Ross, 2006; Walczyk et al., 2007).

Deciphering the precise trajectory of sustained effort is imperiled by inevitable physiological change. Although the majority of our cognitive growth continues indefinitely, some aspects of cognitive development may plateau, decline, or even stop all together (Baltes & Smith, 2003). Researchers have identified *critical periods* when situationally supportive environmental conditions and biological predisposition promote rapid qualitative changes in skill development. You are likely familiar with critical periods based on conventional beliefs that suggest memory declines as we age (Salthouse, 1996), reaction time decreases after age 50 years (Der & Deary, 2006), and children between 3 and 7 years are more adaptive to bilingualism (Huang, 2013; Johnson & Newport, 1989). These examples reveal that many opportunities for competence are subject to biological predispositions, which, in turn, can influence effort and specific task motivation.

We can theoretically debate, when, if, and how development stops, but a common behavioral example easily illustrates the point of developmental stagnation. The most well-known developmental psychologist of the twentieth century, Jean Piaget, posited that children master conservation of volume by about age 8 years and realize that identical amounts of liquid in different shaped glasses may appear dissimilar but, in reality, hold the identical amount of liquid (Piaget, 1964). According to Piaget, young child under the age of 7 years do not have the cognitive capacity to distinguish volume differences and, when given a choice, almost universally choose a tall thin glass over a short wide glass containing the same amount of liquid. These children are operating under the false belief that the shape of the glass determines the volume. To test the theory of developmental plateaus, I encourage you to go out and virtually have a drink on me. Be sure to request the beverage in a wide, short glass and not a tall skinny glass. More often than not, you will receive more Jamba in your juice in the wide container than in the one that is tall and thin (Wansink & van Ittersum, 2005). Apparently, either too many bartenders are developmentally delayed or underage or some aspects of cognitive development do, indeed, plateau.

All the assumptions advanced in Principle #22 suggest that observed differences between individuals are a function of the interaction of biological and environmental factors related to *cognitive* development. Explanations of development that ascribe substantial influence to motivation are surprisingly elusive from these interpretations. A cursory review of a top-selling text describing lifespan development revealed that only 4 pages out of a 625-page text were devoted to the discussion of general motivational influences on development. However, a wealth of multi-disciplinary evidence suggests that many individual aspects of learning and achievement can be predicted by changes in the patterns of motivation relative to chronological age and the context of demonstrated behavior (Heckhausen et al., 2010).

As mentioned in Chapter 3 (p. 69), one way researchers examine the exact influence of context or "nurture" on developmental change is by comparing genetically similar siblings raised in the same or different home environment and culture. Comparison seeks to identify which environments support adaptive growth. While it is unethical to deliberately separate siblings to advance science and enhance your understanding of developmental motivation, examining differences between siblings raised in the same home can provide some interesting and useful information concerning similarities in motivation. In the absence of impractical controlled longitudinal studies that track individuals over lengthy time periods, the MD must resort to methods of convenience to gain insight into how motivated behavior develops. Some might suggest that a starting point is to interview siblings raised in the same home to detect motivational patterns. We next turn to specific and pervasive examples of how particular motivations evolve over the lifespan and how these changes may help predict behaviors in the classroom or workplace.

Motivational Leaders—*Rebecca and Cheryl Hines*

Based upon the interaction between Rebecca and Cheryl Hines, the bond between sisters in arguably incomparable. On the surface, the two appear radically different in profession and demeanor; however, a unique and enduring cerebral connection transcends the superficial differences that often dominate the evaluation of someone you just met.

Rebecca (Becky) Hines is a PhD Professor at the University of Central Florida (UCF) in Orlando, Florida, where she teaches preservice teachers how to teach, specializing in the instruction of exceptional children. Prior to her university position, she was a language arts teacher, a teacher of students with severe emotional challenges, and a middle school co-teacher. Her rich experiences working in and researching inclusive settings have led Rebecca to speak at seminars and conferences globally about her research and classroom experiences. She is the co-author of *Co-Teaching in Secondary Schools*, a guide book of evidence-based strategies supporting the challenges of co-teaching for educators. When not developing future teachers, Rebecca spends time with her family attending to her twin children.

Cheryl Hines is a world-renowned actress, writer, director, and social activist. Cheryl is best known for her twice-nominated Emmy Award role as the irreverent and anguished wife of Larry David in the hit HBO show *Curb Your Enthusiasm*, as well as from the television show *Suburgatory* starring Jane Levy. As a Hollywood staple since 2000, Cheryl has appeared in many hit movies, including *RV*, in which she starred opposite Robin Williams, and *Waitress*. Her 2009 directorial debut of *Serious Moonlight* starred Meg Ryan and Timothy Hutton. Cheryl has recently attracted tabloid attention due to her 2014 marriage to Bobby Kennedy Jr., the third son of the late Senator Bobby Kennedy, brother of US President John F. Kennedy. When not acting or championing the Robert F. Kennedy Center for Justice and Human Rights, Cheryl lives in Malibu, California, with her husband and their combined families.

Could the two sisters be so dramatically different on face value? Cheryl went to West Virginia University for a year before returning home to Tallahassee, where she earned a cosmetology degree and worked to pay her way through school. Rebecca worked her way through school at Florida State University as a paraprofessional at a school for special-needs children. Both ended up in Central Florida because of their brother who moved to the Orlando area. Cheryl landed a job at the Universal theme park in Orlando, and Becky followed to complete her teaching internship. The siblings were very close and roomed together in various configurations throughout their long college careers. Cheryl graduated from UCF and moved to Los Angeles a few years later, as Rebecca moved to the Tampa area to continue her education.

The two sisters, who are obviously different in vocation, social circles, and interests, surprisingly have a lot in common, possibly leading the practitioner to conclude that similar motives can manifest into dramatically different behaviors. Motivationally, Rebecca and Cheryl are closely aligned. Resilience, perseverance, and the realization that failure is a distinct possibility define the sisters' outlook on success. When asked to account for their mutual success, the sisters uniformly agreed they were both "bold risk takers." Cheryl stated, "Things aren't always going to go right; if you recognize this, you will succeed. Part of being an actor is *not* getting the job, but if I don't feel I can get the part, I am wasting everyone's time. There is a confidence factor." (C. Hines, personal communication, May 22, 2014).

Summarizing what leads to a fulfilling and satisfying life, Becky added, "It's not about being motivated to achieve some abstract thing that someone else has defined, it's about waking up and looking forward to every day, and going to bed every night feeling good about my day." Cheryl added, "It's all about your potential, asking yourself, did I reach my potential today? Did I challenge myself intellectually? Did I step outside of my comfort zone?" (Cheryl and Rebecca Hines, personal communications, May 22, 2014). Clearly, Rebecca and Cheryl realize that a combination of optimistic self-beliefs and the expectation of success are two critical factors that spark initiative as well as define motivated behavior.

Principle #23—Academic and competency motives have developmental trajectories

Individuals assign a wide range of value to their endeavors. Some individuals see education as the key to success and actively engage in the pursuit of knowledge as a lifelong endeavor. Others view the process of formal education as burdensome, obligatory, and nothing more than a mandatory stepping stone to hopefully reach some semblance of economic security. If you have a child, know one, or remember being one yourself, it should come as no surprise to you that individual evaluations about the importance of school learning change with maturation and progression through the formal educational process (Wigfield & Eccles, 1992). Evaluations about learning many times are grounded in self-assessments about our personal capabilities and what academic outcomes we expect as a result of our educational efforts. These assessments are so powerful that results from literally hundreds of research studies conclude that evaluations of our academic capabilities may determine the courses we take, the careers we select, and ultimately the socioeconomic status we achieve (Lent, Brown, & Hackett, 1994).

The evolution of academic beliefs usually begins with an enthusiastic and rambunctious child who is anxious to attend school. Children crave the opportunity to demonstrate ability to teachers and parents through their achievements and thus want to attend school. This sense of joy from learning is typically reciprocated and reinforced by attention and recognition from relatives and caregivers. Refrigerator art found in the homes or offices of many proud parents are a strong testament to verify the daily outcomes of early motivated learning and parental pride (see Figure 4.1).

Figure 4.1 Decades later, evidence of academic motivation survives.

Sadly, the initial passion toward formal learning commonly dissipates through the middle-school years, before plummeting during adolescence and high school. Eventually, changes in how students value school and learning lead to acceleration in dropout rates as the student ages (Eccles, 2008). However, even during periods of waning enthusiasm for learning, wide variability exists between how individuals view and approach formal education. The value learners ascribe to learning is closely related to the types of academic challenges individuals will attempt, the energy they are willing to invest in the process of learning, and the persistence displayed when encountering academic obstacles (Schunk & Pajares, 2002). Our goal as MDs is to determine reasons for the radical metamorphosis of academic motivation and understand why the motivations between and within individuals can be so dramatically different at any one time.

The progression of academic motivation is primarily attributed to belief changes as an individual grows and matures. These changing beliefs correlate with chronological age but to a greater extent are influenced by early experiences and feedback received during episodes of learning and performance. When schooling begins, the existing conceptions of competence, ability, intelligence, self-worth, and socialization evolve in children as they navigate the prescribed routines and emerging roles native to elementary education. The adjustment to formal rules and compliance with classroom routines is embedded in the overall teaching process. To encourage adaptation to classroom norms even the most mundane accomplishments are celebrated (Kohn, 1999). For example, children receive praise and recognition for proper bathroom etiquette or for remembering where to hang their coats when entering the classroom. The consistent praise and encouragement from caregivers elevates the child's personal sense of competency and accomplishment while solidifying their belief in attaining specified outcomes. Most children quickly habituate to effortlessly complying with the wishes of teachers and parents in an unwavering attempt to please those around them. Teachers and parents intentionally insulate the child from the stigma of failure by their thoughtful and strategic positive feedback. Negative consequences for undesired behaviors are few, and everyone is given a second chance to show that he or she can comply with the values and expectations deemed desirable by the Cookie Monster, school administrators, and the local classroom culture. Overall, positive feedback and praise cultivate elevated ability beliefs because outcomes of failure are highly improbable.

The child is taught to focus on effort, which, in turn, diminishes the focus on ability perceptions. Children develop naive understandings of academic success, believing that superior outcomes can be achieved when more effort is demonstrated, regardless of ability (Butler, 2005). However, this insulation from failure has unintended evaluative and self-regulatory consequences. Self-awareness may intentionally suffer because the child is taught that anyone who tries hard is rewarded despite the quality of the performance outcome or how long it takes to reach the intended goal. Through the external assurance of success, little need exists for the child to critically examine his or her own performance, resulting in misguided or unregulated self-perceptions (Baumeister & Heatherton, 1996). Children become subliminally convinced of their capability and tend to judgmentally overestimate their cognitive competence under the false belief that everyone has the same skills and abilities, even when the strategies they use do not work (Wigfield et al., 1997). The disturbing trend of overestimation may continue into adulthood, as, unlike the Hines sisters who were highly conscious of their own fallibilities, many adults are poor calibrators of their own abilities and are almost universally convinced that their own performance is better than average (Alicke & Sedikides, 2009). Educators in their quest to instill confidence in the child instead unintentionally set the stage for potential disappointment or failure, as expectancy of superior performance "on demand" radically escalates over the next few years.

By the third grade, the rules begin to change. The compliant behavior previously rewarded is now an expectation. The child is exposed to specific learning challenges, some easily achieved, while others present an academic struggle. Performance variability according to subject and gender begins to appear, and demands gradually increase, with measurable declines in competency beliefs in mathematics and sports in girls and in reading in boys (Wigfield et al., 1997). The instilled optimism of earlier years slowly wanes, as teachers institute quantitative measures of ability, usually in the form of grades. Suddenly, learners become labeled by teachers according to their demonstrated competence. The child reluctantly learns that sometimes even the most dedicated effort may result in performance that does not meet parent or teacher expectations. The overall decline in competency perceptions is associated with changes in performance standards, as the learner is increasingly exposed to a more competitive classroom environment. Parental support and ultimately socioeconomic conditions, such as the availability of study resources, become increasingly important to achieving learning goals. Supportive parents many times unintentionally cultivate classroom competition by ardently involving their offspring in a variety of extracurricular activities that have both winners and losers, leading Wigfield et al. (1997) to conclude that parents are a stronger influence on evolving competency beliefs than teachers. Feedback continues to be an instrumental factor, but the feedback changes from a focus on effort to a focus on understanding the reasons for success or failure. Concurrently, as the child navigates middle school, the source of expectations shifts away from pleasing parents and teachers to attaining required competencies. A strong emphasis on standardized testing evolves. Learners are now required to demonstrate ability under restrictive conditions on demand, bombarded with mandated curriculum requirements and legislated standards of excellence that determine what they learn and when they learn it.

The stakes increase as the child enters the turbulence of adolescence and encounters a series of drastic physiological and psychosocial changes. Grade school enthusiasm and effort are frequently replaced with apathy and systemic contempt, with children showing little value or appreciation for the looming responsibilities and cultural expectations of emerging adults. Instead, the adolescent strives for independence while personifying obstinate and situational resistance to most overtures of authority and direction. The role of control beliefs and self-efficacy become increasingly prominent influencers on the self-concept of the adolescent. *Control beliefs* represent the perception individuals possess concerning how the environment is responsive to their behaviors and interventions (Pintrich & Zusho, 2002). If individuals believe they are in control of life outcomes they exert more effort, persist when encountering obstacles, and achieve more academically (deCharms, 1968). Conversely, learners with the perception of less environmental control are noticeably more passive while exerting less effort to achieve their academic goals.

Self-efficacy beliefs have a similar trajectory and represent the perceptions individuals have concerning their domain-specific skills and abilities to complete a task. These beliefs show gradual and consistent growth through the adolescent years as individuals become more confident in their skill sets which develop over time (Dweck, 1999), reaching an apex at the onset of postsecondary learning. As many of us lament, teenagers are the quintessential repository of knowledge, presumably omniscient (at least more so than their parents) and decidedly confident in their own abilities, although frequently wrong. However, if and when the teenager enters postsecondary education, reality takes hold, and a noticeable drop in competency beliefs ensues. Presumably, when learners encounter more sophisticated and unfamiliar learning contexts their naive perceptions of knowledge recalibrate when they realize their intellectual limitations and academic gaps. Changes in competency beliefs are, indeed, transitory, as elevated competency beliefs are restored as learners master the college curriculum (Pascarella & Terenzini, 2005) and proceed to adulthood.

Academic competence in the adult means a series of highly motivated choices substantiated through career selection, advanced education, and leisurely interests that frequently involve learning. Adult motivation for learning and achievement is more than the next step in development, as motivation to learn is tied to professional interests and contextually influenced by the dynamics of the working environment (Kanfer & Ackerman, 2004). Adult learning is frequently described as *andragogy*, an instructional process that has a bilateral and collective focus whereby knowledge construction is based upon the shared experiences of the learner and instructor. Because learning is frequently a group process, the instructional emphasis goes beyond content and is more socially oriented (McGrath, 2009), since adult learners show distinct preferences for collaborative learning (Kanfer & Ackerman, 2004) in comparison with the individual performance emphasized in earlier education.

Perhaps the most salient and distinctive feature of adult learning compared with learning in earlier periods is enhanced motivation to learn. Older adults tend to set learning goals that have a more realistic probability of attainment. Calibrating appropriate learning targets is strongly related to the trajectory of control beliefs. When learners feel in control of learning outcomes, their competency beliefs increase, and superior engagement ensues (Heckhausen, 1999). Conversely, when the perception of control over educational targets is questionable, adults tend to disengage, demonstrating enhanced sensitivity to contextual conditions that warrant withdrawal. Quite frequently adults will abandon problematic learning goals, if they believe attainment is questionable. Control beliefs are especially important for older adults where control perceptions influence the willingness to engage in tasks and closely correlate with overall physical and psychological well-being (Haynes, Heckhausen, Chipperfield, Perry, & Newall, 2009). When older adults are faced with age-related performance restrictions (e.g., physical bending, memory deficits), individuals with elevated control perceptions will exert more effort and persist longer on tasks. These same individuals almost exclusively report less severity in chronic health conditions and more episodes of positive emotions when exerting task effort than when asking for help or electing to withdraw from a task.

In summary, the trajectory of motivation undergoes substantial change over the course of a lifetime. Although corollaries with age exist, the targets we set and the outcomes we attain are more reliably predicted by the context of learning along with the powerful combination of control and competence beliefs. Regardless of age, learners confident in their abilities to set and reach goals are more likely to exert requisite effort toward their academic challenges, ultimately resulting in superior task performance and increasingly positive ability self-assessments.

Principle #24—Excellence judgments influence effort direction and intensity

Understanding *how* academic motivations change over the lifespan is only part of the solution needed to address motivational challenges. As indicated by Principle #3 (p. 9), if an MD expects to accurately predict behaviors, the *source* of motives must be examined. One particularly useful construct to help determine motivational source is the worldview of an individual. Sue (1978) defined worldviews as "the way in which people perceive their relationship with nature, institutions, and other people. Worldviews constitute our psychological orientation to life and can determine how we think, behave, and make decisions" (p. 452). Worldviews are frequently used in the field of anthropology to describe culture (Koltko-Rivera, 2004) and signify a series of defining principles that determine the direction and intensity of motivated action. Individuals have worldviews on many topics ranging from the type of evidence that constitutes "truth" to how we respond to requests from strangers in need of help. For example, one of my students, Terri, subscribes to the maxim "carpe diem," which she has tattooed on her left wrist. Terri literally seizes the day and capitalizes on opportunities whenever presented. Other individuals, like my colleague Morgana, adhere to a more conservative mantra and "save for a rainy day," by exhibiting caution and deliberation and avoiding impulsive decisions. Worldviews are similar to beliefs, but unlike beliefs, worldviews are a challenge to empirically confirm and are primarily subjective orientations indicating how individuals choose to navigate the challenges of life.

One prominent worldview that evolves substantially over the lifespan is the benchmark or standard that individuals use when determining learning and performance goals. We address the specific impact of academic goal choice and the influence of goal orientations on academics strategies in Chapter 6 (p. 139); however, in this chapter, we seek to understand the derivatives of goal selection. One prominent antecedent of goal choice is based upon the theory of social comparison. The approach stresses the role of self-evaluation as a conduit determining which tasks individuals will approach and which they will avoid. The perspective is insufficient to explain all examples of motivated behavior; however, the view illustrates how the consequences of a worldview explain specific motivations and observed behaviors.

The social comparison view suggests individuals develop normative performance targets based upon comparisons to significant others. The normative approach diminishes the emphasis on performing up to a particular standard but, instead, allows the individual to designate a relative and familiar target to which the individual aspires and believes he or she is capable of achieving. This approach is in contrast to directing effort toward exceeding one's own performance thresholds and/or attaining an external objective standard of mastery unrelated to a particular individual. Interpersonal comparisons develop for many reasons, with lack of task experience and self-serving ego boosting being two common motives underlying social comparison (Wheeler & Suls, 2005). Individuals may either strive toward besting the performance of a rival or protect themselves from deflating consequences and humility by avoiding the performance of a task failed by someone else. Not surprisingly, during self-evaluations, individuals display significantly greater motivation to avoid being perceived as a failure than being recognized for their successes (Lockwood, Sadler, Fyman, & Tuck, 2004).

Several ancillary psychological benefits result from normative comparisons. Favorable comparisons result in positive self-concepts (Marsh, 1987) and help develop ego-boosting self-affirmations that protect the individual from self-doubts about capabilities and performance. Marginalization of self-doubt insulates the individual from the perception of an external threat from others and tempers defensive reactions toward others (Sherman & Hartson, 2011). Individuals may also opt for self-comparison to elevate their emotional status and just feel good (Wood, Taylor, & Lichtman, 1985). Consequently, negative self-evaluations are related to unwillingness for risk taking, negative mood, and fewer feelings of overall well-being (Aspinwall & Taylor, 1993). By example, the irreverent Edward Koch, former New York City mayor, who rescued his city from financial ruin in the 1970s, was an icon of adaptive social comparison. One conventional explanation of Koch's decades-long popularity was his frequent self-portrayal as someone highly positive and vastly more competent than his mayoral predecessors or competitors. Koch's legacy was immortalized by the rhetorical and repeated chants asking constituents "How'm I doin'?" with overwhelmingly positive responses typically reinforcing his optimistic self-views.

Despite the apparent benefits, comparing ourselves to another individual is less effective for fostering adaptive performance motivation than comparison to an absolute standard (Pintrich, 1999; Wolters, Yu, & Pintrich, 1996). Ironically, normative evaluations dominate many commonplace life-changing vocational and personal events. Interpersonal comparisons determine if we are suitable for college based upon SAT scores, influence the choice of our social and romantic partners ("Yes, mother, I realize no one is good enough, *for me*!"), and often social comparisons determine who receives an offer of employment and who does not. The frame of reference process concerning social comparison is best exemplified by Marsh's (1987) seminal study that solidified the colloquial "big fish, little pond" effect. The consensus from numerous longitudinal studies by Marsh and his colleagues across cultures and age groups indicated that individuals of equal ability experience more positive self-evaluations, have higher academic self-concept, and earn higher grades when in "low ability" classrooms compared with when immersed in more demanding and competitive high-ability situations, thus affirming the swamp metaphor. The effect is so pervasive that it lasts beyond formal education and provides a strong foundation of intentionality for the types of environments individuals select for demonstrating their competence

(Marsh, Trautwein, Ludtke, Baumert, & Koller, 2007), with many individuals opting to be the "big fish" in the "small pond" when given a choice.

Social comparison motives are empirically substantiated for children as young as 3 years, presumably as a result of a decrease in egocentrism (Morris & Nemcek, 1982). Around age 4 years, individuals develop "theory of mind" and become aware that others have different perspectives from their own that are used as the basis for reasoning and decision-making (Wellman, Cross, & Watson, 2001). As children mature and progress through formal education, the social comparison motive becomes more distinct, powerful, and influential. The ubiquitous influence of social comparison is found across grades and subjects accounting for observed behaviors related to self-evaluation, self-enhancement, and self-improvement (Dijkstra, Kuyper, Werf, Buunk, & Zee, 2008). Many comparisons are motivated by the desire to fit in with emerging peer groups developed during school. Comparison is more frequently directed toward a similarly performing peer (Vrugt, Oort & Zeeberg, 2002) or a high-achieving target who is similar in race and gender to the person making the comparison (Festinger, 1954).

The subjectivity of ranking continues to escalate during the adolescent years, especially in nonacademic domains, such as music or physical education. Many times, physical competencies relative to other individuals determine adolescent social status, such as who is selected to perform with the high school band or who is designated to be on the football or cheerleading teams. Mastery of particular skills are secondary for inclusion, as, typically, the individuals deemed most competent in comparison with others are selected for important roles despite the potential lack of certain skills or competencies. Several emotional and evaluative consequences emanate from the comparative competency assessments routinely adopted by adolescents. For instance, Weiss and Duncan (1992), in a series of studies investigating assessments of physical competence, determined that peer feedback influenced qualitative impressions of social ability, impacting the views of both teachers and fellow students. A related study (Ntoumanis, Barkoukis, & Thøgersen, 2009) determined that motivational change based upon physical competency assessments differed remarkably among individuals and revealed that overall psychological need satisfaction is inhibited by self-evaluations emanating from social comparisons. For adolescents, absolute performance and competence is largely secondary, as many times pride in individual performance is a direct result of comparing one's own performance with favorable peers (Seidner, Stipek, & Feshbach, 1988).

Research investigating the social comparison motives of adults is less prevalent and reveals more ambiguous findings. Adults, unlike school-aged peers, initiate *downward* social comparisons. Modifications in directionality of comparisons are presumably needed to enhance faltering self-concept that accompanies age-related declines and the physical limitations of adulthood. As adults mature, especially later in life, many perceive a decreased ability to control primary goal strivings. Adults are also faced with restricted relationship choices and limited vocational aspirations as they age and thus have a greater need for positive self-comparisons (Bauer, Wrosch, & Jobin, 2008; Heckhausen et al., 2010). Perhaps this downward comparison may be responsible for the early twenty-first century media phenomenon known as "reality television." While some research indicates that the popularity of reality television is due to a perception of connectedness (Russell, Norman, & Heckler, 2004) or personal gratification received from watching the characters (Barton, 2013), social comparison motives may be a more plausible explanation for the immense popularity of the medium. Viewers lacking in positive self-evaluations enjoy the frustrations and setbacks of the programmed portrayals. Indeed, results from surveys investigating viewer motivation for watching reality television reveal that people watch to escape their mundane lives and to gain satisfaction from watching other people make fools of themselves (Lundy, Ruth, & Park, 2008). Positive psychological benefits emerge from the social comparison despite making comparative judgments about people we hardly know and yet are swift to indisputably evaluate and broadly criticize.

Principle #25—Evolution of values and morality mediate moral motivation

The discussion of reality television prompts a smooth transition to the debate as to whether values and morals change over the lifespan and how morally derived decisions might explain performance motivation. Many reality television programs feature provocative situations that provide a glimpse into the characters' private lives, illustrating the causes and consequences of tacitly derived, but often premeditated, moral decision making. Viewers are frequently privileged to peek into the clandestine minds of the participants on the show as they validate reasons for kicking someone off an island, rationalize why a frumpy singer should be advanced to the next round of a talent contest, or compile reasons for seducing a married neighbor. For example, on a recent episode of "Keeping Up with the Kardashians," a top-rated reality show for over 6 years featuring the escapades of a celebrity family, the characters debated the appropriateness of daughter Kourtney having a second child out of wedlock despite the obvious moral implications in many cultures. These examples illustrate the powerful influence of subjective morality on motivated action, as each choice mentioned above can be influenced by what individuals value and believe to be situationally appropriate behavior.

Evaluation of moral reasoning is usually determined by asking individuals when, if ever, it is appropriate to lie, cheat, or steal. For instance, as a reader of this text, would it be appropriate for you to share the textbook with another student so that he or she can avoid buying the textbook? Keep in mind that the author relies on royalties to feed his seven children and that laws prohibit unauthorized distribution of copyrighted material. You could resolve the hypothetical moral dilemma I just described by simply declaring whether you would or would not lend your text to another person. Although, clearly I would encourage purchasing an additional copy of the textbook for your colleagues, friends, and relatives, it is not *what* you do that matters. Determining the cause or reasons for your decision is what is most important for the MD in order to influence subsequent behavior. In other words, *why* would you share the textbook?

Developmental psychologists typically define moral reasoning as the judgmental and evaluative process used to solve emotionally laden problems that are influenced by individual values. The valence of the decision-making process and what is considered "right" or "wrong" is determined by collectively established laws, rules, and customs that often lead to competing and contradictory answers to moral dilemmas. Morally determined decisions are important because contingent upon an analysis of which factors an individual considers when contemplating action, we can explain or predict subsequent behavior. Morally grounded decisions can influence the degree of attachment and loyalty we have to others (Smetana, 1981), how we respond to social partners (Gilligan, 1982), and can help explain many lifestyle and career choices (Colby & Damon, 2010).

Morality is typically explored by examining the cognitive processes that underlie moral decisions. Cognitive interpretations are primarily based upon the classic developmental theories of Piaget and Kohlberg, who broadly suggested that as individuals mature, they use an increasingly sophisticated and invariant network of ethical considerations when faced with a moral dilemma. At the basic level, the continuum of consideration is grounded in an orderly chronological transition from an exclusively egocentric view. The individual is primarily focused on the personal consequences of a moral decision and ascribes responsibility only to the self. As the individual morally matures, greater consideration is given to universal ethical principles that imply personal gain should be subservient to collective values and follow guidelines that support societal, not individual, prosperity.

Unlike scholarly diatribes determining what constitutes morality and if morality is universal, teachable, or legislated, MDs are concerned with how values and moral reasoning implicate behavioral decisions. Recent theoretical advances have empirically substantiated independent moral reasoning and moral motivation constructs. Moral motivation represents situations where individual preferences and associated actions are superseded by specific morally guided principles. Nunner-Winkler (2007) reasoned that moral motivation can be determined by "the agent's willingness to do what s/he judges to be right, even if that entails personal costs" (p. 401). By example, the employee who feels obligated to work overtime to finish a project she started, even when not specifically required to do so, is demonstrating moral motivation. In this example, the individual makes her decision to work late despite awareness of the personal costs associated with her decision. She realizes that her spouse may chastise her when he is "forced" to eat yet another lonely fast food meal because of his partner's moral motivation. Her morally motivated decision to finish work was premeditated, intentional, and voluntary despite awareness of the associated personal costs.

Various influences dominate moral motivation as the individual matures. Most children under age 4 years are willing to accept rules and guidelines from authoritarian sources and unquestionably follow directions without alteration. As a child matures and hurdles the developmental milestone of *theory of mind* described earlier, the child recognizes that others have different perspectives from their own, which result in diversity of both thought and behavior. By the age of 6 years, children ascribe emotions to decisions and can accurately judge that a wrongdoer who feels happy is problematic, more so than one who shows remorse (Nunner-Winkler & Sodian, 1988).

By the age of 8 years, the influence of moralistic attributions becomes engrained in the decision-making process. In one study, 90% of children realized that breaking a promise for self-serving interests was wrong, leading the author to conclude that individuals can develop an intrinsic morally-influenced personality (Nunner-Winkler, 2007).

Another developmental milestone usually occurs during adolescence when the individual realizes that personal preferences may be subvervient to "morally appropriate responses" and take precedence over individual need satisfaction. In a longitudinal study, Nunner-Winkler (2007) substantiated the upward trajectory of moral motivation, indicating gradual increases in levels of moral motivation up to age 22. As the individual enters adulthood, the moral reasoning process becomes fully integrated into the overall personality of the individual through development of the moral self (Rosenkoetter, 2005). Moral exemplars, such as behaviors related to gratitude (Emmons, Barrett, & Schnitker, 2008), fidelity (Blasi, 1993), and altruism (Wright, 1971), are empirically substantiated as contributing to moral motivation, which is exemplified by prosocial behavior and overall personal responsibility when individuals are faced with moral decisions.

Considering the influential role of moral motivation, it behooves the MD to at least consider how morality may influence individual behavior. The predictive power of moral motivation can be leveraged by understanding the nature of individual moral profiles. The greatest motivational power of morality occurs when moral reasoning is incorporated into an individual's sense of identity (Blasi, 2004). Many times, individuals will voluntarily and enthusiastically reveal their moralistic selves. Some indicators, such as declarations to specific cultural causes, may openly reveal if an individual portrays herself as liberal, conservative, republican, democrat, spiritual, agnostic, environmental, or capitalistic. These declarations and associated symbols can be reliable exemplars of tacit moral motivation helping to understand and predict behavior. Beware of G.R.I.T.S (girls raised in the south) bumper stickers, PETA t-shirts, and employees selling Girl Scout cookies! If the MD can determine how closely an individual is aligned with a greater cause, the information can be very useful to determining moral motivation, which, in turn, helps predict the degree of support or resistance expected for particular learning and performance initiatives.

Principle #26—Gender congruity evaluations substantially influence perceptions of "fit"

Our discussion of moral motivation was based on the fundamental premise that individuals make conscious determinations concerning "right" and "wrong." These evaluative judgments of morality are, in many instances, strongly influenced by a subordinate set of personal beliefs and values. Recognizing the role of moral beliefs is a necessary but insufficient means to effectively diagnose and mediate motivational issues. Personal motivation is better understood when we are also able to compare individual beliefs with the collective beliefs and values attributed to a particular group or segment of society. The comparison of collective and individual beliefs serve as a framework to evaluate if observed behaviors support or refute the underlying belief structure adapted by a particular individual, in a particular culture. If individual beliefs are aligned with expectations endemic to a specific group or culture, we might surmise that motivation to attain culturally reinforcing outcomes would be accelerated by parallel belief structures. Conversely, if the beliefs of an individual are incongruent with societal expectations, maladaptive motivations in the form of personal conflict, resistance, or withdrawal are realistic behavioral consequences.

Gender congruity represents aligning behaviors with the expected gender roles and customs of a particular culture. The degree of congruity between our own gender beliefs and culturally determined practices are particularly salient to the development of our self-identity, which has far-reaching consequences for motivation. Individuals undergo a regular and consistent process of self-reflection to determine degree of perceived "fit" within a culture. The self-evaluations either refute or affirm existing beliefs about the self, ultimately influencing motives and socialization patterns that create opportunities for a positive self-appraisal. Unlike strictly academic or moral motivations, gendered beliefs are described as "diffused" (Diekman & Eagly, 2008, p. 435), suggesting a ubiquitous influence across application contexts. In other words, regardless of the circumstances, our gendered perceptions have a widespread impact on behavior because the culturally universal nature of gender infiltrates most aspects of our development and existence (Egan & Perry, 2001). If you are skeptical about the pervasiveness of gender expectations, try a little experiment. Dress up wearing the clothes of the opposite gender and go shopping; you will quickly see how society responds to atypical gendered expression.

At the most basic applied level, gender congruity is linked to favorability perceptions of women at work (Eagly & Karau, 2002). Depending on the local culture women with career interests and those who are establishing a professional identity may be stigmatized compared with women who pursue utilitarian roles, such as cooking and raising children. Gender perceptions may determine vocational performance judgments and are found to negatively influence supervisory perceptions of female leadership capability (Singh, Nadim, & Ezzedeen, 2012). Not surprisingly, incongruous gender perceptions during the hiring process disadvantage women, as less consideration is given to women for stereotypical male-dominated positions, even when gender ascription is in name only, such as when reviewing employment applications (Keinert-Kisin, Hatzinger, & Koeszegi, n.d.). Gendered expectations are so pervasive that gender concordance accurately predicts how individuals will evaluate retailers, including a direct influence on higher spending based upon exposure to gender-congruent aromas and products (Spangenberg, Sprott, Grohmann, & Tracy, 2006). Even the amount of time a physician will spend with a patient and the degree of thoroughness during physical examinations have gender-congruent implications, with more time spent with individuals who demonstrate stereotypical gendered behaviors (Franks & Bertakis, 2003). Furthermore, the influence of gender congruity has important consequences for overall subjective well-being. Perceptions of life are observed to be more satisfying in women scoring higher on femininity scales and lower on masculinity scales and in men scoring high on masculinity scales and low on femininity measures (Bem, 1993; Wolfram, Mohr, & Borchert, 2009), presumably due to the degree of perceived congruity between gendered behaviors and societal norms.

Gender congruity research suggests that many individuals are highly motivated in situations of gender concordance, implying that males and females have different overall motivational patterns. Diekman and Eagly (2008) made the empirical distinction between categorizing motives as either *agency* or *communal*. Agency motives are more conventionally attributed to men and show an intentional emphasis on mastering one's environment to achieve recognition and prominence. Specific behaviors associated with agency include demonstrating assertiveness, self-reliance, and exhibiting risk tolerance. Communal motives are more traditionally associated with women and focus on the importance of establishing and perpetuating relationships as a means to be supportive of others and achieve personal satisfaction. Communal behaviors include demonstrating affection, sensitivity, and sincerity.

When individuals deviate from gendered traditions and demonstrate behaviors less reflective of their culturally expected roles, a potential self-reflective conflict may arise. Based upon the views of Diekman and Eagly (2008), lack of gender concordance occurs when females assume behaviors affiliated with masculinity and when males exhibit traits typically ascribed to females. Individual gendered perspectives and the degree of concordance may result in the re-evaluation of goal strivings—how much effort one is willing to put forth to reach goals—and can potentially influence how we qualitatively evaluate and reflect on our accomplishments. A significant and troubling consequence develops as individuals may alter courses of action or even abandon outcomes that are minimally supported by self-based values and interests (Sheldon & Elliot, 1999). Goals primarily pursued because of societal expectations are aligned with feelings of guilt and anxiety compared with those goals consistent with self-values (Ryan & Connell, 1989). Additionally, psychological or physiological consequences may develop when goals conflict with self-values. For instance, employees performing tasks that are atypical to established work stereotypes have been found to result in more frequent physiological and affective stress reactions, including increased blood pressure and elevated heart rate compared with the same individuals working in stereotypical roles (Evans & Steptoe, 2003). Consequently, a reality for the MD is to assess the contextual circumstances that potentially might foster gender congruence as a means to avoid conflict and promote maximum investment of focused effort for any particular task.

At least two challenges remain: understanding how gender roles change as the individual matures and calibrating individual self-perceptions against the rapid and progressive nature of evolving cultural expectations that undermine gender concordance. Gender conceptions develop beginning with how parents and teachers interact with and provide gender differentiated feedback to children. In a meta-analysis examining parenting practices Lytton and Rommey (1991) found that gender-related competence differences in children develop based on which behaviors parents encourage, restrict, and discipline, along with parental perceptions of gender-stereotyped characteristics. Not surprisingly, encouragement and positive feedback are more frequently provided to boys participating in traditionally masculine activities, such as playing with trucks and block building. Similarly, girls receive measurably greater encouragement when showing competence in traditional feminine activities, such as playing with doll or when participating in gender-specific household chores. Even in the absence of specific parental promotion of certain activities, children as young as 18 months show conventional toy preferences (Caldera, Huston, & O'Brien, 1989), suggesting both a biological and environmental influence on gender-concordant behaviors.

Teacher and parental support of these early socialization patterns becomes the root of evolving gendered competency differences across domains, primarily with females channeled by teachers and parents to develop linguistic, not mathematical skills, while the opposite is true for boys (Bussey & Bandura, 1999). Strong implications for agency exist as the child becomes accustomed to performing certain tasks that are encouraged, while support for others are dampened. We can generally conclude that regardless of gender, individuals are more motivated to become involved in domain-specific activities when they perceive themselves to be competent than during activities resulting in negative self-evaluations (Bussey & Bandura, 1999). During adolescence, the role of self-evaluation escalates as the teenager strives to establish a clear and positively appraised identity (Eisert & Kahle, 1982), with gender expectations becoming, at least in part, contributory to important motivational decisions. Indeed, many individuals decide upon their vocational choices as a result of gender-influenced interest (Su, Rounds, & Armstrong, 2009) or their perceived competency to perform job responsibilities (Lent et al., 1994), with many occupations labeled as gender preferential, but mostly as a function of socially constructed gender perceptions and stereotyping (Woods & Hampson, 2010).

Gender stereotypes are a particularly egregious concern to the development and perpetuation of gendered beliefs. Stereotyping, "a ubiquitous process to which we all succumb" (Kite, Deaux, & Haines, 2008, p. 206), consists of ascribing traits commonly associated with a particular race or ethnic group to all similarly situated individuals or other group members of a race, nationality, or culture. The labeling process of stereotyping results in assuming that all members of a group have similar traits based solely on association or personal conjecture. Stereotypically, women are viewed as passive and devoted, while men are thought to be more competitive and independent (Kite et al., 2008). Categorically, men and women have both similarities and differences on many traits. Most research refutes stereotypical ascription of traits to particular individuals, such as studies conducted on the nature of intelligence that reveal greater differences within groups of categorized individuals than between individuals (Sternberg, 1996). Actually, researchers have identified over 200 different gender-associated traits (Vonk & Ashmore, 2003), suggesting little, if any, commonality within gender groups.

Kite et al. (2008) contended that stereotypical gendered beliefs inform the uninformed observer not only with views of what men and women are like but also how they should behave. Stereotyped gender roles perpetuate through adulthood as people associate characteristics with individuals based upon the vocational and social roles they occupy. If an individual believes he or she is suitable for a particular role, the person begins to seek out that role, taking on characteristics of the role, and unconsciously perpetuating the stereotype that the individual hopes to avoid! The impact is further exacerbated when individuals begin to adapt beliefs and demonstrate behaviors that coincide with the stereotypical personification. Internal confirmation and self-evaluation occur when the individual performs as the expected stereotype suggests (Cameron & Trope, 2004), giving the person affirmation that the stereotype appears to be true.

The evolution of gendered motivations cannot be accurately examined without recognition of changing societal expectations for men and women. According to the US Bureau of Labor Statistics, in 1950, women comprised only 33% of the workforce compared with 58% in 2011. As of 2011, more women were expected to attend college than men, with 37% of women holding college degrees compared with 11% in 1970 (Bureau of Labor Statistics, 2013). The incidence of reported same-sex couples has doubled in the 10-year period 2002–2012 (www.census.gov). These statistics clearly suggest that the collective values related to gender are changing and likely will continue to evolve.

Consequently, self-assessments of gender congruity and perceptions of an ideal self may evolve even when individual beliefs remain stable. Gender conceptions, similar to many aspects of progressive culture, can undergo significant transitions over time, while individual beliefs remain stagnant. The degree of concordance between personal assessment and cultural expectations can shift, with the individual self becoming more incongruent and isolated, unless the personal shift parallels changing cultural values and norms. Shifting away from cultural mores will find the individual increasingly disenchanted as a culture evolves and progresses. As the role of culture is significantly far reaching and pervasive for motivated action, Chapter 5 is exclusively devoted to identifying the most salient motivational factors that influence performance across cultures.

Chapter summary/conclusions

This chapter illustrated a variety of behavioral changes that individuals experience based primarily upon the evolution of beliefs over the course of a lifespan. Anyone interested in diagnosing the fundamental causes of motivated behavior would be wise to consider personal development and, specifically, what processes an individual uses to reach his or her evaluative decisions. The benchmark for calibration of self-views is often realized through social comparisons with significant others but can range from assessing one's own personal pace of development compared with one's prior accomplishments or with a known benchmark of excellence that is determined by societal judgments and objective standards. Each point of comparison, in essence, is a self-evaluation ultimately used to determine how the individual views personal capabilities and to project the probability of success in reaching personal challenges.

The basis for a large portion of self-development and self-reflection is hypothesized to be a series of predictable physiological changes in conjunction with social influences from parents, teachers, peers, and overall culture. Change, although many times invariable, can vary dramatically between individuals due to the strong influence of environmental conditions on motivated action. To enhance predictability of behavior, the practitioner should examine individual chronology, the conditions present to support or refute belief change, and a host of experience-related factors, for example, the type and quality of academic experiences and the qualitative nature of feedback received from respected sources, such as parents and teachers.

Many times, individual development is significantly influenced by control and outcome beliefs based upon a person's overall perception of personal agency. The degree of concordance individuals perceive concerning such factors as morals and gender can have a profound influence on the goals individuals set, the strategies they use, and the targets they reach. Typically, as individuals mature chronologically, the network of supporting belief structures undergo a parallel change process. The change, although not predictable, can typically be expected to progress toward higher levels of sophistication, with a transition from egocentric valuation to consideration of others and evaluation of an overall fit with a particular organization or group. Individuals who question ability and control beliefs through inferior self-evaluations are highly susceptible to maladaptive motivations, including task deferral, withdrawal, or abandonment.

Next steps

The preceding chapter focused on developmental change within individuals but only briefly alluded to the pervasive role of culture as a mediator of individual behavior. Globalization in education, psychology, and most other aspects of our existence results in creating enormous differences between the standards and expectations of individuals from one geographical region or ethnic group compared to another. Realistically, the MD should expect about as many cultural influences on specific performance and learning motives as there are actual motives to expect! The well-informed MD should broadly assume that strategies effective in one culture must first be empirically validated in another context before generalizing to a different population. Following the important theme of self-evaluation and awareness, we next turn to identifying which factors of concordance and differentiation relate to contextual influence originating from demographic, socioeconomic, and racial or ethnic differences, and how those differences influence resulting motives. Finally, Chapter 5 introduces us to **LaSonya Moore**, an assistant high-school principal, who as a teenager concluded that culture can be highly influential factor on personal motivation and success, perhaps more influential than anything else.

End of chapter motivational minute

Principles covered in this chapter:

22. **Biological change is predictable, motivational change is not**—all individuals undergo motivational change as they mature. Changes in motives are a function of individual beliefs that are strongly influenced by the context of application.
23. **Academic and competency motives have developmental trajectories**—academic beliefs evolve over the lifespan based upon formal school influences along with the degree of confidence individuals have about controlling environmental conditions and orchestrating successful performance outcomes.
24. **Excellence judgments influence effort direction and intensity**—in order to assess one's own performance, individuals frequently use normative comparisons determining their own targets based upon what others have accomplished.

25. **Evolution of values and morality mediates motivation**—egocentric perspectives of morality change as an individual matures, in many cases evolving toward a concern for collective value systems. Moral motivation can develop as a prevailing influence engrained within the personality of the individual.
26. **Gender congruity evaluations substantially influence perceptions of "fit"**—throughout the lifespan, individuals make assessments regarding perceived correspondence with gender-based societal expectations. Gender incongruence can result in the modification of the goals, strategies, and overall well-being of an individual.

Key terminology (in order of chapter presentation)

- **Critical period**—a contextually and biologically opportunistic period when rapid qualitative changes in skill acquisition or development are observed.
- **Control beliefs**—the individual evaluations individuals make concerning their perception of their ability to influence the environment through their behaviors.
- **Self-efficacy beliefs**—perceptions of an individual concerning the ability to reach specific learning goals or attain and master certain skills and abilities.
- **Andragogy**—an instructional process conducive to adult learning whereby the combined experiences of the learners and instructor influence the creation of new knowledge.
- **Worldviews**—a series of defining orientations to life that determine the direction and intensity of motivated action, such as how we think and feel about people and nature.
- **Moral reasoning**—the judgmental and evaluative process used to solve emotionally-laden problems that are influenced by individual values.

References

Alicke, M. D., & Sedikides, C. (2009). Self-enhancement and self-protection: What they are and what they do. *European Review of Social Psychology, 20*(1), 1–48.
Aspinwall, L. G., & Taylor, S. E. (1993). Effects of social comparison direction, threat, and self-esteem on affect, self-evaluation, and expected success. *Journal of Personality and Social Psychology, 64*(5), 708–722. http://dx.doi.org/10.1037/0022-3514.64.5.708.
Baltes, P. B., & Smith, J. (2003). New frontiers in the future of aging: From successful aging of the young old to the dilemmas of the fourth age. *Gerontology, 49*, 123–135.
Barton, K. M. (2013). Why we watch them sing and dance: The uses and gratifications of talent-based reality television. *Communication Quarterly, 61*(2), 217–235. http://dx.doi.org/10.1080/01463373.2012.751437.
Bauer, I., Wrosch, C., & Jobin, J. (2008). I'm better off than most other people: The role of social comparisons for coping with regret in young adulthood and old age. *Psychology and Aging, 23*(4), 800–811.
Baumeister, R. F., & Heatherton, T. F. (1996). Self-regulation failure: An overview. *Psychological Inquiry, 7*, 1–15.
Bem, S. L. (1993). *The lenses of gender—Transforming the debate on sexual inequality*. New Haven, CT: Yale University Press.
Bjorklund, D. F. (2012). *Children's thinking: Cognitive development and individual differences* (5th ed.). Belmont, CA: Wadsworth/Cengage Learning.
Blasi, A. (1993). The development of identity: Some implications for moral functioning. In G. G. Noam & T. E. Wren (Eds.), *The moral self* (pp. 99–122). Cambridge, MA: MIT Press.

Blasi, A. (2004). Moral functioning: Moral understanding and personality. In D. K. Lapsley & D. Narvaez (Eds.), *Moral development, self, and identity* (pp. 335–347). Mahwah, NJ: Lawrence Erlbaum Associates Publishers.

Bureau of Labor Statistics. (2013). *Women in the labor force: A databook.* Retrieved on January 11, 2015 from: <http://www.bls.gov/cps/wlf-databook-2012.pdf>

Bussey, K., & Bandura, A. (1999). Social cognitive theory of gender development and differentiation. *Psychological Review, 106*(4), 676–713.

Butler, R. (2005). Competence assessment, competence, and motivation. In A. J. Elliott & C. S. Dweck (Eds.), *Handbook of competence and motivation* (pp. 202–221). New York, NY: Guilford Press.

Caldera, Y. M., Huston, A. C., & O'Brien, M. (1989). Social interactions and play patterns of parents and toddlers with feminine, masculine, and neutral toys. *Child Development, 60,* 70–76. http://dx.doi.org/10.2307/1131072.

Cameron, J. A., & Trope, Y. (2004). Stereotype-biased search and processing of information about group members. *Social Cognition, 22*(6), 650–672.

Colby, A., & Damon, W. (2010). *Some do care.* Englewood Cliffs, NJ: Simon and Schuster.

Csikszentmihalyi, M. (1997). *Finding flow: The psychology of engagement with everyday life.* New York, NY: Basic Books.

deCharms, R. (1968). *Personal causation: The internal affective determinants of behavior.* New York, NY: Academic Press.

Demetriou, A., Spanoudis, G., & Mouyi, A. (2011). Educating the developing mind: Towards an overarching paradigm. *Educational Psychology Review, 23*(4), 601–663. http://dx.doi.org/10.1007/s10648-011-9178-3.

Der, G., & Deary, I. J. (2006). Age and sex differences in reaction time in adulthood: Results from the United Kingdom Health and Lifestyle Survey. *Psychology and Aging, 21*(1), 62–73. http://dx.doi.org/10.1037/0882-7974.21.1.62.

Diekman, A. B., & Eagly, A. H. (2008). Of men, women, and motivation: A role congruity account. In J. Y. Shah & W. L. Gardner (Eds.), *Handbook of motivation science* (pp. 434–447). New York, NY: Guilford Press.

Dijkstra, P., Kuyper, H., Werf, G., van der Buunk, A. P., & van der Zee, Y. G. (2008). Social comparison in the classroom: A review. *Review of Educational Research, 78*(4), 828–879. http://dx.doi.org/10.3102/0034654308321210.

Dweck, C. S. (1999). *Self-theories: Their role in motivation, personality, and development.* Philadelphia, PA: Taylor & Francis.

Eagly, A. H., & Karau, S. J. (2002). Role congruity theory of prejudice toward female leaders. *Psychological Review, 109*(3), 573–598. http://dx.doi.org/10.1037/0033-295X.109.3.573.

Eccles, J. (2008). *Can middle school reform increase high school graduation rates?* (California Dropout Research Project Report #12). Retrieved on January 11, 2015 from: California Dropout Research Project website <http://www.cdrp.ucsb.edu/pubs_reports.htm>

Egan, S. K., & Perry, D. G. (2001). Gender identity: A multidimensional analysis with implications for psychosocial adjustment. *Developmental Psychology, 37*(4), 451–463. http://dx.doi.org/10.1037/0012-1649.37.4.451.

Eisert, D. C., & Kahle, L. R. (1982). Self-evaluation and social comparison of physical and role change during adolescence: A longitudinal analysis. *Child Development, 53,* 98–104.

Emmons, R. A., Barrett, J. L., & Schnitker, S. A. (2008). Personality and the capacity for religious and spiritual experience. In O. P. John, R. W. Robins, & L. A. Pervin (Eds.), *Handbook of personality theory and research* (pp. 634–653). New York, NY: The Guilford Press.

Ericsson, K. A., & Lehmann, A. C. (1996). Expert and exceptional performance: Evidence of maximal adaptation to task constraints. *Annual Review of Psychology, 47,* 273–305.

Evans, O., & Steptoe, A. (2003). Gender-related psychological characteristics and situational determinants of psychophysiological stress reactivity1. *Journal of Applied Social Psychology, 33*(4), 756–774. http://dx.doi.org/10.1111/j.1559-1816.2003.tb01923.x.

Festinger, L. (1954). A theory of social comparison processes. *Human Relations, 7*(2), 117–140. http://dx.doi.org/10.1177/001872675400700202.

Flavell, J. H. (1988). The development of children's knowledge about the mind: From cognitive connections to mental representations. In J. W. Astington, P. Harris, & D. R. Olson (Eds.), *Developing theories of mind* (pp. 244–267). New York, NY: Cambridge University Press.

Franks, P., & Bertakis, K. D. (2003). Physician gender, patient gender, and primary care. *Journal of Women's Health, 12*(1), 73–80. http://dx.doi.org/10.1089/154099903321154167.

Gilligan, C. (1982). *In a different voice: Psychological theory and women's development* (Vol. 326). Cambridge, MA: Harvard University Press.

Harnishfeger, K. K., & Bjorklund, D. F. (1990). Children's strategies: A brief history. In D. F. Bjorklund (Ed.), *Children's strategies: Contemporary view of cognitive development.* Hillsdale, NJ: Erlbaum.

Haynes, T. L., Heckhausen, J., Chipperfield, J. G., Perry, R. P., & Newall, N. E. (2009). Primary and secondary control strategies: Implications for health and well-being among older adults. *Journal of Social and Clinical Psychology, 28*(2), 165–197. http://dx.doi.org/10.1521/jscp.2009.28.2.165.

Heckhausen, J. (1999). *Developmental regulation in adulthood: Age-normative and sociostructural constraints as adaptive challenge.* Cambridge, UK: Cambridge University Press.

Heckhausen, J., Wrosch, C., & Schulz, R. (2010). A motivational theory of life-span development. *Psychological Review, 117*(1), 32–60. http://dx.doi.org/10.1037/a0017668.

Hoffman, B. (2013). Student perceptions of cognitive efficiency: Implications for instruction. *International Journal of Educational Psychology, 2*(2), 109–143.

Huang, B. H. (2013). The effects of age on second language grammar and speech production. *Journal of Psycholinguistic Research.* http://dx.doi.org/10.1007/s10936-013-9261-7.

Johnson, J. S., & Newport, E. L. (1989). Critical period effects in second language learning: The influence of maturational state on the acquisition of English as a second language. *Cognitive Psychology, 21*, 60–99.

Kalyuga, S., Ayres, P., Chandler, P., & Sweller, J. (2003). The expertise reversal effect. *Educational Psychologist, 38*, 23–31.

Kanfer, R., & Ackerman, P. L. (2004). Aging, adult development, and work motivation. *Academy of Management Review, 29*(3), 440–458. http://dx.doi.org/10.5465/AMR.2004.13670969.

Keinert-Kisin, C., Hatzinger, R., & Koeszegi, S. T. (n.d.). *What's in a name? A personnel selection experiment on gender bias in applicant assessment.* Retrieved on April 9, 2015 from: <http://publik.tuwien.ac.at/files/PubDat_210016.pdf>

Kite, M. E., Deaux, K., & Haines, E. L. (2008). In F. L. Denmark & M. Paludi (Eds.), *Psychology of women: A handbook of issues and theories. Gender stereotypes* (pp. 205–236). Westport, CT: Praeger Publishers.

Kohn, A. (1999). *Punished by rewards: The trouble with gold stars, incentive plans, A's, praise, and other bribes.* Boston, MA: Houghton Mifflin.

Koltko-Rivera, M. E. (2004). The psychology of worldviews. *Review of General Psychology, 8*(1), 3–58.

Kirschner, P. A., Sweller, J., & Clark, R. E. (2006). Why minimal guidance during instruction does not work: an analysis of the failure of constructivist, discovery, problem-based, experiential, and inquiry-based teaching. *Educational Psychologist, 41*(2), 75–86. http://dx.doi.org/10.1207/s15326985ep4102_1.

Lent, R. W., Brown, S. D., & Hackett, G. (1994). Toward a unifying social cognitive theory of career and academic interest, choice, and performance. *Journal of Vocational Behavior, 45*, 79–122.

Lockwood, P., Sadler, P., Fyman, K., & Tuck, S. (2004). To do or not to do: Using positive and negative role models to harness motivation. *Social Cognition, 22*(4), 422–450.

Lundy, L. K., Ruth, A. M., & Park, T. D. (2008). Simply irresistible: Reality TV consumption patterns. *Communication Quarterly, 56*(2), 208–225. http://dx.doi.org/10.1080/01463370802026828.

Lytton, H., & Rommey, D. M. (1991). Parent's differential socialization of boys and girls: A meta-analysis. *Psychological Bulletin, 109*(2), 267–296.

Marsh, H., Trautwein, U., Ludtke, O., Baumert, J., & Koller, O. (2007). The big-fish-little-pond effect: Persistent negative effects of selective high schools on self-concept after graduation. *American Educational Research Journal, 44*(3), 631–669.

Marsh, H. W. (1987). The big-fish-little-pond effect on academic self-concept. *Journal of Educational Psychology, 79*(3), 280–295.

Mayer, R. E. (1998). Cognitive, metacognitive, and motivational aspects of problem-solving. *Instructional Science, 26*, 49–63.

McCombs, B. L., & Marzano, R. J. (1990). Putting the self in self-regulated learning: The self as agent in integrating will and skill. *Educational Psychologist, 25*(1), 51–69.

McGrath, V. (2009). Reviewing the evidence on how adult students learn: An examination of Knowles' model of andragogy. *Adult Learner: The Irish Journal of Adult and Community Education*, 99–110.

Morris, W. N., & Nemcek, D., Jr. (1982). The development of social comparison motivation among preschoolers: Evidence of a stepwise progression. *Merrill-Palmer Quarterly, 28*, 413–425.

Ntoumanis, N., Barkoukis, V., & Thøgersen, E. C. (2009). Developmental trajectories of motivation in physical education: Course, demographic differences and antecedents. *Journal of Educational Psychology, 101*, 717–728.

Nunner-Winkler, G. (2007). Development of moral motivation from childhood to early adulthood. *Journal of Moral Education, 36*(4), 399–414.

Nunner-Winkler, G., & Sodian, B. (1988). Children's understanding of moral emotions. *Child Development, 59*(5), 1323. http://dx.doi.org/10.1111/1467-8624.ep8589378.

Pascarella, E. T., & Terenzini, P. T. (2005). *How college affects students: A third decade of research*. San Francisco, CA: Jossey-Bass.

Passolunghi, M. C., & Siegel, L. S. (2001). Short-term memory, working memory, and inhibitory control in children with difficulties in arithmetic problem solving. *Journal of Experimental Child Psychology, 80*(1), 44–57.

Perfetti, C. A. (1992). The representation problem in reading acquisition. In P. B. Gough, L. C. Ehri, & R. Treiman (Eds.), *Reading acquisition* (pp. 145–174). Hillsdale, NJ: Erlbaum.

Piaget, J. (1964). Part I: Cognitive development in children: Piaget development and learning. *Journal of Research in Science Teaching, 2*(3), 176–186. http://dx.doi.org/10.1002/tea.3660020306.

Pintrich, P. R. (1999). The role of motivation in promoting and sustaining self-regulated learning. *International Journal of Educational Research, 31*(6), 459–470.

Pintrich, P. R., & Zusho, A. (2002). The development of academic self-regulation: The role of cognitive and motivational factors. In A. Wigfield & J. S. Eccles (Eds.), *Development of achievement motivation* (pp. 249–284). New York, NY: Academic Press.

Rosenkoetter, L. I. (2005). Morality's conundrum: A question of motivation. In M. L. Maehr & S. A. Karabenick (Eds.), *Advances in motivation and achievement: Vol. 14. Motivation and religion* (pp. 219–240). Amsterdam: Elsevier.

Russell, C. A., Norman, A. T., & Heckler, S. E. (2004). The consumption of television programming: Development and validation of the connectedness scale. *Journal of Consumer Research*, *31*(1), 150–161.

Ryan, R. M., & Connell, J. P. (1989). Perceived locus of causality and internalization: Examining reasons for acting in two domains. *Journal of Personality & Social Psychology*, *57*(5), 749–761.

Salthouse, T. A. (1996). Constraints on theories of cognitive aging. *Psychonomic Bulletin & Review*, *3*(3), 287–299.

Schraw, G., & Moshman, D. (1995). Metacognitive theories. *Educational Psychology Review*, *7*(4), 351–371.

Schunk, D. H., & Pajares, F. (2002). The development of academic self-efficacy. In A. Wigfield & J. S. Eccles (Eds.), *The development of achievement motivation* (pp. 15–31). San Diego, CA: Academic Press.

Seidner, L. B., Stipek, D. J., & Feshbach, N. D. (1988). A developmental analysis of elementary school-aged children's concepts of pride and embarrassment. *Child Development*, *59*(2), 367–377.

Sheldon, K. M., & Elliot, A. J. (1999). Goal striving, need satisfaction, and longitudinal well-being: The self-concordance model. *Journal of Personality and Social Psychology*, *76*(3), 482–497.

Sherman, D. K., & Hartson, K. A. (2011). Reconciling self-protection with self-improvement: Self-affirmation theory. In M. Alicke & C. Sedikides (Eds.), *The handbook of self-enhancement and self-protection* (pp. 128–151). New York, NY: Guilford Press.

Singh, P., Nadim, A., & Ezzedeen, S. R. (2012). Leadership styles and gender: An extension. *Journal of Leadership Studies*, *5*(4), 6–19. http://dx.doi.org/10.1002/jls.20239.

Smetana, J. G. (1981). Reasoning in the personal and moral domains: Adolescent and young adult women's decision-making regarding abortion. *Journal of Applied Developmental Psychology*, *2*(3), 211–226.

Smith, E. R., & DeCoster, J. (2000). Dual-process models in social and cognitive psychology: Conceptual integration and links to underlying memory systems. *Personality and Social Psychology Review*, *4*(2), 108–131.

Spangenberg, E. R., Sprott, D. E., Grohmann, B., & Tracy, D. L. (2006). Gender-congruent ambient scent influences on approach and avoidance behaviors in a retail store. *Journal of Business Research*, *59*(12), 1281–1287.

Stanovich, K. E. (1986). Matthew effects in reading: Some consequences of individual differences in the acquisition of literacy. *Reading Research Quarterly*, *21*(4), 360–407.

Stanovich, K. E. (2004). *The robot's rebellion: Finding meaning in the age of Darwin*. Chicago, IL: University Press.

Sternberg, R. J. (1996). Myths, countermyths, and truths about intelligence. *Educational Researcher*, *25*(2), 11–16.

Su, R., Rounds, J., & Armstrong, P. I. (2009). Men and things, women and people: A meta-analysis of sex differences in interests. *Psychological Bulletin*, *135*, 859–884.

Sue, D. W. (1978). World views and counseling. *The Personnel and Guidance Journal*, *56*(8), 458–462. http://dx.doi.org/10.1002/j.2164-4918.1978.tb05287.x.

Vonk, R., & Ashmore, R. D. (2003). Thinking about gender types: Cognitive organization of female and male types. *British Journal of Social Psychology*, *42*(2), 257–280.

Vrugt, A., Oort, F. J., & Zeeberg, C. (2002). Goal orientations, perceived self-efficacy and study results amongst beginners and advanced students. *British Journal of Educational Psychology*, *72*(3), 385–397.

Walczyk, J. J., & Griffith-Ross, D. A. (2006). Time restriction and the linkage between subcomponent efficiency and algebraic inequality success. *Journal of Educational Psychology*, *98*, 617–627.

Walczyk, J. J., Wei, M., Griffith-Ross, D. A., Goubert, S. E., Cooper, A. L., & Zha, P. (2007). Development of the interplay between automatic process and cognitive resources in reading. *Journal of Educational Psychology, 99*, 867–887.

Wansink, B., & Van Ittersum, K. (2005). Shape of glass and amount of alcohol poured: Comparative study of effect of practice and concentration. *BMJ: British Medical Journal, 331*(7531), 1512–1514.

Weiss, M. R., & Duncan, S. C. (1992). The relation between physical competence and peer acceptance in the context of children's sport participation. *Journal of Sport and Exercise Psychology, 14*, 177–191.

Wellman, H. M., Cross, D., & Watson, J. (2001). Meta-analysis of theory-of-mind development: The truth about false belief. *Child Development, 72*(3), 655–684. http://dx.doi.org/10.1111/1467-8624.00304.

Wheeler, L., & Suls, J. (2005). Social comparison and self-evaluations of competence. In A. J. Elliott & C. S. Dweck (Eds.), *Handbook of competence and motivation* (pp. 202–221). New York, NY: Guilford Press.

Wigfield, A., & Eccles, J. S. (1992). The development of achievement task values: A theoretical analysis. *Developmental Review, 12*, 265–310.

Wigfield, A., Harold, R. D., Freedman-Doan, C., Eccles, J. S., Yoon, K. S., Arbreton, A. J. A., et al. (1997). Change in children's competence beliefs and subjective task values across the elementary school years: A 3-year study. *Journal of Educational Psychology, 3*, 451–468.

Wolfram, H. F., Mohr, G., & Borchert, J. (2009). Gender role self-concept, gender-role conflict, and well-being in male primary school teachers. *Sex Roles, 60*, 114–127.

Wolters, C. A., Yu, S. L., & Pintrich, P. R. (1996). The relation between goal orientation and students' motivational beliefs and self-regulated learning. *Learning and Individual Differences, 8*(3), 211–238.

Wood, J. V., Taylor, S. E., & Lichtman, R. R. (1985). Social comparison in adjustment to breast cancer. *Journal of Personality and Social Psychology, 49*(5), 1169–1183.

Woods, S. A., & Hampson, S. E. (2010). Predicting adult occupational environments from gender and childhood personality traits. *Journal of Applied Psychology, 95*(6), 1045–1057. http://dx.doi.org/10.1037/a0020600.

Wright, D. (1971). *The psychology of moral behavior*. Harmondsworth, Middlesex, England: Penguin Books.

A rose by any other name: The influence of culture on motivated behavior

Chapter outline

Principle #27—Culture transcends demographics 112
Principle #28—Ethnic identity shapes self-concept and self-relevant motivations 113
Motivational Leader—*LaSonya Moore* 117
Principle #29—Motivational differences exist between individualistic and collectivistic cultures 118
Principle #30—Communication and language patterns are revealing cultural markers 121
Principle #31—Leadership is subjectively interpreted according to culture 126
    Chapter summary/conclusions 130
    Next steps 131
    End of chapter motivational minute 131
References 132

What do Rip Van Winkle, Pauly Shore, and Dr. Who have in common? Celebrities in their own right, the characters are connected by an engaging theme that has amused and captured audiences' attention for centuries: temporal transformation, otherwise known as "time travel." Pauly Shore finds a frozen caveman buried in his backyard in the 1991 comedy cult film "Encino Man"; British TV hero Dr. Who explores galaxies as a time-traveling humanoid alien in his TARDIS; and the iconic Rip Van Winkle slept 20 years, avoiding the American Revolution and the incessant nagging of his shrewish wife. Each fictional character is faced with the dilemma of adjusting his personalized knowledge, values, beliefs, and behaviors as a prerequisite to surviving and prospering in a radically different culture from whence he came.

    The prospect of time travel is reserved for scientists and fictional fantasy. However, the realization that culturally specific behaviors represent disparate motives is an indisputable truth. Interpreting cross-cultural behavior is a challenge for mythical icons and motivational detectives (MDs) alike because the behavior and thought we expect are conditioned upon our own crystallized perceptions of what we consider reality. In practice, unique global socialization patterns mix with environmental influences to produce seemingly unusual and unexpected behaviors in others. What appears familiar to one is alien to another. MDs must be diligent to avoid cultural myopia and mitigate threats of potential prejudice that might inadvertently lead to false conclusions concerning the nature of culturally specific behavior. The initial challenge for interpretive accuracy is twofold: first, a conscious repression of personal experience and subjective bias, followed by an objective recognition that proprietary group values and beliefs may significantly alter individual behaviors.

Although behavioral universals exist across cultures (Triandis & Suh, 2002), there is a strong probability that many motives are contextually dependent and culturally bound. Individuals within cultures use context as a prescriptive guide to determine what is or is not appropriate behavior in a particular situation. When behaviors are aligned with culture, individuals are able to ascribe constancy of meaning to the behaviors, consistent with the framework of their contextual confines (Hofer & Bond, 2008). For instance, any international airport is a goldmine of opportunity to observe cultural conflict. One of the most simplistic of all human behaviors, and something found in every culture, is waiting in line. Watch individuals from any Western culture, and you will quickly observe ample distance, or "personal space," between persons. Westerners would not deliberately brush up against another individual, avoiding at all costs the impression of impropriety. In contrast, many people from Eastern cultures are perfectly comfortable with close physical contact during queuing and conversation. Limited distance between individuals during conversation is the norm and perceived as common and unremarkable. Although cultural deviation may be merely disconcerting for many uninformed or unprepared tourists, for some, it is a traumatic experience and frequently noted as a source of significant anxiety and stress (Ward, Bochner, & Furnham, 2001).

Scripted behaviors and culturally specific practices are beneficial for the individual. The routines serve as a structural foundation, contributing to certainty about the most appropriate ways to interact with others. In many cases, culturally nuanced behaviors are so deeply engrained in the individual that they become instinctual, fast, and automatic, providing the person with a seamless and organized means to navigate familiar environments. This normative behavior serves as an efficient self-regulatory mechanism for the person, as behaviors may completely bypass conscious processing and be perceived as part of everyday life (Cohen, 1997). The behavioral predictability leads to the development of cultural norms, which results in enhanced levels of comfort for those individuals whose behaviors are aligned with the norms (Hofer & Bond, 2008). The sense of comfort an individual receives from group affiliation enhances overall self-perception, as the individual uses the cultural routines and norms as an explicit motivation to justify his or her behavior while also enhancing self-views (Morling & Kitayama, 2008).

Cultural norms are related to the collective beliefs, values, and knowledge that drive culturally specific behaviors. The impact of collective beliefs is enormous and can easily define or dominate the personality of an individual (Triandis & Suh, 2002). As individuals develop, they become *enculturated* whereby the psychological and motivational processes that undermine behavior become aligned, adapted, and embraced to what is perceived to be normative within the culture. Basic behaviors, including eating, sleeping, sex, and concepts of time, follow culturally specific patterns (Morling & Kitayama, 2008). Norms apply to a myriad of motivations as well. Listing all the influences of culture on motivation would take volumes, but some common examples include how we portray and regulate emotions, the degree of openness and flexibility we have toward new ideas, how much independence or autonomy we expect, our tolerance for established rules and traditional ways of thinking, and how we respond to ambiguity.

Cultural norms influence how learners approach and participate in knowledge acquisition and the degree of active participation and effort they are willing to demonstrate during formal learning (Bingham & Okagaki, 2012). For instance, perhaps you have experienced the dilemma of the tardy instructor. Imagine you arrive at your weekly face-to-face "Motivation for Learning and Performance" class only to find that the instructor is not there. After about 10 minutes of waiting, you start to question if the instructor will arrive at all. Should you stay and wait for the instructor to arrive? Would you decide what to do independently, or ask your fellow students? What does the culture of the university or your discipline require? Would you make your decision based upon the gender, age, or rank of your instructor? Do you take the initiative and go to the instructor's office to see if he or she is in, or do you just decide to leave? Students in many North American university cultures might wait the obligatory 15 minutes and bolt, while students from cultures that ascribe a very high personal value to education might actually stay and conduct the class themselves! Any one of these decisions could clearly be related to cultural norms and strongly influence your own personal motivation and behavior.

Considering the wide range of racial and ethnic diversity in most developed nations, it behooves the savvy MD to gain extensive knowledge of cultural practices, beyond those found familiar. In the United States (US) the non-Hispanic white population is still numerically and proportionally the largest major race and ethnic group; however, this segment of the population has also experienced the slowest growth, declining 5% over the 2000–2010 time period (2011, census.gov). Meanwhile, Asian and Hispanic populations in the United States grew by 43% each in the same time period. At the classroom level, as of 2008, 48% of the total student population came from ethnic groups of color, with projections for the year 2021 indicating that ethnically diverse students in US public schools will increase to 52%, leaving those from "traditional" US cultures (i.e., middle-class white kids) in the minority (Aud et al., 2013).

Acknowledging cultural diversity is only part of the solution. Using a repertoire of culturally responsive strategies to address issues of learning and performance is of equal importance for the MD. Instruction that includes culturally relevant pedagogy has emerged at both the classroom and corporate levels as a superior method to connect with diverse learners (Rychly & Graves, 2012). These instructional strategies contend that culturally congruent education is essential for high quality student–teacher relationships and ultimately promotes greater student engagement, more active participation during learning, and eventually leads to more robust performance outcomes (Ladson-Billings, 1995). Culturally responsive education involves embracing the diversity of individuals and engaging cultural differences as a means to develop connections with learners. Unlike multi-cultural education that merely illuminates interpretive differences among cultures, culturally responsive education uses authentic learning examples that emphasize the specific backgrounds and experiences of those learners actually present in the classroom. This highly personalized learning approach demands that educators possess explicit knowledge of cultural nuances across ethnicities, geographic boundaries, and philosophies. It also includes a sensitivity as to what it is like to be a member of a nondominant culture (Rychly & Graves, 2012), with cultural dominance determined by the demographic majority of the specific learners being taught.

The next logical step for the MD is to enhance personal awareness of diverse cultures by developing cross-cultural knowledge. The term "cross-cultural competence" has been coined to describe the ability of individuals and groups to acknowledge that all cultures differ and to use cultural knowledge to effectively assimilate within another culture. Cultural competency requires, in part, the ability to communicate appropriately in intercultural situations based on one's intercultural knowledge, skills, and attitudes (Deardorff, 2006). Descriptions of effective educators (McAllister & Irvine, 2000), individual entrepreneurs (Chen, Liu, & Portnoy, 2012), and profitable global corporations (Johnson, Lenartowicz, & Apud, 2006) are inexorably linked to successful cross-cultural adaptation. Thus, it seems that regardless of personal beliefs or individual motivations, the MD is left with no other option than to know and embrace culturally responsive approaches to learning and performance.

Cultural sensitivity and awareness of multi-cultural values, customs, and norms are necessary, yet insufficient. As MDs we must also consider which culturally nuanced behaviors, including our own, have motivational implications. Cross-cultural success is predicated upon acknowledging and suspending any existing prejudices or biases we may hold toward different groups and ethnicities. Individual bias may be acknowledged; however, in some cases, prejudice can be largely implicit and beyond individual consciousness (Greenwald, McGhee, & Schwartz, 1998). Self-awareness and objective evaluation of existing beliefs will help the MD determine the degree of self-motivation to use cross-cultural knowledge, once acquired. We examine both of these important factors later; but first, let's see how you evaluate your own cross-cultural intelligence by answering questions about your experiences and beliefs. Take the culture competency survey below, and assess your knowledge and adaptability to different cultures. Carefully read each statement, and select the response that honestly best describes your perceptions or capabilities. Using a ranking scale of 1 = strongly disagree through 7 = strongly agree, provide a response for each item below. After answering all items, add your scores and calculate a total score, the read on for interpretative information.

So, how did you do? Although without standardized administration of the survey, your results cannot be considered scientific evidence, your total score should give you a good idea of your cross-cultural capabilities. High scores (above 70) likely mean you should book a trip overseas or apply to the State Department for an ambassadorship because you are culturally gifted. Low scores (under 42) suggest you should consider immediately ordering *Rosetta Stone* language-learning software and start watching *La Dolce Vita* before you dare speak to anyone unlike you. Scores in the mid-range (43–69) signify a base level of confidence and knowledge concerning your cultural awareness and adaptability.

On a more serious note, you may have realized that the statements above were measuring a number of different constructs in a number of different ways. First, your adaptive abilities and openness to changing your behavior to function effectively in

Item	Your rating (1–7)
I adjust my cultural knowledge as I interact with people from a culture that is unfamiliar to me.	
I check the accuracy of my cultural knowledge as I interact with people from different cultures.	
I know the legal and economic systems of other cultures.	
I know the rules (e.g., vocabulary, grammar) of other languages.	
I know the cultural values and religious beliefs of other cultures.	
I know the marriage systems of other cultures.	
I know the rules for expressing nonverbal behaviors in other cultures.	
I am confident that I can socialize with locals in a culture that is unfamiliar to me.	
I am sure I can deal with the stresses of adjusting to a culture that is new to me.	
I am confident that I can get accustomed to the shopping conditions in a different culture.	
I change my verbal behavior (e.g., accent) when a cross-cultural interaction requires it.	
I use pause and silence differently to suit different cross-cultural situations.	
I change my nonverbal behavior when a cross-cultural situation requires it.	
I alter my facial expressions when a cross-cultural interaction requires it.	

Source: Reprinted with permission of the Cultural Intelligence Center. © Cultural Intelligence Center 2005.
Note: Use of this scale granted to academic researchers for research purposes only.

culturally diverse settings was measured. Are you one of those people who insists on using a fork in Asian restaurants, or are you willing to make accommodations and adapt to the customs and practices demanded of the situation? Effective adaptation is related to aspects of affiliation, such as the ability to form quality relationships and perform on culturally diverse work teams (Matsumoto & Hwang, 2013). Second, emotional and affective reactions experienced during adaptation to diverse environments were measured. When your spouse or partner insists that you pitch the fork for the chopsticks, do you get grumpy and sulk, or do you try enthusiastically? How you respond to the situation is described as adjustment, which is related to your overall cultural self-awareness. Individuals resistant to culture adaptation have been found to lack self-confidence and self-esteem and, in extreme cases, may be more susceptible to bouts of depression and anxiety (Matsumoto & Hwang, 2013). Conversely, embracing cultural differences is positively related to overall subjective well-being, including feelings of joy and happiness (Diener, 2012).

By now you may have concluded that when faced with an unfamiliar situation, cultural knowledge and reactivity will influence underlying motivations. You may have also surmised that some of the survey questions targeted motivational constructs related to learning and performance, such as your perceptions of confidence, enjoyment, and interest when encountering novel situations. Earley and Ang (2003) suggested that cultural intelligence includes specific motivational and reflective components that both individuals and groups evaluate when planning, implementing, and deliberating upon cross-cultural experiences. Although we cannot possibly explore all group differences in motivational variables that change based upon culture of origination, we do investigate specific contextually influenced variables that have psychological implications for performance, particularly those that individuals are likely to encounter when removed from familiar and comfortable social and learning situations.

Principle #27—Culture transcends demographics

What exactly is culture, and how is it determined? Culture can be defined as the "the knowledge, skills, rules, traditions, beliefs and values that guide behavior in a particular group" (Woolfolk, 2010, p. 158). Culture is exemplified by the artifacts, reputations, and legacies produced by a group. Kluckhohn (1954) suggested that culture is imbued with the collective memories of a particular society, akin to the episodic or personal memory of individuals. Proprietary representations of how the world operates are exclusive to cultures, with no two cultures representing the world in exactly the same way. For instance, different cultures have diverse interpretations and representations of the meaning of success, and what may appear as a great accomplishment in one culture may be vilified in another. Further, one of the most variable indicators among cultures is how people view themselves, specifically emphasizing self-views of intelligence. Robert Sternberg, during his presidential address to the American Psychological Association, informed the audience that "behavior that in one cultural context is smart may be, in another cultural context, stupid. Stating one's political views honestly and openly, for example, may win one the top political job, such as the presidency, in one culture and the gallows in another" (Sternberg, 2004, p. 325).

Although consensus on the definition and meaning of culture is broadly contested (Triandis & Suh, 2002), scholars, researchers, and MDs should rarely debate the certainty that conceptions of culture transcend the demographic boundaries of gender, race, religion, color, and ethnicity. Cultural belonging can be assumed based upon other fixed categories, such as individuals with disabilities, similar socioeconomic status (SES), or particular beliefs (e.g., animal activists). However, culture is an affiliative variable, with much attention given to how individuals relate to each other and what they have in common. Culture can be established according to peer groups (Ryan, 2001); be socially determined based entirely upon beliefs, such as political affiliation; or by individual identification with particular nationalities, religions, and genders despite conflicting or nonconforming physical attributes (think of the popular Caucasian rapper Eminem, who uncharacteristically represents the hip-hop culture). Cultural labels are ascribed to specific generations (X, Y, Z, Echo Boomers, and Millennials), and culture can even be represented by the commonality of using communication tools. Research affirms Facebook, Twitter, and SMS as definable and prevailing cultural influences on users, affecting not only how individuals communicate but also how their personalities are defined and develop as a result of participation in online cultures, even suggesting that cyber culture is directly related to the development of particular personality traits, such as narcissism (Davenport, Bergman, Bergman, & Fearrington, 2014).

Culture is a strong determinant of how individuals value education and the importance they ascribe to learning. Nuances in academic culture can define how much effort is invested toward a particular task, the degree of openness, the prevalence of individual versus group work, and the extent of emphasis on student-centered versus teacher-centered instruction. Academic culture is responsible for the colorful names ascribed to some students, as many of us know the most focused learners represent the "nerd" culture, while their technologically-gifted peers are affectionately referred to as "geeks." Cultures can be nested within each other, such as when multi-national corporations or expansive universities have a distinctive overall culture, while units and regional operations have a culture of their own. Culture is an intricately matrixed variable, with such factors as childrearing practices, gender roles, and sociopolitical norms significantly influencing the goals individuals set and the strategies they use to attain goal strivings.

Measuring culture is an imprecise science. Researchers typically employ self-reports of attitudes, values, and traits, or use qualitative techniques, such as ethnographies, as methods to determine the meanings individuals ascribe to particular cultures (Morling & Lamoreaux, 2008). Self-reports are conducted primarily through survey completion and interviews and are subject to significant measurement error due to self-report bias and the social desirability of responses (Chen & West, 2008), with individuals frequently reporting what they believe researchers would like to hear, or by representing their group affiliations in the most positive light possible. Group effects are also an important measurement concern, as individuals frequently use their own group affiliation as a primary reference point when describing their cultures (Heine, Lehman, Peng, & Greenholtz, 2002). For example, your assessment of what it means to be rich may be quite different from the concept of "rich" described by Donald Trump because wealth representations are frequently relative to existing finances and based upon normative standards. Give a young child $5 and he or she will quickly proclaim to be wealthy! Researchers use both cross-sectional and longitudinal designs to assess culture. Cross-sectional designs are appropriate to measure cross-cultural differences, while longitudinal designs are particularly helpful to see the evolution of cultural variables over time. In total, these measurement concerns and liabilities suggest that interpretation of cultural data should be approached with caution. Those studies using multiple methodologies will have a higher probability of explanatory power, including the ability to generalize inferences to other populations with greater reliability and with a higher degree of predictive value concerning cultural practices (Heine et al., 2002).

Principle #28—Ethnic identity shapes self-concept and self-relevant motivations

About 10 years ago, I experienced what Freud termed a *catharsis*, an awaking of the emotions and a conscious realization that I likely should have had far sooner. I was visiting a low SES high school in Las Vegas, Nevada, with a highly disadvantaged student population, to determine whether grouping students based on gender had any bearing on learning or socialization. While observing student behavior in a coeducational Algebra class, I noticed that only 6 out of 30 students were actually paying attention to the teacher, who was trying to conduct a lesson on fractions. Students were goofing off and were talking to each other; some girls were putting on makeup, and several of the boys were actually asleep. My experience was shocking because the culture of my pristine homogenous education was radically different. In my idealistic world, all students actually paid attention and were committed to learning. On my next visit to the same classroom, I observed graded tests being returned to the students. To my chagrin, and in direct contrast to my own values, expectations, and beliefs, students earning high test scores were openly teased and humiliated, while those earning low scores actually celebrated with high-fives and boasted about who earned the lowest grade! Although I did not fully grasp the meaning of the behavior at the time, my research immersed me in a culture where academic accomplishment was stigmatized and, unbeknownst to me, success was determined by a variety of other cultural and social factors that had little connection to learning.

So, what motivated the students to celebrate failure? You might assume that since the classroom was dominated by African-American and Hispanic students that inferior academic motivation typically ascribed to minority students explained the observed behavior. After all, isn't it true that students from disadvantaged environments have low self-concepts and low self-esteem when it comes to academics? Why would students be interested in learning, when for many, failure was expected? This stereotypical assumption is, for the most part, wrong. Although sociocultural differences among diverse groups of students are frequently explained as important influences on classroom behavior (Hickey, 1997), and many times beliefs about academic competence show racial and ethnic parallels (Graham & Hudley, 2005), behavior patterns both inside and outside of school are better explained by examining broader cultural influences.

Assessing the degree of *ethnic identity* is an important first step toward understanding the reasons for isomorphic culture-influenced behavior. Ethnic identity reveals which factors are considered important by in-group members when ascribing value and meaning to a particular context or series of events, as well as the comparative influence of ethnic and racial group affiliation on the formation of identity and self-concept. However, two preemptive cautions should guide the interpretation of ethnic identity. First, we should operate under the important premise that all members of a particular ethnic or racial culture do not have the same values, beliefs, or behaviors (Torres, 2004). Such factors as parenting styles (Chao & Kanatsu, 2008), educational choices (Nuñez & Crisp, 2012), and student–teacher relationships (Decker, Dona, & Christenson, 2007) show distinct variability *within* ethnic and minority subgroups. For instance, significant in-group contrasts related to academic beliefs are observed between Mexicans and Central Americans, who are usually aggregated as Hispanic, while many Asian populations, including individuals from Japan, China, Korea, and the Philippines are erroneously perceived as having similar academic values and beliefs.

Second, how ethnic identity develops is an enigma. The goal here is not to assemble a list of what traits are associated with specific ethnicities (otherwise known as stereotyping) but to understand the influence of culture on the psychological processes that result in identity formation. Complicating the analysis is the reality that identity formation is relatively benign and largely implicit. Typically, values and beliefs are gradually formed as individuals interact within their broader general culture (sometimes described as the "dominant culture") and beliefs are refined when people affiliate with like-minded individuals and groups holding similar principles and values (often described as the "in-group"). In-group members include family, friends, and others with similar secular, political, and ideological beliefs and interests. As social development and maturation occur, the in-group members affirm and solidify individual beliefs, while providing a sense of group inclusion and belonging. The in-group beliefs gradually become part of the individual's overall self-concept and identity manifesting in ethnically oriented activities and behaviors, including in-group nationalism, language development, and holiday recognition (Rubin & Chung, 2006).

Individuals will demonstrate willingness to either embrace or suppress dominant cultural beliefs and determine the extent of ethnic identity as the prominent force that regulates self-views, personality, and motives. Phinney (1990) proposed a three-stage model that specifically explains how culture influences the formation of ethnic identity. Stage one of the model indicates that belief formation is implicit, and in many cases, a steadfast ethnic identity does not automatically develop, as many of the committed values and customs of diverse ethnicities align with the beliefs of the mainstream culture. However, some individuals, even when embracing the perspective of the dominant culture, may equally or more positively be inclined to adopt ethnic beliefs, in part because of the frequency of ethnic environmental influences, such as schooling with similar peers and interactions with parents and relatives.

Stage two of the model assumes that individuals eventually become more aware of their own ethnicities and are unable to consciously resist developing interest and pride in their own cultures. The cultural comparisons may result in questioning the validity of the dominant culture's beliefs. During adolescence, diversification increases as the individual becomes more actively involved in culturally-nuanced activities, such as social events, family celebrations, and holidays. During the evaluation process, some individuals may tacitly begin to reject mainstream cultural views and rely more heavily on their ethnic-specific values and beliefs. Alternatively, individuals may tacitly reject the in-group beliefs and values. Cultural rejection may come at the expense of ridicule, alienation, and deleterious psychosocial outcomes, such as when African-Americans are accused of "acting white" when seeking career advancement and educational opportunity (Murray, Neal-Barnett, Demmings, & Stadulis, 2012).

During stage three, a raging psychological battle with regard to intercultural beliefs may envelop the individual, resulting in major dissonance in comparing the suitability of ethnic beliefs with those of the dominant culture. Major conflicts develop if the individual has the perception that the sociocultural status of the in-group is perceived as less favorable than the socially or economically advantaged dominant culture. As a result, ethnic identity solidifies, and self-perceptions of individuals may give rise to beliefs that provide the individual with favorable in-group comparisons.

In extreme cases, as referenced by the many instances of global conflict and secular isolationism, ethnic identity culminates through the development of anger and hostility toward those perceived to violate the culture and values of the in-group (Rosenblatt, Greenberg, Solomon, Pyszczynski, & Lyon, 1989). The psychological protection afforded by in-group affiliation, although potentially positive for individual self-evaluations, comes at a hefty price because individuals often see outsiders as a source of anxiety and conflict, based upon the perception of immutable differences in values and beliefs (Kesebir & Pyszczynski, 2011).

The story of LaSonya clearly represents the conflict some individuals experience when struggling with the differences between a dominant culture and desired in-groups. LaSonya indicated, "First and foremost I am an African-American female in a Caucasian world. I have run into tons of biases, but I chose to be who I am" (L. Moore, personal communication, February 19, 2014). LaSonya consciously and actively distinguished between two types of "worlds," as she described them, developing an ethnic identity that incorporates important cross-cultural values, such as hard work and a willingness to help others be successful. LaSonya added that she has taught her sons that they must be comfortable in both worlds. Her cultural views are not an all-or-nothing proposition. She does not adhere to a strict ethnic or racially-biased dogma but, instead, embraces an ethnic identity based upon a culture of success. In many ways, LaSonya personifies cross-cultural awareness and sensitivity, as she stated, "I understand how to bridge the cultural divides." When asked how to instill an understanding in others that racial stereotypes can be broken, LaSonya suggested, "First and foremost, academic motivation is enhanced by talking to parents, to let them know that you care." She added, "The key to the cultural bridge is building authentic relationships with both the family and the student. No one is trapped, but we have to offer help to make it happen" (L. Moore, personal communication, February 19, 2014).

It is also important for the MD to realize that acceptance or rejection of ethnic identity may directly influence beliefs about learning and school. Unfortunately, the development of ethnic identity does not explain why the Algebra students I observed were so celebratory when earning miniscule test scores. First, we can reasonably conclude that the students I observed ascribed low value to academic success, at least with regard to Algebra. However, even if the premise about the devaluing of Algebra is accurate and those students were not motivated by academics, we should not automatically assume that they were motivated by failure.

One plausible explanation for academic disengagement is the role of self-verification motives. This perspective contends that people philosophically and behaviorally align themselves with others who judge them as they judge themselves. A strong component of the self-verification view is the assumption that people seek out and attend to feedback that confirms their own beliefs and behaviors. This phenomenon prevails whether or not the self-evaluations are favorable or unfavorable (Swann, Pelham, & Krull, 1989). Specifically, the verification of self-evaluations becomes a motivational force to continue the behavior and substantiate the underlying beliefs. Regardless the merit of the belief structure in comparison with the dominant culture, in-group individuals seek and need affirmation of their beliefs, which, in many cases, cannot be confirmed

Motivational Leader—*LaSonya Moore*

LaSonya Moore is a 39-year-old African-American female, who for many is regarded as an exceptional role model. However, based on Phinney's (1990) model of identity formation, others may perceive LaSonya as an ethnic anomaly. LaSonya dispels the cultural stereotype often erroneously ascribed to people from a particular ethnic group. She grew up in an inner-city urban environment, or in what LaSonya and most other people call "the ghetto." As a young girl growing up in the projects, it was difficult for LaSonya to have big dreams because she claimed her life appeared so small. She had the first of her two sons while still in high school, but motherhood did not temper her drive and ambition. LaSonya refused to become what society considered "another statistic" because of the color of her skin or because of what she did not have (L. Moore, personal communication, February 19, 2014).

Seeking challenge and overcoming adversity are routine for LaSonya. After high school, while raising her son, she worked full-time to pay for school, earning a Child Development Associate certificate that allowed her to become a Head Start teacher in Pinellas County, Florida. Challenging herself even more, she continued to finance her own education, earning a Bachelor of Science degree. She then became a high school teacher and worked with emotionally and behaviorally disturbed students who were extremely challenging—you know the kind, the ones they call "deviant"; however, LaSonya never saw them that way. Her passion for helping the disadvantaged continued as she opened the first alternative school in Pinellas County, Florida, where she helped aged-out students and juvenile offenders increase their possibilities of earning a high school diploma. Along the way, LaSonya completed her graduate studies in Educational Leadership and Administration at the University of South Florida.

Today, LaSonya is a proud mother of two sons and a devoted wife. She has been an educator since 1995 and is currently employed with Pinellas County Schools on Florida's gulf coast as an Assistant Principal and she supervises a variety of faculty and staff, as well as providing support to over 1000 students. She regularly coordinates training and meetings for programs, such as Response to Intervention (RTI), Positive Behavior Support (PBS), Pinellas County Girlfriends, Character Education, and Safe Schools. In addition to organizational training, she oversees and conducts extracurricular mentoring and tutoring programs, as well as business and community partnerships. Oh yes, one more thing, LaSonya is now studying for her Ed.D in Educational Leadership at the University of Central Florida, which she will complete in 2015.

elsewhere. The confirmation of beliefs provides the context whereby individuals develop a "support group" to perpetuate their values. The support that individuals experience provides, in turn, a level of predictability and comfort that is derived from many social situations. The supportive feedback from in-group members contributes to feelings of control over one's environment, which then increases positive self-views, since the individuals subsequently evaluate themselves as capable and confident. Conversely, the dominant group culture becomes a target for within group animosity because of the perception of conflicting beliefs. The underlying valence of the motives, emotions, or behaviors is secondary, as long as there is group calibration of self-beliefs.

Returning to my high school catharsis, according to self-verification theory, the group behavior exhibited by the students in the classroom resulted in a sense of in-group security because of affirmations from group members. Low test scores did not interfere with positive assessments of their own identity. The anxiety typically associated with academic failure was arguably not part of the students' self-concepts or self-relevant motivations. According to English, Chen, and Swann (2008), individuals develop a sense of in-group belonging, as "self-verification fosters harmonious interactions and lasting relationships" (p. 124), apparently propagating the maxim "misery loves company." Swann and colleagues do acknowledge that the nature of self-verifications change across cultures, but provide ample evidence to support the universality of the self-verification process among cultures.

In summary, individuals make choices to either affiliate with or disengage from the values and beliefs of the dominant group culture. When an individual perceives group inclusion, positive affect is generated, resulting in perceptions of control and stability not readily found outside the in-group. Belief affirmation accelerates confidence, providing a forum to demonstrate motives and behaviors that support and confirm belief structures. Stability strivings are a powerful force for individuals, irrespective of affective valence. The MD who can effectively orchestrate contextual conditions that foster stability and acceptance has a decisive advantage. Acknowledging beliefs while providing a stable and supportive learning context may result in the creation of a performance culture that can be successful regardless of the extent of ethnic identity. In this culture, individuals realize that in-group beliefs can function in harmony with those of the dominant culture, in the same way articulated by LaSonya Moore. The foundation of affirmation and integration then provides a basis for channeling effort toward goals and outcomes that do not oppose, but rather contribute to learning and performance gains.

Principle #29—Motivational differences exist between individualistic and collectivistic cultures

One of the most deeply engrained and prevailing beliefs associated with Western culture is the seemingly inalienable right to demonstrate free will and exercise the privileges of independence and autonomy. The degree of independence individuals value, seek, or desire varies by culture and can radically influence motivation and performance behavior. Independence can manifest in many ways, including what tasks or activities a person prefers, how meaningful the task is perceived to be, and how task success is evaluated and measured. Self-determination theory, one of the most frequently cited and accepted explanations of motivated behavior in education and psychology (see Principle #4, p. 11), indicates that the need for autonomy is "essential for facilitating optimal functioning of the natural propensities for growth and integration, as well as for constructive social development and personal well-being" (Ryan & Deci, 2000, p. 68). The sanctity of the need for autonomy cannot be more palpable than in the United States, where Independence Day commemorates individual rights and personal freedom.

Although autonomy and independence are not identical constructs, together these attributes are highly correlated and help influence motivated behavior that is described as individualistic. Individualism is generally defined as a worldview that positions the individual self at the center of a person's universe. Egocentric self-appraisals act as a barometer of guided cognition and motivated action. Individualism posits that people are self-serving creatures, focused on how the exterior world impacts their personal growth and prosperity, serving their own needs and the needs of their immediate family. Under the individualistic mindset, formalized groups, such as employers and governments, are entities perceived to exist and function in service to the individual, existing primarily to advance the personal goals of the individual, with group success and group performance subordinate to individual prosperity (Triandis, 1995).

American culture is replete with examples of individualism. My own children attended a preschool named "All about Me," where Miss Connie and the staff diligently attended to the children's personalized social and recreational needs. Montessori education programs (2014), highly popular in the United States, encourage learners to pursue individual interests and choose the academic activities they prefer most. Sports heroes vie for the most valuable player award, while ideologues who run for political office court your vote under the guise of being able to single-handedly solve the needs of a vast constituency. In business, workers take personal days to attend to family issues, and bonuses are awarded to top performers whose personal accomplishments best exemplify corporate expectations, while auto sales people and real estate agents tout who sold the most or closed the top deals in a particular month.

In contrast, a collectivist orientation, typically but not exclusively associated with many Asian cultures, emphasizes group belonging, group processes, and group participation as the focal point of motivated action. *Collectivism* represents a set of meanings and practices that define the individual in relation to his or her in-group (Mesquita, 2001). Individuals with a collectivist orientation follow a more structured social hierarchy, where individual desires are suppressed in a conscious and deliberate effort to be accepted as part of a group. In many cases, the individual defines the self not by his or her own personal accomplishment but by the degree of contribution to group goals and overall ability to fit in seamlessly with a group. Unlike the individualist who primarily uses an internal system of personal self-assessment, individuals espousing a collectivist orientation evaluate themselves based upon the perceptions and judgments of others (Heine, Lehman, Markus, & Kitayama, 1999), with modesty a vital consideration for self-representation (Sedikides, Gaertner, Luke, O'Mara, & Gebauer, 2013).

The valence of self-evaluations is also culturally nuanced. Self-evaluations include assessments of how self-esteem is developed, how people view themselves in comparison with others, and what factors individuals consider when describing an ideal member of a particular culture. North Americans are typically found to demonstrate an elevated sense of self-appraisal bias, consistently feeling better about themselves in comparison with Asians (Heine et al., 1999). Visions of personal success in individualist cultures embrace the perceived universality of human uniqueness, with practically everyone thought to have a particular talent or ability and everyone capable of making a meaningful and diverse contribution to societal prosperity (Gardner, 1985). In contrast, success profiles in eastern cultures require the conscious repression of displays of individuality and, instead, emphasize a far greater focus on cultural acceptance and belonging, forging a self-view that is strongly influenced by the degree of connectivity one has with others (Kim & Chu, 2011). Whereas the individualistic culture encourages expression and demonstrating competence, public behaviors in collectivist cultures are noticeably more passive, with far greater importance given to remaining silent until asked, or being certain that one does not lose "face" through demonstrating beliefs or behaviors that might be negatively evaluated by significant others (Heine, 2007).

With regard to emotions, individual exuberance is tempered in collectivist cultures, with conscious effort focused on deliberately avoiding attention to the self or standing out in comparison with others. Emotion is hallmarked by the suppression of inner feelings in collectivist cultures, where the lack of exhibited expression is valued even in the face of strong emotions, including anger, fear, or nervousness. For instance, Kitayama, Mesquita, and Karasawa (2006) sought to determine if priming emotions during similar social situations resulted in multi-cultural differences. Comparison between Americans and Japanese individuals revealed that individuals from the United States were more likely to display socially disengaging emotions (e.g., pride and anger) in positive social situations, while Japanese participants frequently exhibited socially engaging emotions, such as friendly feelings toward others, in the same types of situations. The strength of emotions was also related to cultural orientation, as the intensity of socially engaging emotions was greater for Japanese individuals, while Americans showed more passion when displaying socially disengaging emotion. Cultural differences in emotion are also substantiated by neurological evidence. Several studies have indicated moderated brain activity in individuals from collectivist cultures during episodes of suggested emotional suppression, when understanding the perspectives of others, and when a social situation suggested the need for emotional empathy. Individuals with an espoused individualistic orientation had comparatively lower levels of brain activity in similar situations (Kim & Sasaki, 2014).

The performance implications of cultural orientation are profound, affecting personal values, cognitive processes, and, of course, motivations (Oyserman & Lee, 2008). Consider a routine situation found in many classrooms and corporate training arenas: individuals working together on a project. The first step in group work is usually to elect a team leader or spokesperson. Individualistic cultures encourage volunteering and the desire to assume a leadership role. Conversely, the emphasis on social hierarchy in the collectivist culture would suggest leader appointment to be a group process, with the leadership role assumed by the individual with the highest perceived social stature. Typical project participation in the individualist culture would involve brainstorming, with team participants readily volunteering ideas; in the collectivist culture, norms dictate that participants take direction from the leader and volunteer suggestions only when asked. Other group behaviors endemic to school and work teams, such as how individuals react to role models (Phinney, 2000), the willingness individuals demonstrate to offer help (Gelfand, Erez, & Aycan, 2007), and openness to convey punishment on others (Henrich et al., 2006), all show distinct cultural differences.

If you have the impression that you can accurately predict behavior based upon cross-cultural assessments of individualism and collectivism, temper your confidence. First, stereotypical behavior is not a basis for evaluation or assessment. Second, not all individuals from Western populations embrace individualism and egocentric behaviors to the same extent, nor do all Asians display collectivist tendencies. Third, we must acknowledge that even within the same context, there will be a range of exhibited behaviors, as individuals do not act in identical ways within cultures (Markus, Mullally, & Kitayama, 1997). Fourth, many studies related to assessment of cultural orientation are correlational. These studies do not take into account other variables that influence or cause cultural differences, such as national wealth, social justice orientation, personal resources, and civil liberties (Oysterman & Lee, 2008). These variables, individually or collectively, may have an equally compelling influence on overall cultural assessments, thus moderating any statistically significant within-group differences.

Principle #30—Communication and language patterns are revealing cultural markers

One of the most enduring symbols of our cultural existence is how we interact and communicate with each other. Our communication choices portray what we believe to be culturally warranted and situationally appropriate behavior. For instance, we already know that people from individualist cultures, compared with collectivist cultures, are more likely to freely volunteer opinions and speak up in public. However, many other communication preferences provide clues that potentially reveal culturally induced motives. Such factors as choice of words and how idiomatic expressions are used, the importance placed on listening instead of talking, the pace and tone of speech, and the preferences for and reliance upon technology are just a few of the many symbolic communicative behaviors that provide cultural clues.

To illustrate this point, what could we infer about a corporate culture where email is used in greater frequency than face-to-face communication (Golden, Veiga, & Dino, 2008)? Does the consistent use of polite or derogatory language provide sufficient evidence to make inferences about a person's social rank or emotional disposition (Karasawa & Maass, 2008)? Are self-verbalizations reliable predictors of a person's self-confidence or self-worth (Sherman & Cohen, 2002)? These types of inquiries seek to determine how variations in communication patterns explain motivated action. Answers to questions like these are not only useful to determine underlying cultural norms but also helpful to understand the frequency, type, and emphasis of communication patterns.

The diversity of spoken language is the foundation of many cultures. Through language, common bonds are created among speakers that signify the shared meanings of the culture. *Lexical analysis*, the process of ascribing meaning to words, not only allows linguists to make conclusions about the representational and semantic qualities of the spoken word but also helps generate evidence regarding the intention and motive for the use of specific words. For example, an enduring Internet lexical meme is the fascination for words used by Eskimos to describe snow and ice. By some accounts, in Inuit and Yupik, the languages of many polar region dwellers, there are supposedly up to 400 different ways to describe crystalline water (Pullum, 1991). Empirical scrutiny of word choice indicates that only about a dozen words are actually used to describe the various forms of snow and ice. However, despite the disparity between conventional wisdom and scientific reality, we can make a plausible conclusion that polar ice conditions are highly interesting to Eskimos (and to people interested in climate change and the Arctic region). Regardless of reality, lexical analysis supports an understanding of what is valued and important in the culture and potentially motivating for the individual.

Some other etymological considerations illustrate how communication patterns help identify culturally-influenced motives. If you are a teacher, pick up any student essay; if you are in business, find a random email; then, count the likely excessive use of the pronoun "I," the frequently preferred perspective of gregarious Americans. The use of "I" is measurably greater in spoken English in comparison with the speaking patterns of many other languages. Some romance languages, such as Italian and Spanish, as well as the Japanese language employ the anophoric pronoun drop (Kashima & Kashima, 1998), which means that during speech, the subject of a sentence is inferred through contextual meaning and not explicitly stated through pronoun use. For example, the sentence "I read this book" in Italian is spoken as "leggo questo libro," literally translated as "read this book." There is no direct mention of who is reading the book. The "drop" shifts the emphasis from the individual to the situation, alluding to a cultural de-emphasis of the individual found in many Eastern cultures. Further, in many languages, there is no capitalization of the pronoun "I," unless at the start of a sentence. Similarly, many romance languages have both formal and informal references for the pronoun "you" depending on the usage context. Use of "you" is determined based upon social hierarchy, illustrated by familiar and formal variations of the pronoun in many languages (except English). In other words, language as a symbolic representation of culture reflects normative behavior of the speaker, which, in turn, reveals important clues that help determine motives.

The rate of speech is also a cultural indicator. Lee and Boster (1992) investigated cultural language differences between Koreans and Americans while also considering the influence of gender on self-reported credibility assessments. Credibility assessments consisted of self-ratings of competence, trustworthiness, and social attractiveness. The study revealed that rapid speech contributed to positive perceptions of speaker credibility for all Americans and for Korean females. A faster speech pace was related to lower credibility ratings and negative appraisals for only Korean males.

Since the pace of diction was a significant factor moderating likability, the authors concluded that diction can influence perceptions of cultural fit. From a motivational perspective, individuals with lowered perceptions of credibility and reduced feelings of belongingness would tend to feel alienated from their culture. Their negative perceptions may lead to social withdrawal and avoidance of tasks challenges that might confirm negative credibility beliefs. Negative self-credibility assessments may also result in the deliberate withholding of effort on tasks due to feelings of incompetency or questionable ability to complete a particular task.

Motives can also be examined by investigating how people perceive and use print and electronic media. If you examine publications in the fields of literacy, anthropology, or social psychology, you will quickly notice many forecasts of impending societal doom, instigated by the invention and use of communication tools and technology. The deleterious effects of progressive communications have resulted in media hysteria about the latest communication fads for over 2,000 years, predicting a populace of illiterate zombies stalking the earth, lacking the ability to communicate and losing interest in all things academic. Plato predicted massive memory erosion and warned his protégés that the newfound invention of "writing" would contribute to massive misunderstandings and minimal conversation because of an overreliance on the written word. Author Conrad Gessner, typically credited with inventing the bibliography, offered grave warnings to his readers, predicting that the effects of information overload were "confusing and harmful" (HarrisInteractive, 2013). Oddly, this prediction was made in 1453 based upon the invention of the Guttenberg press and the emerging popularity of printed books! A more recent survey of over 2000 adults indicated that "technology is creating a lazy society (76%) and is corrupting interpersonal communications (68%)" (HarrisInteractive, 2013). Another arcane study found that 77% of individuals who used electronic media for communication purposes actively used their devices in the toilet (not literally), with over 50% indicating that the use of mobile technology in public restrooms was socially acceptable (Kientz, Choe, & Truong, 2013). Clearly, learning can take place anywhere, but communication patterns have changed. In the minds of many, technology has created a cultural metamorphosis, but does technology change motivation toward how we communicate or how we respond to different forms of communication?

Debate persists concerning the sustainable impact of technology on communication, and precisely how recent innovations influence learning motivation. Assmann (2006), dramatized the digital age as a "culture of attention" (p. 11) that changes the way people approach knowledge and, thus, communicate. This philosophical orientation of attention suggests a bilateral cultural framework that perpetuates and integrates *providers* of knowledge and *users* of knowledge. Attention providers strive to create a compelling reason for users to persist and want more, thus satisfying the capitalistic motives of the creators while fulfilling the attention needs of the user. Assmann pondered,

> *The art of gaining and paying attention is presented as the new economy of the age of information. In a world that is more and more transformed into and inscribed with information, attention, as the capacity of selecting information and endowing it with value, has become the most important and scarcest of resources (p. 16).*

At face value, the process of attention may seem antithetical to cultivating motivation to learn. Attention results in a new paradigm of learning where individuals place limited emphasis on memorizing factual information because of the vast availability of knowledge provided by technology-rich resources. Instead, the view advanced by Assmann (2006) transcends the historical conception of learning as a process of knowledge acquisition and application to one that focuses on the identification and organization of knowledge. Organization, in turn, affects how information is stored, resulting in a paradigm shift from primordial internal storage of knowledge to externally compartmentalized knowledge storage, both because of and perpetuated by the culture of the Internet and digital technology. How many times have you heard "Google it"?

Shifting to the incentive or motivation to learn, the culture of attention described suggests a diminished focus by the individual on actual content mastery specifically due to readily available "on demand" information. The identification of resources and knowledge about where and how information is organized and stored is deemed sufficient to meet many new-age learning goals. In fact, many of the current methods used to convey and assess knowledge, such as the proliferation of web-based high schools and online universities, operate under the presumption that learners must use technology tools to appear competent and specifically to boost knowledge creation and accelerate test performance (Bennett, 2006). In other words, prerequisite knowledge of technology, developed through the evolving communication patterns, is a necessary prerequisite for learning. Of course, the idea of reallocation of learning resources and shifting motives from mastery to attention and organization are not new or even novel. One of the most famous, yet hackneyed, quotes attributed to the individual whom many acknowledge as the most intelligent person of the twentieth century, Albert Einstein, declared "I do not carry information in my mind that is readily available in books ... The value of a college education is not the learning of many facts but the training of the mind to think." Apparently, Einstein was prophetic as well as innovative. If you believe that the knowledge reallocation model just described is conjecture, perhaps some empirical evidence may sway your opinion that technology usage patterns are, indeed, reliable predictors of motivation.

Another example of how technology (and the motivation to use the resources) can be garnered by examining variation in website design across cultures. Cultural modifications in technology indicate that users qualitatively rate websites differently depending on their native country, region, age, SES, and gender (Burgmann, Kitchen, & Williams, 2006; Kim, Coyle, & Gould, 2009; Sears, Jacko & Dubach, 2000). Design elements, such as text size, the use of icons, formats for the display of numbers and symbols, navigation rhythms, and even font type and color, are all related to regional user preferences. Although outlining the design variations across cultures is beyond the scope of assessing motivations, findings generally reveal that individuals from individualistic cultures, compared with collectivists, are less concerned about organization and site navigation and are more open to designs that appear less formal and structured.

Kim et al. (2009) tested various hypotheses related to online presence, with predictions suggesting that individuals in eastern cultures are more tolerant of online interference. The study results indicated that individuals from a collectivist culture (South Korea) showed stronger preferences for technological intrusions, such as rollovers, navigation bars, pop-ups, and splash pages, compared with US participants. The results were explained as a function of individuals in collectivist cultures being more open to multi-tasking and polychronic time organization (tolerance for more things happening at once), while individualists preferred focusing on one task at a time with a monochronic time orientation, where interruptions are deemed distracting and more intrusive. Although tolerance is one small part of the collectivist profile, the tolerance for technology intrusions may, at least partially, explain why so many technological innovations emerge from collectivist economies, such as the countries of Japan, China, and Korea (Forbes & Wield, 2013).

Few discussions of communication, language, and media can be considered complete without mentioning social media usage. Social media comprises a variety of Internet sites, such as Facebook and Twitter, which meet the social needs of users. Social networks have evolved into a unique cultural paradigm that transcends geographical boundaries because of ease of accessibility, regardless of the physical location of the user. Most studies regarding social media usage are one-dimensional and do not focus on cross-cultural differences in communication patterns. No studies have drawn quantitative cross-cultural conclusions. The few qualitative studies reveal more similarities between geographical cultures than disparities, likely because online behavior alone is considered a defining culture with a distinctive framework that moderates typical cultural influences of geography, race, and ethnicity.

The few studies that have been conducted reveal that users prefer content developed within their own geographical culture to media that has been produced elsewhere. When considering online culture, however, the nature of what is considered a culture transcends geographical boundaries and, instead, incorporates the similarities in online behavior as part of a collective online cultural framework (Rohn, 2014). Communication distinctions broadly follow the collectivist–individualist dichotomy discussed earlier, with collectivists preferring a smaller network of individuals with a more compact group of friends both online and offline and individualists, such as Americans, having a more heterogeneous social network, unrelated to offline relationships. Americans are more open to sharing personal information but are selective in what they disclose, refraining from sharing detailed descriptions of themselves. Koreans overall appear to disclose less, under the pretense of not wanting to lose "face" or having to defend the details of their personal lives, which may be inconsistent with local offline culture (Cho & Park, 2012). Summarily, individuals immersed in online cultures have normative expectations consistent with the context of discourse and employ social boundaries and limitations that are influenced by their offline culturally determined practices.

Taken together, the communication and language patterns discussed reveal a variety of socially constructed and situationally accepted behaviors and traits that provide clues to underlying motives. Many of the behaviors discussed, such as how we speak, what tools we use to communicate our ideas, and how we approach technology, are determined by our culture of affiliation. In most cases, our communication tools are socially constructed and highly influenced by contextual variations. Any analysis of specific behaviors must identify and take into account the many critical variables associated with each respective setting. Motives are not determined by cultures alone but also by how individuals interact with and within the culture. What an analysis of language and communication does provide is a greater understanding of the types of circumstances that may promote resistance and withdrawal and which will stimulate approachability and action. Again, although glaring generalities are, indeed, a mistake, what people say and how they say it may provide a very clear indication as to why they approach or avoid certain tasks and opportunities to demonstrate behavior.

Principle #31—Leadership is subjectively interpreted according to culture

The definition of what constitutes effective leadership varies considerably contingent upon the culture and philosophical orientation of the definer. In his seminal book *In Search of Excellence*, organizational development guru Tom Peters described leadership as a combination of skills resulting in "the development, the inducement of people to grow, to go way beyond where they believe they could go" (n.d.). Peters' definition, while noticeably vague, was solidified in context when he described how Hollywood director Robert Altman, who, after winning a lifetime achievement Oscar award, proclaimed, "The role of the director is to provide a space where people can become…more than they ever dreamed of being." These descriptions of leadership intimate that conceptually, leadership is a cultural universal, applicable across all cultures, and primarily focused upon the development of others.

The GLOBE research project (2007), dubbed as the "most large scale international management research project that has ever been undertaken" (p. xiii), surveyed 17,300 middle managers from 950 organizations in 62 countries to develop a consensus definition of leadership, taking into account input from 25 of the 62 surveyed countries. The authors of the study concluded that leadership was "the ability of an individual to influence, motivate, and enable others to contribute toward the effectiveness and success of the organizations of which they are members" (House & Javidan, 2004, p. 15). These generic descriptions show a broad emphasis on the motivational capabilities of a leader and suggest an overall collectivist slant to describing leadership behaviors. Perhaps the best definition that incorporates a firm emphasis on personal development comes from the mind of the irreverent author Mark Twain, who decreed, "The best way to cheer yourself is to try to cheer someone else up." Twain's comments imply that a leader's needs are secondary to the needs of those being led and that leadership involves an intimate understanding of what motivates both the self and others.

These generic descriptions of leadership do not take into account behaviors that may be influenced by culturally specific leadership norms. Leadership and the behaviors associated with leading are not culture-free. In Russia, effective leaders are described as "administratively competent with abilities to think strategically, capable to make serious decisions and inspire his [yes, *his*] followers to meet performance targets" (Grachev, Rogovsky, & Rakitski, 2007, p. 822). Leadership in Japan is comparatively more collectivist than other similarly economically situated countries, such as the United States and China (Von Glinow, Huo, & Lowe, 1999). Japanese leaders emphasize building consensus and avoiding favoritism and contend that vast experience is essential to be considered a successful leader. Leaders in China place heavy emphasis on Confucian principles and collectivist ideals stressing kinship and relationships, a vision of the future, and the behaviors of consistency and compassion (Selvarajah & Meyer, 2008). Collectively, these descriptions of leadership imply that what may be optimal leadership in one culture may be unwelcome in another. Subsequently, contradictory conceptions of leadership imply that different strategies are necessary to reach culturally defined leadership goals, which will ultimately impact how superior performance is motivated. Diverse motivational strategies suggest that the corresponding leadership behaviors will also vary considerably between cultures.

Discussing all of the cultural consequences of leadership style would take more volumes than you have time to read and is beyond the scope of this book. The purpose here is to illuminate how differences in leadership culture may influence the motivations of those being led, not to outline the multitude of cross-cultural differences related to encouraging performance (for a specific discussion of workplace motivation see Chapter 11, p. 312). The previously mentioned GLOBE project identified six universal dimensions that were considered instrumental and psychometrically reliable predictors of global leadership behaviors, regardless of country. These characteristics included (1) the relative degree of charisma a leader demonstrates, (2) the degree of self-protection exhibited toward those being lead, (3) the extent of humanistic orientation shown during leadership, (4) a team-based orientation, (5) the prevalence of participative management, and (6) the degree of autonomy afforded to subordinates (Chhokar, Brodbeck, & House, 2007). How leaders operationalize these desired traits and what behaviors they exhibit in practice help define the between-culture conceptions of the leader.

For example, consider the very frequent situation where a leader is skeptical about the quality of a subordinate's work. This commonplace situation usually demands that different mediation strategies be evaluated and implemented. Faced with this performance dilemma, the leader has four possible choices; (1) ignore the behavior hoping it will improve, (2) coach the individual by providing alternative strategies to enhance work quality, (3) assign the work to another person, or (4) complete the work himself or herself. The leader who elects to coach and delegate work to the subordinate and subsequently holds the individual accountable for her task success would send a much different motivational message than the leader who shows reluctance to delegate tasks and instead decides to do the work himself or herself. The former strategy would likely cultivate feelings of autonomy and personal accountability, communicating a motivational message of trust and competence, incentivizing the employee. However, the leader electing to complete the work on his or her own would likely cultivate differential motivational consequences. In an individualistic culture, the worker relinquishing work to a supervisor could be interpreted as a personal failure, with the worker questioning his or her own ability to be successful on subsequent tasks. In contrast, in a collectivist culture that emphasizes group performance, a leader offering help to a struggling subordinate could be interpreted as committing a selfless act of gratitude, motivated by altruism, saving the worker from embarrassment and ridicule for the inability to complete a work task independently. Thus, leadership behavior exhibited is contingent upon not only the performance context, but also based on the cultural context and organizational norms.

In many ways, the variability of leadership behaviors described parallels the distinction between what many organizational development scholars consider the difference between managing and leading. This important distinction, empirically supported by cross-cultural research (Zaleznick, 1977), suggests that multi-cultural descriptions of organizational behavior operate along a continuum, distinguished by the degree of autonomy afforded to individuals. In dependent, hierarchical, and top-down organizations, traditional managers exhibit behaviors focused on planning, organizing, and directing individuals, offering workers limited opportunities for discretionary behavior while affirming a culture of compliance. Conversely, in flat, bottom-up, empowered organizations, visionary leaders encourage innovation and group autonomy, while providing subordinates opportunities to make decisions and choose how work is completed. This defining dimension of leadership results in radical behavioral differences in leaders and broad psychological consequences for workers based upon how the organizational strategy is executed. Table 5.1 outlines differences between managers and leaders that are not purported to be exclusively a function of geography or philosophy but, instead, are based upon culturally diverse organizational behavior.

As individuals consistently demonstrate the behaviors listed in Table 5.1, the organizational culture is operationalized and reinforced, creating organizationally specific behavioral norms. Norms establish prototypical ideas as to what work should be done, how it should be completed, and how it will be evaluated. Such factors as individual conceptions of work, the social climate among co-workers, and evaluative decision making are all influenced by the leadership culture (Gelfand et al., 2007). The normative process gradually begins to influence worker motivation as subordinates either emulate or resist their behavioral leadership models. Individuals undergo a series of conscious deliberations, assessing their own degree of organizational fit while evaluating their overall willingness to align with the organizational culture. In situations of belief compatibility between individual and organization, individual behaviors are adopted by modeling successful others. In situations of belief inconsistency, resistance and psychological conflict develop with potentially devastating motivational consequences. Motivational incompatibility between the organization and the individual results in resistance, individual apathy, and dissension toward organizational goals. Behaviorally, the individual demonstrates indifference to creativity, unwillingness to take risks, or displays passive conformity to the normative guidelines established and reinforced by the organization.

Individual motives that develop as a result of cultural differences in leadership style can be further explained by borrowing some of the underlying principles of the Prototype Willingness Model (PWM, Litt & Lewis, 2013). The PWM is typically

Table 5.1 A comparison of management and leadership behaviors

Managerial behaviors	Leadership behaviors
Directs energy toward goals, resources, organizational structure, and determining the problems to be solved.	Directs energy toward guiding people toward solutions that resolve business issues in a proactive manner.
Operates in a congenial style and likes to be perceived as fair by staff.	Cultivates vigorous debate on business issues. Challenges the routine, while supporting diversity of opinion.
Changes process by redesign of existing methods.	Innovates through flashes of insight or intuition, willing to take a calculated risk.
Views work as an enabling process, involving a combination of ideas, skills, timing, and people.	Views work as developing fresh approaches to old problems or finding new options for old issues.
Deals with the soft side of a business and therefore may not be directly accountable.	The impact on business results can and must be measured. Results are translated into financial performance.
Has an instinct for survival; seeks to minimize risks and tolerate the mundane.	Approaches the mundane and routine as an opportunity for change and innovation.
Has a low level of emotional involvement in his or her work.	Demonstrates emotional regulation, understanding emotional signals from others, using positive emotions to enhance relationships with others; is often passionate about his or her work.
Focuses on *how* things need to be done.	Focuses on *what* needs to be done, leaving decisions to people involved.
Focuses attention on procedure.	Focuses attention on strategy.
Finds harmony in living up to society, company, and family expectations.	Finds self-esteem through self-reliance and personal expression. Takes control of personal development and growth.

used to predict the willingness of individuals to engage in reasoned modes of risky behavior, such as when adolescents contemplate engaging in behaviors with potential health risks, including drinking, smoking, or unsafe sex. The model purports that individuals undergo a deliberate process of reasoning and evaluations incorporating expectations of anticipated outcomes before making a decision to engage in particular behaviors. The model is based upon the assumptions that individuals are active agents, crafting their own destinies by evaluating both contextual and social circumstances before acting on a decision. Further, the model suggests that individuals evaluate three important antecedents before engaging in behavior: the people who exhibit the behavior, socially determined norms, and personal vulnerability to negative consequences and outcomes.

Reconciliation of internal conflict, which is created when personal and organizational beliefs clash, in many ways mirror the same cognitive dissonance individuals experience when contemplating the consequences of unhealthy or risky social behavior. This inference is based on the assumption that leadership style ultimately determines normative organizational behavior and is, at least in part, socially constructed due to the inherent nature of group dynamics and supervisor–subordinate relationships. The PWM explains how people resolve the ambivalence individuals encounter as they undergo a series of frequent reasoned and repetitive assessments evaluating their overall organizational fit. When individual beliefs are perceived as inconsistent with established organizational norms, individuals become highly vulnerable to the psychological and emotional consequences of misalignment. The individual is ultimately faced with a choice. The first option is to embrace the organizationally preferred behavior. Compliance with organizational norms that are inconsistent with personal beliefs, although psychologically challenging, may be perceived as socially appropriate and financially prudent. The alternative is to resist and rebuke organizational norms but suffer the potentially detrimental consequences of organizational derailment and the possibility of compromising one's job, social standing, and financial security for the sake of personal beliefs.

As the individual wrestles with resolution of the dilemma, an internal or external focus prevails. If the individual elects to align with organizational expectations the decision-making process becomes externally referenced. In this instance, the individual consciously decides to modify personal beliefs to align with those expected by the organization thereby smoothly assimilating into the organizational culture. Conversely, an individual may adapt an internally focused decision-making process. In this instance, the person is unwilling to compromise personal beliefs for the sake of organizational fit and is consciously willing to accept the potential negative organizational consequences in order to maintain the integrity of his or her personal belief conceptions.

Ultimately, the individual's motivations are dominated by either an external perspective and a desire to adapt and conform or an internal perspective minimizing the need for personal belief change. Regardless of which orientation an individual chooses, no best approach prevails. Organizational "fit" comes in many sizes and shapes, and the role of culture is both innocuous and neutral. One person's rose can be another's thorn. Where and how the person decides to plant their motivational seed is a formula known only to the metaphoric florist, who invariably changes her arrangement according to the season.

Chapter summary/conclusions

Culture is a prevailing influence upon how we view the world. Individuals may or may not consciously recognize that culture is instrumental in the overall development of their beliefs and instrumental in guiding daily behaviors. Many times, individuals adopt the culturally accepted behaviors of their dominant geographical culture, but not always. Frequently, overall identities are formed and more readily influenced by the values and beliefs of in-groups, primarily based upon an individual's ethnicity, race, or philosophical leanings. In-group affiliation becomes a strong motivator of performance, as positive self-views develop when individuals experience a sense of belonging and bonding that evolves when like-minded individuals reinforce group behavior.

Recognizing the influence of culture is only one part of understanding how culture affects motivation. The MD must be vigilant to critically analyze his or her own motivations and behaviors, avoiding the trap of cultural bias and prejudice when assessing the motives of others. A focused effort on understanding multi-cultural values and customs is an important means to mediate issues of motivation and performance as the degree of culturally responsive pedagogy can significantly influence performance outcomes. Culture, as an all-encompassing variable, influences how individuals focus attention, what goals they set for themselves, and the degree of individuality or group affiliation they demonstrate. Evidence shows that symbolic representations of culture, such as language, communication patterns, use of technology and demonstrations of leadership, are all culturally-nuanced behaviors. Culture guides many aspects of teaching, learning, and performance because what may seem appropriate in one learning context can be highly detrimental in another. Any decision involving the implementation of learning or performance strategies must consider the role of culture or the MD may quickly surmise that what they are calling a rose is actually nothing but a very prickly thorn.

Next steps

Much of this chapter was based on illuminating the influence of worldviews that frequently operate along a continuum, with most emphasis given to dichotomous anchors, which tend to polarize differences between one theoretical lens and another. We have learned that many values, traits, and behaviors represent either an individualistic or a group focus, and workplace behaviors emphasize a management or a leadership perspective. Since the foundation of many worldviews is broadly influenced by personal orientation, it is not uncommon for some individuals to closely scrutinize their inner selves for motivational guidance and corresponding agency. Others adopt a more external frame of reference, relying upon outsiders' signals when contemplating how they should act. The internal–external paradigm is highly influential for many of our goals, motives and the strategies we use to navigate our lives. Next, we turn to the powerful continuum of intrinsic and extrinsic motivation as determinants of what we do and why we do it, while meeting amicable **Nick Holes**, a gentleman who clearly knows his preferential path.

End of chapter motivational minute

Principles covered in this chapter:

27. **Culture transcends demographics**—Culture can be determined by demographic categories, but also is demonstrated by adaptation and alignment with specific groups that have normative shared philosophies, values, and communication practices.
28. **Ethnic identity shapes self-concept and self-relevant motivations**—Ethnic identity develops as individuals reject dominate culture beliefs and affiliate closely with their own in-groups based upon heritage, race, ethnicity, or religion.
29. **Motivational differences exist between individualistic and collectivistic cultures**—Individualistic cultures support the development of the individual as a dominant focus

of motivated action. The focus of collectivist cultures is centered on group process and performance, with the individual seen as integral to the success of the in-group.
30. **Communication and language patterns are revealing cultural markers**—The way individuals communicate is symbolic of accepted cultural practice and can reveal underlying motives. Language pace, diction, tone, and technology provide many context clues to determine cultural affiliation of an individual or group.
31. **Leadership is subjectively interpreted according to culture**—Individuals can provide direction to others by using strategies of management or leadership. Each approach sets an organizational tone that facilitates conforming or empowering motives in others.

Key terminology (in order of chapter presentation):

- **Enculturated**—changing one's normative psychological, motivational, and behavioral processes to align with the norms expected in another less familiar environment.
- **Culturally responsive strategies and pedagogy**—instructional and motivational strategies that account for the diverse backgrounds, languages, and dispositions of learners.
- **Cross-cultural competence**—the ability of individuals and groups to gain knowledge about unfamiliar cultures and effectively assimilate within them.
- **Catharsis**—a realization of one's owns emotions or cognitions that previously may have been repressed or were not within the stream of consciousness.
- **Ethnic identity**—the process of individual identity formation and evaluations of self-concept that are influenced by perceptions of ethnic and racial group belonging.
- **Individualism**—a worldview that suggests that society exists to satisfy individual needs. Individual identity is based upon success achieved by fulfillment of needs, desires, and actions that support individual growth and development.
- **Collectivism**—a worldview that suggests that individuals exist to serve group goals and accelerate group performance. Individual identity is based upon a representative set of meanings and practices that define the individual in relation to his or her in-group.
- **Lexical analysis**—the process of ascribing meaning to words.

References

Ang, S., Van Dyne, L., Koh, C., Ng, K. Y., Templer, K. J., Tay, C., et al. (2007). Cultural intelligence: Its measurement and effects on cultural judgment and decision making, cultural adaptation and task performance. *Management and Organization Review, 3*(3), 335–371. http://dx.doi.org/10.1111/j.1740-8784.2007.00082.x.

Assmann, A. (2006). The printing press and the internet: From a culture of memory to a culture of attention. In N. Gentz & S. Kramer (Eds.), *Globalization, cultural identities, and media representations* (pp. 11–25). Albany, NY: SUNY Press.

Aud, S., Wilkinson-Flicker, S., Kristapovich, P., Rathbun, A., Wang, X., Zhang, J., & National Center for Education Statistics (ED), (2013). *The condition of education 2013. NCES 2013-037*. National Center for Education Statistics.

Bennett, R. (2006). Inexorable and inevitable: The continuing story of technology and assessment. In D. Bartram & R. K. Hambleton (Eds.), *Computer-based testing and the internet: Issues and advances* (pp. 201–217). New York, NY: John Wiley & Sons Ltd.

Bingham, G. E., & Okagaki, L. (2012). Ethnicity and student engagement. In S. L. Christenson, A. L. Reschly, & C. Wylie (Eds.), *Handbook of research on student engagement* (pp. 65–95). New York, NY: Springer Science. http://dx.doi.org/10.1007/978-1-4614-2018-7_4.

Burgmann, I., Kitchen, P. J., & Williams, R. (2006). Does culture matter on the web? *Marketing, Intelligence & Planning, 24*(1), 62–76.

Chao, R., & Kanatsu, A. (2008). Beyond socioeconomics: Explaining ethnic group differences in parenting through cultural and immigration processes. *Applied Developmental Science, 12*(4), 181–187. http://dx.doi.org/10.1080/10888690802388102.

Chen, F. F., & West, S. G. (2008). Measuring individualism and collectivism: The importance of considering differential components, reference groups, and measurement invariance. *Journal of Research in Personality, 42*(2), 259–294.

Chen, X.-P., Liu, D., & Portnoy, R. (2012). A multilevel investigation of motivational cultural intelligence, organizational diversity climate, and cultural sales: Evidence from U.S. real estate firms. *Journal of Applied Psychology, 97*(1), 93–106. http://dx.doi.org/10.1037/a0024697.

Chhokar, J. S., Brodbeck, F. C., & House, R. J. (2007). Methodology. In R. J. House, F. C. Brodbeck, & J. S. Chhokar (Eds.), *Culture and leadership across the world: The GLOBE book of in-depth studies of 25 societies* (pp. 17–32). Mahwah, NJ: Lawrence Erlbaum Associates.

Cho, S. E., & Park, H. W. (2012). A qualitative analysis of cross-cultural new media research: SNS use in Asia and the West. *Quality & Quantity, 47*(4), 2319–2330.

Cohen, D. (1997). Ifs and thens in cross-cultural psychology. In R. S. Wyer Jr. (Ed.), *The automaticity of everyday life* (pp. 121–131). Mahwah, NJ: Erlbaum.

Davenport, S. W., Bergman, S. M., Bergman, J. Z., & Fearrington, M. E. (2014). Twitter versus Facebook: Exploring the role of narcissism in the motives and usage of different social media platforms. *Computers in Human Behavior, 32*, 212–220. http://dx.doi.org/10.1016/j.chb.2013.12.011.

Deardorff, D. K. (2006). Identification and assessment of intercultural competence as a student outcome of internationalization. *Journal of Studies in International Education, 10*(3), 241–266.

Decker, D. M., Dona, D. P., & Christenson, S. L. (2007). Behaviorally at-risk African American students: The importance of student-teacher relationships for student outcomes. *Journal of School Psychology, 45*, 83–109.

Diener, E. (2012). New findings and future directions for subjective well-being research. *American Psychologist, 67*(8), 590–597. http://dx.doi.org/10.1037/a0029541.

Earley, P. C., & Ang, S. (2003). *Cultural intelligence: Individual interactions across cultures*. Stanford, CA: Stanford University Press.

English, T., Chen, S., & Swann, W. B., Jr. (2008). A cross-cultural analysis of self-verification motives. In R. M. Sorrentino & S. Yamaguchi (Eds.), *Handbook of motivation and cognition across cultures* (pp. 119–142). San Diego, CA: Academic Press.

Forbes, N., & Wield, D. (2013). *From followers to leaders: Managing technology and innovation*. New York, NY: Routledge.

Gardner, H. (1985). *Frames of mind: The theory of multiple intelligences*. New York, NY: Basic Books.

Gelfand, M. J., Erez, M., & Aycan, Z. (2007). Cross-cultural organizational behavior. *Annual Review of Psychology, 58*, 479–514. http://dx.doi.org/10.1146/annurev.psych.58.110405.085559.

Golden, T. D., Veiga, J. F., & Dino, R. N. (2008). The impact of professional isolation on teleworker job performance and turnover intentions: Does time spent teleworking, interacting face-to-face, or having access to communication-enhancing technology matter? *Journal of Applied Psychology, 93*(6), 1412–1421. http://dx.doi.org/10.1037/a0012722.

Grachev, M. V., Rogovsky, N. G., & Rakitski, B. V. (2007). Leadership and culture in Russia: The case of transitional economy. In R. J. House, F. C. Brodbeck, & J. S. Chhokar (Eds.), *Culture and leadership across the world: The GLOBE book of in-depth studies of 25 societies* (pp. 803–831). Mahwah, NJ: Lawrence Erlbaum Associates.

Graham, S., & Hudley, C. (2005). Race and ethnicity in the study of motivation and competence. In A. Elliot & C. Dweck (Eds.), *Handbook of competence and motivation* (pp. 392–413). New York, NY: Guilford.

Greenwald, A. G., McGhee, D. E., & Schwartz, J. L. K. (1998). Measuring individual differences in implicit cognition: The implicit association test. *Journal of Personality and Social Psychology, 74*, 1464–1480.

HarrisInteractive (2013). The not-so-United States of technology. Retrieved on February 26, 2014 from: <http://www.harrisinteractive.com>

Heine, S. J. (2007). Culture and motivation: What motivates people to act in the ways that they do? In S. Kitayama & D. Cohen (Eds.), *Handbook of cultural psychology* (pp. 714–733). New York, NY: Guilford Press.

Heine, S. J., Lehman, D. R., Markus, H. R., & Kitayama, S. (1999). Is there a universal need for positive self-regard? *Psychological Review, 106*(4), 766–794.

Heine, S. J., Lehman, D. R., Peng, K., & Greenholtz, J. (2002). What's wrong with cross-cultural comparisons of subjective Likert scales? The reference-group effect. *Journal of Personality and Social Psychology, 82*(6), 903–918.

Henrich, J., McElreath, R., Barr, A., Ensminger, J., Barrett, C., Bolyanatz, A., et al. (2006). Costly punishment across human societies. *Science, 312*(5781), 1767–1770.

Hickey, D. T. (1997). Motivation and contemporary socio-constructivist instructional perspectives. *Educational Psychologist, 32*(3), 175–193.

Hofer, J., & Bond, M. H. (2008). Do implicit motives add to our understanding of psychological and behavioral outcomes within and across cultures?. In R. M. Sorrentino & S. Yamaguchi (Eds.), *Handbook of motivation and cognition across cultures* (pp. 95–118). San Diego, CA: Academic Press.

House, R. J., Brodbeck, F. C., Chhokar, J., & Global Leadership and Organizational Behavior Effectiveness Research, (2007). *Culture and leadership across the world: The GLOBE book of in-depth studies of 25 societies*. Mahwah, NJ: Lawrence Erlbaum Associates.

House, R. J., & Javidan, M. (2004). Overview of GLOBE. In R. J. House, P. J. Hanges, M. Javidan, P. Dorfman, V. Gupta GLOBE Associates (Eds.), *Leadership, culture, and organizations: The GLOBE study of 62 societies* (pp. 102–121). Thousand Oaks, CA: Sage.

Johnson, J. P., Lenartowicz, T., & Apud, S. (2006). Cross-cultural competence in international business: Toward a definition and a model. *Journal of International Business Studies, 37*(4), 525–543.

Karasawa, M., & Maass, A. (2008). The role of language in the perception of persons and groups. In R. Sorrentino & S. Yamaguchi (Eds.), *Handbook of motivation and cognition across cultures* (pp. 317–341). San Diego, CA: Academic Press.

Kashima, E., & Kashima, Y. (1998). Culture and language: The case of cultural dimensions and personal pronoun use. *Journal of Cross-cultural Psychology, 29*, 461–486.

Kesebir, P., & Pyszczynski, T. (2011). The role of death in life: Existential aspects of human motivation. In R. M. Ryan (Ed.), *The Oxford handbook of human motivation* (pp. 43–64). New York, NY: Oxford University Press.

Kientz, J., Choe, E. K., & Truong, K. (2013). *Texting from the toilet: Mobile computing and acceptance in private and public restrooms*. Retrieved on April 10, 2015 from: <https://tspace.library.utoronto.ca/bitstream/1807/35207/1/TechKMD-2013-1.pdf>

Kim, H., Coyle, J. R., & Gould, S. J. (2009). Collectivist and individualist influences on website design in South Korea and the U.S.: A cross-cultural content analysis. *Journal of Computer-Mediated Communication, 3*, 581. http://dx.doi.org/10.1111/j.1083-6101. 2009.01454.x.

Kim, H. S., & Chu, T. Q. (2011). Cultural variation in the motivation of self-expression. In D. Dunning (Ed.), *Social motivation* (pp. 57–77). New York, NY: Psychology Press.

Kim, H. S., & Sasaki, J. Y. (2014). Cultural neuroscience: Biology of the mind in cultural contexts. *Annual Review of Psychology, 65*, 487–514.

Kitayama, S., Mesquita, B., & Karasawa, M. (2006). Cultural affordances and emotional experience: Socially engaging and disengaging emotions in Japan and the United States. *Journal of Personality and Social Psychology, 91*(5), 890–903.

Kluckhohn, C. (1954). Culture and behavior. In G. Lindzey (Ed.), *Handbook of social psychology* (pp. 921–976). Cambridge, MA: Addison-Wesley.

Ladson-Billings, G. (1995). Toward a theory of culturally relevant pedagogy. *American Educational Research Journal, 32*(3), 465–491.

Lee, H. O., & Boster, F. J. (1992). Collectivism–individualism in perceptions of speech rate: A cross-cultural comparison. *Journal of Cross-Cultural Psychology, 23*, 377–388.

Litt, D. M., & Lewis, M. A. (2013). The prototype willingness model. In J-P. Assailly (Ed.), *Psychology of risk-taking* (pp. 83–98). New York, NY: Nova Science Publishers, Inc.

Markus, H. R., Mullally, P. R., & Kitayama, S. (1997). Selfways: Diversity in modes of cultural participation. In U. Neisser & D. Jopling (Eds.), *The conceptual self in context* (pp. 13–61). New York, NY: Cambridge University Press.

Matsumoto, D., & Hwang, H. C. (2013). Assessing cross-cultural competence: A review of available tests. *Journal of Cross-Cultural Psychology, 44*(6), 849–873. http://dx.doi.org/10.1177/0022022113492891.

McAllister, G., & Irvine, J. J. (2000). Cross cultural competency and multicultural teacher education. *Review of Educational Research, 70*, 3–24.

Mesquita, B. (2001). Emotions in collectivist and individualist contexts. *Journal of Personality and Social Psychology, 80*(1), 68–74.

Montessori, M. (2014). *The Montessori method*. New Brunswick, NJ: Transaction Publishers.

Morling, B., & Kitayama, S. (2008). Culture and motivation. In J. Y. Shah, W. L. Gardner, J. Y. Shah, & W. L. Gardner (Eds.), *Handbook of motivation science* (pp. 417–433). New York, NY: Guilford Press.

Morling, B., & Lamoreaux, M. (2008). Measuring culture outside the head: A meta-analysis of individualism—collectivism in cultural products. *Personality and Social Psychology Review, 12*(3), 199–221. http://dx.doi.org/10.1177/1088868308318260.

Murray, M. S., Neal-Barnett, A., Demmings, J. L., & Stadulis, R. E. (2012). The acting White accusation, racial identity, and anxiety in African American adolescents. *Journal of Anxiety Disorders, 26*(4), 526–531. http://dx.doi.org/10.1016/j.janxdis.2012.02.006.

Nuñez, A. -M., & Crisp, G. (2012). Ethnic diversity and Latino/a college access: A comparison of Mexican American and Puerto Rican beginning college students. *Journal of Diversity in Higher Education, 5*(2), 78–95. http://dx.doi.org/10.1037/a0026810.

Oyserman, D., & Lee, S. W. (2008). A situated cognition perspective on culture: Effects of priming cultural syndromes on cognition and motivation. In R. M. Sorrentino & S. Yamaguchi (Eds.), *Handbook of motivation and cognition across cultures* (pp. 237–265). San Diego, CA: Academic Press.

Peters, T. (n.d.). Definition of leadership. Retrieved on March 6, 2014 from: <http://www.tompeters.com/blogs/freestuff/uploads/Definition_Leadership052908.pdf>

Phinney, J. S. (1990). Ethnic identity in adolescents and adults: Review of research. *Psychological Bulletin, 108*(3), 499–514.

Phinney, J. S. (2000). Identity formation across cultures: The interaction of personal, societal, and historical change. *Human Development, 43*(1), 27–31. http://dx.doi.org/10.1159/000022653.

Pullum, G. K. (1991). *The great Eskimo vocabulary hoax, and other irreverent essays on the study of language*. Chicago, IL: University of Chicago Press.

Rohn, U. (2014). Social networking sites across cultures and countries: Proximity and network effects. *Qualitative Research Reports in Communication, 14*(1), 28–34. http://dx.doi.org/10.1080/17459435.2013.835339.

Rosenblatt, A., Greenberg, J., Solomon, S., Pyszczynski, T., & Lyon, D. (1989). Evidence for terror management theory: The effects of mortality salience on reactions to those who violate or uphold cultural values. *Journal of Personality and Social Psychology, 57*(4), 681–690.

Rubin, K. H., & Chung, O. B. (2006). *Parenting beliefs, behaviors, and parent-child relations: A cross-cultural perspective*. Florence, KY: Psychology Press.

Ryan, A. M. (2001). The peer group as a context for the development of young adolescent motivation and achievement. *Child Development, 72*, 1135–1150.

Ryan, R. M., & Deci, E. L. (2000). Self-determination theory and the facilitation of intrinsic motivation, social development, and well-being. *American Psychologist, 55*(1), 68–78. http://dx.doi.org/10.1037/0003-066X.55.1.68.

Rychly, L., & Graves, E. (2012). Teacher characteristics for culturally responsive pedagogy. *Multicultural Perspectives, 14*(1), 44–49. http://dx.doi.org/10.1080/15210960.2012.646853.

Sears, A., Jacko, J. A., & Dubach, E. M. (2000). International aspects of world wide web usability and the role of high-end graphical enhancements. *International Journal of Human-Computer Interaction, 12*(2), 241–261.

Sedikides, C., Gaertner, L., Luke, M. A., O'Mara, E. M., & Gebauer, J. E. (2013). A three-tier hierarchy of self-potency: Individual self, relational self, collective self. *Advances in Experimental Social Psychology, 48*, 235–295.

Selvarajah, C., & Meyer, D. (2008). Profiling the Chinese manager: Exploring dimensions that relate to leadership. *Leadership & Organization Development Journal, 29*(4), 359–375. http://dx.doi.org/10.1108/01437730810876159.

Sherman, D. K., & Cohen, G. L. (2002). Accepting threatening information: Self-affirmation and the reduction of defensive biases. *Current Directions in Psychological Science (Wiley-Blackwell), 11*(4), 119–123.

Sternberg, R. J. (2004). Culture and intelligence. *American Psychologist, 59*(5), 325–338.

Swann, W. B., Jr., Pelham, B. W., & Krull, D. S. (1989). Agreeable fancy or disagreeable truth? Reconciling self-enhancement and self-verification. *Journal of Personality and Social Psychology*, (5), 782–791.

Torres, V. (2004). The diversity among us: Puerto Ricans, Cuban Americans, Caribbean Americans, and Central and South Americans. *New Directions for Student Services, 105*, 5–16.

Triandis, H. C. (1995). *Individualism and collectivism*. Boulder, CO: Westview Press.

Triandis, H. C., & Suh, E. M. (2002). Cultural influences on personality. *Annual Review of Psychology, 53*(1), 133–160.

Von Glinow, M. A., Huo, Y. P., & Lowe, K. (1999). Leadership across the Pacific Ocean: A tri-national comparison. *International Business Review, 8*(1), 1–15.

Ward, C. A., Bochner, S., & Furnham, A. F. (2001). *The psychology of culture shock*. Hove, UK: Routledge.

Woolfolk, A. (2010). *Educational Psychology*. Upper Saddle River, NJ: Merrill.

www.census.gov. (2011). *2010 Census shows America's diversity*. Retrieved on April 10, 2015 from: <https://www.census.gov/2010census/news/releases/operations/cb11-cn125.html>

Zaleznik, A. (1977). Managers and leaders: Are they different? *Harvard Business Review, 55*(3), 67–78.

Part II

The powerful role of individual differences and self-beliefs

You say to-may-toe, I say to-mah-toe: Individual differences in motives guide focus and effort

Chapter outline

Principle #32—The source of motives determines goal emphasis and strategy choice 144
Motivational Leader—*Nick Holes* 148
Principle #33—Individual reaction to incentives is variable, and predictable 149
Principle #34—Goal type and orientation are reliable and accurate predictors of behavior 154
    Achievement goals: Mastery, normative, or multiple? 157
    Organizational promotion or prevention? 161
Principle #35—Interest is a multi-faceted contributor to motivational intensity 164
    Chapter summary/conclusions 167
    Next steps 168
    End of chapter motivational minute 168
References 169

Welcome to Part II. First, let's recap. Thus far, we have explored several foundational principles to interpret the antecedents of performance motivation. Some motivational myths were debunked, the influence of biopsychology on motivation was described, and the evolving nature of motivation over the lifespan was explained. The pervasive influence of culture when diagnosing and mediating motivational challenges was revealed. Next, we turn to three paradoxical, but central. types of evidence critical to understanding optimal motivation: (1) individual differences in how rewards sway and modify performance effort, (2) factors that contribute to setting and attaining goal targets, and (3) a discussion on how domain-specific interest develops, fluctuates, and influences our attentional focus and corresponding strategy choices.

Now, imagine it is the first day of the semester, or recall your first day on a new job. Like the start of the baseball season, hope springs eternal, and individual confidence abounds. As the naive optimism prevails, you are suddenly offered an intriguing proposition. In the classroom, students hear the instruction, "Line up against the wall." During corporate orientation, I say, "Sign here" and point to a tiny square box that reads, "I agree to all terms and conditions of employment." No, I am not taking attendance or measuring compliant organizational behavior. I am beginning to assess how people are motivated. My academic voice rings out: "How many of you would like an 'A' for the course without needing to attend the next six classes?" Hands dart up. My corporate voice mirrors the similar academic intention: "Who wants to participate in the executive bonus plan? You don't have any specific goals to meet; merely come to work every day!" Suddenly, the tired eyes of students open wide and the workers' eyebrows take a dubious shift. Invariably, responses to these offers are first met with laughter and then skepticism, as people wonder if these overtures could possibly be sincere. After a few minutes of probing questions, about 80% of the respondents assume their positions against the wall or check the little box, all indicating their willingness to either earn grades or pay, with little, if any, investment of effort. Yet 20% of individuals turn my offer down, but why?

The disparity between accepting an unearned "A" and taking pay for minimal effort, in comparison with rejecting the offer is stark evidence that individual differences exist in ascribing values to tasks, determining what goals are worthy of pursuit, and what people find interesting. Each choice described has broad and powerful motivational implications. The variability of individual need and choice suggests that what is perceived as satisfying by one individual may be disparaged by another. The reasons for choices are robust indicators of individual commitment and symptomatic of the value individuals place on various learning objectives and performance targets. Frequently, we hear friends and co-workers lament their choices and obligations, using terminology, such as "wanting," "needing," or being "obligated," as the prevailing rationale that determines how much time, focus, or effort is invested in a particular endeavor. Broadly, these exclamations represent how individuals qualitatively evaluate various aspects of their decisions, choices which ultimately influence how they apply and regulate their motivation. Individuals make clear assessments and distinctions between what is considered "work" or "play" (Lepper & Henderlong, 2000), and if they approach tasks because of "desire" or a perceived "necessity" (Sansone & Smith, 2000). It is these dimensions, typically described in research as the difference between intrinsic and extrinsic motivation, that motivational detectives (MDs) can use to make some preliminary and significant diagnostic inferences concerning the conditions and contingencies related to cultivating optimal performance.

Conceptions of motivation vary broadly, yet most researchers agree that individuals assume one of two motivational dispositions when contemplating the goals they set and the tasks they are willing to pursue. Although at times people embrace dualistic motives, frequently individuals have either intrinsic or extrinsic motives (Vallerand & Ratelle, 2002). Intrinsic motivation, from a learning or performance perspective, suggests that individuals possess a predisposition to engage in the pursuit of knowledge and seek opportunities to demonstrate competence. When intrinsically motivated, individuals gain pleasure and satisfaction merely from the process of reaching a learning or performance target (Stipek, 1998). Intrinsic motivation implies that the impetus to achieve is cultivated without consideration or expectation of external recognition or reward. The purposeful and intentional process of goal pursuit is emotionally perceived as positive for the intrinsically motivated (White, 1959), presumably because the individual ascribes personal value and utility to reaching the intended goal. Successful goal attainment cultivates a sense of competency and nurtures positive efficacy perceptions, primarily because the individual is able to reach the desired target.

Conversely, when extrinsically motivated, individuals pursue goal targets chiefly because reaching the desired goal results in attaining specific incentives or reinforcements, jointly described as "contingencies." Learning contingencies represent desired short-term outcomes, such as earning good grades or receiving teacher and parent praise for academic achievements. Long-term learning contingencies include making incremental progress toward career goals, earning positive social evaluations from others, or realizing personal definitions of economic success, if and when goal targets are met. Performance-related contingencies provide similar materialistic inducements, affording recognition of accomplishments or gaining elevated social status because of one's talents and abilities. Avoidance of negative consequences may also incentivize the extrinsically-motivated individual by thwarting the appearance of incompetence and by evading tasks that might bring about self-doubt (Bandura, 1991).

The key difference between individuals with intrinsic versus extrinsic orientations are the purported justifications and reasons for pursuing exhibited behavior. When contemplating goal setting and task engagement, individuals undergo a series of intrapsychological evaluations. Broadly, individuals assess whether task pursuits are undertaken for reasons external to the psychic self or to satisfy the inner psychological strivings of the core self (Ryan, Sheldon, Kasser, & Deci, 1996). This assessment process implies that individuals have a dominant phenomenological orientation that is either internally or externally anchored, sometimes referred to as the *locus of control* (deCharms, 1968). Individuals with an internally controlled locus are primarily intrinsically motivated. When considering task engagement, they will assess tasks relative to their personal interests and beliefs. These individuals will consider task relevance, personal importance placed upon completing the task, and the overall value or worth associated with task, including how task completion will make them feel emotionally. Positive appraisals result in task pursuit. For instance, intrinsically-motivated individuals given the opportunity to explain *why* they exercise, often report reasons, such as having fun, personal challenge, and enjoyment (Ryan, Frederick, Lepes, Rubio, & Sheldon, 1997), and their exercise frequency is positively correlated with the individual degree of self-focus they profess (Lewis & Sutton, 2011). Similar self-reflective rationales are reported by intrinsically-motivated individuals during other episodes of highly focused goal-directed behavior, including weight loss (Mata et al., 2011), superior athletic performance (Gillet, Vallerand, Amoura, & Baldes, 2010), and tobacco abstinence (Williams et al., 2006). Summarily, individual self-views and personal interest strongly influence the attention and effort of the intrinsically oriented individual.

Extrinsically-motivated individuals are also interested in reaching goal targets, albeit for different reasons. Psychologically, a person with an external locus of control makes a conscious and deliberate distinction between behaviors pursued strictly for the purpose of self-gratification, and those tasks attempted with the anticipation of a materialistic outcome or a psychological payoff. Unlike their intrinsic peers, extrinsically oriented individuals have differently weighted dualistic motives, whereby goal attainment is subordinate to goal contingencies or the benefits reaped as a result of goal attainment. Benefits include materialistic outcomes or valued incentives but may also consist of positive social comparisons inherent to task choice and completion. Attaining the "reward," or avoiding negative perceptions when not reaching the goal takes precedence and becomes a more meaningful reason to pursue a goal when motives are extrinsically dominated and focused.

Abundant educational and psychological evidence supports the power of extrinsic motivation for optimal performance, with limitations (Ryan & Deci, 2000). Perhaps the best-known example of extrinsic motivation and the blatant coercion of learners based upon incentives is the Pizza Hut "Book It!" reading program created in 1985. Commercialism aside, the goal of the program is to motivate and increase children's reading frequency and enjoyment. The mass appeal of incentive motivation is evidenced by the more than 14 million young readers who were expected to participate in the ongoing program in 630,000 classrooms during the 2014–2015 school year (Pizza Hut, 2015). According to an independent survey (University of Rhode Island, 1986 as cited in Flora & Flora, 1999) a strong majority of teachers involved in the program claimed that historically, the program increased reading interest, reading level, and reading enjoyment (and probably the unmeasured variable, reader waist size)! Although perpetuating pizza parties may increase certain behavior frequencies, under closer scrutiny, a strictly extrinsic reward focus can have profound motivational consequences and influence how students view ongoing learning and performance tasks, which, under certain circumstances, may decrease task motivation (Deci, Koestner, & Ryan, 2001; see Principle #33, p. 149).

Despite that apparent dichotomous nature of motivational orientation, categorizing motives is not an all-or-nothing proposition. Intrinsic and extrinsic orientations are neither antagonistic nor orthogonal and may peacefully coexist in the same person (Covington & Müeller, 2001). Although there may be a dominant influence on behavior, other factors discussed in this chapter, including goal orientation, the performance context, and various social mediators, can radically alter situational motives (Lepper & Henderlong, 2000), inhibiting a precise temporal interpretation of what drives behavior. Imagine the intrinsically motivated, highly ambitious, energized student of college statistics, fully confident in her ability to conquer a formidable class at the semester's launch, who is gradually transformed into a lethargic, work avoidant, grade junkie as the semester wanes and academic pressures mount. Realistically, competing goals and practical considerations will mandate that individuals prioritize goals. Individuals, invariably, will differ in the strength and degree of commitment and intentionality toward attaining goal targets. Initial mastery intentions may ultimately be masked and pursued solely for the perceived payoffs as contextual conditions change. Further, dual performance motives may concurrently exist, such as when the highly paid athlete with the long-term contract excels, not exclusively for money but for pride and personal accomplishment.

Before illuminating the etiology and consequences of motivational orientation, I would like to introduce you to the motivational enigma known as Alec Torelli, who is profiled in detail in Chapter 9 (p. 251). Before I met Alec, his wife Ambra informed me that "Alec regularly travels the world following high-stakes poker action" (A. Meda, personal communication, November 20, 2013). On any given day, Alec can be found in one of the many opulent casinos throughout the world, playing in lucrative tournaments in exotic locales, such as Macau, China, or Monaco (in Monte Carlo's Grand Casino of James Bond fame). As a professional gambler, you might quickly surmise that Alec is highly extrinsically motivated, especially considering that he has twice played at the finals table in the famed Las Vegas World Series of Poker, where the payout to the winner is over $10,000,000! As emphasized in Chapter 1, however, snap judgments and quick inferences concerning the meaning of behaviors should always be tempered. In this case, the extrinsic inference concerning Alec is only marginally true.

I described Alec as "enigmatic" because contrary to intuition, he does not play in high-risk, high-reward poker tournaments for money alone. When asked why he participated, Alec emphasized the opportunity for perfect play and the potentially boosting feelings of efficacy as strong motivators of his behavior. Alec stated,

> *When I am at the table, I feel I am in control of my own destiny. Win or lose, nothing or no one gets in my head. I am totally focused on the outcome. I decide if I should fold, raise, or pass; it's my choice. I use my advanced knowledge of mathematics and assess the probability of winning; what decision should be made is usually crystal clear. Obviously, winning is important for my career, but being right is more important for my state of mind.*
>
> A. Torelli, personal communication, May 13, 2014

He added, "Losing is part of the game. Over time, everyone gets dealt the same hands; knowing when to fold is the difference between the ultimate winners and losers."

Analyzing Alec's motives for immersing himself in the risky career of a tournament poker player shows an obvious connection to extrinsic factors. Would Alec play if there were no promise of economic gain? Probably not. Does he engage in the behavior for extrinsic reasons alone? Also unlikely. While the monetary gains from winning tournaments are immense, Alec realizes his quest for control by consciously regulating his willingness to engage in playing and by making in-game tactical decisions. Alec's behavior can be best understood through the broad theoretical lens of self-determination theory (SDT; Ryan & Deci, 2000) introduced in Chapter 2 (p. 36). SDT contends that individuals strive to create a unified view of the self that integrates with their perceptions of their conceptual and social world. Individuals elect to immerse themselves in environments that may either impede or accelerate integration. The foundation of organismic integration (one component of SDT) suggests that reciprocal and harmonious relationships between the psychic self and the external world are based upon the satisfaction of three basic psychological needs: autonomy, competence, and relatedness (Deci & Ryan, 2002; also see Principle #11, p. 35). For Alec, the needs for autonomy and competence are revealed in his answer to the "why do you play" question. When Alec plays, he presumes to be in control of his environment. His choice of vocation provides the social context that allows him the opportunity to fulfill his needs while concurrently allowing him to develop more positive views of the self as he meets his playing objectives (aka, winning). Alec feels competent when his choices are correct; he feels autonomous because he believes it is his own volition, not the cards, that ultimately determines his seemingly extrinsically-focused destiny. Alec's orientation, although perhaps statistically infrequent, is supported by neurological evidence indicating that individuals exhibit similar biopsychological reactions to materialistic reward as they do when having the perception of making a correct choice (Satterthwaite et al., 2012).

While Alec's behavior may seem circumstantially logical, according to SDT, motives are not fixed but, instead, operate under a continuum that predicts a range of behaviors. Knowing under what circumstances innately intrinsic motivation shifts to an extrinsic focus is of great value to the practitioner. Knowledge of the motive source can influence not only what goals individuals will set but also what strategies they will choose as the mechanism to attain their goals. Although some ambiguity exists, an abundance of research supports the view that when it comes to cultivating superior learning and performance outcomes, intrinsic motives are highly coveted and beneficial (Pintrich & De Groot, 1990; Ryan & Deci, 2000). What remains elusive are the specific cognitive triggers that influence motivational orientation and how orientation can be used as a reliable predictor to determine which goal attainment strategies individuals will use.

Principle #32—The source of motives determines goal emphasis and strategy choice

When individuals set targets, they undergo a series of largely implicit cognitive evaluations ascribing a degree of relative importance, value, interest, and utility to the tasks under consideration. Goal setting criteria vary among individuals and are contingent upon a variety of task-related beliefs, contextual circumstances, and the perceived social climate of application. The factors individuals consider during task appraisal will vary according to the nature of the task, the individual's ability perceptions, and the perceived benefits derived, if and when the task is completed. In other words, individual differences in the perception and evaluation of task goals influence the type of goals set, the degree of challenge one is willing to accept, the level of commitment or effort devoted toward reaching a goal, including which strategies will be employed during goal pursuit.

Perhaps the best example of the variety of factors individuals consider when setting goals is the classic case of a learner studying for an examination. Some learners exhibit organized and methodical approaches when planning and executing study strategies, setting lofty goals, such as attaining a perfect test score. Take Jerry from Chapter 1, for example. Jerry considers where he will study, which specific material he will study, and with whom he will share his study efforts. Jerry's study strategy varies based upon how well he already knows the material and the relative importance of the examination to his overall academic success. The more important the test, the more he studies. Ginny's study strategy is radically different. Ginny waits until the last minute to even think about the examination. As a procrastinator, she undergoes a cognitive evaluation similar to her highly organized brother, yet Ginny ascribes little value to test outcomes, lacks interest in the test subject (for instance, earth science), and believes that the amount of time invested in studying will likely have little, if any, bearing on her test score. We might conclude that the degree of commitment and value when studying for an earth science test is profoundly different between siblings. These dichotomous approaches to studying in many ways mirror the diversity of strategies individuals use when striving toward meeting many learning and performance goals. Logically, if we understand the nature of strategy choices, we can potentially identify the antecedents of behavior (i.e., motives). This "bottom-up" approach of examining strategies aids in understanding the relationships between motives and strategies and also allows us to consider what factors individuals evaluate when contemplating the direction and regulation of their own behaviors.

Returning to SDT as a broad theoretical lens for examining performance behavior, one core aspect of SDT, Organismic Integration Theory (OIT), deserves additional investigation. This component of SDT posits that individuals have an innate tendency either to integrate task goals as an integral part of their self-perceptions and self-identity or to conceptually reject tasks inconsistent with core perceptions of the self (Deci & Ryan, 2002; Koestner & Losier, 2002). External stimuli, if perceived as congruent with organismic self-perceptions, will be evaluated as meaningful and thus intrinsically motivating. Conversely, external stimuli assessed as incongruent with self-views are likely pursued for extrinsically motivated reasons, or in the language of SDT, a "separable payoff."

For instance, consider that over 1,000,000 animals are killed per year as a result of being run over by vehicles (Highcountrynews.com, 2014). I have a tendency to stop in the middle of the road when I see turtles in peril, a common occurrence in my home state, Florida. I frequently view myself as a turtle whisperer, with the highly internalized belief that humans are obligated to care for animals because many animals do not have the cognitive capacity to reason accurately and make informed decisions. In other words, turtles' skills in calculating the relationship between personal speed and vehicular velocity are often flawed, causing them to risk their lives crossing highways in search of food and water. When I see a turtle, I stop the car and pick up the turtle. I do not need a "payoff" to prompt my action: in the vernacular of SDT and OIT, I am self-determined.

Alternatively, I could continue driving while leaving the turtle vulnerable to drivers who have no concern or interest in turtles, people who would run them over and use them as an ingredient in soup (another common Florida occurrence). We might say that for some drivers, saving turtles lacks intrinsic appeal. Some sort of incentive is necessary to motivate prospective turtle crushers to stop driving and rescue turtles. Clearly, those who do not stop are not motivated by aspirations of becoming a reptilian savior. I could offer the turtle crusher an incentive, such as $20, to change his or her behavior, but would $20 really change perceptions of turtle preservation? Or would the driver stop just to get the cash? Psychologically, stopping for a cash payoff or stopping for the turtle's sake have very different motivational antecedents, which are explained more fully by Principle #34 (p. 154).

OIT outlines a continuum of task commitment, or personal endorsement, described as the degree to which individuals *internalize* a task. The continuum of internalization identifies six variations among the type of effort and commitment individuals are willing to devote to a task. Table 6.1 identifies the continuum of internalization and some of the strategies that align with enacting a particular task orientation. With a greater degree of internalization comes a higher probability that an individual will experience self-determination. Applying the turtle example to the chart, a person taking $20 would likely be classified as having a fully external internalization, according to OIT. Meanwhile, self-righteous rescue behavior would classify me as fully internal, but only when it comes to turtle rescue tasks, and not my behavior in general because the degree of internalization usually changes based on the task.

Internalization differs from intrinsic motivation: unlike intrinsic motivation, when individuals internalize a task previously perceived as introjected, meaning is derived primarily based upon social influence. For example, an individual with low intrinsic task motivation might agree to complete a potentially boring task based upon the perception of social acceptance or a moral obligation to respond affirmatively. I am reminded of the time I asked my son to assume the dismal task of looking up "doi" numbers (an alpha-numeric document identifier) as seen in the reference section of

Table 6.1 The spectrum of internalized motivation according to SDT

Degree of internalization	Valence of motivation	Associated behaviors
None	Amotivated	Task avoidance or resistance
Fully external	Fully extrinsic	Controlled behavior and passive task acceptance motivated by outcomes only
Introjected	Partially extrinsic	Internalized behavior usually to avoid guilt or anxiety, or ego boosting
Identified	Partially intrinsic	Personally valued but externally motivated behavior
Integrated	Mostly intrinsic	Self-aligned, but with dualistic motives; important, but separable payoff required
Fully internal	Fully intrinsic	Completely interested and satisfying; strong task effort without incentive

this and many other texts. Although his intrinsic motivation was non-existent for the actual task, he cheerfully volunteered for this mundane opportunity and delivered a flawless performance with robust enthusiasm, primarily to stay in my good graces. Did he embrace and internalize the "doi" task as one of his own? Probably not, but he completed the task despite an overall lack of commitment and interest. He did not seek me out for similar tasks after the first assignment. In this example, little intrinsic motivation resulted from performing the actual task, but we might conclude that internalization has *potential* to influence intrinsic motivation (Koestner & Losier, 2002) if task engagement is perceived as challenging, experienced positively, and found to be personally rewarding and important. The greater the perception that a task aligns with personal beliefs and values, the more likely the task will be perceived as integrative. In the absence of task commitment and value found in boring mundane tasks, little, if any, self-integration would be expected and likely not experienced.

Clearly, these examples reveal that *what* you do is important; however, the motives for setting particular goals and striving toward goal attainment are even more critical. The continuum of task orientation can, in many ways, predict *how* a task will be completed. Research identifies variable cognitive, affective and socioemotional consequences for individuals who engage in a task for reasons external to the self. When tasks are completed for obligatory reasons, learners tend to show motivational apathy, negative affect, and occasionally, open resistance to the actual task as well as the perceived originating source of the task (i.e., the "boss"). Commenting upon the feelings associated with completing a task when not fully self-determined, and demonstrating an introjected task orientation, Koestner and Losier (2002) indicated "…the person feels pressured to do the activity in order to feel good about himself or herself, but would rather not have to do it" (p. 104). This disturbing scenario potentially results in compliant individuals feeling coerced into completing tasks that are potentially in conflict with their preferred desires and interests. In turn, introjection also places individuals at risk for impeding the basic foundation of self-determined motivation: feeling autonomous, specifically because the choice and independence of free will are replaced with obligation and guilt.

At a minimum, the degree of internalization is a reliable predictor of effort across domains. The absence of intrinsic motivation and a dominant introjected regulatory style are related to the investment of lower task effort and the use of more shallow processing strategies during learning. In a study investigating self-reported behavioral intentions to perform physical exercise, introjected participants ascribed less effort, lower importance, and less intention to exercise compared with participants indicating a more identified behavioral regulation (Wilson, Rodgers, Fraser, & Murray, 2004). Organismic orientation also predicted exercise frequency 4 months later. Integrated regulation of behavior has also been linked to investing more effort in work activities (Dysvik & Kuvaas, 2013) and feeling more autonomous during educational endeavors (Ratelle, Guay, Vallerand, Larose, & Senécal, 2007; Williams & Deci, 1996) and can even predict the extent of listening proficiency (Vandergrift, 2005).

Motivational Leader—*Nick Holes*

Nicholas Formato (aka Nick Holes) is the personification of integrated task orientation. Nick was born and raised in Elmont, New York, a sleepy bedroom community about 30 miles east of New York City. Nick graduated from high school in 2001 and went on to earn a Business Management degree from Five Towns College in 2005. In February 2005, a few months before he graduated college, Nick received a fantastic opportunity, a piercing apprenticeship. Piercing involves "puncturing or cutting a part of the human body and creating an opening in which jewelry may be worn" (FloridaHealth, 2015, para 1).
Piercing is a regulated and licensed occupation in many states. Minimally, a piercing career requires completion of a certification course verifying ability, including knowledge of safe and sanitary procedures.

Nick dreamed of becoming a piercer since he was 16. At the time, he thought it would be an interesting and fun profession. Today, he realizes his passion is much more rewarding than he ever imagined because Nick is highly content with his career choice, having few regrets in what some people might despise as an "alternative lifestyle." In addition to his professional skill, Nick has over 20 piercings and has endured hundreds of hours of intricate tattooing, but for him, piercing is not just about making money, passing time, or doing something he likes. Nick sees his work as meaning much more than just piercing people. Nick explained, "I help transform them." He added, "There are many people out there who get piercings for purely aesthetic reasons. Then there are people who are doing it for a deeper meaning" (N. Holes, personal communication, December 28, 2013). For nearly as long as he can remember, Nick felt reticent about his life. For Nick, being pierced or tattooed was a metaphysical catharsis, akin to solving a mystery by recovering some of the pieces he thought were missing in his life. As he became more accomplished in his craft, his views of personal satisfaction and contentment significantly increased.

Nick also engages in body suspensions and flesh pulls, along with a scarification. For a moment, visualize Nick dangling from the ceiling with four hooks his back. He knows for most people, these rituals all sound painful and weird, but according to Nick, "once you realize that you are in charge of what your body is going through, that changes everything. You never really know what you are capable of until you challenge yourself." "These marks (referring to his scarification)," he says, "you have to earn them" (N. Holes, personal communication, December 28, 2013).

As of 2015, Nick has been piercing for 10 years. Even now, he explained, "I still get a big rush when I pierce someone. I can't think of any other profession that could give me that same feeling" (N. Holes, personal communication, December 28, 2013). Nick also loves animals and the outdoors. In his spare

> time, he enjoys running, hiking, camping, and practicing outdoor skills. He has competed in several marathons and obstacle courses and plans on taking his physical abilities to the limits even more in the near future.
>
> Don't let Nick scare you. He is one of the most genuine, gentle, and congenial individuals you could ever hope to meet. When asked about his eventual goal, Nick responded he wanted to "live off the land and do as much for myself as I can, without depending on other people" (N. Holes, personal communication, December 28, 2013). Nick currently lives in in Brunswick, Maine, and pierces at Vibes Tattoo. Stop in and see him for a stabbing sometime.

The story of Nick Holes is highly reflective of an integrated task orientation for several reasons. Nick, who has a business degree and great communication skill, has the ability to earn much more in a different profession. He receives minimal social benefits from his profession and lifestyle and admits that his unorthodox appearance can sometimes frighten or intimidate the uninformed observer. His vocation offers little opportunity for the "separable payoff" that often compels individuals with an introjected orientation to persist in meaningless jobs and stay in unfulfilling careers far longer than they likely should. Nick exemplifies internalization because piercing satisfies his psychological strivings and provides a meaningful and purposeful life. Nick sees his craft as one that does much more than just adorn people with body art. His career provides many opportunities for him to transfer his highly evident positive energy to other people and to help others move closer to a mental state that offers the same inner peace and subjective well-being that he experiences almost every day.

Considering the confluence of evidence, it seems both important and necessary that educators and leaders strive to cultivate familial, classroom, and organizational cultures that openly promote internalized regulation of behavior. In many cases, overall psychological well-being is highly related to the degree of success individuals experience when internalizing values during task performance (Vallerand, 1997). Creating value-laden opportunities that offer discretion and choice, rather than instigating those made through mandate or decree, invariably leads to the more probable adaptation of identified regulatory styles because individuals perceive the presence of autonomy. Nevertheless, a conundrum exists. Autonomy is typically associated with high degrees of intrinsic motivation, yet many learning and performance environments, such as school and work, operate under the diametrically opposed deterministic principle that the extrinsic rewards represented by grades and incentives motivate individuals.

Principle #33—Individual reaction to incentives is variable, and predictable

Historically, determining the optimal conditions necessary to leverage the powerful but tenuous influence of rewards on motivation is the metaphoric equivalent of gaining consensus on hairstyle or trouser flare. The chic Bardot Bouffant and trendy elephant bells of the 1970s are no longer quite in vogue. Like fashion, the convoluted annals of psychological and educational research over the past 100 years have seen varying degrees of emphasis on the potency and packaging of incentives as catalysts for accelerated performance. Incentives, defined as contingencies that increase the frequency or quality of learning or performance outcomes, are generally thought to perpetuate extrinsic motivation. Incentives are both lionized and demonized as bosses and educators worldwide wrestle with the dilemma of determining the precise blend of personalized rewards that will accelerate individual performance while concurrently circumventing the demotivating consequences of incentives on interest and intrinsic motivation.

Many prominent behavioral researchers and a plurality of educators laud the apparent benefits of incentives to prompt and accelerate performance. Beginning with Taylor's (1911) publication of the *Principles of Scientific Management* and his goal of fostering "maximum prosperity" (p. 9) in individuals, incentives were deemed the primary method to accelerate "a large gain in the quantity of work done and at the same time a marked improvement in quality" (p. 93). Taylor theorized that every worker possessed a "personal coefficient" (p. 89) that represented an amalgamation of speed and production metrics that could be calculated as a proxy to predict anticipated effort invested toward a particular task. Although Taylor lamented about the need for the judicious use of incentives and the necessity of patience as a prerequisite for a change in "mental attitude" (p. 101), his efforts spawned the universal adaptation of extrinsic rewards to motivate performance in the workplace.

The ubiquitous view of the power of incentives as a utopian performance catalyst continued unabated for almost 60 years, led, in part, by twentieth century educational pioneers, including Thorndike, Watson, and Skinner, all touting evangelic incentives as the means to direct and maintain task interest and effort. White (1959), primarily commenting on the monkey experimentation of his colleagues, posited that something more was responsible for the drives and interests augmented by rewards. He wrote, "Contact with the environment seem to be sought and welcomed, in which raised tension and even mild excitement seem to be cherished, and in which novelty and variety seem to be enjoyed for their own sake" (p. 58). White's ideas implied that motives were, at least in part, internally derived, and his conceptions are close cousins of the current empirically supported definitions of intrinsic motivation, which contend that interest and inherent task value alone are sufficient to motivate performance.

As the cognitive revolution unfolded during the 1960s and 1970s, interest in intrinsic motives increased and reward contingencies were scrutinized, discounting and qualifying the auspicious role of incentives as potentially *demotivating*. Lepper, Greene, and Nisbett (1973) found that when children were provided incentives to complete a task they enjoyed, future performance and task interest suffered when the incentive was removed. Intrinsic motivation was measured by lower levels of discretionary time devoted to a puzzle completion task subsequent to being rewarded, in comparison with higher interest and more puzzle building for children not initially rewarded. The Lepper et al. (1973) study and others (Deci, Koestner, & Ryan, 1999, Deci et al., 2001; Vallerand, 1997) initiated a shift in the universal applicability of rewards to a staunch stance that suggested incentives inhibited intrinsic motivation because "reward contingencies undermine people's taking responsibility for motivating or regulating themselves" (Deci et al., 1999, p. 659). In other words, incentives and rewards were considered as potentially controlling individual performance; in the minds of many researchers, incentives were downright evil (Kohn, 1999). Viewed through SDT, rewards were thought to manipulate individuals, stymie the ability to exercise free will, and inhibit satisfaction of the basic human need for autonomy.

The primary dilemma persists: Can autonomy and extrinsic reward coexist productively? Despite the apparent and persistent denigrating influence of incentives on performance perpetuated by some consultants and scholars (Firestone, 2014; Kohn, 1999; Pink, 2011), under the optimal set of circumstances, individuals can embrace extrinsic rewards while concurrently forestalling the perception of control, inducing feelings of autonomous self-determination. Motivational pioneers Deci and Ryan (2002), the originators of SDT, emphatically maintained that contrary to the claims of many researchers, "it is possible to be autonomously extrinsically motivated" (p. 15). Thus, the challenge shifts from "if" extrinsic rewards are motivating to determining a clear representation about those circumstances in which incentives can concurrently promote performance while eluding the negative intrinsic motivational consequences.

The primary obstacle inhibiting intrinsic motivation and the associated autonomy achieved through self-determination of performance is the perception of control. Extrinsic rewards may be experienced as controlling when individuals set and strive toward goals merely for the anticipated payoff of attaining a reward or avoiding the negative consequences of not completing a task successfully. When performance is enacted exclusively for externally motivated incentive reasons, individuals are reluctant to integrate task attainment as a representation of their defined selves: They perceive the value or utility of achieving the task outcome as functionally meaningless *except* to earn the anticipated incentive. However, some tasks are pursued for dualistic motives: first to earn the incentive but also because the individual ascribes value and worth to the process of attaining the predetermined goal. Only when the individual has the perception that *both* the incentive and the process of earning the incentive are worthy of attainment will the individual feel self-determined.

When the extrinsically-motivated individual is faced with the possibility of goal failure, we might predict that psychological conflict would develop. Intuitively, if an individual is motivated by incentives, then the inability to attain the incentive or removal of the incentive should automatically decrease drive and effort invested toward reaching the goal target. However, effort decrements do not always occur when reward contingencies are changed. Prosperous performance is decidedly more probable when incentives are not given at regularly scheduled intervals. Like the Las Vegas gambler who hits big on the slot machine and walks away, humans have an innate tendency to redirect learning and performance effort once the incentive is realized. Alec Torelli has reiterated many times that regardless of winning or losing and despite being on streaks of luck, he routinely sets targets and walks away from the table as a means to monetarily regulate his play.

Although effort regulation can be strongly influenced by reward removal, many other contingencies are considered by the extrinsically-motivated individual when appropriating effort toward goal targets. Such factors as the degree of task complexity, the value associated with the task reward, reasons why the reward is provided or removed and, of course, overall task interest are important considerations that help predict the performance of an extrinsically-motivated individual. Many times, however, task value and commitment are promoted as a result of social factors. When activities are deemed important by peers, the probability of task internalization grows, and individuals are more inclined to associate value to tasks perceived as important and useful to others. Additionally, when a performance evokes affirmations of confidence in one's ability, the effectiveness of incentives is increased (Deci et al., 1999).

Torelli's persona reveals how a person can be driven to attain a valued external task outcome and concurrently realize the benefits associated with intrinsic motivation. In the absence of a predictable playoff, Alec takes great pride in his expert card play. He views his own strategic choices as a source of contentment and pleasure (i.e., those confidence feelings). Although Alec realizes that ultimately the fate of his card playing is a function of mathematical probability, his task effort and commitment to the process of goal attainment remain constant, whether he wins or loses. Of course, Alec is dissatisfied when dealt an obviously losing hand because his materialistic goals are thwarted. However, Alec believes he has control of his own destiny. His volition is not encumbered because *he* decides whether to play or fold. While the cards will ultimately determine his destiny, and whether Alec's decisions were right or wrong, his choices are personally meaningful and likely to instill competence attributions, even when he loses. In short, Alec is self-determined based upon perceptions of controlling outcomes; thus, he experiences a high degree of autonomy.

Unfortunately, many of us do not lead the dualistically motivating, glamorous life of Alec Torelli. Educators and leaders are typically charged with accelerating achievement or motivating lethargic individuals to complete mundane learning or boring performance tasks at school and work. Despite the erratic effectiveness of incentives, reward programs proliferate in classroom and organizational cultures and are conventionally perceived as effective in accelerating performance. In reality, teacher candidates frequently inform me about the various gyrations of incentives used in the classroom to control performance, including the use of "treasure boxes," "traffic light" systems, or making students run track laps (yes, that still really happens) when task-contingent goals are not met. In business, sales contests and incentive bonuses are the foundation of many corporate compensation programs. The power of incentives in many ways define individualistic Western cultures, with materialistic incentives provided for activities as varied as weight loss, smoking cessation, blood donations, and, yes, even school attendance (Gneezy, Meier, & Rey-Biel, 2011). It is improbable that these remedies instill little, if any, internalization of task value, inhibiting much hope of creating intrinsic motivation and sustained performance once the reward is removed.

Instead, MDs are faced with a number of potentially debilitating performance and learning situations that can undermine intrinsic motivation. Many times, learners are presented with performance contingencies designed to assist effort in reaching specific targets, such as finishing a certain portion of homework or the corporate equivalent of homework, completing a work project by a specific deadline. Other times, incentives are not task contingent, with few, if any, quality considerations, such as the promise of rewards, points, or recognition for class attendance or group project participation. These contingent situations typically redirect focus from the task to the outcome, leaving individuals highly susceptible to perceptions of control. Frequently, the incentive that was designed to be a performance catalyst reduces autonomy perceptions and deflates intrinsic drive because little emphasis is on the process of goal attainment, and only the outcome is perceived as valued.

Knowing how intrinsic motivation dissipates and realizing when task internalization is less probable are two of the many prerequisites necessary to mediate the motivational consequences of incentives. However, implementing strategic remedies is decidedly more valuable. First, effort should be devoted to fostering autonomy-supportive learning and performance contexts. Reeve (2009) recommends specific strategies educators can use to promote autonomy, including providing learners with explanatory rationales, acting patiently, and accepting expressions of negative affect in the classroom. Autonomy-supportive environments accelerate performance across diverse domains, including academic achievement strivings (Bonneville-Roussy, Vallerand, & Bouffard, 2013; Reeve, 2013), child rearing (Marbell & Grolnick, 2013), and superior athletic ability cultivation (Conroy & Coatsworth, 2007).

Second, in order to realize adaptive motivation that is beneficial to performance, MDs should leverage the power of choice. Individuals crave choices that foster perceptions of autonomy and control. In the classroom, autonomy is promoted by involving students in decisions related to instructional content, teaching methods, and types of assessment. Providing choice, however, is a precarious proposition. When improperly implemented, choice can be debilitating. Learners should be offered choices that instill competence in them as they strive toward reaching learning and performance goals but do not evoke undue psychological conflict or anxiety as a result of needing to make a choice (Patall, 2012). To be instrumental in promoting intrinsic motivation, choices should not be perceived as overly stressful, effortful, or restrictive (Patall, Cooper, & Robinson, 2008). Foremost, precautions should be taken so that perceived responsibility for choice outcomes is shared between the learner and the educator. If an individual perceives full responsibility for a choice and the choice does not work out as planned, the responsibility may inadvertently result in reluctance to make future choices under the perception of potential task failure (Moller, Deci, & Ryan, 2006).

Third, research suggests that performance-contingent rewards and intrinsic motivation can coexist peacefully by following a prescriptive model that starts with a clear distinction between the reward offer and the reward outcome (Harackiewicz & Sansone, 2000). According to the model, in order to avoid undermining interest and intrinsic motivation, individuals must know that rewards can only be achieved through the demonstration of specific competencies. Feedback should be provided to learners during task effort that guides the individuals toward successful task completion. Additionally, the reward–task distinction must be implemented with effective monitoring and a conscious realization that some tasks for some learners may promote anxiety that ultimately reduces task interest. Intrinsic motivation can be retained *if* and *only if* feelings of competence are instilled concurrent to attaining the incentive. Despite the contingencies, the Harackiewicz and Sansone model, when properly implemented, suggests that intrinsic motivation under optimal conditions can actually be *increased* through the availability of task-contingent extrinsic rewards.

In summary, using incentives to promote learning and performance is, at best, tricky business. The use of a prescriptive model as described above that accounts for the impact on both intrinsic and extrinsic motives is an important consideration. Not everyone is an Alec Torelli with fully declared dualistic motives. Even when motives are recognized, motivational orientation can change drastically within individuals based upon the person, task, and context of implementation (remember Principle #32, p. 144). However, under controlled circumstances, individuals will follow a pattern of predictable behavior revealing important clues about their motivational orientations. Unfortunately, there is one special caveat: Not all individuals value academic success and superior performance. Others have little concern for learning and put forth minimal effort or just enough to get by, perhaps because they value other things as more important for success, such as friendship, social status, or their own ethnicity (Stipek, 1998). Even worse, some individuals may not realize or understand why or how their effort is directed because they do not fully recognize or appreciate their own goals and intentions. We next examine the elusive nature of goals and explore how and why individuals strive toward goal targets and the manner by which those targets help predict the strategies individuals will use to reach their desired outcomes.

Principle #34—Goal type and orientation are reliable and accurate predictors of behavior

> *There was an old lady from Kent, Whose nose was most awfully bent. She followed her nose One day, I suppose, and no one knows which way she went.*
>
> *Anonymous*

Some might contend that everything we do in life has a purpose, and for every purpose, there is a reason. While the "bent" of some individuals is as plain as the nose on a face, for others, knowing and understanding our directional destiny and which road will lead us to our desired destination is more mysterious than deciphering the origin of ancient limericks. Allegory aside, the goals we set and the paths we take are robust indicators that illuminate our inner motives. All goals have a source of origination, with most conventional goal theories operating under the dichotomous premise that goal formation emanates from either internal evaluations of our core values and beliefs (Ryan et al., 1996) or through socially derived external expectations or pressures (Heider, 1958). Unlike the generalized orientation of *locus of control* (pp. 141–142), goal emphasis in most cases is domain specific, with noticeable individual differences existing within and between persons according to the task. The specific degree of goal challenge and the relative importance ascribed to goals are subject to change in valence and strength based upon a variety of situational factors to be discussed. Most importantly, goal choice and particularly goal orientations have well-defined motivational and self-regulatory trajectories that help predict the degree of individual task engagement and the preferred strategies individuals will use in their quest to reach goal targets.

Distinct differences exist between *goals* and *goal orientations*, with goals representing *what* an individual intends to accomplish, in comparison with goal orientations that are typically associated with achievement motives and representing *why* (i.e., the motive) individuals set and pursue a particular target. The distinction between goal targets and intent is important because individuals with identical targets may exhibit radically different behaviors to attain their goals. Between-person comparisons, such as the reasons for career choice, illuminate the eclectic nature of goal choice. For instance, in academia, some individuals pursue university faculty positions specifically for the sometimes misconceived notion of ample materialistic benefits. Others seek to make meaningful scientific contributions to advance their chosen field. Yet others elect an academic career path for the serenity of the university lifestyle, or the opportunity to influence the development of young minds and nascent scholars. All four of these examples illustrate similar behaviors and the election of the same career goal, albeit for vastly different motives.

The precise and consensual operational definition of goals is idiosyncratic, with variations in definition based upon theorist, discipline of origin, or context of application. Some definitions prescribe a focus based on the emotional valence of a goal, describing intent as "representations of future states that are accompanied by some desire or affect" (Ryan et al., 1996, p. 21), while others ascribe a cerebral and achievement emphasis indicating that goals are "the cognitive representations we hope to accomplish" (Barron & Harackiewicz, 2000, p. 231). Some adopt a dualistic focus, defining goals as the confluence of "internally represented desired states ranging from biological set points for internal processes (e.g., body temperature) to complex cognitive depictions of desired outcomes" (Austin &Vancouver, 1996, p. 338). The commonality among these definitions implies that goal attainment is typically an effortful, largely conscious, agentic satisfaction of a need or desire, which transitions an individual from one motivational state to a discrepant other.

Although the goals we set permeate most aspects of our lives (Ford, 1992), goal orientation provides revealing evidence about *how* we prefer to reach our goals. Orientation is a strong predictor of effort invested in a task and persistence to complete the task, and is indicative of the types of strategies individuals will use to attain their goals (Senko, Hulleman, & Harackiewicz, 2011). The individual goal choices and the pathways we elect to reach our goals have critical implications for the quantity, quality, and efficiency of learning and performance outcomes (Hoffman & Schraw, 2010). In other words, all goals are *not* created equal (Ryan et al., 1996), and as such, we should recognize that each goal target is engulfed with potentially diverse motivational costs and benefits. Individuals may not only enact adaptive and self-regulatory strategies, such as planning and reflection, to enhance the probability of reaching targets but may also be susceptible to hurdles that interfere with task success. If the perception of reaching a goal is doubtful, individuals often evoke goal inhibiting strategies, such as when a student sets unrealistic goals or waits until the last minute to study for an important examination (Alderman, 2004).

Determining optimal goal orientation for a particular individual and task involves acknowledgment of at least four universal interpretative concerns. First, not all goal pursuits are within the realm of individual consciousness. Although many goal-directed behaviors involve explicit intentionality, individuals may indiscriminately pursue objectives under the guise of habit or cognitive automaticity. For instance, when individuals are exposed to certain food choices, the choices automatically evoke emotionally laden reactions (Shiv & Fedorikhin, 2002) similar to the pleasurable neurological responses observed when people anticipate financial reward (Knapp & Kornetsky, 2009, see Principle #17, p. 57). In turn, these automatic affectively laden choices lead to optimistic mental representations, which subsequently increase goal intensity (Bargh, 2006). These "psychological transactions" are frequently unknown to the individual and direct behaviors toward certain targets as people navigate their daily lives.

Individuals can also be deliberately "primed" to pursue different goals. Priming studies require individuals to complete an explicit task while they are simultaneously, but subliminally, given suggestive ideas designed to unconsciously influence their behaviors. Priming can be accomplished through environmental manipulations as innocuous as leaving a leather briefcase in view of participants in an experimental office setting, which, when clearly visible, evokes more competitive behavior in individuals than when hidden (Kay, Wheeler, Bargh, & Ross, 2004). Priming can also affect motivation though subliminally suggestive words. For example, individuals consume more beverages after being exposed to words that evoke positive affective responses (e.g., wet, cold) compared with neutral words despite no conscious awareness of the words being primed (Strahan, Spencer, & Zanna, 2002).

Second, the specificity and transience of goal orientation is important. While some evidence supports generalized goal orientations (Elliot & Murayama, 2008), more often goal orientations fluctuate based upon specific task requirements, or the circumstances influencing performance outcomes (Duda & Nicholls, 1992). Revision may occur in stages, with modulation of orientation based upon insights of task progress, including evaluations of potential success or impending failure. Consider the elite runner who first intends to achieve a personal best but exerts less effort when she realizes there is little or no hope of winning a race. Similarly, many classroom cues may influence task engagement. For instance, when students engage in classroom competitions, they may initially intend to demonstrate superior knowledge through avid participation. After a series of wrong answers, competency strivings may quickly evaporate, resulting in motives shifting from demonstrating high achievement to avoiding the embarrassment associated with fear of failure or public humiliation when wrong (Elliot, 2006).

Third, a compendium of goal theories imply that individual goal orientation is one-dimensional and polarized, sometimes pitting one dimension against the other, falsely suggesting mutual exclusivity of underlying motives. Theorists have contended that we are either driven to achieve gains or forestall losses (Freund & Ebner, 2005), relish pleasure yet detest pain (Kringelbach & Berridge, 2010), enthusiastically approach some goals but aggressively avoid others (Elliot, 2006), demonstrate vigilance, or enact eagerness (Higgins, 1997). However, contrary to these apparently polarized historical conceptions of orientation, goal dimensions are not dichotomous;

many times, individuals will concurrently adopt multiple goal orientations (Senko et al., 2011). In practice, goal orientations are more like attitudes, moods, and opinions that situationally shift and operate on a continuum based upon factors, including individual differences, task beliefs, emotion, and the social context of goal pursuit (see Principle #4, p. 11).

Finally, a point of potential misunderstanding for many is the overlapping terminology used to describe achievement–goal paradigms. Historically, many conceptually similar constructs with related motivational trajectories are described using different names, as illustrated in Table 6.2. Much of the terminology emanates from the underlying dualistic premise that individuals pursue goals from either a normative perspective, comparing themselves with others, or a mastery perspective, pursuing knowledge or performance targets for their own sake, similar to the approach used by Nick Holes. Each particular orientation is aligned with relatively predictable cognitive, affective, or motivational manifestations. Although individuals may frequently adopt one specific orientation, in some cases, a multiple goal perspective is more probable (Senko et al., 2011). All frameworks outlined differentiate reasons (i.e., motive) for why and how an individual pursues a goal, which are distinct and separable from the specific goal target.

Considering the abundance of research examining achievement-goal orientation (for a review, see Murayama, Elliott, & Friedman, 2012; Senko et al., 2011), I avoid a detailed examination of each classification in Table 6.2 but, instead, feature two particularly useful and applied approaches that subsume many issues of learning and performance. First, the evolving mastery–performance and approach–avoidance paradigms that are most frequently used to explain individual differences in academic outcomes and study strategies are described (Dweck, 1986; Elliot, 1999; Hulleman, Schrager, Bodmann, & Harackiewicz, 2010; Pintrich, 2000). Next, the promotion and prevention orientations of Regulatory Focus Theory that are particularly useful in organizational settings are advanced (Scholer & Higgins, 2012). Both interpretations are designed to illuminate a dominant approach to goal striving that individuals adopt to reach their intended learning or performance targets.

Achievement goals: Mastery, normative, or multiple?

The achievement-goal approach to understanding academic motivation suggests that learners set goals for one of two reasons. Some learners have a dominant mastery orientation. These learners are motivated to achieve for such reasons as intellectual curiosity or topic interest. For these *mastery-oriented learners*, gaining knowledge or meeting task-specific goals is sufficient motivation to engage in the process of learning, with few, if any, additional incentives needed. The mastery learner generally believes that knowledge creation is deliberate and malleable, operating under the assumption that intellectual ability can change in response to the degree of commitment and engagement devoted toward the learning process (Dweck, 1986).

In contrast, learners who assume a more normative approach to learning view academics as an intermediary, but necessary, step to achieving more important primary goals. *Normative-oriented learners* strive toward reaching academic targets not for

Table 6.2 Clarifying academic goal orientation

Terminology	Theoretical interpretation	Strategy implication	Source
Learning or performance goals	Learners have implicit and relatively stable beliefs concerning ability and effort, which may provide a strong orientation toward learning. *Learning* goals are motivated by topic mastery, while *performance* goals are motivated by favorable social comparisons.	Learners with similar abilities respond differently to learning if they believe knowledge acquisition is fixed and unrelated to effort. Fixed views of competence are detrimental to intellectual growth and may result in reduced effort and/or failure attributions.	Dweck and Leggett (1988), Elliott and Dweck (1988)
Task or ego involvement goals	Young children (<12) have difficulty distinguishing the source of academic success because of the inability to differentiate between task effort and task ability. *Task* involvement implies an adaptive and intrinsically motivating orientation. *Ego* involvement contributes to selecting easier task goals.	Differentiated or undifferentiated views of learning are related to the degree of concurrent learning and effort. Those with an undifferentiated view tend to strive toward eclipsing the performance of others, while those with a differentiated view of learning distinguish effort from ability.	Maehr and Nicholls (1980), Nicholls (1984)
Approach or avoidance goals	Individuals possess biological temperaments conducive to seeking positive outcomes while avoiding those deemed negative. Goal attainment is intentional and strategic.	Psychological or physiological "movement" is evolutionary and energizes individuals to attain or avoid goal targets. Individual valance guides the nature of self-regulation.	Elliot (2006)
Mastery or performance goals	Learner competency is a combination of the approach–avoidance distinction, coupled with effort directed toward positive, normative comparisons and/or a deliberate focus on content mastery. A multiple goal focus is sometimes likely and helpful for learning.	Although mastery-approach goals are typically thought preferential, and strictly performance goals may lead to shallow learning (but normative superiority), few achievement differences are observed. A dual focus on normative competence and content mastery is beneficial.	Pintrich (2000), Senko et al. (2011)

the obligatory sake of knowledge but for socially constructed and extrinsically motivated reasons. Many normative learners view ability as relatively fixed and stable, generally withholding or avoiding greater investment of academic effort, under the belief that the investment of extra effort is often fruitless (Dweck, 1986). Normative learners seek positive competence evaluations from others, and the extrinsic incentive of good grades is usually a sufficient benchmark to connote academic prowess, regardless of actual or sustained content mastery.

In addition to a primary mastery or normative orientation, learners conceptually frame their approach toward learning in one of two ways. Learners strive either to gain the positive consequences of their mastery or normative orientation or to avoid the negative consequences they presume likely when academic targets are not met. Regardless of a mastery or normative orientation, academic energy and resultant knowledge acquisition strategies are either invested toward *attaining* a competence goal or, if academic efforts are derailed, directed toward *avoiding* the appearance of lower ability or questionable talent in comparison with others. Elliot (2006) described the avoidance-approach valence of goals as "one of the oldest ideas in the history of psychological thinking about organisms" (p. 111). The approach–avoidance distinction suggests mutual exclusivity of motives. Individuals are energized to intentionally and deliberately seek goals in the hope of attaining desired positive outcomes or are alternatively driven to avoid the negative contingencies associated with goal failure. Table 6.3 aggregates selective behavioral examples from our motivational leaders using a "2 × 2" goal orientation framework as a means to decipher underlying academic motives by evaluating goal orientations.

The orientation matrix below illustrates the nexus of academic orientation in conjunction with the motivational valence of a learner, suggesting that academic goals are pursued for one of four reasons. A *mastery-approach* orientation is demonstrated by learners who seek knowledge under the presumption of personal improvement. The mastery-approach orientation is generally deemed preferential for adaptive and sustained learning. Learners espousing this approach are typically more interested in

Table 6.3 Behavioral and motivational examples of academic goal orientation

Goal orientation	Approach	Avoid
Mastery	*LaSonya Moore* Has personal goal strivings that are largely intrinsic and focused on self-improvement.	*Alec Torelli* Desires to make performance decisions that maintain psychological equilibrium and behavioral regulation.
Normative	*Alex Dixon* Sets performance benchmarks based upon the abilities that her peer group exhibits.	*Robert Hoffman* (author's son) Completes requested "doi" task only under the coercion of his father; minimal cognitive task engagement or integration.

academics, approach learning strategically, and persist in the face of academic obstacles (Pintrich & De Groot, 1990). Mastery-approach learners are more open to changing existing belief conceptions (Johnson & Sinatra, 2014), demonstrate higher levels of self-regulation (Burnette, O'Boyle, VanEpps, Pollack, & Finkel, 2013), and associate positive emotions with the learning process (Mega, Ronconi, & De Beni, 2014).

Mastery-avoid learners also focus on achieving positive learning outcomes but seek to avoid the appearance of poor performance, especially in comparison with their own successful past achievements. A mastery-avoid orientation is particularly prevalent in older individuals who seek to avoid perceptions of diminished control, which increases with age (Heckhausen, Wrosch, & Schulz, 2010). Many individuals with a mastery-avoid orientation show deliberate, focused attention, and assertively seek performance feedback (Baranik, Lau, Stanley, Barron, & Lance, 2013). This task-directed focus can lead to vigilant information processing, presumably because mastery-avoid learners want details to assist in circumventing the self-referent impressions of academic failure that often drive their motivation (Förster, Friedman, & Liberman, 2004).

Unlike their mastery-oriented peers, learners with a *normative-approach* orientation exhibit an intentional focus grounded in social comparison. The primary goal of the normative-approach learner is to project the perception of relative academic superiority, irrespective of content mastery. Researchers deliberate as to whether normative-approach learners are primarily motivated by competence strivings, by achieving social superiority, or by a combination of both (Senko et al., 2011). Nevertheless, normative-approach learners are keenly attuned to what strategies are most effective to earn high grades (Elliot & Moller, 2003; Mouratidis, Vansteenkiste, Michou, & Lens, 2013) and how to direct their academic effort (Bouffard, Boisvert, Vezeau, & Larouche, 1995), and the normative-approach learner clearly understands and strives toward the competencies that are valued by instructors (Senko & Miles, 2008).

Universally, *performance-avoid* learners are demonized in comparison with other orientations because they seek to avert looking less capable in comparison with peers at all costs, exhibiting highly external self-referent evaluations. These learners tend to alienate themselves from academics, show low task commitment, and devalue the importance of academic success (Senko et al., 2011). The performance-avoid orientation is positively correlated with a number of academically undesirable behaviors, including lack of cooperation and not helping others (Poortvliet & Darnon, 2014), cheating (Van Yperen, Hamstra, & van der Klauw, 2011), and self-sabotage through the use of academic self-handicapping strategies (Urdan, 2004). The performance-avoid learner frequently exhibits a self-preservation motive tending to evade academic challenges that might reveal lack of knowledge or ability (Pajares, Britner, & Valiante, 2000; Skaalvik, 1997).

A number of inconsistent generalizations and broad misconceptions overshadow the practical implications of goal orientation. First, some researchers and practitioners unequivocally advocate the superiority of a mastery orientation for learning, in conflict with a substantial body of evidence that indicates a mastery orientation is *unrelated* to achievement, whereas normative performance goals are positively correlated with achievement outcomes (Hulleman et al., 2010). A normative orientation is preferential for learners seeking performance attainment and classroom help and is positively correlated with individual self-efficacy and effort investment (Elliot & Moller, 2003), likely because normative learning is highly focused on earning grades and the qualitative markers necessary to claim academic success (Midgley, Kaplan, & Middleton, 2001). Second, substantial research asserts that normative learners adapt shallow processing strategies, such as rote memorization; however, meta-analytic reviews show that little evidence exists differentiating the strategies used by mastery and normative learners when preparing for examinations (Hulleman et al., 2010; Senko et al., 2011). Third, the study strategies of normative learners are, at times, contributory to preferential learning outcomes because normative learners are better at deciphering the key content that should be studied, unlike mastery learners who usually concentrate only on the content they perceive to be interesting (Shell & Husman, 2008). The normative learner with focused task concentration is advantaged with an "academic sonar" and thus is able to detect exactly what it takes to reach a desired performance goal.

Senko et al. (2011) advocated a multiple goals approach based upon close scrutiny of empirical findings related to the positive benefits of a combined normative and mastery orientation. Their multiple goals perspective suggests that learners can adopt multiple goal orientations concurrently, leveraging the high interest associated with mastery learners and the preferential performance attainment strategies typically used by normative learners. The approach is substantiated by positive correlations between normative and mastery goals, and the apparent shift in goal priorities students exhibit as they navigate coursework over a semester (Hulleman et al., 2010). Recent school-based research indicates that a multiple goals approach can result in enhanced achievement and adaptive motivation. Mason, Boscolo, Tornatora, and Ronconi (2013) observed increased subject specific self-efficacy in elementary students adapting a multiple-goals approach, while Luo, Paris, Hogan, and Luo (2011) found that in addition to improved mathematics scores, high school learners employing dual mastery and normative goals showed increased class engagement, improved time management, and greater self-regulation compared with other goal orientation combinations. In business, a multiple goals orientation has been found related to superior individual workplace performance (Van Yperen & Orehek, 2013), while organizations advocating a dualistic goal orientation are positively correlated with elevated innovation and lucrative corporate profitability (Che-Ha, Mavondo, & Mohd-Said, 2014). Although more research is needed, these findings show promising evidence that the concurrent adoption of mastery- and normative-approach goals is an optimal and powerful combination that may enhance both individual and organizational performance.

Organizational promotion or prevention?

Operating under the fundamental and dualistic premise that individuals strive to either approach or avoid goal targets and that motives are distinct from goal orientations, Scholer and Higgins (2012) suggested that individuals navigate life under the compulsion of either amassing accomplishments or avoiding the liabilities of prospective goal failure. Described as the *regulatory focus* theory, motives operate under the presumption that emotional trade-offs will always occur between the coexisting motivational systems of promotion and prevention. Individuals with a *promotion orientation* are opportunistic and seek out authentic experiences as incentives to set action-oriented goals, which are a prerequisite to achieving results. Individuals with a promotion focus colloquially see the world as a half-filled glass in need of bubbling overflow. Promotion-oriented individuals thrive on progress and enjoy recognition of accomplishment. Conversely, individuals with a *prevention orientation* are cautiously optimistic and perceive the maintenance of status quo and avoidance of negative outcomes as their defining and dominant motive. Prevention-oriented individuals show less risk tolerance and, instead, are motivated by psychological safety and security, evidenced by emotional calm and contentment. The prevention-oriented individual thrives when stability is assured and negativity is controlled. Regulatory focus suggests that each orientation is philosophically antithetical to the other and goal attainment is accomplished through a unique blend of emotional balance, task commitment, and successful performances that are moderated by the respective orientations.

Regulatory focus is a particularly useful motivational model to describe organizational behavior because many organizations and corresponding cultures align with a strategic vision emphasizing either growth or preservation, similar to the personal valences exhibited by individuals with a promotion or prevention orientation. Like individuals, some organizations may become complacent, showing resistance to change, while others aggressively pursue a corporate agenda rooted in the philosophy of perpetual organizational transformation as part of growth and prosperity. Operationalizing the promotion focus, we may describe individuals exhibiting a promotion-influenced orientation as those who seek accomplishment through taking risks, living by the maxim "Nothing ventured, nothing gained." These individuals exemplify the virtues of advancement and assertion, eager to question authority or challenge tradition. In contrast, the prevention-influenced individual follows a conservative and secure dogma of self-preservation, operating under the mantra "If it ain't broke, don't fix it" (Scholer & Higgins, 2012, p. 71). These individuals value organizational behaviors, such as loyalty and vigilance, while nurturing group cohesion and collective work teams.

Considering the diversity of motives, prevention- and promotion-oriented individuals use a vastly different repertoire of strategies to accomplish their objectives. Different strategies are engaged because the outcomes valued by promotion and prevention orientations are different. The promotion orientation values progress, and thus these individuals will have goals grounded in precise action, not maintenance of a current state. They will use strategies involving discreet planning and steadfast evaluation of incremental success. For instance, recall the adolescent dilemma of LaSonya Moore, who had a child before graduating high school. Demonstrating a promotion orientation, LaSonya perceived her circumstances not as the reason to curtail or plateau her career growth, but as an opportunity to demonstrate her personal drive and ambition. Through a series of calculated and carefully designed steps, LaSonya continued her education as a means of reaching her personal goal of independence, discounting negative ruminations while refuting the racial stereotypes she so fervently rejected. Had LaSonya exhibited a more dominant prevention orientation, she may have used her circumstances as the justification for not finishing her education, perhaps striving to only finish high school, seeking a safe haven, and avoiding conflict.

Higgins (1997) noted that regulatory focus and corresponding orientations have strong emotional consequences and performance implications. Promotionally focused individuals will set more aggressive goal targets, perhaps learning new skills or immersing themselves in unfamiliar social situations. The emotional consequences of success for the promotion individual are feelings of accomplishment and elation, but the emotional ramifications of failure can be devastating: dejection, sadness, and disappointment. Conversely, prevention-focused individuals with a more guarded task approach will appear more judicious in their strategy use, showing an even-tempered disposition, calculating and planning their every move. The emotional contingencies of the prevention orientation are serenity and feelings of overall well-being when successful. One of the primary goals of the prevention orientation is minimizing mistakes and being more satisfied with safe and secure alternatives (Zhang & Mittal, 2007). However, prevention individuals are susceptible to anxiety, nervousness, and guilt, based upon the insecurity associated with potentially negative outcomes.

The nature of regulatory focus to understand behavior is ubiquitous, with the model applied broadly across disciplines. A regulatory focus has been used to examine how physicians respond to feedback in a clinical setting (Watling, Driessen, van der Vleuten, Vanstone, & Lingard, 2012), to determine what factors managers consider when making ethical decisions in the workplace (Neubert, Wu, & Roberts, 2013), and research reveals how regulatory orientation influences labor negotiations and bargaining concessions (Troetschel, Bundgens, Huffmeier, & Loschelder, 2013). Regulatory orientation can also assist in predicting behavioral intentions, such as which information consumers consider when making buying decisions (Pham & Chang, 2010), understanding how much a person is willing to pay for an item (Avnet & Higgins, 2006), or what factors are considered when engaging in healthy behavior (Keller, 2006).

Generally, these findings reveal that both prevention and promotion orientations will instill successful performance; however, individuals with a promotion focus are regarded as more creative, abstract oriented, and quick thinking. In contrast, prevention-oriented individuals are deemed more analytical, detail-oriented, and methodical thinkers. Scholar and Higgins (2012) suggested that what seems to matter most is effective calibration of regulatory fit with specific task goals. In other words, individuals should be encouraged and directed to play the right position within organizations in order to leverage their strengths. By analogy, in American football the quarterback position requires a nimble athlete capable of instant decisions and perceptive field awareness, unlike the brawny lineman who must protect the quarterback through brute strength, individual vigilance, and focused attention on his defensive counterpart. Linemen make terrible quarterbacks, as poor as most quarterbacks are in making tackles. Thus, at minimum, we can conclude that across contexts, position compatibility is key, and assessment of regulatory fit is an essential step when striving to cultivate optimal task motivation.

Principle #35—Interest is a multi-faceted contributor to motivational intensity

Disputing the influence of interest on performance motivation is akin to suggesting that basking for hours under a searing-hot sun is a cure for sunburn. Evidence suggests that interest, as an independent influence on learning outcomes, accounts for between 11% and 38% of unique variability between individuals when learning is measured by information retention, grades, or achievement test scores (Alexander & Murphy, 1998; Krapp & Prenzel, 2011; Linnenbrink-Garcia, Patall, & Messersmith, 2013; Schiefele, Krapp, & Winteler, 1992). As such, interest strongly influences the activities we choose and the degree of our overall task engagement. Interest is a reliable predictor of how much attention we give to the educational process and the educational goals we set (Pintrich & Zusho, 2002), including the degree of self-regulation students use when learning such subjects as mathematics, science, and English (Lee, Lee, & Bong, 2014). Interest is also a mediating factor influencing the choice of academic majors (Lapan, Shaughnessy, & Boggs, 1996), degree of college completion (Larson, Pesch, Bonitz, Wu, & Werbel, 2013), and career choice (Tracey, 2010). After employment, interest is highly influential in determining vocational success and can predict employee turnover. A meta-analysis of vocational literature revealed validity estimates of .23, correlating results on interest inventories with job performance, while interests are moderately, but negatively (.22), predictive of employee turnover (Van Iddekinge, Roth, Putka, & Lanivich, 2011).

The pervasive influence of interest cannot be denied; however, "disparate conceptualizations" (Renninger & Hidi, 2011, p. 168) have plagued the precise meaning and interpretation of interest since Dewey (1913) declared in his seminal publication that interest was "the sole guarantee of attention" (p. 1). The relative effect of interest on performance at any specific time is contingent upon the type of content or task attempted, individual developmental factors, and the trajectory of the interest. Most researchers describe the trajectory of interest as beginning with a genetic predisposition for certain topics, followed by either a self-generated or situational "trigger," emanating from an environmental-based cognitive or emotional stimulus, that subsequently promotes individual willingness to engage in a task (Hidi & Renninger, 2006). Interest is maintained if and when the individual believes the knowledge, or experience gained, from task participation is personally valuable, useful, or socially rewarding. Recent neurological evidence supports behavioral observations of interest and suggests that individuals show similar biopsychological reactions during performances accompanied by sustained self-reported interest and curiosity as when receiving monetary or other pleasurable rewards (Corr, DeYoung, & McNaughton, 2013; Kang et al., 2009; Ulrich, Keller, Hoenig, Waller, & Grön, 2014).

Interest is generally categorized in one of two ways: either as personal (also referred to as "topical" or "individualized"), or situational (Ainley, Hidi, & Berndorff, 2002). *Personal interest* represents interest that is primarily cognitively grounded, enduring, individually valued, and usually topic specific, while *situational interest* is affectively induced, transient, environmentally activated, and typically not premeditated (Schraw

& Lehman, 2001). Frequently, personal interest represents an internal striving that behaviorally results in re-engagement of behavior, such as voluntarily reading all books about motivation, whereas situational interest occurs during instances, such as the familiar leisurely pastime of channel surfing, when attention is drawn toward a particular program not actively being sought, which subsequently engages the individual's attention. Considering the emphasis here on learning and performance, interest is operationalized as "a psychological state and a predisposition to re-engage [in] particular disciplinary content over time" (Renninger & Hidi, 2011, p. 170).

Two key points underlie the interpretation of interest. First, a key moderator of interest is biological sex and gender (Ainley et al., 2002; Lee et al., 2014; Su, Rounds, & Armstrong, 2009). Consistent findings across cultures suggest male preferences for mathematics and science, whereas females prefer and demonstrate greater language arts proficiency and interest in social and artistic domains. Despite the broad generalizations concerning subject matter preferences, the relationship between gender and interest can be spurious. For instance, when interpreting the contributory influences of interest and gender on science learning and career expectations, gender norms are more influential and important than personal interest (Buccheri, Gürber, & Brühwiler, 2011). Despite declining interest based upon purported stereotypic threat, whereby learners base important decisions on presumed social norms, ambiguous results across domains suggest that the majority of gender differences ascribed to interest may be more of a function of gender differences in self-beliefs, such as self-efficacy, than those due to domain-specific interest (Krapp & Prenzel, 2011).

Second, unlike many motivational influences that are primarily derived from cognitive self-perceptions, interest is conceptualized to include both cognitive and affective components. Interest targets are typically activated by either a positively or negatively charged environmental trigger or a preconceived emotional valence held toward a learning target or impending task (Hidi, 1990). The affective nature of interest is grounded in individualistic self-beliefs that contend that certain tasks hold more value and utility for some individuals than for others. When evaluating their engagement opportunities, individuals undergo continuous qualitative assessments that calibrate and associate worth for a particular subject or activity, such as learners do when they evaluate their personal interest and the usefulness of learning science (Nadelson et al., 2014). Interesting material is perceived as exciting! When task valence is deemed positive, the individual will engage, and potentially re-engage, in the activity, provided the task is perceived as meaningful and offers sufficient cognitive and intellectual stimulation to hold his or her interest (Harackiewicz, Barron, Tauer, Carter, & Elliot, 2000; Mitchell, 1993). Conversely, if a negative affective valence is associated with a task, disengagement is likely to follow (Skinner, Furrer, Marchand, & Kindermann, 2008), superseding evaluations of cognitive suitability. The pervasive affective component of interest is supported by substantial neurological evidence that confirms self-reported and behavioral engagement of interest. The evidence suggests that both cognitive and affective evaluations occur during task choice, with conceptually distinct brain localization patterns observed when individuals express interest and when they do not (Hidi & Renninger, 2006; Ulrich et al., 2014).

Keeping with our applied emphasis, I shift to determining how experience contributes to the development of sustained personal interest, along with suggesting specific strategies that are useful to promote interest related to learning and performance. Krapp and Prenzel (2011) and Hidi and Renninger (2006) indicated that personal interest develops primarily when positive associations are ascribed to situationally engaging experiences. Interest for learning develops, in part, through the socialization process, which, in some cases, is concurrent with the evolution of individual and idealistic self-views. As children interact with their environment, they encounter situations that are potentially positive and rewarding, or negative and debilitating. During task performance, the inherent interest in topical learning is either reinforced or discouraged by significant others. Feedback, embedded in the process of environmental exploration and socialization, is offered first by parents and teachers and then by peers. If external evaluations and personal perceptions of the learning experience are commensurate with skill, personally valued, and self-relevant, individuals will internalize topical interest and incorporate task participation as part of their overall performance self-identity. Over time, repeated performances coupled with ongoing self-evaluations become deeply internalized, resulting in the development of positive self-beliefs about the task, including outcome beliefs concerning the ability to complete the task successfully (Bandura, 1989). Prospectively, when a child encounters task success, the feat is accompanied by feedback and positive social support, contributing to interest growth. Conversely, the combination of task failure, social stigma, or lack of positive feedback will impede or divert interest development from the task at hand and, instead, lead the individual to pursue more palatable alternatives to satisfy the intellectual curiosity inherent in most individuals.

Capitalizing on curiosity, situational interest, or nascent personal interest can be facilitated by using a variety of interest-evoking strategies. First, a combined emphasis on both the cognitive and affective components of interest is a prerequisite to foster interest development. Individuals need to believe the targeted task is within their cognitive and academic capability. The task should leverage a "knowledge thirst," able to close an information gap (Rotgans & Schmidt, 2014, p. 37), and provide sufficient, but not overwhelming, challenge in order to generate positive affective evaluations to accompany task performance (Lee et al., 2014). Next, educators should provide ongoing opportunities and continued social support for activities valued by the learner. In a 4-year longitudinal qualitative study examining student perception of science, Logan and Skamp (2013) determined educators promoted science interest when learners believed that the content being taught was relevant and had direct implications for their daily lives. Pedagogically, in the same study, students indicated that educators with a sense of humor, those who avoided the requirement of extensive note taking, and those able to align instructional content with student perceptions of their "ideal self-concept" (p. 2881) contributed to their sustained interest in science learning.

Linnenbrink-Garcia et al. (2013) described a number of contextual conditions conducive to leveraging situational interest and transforming transient learner focus into more stable and enduring individual interest. First, consistent with SDT (see Principle #32, p. 144), educators should strive toward creating autonomy-supportive learning environments. When learners experience autonomy, they believe their individual interests are self-promoted and voluntarily pursued, as opposed to feeling controlled by instructor directives or curricular mandates. Next, educators should strive to be perceived as "friendly, approachable, and supportive of a social relationship with students" (p. 595). By appearing approachable, learners are more likely to ask questions and become part of the learning process than when they experience instructor alienation (Jennings & Greenberg, 2009). Third, learners should be provided with opportunities for hands-on exploration of learning content. Pedagogical strategies, such as guided inquiry and jigsaw, are especially useful in the domain of science and have been found to promote enhanced interest and learner motivation (Furtak, Seidel, Iverson, & Briggs, 2012).

Finally, we must address the all too common enigma of learner amotivation, cognitive apathy, and behavioral lethargy. Many times, the academic engagement of learners may appear fleeting or non-existent at face value. One promising interest-generating strategy, primarily confined to generating interest in reading content, is the use of seductive details. Texts that include vivid imagery on such topics as sex, religion, politics, and death are highly interesting, and described as seductive, but frequently impede knowledge building because the learner focuses on unessential aspects of the narrative content. Although historically research on the use of seductive details has been broadly inconsistent and resulted in pedagogically vilified outcomes (Abercrombie, 2013; Schraw & Lehman, 2001), under certain circumstances, seductive details will capture learner interest.

Park, Flowerday, and Brünken (2014), using multi-media science learning, found that under conditions of low cognitive load, seductive details were more motivating and actually enhanced learning in comparison with topically similar high-load conditions, replicating previous findings using biology learning (Park, Moreno, Seufert, & Brünken, 2011). Similarly, animations that appear more lifelike, illustrating the emotions of surprise, fear, and sickness, promoted learning about the development of rhinovirus in comparison with simple, unemotional, black-and-white drawings (Mayer & Estrella, 2014). Although more research is needed, these findings suggest that even when controlling for existing interest, judicious use of vividness and seductive details may be a promising strategy to induce interest, even in the most aloof learners.

Chapter summary/conclusions

Evidence described in this chapter revealed that goal-directed behaviors are influenced by the *source* of motivation. Individuals have a demarcated locus of control, internalize task value along a continuum, have dominant but varying goal orientations, and are prone to a number of influences that determine and direct situational and enduring interests. Evaluation of the examples from individuals, classrooms, and organizations supports the contention that finding the source of a motive can be highly beneficial in assessing which particular mediation strategy or strategies will be most effective to guide a particular individual or work team.

Assessing locus of control is an important first step to determining if an individual is prone to self-internalizing tasks that foster intrinsic motivation or if separable, externally-focused contingencies that are based upon social comparison or incentives are instrumental in energizing behavior. Although some positive correlations exist between intrinsic motives and goal orientation, individuals predominantly actualize their goal intentions for reasons of self-determined mastery or to appear competent based upon past performance or in the eyes of others. Categorizing individuals is a risky proposition, but success strivings and avoidant behaviors can easily be observed and detected in most individuals by examining which choices are made and probing to determine the degree of personal investment and task commitment.

Variations in individual interest are guided by cognitive and affective influences that are both fleeting and enduring. All interests have a developmental trajectory and may change from situational to personal, based on the social and contextual influences that align with a particular interest. MDs can influence interest development and longevity by providing incentives, choices, and authentic task-based feedback as a means to cultivating interest in academically or organizationally productive ways.

Next steps

Throughout the chapter, I identified numerous sources that influence the direction and intensity of our motivational efforts. Although not specifically articulated as a distinct and prevailing basis for motivation, one common theme continues to persist: the strong and immutable influence of social factors on motivated action. For some individuals, nothing has a greater influence on behavior than how they perceive themselves in relation to others. Social factors determine, modify, and localize our behaviors as we seek outlets to demonstrate who we are and what we are capable of accomplishing. A key determinant of social behavior is how we think about ourselves in relation to others, often described as socialized self-beliefs. The next step is an extensive examination of the socialized nature of motivation, and understanding which self-beliefs are most instrumental in directing our performance efforts. Chapter 7 also features a legendary performer, **Nick Lowery**, who when he retired from the National Football League held practically every kicking record in the history of the sport!

End of chapter motivational minute

Principles covered in this chapter:

32. **The source of motives determines goal emphasis and strategy choice**—individuals pursue goals and exhibit goal-specific behaviors along a continuum of internalization that identifies six variations among the type of effort and commitment individuals are willing to devote toward a task. Each variation in motive is aligned with certain preferred motivational and behavioral regulation strategies.
33. **Individual reaction to incentives is variable, and predictable**—incentives, when judiciously administered, promote superior performance, especially when the incentive is task contingent and variable or used to generate interest in a boring task. Incentives perceived as promoting task internalization and providing perceptions of autonomy and choice are more conducive to developing intrinsic motivation.
34. **Goal type and orientation are reliable and accurate predictors of behavior**—individuals pursue goals for specific reasons that fluctuate based upon task and circumstance. Some

learners actively strive toward goals to satisfy motives of personal accomplishment and knowledge building. Others goal strivings are pursued to demonstrate competence to peers or for other separable incentives. Multiple goal orientations are highly probable and typically result in superior performance outcomes.
35. **Interest is a multi-faceted contributor to motivational intensity**—interests are a catalyst for motivated behavior, predicting the degree of intensity an individual is willing to invest in a task. Individuals demonstrate interests on both a personal (recurring) and situational (transitory) basis. Strategies, such as feedback, incentives, and autonomy-supportive environments, can either promote or impede interest depending upon the learner, context, and the developmental trajectory of interest.

Key terminology (in order of chapter presentation):

- **Contingencies**—often the target of extrinsically-motivated individuals, contingencies are the catalysts of motivated behavior and represent the incentives and reinforcements gained when reaching desired learning or normative goals.
- **Locus of control**—a phenomenological orientation that classifies individuals based upon what they consider when setting goals and making task decisions. Individuals with an internal locus pursue tasks relative to their own personal interests and beliefs, while individuals with an external locus consider the materialistic or social contingencies associated with task pursuit.
- **Internalization**—the process of accepting the value of an activity as part of the identified self, resulting in high engagement and inherent reward.
- **Goals**—the typically conscious objectives set by individuals as the targets of their active motivational strivings, otherwise described as *what* an individual intends to accomplish.
- **Goal orientations**—the underlying reason associated with individual goal strivings, which may be tacit to the individual or actively recognized. Goal orientations are empirically valid indicators of why an individual seeks certain goal targets.
- **Mastery-oriented learners**—a goal striving grounded in the motive of gaining knowledge or meeting task-specific goals primarily to satisfy intellectual curiosity. These learners presumably are not motivated by separable outcomes unrelated to learning.
- **Normative-oriented learners**—a goal striving grounded in the motive of favorable social comparison or goals pursued for a separable outcome (e.g., grades, money). These learners presumably need incentives to energize motivational strivings.
- **Personal interest**—cognitively activated and valued internal strivings that behaviorally result in re-engagement of behavior directed toward a specific activity or target.
- **Situational interest**—transitory focus of attention that is affectively induced, environmentally activated, and typically not premediated.

References

Abercrombie, S. (2013). Transfer effects of adding seductive details to case-based instruction. *Contemporary Educational Psychology*, *38*(2), 149–157. http://dx.doi.org/10.1016/j.cedpsych.2013.01.002.

Ainley, M., Hidi, S., & Berndorff, D. (2002). Interest, learning, and the psychological processes that mediate their relationship. *Journal of Educational Psychology*, *94*(3), 545–561. http://dx.doi.org/10.1037//0022-0663.94.3.545.

Alderman, M. K. (2004). *Motivation for achievement: Possibilities for teaching and learning* (2nd ed.). Mahwah, NJ: Lawrence Erlbaum Associates.

Alexander, P. A., & Murphy, P. K. (1998). Profiling the differences in students' knowledge, interest, and strategic processing. *Journal of Educational Psychology, 90*, 435–447.

Austin, J. T., & Vancouver, J. B. (1996). Goal constructs in psychology: Structure, process, and content. *Psychological Bulletin, 120*(3), 338–375.

Avnet, T., & Higgins, E. T. (2006). How regulatory fit affects value in consumer choices and opinions. *Journal of Marketing Research, 43*(1), 1–10.

Bandura, A. (1989). Regulation of cognitive processes through perceived self-efficacy. *Developmental Psychology, 25*(5), 729–735.

Bandura, A. (1991). Self-regulation of motivation through anticipatory and self-reactive mechanisms. *Perspectives on Motivation: Nebraska Symposium on Motivation, 38*, 69–164.

Baranik, L. E., Lau, A. R., Stanley, L. J., Barron, K. E., & Lance, C. E. (2013). Achievement goals in organizations: Is there support for mastery-avoidance? *Journal of Managerial Issues, 25*(1), 46–61.

Bargh, J. A. (2006). What have we been priming all these years? On the development, mechanisms, and ecology of non-conscious social behavior. *European Journal of Social Psychology, 36*(2), 147–168.

Barron, K. E., & Harackiewicz, J. M. (2000). Achievement goals and optimal motivation: A multiple goals approach. In C. Sansone & J. M. Harackiewicz (Eds.), *Intrinsic and extrinsic motivation: The search for optimal motivation and performance* (pp. 229–256). San Diego, CA: Academic Press.

Bonneville-Roussy, A., Vallerand, R. J., & Bouffard, T. (2013). The roles of autonomy support and harmonious and obsessive passions in educational persistence. *Learning and Individual Differences, 24*, 22–31. http://dx.doi.org/10.1016/j.lindif.2012.12.015.

Bouffard, T., Boisvert, J., Vezeau, C., & Larouche, C. (1995). The impact of goal orientation on self-regulation and performance among college students. *British Journal of Educational Psychology, 65*, 317–329.

Buccheri, G., Gürber, N. A., & Brühwiler, C. (2011). The impact of gender on interest in science topics and the choice of scientific and technical vocations. *International Journal of Science Education, 33*(1), 159–178. http://dx.doi.org/10.1080/09500693.2010.518643.

Burnette, J. L., O'Boyle, E. H., VanEpps, E. M., Pollack, J. M., & Finkel, E. J. (2013). Mindsets matter: A meta-analytic review of implicit theories and self-regulation. *Psychological Bulletin, 139*(3), 655–701. http://dx.doi.org/10.1037/a0029531.

Che-Ha, N., Mavondo, F. T., & Mohd-Said, S. (2014). Performance or learning goal orientation: Implications for business performance. *Journal of Business Research, 67*(1), 2811–2820.

Conroy, D. E., & Coatsworth, D. J. (2007). Assessing autonomy-supportive coaching strategies in youth sport. *Psychology of Sport and Exercise, 8*(5), 671–684. http://dx.doi.org/10.1016/j.psychsport.2006.12.001.

Corr, P. J., DeYoung, C. G., & McNaughton, N. (2013). Motivation and personality: A neuropsychological perspective. *Social and Personality Psychology Compass, 7*(3), 158–175. http://dx.doi.org/10.1111/spc3.12016/abstract.

Covington, M. V., & Müeller, K. J. (2001). Intrinsic versus extrinsic motivation: An approach/avoidance reformulation. *Educational Psychology Review, 13*(2), 157–176.

deCharms, R. (1968). *Personal causation: The internal affective determinants of behavior*. New York, NY: Academic Press.

Deci, E. L., Koestner, R., & Ryan, R. M. (1999). A meta-analytic review of experiments examining the effects of extrinsic rewards on intrinsic motivation. *Psychological Bulletin, 125*(6), 627–668.

Deci, E. L., Koestner, R., & Ryan, R. M. (2001). Extrinsic rewards and intrinsic motivation in education: Reconsidered once again. *Review of Educational Research, 71*(1), 1–27.

Deci, E. L., & Ryan, R. M. (2002). An overview of self-determination theory: An organismic-dialectical perspective. In E. L. Deci & R. M. Ryan (Eds.), *Handbook of self-determination research* (pp. 3–36). Rochester, NY: University Rochester Press.

Dewey, J. (1913). *Interest and effort in education*. Boston, MA: Riverside.

Duda, J. L., & Nicholls, J. G. (1992). Dimensions of achievement motivation in schoolwork and sport. *Journal of Educational Psychology, 84*(3), 290–299.

Dweck, C. S. (1986). Motivational processes affect learning. *American Psychologist, 41*, 1040–1048.

Dweck, C. S., & Leggett, E. L. (1988). A social-cognitive approach to motivation and personality. *Psychological Review, 95*(2), 256–273.

Dysvik, A., & Kuvaas, B. (2013). Intrinsic and extrinsic motivation as predictors of work effort: The moderating role of achievement goals. *British Journal of Social Psychology, 52*(3), 412–430. http://dx.doi.org/10.1111/j.2044-8309.2011.02090.x.

Elliot, A. J. (1999). Approach and avoidance motivation and achievement goals. *Educational Psychologist, 34*, 169–189.

Elliot, A. J. (2006). The hierarchical model of approach-avoidance motivation. *Motivation and Emotion, 30*(2), 111–116. http://dx.doi.org/10.1007/s11031-006-9028-7.

Elliot, A. J., & Moller, A. C. (2003). Performance-approach goals: Good or bad forms of regulation? *International Journal of Educational Research, 39*(4-5), 339–356. http://dx.doi.org/10.1016/j.ijer.2004.06.003.

Elliot, A. J., & Murayama, K. (2008). On the measurement of achievement goals: Critique, illustration, and application. *Journal of Educational Psychology, 100*(3), 613–628. http://dx.doi.org/10.1037/0022-0663.100.3.613.

Elliott, E. S., & Dweck, C. S. (1988). Goals: An approach to motivation and achievement. *Journal of Personality and Social Psychology, 54*(1), 5–12.

Firestone, W. A. (2014). Teacher evaluation and conflicting theories of motivation. *Educational Researcher, 43*, 100–107. http://dx.doi.org/10.3102/0013189X14521864.

Flora, S. R., & Flora, D. B. (1999). Effects of extrinsic reinforcement for reading during childhood on reported reading habits of college students. *The Psychological Record, 49*(1), 3–14.

FloridaHealth (2015). Body piercing. Retrieved on January 13, 2015 from: <http://www.floridahealth.gov/%5C%5C/environmental-health/body-piercing/index.html>

Ford, M. (1992). *Motivating humans: Goals, emotions, and personal agency beliefs*. Newbury Park, CA: Sage.

Förster, J., Friedman, R. S., & Liberman, N. (2004). Temporal construal effects on abstract and concrete thinking: Consequences for insight and creative cognition. *Journal of Personality and Social Psychology, 87*, 177–189.

Freund, A. M., & Ebner, N. C. (2005). The aging self: Shifting from promoting gains to balancing losses. In W. Greve, K. Rothermund, & D. Wentura (Eds.), *The adaptive self: Personal continuity and intentional self-development* (pp. 185–202). Ashland, OH: Hogrefe & Huber.

Furtak, E. M., Seidel, T., Iverson, H., & Briggs, D. C. (2012). Experimental and quasi-experimental studies of inquiry-based science teaching a meta-analysis. *Review of Educational Research, 82*(3), 300–329. http://dx.doi.org/10.3102/0034654312457206.

Gillet, N., Vallerand, R. J., Amoura, S., & Baldes, B. (2010). Influence of coaches' autonomy support on athletes' motivation and sport performance: A test of the hierarchical model of intrinsic and extrinsic motivation. *Psychology of Sport and Exercise, 11*(2), 155–161.

Gneezy, U., Meier, S., & Rey-Biel, P. (2011). When and why incentives (don't) work to modify behavior. *The Journal of Economic Perspectives, 25*(4), 191–209.

Harackiewicz, J., Barron, K., Tauer, J., Carter, S., & Elliot, A. (2000). Short-term and long-term consequences of achievement goals: Predicting interest and performance over time. *Journal of Educational Psychology, 92*(2), 316–330.

Harackiewicz, J. M., & Sansone, C. (2000). Rewarding competence: The importance of goals in the study of intrinsic motivation. In C. Sansone & J. M. Harackiewicz (Eds.), *Intrinsic and extrinsic motivation: The search for optimal motivation and performance* (pp. 79–103). New York: Academic.

Heckhausen, J., Wrosch, C., & Schulz, R. (2010). A motivational theory of life-span development. *Psychological Review, 117*(1), 32–60. http://dx.doi.org/10.1037/a0017668.

Heider, F. (1958). *The psychology of interpersonal relations*. New York, NY: Wiley.

Hidi, S. (1990). Interest and its contribution as a mental resource for learning. *Review of Educational Research, 60*(4), 549–571.

Hidi, S., & Renninger, K. A. (2006). The four-phase model of interest development. *Educational Psychologist, 41*(2), 111–127.

Higgins, E. T. (1997). Beyond pleasure and pain. *American Psychologist, 52*(12), 1280–1300.

Highcountrynews.com. (2014). Roadkill statistics. Retrieved on March 19, 2014 from: <www.wildlifecrossings.info/beta2.htm>

Hoffman, B., & Schraw, G. (2010). Conceptions of efficiency: Applications in learning and problem-solving. *Educational Psychologist, 45*, 1–14. http://dx.doi.org/10.1080/00461520 903213618.

Hulleman, C. S., Schrager, S. M., Bodmann, S. M., & Harackiewicz, J. M. (2010). A meta-analytic review of achievement goal measures: Different labels for the same constructs or different constructs with similar labels? *Psychological Bulletin, 136*(3), 422–449.

Jennings, P. A., & Greenberg, M. T. (2009). The prosocial classroom: Teacher social and emotional competence in relation to student and classroom outcomes. *Review of Educational Research, 79*(1), 491–525. http://dx.doi.org/10.3102/0034654308325693.

Johnson, M. L., & Sinatra, G. M. (2014). The influence of approach and avoidance goals on conceptual change. *The Journal of Educational Research, 107*(4), 312–326. http://dx.doi.org/10.1080/00220671.2013.807492.

Kang, M. J., Hsu, M., Krajbich, I. M., Loewenstein, G., McClure, S. M., Wang, J. T., et al. (2009). The wick in the candle of learning: Epistemic curiosity activates reward circuitry and enhances memory. *Psychological Science, 20*(8), 963–973. http://dx.doi.org/10.1111/j.1467-9280.2009.02402.x.

Kay, A. C., Wheeler, S. C., Bargh, J. A., & Ross, L. (2004). Material priming: The influence of mundane physical objects on situational construal and competitive behavioral choice. *Organizational Behavior and Human Decision Processes, 95*(1), 83–96.

Keller, P. A. (2006). Regulatory focus and efficacy of health messages. *Journal of Consumer Research, 33*(1), 109–114.

Knapp, C. M., & Kornetsky, C. (2009). Neural basis of pleasure and reward. In G. G. Berntson & J. T. Cacioppo (Eds.), *Handbook of neuroscience for the behavioral sciences* (pp. 781–806). Hoboken, NJ: John Wiley & Sons, Inc..

Koestner, R., & Losier, G. F. (2002). Distinguishing three ways of being highly motivated: A closer look at introjection, identification, and intrinsic motivation. In E. L. Deci & R. M. Ryan (Eds.), *Handbook of self-determination research* (pp. 101–122). Rochester, NY: University Rochester Press.

Kohn, A. (1999). *Punished by rewards: The trouble with gold stars, incentive plans, A's, praise, and other bribes*. Boston, MA: Houghton Mifflin.

Krapp, A., & Prenzel, M. (2011). Research on interest in science: Theories, methods, and findings. *International Journal of Science Education, 33*(1), 27–50. http://dx.doi.org/10.1080/09500693.2010.518645.

Kringelbach, M. L., & Berridge, K. C. (2010). *Pleasures of the brain*. Oxford, England: Oxford University Press.

Lapan, R., Shaughnessy, P., & Boggs, K. (1996). Efficacy expectation and vocational interests as mediators between sex and choice of math/science college majors: A longitudinal study. *Journal of Vocational Behavior, 49*, 277–291.

Larson, L. M., Pesch, K. M., Bonitz, V. S., Wu, T., & Werbel, J. D. (2014). Graduating with a science major: The roles of first-year science interests and educational aspirations. *Journal of Career Assessment, 22*(3), 479–488. http://dx.doi.org/10.1177/1069072713498680.

Lee, W., Lee, M.-J., & Bong, M. (2014). Testing interest and self-efficacy as predictors of academic self-regulation and achievement. *Contemporary Educational Psychology, 39*, 86–99. http://dx.doi.org/10.1016/j.cedpsych.2014.02.002.

Lepper, M. R., Greene, D., & Nisbett, R. E. (1973). Undermining children's intrinsic interest with extrinsic reward: A test of the "overjustification" hypothesis. *Journal of Personality and Social Psychology, 28*, 129–137.

Lepper, M. R., & Henderlong, J. (2000). The role of interest in learning and self-regulation. In C. Sansone & J. M. Harackiewicz (Eds.), *Intrinsic and extrinsic motivation: The search for optimal motivation and performance* (pp. 257–310). San Diego, CA: Academic Press.

Lewis, M., & Sutton, A. (2011). Understanding exercise behaviour: Examining the interaction of exercise motivation and personality in predicting exercise frequency. *Journal of Sport Behavior, 34*(1), 82–98.

Linnenbrink-Garcia, L., Patall, E. A., & Messersmith, E. E. (2013). Antecedents and consequences of situational interest. *British Journal of Educational Psychology, 4*, 591–614.

Logan, M., & Skamp, K. (2013). The impact of teachers and their science teaching on students' "science interest": A four-year study. *International Journal of Science Education, 35*(17), 2879–2904.

Luo, W., Paris, S. G., Hogan, D., & Luo, Z. (2011). Do performance goals promote learning? A pattern analysis of Singapore students' achievement goals. *Contemporary Educational Psychology, 36*(2), 165–176. http://dx.doi.org/10.1016/j.cedpsych.2011.02.003.

Maehr, M. L., & Nicholls, J. G. (1980). Culture and achievement motivation: A second look. In N. Warren (Ed.), *Studies in cross-cultural psychology* (Vol. 3, pp. 221–267). New York, NY: Academic Press.

Marbell, K. N., & Grolnick, W. S. (2013). Correlates of parental control and autonomy support in an interdependent culture: A look at Ghana. *Motivation and Emotion, 37*(1), 79–92. http://dx.doi.org/10.1007/s11031-012-9289-2.

Mason, L., Boscolo, P., Tornatora, M. C., & Ronconi, L. (2013). Besides knowledge: A cross-sectional study on the relations between epistemic beliefs, achievement goals, self-beliefs, and achievement in science. *Instructional Science, 41*(1), 49–79. http://dx.doi.org/10.1007/s11251-012-9210-0.

Mata, J., Silva, M. N., Vieira, P. N., Carraça, E. V., Andrade, A. M., Coutinho, S. R., et al. (2011). Motivational "spill-over" during weight control: Increased self-determination and exercise intrinsic motivation predict eating self-regulation. *Sport, Exercise, and Performance Psychology, 1*(S), 49–59. http://dx.doi.org/10.1037/2157-3905.1.S.49.

Mayer, R. E., & Estrella, G. (2014). Benefits of emotional design in multimedia instruction. *Learning and Instruction, 33*, 12–18. http://dx.doi.org/10.1016/j.learninstruc.2014.02.004.

Mega, C., Ronconi, L., & De Beni, R. (2014). What makes a good student? How emotions, self-regulated learning, and motivation contribute to academic achievement. *Journal of Educational Psychology, 106*(1), 121–131.

Midgley, C., Kaplan, A., & Middleton, M. (2001). Performance-approach goals: Good for what, for whom, under what circumstances, and at what cost? *Journal of Educational Psychology, 93*(1), 77–86.

Mitchell, M. (1993). Situational interest: Its multifaceted structure in the secondary school mathematics classroom. *Journal of Educational Psychology, 85*, 424–436.

Moller, A. C., Deci, E. L., & Ryan, R. M. (2006). Choice and ego-depletion: The moderating role of autonomy. *Personality and Social Psychology Bulletin, 32*(8), 1024–1036.

Mouratidis, A., Vansteenkiste, M., Michou, A., & Lens, W. (2013). Perceived structure and achievement goals as predictors of students' self-regulated learning and affect and the mediating role of competence need satisfaction. *Learning and Individual Differences, 23*, 179–186. http://dx.doi.org/10.1016/j.lindif.2012.09.001.

Murayama, K., Elliot, A. J., & Friedman, R. (2012). Achievement goals. In R. M. Ryan (Ed.), *The Oxford handbook of human motivation* (pp. 191–207). New York, NY: Oxford University Press.

Nadelson L. S., Cornell, K., Hustings, V., Jarrett-Smith, M., Jorcyk, C., Matson, S., et al. (in press). What good is it for me? The development and validation of the Science Usefulness Survey – the SUS. *Journal of Higher Education Theory and Practice, 15*(3).

Neubert, M. J., Wu, C., & Roberts, J. A. (2013). The influence of ethical leadership and regulatory focus on employee outcomes. *Business Ethics Quarterly, 23*(2), 269–296. http://dx.doi.org/10.5840/beq201323217.

Nicholls, J. G. (1984). Achievement motivation: Conceptions of ability, subjective experience, task choice, and performance. *Psychological Review, 91*(3), 328–346.

Pajares, F., Britner, S. L., & Valiante, G. (2000). Relation between achievement goals and self-beliefs of middle school students in writing and science. *Contemporary Educational Psychology, 25*(4), 406–422. http://dx.doi.org/10.1006/ceps.1999.1027.

Park, B., Flowerday, T., & Brünken, R. (2014, April). *Cognitive and affective processing in multimedia learning*. Paper presented at the annual meeting of the American Educational Research Association, Philadelphia, PA.

Park, B., Moreno, R., Seufert, T., & Brünken, R. (2011). Does cognitive load moderate the seductive details effect? A multimedia study. *Computers in Human Behavior, 27*, 5–10. http://dx.doi.org/10.1016/j.chb.2010.05.006.

Patall, E. A. (2012). The motivational complexity of choosing: A review of theory and research. In R. M. Ryan (Ed.), *The Oxford handbook of human motivation* (pp. 248–279). New York, NY: Oxford University Press.

Patall, E. A., Cooper, H., & Robinson, J. C. (2008). The effects of choice on intrinsic motivation and related outcomes: A meta-analysis of research findings. *Psychological Bulletin, 134*(2), 270–300. http://dx.doi.org/10.1037/0033-2909.134.2.270.

Pham, M. T., & Chang, H. (2010). Regulatory focus, regulatory fit, and the search and consideration of choice alternatives. *Journal of Consumer Research, 37*(4), 626–640. http://dx.doi.org/10.1086/655668.

Pink, D. H. (2011). *Drive: The surprising truth about what motivates us*. New York, NY: Riverhead Books.

Pintrich, P. R. (2000). An achievement goal theory perspective on issues in motivation terminology, theory, and research. *Contemporary Educational Psychology, 25*(1), 92–104.

Pintrich, P. R., & De Groot, E. V. (1990). Motivational and self-regulated learning components of classroom academic performance. *Journal of Educational Psychology, 82*, 33–40.

Pintrich, P. R., & Zusho, A. (2002). The development of academic self-regulation: The role of cognitive and motivational factors. In A. Wigfield & J. S. Eccles (Eds.), *Development of achievement motivation* (pp. 249–284). New York, NY: Academic Press.

Pizza Hut (2015). Pizza Hut® recognizes 30 years of book it!®. Retrieved on April 14, 2015 from: <http://www.bookitprogram.com/pressroom/>

Poortvliet, P. M., & Darnon, C. (2014). Understanding positive attitudes toward helping peers: The role of mastery goals and academic self-efficacy. *Self and Identity*, *13*(3), 345–363. http://dx.doi.org/10.1080/15298868.2013.832363.

Ratelle, C. F., Guay, F., Vallerand, R. J., Larose, S., & Senécal, C. (2007). Autonomous, controlled, and amotivated types of academic motivation: A person-oriented analysis. *Journal of Educational Psychology*, *99*(4), 734–746. http://dx.doi.org/10.1037/0022-0663.99.4.734.

Reeve, J. (2009). Why teachers adopt a controlling motivating style toward students and how they can become more autonomy supportive. *Educational Psychologist*, *44*(3), 159–175. http://dx.doi.org/10.1080/00461520903028990.

Reeve, J. (2013). How students create motivationally supportive learning environments for themselves: The concept of agentic engagement. *Journal of Educational Psychology*, *105*(3), 579–595.

Renninger, K. A., & Hidi, S. (2011). Revisiting the conceptualization, measurement, and generation of interest. *Educational Psychologist*, *46*(3), 168–184. http://dx.doi.org/10.1080/00461520.2011.587723.

Rotgans, J. I., & Schmidt, H. G. (2014). Situational interest and learning: Thirst for knowledge. *Learning and Instruction*, *32*, 37–50. http://dx.doi.org/10.1016/j.learninstruc.2014.01.002.

Ryan, R. M., & Deci, E. L. (2000). Self-determination theory and the facilitation of intrinsic motivation, social development, and well-being. *American Psychologist*, *55*, 68–78.

Ryan, R. M., Frederick, C. M., Lepes, D. D., Rubio, N. N., & Sheldon, K. M. (1997). Intrinsic motivation and exercise adherence. *International Journal of Sport Psychology*, *28*(4), 335–354.

Ryan, R. M., Sheldon, K. M., Kasser, T., & Deci, E. L. (1996). All goals are not created equal: An organismic perspective on the nature of goals and their regulation. In P. M. Gollwitzer & J. A. Bargh (Eds.), *The psychology of action: Linking cognition and motivation to behavior* (pp. 7–26). New York, NY: Guilford Press.

Sansone, C., & Smith, J. L. (2000). Interest and self-regulation: The relation between having to and wanting to. In C. Sansone & J. M. Harackiewicz (Eds.), *Intrinsic and extrinsic motivation: The search for optimal motivation and performance* (pp. 343–374). San Diego, CA: Academic Press.

Satterthwaite, T. D., Ruparel, K., Loughead, J., Elliott, M. A., Gerraty, R. T., Calkins, M. E., et al. (2012). Being right is its own reward: Load and performance related ventral striatum activation to correct responses during a working memory task in youth. *NeuroImage*, *61*(3), 723–729. http://dx.doi.org/10.1016/j.neuroimage.2012.03.060.

Schiefele, U., Krapp, A., & Winteler, A. (1992). Interest as a predictor of academic achievement: A meta-analysis of research. In K. A. Renninger, S. Hidi, & A. Krapp (Eds.), *The role of interest in learning and development* (pp. 183–212). Hillsdale, NJ: Erlbaum.

Scholer, A. A., & Higgins, E. T. (2012). Too much of a good thing: Trade-offs in promotion and prevention focus. In R. M. Ryan (Ed.), *The Oxford handbook of human motivation* (pp. 65–84). New York, NY: Oxford University Press.

Schraw, G., & Lehman, S. (2001). Situational interest: A review of the literature and directions for future research. *Educational Psychology Review*, *13*, 23–52.

Senko, C., Hulleman, C. S., & Harackiewicz, J. M. (2011). Achievement goal theory at the crossroads: Old controversies, current challenges, and new directions. *Educational Psychologist*, *46*(1), 26–47. http://dx.doi.org/10.1080/00461520.2011.538646.

Senko, C., & Miles, K. M. (2008). Pursuing their own learning agenda: How mastery-oriented students jeopardize their class performance. *Contemporary Educational Psychology*, *33*(4), 561–583.

Shell, D. F., & Husman, J. (2008). Control, motivation, affect, and strategic self-regulation in the college classroom: A multidimensional phenomenon. *Journal of Educational Psychology*, *100*(2), 443–459.

Shiv, B., & Fedorikhin, A. (2002). Spontaneous versus controlled influences of stimulus-based affect on choice behavior. *Organizational Behavior and Human Decision Processes*, *87*(2), 342–370. http://dx.doi.org/10.1006/obhd.2001.2977.

Skaalvik, E. M. (1997). Self-enhancing and self-defeating ego orientation: Relations with task and avoidance orientation, achievement, self-perceptions, and anxiety. *Journal of Educational Psychology*, *89*(1), 71–81.

Skinner, E., Furrer, C., Marchand, G., & Kindermann, T. (2008). Engagement and disaffection in the classroom: Part of a larger motivational dynamic? *Journal of Educational Psychology*, *100*(4), 765–781.

Stipek, D. (1998). *Motivation to learn: From theory to practice*. Needham Heights, MA: Allyn and Bacon.

Strahan, E. J., Spencer, S. J., & Zanna, M. P. (2002). Subliminal priming and persuasion: Striking while the iron is hot. *Journal of Experimental Social Psychology*, *38*(6), 556–568. http://dx.doi.org/10.1016/S0022-1031(02)00502-4.

Su, R., Rounds, J., & Armstrong, P. I. (2009). Men and things, women and people: A meta-analysis of sex differences in interests. *Psychological Bulletin*, *135*(6), 859–884. http://dx.doi.org/10.1037/a0017364.

Taylor, F. W. (1911). *The principles of scientific management*. New York, NY: Harper Brothers.

Tracey, T. J. G. (2010). Relation of interest and self-efficacy occupational congruence and career choice certainty. *Journal of Vocational Behavior*, *76*(3), 441–447.

Troetschel, R., Bundgens, S., Huffmeier, J., & Loschelder, D. D. (2013). Promoting prevention success at the bargaining table: Regulatory focus in distributive negotiations. *Journal of Economic Psychology*, *38*, 26–39.

Ulrich, M., Keller, J., Hoenig, K., Waller, C., & Grön, G. (2014). Neural correlates of experimentally induced flow experiences. *NeuroImage*, *86*, 194–202. http://dx.doi.org/10.1016/j.neuroimage.2013.08.019.

Urdan, T. (2004). Predictors of academic self-handicapping and achievement: Examining achievement goals, classroom goal structures, and culture. *Journal of Educational Psychology*, *96*(2), 251–264. http://dx.doi.org/10.1037/0022-0663.96.2.251.

Vallerand, R. J. (1997). Toward a hierarchical model of intrinsic and extrinsic motivation. In M. P. Zanna (Ed.), *Advances in experimental social psychology* (Vol. 29, pp. 271–360). San Diego, CA: Academic Press.

Vallerand, R. J., & Ratelle, C. F. (2002). Intrinsic and extrinsic motivation: A hierarchical model. In E. L. Deci & R. M. Ryan (Eds.), *Handbook of self-determination research* (pp. 37–63). Rochester, NY: University of Rochester Press.

Vandergrift, L. (2005). Relationships among motivation orientations, metacognitive awareness and proficiency in L2 listening. *Applied Linguistics*, *26*(1), 70–89.

Van Iddekinge, C. H., Roth, P. L., Putka, D. J., & Lanivich, S. E. (2011). Are you interested? A meta-analysis of relations between vocational interests and employee performance and turnover. *Journal of Applied Psychology*, *96*(6), 1167–1194. http://dx.doi.org/10.1037/a0024343.

Van Yperen, N. W., Hamstra, M. R. W., & van der Klauw, M. (2011). To win, or not to lose, at any cost: The impact of achievement goals on cheating: Achievement goals and cheating. *British Journal of Management*, *22*, S5–S15. http://dx.doi.org/10.1111/j.1467-8551.2010.00702.x.

Van Yperen, N. W., & Orehek, E. (2013). Achievement goals in the workplace: Conceptualization, prevalence, profiles, and outcomes. *Journal of Economic Psychology*, *38*, 71–79. http://dx.doi.org/10.1016/j.joep.2012.08.013.

Watling, C., Driessen, E., van der Vleuten, C. P. M., Vanstone, M., & Lingard, L. (2012). Understanding responses to feedback: The potential and limitations of regulatory focus theory. *Medical Education, 46*(6), 593–603. http://dx.doi.org/10.1111/j.1365-2923.2012.04209.x.

White, R. W. (1959). Motivation reconsidered: The concept of competence. *Psychological Review, 66*(5), 297–333.

Williams, G. C., & Deci, E. L. (1996). Internalization of biopsychosocial values by medical students: A test of self-determination theory. *Journal of Personality and Social Psychology, 70*(4), 767–779. http://dx.doi.org/10.1037/0022-3514.70.4.767.

Williams, G. C., McGregor, H., Sharp, D., Kouides, R. W., Lévesque, C. S., Ryan, R. M., et al. (2006). A self-determination multiple risk intervention trial to improve smokers' health. *Journal of General Internal Medicine, 21*(12), 1288–1294. http://dx.doi.org/10.1111/j.1525-1497.2006.00621.x.

Wilson, P. M., Rodgers, W. M., Fraser, S. N., & Murray, T. C. (2004). Relationships between exercise regulations and motivational consequences in university students. *Research Quarterly for Exercise and Sport, 75*(1), 81–91. http://dx.doi.org/10.1080/02701367.2004.10609136.

Zhang, Y., & Mittal, V. (2007). The attractiveness of enriched and impoverished options culture, self-construal, and regulatory focus. *Personality and Social Psychology Bulletin, 33*(4), 588–598.

Mount Rushmore: Bedrock theories of applied motivation

Chapter outline

Principle #36—Past performance guides future motivation   182
Motivational Leader—*Nick Lowery*   188
Principle #37—Certain motives are extraordinarily difficult to suppress   189
Principle #38—After ability, self-efficacy explains more performance variation than any other motivational self-belief   192
Principle #39—Motivational theory is applied temporally and situationally   197
    Chapter summary/conclusions   201
    Next steps   201
    End of chapter motivational minute   202
References   203

Thinking back to Chapter 1, you may recall that Reeve (2009) indicated that at least 24 different theories have been empirically advanced to substantiate agentic behavior. A select few theories are conceptualized as the "grand" theories of motivation. The "grand" moniker purports that these theories do more than explain particular influences on behavior; instead, they have expansive explanatory power regarding how people control and regulate their lives. For example, the principle of operant conditioning rooted in behavioral learning theory (see Principle #33, p. 149) and Freud's Drive Theory (1922) were once thought by many scholars to be consummate approaches to understanding human behavior. Subsequently, each theory has been debunked as all-encompassing: operant conditioning due to minimal consideration of personal beliefs and nuanced reasoning, while psychoanalytic approaches were rejected due to the highly introspective and untestable nature of Freud's proclamations.

Today, grand theories are historical relics that have acquiesced to prominent mini-theories, which "analyze specific areas of motivated behavior" (Graham & Weiner, 1996, p. 63). Mini-theories typically target one aspect of personal agency, such as goal setting or emotional arousal, and frequently generalize applicability of theoretical premises to specific populations or contexts of application. For instance, we previously learned about the role of self-determination as instrumental in indicating the degree of commitment and type of motivation individuals may exhibit toward a task. Three other prominent mini-theories that provide significant explanatory power and utility to describe learning, achievement, and performance motivation across contexts are the attributions, or causes, that individuals use to account for their academic success or failure; the importance, value, and usefulness individuals ascribe to particular tasks; and the beliefs individuals hold concerning personal effectiveness.

Prolific researchers, such as Bandura (self-efficacy), Weiner (attributions), and a host of scholars, including Rotter, and Wigfield/Eccles (expectancy-value), have spawned literally thousands of cross-disciplinary and multi-cultural research studies revealing specific cognitive and affective evaluations originating in personal task beliefs, which are strong predictors of the challenges individuals are willing to pursue, and, ultimately, how and why they are energized to reach their goals.

The common bond among the three iconic theories briefly described above rests upon the defining premises of social cognitive theory, which contends that learning, performance, and achievement motivations are contingent upon a causal and reciprocal interdependence among personal expectations and values, intentional behaviors, and environmental influences. The interdependent phenomena suggest that human behavior is mediated by cognition and *reciprocally determined* by a series of bi-directional, differentially weighted influences, rooted in human sociocultural interaction. Individuals use a personal framework, akin to a set of rules that they act upon, to accomplish their motivational goals. The relative influence of each pillar of the triadic social cognitive model fluctuates, based upon proactive judgments and the action being contemplated by the individual. As Bandura (1997) eloquently indicated when describing self-reflective action, "people analyze the situations that confront them, consider alternative course of action, judge their abilities to carry them out successfully, and estimate the results the actions are likely to produce" (p. 5). The social cognitive model does not purport to be the sole determinant of individual action but, instead, provides a process of systemic, reflective guidance promoting ongoing appraisals of personal values, situational determinants, and probabilistic outcomes used by the individual to make behavioral decisions. In all cases, individuals see themselves as part of a larger, socially constructed system that is frequently a prevailing influence on behavior.

A practical example of the socially guided nature of reciprocal determination was provided by former National Football League (NFL) star, Guillermo C. "Bill" Gramática. Bill, who as a teenager along with his brothers Martin and Santiago, made the culturally defiant, life-changing decision to give up promising and predictable careers as professional soccer players. Instead, the brothers collectively decided to attempt to make a living kicking field goals despite lack of proven skills and the unpredictable and more dangerous life of a professional NFL football player. When asked about what influenced the decision to leave the relative safety, security, and culturally expected game of playing soccer, Bill stated,

> As a kid in Argentina, the first thing you get is a soccer ball and a jersey, and you play ALL the time, you love it so much, it's a passion. My brother, Martin, was like a father to us; he gave up his childhood for us. I decided to pursue college football instead of soccer because of him. I wanted to be successful, and I wanted to follow in my brother's footsteps and not disappoint him.
> B. Gramática, personal communication, October 13, 2013.

Bill revealed that place kicking was very different from playing soccer, and he was not entirely sure of what would happen upon giving up soccer: yet he decided to pursue a football career in spite of the uncertainty. Bill added, "Whatever it is, you don't want to go in half-way. I wanted to take it to the next level; I grew up that way. You set a level or a goal and go for it, nothing gets in the way of reaching the goal" (B. Gramática, personal communication, October 13, 2013). Nothing did get in the way of success for Bill or Martin, as both become highly decorated, record-holding college field-goal kickers. The brothers went on to be Pro-Bowl–caliber NFL stars: Martin playing for over 10 years, including playing in a Super Bowl game, while Bill's career was cut short after 4 years by a series of debilitating injuries.

We can quickly detect the social influence of Bill's family upon his career choices. Bill was primarily motivated by his desire to model his older brother's behavior and show Martin that his fraternal guidance was instrumental in his choices. A closer examination of Bill's remarks reveals that a series of beliefs about success, goal setting, and contextual evaluations were also part of his career decision. Bill was initially skeptical that his soccer skill could be transferred to football, but he was willing to take a calculated risk and attempt place kicking based upon his past performances and highly successful soccer playing. In other words, Bill questioned the outcome he might realize based upon his existing skill, his perceived athleticism, and his focused drive and ambition. His decision, in part, was based upon evaluating his own competency strivings and the extent of feeling confident and capable about past performances. Further, Bill surmised that a kicking career was potentially lucrative, but he worried about the added risk of injury. Despite his physical trepidation, Bill was willing to assume the risk of career transition because of the potential notoriety and payoff associated with being a Pro-Bowl–caliber NFL football player. Finally, we can see from Bill's reasoning that environmental factors, although a consideration, were relatively inconsequential for his career choice in the United States; however, we could speculate that if Bill had remained in his native Argentina, environmental influences would have been a much more heavily weighted consideration, since the probability of playing American style football was nil, regardless of his self-beliefs or career aspirations.

We can see from Gramática's decision-making process that Bill's motives were influenced by many different types of personal appraisals. Through deductive reasoning and reflective thinking, and using his brother as a behavioral model, Bill evaluated his past performance, current abilities, and future aspirations, making an informed decision that was guided by his overall beliefs about family and commitment. He made performance assessments based upon generalized impressions of his previously demonstrated athletic skills. He evaluated potential career options, comparing the relative degree of worth and importance to ancillary factors, such as pursuing higher education while playing college football. He considered the prospect of committing to a goal that his brother would expect him to achieve, and he contemplated the probabilities of when, where, and how to reach his desired outcome of personal, familial, and career satisfaction.

The perceptive motivational detective (MD) and the motivation scholar will likely detect elements of many theories of motivation intermingled with the previous analysis and entrenched within Gramática's evaluative judgments and decision-making processes. Reflecting on past performances to make future decisions illustrates an attributional approach to motivation. Evaluating the potential rewards and liabilities of becoming a college place kicker demonstrates consideration of task values and expectancies. Contemplation of current abilities to predict future performance and probabilistic outcomes shows a cognitive evaluation of personal efficacy. However, by now the astute MD realizes that each approach to explain motivated behavior must be evaluated at different levels of detail, specificity, and temporality to be fully understood. It is prudent to understand not only what decisions are made but also the reasons behind the decision-making process.

When contemplating a performance or academic task, individuals undergo a series of evaluations and reflective judgments to determine task choice, while assessing the degree of effort and commitment they are willing to invest toward reaching their intended goals. Understanding the source of information for evaluative judgments is an important first step in predicting which behaviors will manifest as a result of a choice and which strategies the individual will use to progress toward his or her goals. Social cognitive theory suggests that evaluative decisions are based, in part, upon a variety of interdependent cognitive, affective, and contextual factors that collectively influence behavior; logic does not always prevail. The important and variable role of affect and emotional valence on task choice and devotion of effort should not be underemphasized and is discussed extensively in Chapter 9 (p. 237). Now, I turn to identifying and assessing the relative influence of *cognitive* factors used in determining personal agency.

Principle #36—Past performance guides future motivation

Visualize a recurrent task or challenge that you usually execute flawlessly. Maybe you excel at playing tennis, are a whiz at solving mental multiplication problems, or have a reputation for being the life of the party. The types of tasks you could select are infinite but essentially inconsequential. Regardless of the task or challenge, whenever you contemplate motivated action, you make both implicit and explicit cognitive judgments about how successful you might be at performing the task while likely visualizing the probable outcomes resulting from your task-based decision. In all likelihood, the task you consider and the one you eventually select will be motivated by the reasonable prospect of being able to do the task well. So, which task did you choose?

Scholars might contest the antecedents of your task-selection thought process. Some would contend that your choices and subsequent performances were based upon overall enjoyment and interest. Others might deduce that the visualization of a successful outcome was the main reason for your task choice, with the prospect of an impeccable performance strengthening your existing interest and influencing your choice. Regardless of what ignites task engagement, the potential for a positive outcome attracts individuals toward attempting and completing tasks, while the anticipation of negative results usually inhibits task desirability and accelerates task avoidance (Eccles & Wigfield, 1995; Schultheiss & Brunstein, 2005). Unless the task is something never previously attempted, more often than not, during task selection, you will make a series of evaluative cognitive judgments concerning the degree of challenge you are willing to accept, an appraisal of *how* you will complete the task, and a projection of potential task outcomes, including how completing the task will make you feel. Each task-relevant judgment involves a series of personal calibrations, resulting in the assumed alignment of your perceptions of task competence to the anticipated task demands. Ultimately, your task choice and associated engagement strategies are grounded in task-related personal beliefs, based, in part, on competence perceptions, which emanate from results on similar past performances.

Assessments of past performance as a barometer of future task choice and potential task engagement are based upon the core principles of attribution theory, which suggests that individuals seek justified explanations that guide future effort investments. Grounded in the seminal work of Rotter (1966) and popularized by Weiner (1979, 2012), attribution theory suggests that positive task consequences are insufficient to explain future task choice and engagement. Critical to attribution theory is an understanding of the powerful role of individual beliefs concerning perceived retrospective reasons for past success or failure, which are thought to be highly instrumental in determining future task orientation and motivated effort. In other words, individuals possess an inherent curiosity and evoke a deliberate conscious affinity toward knowing and understanding how accomplishments are attained as a means to assess, calibrate, and validate personal values and future intentions (Baumeister & Finkel, 2010).

Attributional musings remind me of a time when I contemplated the ludicrous notion that I could bake a carrot cake from scratch. Although not an "Iron Chef" by any account, I know the difference between a fork and chopsticks, and in spite of being a stereotypical male, I can follow recipe directions, even without pictures. I methodically added the ingredients as instructed, preheated the oven, and mixed the batter to a fine lumpy consistency. The result was a slightly fluffy concoction resembling a burnt pancake, charred on the outside, wet and sagging in the middle, and bearing a striking visual resemblance to rotting squash. Maybe I should not have used frozen carrots? But why did I really fail, or more realistically, why did I *believe* I failed at the baking task? Having heard a litany of student attributions for poor performance over the past 10 years, I was well equipped to rationalize the reasons for my own catastrophic cake. I quickly concluded that the recipe was far too complicated, the baking temperature of my oven was obviously miscalibrated, and my ingredients were apparently inferior. I attributed my failure to a variety of factors beyond my personal control that would likely remain unchanged, if I ever dared to bake again. In any event, who wants to waste time baking a cake when one can easily be purchased at a bakery for half the cost? I concluded that baking is reserved for others with greater culinary skills, which clearly excluded me.

Although my cake disaster was not an academic achievement (although I tacitly learned how NOT to bake a cake), the *espoused* rationale for my failure exemplified specific attributions, or self-assessed causes, as to why I failed. Attributions are best understood by examining three specific underlying dimensions related to interpreting task outcomes. First, assessment of *causal locus* provides evidence as to the source of responsibility for the achieved outcome. Individuals generally rationalize why they succeeded or failed, ascribing responsibility for outcomes based on either internal self-strivings, or like me, attributing outcomes to external causes unrelated to the self. In other words, I rejected the notion that my personal ability or effort was the reason for my failed cake. Instead, I concluded that a variety of contextual factors were responsible for the outcomes I achieved, including the recipe being too hard to follow, a defective oven, and the need for better ingredients, all factors unrelated to my personal skills or the degree of effort I had invested. Alternatively, I might have concluded that my failure was the result of internal deficiencies, including the apparent absence of the baking gene in my genetic code, poor planning, questionable ability, or lack of personal effort and attention devoted to the baking process.

In addition to having an internal or external antecedent, attributions are based on perceptions of personal *ability* or on the degree of *effort* invested in a task (Weiner, 1979). Ability attributions suggest the depth of skill and extent of talent determine task results. When an individual fails, ability attributions leave learners vulnerable to feelings of despair, lower self-esteem, and promote negative ruminations, as the individual, in many cases, may believe that deficient skills will limit future success on similar tasks. Subsequently, motivation to complete the task decreases. In contrast, effort attributions inspire more encouraging performance expectations, as the individual believes that there is a direct connection between the amount of effort invested in a task and the quality or efficiency of task results. When effort attributions prevail, the individual is likely to muster additional resources when presented with a similar opportunity, fostering feelings of optimism, hope, and potential pride, leading to robust adaptive motivation on similar subsequent tasks.

Assessments of stability or the perceptual permanence of attributions are an important second causal dimension of task-directed behavior. Weiner (2010) suggested that the perception of stability, or the predictability of outcomes, was as instrumental in performance domains as causal locus. Attributions are perceived by individuals either to persist over time, showing consistency between similar tasks, or to be unstable and malleable. Outcomes lacking perceived stability suggest that each occurrence or opportunity presents an additional chance for the individual to demonstrate competency and reassess the source of success or failure. Sadly, I believe my cake-making ability is immutable: I doubt that any cooking class would improve my baking skills, suggesting a highly stable ability-based attribution. It is extremely unlikely that I will ever raise a spatula again! In the vernacular of attribution theory, I exemplify learned helplessness, since I have been conditioned to expect baking failure. I am unwilling to devote additional effort to baking because I believe that any effort to improve my baking skill will be fruitless, especially if baking a carrot cake. When it comes to cake baking, I have surrendered psychologically because I am unwilling to expose myself to additional humiliation. From a motivational perspective, I have abdicated effort and responsibility for my task outcome because I believe there is minimal probability that anything will reverse my baking misfortunes.

Controllability is the third dimension influencing causal attributions. Controllability implies that the individual believes that they are able to orchestrate the nature and quality of performance outcomes. Most individuals actively strive to control the outcomes of the challenges they elect to pursue. If an individual believes he or she has influence over outcomes and then experiences success, the person will also believe that effort expenditures are warranted and worth the necessary cognitive investment. When the same individual encounters formidable obstacles or task failure, he or she may attribute performance decrements to lack of effort, such as when low grades are earned because of not studying enough for an important examination. Individuals who achieve success when harboring deficient control beliefs usually attribute positive outcomes to either a stroke of luck or to the apparent ease of the task. Questionable control beliefs are prone to decrease the effort invested in a task because the person sees little relation between effort and outcomes. An external causal locus and minimal controllability beliefs constitute a particularly lethal combination, usually resulting in attributions equivalent to believing in bad karma or a questionable horoscope, such as the feelings I experienced during my colossal cake caper.

Most salient to the MD are the behavioral implications of various attributions and the expectation that certain attributions will likely result in a set of highly probable corresponding behaviors and emotions. When individuals expect success, they will enthusiastically pursue task goals, exerting cognitive energy in the optimistic anticipation of a positive result. Conversely, when negative outcomes are anticipated, lethargy, procrastination, or deliberate task avoidance is likely to follow (Atkinson, 1964). In turn, the behavior produces a corresponding set of emotions associated with success or failure. Negative expectations generate undesirable feelings and a corresponding decrease in task engagement, resulting in maladaptive motivation and reduced effort. Consequently, if the individual presumes a positive outcome, a corresponding positive affective valence will be associated with the task, and likelihood of sustained effort or task re-engagement will increase. Table 7.1 illustrates the relationship among perceived causality and the attributional and emotional consequences associated with each task orientation, as well as the likelihood of task re-engagement.

Weiner (2012) emphasized that causal cognitive ruminations generate feelings, but that attributions alone do not propel individuals to act in a certain way or point the individual in a specific affective direction. The emotional consequences of individual attributions do not evolve in social isolation but, instead, are socially influenced. Like many emotional triggers, the development, evolution, and display of emotion is frequently contextually bound and based upon self-referent comparison and anticipated reaction from others. Imagine the academically unsuccessful student or the forlorn co-worker explaining how their poor planning or procrastinating nature resulted in a pitiful test performance or project failure. If significant others determine that the poor performance was within the control of the individual, indifferent responses to the individual are almost guaranteed. Conversely, if a justifiable circumstance inhibited successful performance, sympathy and understanding would likely result.

Devoid of the need for justification, individuals are more prone to ascribing negative self-appraisals to external factors in order to avoid feelings of personal demoralization. Frequently, "self-serving" bias is observed, whereby success is often justified as internally derived, but task failure is attributed to external ascriptions (McClure et al., 2011). Although feelings of pride, shame, guilt and anger can be self-induced and based strictly upon self-impressions, quite often, individuals ascribe personal worth and expectations based upon societal, gender, and cultural norms. In school, a

Table 7.1 Selective causal attributions and associated dimensional likelihoods

Attributions	Outcome	Probable locus	Stability	Control	Emotion generated	Probability of task re-engagement
Ability	Success	Internal	Stable	Low	Surprise, Happy	High
Ability	Failure	Internal	Stable	Low	Humiliation	Low
Effort	Success	Internal	Unstable	High	Pride	Very high
Effort	Failure	Internal	Unstable	High	Shame, guilt, anger	High
Low difficulty task	Success	External	Stable	Low	Pride, grateful	High
High difficulty task	Failure	External	Stable	Low	Hopelessness	Very low
Luck	Success	External	Unstable	Low	Relief	Moderate
Luck	Failure	External	Unstable	Low	Surprise, contempt	Moderate

Source: Based on Weiner (2012).

substantial portion of students' attributional information is based upon teacher judgments and expectations (Dompnier, Pansu, & Bressoux, 2006; Sudkamp, Kaiser, & Moller, 2012). Similarly, in organizations, performance feedback to employees is strongly influenced by how supervisors assess worker attributions (Martinko, Douglas, & Harvey, 2006), with assessments influencing pay and compensation (Reb & Greguras, 2010).

Finally, the social nature of attributions is emphasized by examining cross-cultural and gender differences. Generally, studies conclude that individuals with a collectivist orientation (see Chapter 5, p. 118) ascribe causality for achievement to externally derived socially influenced sources, whereas people in individualist cultures have more intrinsic attributions, as well as the belief that their attained outcomes are more controllable (Zusho, Pintrich & Cortina, 2005). As for gender, stereotypical patterns are usually observed both within and between cultures, with females often attributing performance excellence to the exertion of greater effort, while subpar performances are attributed to poor ability, more so than their male counterparts (McClure et al., 2011). However, some attributional phenomena are constant, regardless of culture or gender. In a comprehensive meta-analysis, Mezulis, Abramson, Hyde, and Hankin (2004) substantiated the ubiquitous, self-serving bias that permeates all cultures, with individuals universally attributing success to more internal and stable causes, rather than taking deliberate and intentional personal responsibility for their own paltry performances.

One person with easily recognized internal, highly stable, and controllable effort attributions is former NFL superstar Nick Lowery. Seven times an "All Pro," Nick was selected to the Pro-Bowl three times and was inducted into the Kansas City Chiefs Hall of Fame in 2009. At the time of his retirement, he was the most accurate and prolific field-goal kicker in NFL history. Nick set four all-time NFL records all *after* being cut 11 times by eight NFL teams! I asked Nick how he felt when 60,000 manic fans were screaming at him and he missed a potential game-winning field goal because of a wayward kick. Nick explained that taking personal responsibility for performance outcomes is inherent to anything he has ever attempted or done, including field-goal precision. He enthusiastically responded, "If I go through life thinking that I need things that are outside my locus of control (i.e., me), then I will always feel some kind of void that I don't have what it takes. It comes down to realizing we control our destinies. Always, always, always, it is necessary to give ourselves the permission to learn. With that assumption then mistakes become part of the overall plan, rather than an exception." Nick added, "All I can do is learn and to be sure I will never make the same mistake again. I was in a game in Buffalo when an 80-year old lady was hurling verbal and visual obscenities at me like an angry trucker. The wind was blowing at 20 mph, and the wind chill was five degrees below zero, but I knew I couldn't control her or the weather, all I could do was learn. I was thinking, what would I do to ensure that this [failing] never happens again?" (N. Lowery, personal communication, January 2, 2014). Nick's attributional approach to kicking field goals applies to most other aspects of his extraordinary career, suggesting that at least by his example, casual attributions and personal beliefs concerning past performance generalize to the future challenges a person is willing to consider.

Motivational Leader—*Nick Lowery*

There is so much more to the Nick Lowery story than just football. Nick transcends any simple category. He is a Kansas City Hall of Fame athlete, Ivy-League scholar, a former presidential aide, poet, teacher, motivational speaker, and philanthropist. Nick's life is about persistence, focus, and passion, regardless of where he dedicates his energy.

He is the only person to work for both Presidents George H. W. Bush and Bill Clinton in the White House Office of National Service. In 2002, Lowery became the first pro athlete with both a Master's degree and a fellowship from the Harvard University Kennedy School of Government. He founded *Champions for the Homeless* in 2006, giving food and gifts to the less fortunate on Thanksgiving, Christmas, and Easter each year. Nick's *Champions Against Bullying* program may be the next major program adopted by the NFL, and the program is currently helping 81 schools across the country combat bullying. His latest national philanthropic program *Taking Control: Safe Healthy and Empowered Campuses* is designed to counter sexual assault and domestic abuse on campus, with an expected kickoff during fall 2015 at Arizona State University.

Nick's lifetime of work is about giving power and voice to the youth and to all people looking to find their true purpose. According to Nick, "We live in a post-governmental era where government cannot fully solve any of the crucial problems of our day. In this vacuum, youth are not our future; they are our PRESENT!" (N. Lowery, personal communication, November 7, 2014). Lowery was instrumental in the passage of AmeriCorps in 1993 for President Bill Clinton and was recently recognized by the five living Presidents at the White House for the 20th anniversary of the AmeriCorps program.

In addition, the Nick Lowery Youth Foundation (www.nickloweryfoundation.org), founded and managed by Nick, thrives by supporting many national and community-based programs, including creating the *Adult Role Models for Youth* (ARMY) program, now called *Youthfriends*, celebrating its 24th year with over 5,000 volunteers working to help 20,000 at-risk youth! The foundation also supports the *Native Vision* program along with the Johns Hopkins Center for American Indian Health and the NFL Players Association. Nick was also instrumental in creating the Nation Building for Native Youth (NBNY) program, now in its 14th year, featured on PBS in the documentary "Hungry Minds," a national leadership program that has served hundreds of youth from over 50 tribes. Nick is the Founding Director of the *National Fund for Excellence in American Indian Education* and has twice testified before the US Senate on problems facing Native-American youth and education.

Nick is a recipient of the NFL's foremost humanitarian award, the Byron "Whizzer" White award, an honor dedicated to former football star and US Supreme Court Justice White and is annually awarded to the player who best serves his team, community, and country through dedicated service to helping others. In addition, Nick has also won the US Jaycees' "Ten Outstanding Young Americans Award," an honor also bestowed upon Elvis Presley and the late US President John F. Kennedy. Now in Arizona, Nick continues to devote many waking hours improving the lives of others and, not surprisingly, is a highly coveted, internationally desired motivational speaker.

Principle #37—Certain motives are extraordinarily difficult to suppress

In addition to qualitatively examining our past performances as a source of task-relevant information guiding future engagement decisions, individuals also make ongoing, real-time cost–benefit evaluations as to how they want to direct and invest their available cognitive resources. Originating in the formulaic "approach and avoid" models of Atkinson (1964) that sought to predict the probability of task engagement and popularized by the application of expectancy incentives to school achievement (Wigfield & Eccles, 2000), expectancy-value approaches suggest that when individuals contemplate task engagement, they make a series of culturally-nuanced weightings and assign personal priorities to different task aspects while concurrently ascribing relative value and worth to prospective task outcomes. Expectancy-value theory is frequently used to explain how idiosyncratic incentives are instrumental in achievement motivation; however, the approach is also used to answer broad and varied research questions across domains and cultures (Wigfield, Tonks, & Klauda, 2009). Some applied research questions that have been answered using an expectancy-value lens include: under what conditions do individuals demonstrate organizational trust (Viklund & Sjöberg, 2008), which factors undermine the willingness of individuals to exercise (Yli-Piipari & Kokkonen, 2014), and what type of information influences science career aspirations (Nagengast et al., 2011)?

Perhaps the best example of the practical utility of expectancy-value theory can be drawn from one of the supreme moments in movie history, evoking one of the most memorable and powerful lines of all time from *The Godfather*, when underworld boss Don Corleone (played by Best Actor winner Marlon Brando) said, "I'm gonna make him an offer he can't refuse." Brando was alluding to his highly successful ability to persuade individuals to agree with his desires. In this instance, he convinced a recalcitrant Hollywood producer to cast his godson Johnny Fontaine (played by Al Martino), a fading star, in a leading movie role. The producer, who was originally adamant in his resistance to casting Johnny, finally realized the value and importance of changing his decision when he woke up in bed drenched in blood from the decapitated head of his prized racehorse, which was strategically placed under his blanket while he slept as an incentive to change his mind. While the factors we evaluate and the magnitude of the decisions we face are far less graphic and sensational, we regularly make judgments about the importance of task-relevant criteria and evaluate the physical and psychological incentives and consequences of task engagement.

Like other stalwarts on the motivational Mount Rushmore, the foundation of expectancy-value theory rests heavily on the role of personal competency beliefs and the presumptions individuals have about prospective task outcomes. When evaluating task choice through an expectancy-value lens, individuals first appraise the incentive value of a task, which is based upon four evaluation criteria: attainment value, intrinsic value, utility value, and cost (Eccles et al., 1983). Attainment value represents the degree of relative importance the individual places on the contemplated task. Intrinsic value is measured by how much an individual subjectively enjoys doing and completing the task. Utility value represents the degree of usefulness afforded to doing or mastering the task from an applied perspective; a task high in utility value would be valued or perceived as proximal and instrumental to achieving longer-term goals, such as taking a course to enhance one's career development. Alternatively, utility value can be perceived as low, or even negative, if the task is deemed unnecessary to advance individual long-term goals. Cost represents the subjectively determined, personal, and/or psychological consequences associated with task engagement, including, but not limited to, the inability to perform other more desirable tasks, the degree of cognitive effort invested in the task, or the social stigmas associated with reaching perceived task outcomes.

Expectancy-value approaches are an effective means of examining the choices individuals make in both the classroom and a variety of other domains. Understanding how learners evaluate academic tasks can help predict what courses they will take and what assignments they will do (Simpkins, Davis-Kean, & Eccles, 2006) and may assist in determining when and if they will develop intrinsic motivation and interest for a particular task (Wigfield & Cambria, 2010). Value assessments can be highly stable and psychologically durable. In one longitudinal study, Durik, Vida, and Eccles (2006) found that subject judgments made in grammar school were so enduring that they accurately predicted the frequency of future literacy choices 6 years later. Outside of the classroom, expectancies are strong indicators of the willingness of individuals to engage in and perform a diverse set of behaviors, such as the degree of effective self-management employees demonstrate at work (Lord, Diefendorff, Schmidt, & Hall, 2010), when, if, and how online learners use wiki-tools to enhance collaboration (Ertmer et al., 2011), and even the intentionality and associated expectations for using a condom (Albarracín, Johnson, Fishbein & Muellerliele, 2001)!

The value and usefulness of expectancy approaches in applied settings requires careful consideration of how individuals make task-relevant judgments. Several interpretive threats challenge the over-reliance on expectancy-value conclusions as a means to explain motives. First, the valuation of expectancies and outcomes relies almost exclusively on individual self-report. The individualized nature of task assessment is both a strength and a weakness of the approach. Asking individuals to evaluate tasks provides an excellent opportunity to glimpse into the introspective nature of causal outcomes and examine the underlying beliefs that influence personal expectancy assessments. However, as described in Chapter 2, individuals are notorious for misinterpreting their own motives and frequently display personal bias, often evaluating task outcomes based upon perceptions of social desirability, including ascribing preferential normative values to certain more desirable tasks and careers. Wigfield, Cambria, and Eccles (2012) recommended using multiple measurements of task expectations and evaluating outcome expectancies *after* task completion as a means to counteract the liabilities of self-report and to solidify subsequent inferences.

Second, we should expect variation regarding which aspects of a task individuals consider when making evaluative judgments. Task demands may be ambiguous, and individuals may not accurately gauge what skills are needed to complete a specific task. Further, the investment of cognitive and motivational effort toward task completion is not a linear process. Vacillations of effort frequently occur, which can result in individuals re-evaluating both task values and outcomes during task engagement. Consider the individual who is optimistic at task start but loses confidence and becomes frustrated from lack of task progress as the task becomes increasingly challenging. Negative anticipatory ruminations may quickly emerge. Try putting together a *do-it-yourself* modular desk or a barbeque grill that requires you to follow convoluted instructions, and you will quickly relate to why and how success beliefs concerning task outcomes may quickly change. Additionally, individuals experience challenges with accurately calibrating effort assessments because those calculations are contextually and temporally bound and are, in part, determined by the influence of expertise (Beckmann, 2010). Individuals frequently miscalculate and misinterpret the degree of mental workload needed to complete a task, thus impeding accurate effort assessments and measurement (Hoffman, 2012).

Third, as with any task judgment, we should consider the stability of assessments, which can change radically over the course of time. Outcomes once highly valued can be frequently recalibrated, resulting in a wide disparity both between and within individuals. In addition, individuals are subject to faulty assessments, especially when ascribing value to a certain outcome (Bandura, 1997). By example, an individual can pursue a college degree for a number of potential reasons, including financial reward, knowledge acquisition, preferential social status, or merely for personal accomplishment. If offered a high-paying job before degree completion, the once highly prized degree can become instantly superfluous, plummeting in perceived value and reducing task engagement. Degree continuance would be subject to the original motive source and the fluctuating perceived value of the diploma, regardless of payoff.

Fourth, task valuations are partly influenced by social dynamics. Sociocultural factors may result in a task being embraced in one context and yet blatantly devalued in another. Attainment value and utility value are not absolute, as a skill deemed desirable in one social setting may be unimportant or even stigmatized in a different context of application. For instance, in some businesses, attitudes toward advanced education, and PhDs in particular, may be negative (Fendt, 2013). The identical credentials can be revered in other venues, such as academics, where a terminal degree is usually an employment prerequisite (Karl & Peluchette, 2013). Therefore, close examination of prevailing social norms is essential when evaluating expectancy motives. Coincidentally, back in 1972, when Marlon Brando won the Best Actor award, in a socially historical moment, he elected to repudiate the award in protest of the treatment of Native Americans in film and television. Apparently, Brando's ascribed value to the honor was inconsistent with the valuation of his peers, who were astonished that he would reject such a coveted honor.

Finally, examination of a compendium of evidence reveals that the variability associated with task outcomes can be more reliably predicted by other self-reflective judgments beyond expectancy considerations. The degree of confidence that individuals ascribe to achieving certain courses of action or outcomes may provide superior explanatory power in understanding motives than expectancies alone. Bandura (1997) indicated that "when variations in efficacy beliefs are controlled statistically, the outcomes expected for a given performance contribute little to the prediction of behavior" (p. 126). Bandura contended that outcome judgments made during the evaluation of expectancies do not account for many causal beliefs that influence performance, including inattention to the deliberate or unintentional self-handicapping strategies individuals employ that may impede goal progress (see Chapter 8, p. 225). Outcome expectations are especially vulnerable in situations where an individual must demonstrate adaptivity and creativity to meet ill-defined task demands, as task demands are far less clear or predictable during exploratory learning. In sum, according to Bandura (1997), the inclusion of self-efficacy when making evaluative judgments of task outcomes provides better support for explaining variations in motivation than merely accounting for task incentives and outcome expectancies. Thus, we next turn to another celebrated cornerstone of the motivational Mount Rushmore and explore the powerful influence of self-efficacy evaluations as a conduit for successful learning and performance.

Principle #38—After ability, self-efficacy explains more performance variation than any other motivational self-belief

When examining the similarities among our motivational leaders, at least one common theme prevails. Each personality articulated a deeply entrenched belief indicating willingness to do whatever it took to attain a desired goal or reach an anticipated outcome. Nick Holes lives by the maxim inscribed on his toes *"Keep moving."* Darren Soto (see Chapter 10, p. 288) affirmed "I work at things that I know I can attain." Alec Torelli alluded to how he competes against his own inner voice stating, "I focus on the things that I can control and get done" (A. Torelli, personal communication, May 13, 2014). Cheryl Hines pronounced, "Brace yourself for the worst, but the worst doesn't usually happen. Just push yourself until you get what you want" (C. Hines, personal communication, May 22, 2014). Ironically, Cheryl was describing how she was rejected three times when auditioning for the same role on the television series "Swamp Thing." On her fourth try, Cheryl finally earned the part and launched her illustrious career, attributing her success to drive and ambition, and demonstrating an emphatic self-belief that she ultimately expected to succeed.

The leaders described a unique blend of distinctive talent and exceptional abilities that contributed to their successes. Conceptions of performance across domains reveal that what we already know, as well as our own performance history, explains about 30% of the variability in future performance outcomes (Sitzmann & Yeo, 2013). In other words, prior experience does contribute to future success. However, 70% of the variability in future performance outcomes is explained by factors other than what we already know or what we have previously accomplished. We might then surmise that the success of our motivational leaders is attributed to their inclination to persevere in the face of obstacles, their lofty aspirations, blind optimism, good looks, or perhaps the perception of being in control of their own destinies. These potential explanations for superior performance are warranted, to some degree, by empirical evidence, but clearly, in aggregate, the most probable explanation for successful performance outcomes, after accounting for existing skills and experience, is domain-specific self-efficacy. The belief in one's capability is a powerful force that assists the individual in organizing and executing courses of action that produce desired results (Bandura, 1997).

According to over 40 years of programmatic research conducted across domains and cultures, after controlling for fundamental ability distinctions, no other variable has greater mediational power over performance outcomes than self-efficacy beliefs. The pervasive and positive influence of self-efficacy on performance is demonstrated in academics (Pajares, 1996), in organizations (Wood & Bandura, 1989), during work performance (Stajkovic, & Luthans, 1998), and in athletic competition (Moritz, Feltz, Fahrbach, & Mack, 2000) and is a catalyst for overall physical activity (Plotnikoff, Costigan, Karunamuni, & Lubans, 2013). Self-efficacy beliefs are not based on a quantitative or qualitative assessment of a repertoire of demonstrated experience or skills. Instead, self-efficacy beliefs are motivational antecedents, consisting of cognitive and affective self-assessments that prime the individual for focused action, based upon what we believe we can accomplish. The strength of beliefs concerning ability perceptions is instrumental in superior performance because the individual believes that he or she has the cognitive horsepower, executable skills, and tangible strategies to produce desired outcomes for a specific task. Armed with a foundation of knowledge and experience, individuals possessing elevated self-efficacy beliefs will consistently outperform their lower self-efficacy peers in domains as varied as writing (Bruning, Dempsey, Kauffman, McKim, & Zumbrunn, 2013), playing musical instruments (McPherson, 2006), using Internet technology to promote learning (Lee & Tsai, 2010), and making assessments unrelated to specific performance metrics, such as seeking sensual pleasure, and anticipatory emotions, such as happiness and hope (Maddux, 2002).

The power of self-efficacy to mediate performance is based, to some extent, on positive associations among elevated self-efficacy levels and key indicators related to learning and performance. The belief in one's abilities exerts both direct influence and incidental influence on outcome perceptions. For instance, as the degree of self-efficacy increases, learners will deliberately elect more formidable classroom challenges when weighing academic goals and contemplating classroom activities (Zimmerman, Bandura & Martinez-Pons, 1992; Zimmerman & Cleary, 2009). Enhanced self-efficacy is related to academic persistence (Wright, Jenkins-Guarnieri, & Murdock, 2013) and resilience when under stress (Benight & Cieslak, 2011) and has strategy implications, as highly efficacious learners are more efficient problem solvers (Hoffman & Schraw, 2009). From an applied perspective, the influence of self-efficacy is broad and ubiquitous. Self-efficacy levels foretell which subjects' learners are willing to study and the career choices they will eventually make (Betz & Hackett, 1983). The degree of self-efficacy also serves as a reliable lifestyle predictor, indicating what types of strategies individuals will or will not use to manage their health and health issues (Plotnikoff, Lippke, Courneya, Birkett, & Sigal, 2008).

Elevated levels of self-efficacy exert indirect positive influences on a variety of performance outcomes and are instrumental in directing individual and collective effort investments. Most notably, enhanced levels of self-efficacy contribute to learners using a broader repertoire of academically productive learning strategies, such as enhanced mental monitoring of accuracy and metacognitive awareness. High self-efficacy learners generally show adaptive motivation during learning by processing information more deeply than their lower-efficacy peers (Wood & Bandura, 1989). Self-efficacy also makes independent contributions to the emotional experiences individuals report when completing tasks (Bandura, 2012), including reducing stress perceptions and moderating anxiety reactions. As self-efficacy levels increase, emotional stability is elevated, while perceived neuroticism decreases (Judge, Jackson, Shaw, Scott, & Rich 2007).

When measured at the group level, collective efficacy reveals interdependent linkages among team members, influencing systemic organizational performances. Like individuals, groups and teams with elevated efficacy levels are typically associated with superior performance outcomes. The profound benefits of collective efficacy are particularly useful to predict teaching effectiveness and achievement gains at the school or district level (Goddard, Hoy, & Hoy, 2004), to positively influence employee job satisfaction (Borgogni, Dello Russo, & Latham, 2011), and to enhance overall organizational and group dynamics (Prussia & Kinicki, 1996; Stajkovic, Lee, & Nyberg, 2009) in both corporate (Murphy, Cooke, & Lopez, 2013) and competitive athletic domains (Chow & Feltz, 2007).

Operating under the presumption that instilling elevated levels of efficacy in the self and others is highly advantageous for learning and performance, the next logical step for the aspiring MD is discovering the sources and useful strategies necessary to cultivate self-efficacy beliefs. The development and accrual of adaptive self-efficacy beliefs starts with providing individuals with opportunities to receive task-relevant feedback that is credible, positive, and integrated within the self. Termed "enactive mastery experiences" by Bandura (1997, p. 80), any exceptional performance outcome that is intentional and perceived to be within the control of the individual will potentially enhance self-efficacy. Mastery requires supportive contextual conditions that provide appropriate structure and guidelines to allow the individual to harness and apply ambitions, skills, and strategies to reach premeditated goals. When the individual surpasses desired performance thresholds and equates success with personal agency, self-efficacy is enhanced. Critical to fostering increases in self-efficacy are mastery experiences that are commensurate with existing talents and ability. Individuals overwhelmed by task demands or those able to meet task goals without cognitive exertion or minimal effort will either see efficacy levels remain stable or decrease. Contemplated tasks must be both attainable and challenging; otherwise self-efficacy will be foiled due to overwhelming complexity and cognitive load or because of minimal cognitive stretch that is insufficient to foster intellectual growth.

To a lesser extent, self-efficacy levels can be enhanced by the actions of others if the other is deemed capable and significant. Bandura (1997) suggested that vicarious experience enhances self-efficacy when one's own performance is mediated by observing the skills of a competent model. When individuals have the opportunity to witness other highly regarded individuals performing contemplative tasks, efficacy beliefs elevate because social comparison aids the individual in visualizing successful personal task completion and feeling confident that the observed performance can be replicated. Grounded in behavioral learning theories, if the physical and emotional consequences of performing a task are perceived as positive, emulation is encouraged. Likewise, if outcomes are perceived as undesirable or are associated with the perception of unwelcomed emotional consequences, a negative model can be psychologically debilitating and adversely impact self-efficacy and an individual's motive to replicate a task.

Verbal encouragement in the form of constructive feedback received from credible others may also enhance self-efficacy. When an individual receives verbal affirmation (Bandura, 1997) originating from a reliable source, the feedback is integrated into his or her personal belief system. The encouragement from others is based on personal faith and designed to reassure the dubious learner of his or her prospective abilities. As the learner integrates the encouragement into individual self-perceptions, efficacy beliefs escalate. An excellent example of the power of verbal persuasion was described by Rebecca Hines, who responded to the repeated laments of frustration from her then-struggling sister Cheryl. When repeatedly discouraged by failed auditions, which stalled her acting career, Cheryl developed personal skepticism concerning her acting ability. Rebecca advised Cheryl that rejection was inherent to the acting profession and that experiencing failure was necessary to achieve success. Although Rebecca had no acting experience, she communicated her faith in Cheryl's abilities even in the face of repeated rejections, which resulted in modifying Cheryl's self-doubts. Cheryl integrated her sister's verbal encouragement into her self-view, becoming more accepting of potential failure but without letting this acceptance impede her motivation to succeed despite the repeated obstacles encountered. One would be remiss in believing that simple encouragement or vicarious performance is sufficient to transform self-efficacy beliefs. Fundamental skill is a necessary prerequisite to maximize belief change, even for the most optimistic individual. Devoid of sufficient skill, the doubting learner would, indeed, be condemned to failure, regardless of the persuasive abilities of a competent mentor or the extent of positive self-beliefs.

Finally, physiological and emotional predispositions can be a catalyst of motivated action and be conducive to modification of existing self-efficacy beliefs. Performance outcomes and corresponding expectations during situations of high stress or anxiety can have either productive or potentially dangerous cognitive consequences. Anyone apprehensive about giving a speech or experiencing stage fright will likely relate to the debilitating effects of cognitive ruminations related to visualizing potential failure. Even the most practiced and integrated skills can be hampered during situations of heightened anxiety. Efficacy beliefs are particularly vulnerable when anticipating negative performance expectations.

Alternatively, heightened arousal can be a catalyst for positive anticipatory performances (Nicholls, Polman, & Levy, 2010). This phenomenon is observable during athletic performances, when athletes are provided the opportunity to display skills and abilities during high-pressure situations, such as during elimination or playoff games. The heightened sense of arousal stimulates physiological and psychological readiness in the individual. Optimal levels of arousal vary among individuals and are subject to vacillation based upon contextual conditions that influence the nature of the performance and subsequent self-efficacy perceptions. As an example, team performance is traditionally superior when teams have the home field advantage, more so than when competing in the opposition's venue (Courneya & Carron, 1992). Optimal efficacy-building environments for one person can be quite unproductive for another, suggesting substantial variability among individuals based upon subjective interpretations of somatic events (Bandura, 1997).

Maximizing the predictive and diagnostic power of self-efficacy requires consideration of at least three critical analytical factors. First, self-efficacy beliefs are domain-specific beliefs and should not be measured at the omnibus level. Generalized beliefs differ from domain-specific self-efficacy beliefs, as the latter are based upon the appraisal of specific task-relevant criteria and the perception of specific skills and abilities individuals envision as being necessary to meet performance goals. Generalized measures, such as academic self-concept (Bong & Skaalvik, 2003), are less accurate in predicting performance outcomes in comparison with self-efficacy, which is most accurately evaluated at the task level (Judge & Bono, 2001).

Second, self-reported beliefs are subjective and can be misinterpreted. Individuals are vulnerable to errors of miscalibration, potentially over- or underestimating the degree of skills, ability, and effort needed to reach successful task outcomes. The accuracy of one's own self-efficacy beliefs can be further impeded by misconstrued task demands that are malleable, temporal, and unstable based upon a variety of individual difference variables. The evaluation of task complexity is contingent upon level of expertise, availability of depletable cognitive resources expended during task completion, and conscious control of emotions experienced during incremental task success or failure.

Third, individuals make plausible assessments of prospective ability, which, in turn, should produce commensurate results. Ability assessments can originate from three sources: normative comparisons (i.e., other people), comparison with criterion thresholds indicative of specific content mastery, or comparison with one's own past performances. Contingent upon the conceptual anchors used by an individual to calibrate self-efficacy beliefs, a broad spectrum of variability may develop in self-efficacy assessments. Individuals lacking sufficient experience or understanding of criterion standards may default to more identifiable socially-referent performance anchors. The nature of social comparison alone can forestall accurate calibrations of assessments. Individuals may fixate on or over-emphasize the affective consequences of performance competition, wanting to best a rival's accomplishments, or align personal performance with that of a favored other, rather than making more reliable self-efficacy judgments on qualitative performance standards necessary to accurately and effectively complete a task.

The panacea of self-efficacy findings should be tempered and approached with caution. Self-efficacy, like many other motivational mediators, is interdependent, with accurate interpretations relying upon the influence of a variety of other individual difference and contextual variables, precluding an absolute or invariant positive affect on behavior (Bandura, 2012). In situations of task or effort miscalibration, self-efficacy may appear to inhibit effort or lead to increased errors (Vancouver, Thompson, Tischner, & Putka, 2002). Logically, overconfident learners may approach tasks with a lackadaisical attitude, deficient mindfulness, or speculating the ease of task completion. However, this calibration gap is not a reflection of the negative or null effects of self-efficacy beliefs but, instead, is predicated upon inaccurate and erroneous self-assessments. Bandura (2012) vehemently and eloquently contests the impotency of self-efficacy beliefs as pervasive and powerful due to methodological compromise and theoretical attenuation of disconfirming research. For MDs, cultivating self-efficacy should be a primarily goal, accomplished by leveraging the multiple sources and number of strategies previously outlined. Summarily, we can conclude that after controlling for performance enhancing influences, such as prior knowledge and experience, higher levels of domain-specific self-efficacy routinely predict beneficial performance outcomes—outcomes that are highly improbable for lower-efficacious peers (Bandura, 2012; Bouffard-Bouchard, 1990).

Principle #39—Motivational theory is applied temporally and situationally

An epigram used by Kurt Lewin (1951) to disseminate his views on social psychology is paraphrased as "There is nothing so practical as a good theory." When evaluating motivation and performance phenomena in applied settings, practicality means that the premises of a theory provide broad explanatory power to understand behaviors, beyond those described during experimental simulations. Each theory discussed in this chapter meets the applied criterion based upon classroom and organizational applicability. A "good" theory is the metaphorical equivalent of grasping the ideal tool from a vast repertoire of options in the carpenter's grandiose toolbox and using the tool properly to make needed repairs. Tools, however, can be rendered useless or harmful if used for purposes that are inappropriate or unintended. I have several scars as evidence of using pliers as a hammer to refute my creative tool theory. Ideally, one specific tool is considered optimal to complete a particular carpentry task. Similarly, the enduring theories of attributions, expectancies, and self-efficacy are best employed as situation- or task-contingent explanations of motivated behavior.

Although each theory is a viable explanation of agentic behavior, the construct emphasis of each view is conceptually different, suggesting that one approach may be more useful or appropriate than another to understand a particular motivational challenge. Relying too heavily on one interpretation of behavior may result in the all too frequent problem of *confirmation bias* whereby individuals exhibit an affinity toward identifying problems or seeking solutions that support their pre-existing notions while implicitly suppressing other plausible explanations of behavior (Greenwald, 2012). Avoiding theoretical bias means that tool selection for the aspiring MD involves a conscious realization that each approach to explain motivated behavior must be evaluated at different levels of detail, specificity, and temporality to be used effectively. Some people may dwell on past performances, while others will focus attention and effort on their current task challenges or demonstrate a focus on future performance goals. Popular diagnostic instruments, such as the Myers-Briggs Type Indicator, were specifically designed and validated to determine, in part, the degree of past, present, and future orientation of individuals as a means to enhancing personal growth and development (Cohen, Cohen, & Cross, 1981). Additionally, diagnostic approaches should be evaluated through a utility lens to answer specific research questions, with the understanding that one approach may be more relevant at a particular time than another. Table 7.2 outlines the main premises, temporality, and utility of each theoretical lens examined in the current chapter, including some suggested application strategies.

Precise determination concerning which interpretive lens is most appropriate to mediate any particular motivational challenge should also include consideration of contextual and individual difference variables that influence task-directed behaviors. Contextual factors include social influences, such as the presence of particular individuals, in-groups, and organizational and cyber cultures that may alter behavior across contexts. Individual difference variables include special consideration of the specific aspects of a task individuals assess, including the realistic probability that people will overestimate abilities or erroneously appraise task requirements. Further, the adaptation of any particular theoretical model should consider how task appraisals change over time, including the evaluation of escalating expertise as learners gain more task experience. Finally, it behooves the MD to identify the source of self-referent evaluations. As will be described in Chapter 8, individuals make task evaluations from a variety of perspectives. Some will focus on their own past performance, others will identify certain skills they intend to master, and many others will approach a task with the hope of bettering their own past performance. The individual's perspective may radically alter the suitability and analytical effectiveness of any one remedy, especially when individuals shift task-directed focus between normative and criterion performance standards.

Table 7.2 Summary, utility, application, and comparison of chapter constructs

Theory	Temporal focus	Underlying concepts	Theoretical explanation	Utility	Performance implications
Attributions	Past performance	People seek explanations for retrospective success and failure in order to understand the self with an overall goal of maintaining a positive self-image. Either effort or ability are the basis for most learning attributions	Attributions explain success and failure using three causal dimensions. First, internal or external locus is considered. Second, causes are evaluated for stability. Third, success and failure are attributed to either controllable (effort/ability) or uncontrollable factors (luck)	Attributions are useful to examine academic performance and social integration. They are particularly helpful to understand academic apathy or learned helplessness. Attributional beliefs are highly focused on personal competency assessments	Educators should provide feedback that focuses on effort. Feedback that uses the self as a performance benchmark is preferred. Educators should also model effort attributions and provide learners with attainable proximal goals
Expectancy-value (EV)	Current and contemplative performance	The strength of goal strivings are evaluated based upon the expectation of incentive outcomes.	Cost-benefit assessments weigh relative task importance, subjective enjoyment, and task usefulness in comparison to costs, such as effort exerted or the inability to pursue other options. EV is helpful to predict effort investments	Highly useful to investigate decision-making and choice. Provides insight into what people value and consider important performance success. EV assessments are highly predictive of future goals and behaviors	Focusing on authentic learning and task relevance is critical. Educators should provide reasons why competencies are important. Individuals should have clarity as to the process for earning incentives and how payoffs are determined

(*Continued*)

Table 7.2 (Continued)

Theory	Temporal focus	Underlying concepts	Theoretical explanation	Utility	Performance implications
Self-efficacy (SE)	Future performance	SE is a belief based on ability perceptions to execute courses of action to meet desired outcomes. SE beliefs include success expectations and the expectation that skills will lead to positive performance outcomes	Social-cognitive theory states personal beliefs, behaviors, and environmental events reciprocally influence task engagement. SE is best derived from masterful performances. SE is also achieved vicariously or modified by verbal persuasion and physiological events	SE is highly predictive of task engagement, persistence, resilience, and opportunistic strategy use. High SE explains variations in performance beyond ability	Modeling of desired behaviors is a key to promoting SE in others. Educators should set attainable goals and provide process feedback. Leaders can create supportive organizational contexts that emphasize skill development and improvement above base performance

Chapter summary/conclusions

Three prominent explanations of performance motivation were described in the current chapter: attributions, expectancies, and self-efficacy. Each explanation affirmed that our thoughts, emotions, and agentic behaviors are influenced, in part, by personal beliefs and values, the context of task implementation, and a variety of social influences, including the physical or psychological presence of others. The reciprocal nature of social cognitive theory suggests that task engagement is based upon the complex interplay of named influences, combined with personal evaluative judgments that determine subjective priorities, which result in differential weightings, ultimately determining what influence dominates any given task motivation. Individuals strive to find explanations for their performance results, as evidence for performance causality is instrumental in the development of self-identity. Most task engagement decisions are strongly influenced by competency beliefs, including micro-level appraisals of particular task-relevant skills and a belief in the ability to use those skills to attain desired performance outcomes. The source of competency appraisals is varied; some are based upon past performance, while others focus on current challenges or on the anticipation of gaining desirable future task outcomes.

Attribution theory uses a retrospective approach to determine the origins of academic success or failure, focusing primarily upon whether the individual believes her ability or effort is instrumental in achieving performance outcomes. The dimensions of locus, stability, and controllability contribute to evaluations of causality as individuals justify outcomes as either a product of their own agency or incongruous with their behavioral or motivational intentions. Expectancy-value approaches are based upon cost–benefit algorithms that assess relative perceptions regarding the degree of task enjoyment, interest, and usefulness individuals ascribe to the process of reaching task goals, while concurrently calculating the physical and psychological liabilities associated with reaching desired outcomes. Self-efficacy affects motivation by providing the individual with a set of entrenched, domain-specific evaluative beliefs that calibrate the adequacy of skills to complete a task. Self-efficacy beliefs also reveal the extent of control and regulation individuals believe they possess to successfully navigate contextual events that may impede the ability to orchestrate desired outcomes.

The interpretative lenses described are not ranked, nor is one preferential to another. Adapting a specific theoretical lens is based upon the judicious evaluation of a myriad of social cognitive factors and best determined by examining the overall patterns of behaviors exhibited by individuals. The self-beliefs described rarely develop from isolated events and, like all other self-beliefs, are influenced by cultural factors and developmental trajectories described in earlier chapters. Despite situational applicability, the masters of the motivational Mount Rushmore are highly effective in understanding academic and performance motivation, and the associated strategies should be well-worn tools in the MD's toolbox.

Next steps

Operating under the premise that individuals universally desire positive self-images, it is not surprising that an important motive for many individuals is actively developing and seeking ways to maintain positive self-impressions. A positive self-image can be achieved in many ways; however, sometimes the behaviors individuals display in their self-affirming quest are not always representative of their precise motives and can be misconstrued by the casual observer. In addition, individuals may intentionally exhibit behaviors that lead to false impressions by others concerning underlying motives in order to preserve positive self-views. Chapter 8 examines several personal motivations and strategies primarily used to achieve the goal of elevated self-worth. Chapter 8 also introduces the reader to country music star **Jessi Colter** who has found that much of her self-esteem and happiness were derived from helping others achieve success and well-being, sometimes at her own expense.

End of chapter motivational minute

Principles covered in this chapter:

36. **Past performance guides future motivation**—reasons concerning the perceived causes of success or failures are instrumental in guiding future performance. Attributional dimensions, including causal locus, stability, and controllability, are useful measures to predict if an individual will engage with a task.
37. **Certain motives are extraordinarily difficult to suppress**—when contemplating task involvement, individuals make ongoing cost–benefit assessments to determine if a task has sufficient merit to justify engagement. Individuals consider task importance, enjoyment, value, and utility as a means of calibrating the materialistic and psychological payoffs associated with task completion.
38. **After ability, self-efficacy explains more performance variation than any other motivational self-belief**—the belief in one's ability to attain desired outcomes is powerful. Elevated self-efficacy beliefs are related to greater persistence, resilience, and setting more challenging learning and performance goals. Most importantly, after controlling for ability, self-efficacy is a reliable predictor of performance.
39. **Motivational theory is applied temporally and situationally**—one explanation of motivation does not mediate all issues of learning and performance. The choice of mediational strategies is based upon individual differences and contextual factors in conjunction with an understanding of overall patterns of behavior.

Key terminology (in order of chapter presentation):

- **Reciprocal determinism**—the interdependent network of personal beliefs and values, behaviors, and environmental factors that influence agentic action according to social cognitive motivational perspectives.
- **Causal locus**—when ascribing attributional sources of success or failure, individuals consider factors internal or external to the self. An external locus suggests that individuals perceive environmental factors or chance as accountable for outcomes, while an internal locus indicates the individual believes ability or effort are the reason for task outcomes.
- **Ability attributions**—internally focused causal beliefs associated with task success or failure, grounded in self-assessed perceptions of talent, skills, and ability.
- **Effort attributions**—internally focused causal beliefs associated with task success or failure, grounded in self-assessed perceptions of engaged effort devoted to a task.

- **Collective efficacy**—self-efficacy can be measured at individual or collective group levels. Elevated collective efficacy is related to enhanced team and group cohesion and frequently associated with highly-functioning team performance.
- **Confirmation bias**—the subjective bias of individuals who seek out confirming evidence for their own theoretical view or opinion, while concurrently avoiding or ignoring falsifying evidence.

References

Albarracín, D., Johnson, B. T., Fishbein, M., & Muellerleile, P. A. (2001). *Theories of reasoned action and planned behavior as models of condom use: A meta-analysis*. CHIP Documents, Paper 8. Retrieved on May 23, 2014 from: <http://digitalcommons.uconn.edu/chip_docs/8>.

Atkinson, J. (1964). *An introduction to motivation*. Princeton, NJ: Van Nostrand.

Bandura, A. (1997). *Self-efficacy: The exercise of control*. New York, NY: Freeman.

Bandura, A. (2012). On the functional properties of perceived self-efficacy revisited. *Journal of Management, 38*(1), 9–44.

Baumeister, R. F., & Finkel, E. J. (2010). *Advanced social psychology: The state of the science*. New York, NY: Oxford University Press.

Beckmann, J. F. (2010). Taming a beast of burden on some issues with the conceptualization and operationalisation of cognitive load. *Learning and Instruction, 20*, 250–264.

Benight, C. C., & Cieslak, R. (2011). Cognitive factors and resilience: How self-efficacy contributes to coping with adversities. In S. M. Southwick, B. Litz, D. Charney, & M. J. Friedman (Eds.), *Resilience and mental health. Challenges across the lifespan* (pp. 45–55). New York, NY: Cambridge University Press.

Betz, N. E., & Hackett, G. (1983). The relationship of mathematics self-efficacy expectations to the selection of science-based college majors. *Journal of Vocational Behavior, 23*(3), 329–345.

Bong, M., & Skaalvik, E. M. (2003). Academic self-concept and self-efficacy: How different are they really? *Educational Psychology Review, 15*(1), 1–40.

Borgogni, L., Dello Russo, S., & Latham, G. P. (2011). The relationship of employee perceptions of the immediate supervisor and top management with collective efficacy. *Journal of Leadership & Organizational Studies, 18*(1), 5–13. http://dx.doi.org/10.1177/1548051810379799.

Bouffard-Bouchard, T. (1990). Influence of self-efficacy on performance of a cognitive task. *The Journal of Social Psychology, 130*, 353–363.

Bruning, R., Dempsey, M., Kauffman, D., McKim, C., & Zumbrunn, S. (2013). Examining dimensions of self-efficacy for writing. *Journal of Educational Psychology, 105*(1), 25–38.

Chow, G. M., & Feltz, D. L. (2007). Collective efficacy beliefs and sports. In M. R. Beauchamp & M. A. Eys (Eds.), *Group dynamics in exercise and sport psychology: Contemporary themes* (pp. 298–316). New York, NY: Routledge.

Cohen, D., Cohen, M., & Cross, H. (1981). A construct validity study of the Myers-Briggs Type Indicator. *Educational and Psychological Measurement, 41*(3), 883–891.

Courneya, K. S., & Carron, A. V. (1992). The home advantage in sport competitions: A literature review. *Journal of Sport & Exercise Psychology, 14*, 13–27.

Dompnier, B., Pansu, P., & Bressoux, P. (2006). An integrative model of scholastic judgments: Pupils' characteristics, class context, halo effect and internal attributions. *European Journal of Psychology Education, 21*(2), 119–133.

Durik, A., Vida, M., & Eccles, J. (2006). Task values and ability beliefs as predictors of high school literacy choices: A developmental analysis. *Journal of Educational Psychology, 98*, 382–393.

Eccles, J. S., Adler, T. F., Futterman, R., Goff, S. B., Kaczala, C. M., Meece, J. L., et al. (1983). Expectancies, values, and academic behaviors. In J. T. Spence (Ed.), *Achievement and achievement motivation* (pp. 75–146). San Francisco, CA: Freeman.

Eccles, J. S., & Wigfield, A. (1995). In the mind of the actor: The structure of adolescents' achievement task values and expectancy-related beliefs. *Personality & Social Psychology Bulletin, 21*(3), 215–225. http://dx.doi.org/10.1177/0146167295213003.

Ertmer, P. A., Newby, T. J., Yu, J. H., Liu, W., Tomory, A., Lee, Y. M., et al. (2011). Facilitating students' global perspectives: Collaborating with international partners using Web 2.0 technologies. *The Internet and Higher Education, 14*, 251–261. http://dx.doi.org/10.1016/j.iheduc.2011.05.005.

Fendt, J. (2013). Lost in translation? On mind and matter in management research. *SAGE Open, 3*(2), 1–13. http://dx.doi.org/10.1177/2158244013481358.

Freud, S. (1922). *Beyond the pleasure principle* (J. Strachey, Trans.). London, UK: Hogarth.

Goddard, R. D., Hoy, W. K., & Hoy, A. W. (2004). Collective efficacy beliefs: Theoretical developments, empirical evidence, and future directions. *Educational Researcher, 33*(3), 3–13.

Graham, S., & Weiner, B. (1996). Theories and principles of motivation. In D. C. Berliner & R. Calfee (Eds.), *Handbook of educational psychology* (pp. 63–84). New York, NY: Macmillan.

Greenwald, A. G. (2012). There is nothing so theoretical as a good method. *Perspectives on Psychological Science, 7*(2), 99–108. http://dx.doi.org/10.1177/1745691611434210.

Hoffman, B. (2012). Cognitive efficiency: A conceptual and measurement comparison. *Learning and Instruction, 22*, 133–144. http://dx.doi.org/10.1016/j.learninstruc.2011.09.001.

Hoffman, B., & Schraw, G. (2009). The influence of self-efficacy and working memory capacity on problem-solving efficiency. *Learning and Individual Differences, 19*, 91–100.

Judge, T. A., & Bono, J. E. (2001). Relationship of core self-evaluations traits—self-esteem, generalized self-efficacy, locus of control, and emotional stability—with job satisfaction and job performance: A meta-analysis. *Journal of Applied Psychology, 86*(1), 80–92. http://dx.doi.org/10.1037/0021-9010.86.1.80.

Judge, T. A., Jackson, C. L., Shaw, J. C., Scott, B. A., & Rich, B. L. (2007). Self-efficacy and work-related performance: The integral role of individual differences. *Journal of Applied Psychology, 92*, 107–127.

Karl, K., & Peluchette, J. (2013). Management faculty perceptions of candidates with online doctorates: Why the stigma? *American Journal of Distance Education, 27*(2), 89–99.

Lee, M. H., & Tsai, C. C. (2010). Exploring teachers' perceived self-efficacy and technological pedagogical content knowledge with respect to educational use of the World Wide Web. *Instructional Science, 38*(1), 1–21.

Lewin, K. (1951). In D. Cartwright (Ed.), *Field theory in social science; selected theoretical papers*. New York, NY: Harper & Row.

Lord, R. G., Diefendorff, J. M., Schmidt, A. M., & Hall, R. J. (2010). Self-regulation at work. *Annual Review of Psychology, 61*, 543–568.

Maddux, J. E. (2002). Self-efficacy: The power of believing you can. In C. R. Snyder & S. J. Lopez (Eds.), *Handbook of positive psychology* (pp. 277–287). New York, NY: Oxford University Press.

Martinko, M. J., Douglas, S. C., & Harvey, P. (2006). Attribution theory in industrial and organizational psychology: A review. In G. P. Hodgkinson & J. K. Ford (Eds.), *International review of industrial and organizational psychology* (pp. 127–187). West Sussex: John Wiley & Sons, Ltd.

McClure, J., Meyer, L. H., Garisch, J., Fischer, R., Weir, K. F., & Walkey, F. H. (2011). Students' attributions for their best and worst marks: Do they relate to achievement? *Contemporary Educational Psychology*, *36*(2), 71–81. http://dx.doi.org/10.1016/j.cedpsych.2010.11.001.

McPherson, G. E. (2006). Self-efficacy and music performance. *Psychology of Music*, *34*(3), 322–336. http://dx.doi.org/10.1177/0305735606064841.

Mezulis, A. H., Abramson, L. Y., Hyde, J. S., & Hankin, B. L. (2004). Is there a universal positivity bias in attributions? A meta-analytic review of individual, developmental, and cultural differences in the self-serving attributional bias. *Psychological Bulletin*, *130*(5), 711–747. http://dx.doi.org/10.1037/0033-2909.130.5.711.

Moritz, S. E., Feltz, D. L., Fahrbach, K. R., & Mack, D. E. (2000). The relation of self-efficacy measures to sport performance: A meta-analytic review. *Research Quarterly for Exercise and Sport*, *71*(3), 280–294.

Murphy, P. J., Cooke, R. A., & Lopez, Y. (2013). Firm culture and performance: Intensity's effects and limits. *Management Decision*, *51*(3), 661–679. http://dx.doi.org/10.1108/00251741311309715.

Nagengast, B., Marsh, H. W., Scalas, L. F., Xu, M. K., Hau, K.-T., & Trautwein, U. (2011). Who took the "×" out of expectancy-value theory? A psychological mystery, a substantive-methodological synergy, and a cross-national generalization. *Psychological Science*, *22*(8), 1058–1066. http://dx.doi.org/10.1177/0956797611415540.

Nicholls, A. R., Polman, R., & Levy, A. R. (2010). Coping self-efficacy, pre-competitive anxiety, and subjective performance among athletes. *European Journal of Sport Science*, *10*(2), 97–102. http://dx.doi.org/10.1080/17461390903271592.

Pajares, F. (1996). Self-efficacy beliefs in academic settings. *Review of Educational Research*, *66*(4), 543–578.

Plotnikoff, R. C., Costigan, S. A., Karunamuni, N., & Lubans, D. R. (2013). Social cognitive theories used to explain physical activity behavior in adolescents: A systematic review and meta-analysis. *Preventive Medicine*, *56*(5), 245–253. http://dx.doi.org/10.1016/j.ypmed.2013.01.013.

Plotnikoff, R. C., Lippke, S., Courneya, K. S., Birkett, N., & Sigal, R. J. (2008). Physical activity and social cognitive theory: A test in a population sample of adults with Type 1 or Type 2 Diabetes. *Applied Psychology*, *57*(4), 628–643.

Prussia, G. E., & Kinicki, A. J. (1996). A motivational investigation of group effectiveness using social-cognitive theory. *Journal of Applied Psychology*, *81*(2), 187–198.

Reb, J., & Greguras, G. J. (2010). Understanding performance ratings: Dynamic performance, attributions, and rating purpose. *Journal of Applied Psychology*, *95*(1), 213–220.

Reeve, J. (2009). *Understanding motivation and emotion* (5th ed.). Hoboken, NJ: John Wiley & Sons.

Rotter, J. (1966). Generalized expectancies for internal versus external control of reinforcement. *Psychological Monographs*, *80*, 1–28.

Schultheiss, O. C., & Brunstein, J. C. (2005). An implicit motive perspective on competence. In A. J. Elliot & C. S. Dweck (Eds.), *Handbook of competence and motivation* (pp. 31–51). New York, NY: Guilford Publications.

Simpkins, S. D., Davis-Kean, P. E., & Eccles, J. S. (2006). Math and science motivation: A longitudinal examination of the links between choices and beliefs. *Developmental Psychology*, *42*(1), 70–83. http://dx.doi.org/10.1037/0012-1649.42.1.70.

Sitzmann, T., & Yeo, G. (2013). A meta-analytic investigation of the within-person self-efficacy domain: Is self-efficacy a product of past performance or a driver of future performance? *Personnel Psychology*, *66*(3), 531–568. http://dx.doi.org/10.1111/peps.12035.

Stajkovic, A. D., Lee, D., & Nyberg, A. J. (2009). Collective efficacy, group potency, and group performance: Meta-analyses of their relationships, and test of a mediation model. *Journal of Applied Psychology, 94*(3), 814–828. http://dx.doi.org/10.1037/a0015659.

Stajkovic, A. D., & Luthans, F. (1998). Self-efficacy and work-related performance: A meta-analysis. *Psychological Bulletin, 124*, 240–261. http://dx.doi.org/10.1037/0033-2909.124.2.240.

Sudkamp, A., Kaiser, J., & Moller, J. (2012). Accuracy of teachers' judgments of students' academic achievement: A meta-analysis. *Journal of Educational Psychology, 104*(3), 743–762.

Vancouver, J. B., Thompson, C. M., Tischner, E. C., & Putka, D. J. (2002). Two studies examining the negative effect of self-efficacy on performance. *Journal of Applied Psychology, 87*(3), 506–516. http://dx.doi.org/10.1037/0021-9010.87.3.506.

Viklund, M., & Sjöberg, L. (2008). An Expectancy-Value approach to determinants of trust. *Journal of Applied Social Psychology, 38*(2), 294–313. http://dx.doi.org/10.1111/j.1559-1816.2007.00306.x.

Weiner, B. (1979). A theory of motivation for some classroom experiences. *Journal of Educational Psychology, 71*, 3–25.

Weiner, B. (2010). The development of an attribution-based theory of motivation: A history of ideas. *Educational Psychologist, 45*(1), 28–36.

Weiner, B. (2012). An attribution theory of motivation. In P. M. Van Lange, A. W. Kruglanski, & E. Higgins (Eds.), *Handbook of theories of social psychology* (Vol. 1, pp. 135–155). Thousand Oaks, CA: Sage Publications Ltd.

Wigfield, A., & Cambria, J. (2010). Students' achievement values, goal orientations, and interest: Definitions, development, and relations to achievement outcomes. *Developmental Review, 30*(1), 1–35.

Wigfield, A., Cambria, J., & Eccles, J. S. (2012). Motivation in education. In R. C. Ryan (Ed.), *Oxford handbook of motivation* (pp. 463–478). New York, NY: Oxford University Press.

Wigfield, A., & Eccles, J. S. (2000). Expectancy–value theory of achievement motivation. *Contemporary Educational Psychology, 25*(1), 68–81. http://dx.doi.org/10.1006/ceps.1999.1015.

Wigfield, A., Tonks, S., & Klauda, S. (2009). Expectancy-value theory. In K. R. Wenzel & A. Wigfield (Eds.), *Handbook of motivation at school* (pp. 55–75). New York, NY: Routledge/Taylor & Francis Group.

Wood, R., & Bandura, A. (1989). Impact of conceptions of ability on self-regulatory mechanisms and complex decision making. *Journal of Personality & Social Psychology, 56*, 407–415. http://dx.doi.org/10.1037/0022-3514.56.3.407.

Wright, S., Jenkins-Guarnieri, M., & Murdock, J. (2013). Career development among first-year college students: College self-efficacy, student persistence, and academic success. *Journal of Career Development, 40*(4), 292–310.

Yli-Piipari, S., & Kokkonen, J. (2014). An application of the expectancy-value model to understand adolescents' performance and engagement in physical education. *Journal of Teaching in Physical Education, 33*(2), 250–268. http://dx.doi.org/10.1123/jtpe.2013-0067.

Zimmerman, B. J., Bandura, A., & Martinez-Pons, M. (1992). Self-motivation for academic attainment: The role of self-efficacy beliefs and personal goal setting. *American Educational Research Journal, 29*, 663–676.

Zimmerman, B. J., & Cleary, T. J. (2009). Motives to self-regulate learning: A social cognitive account. In K. R. Wenzel & A. Wigfield (Eds.), *Handbook of motivation at school* (pp. 247–264). New York, NY: Routledge/Taylor & Francis Group.

Zusho, A., Pintrich, P. R., & Cortina, K. S. (2005). Motives, goals, and adaptive patterns of performance in Asian American and Anglo American students. *Learning and Individual Differences, 15*, 141–158.

Can I see the real me?: The powerful influence of self-beliefs on motivated behavior

Can you see the real me, preacher?
Can you see the real me, doctor?
Can you see the real me, mother?
Can you see the real me, me, me?

Peter Townshend

Chapter outline

Principle #40—The psychological or physical presence of others may alter normative behavior 212
Principle #41—Pro-social behaviors are compliant, adaptive, and predictable 216
Principle #42—Pro-social motives are egoistic and altruistic 220
Motivational Leader—*Jessi Colter* 221
Principle #43—Performance inhibiting strategies augment self-worth 225
    Chapter summary/conclusions 229
    Next steps 229
    End of chapter motivational minute 230
References 231

The rock band the *The Who* were onto something when they chanted the lyrics to the song *The Real Me* as part of the 1973 classic rock opera *Quadrophenia*. The psychodramatic theme of the album, and of the subsequent movie, was about the tribulations of establishing a social identity during the turbulent 1960s in Brighton, England. The story featured the adolescent exploits of Jimmy Cooper, a rebellious and indifferent lad, who was painfully searching for his personal identity among four different and conflicted personalities, none of which satisfied his alienated desires and troubled mind. Unfortunately, Jimmy and songwriter Townsend were operating under the misguided impression that individuals are able to precisely articulate and accurately determine the unique psychological characteristics that comprise identity. As we know from Principle #5 (p. 12), individuals are especially prone to misinterpreting their own motives and frequently cannot accurately describe their cognitive processes (Nisbett & Wilson, 1977). In turn, bias sometimes distorts behavioral meaning due to an overwhelming desire to portray the self in socially acceptable ways (Hyman & Sierra, 2011). Perhaps, the more relevant question for Jimmy Cooper, Peter Townshend, and the aspiring motivational detective (MD), is "Can *you* see the real *you?*"

To decipher the real you, or to "find oneself" (Baumeister, 1987, p. 163), is a process that starts with an introspective and evaluative examination of the beliefs, values, and standards that orchestrate behavior. The self is broadly defined as who we are, a personal representation, symbolic of our underlying motives, which represent purpose, characteristics, interests, and idiosyncratic attributes that comprise the totality of our being. The ability to describe and understand the self is grounded in a self-awareness that enables the individual to understand why certain goals are selected and pursued and why we choose to reach our goals using particular strategies. Self-awareness implies that we have the ability to discern the difference between the external self that we elect to divulge publically through visible action, compared with the often clandestine and social self, which we may deliberately choose to obscure or share only selectively with others (Schlenker, 1980).

Ironically, realizing self-awareness and shaping self-representations many times involve a series of introspective and analytical evaluations based upon our relationships, interactions, and comparisons of ourselves to *others*. Considering that the primary function of the self is to gain social acceptance and enhance social position within desired in-groups (Baumeister, 2010), individuals frequently become highly susceptible to social influence. The slightest indication that certain people will be present, either physically or virtually, to observe or evaluate our actions may cause a radical shift in our behaviors and even change the way we think (Dunning, 2011). As a youth, before making an important decision, you may have been advised to ask yourself, "What would I do if my mother were watching?" as a conscientious check on impending action. Although a maternal conscience may not guide your adult actions, every day we make many significant implicit and explicit evaluations of who we are and how we elect to portray ourselves in comparison with the expectations and ideals of significant others, desired in-groups, and affiliative cultures.

At any given moment, we may consciously choose to modify our external self. Faced with the prospect of engaging with one particular peer group, we may choose to be talkative, optimistic, and helpful, while in another setting we may elect to send a different message and intentionally decide to be inflexible, contrarian, or aloof, based merely on group composition or the specific impressions and reactions we wish to generate from others. Our public face applies to virtual arenas as well, as individuals frequently elect to express different facets of their personas, with variations in exhibited traits contextually determined by the type of virtual environment encountered (Childs, 2011). The changes in how we think and behave when alone versus under the influence of others are so pervasive that psychometricians have designed and validated instruments, such as the Predictive Index (Harris, Tracy, & Fisher, 2011), which measure differences between the qualities that individuals expect or believe they should publically exhibit, as opposed to their actual behaviors. Measureable differences are usually observed, solidifying the contention that individuals calibrate their own behaviors based upon a set of measurable standards determined and expected by others.

Consequently, attaining an accurate and realistic self-portrayal is a complicated, challenging, and potentially stressful process because "nearly every action can carry a social meaning that has implications for what a person is like and how he or she should be treated" (Schlenker, 1980, p. 5). Individuals develop a "relational self" (Brewer & Gardner, 1996, p. 83) that dictates how we want to be perceived. Once the relational self is affirmed, individuals engage in evaluative comparisons of the self to the preferred set of cultural standards or in-group norms, hoping to voluntarily fit in, or alternatively, deliberately stand out. By example, motivational leaders Alec Torelli and LaSonya Moore specifically rebuffed stereotypical standards, setting themselves apart from their peers. LaSonya consciously rejected the typical consequences of having a child at a young age and relying upon social programs for financial assistance. She stated that one of her primary motives was to escape the "hood" at all costs. Alec Torelli mentioned disdain for *Tourney Pros*, who, in addition to craving poker winnings, are highly motivated to developing glamorous television images to secure sponsors, generate publicity, and increase personal notoriety. LaSonya and Alec deliberately elected to stand out, not fit in.

Individuals are motivated to attain consistency between their enacted and desired selves (Higgins, 1987). Psychological vulnerability, primarily in the form of anxiety and negative emotions, results when individuals realize that their actual self is discrepant from their desired self. Unfavorable discrepant self-evaluations often result in feelings that the self is incompetent, insincere, inconsiderate, phony, thoughtless, and unattractive (Baumeister, Tice, & Hutton, 1989). In extreme cases, self-discrepancies result in dramatic self-esteem deficits and may lead to clinical depression (Sowislo & Orth, 2013). Paradoxically, those who best know the self may suffer as heightened self-awareness may contribute to the development of a chronic discrepancy fixation. This sardonic consequence of effective introspection promotes sarcastic and negative ruminations. Author Kafka claimed, "I have the feeling of myself only when I am unbearably unhappy," while occasional celebrity Courtney Love caustically proclaimed, "Only dumb people are happy!" suggesting that a lack of self-awareness is, indeed, a blessing in disguise.

When applying the paradigm of self-awareness to evaluating the superiority of their academic fortunes, individuals are faced with a comparative dilemma. They can associate their most current achievement with their own past performance, identify an objective mastery standard, such as a learning target, or compare themselves to another person deemed similar in ability or temperament. Chapter 4 discussed the developmental trajectory of social comparisons and identified two primary reasons why individuals elect relational benchmarks. First, individuals may not have sufficient experience or past performance or may lack available or understandable task-relevant data to make informed comparisons with a standard of mastery. Second, individuals may be highly motivated to make positive comparisons with others as a means of attaining a self-serving ego boost (Wheeler & Suls, 2005). A third viable explanation for person-to-person appraisals suggests that social comparison fosters positive self-evaluation and serves as a way to validate personal capabilities against societal norms (Buunk, Groothof, & Siero, 2007; Festinger, 1954). In school, many social comparisons are motivated by the desire to fit in with emerging peer groups, which potentially contribute to affirming positive self-images based upon group inclusion (Alderman, 2004). Organizationally, social comparisons serve as a barometer to calibrate and justify leadership styles, set performance standards, and establish organizational norms for social behavior (Greenberg, Ashton-James, & Ashkanasy, 2007), which subsequently helps individuals successfully assimilate within an organizational culture.

Social comparisons are broadly categorized as either upward or downward in trajectory. Upward comparisons can provide useful information for positive self-enhancement (Mussweiler, Gabriel, & Bodenhausen, 2000), suggesting that the individual is motivated by self-improvement, enticed by the prospect of attaining the skills and abilities of a viable and respected behavioral model, perceived to have similar characteristics to the individual (Buunk et al., 2007). Upward comparisons are motivationally adaptive because the individual strives to improve, such as when academically aspiring to earn better grades, or to master content. Upward comparisons are more productive when undertaken anonymously, as individuals are able to physically insulate themselves from the evaluation of others, who, if physically present, may potentially ascribe skill deficits or inferior ability to the individual (Ybema & Buunk, 1993).

Downward comparisons are self-protective and are typically undertaken by individuals lacking the necessary confidence to make upward comparisons, by persons with lower levels of self-esteem, and by those who are worried about what others think of them. Individuals with a downward comparison trajectory tend to have inflated perceptions of their subjective well-being because they believe they are better off in comparison with others (Wills, 1981). The downward comparisons generate positive affect in many individuals because of the presumption that others are more disadvantaged than the individual making the downward comparison. Ultimately, the feeling of superiority enhances the self-esteem of the comparative beneficiary. The phenomenon of downward comparison is especially striking for individuals suffering health complications (Tennen, McKee, & Affleck, 2000). For instance, individuals who perceive themselves as better off than someone else (or who believe that someone else is more ill), independent of physical disability, report higher overall subjective well-being (Buunk et al., 2007) and have greater reductions in the severity of health problems following cancer (Eiser & Eiser, 2000).

The physical, emotional, and cognitive reactions to social comparisons are of critical importance to MDs. Considering that individuals frequently base their self-evaluations on their perceived degree of fit and alignment with significant others, self-esteem and corresponding self-worth contingencies develop during the evaluation process. Individuals will tend to appraise their degree of competence not entirely based upon actual ability and knowledge but will, instead, make personal capability evaluations based upon the presumed competency beliefs others ascribe to the individual. Covington (1984) suggested that evaluation of self-worth is a consequence of academic cultures because competitive academic environments contribute to the self-evaluation of attributes needed for classroom success, primarily realized through ability assessments. According to Covington, "perceptions of ability are critical to the self-protective process, since for many students, the mere possession of ability signifies worthiness" (p. 4). Individuals will naturally tend to seek out environments that generate positive self-esteem, which, in turn, promotes improved perceptions of self-worth. Academic and workplace performance arenas are high-stakes for many individuals. Who we are and the general conception of our competency is based, in part, on instigating outcomes deemed of value to others. As a personal motive, the perception of positive self-worth alone should be a catalyst directing individuals toward performance tasks at which they have a probability of being successful while steering clear of those targets deemed overly challenging or having a high probability of failure.

Unlike the previously discussed motives related to historical attributions and prospective self-efficacy evaluations (Chapter 6, p. 139), the source of self-worth assessments and corresponding competency beliefs does not originate solely from observed results. Criteria-based outcomes are important but are primarily relevant from the perspective of how they are perceived. Many times, individuals stake their self-evaluated academic reputation and their mirrored reputation by others based not upon what they accomplish but on reactions to their achievements. Feasibly, two individuals can achieve identical results but reach entirely different conclusions about the suitability of the outcomes. One person may react positively, resulting in enhancements to self-worth, while the other person views the same results as frustrating and self-defeating, leading to negative ruminations and deteriorating self-worth perceptions.

The differential reactivity phenomenon is naturally observed when the skeptical and marginally competent learner earns a "B" on an examination when expecting a lower score. Emotions resulting from the "B" grade range from ecstasy to surprise, but the "B" outcome is positively perceived because it was better than expected, leading to elevated perceptions of self-worth. Conversely, when the overachieving peer earns the same "B" grade, the learner becomes fraught with anxiety. Perceptions of worthiness are decimated, not because of ability differences but because the overachiever expects more and emphatically stakes self-perceptions on academic ability. The potential that the grade may be perceived as relatively inferior, in light of his or her ability perceptions, threatens self-worth. Individuals not living up to their own expectations will experience feelings of guilt, shame, and humiliation, especially in highly vulnerable situations where substantial effort was expended but anticipated results were not achieved.

The *coup de grâce*, however, is not the academic outcome but the potential that the individual will evaluate and define his or her self based upon the observed results. Self-definition may usurp traditional logic, with worthiness anchored not upon knowledge or results, but on the qualitative consequences of forestalled achievement. Covington cautioned that "one's first priority is to act in ways that minimize the implications of failure, namely, that one lacks ability" (1984, p. 8). Thus, to maintain a positive self-image, individuals will go to great lengths to insulate themselves from threats to self-worth. When individuals perceive a threat to positive aspirations of self-worth, they tend to engage in a series of strategic failure-avoiding manipulations. The strategies are designed to deflect any possible inferences concerning ability and concurrently avoid deterioration of self-worth perceptions. In the words of Covington, "students are likely to choose—if choose they must—to endure the pangs of guilt rather than the humiliation of incompetency" (1984, p. 11). Guilt results from the pain of avoidable failure, while humiliation occurs when invested effort reaps few rewards, promoting anxiety and trepidation based upon the presumption that significant others may believe the individual lacks sufficient ability to succeed. To avoid the stigma of inferior ability, individuals will protect their self-worth perceptions by shifting blame for failure to external or uncontrollable causes, such as downplaying the significance of results or criticizing test integrity (Covington, 2009). The individual assumes little or no responsibility for results, leaving positive self-worth intact.

At least three conclusions can be drawn from the powerful influence of self-worth perceptions. First, individuals change behaviors based on others, and many exhibit a strong proclivity to look good in the vantage of the admirer's eyes. Second, individuals react differently to undesired outcomes, notwithstanding absolute results, because of the consequence of the outcome on self-evaluations. Third, people actively strive to insulate themselves from disparaging and negative self-worth perceptions by engaging in a variety of failure-avoiding strategies. However, the exact influence of other people, the consequences of individual self-worth differences, and the unique set of strategies that individuals use to fortify positive evaluations are of great concern and thus discussed next.

Principle #40—The psychological or physical presence of others may alter normative behavior

Many classic studies in social psychology reveal how the presence of others influences our personal perceptions and the behaviors we are willing to demonstrate in public. In the seminal conformity study, Asch (1956) asked experimental *subjects* (research study participants) to compare two sets of geometric lines for accuracy of length. Under the influence of a group of disagreeable *confederates* (people knowing the actual purpose of the study), subjects repeatedly agreed to obviously wrong answers when comparing a shorter line to a supposedly similar, but actually much longer line. The study illustrated how individuals will knowingly make judgments in contrast to their own personal beliefs and conform to normative behavior based upon suggestions from others. The classic Milgram obedience experiments (1963) revealed that individuals can be pressured into giving another person what appeared to be painful electric shocks of escalating voltage, merely at the suggestions of an authoritative source, in this case a researcher wearing a lab coat. During the experiment, 65% of study participants obeyed the researcher's instructions and were willing to deliver what they believed were 450-volts electric shocks to a study participant who did not correctly recall a specific word in a staged memory experiment.

The presence of others can also tragically result in behavioral lethargy or failure to act. The most salient example of collective apathy is the horrific story of young Kitty Genovese, who, in 1964, was brutally assaulted and raped in an apartment courtyard within earshot of 38 witnesses. Upon questioning from the police immediately after the crime, witnesses indicated that they did not call the police because they expected that someone else would make the call. The phenomenon of inaction resulted in coining the infamous *bystander effect* (Latané & Darley, 1970), which contends that individuals are more willing and likely to offer help when alone, than when part of a group. While some accounts of the Genovese murder were blamed on pluralistic ignorance (Latané & Rodin, 1969), no witness indicated withholding help specifically because of conflicted Samaritan beliefs or due to lack of a presumed obligation to help another person in distress. Instead, enacted behavior was discordant with individual beliefs and blamed on the social influence of others. Although the specifics of the Genovese case are sometimes disputed (Manning, Levine, & Collins, 2007), the general inferences are not; people act differently when others are watching.

The seminal examples described here suggest that individuals are vulnerable to a variety of social and contextual influences and may exhibit certain thoughts and actions contrary to personal beliefs and private behavior. The theories of planned behavior (TPB) and reasoned action (Ajzen, 1991) contend that individuals evaluate their beliefs and attitudes as a prelude to motivated action. Further, TPB indicates that behavioral intentions are mediated by socially acceptable normative beliefs that modify an individual's actions. Normative beliefs undergo scrutiny by the individual, whereby the person assesses the integrative and relative fit of the normative beliefs to their own personal beliefs and behavioral intentions. If the individual is of the presumption that his personal beliefs are weak compared with societal norms and the person believes he can exert control over a situation, social pressure will induce the person to follow normative patterns. In the absence of control, or when personal beliefs are deeply entrenched or strongly conflict with normative beliefs, there is reduced likelihood that the person will exhibit socially desirable behavior. In other words, societal norms and pressures can ignite or diffuse behavioral intentions, influencing behavioral direction and intensity based upon the commitment to one's beliefs. Frequently, people yield to behavioral intentions that conflict with societal norms, resorting to the maxim of "go with the flow," accelerating action based upon the intensity of societal expectations, lukewarm self-beliefs, and the prospect of feeling in control.

When subjected to excessive social pressure, individuals may display a variety of behavioral differences in public and private, primarily as a means of inducing approval from others and strengthening their public identities (Gollwitzer, 1986). The phenomenon of being easily persuaded by the external expectations of others and portraying the self in particular ways to foster social inclusion is termed *self-presentation* or the process of *impression management*, which dictates that individuals actively seek to elicit and control reactions from others (Schlenker, 1980). Personal control may provoke both positive and negative reactions in others based upon the individual's behavioral intentions. If you have ever heard the words, "Are you trying to start an argument with me?" or "What's your problem?" you will quickly realize the power of impression management! Table 8.1 illustrates concrete examples from diverse domains where the presence of others is a catalyst that usually induces normative behavior, sometimes in contrast to, or despite the intensity of, one's convictions or behavior patterns typically displayed when alone.

The contingencies related to *how* individuals exert influence on others transcend behavior. The psychological or physical presence of others motivates change not only in the public domain but also in how we respond to and feel retrospectively about the behaviors we exhibit. The self-assessments generated by the qualitative and affective assessments of our successes and failures are frequently labeled as the degree of *self-esteem* we possess. Self-esteem is generally conceived as a personality variable

Table 8.1 Selected summary of empirical results supporting the influence of sociocultural norms on exhibited behavior

Behavior	Effects of social influence	Evidence
Dieting	Girls begin dieting at younger ages. Norms instill more concerns about appearance resulting in greater body dissatisfaction.	Strahan et al. (2008)
Social eating	Social influences result in greater or reduced consumption based on type of host, group composition, gender, and observer type.	Herman, Roth, and Polivy (2003)
Health screening	Women are more likely to seek breast cancer screenings when supported by spouse, compared with no spousal support.	Steadman and Rutter (2004)
Aggressive driving	Level of aggressive teen driving significantly increases in the presence of peers or decreases based upon extent of parental involvement.	Prato and Kaplan (2013)
Public littering	People are more prone to littering when in the presence of other litterers. Dirt begets dirt.	Cialdini, Reno, and Kallgren (1990)
Academic participation	University students participate less in class because of fear of peer disapproval from other students accounting for large negative self-reported perceptions of participation.	Weaver and Qi (2005)
Gratuities	Patrons give higher tips to servers when the server compliments the patron and when the patron seeks social approval from the server.	Seiter (2007)

(Brown & Marshall, 2006) that influences our ascriptions of overall self-worth. Self-esteem describes the personal evaluations of the self in relation to others or to a set of arbitrary values that are determined by our relationships, contexts of application, or culturally-determined normative standards. The resulting assessments are self-evaluations, or judgments, of our accomplishments that either produce satisfaction or promote disenchantment based upon the subjective appraisal of outcomes in comparison to expectations. While researchers debate whether self-esteem is the cause or the result of self-evaluations (Crocker & Wolfe, 2001), positive assessments elevate levels of self-esteem, while negative evaluations decrease self-esteem. Ultimately, these self-judgments lead to appraisals of self-worth, and many researchers use the terms self-esteem and self-worth interchangeably (Crocker & Wolfe, 2001).

Self-evaluations may correspond with prosperous emotions, such as feelings of fulfillment, elation, and pride, after a positively evaluated achievement, while not meeting self-expectations may lead to feelings of disappointment, shame, guilt, or humility. Ascriptions of self-worth are personal and quite arbitrary, as it is not the event, per se, that determines self-evaluation valence, but the reaction to the event. For instance, Alex Dixon correctly recalling a word when searching the recesses of her vocabulary may be a strong source of satisfaction leading to positive self-esteem, while the same phenomenon for eloquent speaker Nick Lowery would be inconsequential and effectively esteem neutral. Thus, we can infer that self-esteem is grounded in a foundational assessment of our own perceived capabilities, in relation to our anticipated potential. Although assessments are relative to the individual, we should recognize that individuals higher in self-esteem frequently set more challenging goals, have stronger expectancies of goal attainment, and exhibit a higher commitment toward attaining their goals (Hollenbeck & Klein, 1987; Hrabluik, Latham, & McCarthy, 2012).

Self-awareness and degree of self-view positivity are the primary psychological distinctions between individuals described as possessing high self-esteem (HSE) in comparison with low self-esteem (LSE) (Campbell & Lavallee, 1993). Individuals with HSE show consistency and clarity of beliefs characterized by expectations of task-based success, as opposed to LSE individuals who are skeptical of their abilities and uncertain as to what actions would promote successful outcomes (Tice, 1993). Subsequently, the HSE individual seeks ego-inflating opportunities that, if mastered, enhance impressions of self-worth. Consequently, the LSE person will deliberately avoid opportunities that have the potential to result in failure instead taking solace in choosing more conservative and cautious endeavors, exhibiting a self-protection motive and thereby avoiding the risk of possible humiliation or social rejection.

A crucial aspect of the HSE–LSE distinction is manifested in appraisals of ongoing self-worth based on task-based experience. Early life experiences in performance domains, such as athletics, socialization, or academics lead to self-assessments and corresponding evaluations of self-worth. Many times, children will experience early-life emotionally laden triumphs and challenges that expose the child to contextually driven and unsolicited socialized feedback, presumably from parents, caregivers, and teachers. When experiencing success, the developing child hears encouraging remarks, such as "Great effort!" or "Fantastic job!" or "You're the best!" Failure to reach performance goals is met with optimistic reassurances, such as "Try harder," "Don't give up," or "You will improve," to deflect the negative emotionality of falling short of one's goals. These basic task-contingent evaluations contribute to self-identity formation and eventual self-competency conclusions that contribute to evaluations of self-worth in relation to specific tasks. The spiraling evaluation process is recursive and perpetuating as Brown and Marshall (2006) succinctly described:

> *When low self-esteem people encounter negative feedback their self-evaluations become more negative and their feelings of self-worth fall. When high self-esteem people encounter negative feedback they maintain their high self-evaluations and protect or quickly restore their feelings of self-worth (p. 7).*

Eventually, the certainty of emotions aligned with particular tasks becomes cumulative, either forestalling or encouraging future task engagement. The probabilistic emotion supersedes the usual satisfaction of task completion, resulting in either avoidance or shallow task commitment by the LSE individual. Conversely, the HSE person is more resilient and willing to try harder, not easily discouraged from attempting the most challenging tasks, even when suffering humiliation (Baumeister & Tice, 1985).

But the rosy profile of the HSE individual bears many thorns. The relation among elevated levels of self-worth and work performance or academic achievement is, at best, ambiguous (Baumeister, Campbell, Krueger, & Vohs, 2003). Little evidence actually supports the notion that HSE causes accelerated performance or results in learning gains. Individuals high in self-esteem may feel good about themselves, but they are also prone to having exaggerated views of the self. These views, predicated on ignoring important and relevant feedback, may hinder positive socialization and relationships, promote lack of self-regulatory skill, and lead to individuals inflating ability perceptions when skills may be lacking (Crocker & Park, 2004). Regardless of the potential liabilities for the HSE person, we can summarily conclude that normative and social factors exert an enormous influence on individual thoughts and behaviors. The question remains, however, as to why others exert such a tremendous influence on behavior and how MDs can harness knowledge of conformity and socialization to effectively cultivate motivated behavior. We next examine specific social influences and the behavior these influences may potentially cause.

Principle #41—Pro-social behaviors are compliant, adaptive, and predictable

The social affects described thus far suggest that the influence of others can, at times, be disturbing, self-defeating, and clearly inhibit self-determination. Evidence was presented that friends and strangers alike can inflict subtle or direct psychological control over our decisions, akin to manipulating us, despite our common sense, logic, or personal beliefs. The power of others is so pervasive that gullible humans will engage in risky and unhealthy behavior, tolerating danger and tempting fate, despite knowing the harmful consequences of their actions and the likelihood of disastrous outcomes. Motivated by the desire to enhance positive impressions and develop self-worth, individuals will risk skin exposure without sunscreen use, drive recklessly when with friends, be promiscuous and engage in unprotected sex, continue smoking to avoid weight gain, and participate in dangerous sports, such as extreme skiing, risking permanent disability or death, all in the name of admirable self-presentation (Leary, Tchividijian, & Kraxberger, 1994).

While the sordid side of influence cannot be denied, we are also inclined to exhibit a wide variety of supportive, industrious, and gratuitous behaviors *because* of others. The benefits of *prosocial behavior* whereby individuals and groups engage in a variety of helping and cooperative behaviors that are beneficial to others are enormous (Mussen & Eisenberg-Berg, 1977). Our culture abounds with iconic symbols of prosocial behavior, such as traffic lights, group discounts, online music swapping, and self-directed work teams that provide various incentives for us to socialize, collaborate, and work together. In the classroom, pedagogical methods, such as constructivism and guided discovery, are used to engage learners and leverage the positive motivational benefits of working together as a means to master learning and problem solving goals. The myriad of variables that influence prosocial motives and subsequent behavior are far too numerous to comment upon individually. Instead I examine *why* individuals across cultures will frequently offer unsolicited help to seemingly benefit others, volunteer their time and services, and categorically comply with a multitude of requests from arbitrary "superiors," keeping in mind that exhibited behaviors and espoused motives may be a façade and not portray who we truly are or hope to be.

Prosocial behavior can be explained in many ways. Cialdini and Griskevicius (2010) suggested that individuals have innate needs to engage in goal-directed behavior. People prefer to attribute causality of outcomes to personal actions, not random events, and tend to realize an immense satisfaction when achieving desired results. From an evolutionary perspective, reaching premeditated goals is adaptive; During the goal attainment process individuals hone and regulate critical skills necessary for survival, ultimately enhancing personal longevity, *if* successful. Psychologically, goal attainment contributes to positive self-evaluations, solidifying public reputations and giving groups the impression of our value as a group member. Physiologically, prosocial behavior is especially significant among kin and for the perpetuation of one's lineage, based on "promoting the survival of those who share your genetic make-up" (Kassin, Fein, & Markus, 2008, p. 347). Summarily, behavior supporting others provides social, collective, and cultural benefits.

Engaging in prosocial behavior is *personally* beneficial in at least three ways: (1) Being involved in the success of others satisfies our need for affiliation (Correll & Park, 2005); (2) helping others makes us feel good by elevating mood (Wegener, Petty, & Smith, 1995); and (3) assisting others affords us the social and materialistic benefits of group participation (Penner, Dovidio, Piliavin, & Schroeder, 2005). Collectively, these reasons suggest that one important motive for prosocial behavior is our own psychological prosperity; it boosts self-worth evaluations. Unfortunately, many times, awareness of prosocial motives may be unconscious and personally elusive (Penner et al., 2005), inhibiting a person's ability to actually see the real "me." The phenomenon of demonstrating effort to benefit others while actually helping ourselves is known as *egoism* (Batson, Ahmad & Stocks, 2011). Thus, prosocial behavior that may appear to be demonstrated for the service of others can actually be exhibited exclusively for personal gain. The egoism motive is especially instrumental when we are already in a good mood, serving the purpose of perpetuating the positive mood (Piliavin, 2003). However, we also tend to help others when we feel bad about ourselves because the process of helping often leads to a positive mood change and restoration (Carlson & Miller, 1987; Weinstein & Ryan, 2010).

Prosocial behavior manifests in a variety of ways. First, many individuals subscribe to the principle of *reciprocity* whereby individuals feel obligated to respond in kind when they believe others have helped them. The human consciousness is bound in the evaluation and integration of personal and sociocultural equity assessments. When someone does us a favor, we reciprocate. When a favor is unreciprocated, anger and tempestuous reactions may follow because most individuals believe in the restoration of social or materialistic inequity (van Doorn, Zeelenberg, & Breugelmans, 2014). I have mordant memories of inequities resolved during family feuds over the calculation of the appropriate amounts or the value of planned wedding or baby-shower gifts, based exclusively on what was received in a similar situation. Similarly, obligatory debt has social ramifications, such as when my daughter Rebecca accepted an iPod as a gift from a not-so-secret admirer who had hopeful expectations of receiving "something" in return. At times, we feel obligated to socially entertain friends or colleagues, after accepting a similar invitation. The obligatory trend to reciprocate transcends dyads and families, extending to strangers through indirect reciprocity. The *spillover effect* suggests that we are willing to do favors, be "nicer," and help others we do not even know, provided that the person in need has been kind to a mutual friend or relative (Liang & Meng, 2013).

A second social influence whereby individuals are willing to comply with the requests of others, due, at least in part, to enhance positive self-impressions, is the consistency motive (Cialdini & Griskevicius, 2010). Consistency suggests that individuals have espoused values and beliefs that substantiate identity and contribute to the impressions we imprint on others. Consistency becomes important because uniformity of behavior implies commitment, loyalty, and stability, which are highly desirable human qualities (Bendapudi & Berry, 1997; Cialdini, Trost, & Newsom, 1995). Once a philosophical or behavioral commitment has been espoused, such as giving money to a worthwhile charity, consistency principles suggest we are more likely to demonstrate that type of behavior toward affiliated causes. My philanthropic girlfriend, Karen, once made the charitable gesture of donating $10 to an animal rights group, only to receive a barrage of mail order solicitations in the subsequent months, suggesting that she live up to her public commitment to animals by making additional donations to organizations purportedly designed to save dogs, cats, tigers, lions, horses, cattle, and whales. Many of these donation requests included nominal gifts, such as shiny coins, $2 US notes, calendars, address labels, flags, or t-shirts, hoping to take advantage of her admirable kindness by using the social obligatory motives described in the previous paragraph.

A third factor inducing prosocial behavior is individual responses to requests based on actual or purported power. Almost all societies are structured in social hierarchies. Leaders at the hierarchy apex are granted certain rights and privileges as a condition of leadership—advantages that are not readily offered to or assumed by subordinates. Leadership privilege connotes direct and indirect influence of one person on another. *Compliance* implies a purposeful expectation to complete an act under a controlling influence, such as when individuals acquiesce to supervisory demands. Responding affirmatively to a compliance request is oddly comforting for the individual because the correct response means that the individual has attained a proximal reality-based goal (as well as continuing employment). *Conformity* suggests that individuals respond to leadership direction, not by obligation, but based upon perceived norms, expectations, and indirect social influence (Cialdini & Goldstein, 2004). When capitulating to conformity, responses to leadership power are typically motivated in two ways: informational or normative. *Informational* influence suggests that the powerful other is an accurate and trustworthy source of information. People respond affirmatively to informational influence because the individual making the request is perceived as a qualitatively superior source of information, possessing greater knowledge than the uninformed or inexperienced individual conforming to the informational influence. Conformity under *normative* influence is motivated by social approval, as many individuals conform because they prefer to align with others and avoid the perception of social defiance, which frequently results in being ostracized for recalcitrant and uncooperative behavior, especially in organizations (Begley, Lee, & Hui, 2006).

Despite power hierarchies and conformity pressure, some individuals will dissent, dispute authority, be disobedient, and rebuff compliant behavior, but why? First, we should operate under the understanding that based upon contextual conditions, such as the proximity and strength of the conformity influence (Latané, 1981), individuals will situationally exhibit a range of behaviors from fully compliant to fully defiant. Recalling the classic Milgram experiment (1963), 35% of the participants ignored the researcher's instructions to continue to shock the confederate with up to 450 volts of electricity and, instead, quit the experiment despite the researcher's multiple stern warnings that stopping was not allowed. In the Milgram study, the experimental subject could not physically see (but could hear) the confederate actor grimacing in imaginary pain from the pretend shocks, thus lessening exposure. Second, the experimenter had a high degree of authoritarian strength that was intensified by wearing a lab coat. Although you may be skeptical that a lab coat or the social status of an individual can encourage people to give electric shocks, Bushman (1988) found that individuals are more likely to follow orders given by someone dressed as a security guard, compared with the same person being dressed in regular work clothes, even when the request has nothing to do with the security guard's position (e.g., picking up garbage in the street). Third, Milgram's groundbreaking experiment was criticized for some methodological imprecision that may have biased the results (Reicher & Haslam, 2011), suggesting that perhaps other explanations for disobedience are warranted and justified. Specifically, Reicher and Haslam proposed that *social identity* was a prevailing variable in dissention. Once individuals formed a relationship with another study participant, social pressure to dissent increased because the individuals wanted to be seen positively in the eyes of other participants, again suggesting that our own self-worth evaluations and how we want to be perceived by others are socially grounded and instrumental in mediating compliant and conforming behavior.

We can reasonably infer that individuals with deeply entrenched beliefs, high domain-specific knowledge, and HSE are more willing to reject normative behavior because of high ascriptions of self-worth. Pitesa and Thau (2013) studied espoused reasons for resisting and rejecting overtures of unethical organizational behavior. The researchers hypothesized that individuals who directed more attention to themselves and those who exhibited a "private self-focus" would be less likely to make unethical decisions. Self-focus was defined as "the attentional state of being aware of personal thoughts and feelings" (Fenigstein, 1979, p. 76). Individuals with higher "self-focus" paid less attention to work environmental factors and, instead, relied more heavily on self-perceptions to make their ethical decisions. The results of the study concluded that individuals using an introspective focus mediated the effects of power on behavior, suggesting that at a minimum, self-awareness and self-perceptions in relation to authority figures can radically influence organizational cohesiveness and behavior.

While knowing *why* people are socially responsive is one part of the MD's challenge, application of that knowledge is highly useful. The practical aspects of how adaptive prosocial behavior impacts individuals is perhaps best illustrated by a workplace study conducted by Thau, Tröster, Aquino, Pillutla, and De Cremer (2013) who investigated how the leadership behavior of supervisors influenced employee self-worth perceptions and intergroup dynamics among co-workers. Thau and colleagues hypothesized that preferential treatment from supervisors led to employees initiating social comparison with co-workers, which ultimately influenced evaluations of their own self-worth based on perceptions of preferred comparative treatment. When supervisory treatment was manipulated, participants who were treated best rated their self-worth higher than those employees treated less favorably. In two related studies, preferential supervisor treatment predicted greater adherence to normative and desired organizational behavior (e.g., not stealing company property), as well as encouraging a greater willingness in employees to engage in gratuitous behaviors beneficial to others. In essence, a conscious and deliberate emphasis on variations of kind and considerate leadership style supported individual psychological growth and overall group cohesion. Additionally, the perception of better treatment from supervisors led to higher ascriptions of self-worth in the individuals. These findings suggest that it is possible to concurrently orchestrate contextual environments and influence self-evaluations that promote adaptive motivation, result in congenial behavior, and support the egoistic prosocial motives that are highly useful to promote cooperation in others.

Principle #42—Pro-social motives are egoistic and altruistic

Reflecting on the antecedents of cooperative behavior, it may seem that egoistic motives and self-satisfaction of psychological or materialistic needs underlie most instances of prosocial behavior. While an egoistic interpretation is frequently viable and accurate, the explanation is insufficient to explain the full spectrum of prosocial behaviors. Sometimes, we are specifically motivated to help others with no expectation of intended benefits in return. In these cases, individuals exhibit *altruism*, a special form of cooperative and gratuitous behavior, primarily motivated by "the expenditure of the self in the service of others" (Cavalier, 2000, p. 68). Altruism differs from other types of prosocial behavior because when motives are exclusively altruistic, personal needs become subordinate, suppressed, or deferred in order to satisfy the needs of others. Although frequently individuals receive egoistic benefits from instances of altruism, self-benefits are unintended consequences of the helping process (Batson et al., 2011). Altruistic motives are endemic to many professions where people, sometimes referred to as "superheroes," regularly exhibit self-sacrifice for the benefit of others. Individuals demonstrating unadulterated altruism run into burning buildings, spontaneously perform Samaritan acts, or potentially risk their own psychological harm while helping those less fortunate or in need, such as the frequent challenges experienced when working in the first responder, medical, or teaching professions.

One such person is country music star Jessi Colter. Although not a doctor or teacher, from an altruistic perspective Jessi is a prototypical model of someone who forestalled personal gain to unselfishly help others. Like many family matriarchs, Jessi elected to devote much of life to her husband and now is dedicating her time, partly, to helping her son be as successful as possible. Considering that Jessi was married to country music pioneer and icon Waylon Jennings for over 30 years, the evidence speaks loudly in her favor. Jessi indicated, "I believe that you live so that others can believe in you. It starts by asking yourself, how can I help in this situation?" (J. Colter, personal communication, August 15, 2014). Jessi downplayed her persuasive abilities and her personality is notably reserved and highly spiritual, but she readily admitted that helping others starts with leading by example. Despite her reserved nature, many people give Jessi credit for keeping her superstar husband alive through turbulent times while navigating the pitfalls of fame and fortune. She described the challenges of resisting hedonistic temptation that often occurs when traveling on the road 300 days a year. Several times, she stressed the importance of stability and commitment to one's own self-values as the key to leading a fulfilling life and being able to give unto yourself in the service of others.

Motivational Leader—*Jessi Colter*

One might not figure how a lovely girl from a strict Pentecostal family would become a leading lady "Outlaw," but Jessi Colter is not your average woman. Born Mirriam Johnson in Phoenix, Arizona, to a race car builder father and a preacher mother, Jessi Colter was anything but ordinary, starting her career as a church pianist at the age of 11 years. Soon after, Jessi was in demand to play her piano and sing at talent shows, local television shows, school assemblies, school dances, and weddings. At 18 years, she appeared on *Dick Clark's American Bandstand* singing *Lonesome Road*.  It did not take long for Mirriam Johnson, as she was called back then, to be noticed, and she caught the eye of Rock and Roll Hall of Fame guitarist Duane Eddy, who she married in 1963 in lavish ceremony in Las Vegas with Dick Clark serving as best man! After 6 years of marriage, the two separated and eventually divorced, but for this talented, young singer-songwriter, the best was yet to come.

After her divorce Jessi returned to Phoenix and met Waylon Jennings, who was so taken with her voice that he invited her to record a duet with him. Waylon helped Jessi secure an RCA record deal and co-produced the tracks for her first album titled *A Country Star Is Born*. By the time the record was released, the couple were married. At the suggestion of RCA's Chet Atkins, Mirriam changed her stage name to Jessi Colter in honor of her great grandfather, Jesse Colter, who was rumored to be a member of the Jesse James' outlaw gang.

In 1975, Jessi recorded her debut single, *I'm Not Lisa* The song was an instant success and reached #1 on the Billboard Country Chart and the song peaked at #4 on Billboard's US Pop Chart. In 1976, she recorded another hit *What's Happened to Blue Eyes*, and soon after completed two more highly successful albums, *Jessi* and *Diamond in the Rough*. The beautiful singer-songwriter continued to enjoy burgeoning fame and charting singles, but she also found success working with her husband Waylon. Colter appeared on the double-platinum album *Wanted! The Outlaws* along with Jennings, Tompall Glaser, and Willie Nelson.

Colter and Jennings released their first formal duets album, *Leather and Lace*, in February 1981. After taking many years off to raise her son, in 1996, Jessi recorded a children's album entitled, *Jessi Colter Sings Songs for Kids: Songs from Around the World*. This album also included a video, which she starred in, along with her husband Waylon Jennings and her old songwriting partner, Basil McDavid. This album had 21 tracks, which include children's music from different parts of the world, including Europe and Latin America.

Jessi Colter continued to record and perform after Waylon's death in February 2002. She has done many tribute compilations to her late husband's career. She frequently performs around the country, often on the same stage as her country-music star son, Shooter, appearing at major venues and music festivals such as Austin's annual SXSW event. Jessi and Steven Van Zandt, famed member of the Bruce Springsteen band and star of HBO drama, *The Sopranos*, launched Sirius Radio's, *Outlaw Country*, station during 2004 in Scottsdale Arizona. In 2006, Jessi released her most recent Grammy-nominated album *Out of the Ashes* to wide critical acclaim.

Jessi continues to perform, frequently appearing at major philanthropic and charity events. Soon you will see and hear Jessi tell the behind-the-scenes story of the *Outlaw Era*, when she appears on Ken Burns' documentary, *Study of Country Music*, to be aired on PBS. The award-winning director/writer is chronicling country music history from the 1920s to the present and appropriately includes Jessi for her lifetime of industry contributions and musical achievement.

It may be difficult to tell from Jessi's brief biography what really matters to her. Jessi exemplifies the empathetic style of altruism described below. If she had not put the needs of others before her own, her music career may have turned out much differently. She intentionally deviated from her own career path for her late husband and continues to do so for her son Shooter Jennings, who, under her tutelage, has emerged as a star performer. Jessi explained, "I pursue what my heart is stirred to do, I have been on the bench so to speak, but I pick my moments. She added, I express what my heart feels, there is a dark side to life that has opened my heart to love more and be compassionate of others and their weaknesses" (J. Colter, personal communication, August 15, 2014). While the magnitude of Jessi's influence on others is scientifically immeasurable, many of her self-views and her enacted behaviors originated through consideration of how her life intertwined with those around her. She often subjugated her own needs for what she believes was a greater purpose and continues the practice to this day.

More mundane, yet common, behavioral examples of expressing altruistic motives include buying unneeded Girl Scout cookies, pasting bumper stickers on vehicles broadcasting allegiance to certain candidates or social concerns, preparing "blessing bags" for the homeless, or volunteering our cherished discretionary time to selective charities: behaviors devoid of any expectation in return. While one could argue that helping behaviors are primarily motivated by the goal of boosting our mood or self-esteem or by other self-serving concerns, evidence supports an altruistic interpretation of the described behaviors. One justification for altruistic motives is the empathy arousal hypothesis (Batson, 2010a,b), which contends that individuals will assume the feelings of others and be personally motivated to action by restoring others to a state of physical or psychological comfort. Energized by the goal of reducing personal distress, an empathy arousal interpretation assumes that the helper makes an emotional connection with the distressed individual, provoking personal empathy, whereby the spontaneous needs of the empathetic person cannot be relieved until the assumed perils of the person in distress are overcome. This empathy motive likely explains the behavior of Jessi Colter.

Sometimes, the phenomena of reducing peril is described as orchestrating a state of negative relief, typically characterized by one of four psychological determinants used to connect with the distressed individual. Empathy can be realized by taking the self-perspective of the other person and imagining how he or she thinks, conceiving how the self would think under similar circumstances, feeling like the person in distress through emotional matching, or through empathetic concern where the helper envisions how the self would feel under similar circumstances. Each state of empathy assumes that an emotional or cognitive connection is made with the distressed individual and the perspective of that person can be assumed either psychologically or emotionally (Batson & Ahmad, 2009).

Empirical support for the negative state relief model exists but is often debated on the grounds that pure altruism is a philosophical possibility but a pragmatic illusion (de Waal, 2008). Supporters of empathetic altruism contend that empathy can be experimentally induced by exposing research participants to the distressed condition of another person, followed by the opportunity for the participant to mediate the distress (Piliavin & Charng, 1990). Contingent upon the type of help provided, and if the research participant voluntarily elects to continue to offer help given the opportunity to withdraw, the tenability of the *ease of escape* hypothesis can be tested (Batson, 2010a, p. 112). Many studies reveal that even when given the opportunity to quit without stigma or consequence during an experimental situation, altruistic-empathy motives support behavioral persistence (Batson, 2010a,b). Biopsychological evidence confirms that helping another person and relieving the pain of others when using an empathy motive have similar brain localization in the left anterior insula and complementary neurological responses to relieving our own pain (Fan, Duncan, de Greck, & Northoff, 2011). However, neurological evidence has not empirically confirmed whether empathetic altruism is initiated only when a dualistic threat to the self and others is perceived, or if the perception of stress in others alone is sufficient to motivate altruistic action and activate the insula.

Altruistic behavior should not be ontologically relegated to strictly crisis interventions or viewed only through a catastrophic lens. Peer kindness and benevolence can be exhibited in learning and performance contexts through volunteerism, where individuals devote their time and energy to meet interpersonal, group, or organizational goals. Volunteering is defined as a deliberate, intentional, and non-obligatory form of helping (Aydinli, Bender & Chasiotis, 2013). The precise motive for volunteering across cultures and contexts is unclear; however, typically one of three motives explains individual and organizational volunteerism: Individuals usually volunteer (1) out of empathetic concern for others; (2) under the pretense of reciprocal altruism, where they expect something in return; or (3) for strictly egoistic reasons, including materialistic gain (Omoto & Snyder, 1995). The most commonly observed organizational motive for volunteerism is to strategically promote a company ideology of social responsibility, enhancing a company's image to employees, consumers, and the general community (Grant, 2012).

Pragmatically, understanding volunteerism motives is secondary to cultivating an organizational climate that is conducive to helping and cooperation. Many individuals perceive volunteerism as an effective way to develop marketable job skills, as many organizations consider individual volunteerism as a basis to evaluate prospective employees (Deloitte, 2013). The MD can initiate practical steps to cultivate a prosocial disposition among workers and students, promoting altruistic behaviors and volunteerism alike, by designing work and learning cultures where supporting others is a learned and valued personal attribute. Brief and Motowidlo (1986) outlined several steps leaders can take to cultivate organizational altruism. First, leaders should exhibit behavioral and emotional consistency across all individuals, integrate cooperation into project planning, and include sharing and helping as foundational components of performance or behavior assessment. In addition, the development of a prosocial work culture is accomplished by leaders exhibiting a concerted effort to validate the importance of individuality, concurrent with a focus that organizational growth is contingent upon individuals modeling prosocial behavior throughout all facets of an organization.

Finally, knowing *how* to induce cooperative and gratuitous behavior is critical but is only part of the solution. Frequently, when individuals are contemplating assistance to others, they undergo a cost–benefit analysis calculating the personal rewards of helping, as well as the psychological and physical drawbacks of offering help. If the emotional costs are deemed too high, such as when individuals feel overly threatened, insecure, or not personally accountable for offering help, they will be far less inclined to exhibit adaptive helping behavior (Dovidio, Piliavin, Gaertner, Schroeder, & Clark, 1991).

A robust field of research indicates *when* people are willing to offer help. First, people are much less compassionate and less inclined to offer assistance to others when part of a group in comparison with when alone (Cameron & Payne, 2011), unless the helping context offers cues that the individual has a social or legal responsibility to help, as exemplified by Samaritan laws in many countries (van Bommel, van Prooijen, Elffers, & Van Lange, 2012). Individuals help more when the psychological cost of helping is low, *and* the need of the person needing help is considered to be substantial. Altruistic motives are attenuated when we believe the person in distress could have preempted the problem through proactive and decisive action of his or her own, justifying lower empathy and discounting negative social evaluation from others (Batson, 2010a,b). Unfortunately, willingness to assist others is also a function of many superficial associations between the helper and the person needing help, such as the perceived degree of physical, intellectual, racial, and gender similarities (Mallozzi, Mcdermott, & Kayson, 1990), as well as perceptions of in-group membership (Stürmer, Snyder, & Omoto, 2005). Although many of the factors above are only indirectly related to performance motivation, the helping contingencies described suggest that many altruistic behaviors are motivated by self-interest, how we see ourselves in relation to others, or an external standard of personal accountability.

The preceding narrative primarily focused on people taking specific actions to either deliberately, or unintentionally, boost their self-evaluations and subsequent self-worth. However, not all individuals are primed for action and willing to take specific steps to invigorate self-worth perceptions. Instead, many times individuals will appear apathetic and aloof, intentionally electing *inaction*. By using a series of complex, self-protection strategies, the individual can insulate the self and avoid the demoralizing prospect that others may think the individual has insufficient resources to meet learning and performance goals. We next examine which strategies learners employ to maintain elevated competency beliefs, motivated by the strong desire to protect the individual from harmful self-intrusions and public repudiation.

Principle #43—Performance inhibiting strategies augment self-worth

Some individuals, especially adolescent students (Alderman, 2004), are highly motivated by the goal of worthiness. Superficially, these individuals portray a confident façade when staring into the metaphoric mirror; they want to be perceived as Herculean in the eyes of their beholders. Looking good requires positive self-affirmations coupled with encouraging feedback from others, asserting that the individual is competent and capable: someone who is able to overcome academic hurdles and master challenging performance goals. But sometimes, during the iterative process of self-evaluation, even the most confident individuals become highly self-critical, questioning the legitimacy of their knowledge and ability. The emotional conflict of self-doubt and uncertainty may lead to psychological ruminations concerning the precise caliber of their competency perceptions. In extreme cases, and despite actual ability, these individuals may come to believe they do not have the necessary talent or requisite skills to be academically, socially, or vocationally adept, leading to feelings of unworthiness (Covington, 2009). In order to quell anxiety and sustain a positive self-image, individuals will frequently use self-protective strategies to preserve their positive affirmations: concealing or forestalling any aspersions of performance inadequacy or academic impotence. Although these strategies are self-protective of ability attributions, the approaches are frequently counterproductive, resulting in performance deficits on tasks and are thus categorized as *self-handicapping strategies* (SHS).

Deliberate handicapping is an active process designed "to diminish the threat of failure by obscuring low ability as the reason for the failure" (Brown & Kimble, 2009, p. 609). SHS serve three main purposes for the individual. First, the strategies allow the person to justify undesirable performances and "save face" by shifting responsibility for any negatives outcomes from the internal self to external causes (Schlenker, 1980; Warner & Moore, 2004). Second, SHS insulate the individual from their own negative self-perceptions, enhancing self-esteem, and thus sustaining or increasing individual self-worth (Berglas & Jones, 1978; De Castella, Byrne, & Covington, 2013). Third, the use of SHS sometimes results in self-enhancement, when positive task outcomes are achieved *despite* the use of the failure-avoiding, performance-damaging strategies (Tice, 1993).

The variability of SHS is broad, primarily determined by the context of application. Most SHS research focuses on academic performance, when strategies thwart attributions of low ability and protect academic self-esteem (Schwinger, Wirthwein, Lemmer, & Steinmayr, 2014). To a lesser extent, researchers investigate the impact of SHS on organizational behavior, where strategies are designed to protect organizational image and enhance business integrity, such as when a company rationalizes an environmentally unsound decision as necessary to help improve people's lives (Higgins & Snyder, 1989). Self-handicapping also has significant interpersonal implications. Individuals use SHS when subjected to episodes of social exclusion, most notably from soured relationships or in response to devastating personal milestones, such as bereavement for a close friend or spouse. Frequently, these personal events trigger a variety of self-defeating behaviors, including excessive food consumption, drunkenness, or drug use. Although SHS are self-deprecating, the strategies provide the individual with an outlet for situational relief, leading to a state of limited self-awareness, temporarily insulating the person from the reality of his or her loss (Twenge, 2007).

In regard to learning and performance, the primary benefit of using SHS is to promote positive perceptions of the self by others and obscure any connection between negative results and personal lack of ability. The most common contingencies resulting from the use of SHS are the perception that external reasons justify episodes of inferior performance, shifting blame away from the individual and artificially insulating the self from intrusive and disturbing self-perceptions, which are equated with decreases in self-worth. The motivation to avoid failure prompts the use of techniques, such as procrastination, setting unattainable goals, or deliberately withholding task effort. Although these strategies may appear to accelerate failure, in the mind of the actor they serve a self-protection motive, designed to increase, not decrease self-worth. By using SHS the individual has a viable rationalization, or a seemingly justified excuse, in the event that performance suffers. Individuals can attribute any negative outcome to the use of the strategies, not to the self, and effectively avoid the psychologically decimating prospect that they actually have low ability. In the eyes of the individual, it is considerably easier and much more palatable to acknowledge that you could have done better if you had tried harder or had not waited until the last minute than to admit to yourself and others that you might have limited ability. Table 8.2 lists some of the more common academic SHS, along with the potential negative performance consequences associated with each type of strategy use.

Although the examples provided in Table 8.2 suggest that most instances of SHS are barriers to successful performance, at times, SHS can be adaptive and situationally

Table 8.2 The potential liabilities of academic self-handicapping

Strategy	Description	Negative performance consequences	Evidence
Procrastination	Intentional deferral or delay of work that individuals perceive as important to complete	Irritability, fatigue, stress, guilt	Schraw, Wadkins, and Olafson (2007)
Unattainable goals	Setting overly aggressive or impossible goals	Low effort, poor self-regulation, reduced subjective well-being	Wrosch, Scheier, Miller, Schulz, and Carver (2003)
Boundary goals	Setting goals that can be reached with little effort, low levels of aspiration	Performance avoidant goals, reduced effort expenditures, high expectations for success	Corker and Donnellan (2012)
Low effort	Lack of attention to academics, ineffective use of study time, poor preparation and not trying hard in school	Self-deprecation, negative attitudes toward education, ego-oriented goals, and low grades	Midgley, Arunkumar, and Urdan (1996)
Defensive pessimism	Setting low expectations for the self to avoid disappointing learning outcomes	High task avoidance with strong failure expectations	Martin, Marsh, and Debus (2001)
Minimal practice	Reduced study hours, inefficient studying	Inferior learning outcomes, lack of effective coping	Warner and Moore (2004)
Academic wooden leg	Using a specific excuse such as test anxiety to justify outcomes and escape responsibility for actions	External attributions of failure, anxiety, low effort	Smith, Snyder, and Handelsman (1982)

support academic prosperity. In instances when an individual uses SHS and unexpectedly observes positive consequences *despite* the strategy use, increases in academic self-esteem typically follow (Tice, 1993). For instance, when a procrastinating student deliberately delays a semester-long project by waiting until the last minute to start work, academic efficiency is realized because the student is able to complete more work in less time than when the project is started several weeks in advance of the deadline (Schraw et al. 2007). Setting lofty goals may also have positive implications. Individuals who set unattainable goals, upon realization of the low probability of reaching their goals, disengage from the lofty goals, then re-engage, by setting more practical expectations for themselves. Goal recalibration results in stress reductions, fewer reported depression symptoms, and overall higher optimism concerning life experiences (Wrosch et al., 2003).

Organizationally, *social loafing*, which occurs when individuals exhibit lower effort when working in groups than when working independently, can be motivationally adaptive (Shepperd, 1993). During group work, individuals doubting their own abilities often deliberately withhold effort as a self-protective strategy, preferring criticism of their low effort to negative evaluations of their work performance. Known as the *free-rider effect*, individuals may potentially enhance their academic self-esteem through group affiliation, if positive group results are achieved, leading to positive team praise or materialistic group benefits for the individual despite questionable individual contribution. Unfortunately, self-protection motives and associated SHS more frequently result in performance decrements, as evidenced by Table 8.2, because strategies are often counterproductive to meeting learning objectives. In a recent meta-analysis, Schwinger et al. (2014) observed a mean negative correlation between academic performance and use of self-handicapping of −.23, indicating that as the frequency of SHS increases, academic performance declines.

While performance reductions and inferior results are easily measured, mediation of behavioral self-handicapping is not. Schwinger et al. (2014) lamented that empirically supported interventions that address SHS are "barely available" (p. 14). Complicating implementation of remedies is the recurring obstacle that many individuals may not realize or understand the rationale for their own actions (see Principle #5, p. 12). Perception and use of SHS may be implicit, below the direct consciousness of the individual. Thus, the MD is faced with a formidable triple-threat challenge. First, the individual must acknowledge the futility of the failure-avoidance motive and the potentially disruptive consequences of using SHS. Second, upon realization of strategy implications, the individual must recognize *when* SHS are used. Finally, maladaptive SHS must be replaced with adaptive strategies, which concurrently address performance challenges while instilling self-esteem and supporting enhancement of overall self-worth.

The few interventions found to reduce SHS focus on cognitive restructuring, including instilling in learners a greater emphasis on the value of education and why using self-regulation strategies, such as monitoring and planning, typically result in learners adopting mastery-approach goal orientations (Martin, 2005). However, considering that the primary motive for using SHS is to avoid failure and sustain self-worth, it is essential that habitual SHS users realize that expertise is effortful and deliberate and that failure is a malleable part of the learning and performance process, not an immutable, personal flaw. As Nick Lowery reminded us in Chapter 7, we must always give ourselves permission to learn. The origination of SHS is largely a function of psychological frailty, partly fueled by a strong emphasis on individualism. In order to jettison nonproductive SHS, learners and workers alike must believe that the "real me" can be respected and valued at all times, even when results occasionally fall short of expectations. Leadership actions and organizational programs that focus on incremental skills development, debunking the misconception of rigid ability, will shift the individual from a fixation on the self and, instead, impart a focus on what can be attained with effort, deliberation, and dedicated practice.

Chapter summary/conclusions

Individuals may not realize or understand the rationale for their own actions. The implicit nature of many motivational beliefs obscures the individual from making accurate and definitive assessments of the self or clearly understanding who is "the real me." Lacking criterion evidence, individuals often resort to social comparisons by paralleling themselves to meaningful others or to normative standards. Once personal benchmarks are defined, individuals conduct introspective self-evaluations, assessing consistency between their enacted and desired selves. Positive judgments produce satisfaction, elevated self-esteem, and escalating self-worth, while negative discrepancies promote disenchantment and angst, as individuals struggle to understand their relational value and assess their comparative self-worth.

The presence of others is a powerful motive that induces individuals to display different behaviors in public than in private, based upon who is watching, the intensity of personal beliefs, normative expectations, and the type of impressions we wish to make. Social influence determines if we conform or disobey, participate or withdraw, reciprocate or oblige, and when and why we are willing to exhibit prosocial behaviors to serve and cooperate with others. Sometimes, we help to satisfy our own egoistic needs, motivated by the quest to create positive impressions and develop self-worth. Other times, we volunteer in the name of altruism, motivated by empathetic concern and a genuine unsolicited desire to satisfy the needs of others before we satisfy our own. Competency perceptions trump all self-beliefs, and perhaps are the strongest motive of all. Individuals will employee radical SHS, such as procrastination and setting impossible goals as a subterfuge to sustain positive self-worth, having others believe that our personal misfortunes are inevitable consequences of our efforts, but only circumstantial evidence, unrelated to who we are or what we might want to be.

Next steps

Assessing personal and normative fit requires that we consider mountains of belief, contextual, and behavioral evidence. The evaluative decisions help determine perceptions of our identity and self-worth, which, in turn, trigger a corresponding series of feelings, often interpreted as emotions. Success may breed pride, joy, and optimism. Failure may portend anger, humiliation, guilt, and depression. Every emotion is a powerful, subjective reaction to what we experience that frequently determines how we think and feel but, more importantly, what we do next. Chapter 9 examines the world of moods, dispositions, and emotions, revealing how our feelings radically alter the tasks we consider and what we are willing and able to accomplish. **Alec Torelli** returns in Chapter 9, as we learn that one key to optimal performance is an exceptional ability to regulate emotions, even when things do not turn out as planned.

End of chapter motivational minute

Principles covered in this chapter:

36. **The psychological or physical presence of others may alter normative behavior**—people are influenced by others and act differently in public versus in private. Typically, normative behavior is demonstrated to satisfy motives of social acceptance and group inclusion.
37. **Prosocial behaviors are compliant, adaptive, and predictable**—individuals are willing to help others for reasons of personal satisfaction; because of the perceived needs of fairness, reciprocity, and consistency; or out of obedience in respect of power.
38. **Prosocial motives are egoistic and altruistic**—some individuals offer to help to others for egoistic reasons that are motivated by a desire to satisfy one's personal psychological needs. Altruistic helping is motivated by the genuine desire to assist others based upon empathetic thoughts and feelings about the person in need.
39. **Performance inhibiting strategies augment self-worth**—protecting the self is a decisive motive based upon the prospect of looking good and avoiding failure. Self-worth can be protected by the use of SHS that shift blame for failure to external factors unrelated to ability perceptions.

Key terminology (in order of chapter presentation):

- **Subjects**—research participants in a research study that do not have explicit awareness of the purpose of the research.
- **Confederates**—individuals who participate in a research study and are aware of the purpose of the study and primarily participate to induce behavioral changes in actual study subjects.
- **Bystander effect**—the phenomenon whereby the public helping behavior of an individual is influenced by the presence of others.
- **Impression management**—the process used by individuals to generate and control desired opinions in others.
- **Prosocial behavior**—gratuitous and cooperative behaviors usually initiated to help and assist other individuals or groups in meeting desired goals.
- **Egoism**—the demonstration of cooperative and helping behaviors primarily motivated by the desire to enhance one's own psychological, materialistic, or social needs.
- **Reciprocity**—the prevailing belief in many cultures that obligates individuals to return help when others have helped the individual.
- **Spillover effect**—the obligatory tendency to offer help to friends of friends.
- **Altruism**—the demonstration of cooperative and helping behaviors primarily motivated by a desire to help meet the needs of others.
- **Self-handicapping strategies**—idiosyncratic performance damaging approaches used by individuals to diminish or conceal self-perceptions of failure believed to be caused by low ability.
- **Social loafing**—the phenomenon of individuals exhibiting lower effort when working in groups than when working independently.
- **Social identity**—the process of establishing and communicating one's beliefs, individuality, and self-concept to another person based upon social interaction.

References

Ajzen, I. (1991). The theory of planned behaviour. *Organizational Behavior and Human Decision Processes, 50*, 179–211.

Alderman, M. K. (2004). *Motivation for achievement: Possibilities for teaching and learning* (2nd ed.). Mahwah, NJ: Lawrence Erlbaum Associates.

Asch, S. E. (1956). Studies of independence and conformity: I. A minority of one against a unanimous majority. *Psychological Monographs: General and Applied, 70*(9), 1–70. http://dx.doi.org/10.1037/h0093718.

Aydinli, A., Bender, M., & Chasiotis, A. (2013). Helping and volunteering across cultures: Determinants of prosocial behavior. *Online Readings in Psychology and Culture, 5*(3) Retrieved on July 7, 2014 from: http://dx.doi.org/10.9707/2307-0919.1118.

Batson, C. D. (2010a). *Altruism in humans*. Oxford, UK: Oxford University Press.

Batson, C. D. (2010b). Empathy-induced altruistic motivation. In M. Mikulincer & P. R. Shaver (Eds.), *Prosocial motives, emotions, and behavior: The better angels of our nature* (pp. 15–34). Washington, DC: American Psychological Association.

Batson, C. D., Ahmad, N., & Stocks, E. L. (2011). Four forms of prosocial motivation: Egoism, altruism, collectivism, and principlism. In D. Dunning (Ed.), *Social motivation* (pp. 103–126). New York, NY: Psychology Press.

Batson, C. D., & Ahmad, N. Y. (2009). Using empathy to improve intergroup attitudes and relations. *Social Issues and Policy Review, 3*(1), 141–177.

Baumeister, R. F. (1987). How the self became a problem: A psychological review of historical research. *Journal of Personality and Social Psychology, 52*(1), 163–176. http://dx.doi.org/10.1037/0022-3514.52.1.163.

Baumeister, R. F. (2010). The self. In R. F. Baumeister & E. J. Finkel (Eds.), *Advanced social psychology: The state of science* (pp. 139–175). New York, NY: Oxford University Press.

Baumeister, R. F., Campbell, J. D., Krueger, J. I., & Vohs, K. D. (2003). Does high self-esteem cause better performance, interpersonal success, happiness, or healthier lifestyles? *Psychological Science in the Public Interest, 4*(1), 1–44. http://dx.doi.org/10.2307/40062291.

Baumeister, R. F., & Tice, D. M. (1985). Self-esteem and responses to success and failure: Subsequent performance and intrinsic motivation. *Journal of Personality, 53*(3), 450–467.

Baumeister, R. F., Tice, D. M., & Hutton, D. G. (1989). Self-presentational motivations and personality differences in self-esteem. *Journal of Personality, 57*, 547–579.

Begley, T. M., Lee, C., & Hui, C. (2006). Organizational level as a moderator of the relationship between justice perceptions and work-related reactions. *Journal of Organizational Behavior* (6), 705–721.

Bendapudi, N., & Berry, L. L. (1997). Customers' motivations for maintaining relationships with service providers. *Journal of Retailing, 73*(1), 15–37.

Berglas, S., & Jones, E. E. (1978). Drug choice as a self-handicapping strategy in response to noncontingent success. *Journal of Personality and Social Psychology, 36*, 405–417.

Brewer, M. B., & Gardner, W. (1996). Who is this "we"? Levels of collective identity and self-representations. *Journal of Personality and Social Psychology, 71*, 83–93.

Brief, A. P., & Motowidlo, S. J. (1986). Prosocial organizational behaviors. *Academy of management Review, 11*(4), 710–725.

Brown, C. M., & Kimble, C. E. (2009). Personal, interpersonal, and situational influences on behavioral self-handicapping. *Journal of Social Psychology, 149*(6), 609–626.

Brown, J. D., & Marshall, M. A. (2006). The three faces of self-esteem. In M. H. Kernis (Ed.), *Self-esteem issues and answers: A sourcebook of current perspectives* (pp. 4–10). New York, NY: Psychology Press.

Bushman, B. J. (1988). The effects of apparel on compliance: A field experiment with a female authority figure. *Personality and Social Psychology Bulletin, 14*(3), 459–467. http://dx.doi.org/10.1177/0146167288143004.

Buunk, A. P., Groothof, H. A., & Siero, F. W. (2007). Social comparison and satisfaction with one's social life. *Journal of Social and Personal Relationships, 24*(2), 197–205.

Cameron, C. D., & Payne, B. K. (2011). Escaping affect: How motivated emotion regulation creates insensitivity to mass suffering. *Journal of Personality and Social Psychology, 100*(1), 1–15. http://dx.doi.org/10.1037/a0021643.

Campbell, J. D., & Lavallee, L. F. (1993). Who am I? The role of self-concept confusion in understanding the behavior of people with low self-esteem. In R. F. Baumeister (Ed.), *Self-esteem: The puzzle of low self-regard* (pp. 3–20). New York, NY: Plenum Press.

Carlson, M., & Miller, N. (1987). Explanation of the relation between negative mood and helping. *Psychological Bulletin, 102*, 91–108. http://dx.doi.org/10.1037/0033-2909.102.1.91.

Cavalier, R. P. (2000). *Personal motivation: A model for decision making*. Westport, CT: Praeger Publishers.

Childs, M. (2011). Identity: A primer. In A. Peachey & M. Childs (Eds.), *Reinventing ourselves: Contemporary concepts of identity in virtual worlds* (pp. 13–31). London: Springer-Verlag.

Cialdini, R. B., & Goldstein, N. J. (2004). Social influence: Compliance and conformity. In S. T. Fiske, D. L. Schacter, & C. Zahn-Wexler (Eds.), *Annual Review of Psychology* (55, pp. 591–621). Palo Alto, CA: Annual Reviews.

Cialdini, R. B., & Griskevicius, V. (2010). Social influence. In R. F. Baumeister & E. J. Finkel (Eds.), *Advanced social psychology: The state of the science* (pp. 385–417). New York, NY: Oxford University Press.

Cialdini, R. B., Reno, R. R., & Kallgren, C. A. (1990). A focus theory of normative conduct: Recycling the concept of norms to reduce littering in public places. *Journal of Personality and Social Psychology, 58*(6), 1015–1026.

Cialdini, R. B., Trost, M. R., & Newsom, J. T. (1995). Preference for consistency: The development of a valid measure and the discovery of surprising behavioral implications. *Journal of Personality and Social Psychology, 69*, 318–328.

Corker, K. S., & Donnellan, M. B. (2012). Setting lower limits high: The role of boundary goals in achievement motivation. *Journal of Educational Psychology, 104*(1), 138–149. http://dx.doi.org/10.1037/a0026228.

Correll, J., & Park, B. (2005). A model of the in-group as a social resource. *Personality and Social Psychology Review, 9*(4), 341–359.

Covington, M. (2009). Self-worth theory: Retrospection and prospects. In K. R. Wentzel & A. Wigfield (Eds.), *Handbook of motivation at school* (pp. 141–169). New York, NY: Routledge.

Covington, M. V. (1984). The self-worth theory of achievement motivation: Findings and implications. *The Elementary School Journal, 85*(1), 5–20.

Crocker, J., & Park, L. E. (2004). The costly pursuit of self-esteem. *Psychological Bulletin, 130*(3), 392–414. http://dx.doi.org/10.1037/0033-2909.130.3.392.

Crocker, J., & Wolfe, C. T. (2001). Contingencies of self-worth. *Psychological Review, 108*(3), 593–623. http://dx.doi.org/10.1037/0033-295X.108.3.593.

De Castella, K., Byrne, D., & Covington, M. (2013). Unmotivated or motivated to fail? A cross-cultural study of achievement motivation, fear of failure, and student disengagement. *Journal of Educational Psychology, 105*(3), 861–880. http://dx.doi.org/10.1037/a0032464.

Deloitte (2013). *Executive summary: 2013 Deloitte volunteer IMPACT survey*. Retrieved on July 5, 2014 from: <http://www.deloitte.com/assets/DcomUnitedStates/Assets/Documents/us_VolunteerIMPACTSurveyExecutiveSummary_2013.pdf>

de Waal, F. B. M. (2008). Putting the altruism back into altruism: The evolution of empathy. *Annual Review of Psychology*, *59*, 279–300.

Dovidio, J. F., Piliavin, J. A., Gaertner, S. L., Schroeder, D. A., & Clark, R. D. I. (1991). The arousal: Cost-reward model and the process of intervention: A review of the evidence. In M. S. Clark (Ed.), *Prosocial behavior* (pp. 86–118). Thousand Oaks, CA: Sage Publications, Inc.

Dunning, D. (2011). *Social motivation*. New York, NY: Psychology Press.

Eiser, C., & Eiser, J. (2000). Social comparisons and quality of life among survivors of childhood cancer and their mothers. *Psychology & Health*, *15*(3), 435–450.

Fan, Y., Duncan, N. W., de Greck, M., & Northoff, G. (2011). Is there a core neural network in empathy? An fMRI based quantitative meta-analysis. *Neuroscience and Biobehavioral Reviews*, *35*(3), 903–911. http://dx.doi.org/10.1016/j.neubiorev.2010.10.009.

Fenigstein, A. (1979). Self-consciousness, self-attention, and social interaction. *Journal of Personality and Social Psychology*, *37*, 75–86.

Festinger, L. (1954). A theory of social comparison processes. *Human Relations*, *7*, 117–140. http://dx.doi.org/10.1177/001872675400700202.

Gollwitzer, P. M. (1986). Striving for specific identities: The social reality of self-symbolizing. In R. Baumeister (Ed.), *Public self and private self* (pp. 143–159). New York, NY: Springer-Verlag.

Grant, A. M. (2012). Giving time, time after time: Work design and sustained employee participation in corporate volunteering. *Academy of Management Review*, *37*(4), 589–615. http://dx.doi.org/10.5465/amr.2010.0280.

Greenberg, J., Ashton-James, C. E., & Ashkanasy, N. M. (2007). Social comparison processes in organizations. *Organizational Behavior and Human Decision Processes*, *102*(1), 22–41. http://dx.doi.org/10.1016/j.obhdp.2006.09.006.

Harris, T. D., Tracy, A. J., & Fisher, C. C. (2011). *The predictive index®: Technical overview*. Wellesley Hills, MA: Praendex, Inc.

Herman, C. P., Roth, D. A., & Polivy, J. (2003). Effects of the presence of others on food intake: A normative interpretation. *Psychological Bulletin*, *129*(6), 873–886. http://dx.doi.org/10.1037/0033-2909.129.6.873.

Higgins, E. T. (1987). Self-discrepancy: A theory relating self and affect. *Psychological Review*, *94*, 319–340. http://dx.doi.org/10.1037/0033-295X.94.3.319.

Higgins, R. L., & Snyder, C. R. (1989). The business of excuses. In R. A. Giacalone & P. Rosenfeld (Eds.), *Impression management in the organization* (pp. 73–85). Hillsdale, NJ: Lawrence Erlbaum Associates, Inc.

Hollenbeck, J. R., & Klein, H. J. (1987). Goal commitment and the goal-setting process: Problems, prospects, and proposals for future research. *Journal of Applied Psychology*, *72*(2), 212.

Hrabluik, C., Latham, G. P., & McCarthy, J. M. (2012). Does goal setting have a dark side? The relationship between perfectionism and maximum versus typical employee performance. *International Public Management Journal*, *15*(1), 5–38. http://dx.doi.org/10.1080/10967494.2012.684010.

Hyman, M. R., & Sierra, J. J. (2011). Adjusting self-reported attitudinal data for mischievous respondents. *International Journal of Market Research*, *54*(1), 129–145. http://dx.doi.org/10.2501/IJMR-54-1-129-145.

Kassin, S., Fein, S., & Markus, H. R. (2008). *Social psychology* (7th ed.). Belmont, CA: Wadsworth.

Latané, B. (1981). The psychology of social impact. *American Psychologist*, *36*(4), 343–356.

Latané, B., & Darley, J. M. (1970). *The unresponsive bystander: Why doesn't he help?* New York, NY: Appleton-Century Crofts.

Latané, B., & Rodin, J. (1969). A lady in distress: Inhibiting effects of friends and strangers on bystander intervention. *Journal of Experimental Social Psychology, 5*(2), 189–202. http://dx.doi.org/10.1016/0022-1031(69)90046-8.

Leary, M. R., Tchividijian, L. R., & Kraxberger, B. E. (1994). Self-presentation can be hazardous to your health: Impression management and health risk. *Health Psychology, 13*(6), 461–470. http://dx.doi.org/10.1037/0278-6133.13.6.461.

Liang, P., & Meng, J. (2013). *Love me, love my dog: An experimental study on social connections and indirect reciprocity.* Retrieved on June 25, 2014 from: <http://mpra.ub.uni-muenchen.de/45270/1/MPRA_paper_45270.pdf>

Mallozzi, J., Mcdermott, V., & Kayson, W. A. (1990). Effects of sex, type of dress, and location on altruistic behavior. *Psychological Reports, 67*(3), 1103–1106.

Manning, R., Levine, M., & Collins, A. (2007). The Kitty Genovese murder and the social psychology of helping: The parable of the 38 witnesses. *American Psychologist, 62*(6), 555–562.

Martin, A. J. (2005). Exploring the effects of a youth enrichment program on academic motivation and engagement. *Social Psychology of Education, 8*(2), 179–206.

Martin, A. J., Marsh, H. W., & Debus, R. L. (2001). Self-handicapping and defensive pessimism: Exploring a model of predictors and outcomes from a self-protection perspective. *Journal of Educational Psychology, 93*(1), 87–102.

Midgley, C., Arunkumar, R., & Urdan, T. C. (1996). "If I don't do well tomorrow, there's a reason": Predictors of adolescents' use of academic self-handicapping strategies. *Journal of Educational Psychology, 88*(3), 423–434. http://dx.doi.org/10.1037/0022-0663.88.3.423.

Milgram, S. (1963). Behavioral study of obedience. *Journal of Abnormal & Social Psychology, 67*(4), 371–378.

Mussen, P., & Eisenberg-Berg, N. (1977). *Roots of caring, sharing, and helping: The development of pro-social behavior in children.* Oxford, England: W. H. Freeman.

Mussweiler, T., Gabriel, S., & Bodenhausen, G. V. (2000). Shifting social identities as a strategy for deflecting threatening social comparisons. *Journal of Personality & Social Psychology, 79*(3), 398–409. http://dx.doi.org/10.1037//0022-3514.79.3.398.

Nisbett, R. E., & Wilson, T. D. (1977). Telling more than we can know: Verbal reports on mental processes. *Psychological Review, 84*(3), 231–259.

Omoto, A. M., & Snyder, M. (1995). Sustained helping without obligation: Motivation, longevity of service, and perceived attitude change among AIDS volunteers. *Journal of Personality & Social Psychology, 68,* 671–687.

Penner, L. A., Dovidio, J. F., Piliavin, J. A., & Schroeder, D. A. (2005). Prosocial behavior: Multilevel perspectives. *Annual Review of Psychology, 56*(1), 365–392. http://dx.doi.org/10.1146/annurev.psych.56.091103.070141.

Piliavin, J. A. (2003). Doing well by doing good: Benefits for the benefactor. In C. L. Keyes & J. Haidt (Eds.), *Flourishing: Positive psychology and the life well-lived* (pp. 227–247). Washington, DC: American Psychological Association.

Piliavin, J. A., & Charng, H. -W. (1990). Altruism: A review of recent theory and research. *American Sociological Review, 16,* 27–65.

Pitesa, M., & Thau, S. (2013). Compliant sinners, obstinate saints: How power and self-focus determine the effectiveness of social influences in ethical decision making. *Academy of Management Journal, 56*(3), 635–658. http://dx.doi.org/10.5465/amj.2011.0891.

Prato, C. G., & Kaplan, S. (2013). Driving on the edge: The motivational factors of risk-taking among teen drivers. In J. -P. Assailly (Ed.), *Psychology of risk-taking* (pp. 115–137). Hauppauge, NY: Nova Science Publishers.

Reicher, S., & Haslam, S. A. (2011). After shock? Towards a social identity explanation of the Milgram "obedience" studies: Social identity and the Milgram studies. *British Journal of Social Psychology, 50*(1), 163–169. http://dx.doi.org/10.1111/j.2044-8309.2010.02015.x.

Schlenker, B. R. (1980). *Impression management: The self-concept, social identity, and interpersonal relations*. Monterey, CA: Brooks/Cole Publishing Company.

Schraw, G., Wadkins, T., & Olafson, L. (2007). Doing the things we do: A grounded theory of academic procrastination. *Journal of Educational Psychology, 99*(1), 12–25.

Schwinger, M., Wirthwein, L., Lemmer, G., & Steinmayr, R. (2014). Academic self-handicapping and achievement: A meta-analysis. *Journal of Educational Psychology, 106*(3), 744–761. http://dx.doi.org/10.1037/a0035832.

Seiter, J. S. (2007). Ingratiation and gratuity: The effect of complimenting customers on tipping behavior in restaurants. *Journal of Applied Social Psychology, 37*(3), 478–485.

Shepperd, J. A. (1993). Productivity loss in performance groups: A motivation analysis. *Psychological Bulletin, 113*(1), 67–81.

Smith, T. W., Snyder, C. R., & Handelsman, M. M. (1982). On the self-serving function of an academic wooden leg: Test anxiety as a self-handicapping strategy. *Journal of Personality and Social Psychology, 42*(2), 314–321. http://dx.doi.org/10.1037/0022-3514.42.2.314.

Sowislo, J. F., & Orth, U. (2013). Does low self-esteem predict depression and anxiety? A meta-analysis of longitudinal studies. *Psychological Bulletin, 139*(1), 213–240. http://dx.doi.org/10.1037/a0028931.

Steadman, L., & Rutter, D. (2004). Belief importance and the theory of planned behaviour: Comparing modal and ranked modal beliefs in predicting attendance at breast screening. *British Journal of Health Psychology, 9*, 447–463.

Strahan, E. J., Lafrance, A., Wilson, A. E., Ethier, N., Spencer, S. J., & Zanna, M. P. (2008). Victoria's dirty secret: How sociocultural norms influence adolescent girls and women. *Personality & Social Psychology Bulletin, 34*(2), 288–302. http://dx.doi.org/10.1177/0146167207310457.

Stürmer, S., Snyder, M., & Omoto, A. M. (2005). Prosocial emotions and helping: The moderating role of group membership. *Journal of Personality and Social Psychology, 88*(3), 532–546.

Tennen, H., McKee, T. E., & Affleck, G. (2000). Social comparison processes in health and illness. In J. Suls & L. Wheeler (Eds.), *Handbook of social comparison: Theory and research* (pp. 443–483). Dordrecht, Netherlands: Kluwer.

Thau, S., Tröster, C., Aquino, K., Pillutla, M., & De Cremer, D. (2013). Satisfying individual desires or moral standards? Preferential treatment and group members' self-worth, affect, and behavior. *Journal of Business Ethics, 113*(1), 133–145.

Tice, D. M. (1993). The social motivations of people with low self-esteem. In R. F. Baumeister (Ed.), *Self-esteem: The puzzle of low self-regard* (pp. 37–54). New York, NY: Plenum Press.

Twenge, J. M. (2007). Social exclusion, motivation, and self-defeating behavior: Why breakups lead to drunkenness and ice cream. In J. Y. Shah & W. L. Gardner (Eds.), *Handbook of motivational science* (pp. 508–517). New York, NY: Guilford Publications.

van Bommel, M., van Prooijen, J.-W., Elffers, H., & Van Lange, P. A. M. (2012). Be aware to care: Public self-awareness leads to a reversal of the bystander effect. *Journal of Experimental Social Psychology, 48*(4), 926–930. http://dx.doi.org/10.1016/j.jesp.2012.02.011.

van Doorn, J., Zeelenberg, M., & Breugelmans, S. M. (2014). Anger and prosocial behavior. *Emotion Review, 6*(3), 261–268. http://dx.doi.org/10.1177/1754073914523794.

Warner, S., & Moore, S. (2004). Excuses, excuses: Self-Handicapping in an Australian adolescent sample. *Journal of Youth Adolescence, 33*(4), 271–281.

Weaver, R. R., & Qi, J. (2005). Classroom organization and participation: College students' perceptions. *Journal of Higher Education, 76*(5), 570–601. http://dx.doi.org/10.1353/jhe.2005.0038.

Wegener, D. T., Petty, R. E., & Smith, S. M. (1995). Positive mood can increase or decrease message scrutiny: The hedonic contingency view of mood and message processing. *Journal of Personality and Social Psychology, 69*(1), 5–15.

Weinstein, N., & Ryan, R. M. (2010). When helping helps: Autonomous motivation for prosocial behavior and its influence on well-being for the helper and recipient. *Journal of Personality and Social Psychology, 98*(2), 222–244. http://dx.doi.org/10.1037/a0016984.

Wheeler, L., & Suls, J. (2005). Social comparison and self-evaluations of competence. In A. J. Elliott & C. S. Dweck (Eds.), *Handbook of competence and motivation* (pp. 202–221). New York, NY: Guilford Press.

Wills, T. A. (1981). Downward comparison principles in social psychology. *Psychological Bulletin, 90*, 245–271.

Wrosch, C., Scheier, M., Miller, G., Schulz, R., & Carver, C. (2003). Adaptive self-regulation of unattainable goals: Goal disengagement, goal reengagement, and subjective well-being. *Personality and Social Psychology Bulletin, 29*(12), 1494–1508.

Ybema, J. F., & Buunk, B. P. (1993). Aiming at the top? Upward social comparison of abilities after failure. *European Journal of Social Psychology, 23*(6), 627–645.

No place to hide: Motivation and emotion

Chapter outline

Principle #44—Emotional reactions are localized, subjective, and learned 240
Principle #45—Anxiety and boredom are performance-restricting culprits 245
   Anxiety 245
   Boredom 247
Principle #46—Positive affect is a powerful performance determinant 250
Motivational Leader—*Alec Torelli* 251
Principle #47—Individuals restructure affect to regulate their emotions 253
   Chapter summary/conclusions 259
   Next steps 260
   End of chapter motivational minute 260
References 261

Times are tough: Read the news and you will quickly conclude that global economic stability and financial security are, at best, cyclical. Prosperity is often challenging and elusive. If you are a college student, an aspiring entrepreneur, someone starting a career, or a worker on a fixed hourly or monthly income, you may need to conserve your resources as much as possible to survive. If you need to save money, I have some great advice for you. Actually, my tip is borrowed from author Abbie Hoffman (no relation), who outlined how to get things for free in his counter-culture manifesto *Steal This Book*. Along with listing hundreds of ways to exploit government, scam law enforcement, and be a highly qualified, subversive hippy, Hoffman, Haber, and Cohen (1971) recommended getting someone else to pay for your expenses. For example, try the Hoffman approach to clean clothes. Go to a laundromat, and find someone with a light load of wash, ask to share their washing machine to get your laundry done for free. After overcoming the odd looks you will likely receive from your audacious request, the person will probably tell you to "get lost" or attempt to convey the same idea to you using more descriptive and colorful terminology. If the light loader resists your requests, shame him through verbal assault, calling him "cheap," "self-centered," and a "capitalist pig." Then, assess the person's emotional reaction.

If no significant reaction is observed at the laundromat, or if public laundering is not your style, escalate your obnoxious emotion-inducing behavior. Find a pregnant woman, who, if you are strategic, may be found at the laundromat. Approach the woman and ask politely, "Instead of getting pregnant, why didn't you adopt one of the thousands of orphaned children who desperately need a loving home?" Even if you avoid assault and are not arrested for vagrancy or loitering, your outrageous behavior will most likely be critically evaluated by the target of your intentions, eliciting a response ranging from uncontrollable anger to belligerent contempt. In all likelihood, you will have triggered a subjective *emotional episode* (Moors, 2010), typically defined as the motivational and emotional consequences generated when an individual interacts with his or her surrounding environment. Before you leave the laundromat, be sure to tell the unsuspecting victim that your questions were asked in the name of advancing motivational science!

Unlike clandestine motives, which underlie behaviors designed to protect self-worth and the public scrutiny of private behavior, these emotion-evoking examples are based upon a very clear objective: actively providing a context for others to express their feelings. Although the emotional triggers described were suggested in jest, the deliberate and intentional cultivation of emotions is a common manipulative strategy used by lawyers, politicians, salesmen, and advertisers. The goal of these cunning individuals is to trigger snap judgments or to prompt impulsive buying decisions; deliberate strategies designed to circumvent objective deliberation and reason (Petty, Fabrigar, & Wegener, 2003). Suppressing emotional reactions is tenuous at best and minimally unhealthy. Actually, forestalling an emotional response and disguising behaviors is extremely challenging for many individuals, while for others, hiding emotions is a product of a conditioned brain and some crafty experience. Regardless, the deliberate repression of raging emotions is linked to detrimental psychological consequences, including depression. Further, the intentional repression of emotion inhibits both accurate sensory perception and efficient cognitive processing (Gross & Levenson, 1997).

The overt nature of emotional episodes is both helpful and agnostic in fostering understanding of emotion and reactive behavior. The unique and obvious symptoms that accompany some emotions are readily observed and easily identified (Russell, 1994). Universally, the expressive symptoms of anger, disgust, fear, happiness, sadness, and surprise are consistently portrayed and accurately interpreted across cultures (Ekman, 1993), with evidence suggesting that many basic emotions are innate and evolutionary (Izard, 1994). People cry when they are sad, tremble in fear, laugh and smile when happy, and frown when angry. Each major emotion aligns with relatively stable and predictive behavioral patterns, such as the unmistakable resistive passion, raised voice, and flushed face of an individual when expressing the most common emotion: anger.

One reason individuals are unsuccessful at hiding visible, auditory, and affective symptoms are the inevitable somatic (bodily) and physiological responses associated with many emotions. Early theories of emotion, such as that of James-Lange (Lang, 1994) and the facial-feedback hypothesis (Buck, 1980; Izard, 1994), contended that emotions and biology share an intricately entwined, symbiotic relationship: One cannot exist without the other. These unitary historical views of emotion implied that nonverbal antecedents activated or accompanied the expression of emotions and were prompted by bodily changes in the individual. The temporality of emotional reactions was and still is debated, with various perspectives asserting that individuals first evaluate a situation and ascribe contingencies to what they experience, or conversely, bodily change precedes behavior and predicts your emotional expression.

Pragmatically, temporality does not matter. It makes little practical difference if you shudder at the sight of hungry, saw-toothed, drooling grizzly bear because you are afraid or if the fear is instigated by bodily changes, such as adrenal secretion or wet pants. As the aspiring and practical MD knows by reading the previous eight chapters, when confronting a bear, it only matters whether or not you can outrun the bear.

Some emotions are not easily identified or well defined (Parkinson, 1995), and like many other motivational constructs, operational consensus of what constitutes an emotion is contentious. For instance, are you able to readily distinguish or articulate qualitative differences in feelings when embarrassed, humiliated, or mortified? Probably not. In aggregate, most scholars define emotions as event-driven episodes accompanied by biological changes that lead to culturally contingent "expressive behavior" (Moors, 2010, p. 1), also referred to as intentional action or "motivated action" (Parkinson, 1995, p. 8). These definitions imply that emotional action is goal directed with a measurable starting and end point. Once you kill the annoying fly buzzing around your head, your fly-induced anger will subside. Emotions differ from moods, dispositions, and attitudes, which are transient, involve multiple, deliberate cogitations and are usually associated with series of events. Unlike an emotion, moods may not have a singular identifiable target of origination or an easily identified cause. *Affect* is also frequently used as a term to describe emotions and is sometimes used interchangeably. Affect is distinguished as the neurophysical state associated with particular subjective feelings during an emotional event (Russell, 2003). In practical terms, affect is typically an evaluative function indicating how we feel, while emotion is the expression and result of the subjective evaluation of the feeling.

Ironically, emotional expressions that are incredibly easy to describe with examples (e.g., "OMG he is so sad, he can't stop crying") are particularly challenging to interpret through indisputable behavioral and neurological evidence. Recall from chapter three and Principle #14 (p. 50) the multi-level, hierarchical nature of neurological activation, occurring systemically or individually and interdependently at five activity levels: genetic, synaptic, autonomic, skeletal, and cognitive. This means different emotions can have identical somatic and behavioral markers, the same emotions can activate different reactions between individuals, and the same individual can exhibit different behaviors while reacting to the same emotion! Beside definitions, scholars and philosophers debate what is necessary or sufficient to be considered an emotional episode, what does or does not constitute an emotion, and the sequential or discontinuous etiology of emotional paths (Moors, 2010). Additional concerns examine the automatic and implicit nature of emotion and what is responsible for individual differences in emotional behavior. For example, when does the dislike of a person evolve into the emotion of hate? Remedially, when do emotions result in stable belief change and can the belief change be reversed? While many of these questions have been answered through empirical research, as MDs, we care less about these philosophical and rhetorical musings and more about practicality.

Pragmatically, knowledge of emotion is helpful to the MD for at least three reasons. First, emotion helps diagnosis motivational issues. Emotion and motivation are both influenced by the relationship between the individual and his or her physical and psychological surroundings (Parkinson, 1995). From a causal perspective, excluding evaluation of emotion may skew the interpretation of motivated behavior. Second, inferences based upon emotional episodes and emotional expressions reveal the substance of motivational beliefs. By example, if you observed a person being assaulted in public and the bystanders elected not to intervene, you might contend that the bystanders lacked the physical ability to help, had little empathy for the victim, or held the belief that people should fend for themselves. Alternatively, you might have surmised that the bystanders had exceptional ability to regulate emotion. Although the precise bystander motive would be unknown, clearly you could rule out courage and bravery as compelling motives of the bystanders. Third, although research and corresponding inferences frequently focus on how to mediate performance-inhibiting emotions, such as anger and anxiety, many positive emotions, including happiness and pride, are contextually bound and result in performance enhancements. Knowledge of the circumstances and conditions necessary to promote positive emotions are a valuable addition to the MD's strategic repertoire, especially when responsible for enhancing the knowledge or productivity of others.

Awareness of the signs and symptoms of many emotions is key to diagnostic precision; however, the ongoing focus here is on why and how emotion-provoking events are appraised differently among individuals leading to wide performance and behavior fluctuations. The remainder of the chapter emphasizes the subjective appraisal of contextual and social variables motivating the individual to express actionable behavior that may differ in both intensity and direction. I concentrate on the critical question of which factors individuals consider when evaluating their environments, leading to a variety of motives for their ensuing emotional expression. Last, the role of emotional regulation is discussed, including how to orchestrate contexts that promote adaptive self-regulation of emotion to enhance learning and performance.

Principle #44—Emotional reactions are localized, subjective, and learned

"There are good days and there are bad days, and this is one of them."
Lawrence Welk

"In the hopes of reaching the moon, men fail to see the flowers that blossom at their feet."
Albert Schweitzer

Emotions are powerful motives that prompt us to take actions that might be suppressed in absence of the emotion. The emotionally instigated behaviors we exhibit are frequently in direct response to contextual cues emanating from our surrounding virtual and physical environments. We evaluate our surroundings by making cognitive appraisals and judgments, often based on our implicit values and beliefs. Through selective attention to goal-directed and personally salient cues, individuals subjectively discriminate and instantly appraise the people, places, and things they encounter. Perceptions of the affective quality of an event occur as quickly as within

25 milliseconds of evaluating an environmental stimulus (Bargh, 1997). However, *what* we perceive varies remarkably among individuals.

For instance, when entering a workplace meeting or university classroom, we must decide where to sit. We likely choose a spot based upon who is in the room, the impression we want to give to others, and the degree of comfort we have contributing to the impending discussion. Imagine seeing chairs lined up along the perimeter walls with one big table in the middle of the room. For some, this scenario might be appraised as an opportunity to sit back, be passive, and blend in with the crowd. A radically different perception would result when encountering a cluster of four chairs around small oval tables. The more intimate set-up may evoke an appraisal of apprehension and anxiety for some individuals, while instilling opportunities to excel in others. Based upon our cultural perspectives, social proclivities, past experiences, and contextual emotions, environments will be perceived as contributory or inhibitory to our objectives, assisting or forestalling progress toward desired personal goals. Ultimately, some individuals will favor perimeter positions at a large table, avoiding interaction as much as possible, while others will relish in the intimacy of quad seating. For some, the seating arrangement is opportunistic, contributing to feelings of pride, egoism, and enhanced efficacy. Others might cringe, riddled with trepidation and disdain, as the quad configuration could lead to unwanted attention, obligatory participation, and possibly result in embarrassment and shame for conceptual mistakes or social blunders.

Brosch, Pourtois, and Sandler (2010) described the evaluation of perceptions as the process of "categorization," or creating an internal mental representation that "activates certain categories in the mind" (p. 378). The categorical appraisals we develop about stimuli are largely consistent with our current mood and emotional states (Tamir & Robinson, 2007). Each emotion is aligned with a set of personally appraised consequences and contingencies varying between and within individuals. Categorization of emotions ranges from the simplistic "approach or avoid" designations that we make (Nesse & Ellsworth, 2009) to a long list of naturally occurring, culturally universal emotions (Barrett, 2006). Most contemporary approaches suggest a phylogeny of at least 12 primary emotions (see Table 9.1) that broadly represent dozens of discrete subordinate feelings with corresponding behavioral implications (Neese, 2004).

However, activating affect is not as simplistic as making a choice between two dichotomous attributes. Affect exists along a continuum of appraisals, which are not mutually exclusive. The absence of negative ruminations does not necessarily imply the presence of positive affect, nor does a dominantly pessimistic outlook exclude the probability of positivity. Instead, emotions fluctuate and evolve along at least two dimensions: potency and frequency. *Potency* is the subjective experience of emotional intensity and operates independent of *frequency*, which refers to the amount or prevalence of a particular emotion. Differences in potency suggest, for instance, that you may be conspicuously more afraid and take quicker and more decisive avoidant action when encountering a vicious stare from a drooling lion than when being watched through the eyes of a harmless housefly. Conversely, the types of reactions we exhibit to similar stimuli are fairly consistent and predictable. People who experience high

Table 9.1 Naturally occurring emotions and behavioral implications

Emotional catalyst	Valence	Behavioral implication
Desire	Positive	Approach
Physical pleasure	Positive	Approach
Love	Positive	Approach
Friendship	Positive	Approach
Pride	Positive	Approach
Shame	Negative	Avoid
Guilt	Negative	Avoid
Grief	Negative	Avoid
Jealousy	Negative	Avoid
Sadness	Negative	Avoid
Anxiety	Negative	Avoid
Pain	Negative	Avoid or Approach

Based on Nesse and Ellsworth (2009).

positive emotional intensity also frequently experience high negative intensity. For example, when analyzing the nature of positive affect, Diener, Larsen, Levine, and Emmons (1985) concluded:

> *Those who are high in frequency of positive affect and high in intensity tend to feel exuberance and joy, whereas those high in frequency but low in intensity experience contentment and serenity. Those who are low on frequency and high in intensity often experience depression. Low-frequency persons who are also low in intensity experience affect characterized by mild unhappiness (p. 1263).*

Consequently, we may reasonably assume that the ontological consistency of some primary emotions may yield stereotypical behaviors (Brosch et al., 2010). By example, angry people almost always yell and get red in the face. The predictability of biological and behavioral correlates of some emotions has led some researchers to conclude that emotion is trait-like (Frick & White, 2008; Petrides, Pita, & Kokkinaki, 2007). However, even when emotional expression is engendered in personality, variability in behavior is often observed (Kaspar & König, 2012). The categorical consistency of emotion is a function of *intensity*. When intensity is experimentally removed from the emotional equation, significant negative correlations between positive and negative affect result (Denier et al., 1985): Reactions to the same stimuli may differ within the same individual, and different responses to identical stimuli are often observed between individuals. Unfortunately for the MD, there is no convenient chart or fixed list of behaviors associating particular emotions with a triggered response (Moors, 2010). The more relevant question is this: What triggers a particular emotion in a particular person, and how do individuals evaluate information that results in emotionally-charged behavior?

Scholars vigorously debate the temporality of emotional reactions, with one perspective suggesting that initial physiological reactions to an environmental event precede any emotional expression, while an alternative view champions the primacy of antecedent emotions as the trigger for physiological change. Regardless of sequence, the trajectory of emotional expression arguably follows a predictable and learned pattern. First, almost all emotional events are preceded by a definable interaction between the person and the environment. Second, a subjective and localized cognitive appraisal occurs based on the situational nature and circumstances of the environmental event. The appraisal process consists of assigning emotions and a set of emotional responses to the event. The valence of the emotional ascription is influenced primarily by specific semantic and affective memories associated with a similar circumstance. During the appraisal process, individuals differentiate and evaluate historical representations of the event. Individuals will be motivated to avoid or escape environmental triggers that previously either resulted in negative feelings or outcomes or when the individual perceives the emotional trigger to be inconsistent with his or her cultural values and idiosyncratic beliefs. Conversely, individuals may be motivated to strive toward approaching environmental targets when similar past experience has been personally rewarding or pleasantly evaluated.

Third, bodily responses will accompany the emotional activation. Changes in physiology may be at the obvious behavioral level as evidenced by radical shifts in facial expression; body language or dyspnea, such as when someone is crying from shame or humiliation; or gloating with pride and ambition after winning a competitive event. Other bodily changes may have less obvious somatic markers, such as heart rate escalation, pupil dilation, or fluctuations in breathing patterns, such as when a person experiences anxiety or fear. Physiological arousal will also occur at the concealed neurological and synaptic levels, as changes in hormonal levels and neurotransmissions will occur in the sympathetic nervous system, as the brain and the mind coordinate the appropriate response to the emotionally activated event.

Finally, the congenial partnership of mind and body activates emotional expression and a corresponding motor response, as the individual actively seeks to physically or psychologically approach or avoid the target of their desire. Sometimes referred to as "core affect" (Russell, 2003), the resultant behavior is energized by the target, leading to a conscious continuum of emotional expression based upon fluctuating feelings determined through subjective experience. The premise of core affect implies that certain emotions lead to culturally predictable, prototypical behaviors with minimal variation of expression across individuals. For example, across cultures, jealousy imbues insecurity, while love begets joy. Through consistent and rapid appraisal and vigilance, core affect propels the individual to take action, until the emotionally catalyzed goal is satisfied. In total, the individual experiences an affectively-induced cycle that is sequential, perceptual, evaluative, and discriminatory. The cycle is largely conditioned through personal experience, but mediated by the social norms and contextual conditions that precipitated the emotional event.

Ambiguous or unfamiliar stimuli present a host of integrative responses that are far less predictable of affective valence or ensuing behavior. When an individual lacks a clear mental representation of how event causality leads to certain emotional and behavioral progressions, the concrete appraisal algorithm used with familiar stimuli is no longer a viable reconciliation method. Instead, individuals proceed guardedly, and sometimes automatically, when evaluating the salient and existing mental representations of an environmental event. Contextual appraisals are guided, in part, by attitudinal bias toward a target, situational goals, personal risk propensity, and overall domain knowledge (Rubio, Hernández, and Márquez, 2013). The specific contingencies to which a person attends are governed by the characteristics of the person and the situation and also by the strength with which potential emotions might influence subsequent behavior. Individuals have a proclivity to focus more attention, and show less ability to ignore, those factors that imply threat than to disregard neutral or positive stimuli (Rothermund, Wentura, & Bak, 2001).

A caveat to the universal sequential and serial path of emotional expression is the reality that some emotions may be triggered subconsciously, with no active awareness of what caused the emotional response (Berridge & Winkielman, 2003). Automatic responses occur when individuals merely consider the perceptual features of a stimulus or when spontaneous thinking occurs. Automatic responses can be innate and impulsive, such as the automatic fleeing behavior exercised in the face of danger. Strong evidence suggests that even with seemingly emotionally neutral objects and events, we are predisposed to certain biased judgments and make implicit affective evaluations in order to make sense of our surrounding environments. Using simulated measures, such as the Emotional Stroop test (McKenna & Sharma, 1995), which consists of naming the font color of a word irrespective of the word meaning, shows that individuals rely heavily on implicit cues and unconscious evaluations when making emotionally-laden appraisals. The Emotional Stroop test results show consistent patterns of longer response latency for color naming of threat-related words, such as "abuse," "gloom," and "evil," more so than for neutral words, such as "bank," "marble," or "dirt." Results of this nature support the conclusion that seemingly neutral objects and experiences are infused with an "emotional flavor" that potentially influences perceptions and impacts the focus and efficiency of cognition. In other words, affective ascriptions have cognitive consequences, which the seasoned MD knows are often associated with corresponding motivational implications.

Most importantly, intense emotion influences attentional focus and memory (Levine & Edelstein, 2010). Although results vary across studies, typically heightened levels of attention are associated with elevated levels of emotional experience. However, focused attention does not guarantee learning or knowledge retention. During affective arousal, individuals have a tendency to remember main ideas, sometimes referred to as "the gist," but have difficulty recalling peripheral details associated with a task or event (Kensinger, Garoff-Eaton, & Schacter, 2007). Many explanations for the qualitative influence of emotion on attentional resources and downstream memory processing suggest better memory of central ideas results from heightened arousal, but at the cost of a narrowing cognitive focus that usurps precious working-memory resources, limiting memory capacity needed to recall details. Emotional valence also has cognitive implications. Unified behavioral observation and biopsychological evidence confirm that negative events are recalled more accurately than positive ones (Kensinger, 2009), with differences between emotional type exerting the greatest influence on what is remembered and why. Ultimately, the influence of emotion on performance motives is undeniable; however, in order to use emotional cues as a mediating strategy tool, specific emotions should be considered.

Principle #45—Anxiety and boredom are performance-restricting culprits

Anxiety

The irrefutable outcome of emotional appraisal is motivated action. The emotional valence associated with a particular context, person, or task will empower individuals to actively seek and pursue certain positively evaluated targets while vehemently avoiding negative others. While most emotions have motivational consequences, those emotions empirically shown to enhance or inhibit performance motivation, especially those emotions that may be within the jurisdiction of the MD's influence and control, are of greatest interest. Emotions, such as jealousy, greed, or grief, are vital to understanding human behaviors but are beyond the scope of feasible intervention by the MD. In lieu of the dozens of reviews and meta-analyses completed on specific or contextual emotions (Baas, De Dreu, & Nijstad, 2008; Pekrun, Goetz, Titz, & Perry, 2002; Stankowich & Blumstein, 2005; Wittouck, Van Autreve, De Jaegere, Portzky, & van Heeringen, 2011), the focus here is on two of the greatest classroom culprits contributing to disengagement and mediocre academic performance; anxiety and boredom. Despite the seemingly antithetical nature of these two sentiments, both avoidance emotions are perpetuated by maladaptive motives, albeit for vastly different reasons.

Anxiety, the most frequently researched performance inhibitor (Beck, 2004), is an affective response exemplified behaviorally by uneasiness or nervousness as a result of an encountered stimulus or event perceived as threatening or unpleasant. Anxiety can originate from multiple sources, but frequently, performance anxiety develops based on a recurring history of task failure or unrealistic performance expectations from parents or teachers (Wigfield & Eccles, 1989). Heritability of anxiety-related personality traits is common, with 40% of anxiety occurrence attributed to genetic variations, as evidenced by studies of genetic twins (Hettema, Neale, & Kendler, 2001). Individuals also exhibit environmentally-induced genetic susceptibility to anxiety through hyperexcitability to aversive stimuli, coupled with increased activity in the fear receptors of the brain (Gross & Hen, 2004). Behaviorally, anxiety occurs most often when negative outcomes are anticipated during a performance task. Anxiety may develop during an actual threat encountered by an individual, or anxiety can be triggered merely by the expectation of a threat, in the absence of a specific environmental peril (Bandura, 1988).

Identifying sources of anxiety is relevant for potential mediation of anxiety. State anxiety is situational in nature, environmentally triggered, and often experienced when encountering unfamiliar performance contexts, when facing tasks deemed overly complex, or when attempting challenges beyond one's perceived skill level (Onwuegbuzie & Wilson, 2003). State anxiety is a malleable and predictable form of anxiety, since similar contextual conditions evoke prototypical behaviors and affect, such as the sweaty palms and stomach cramps that accompany worry and apprehension. By example, a person who habitually fears any computer-related task or an otherwise academically successful student who freezes at the thought of certain types of calculus problems would be characterized as exhibiting state anxiety. Trait anxiety is both static and stable, akin to an enduring personality characteristic, and is less amenable to intervention than state anxiety (Chen, Gully, Whiteman, & Kilcullen, 2006). Individuals with trait-like anxiety have nonspecific, generalized anxiety across multiple performance domains. Trait-like anxiety can be especially devastating for performance because irrespective of skill or competency beliefs, individuals plagued with stable and recurring trait anxiety will routinely exhibit inferior performance, especially during higher-order and creative thinking tasks, which are integral to performance success in many domains (Byron & Khazanchi, 2011).

Regardless of source, anxiety inhibits optimal performance for at least three reasons, which directly correspond with plummeting performance motivation. A primary consequence of anxiety is excessive worry, defined as "any cognitive expression of concern about one's own performance" (Liebert & Morris, 1967, p. 975). Preoccupation with worry results in intrusive thoughts concerning the self and self-criticism of competence, leading to attributions of failure based on low ability (Covington, 2009). Anxiety is causally linked to lower self-efficacy, leading to performance apathy and task avoidant motivation due to the anticipation of aversive task consequences (Bandura, 1988; Hoffman, 2010). Second, highly anxious individuals have little choice but to allocate finite working-memory resources to anxiety reduction, in turn limiting the allocation of cognitive resources toward effortful learning and performance (Eysenck & Calvo, 1992). Third, highly anxious individuals use less efficient and productive learning strategies, relying instead on cognitively costly working-memory dependent strategies, such as basic rehearsal (Pekrun et al., 2002). Presumably, the highly anxious individual has a decreased ability to self-monitor and is easily distracted by personal ruminations leading to an altered focus on task-relevant cues needed to resolve academic and performance concerns (Pintrich & DeGroot, 1990). In aggregate, anxiety generates numerous cognitive consequences, interfering with the ability to maintain a clear task focus.

Fortunately, not all performance anxiety is debilitating. A moderate amount of anxiety can actually *enhance* performance outcomes in many domains due to a heightened state of arousal that directs attention to salient task demands (Wilson, 2012). The familiar "clutch performances" typically observed in athletic and military arenas illustrate the benefits of performance under stressful evaluative conditions. Anxiety advantages are realized when an individual demonstrates the ability to regulate and focus attentional resources during a performance episode (Janelle & Hatfield, 2008). Performance is thought to be enhanced under conditions of moderate anxiety because some individuals are better able to monitor and address the heightened arousal that is promulgated by their anxiety. These individuals use the moderate anxiety as a motivational catalyst to increase effort because they believe they have the ability and control to use moderate anxiety as a coping strategy to enhance performance outcomes (Carver & Scheier, 1988). Anxiety-controlling advantages are typically realized by individuals with greater domain expertise and more expansive working-memory capacity (Eysenck & Calvo, 1992; Hoffman & Schraw, 2009), as these individuals are more efficient managers of the increased cognitive load that accompanies demanding performance challenges. Unfortunately, individuals with less expertise, those lacking focused attentional resources, or those perceiving a lack of control over their performance context, succumb to the debilitating effects of performance anxiety. Corroborating biopsychological and behavioral evidence suggests that physiological and cognitive arousal reaches a point of diminishing returns, with optimal performance across performance tasks generally observed at 60% to 70% of maximum arousal (Arent & Landers, 2003; Wilson, Smith, & Holmes, 2007). Once the threshold of manageable anxiety is surpassed, performance suffers even for the most experienced and skilled performers and athletes.

Operating under the generalized conclusion that as levels of anxiety increase, performance accuracy and relative efficiency suffer, it behooves educators to take proactive actions to discount or eliminate the perception of threat and ensuing anxiety. Straightforward instructional approaches, such as creating clarity in learning objectives, welcoming mistakes during learning, and giving learners the ability to self-pace knowledge building, are some of the many well-supported strategies that can temper the impact of academic anxiety (Stipek, 1998). Hallett and Hoffman (2014), in a review of optimal performance strategies in business domains, revealed that through a series of proactive routines and rituals, individuals can quell performance anxiety and mitigate the anxious feelings that accompany high-pressure performance demonstrations. By using pretask visualization of the performance process, monitoring on-board effectiveness of performance, and employing a structured methodology to know in advance what might go awry, the probability of an anxiety-neutral peak performance is improved. Further, Graesser and D'Mello (2012), in a series of studies using the intelligent tutoring system "AutoTutor" for complex learning, found that the computerized monitoring of facial expressions and body language can easily detect instances of educational "impasse" (p. 189), which are essentially instances of escalating emotion (i.e., anxiety) that frequently lead to cognitive disengagement. These innovative emotion-sensitive technologies show substantial promise to not only seamlessly detect emotions during computer-based learning, but also to automatically modulate content difficulty based on emotional cues as a means to reduce anxiety and forestall learner disengagement.

Boredom

The heightened arousal realized during many anxiety-ridden performances is, perhaps, the antithesis of the disengagement experienced during bouts of instructional boredom—one of the few emotions to be experienced more frequently than anxiety in school (Goetz, Frenzel, Pekrun, Hall, & Lüdtke, 2007). When individuals encounter learning content or performance opportunities that they subjectively perceive as unpleasant, indifferent, lacking value, or useless, cognitive and/or behavioral disengagement typically follows. Feelings that accompany boredom include a deactivating cognitive focus, memory lapse, distractibility, apathy, lethargy, and the physical desire to extricate one's self from the aversive source of boredom (Nett, Goetz, & Hall, 2011; Pekrun, Goetz, Daniels, Stupnisky, & Perry, 2010; Pekrun, Hall, Goetz, & Perry, 2014). Surprisingly, boredom is highly correlated with anger, but unlike anger that usually triggers motivation toward the egregious target, boredom is a negative emotion highly related to avoidance and escape motives and behavior (Goetz et al., 2007).

The effects of boredom are pervasive and severe. In a study using the experience sampling approach, which intermittently asks individuals to report how they feel and what they are doing at predetermined time intervals, 58% of students reported some degree of boredom during instruction, while only 6% indicated never being bored (Goetz et al., 2014). Contingent upon the source and culture of investigation, boredom is an instigating factor in 32% to 50% of individuals who drop out of school (Larson & Richards, 1991; Wegner, Flisher, Chikobvu, Lombard, & King, 2008). The incidence, severity and consequence of boredom are further echoed in nonacademic domains. Work and organizational boredom has been reported in as high as 87% of the workforce, and boredom is linked to organizational malcontent, reduced work effort, high turnover, and lowered perceptions of organizational support (van Hooff & van Hooft, 2014). Workers are hard pressed to conceal the emotional malaise of boredom, as the emotion is related to feelings of "underemployment" and individuals self-reporting boredom consistently earn lower performance ratings from their supervisors (Watt & Hargis, 2010). Boredom is not only experienced in obligatory ventures, such as work and school; it is experienced far more frequently in leisure activities than in work (Csikszentmihalyi, 1997). The apathy of adolescence, which many times is a derivative of boredom, leads to risky and unhealthy behaviors, such as substance abuse and delinquency (Wegner & Flisher, 2009). Perhaps an even more revealing consequence of boredom is the disturbing incidence of higher degrees of boredom in psychiatric and neurologically challenged populations (Goldberg, Eastwood, LaGuardia, & Danckert, 2011), which suggests that boredom may be contributory to mental illness.

Boredom differs from lack of interest, based upon the polarity of the emotional valence. The avoidant behaviors associated with boredom are actually the converse of the approach behaviors associated with interest (Pekrun et al., 2014). Learners actively seek out domains found to be of interest and value while *passively* ignoring topics lacking interest. Bored learners do not loathe uninteresting topics but, instead, find little value or meaning in many of their academic endeavors. Tilburg and Igou (2012) investigated the unique experiential nature of boredom by asking learners to describe and rate their feelings during instances of boredom. Analysis of results showed a consistent pattern of feelings of questionable utility and lower perceived value of knowledge, leading to the conclusion that "boredom—experienced in educational settings, work settings, leisure contexts, and while being alone—involves feeling restless and unchallenged at the same time, while thinking that the situation serves no purpose" (p. 191).

A preponderance of evidence indicates that bored learners achieve less, have lower academic engagement, and exert less effort (Linnebrink, 2007). However, contrary to some misconceptions, the occurrence of boredom is not relegated to only those learners with exceptional ability. Instead, most studies suggest that boredom is more frequently observed in *low-achieving students*, and after controlling for other variables, such as prior achievement, gender, and age, boredom and achievement show significant reciprocal relations (Pekrun et al., 2014). In other words, a dual relationship exists between boredom and academic achievement. Boredom may cause lower achievement, and conversely inferior academic performance may be the catalyst for boredom. Regardless of temporality, academic performance suffers when learners are bored.

Boredom originates from a number of sources that are within the direct control and influence of educators. Learners report boredom during monotonous teacher-centered instruction (Larson & Richards, 1991) and in situations where teachers tend to dominate instruction by using a top-down pedagogical style, such as typically observed during direct instruction, thus limiting the extent of learner involvement with instructional choices and content (Fallis & Opotow, 2003). Student–teacher relationships and the extent of positive attitudes toward content may also become a catalyst for boredom. Disengagement and boredom are highly probable when students dislike their teacher or when they appraise a teaching style unfavorably. Boredom is rampant when content is perceived as particularly challenging or irrelevant, such during advanced mathematics instruction (Daschmann, Goetz, & Stupnisky, 2011). The control-value theory of academic emotions (Pekrun et al., 2002; Pekrun et al., 2014) suggests that students with perceived low levels of control over their instructional fates are especially vulnerable to episodes of boredom. Reduced control means that learners believe they have limited influence over the nature of instructional challenges and outcomes. Incongruence between learners and instructors results in boredom when material is perceived as overly demanding, resulting in cognitive disengagement due to complexity, while being underchallenged may imply minimal demands on learners, resulting in questionable teacher "withedness," which occurs when instructors are disconnected from the necessary pace or activity levels needed by their learners (Kounin, 1970).

Considering the deleterious outcomes of boredom, conscious effort toward eliminating circumstantial factors that contribute to boredom should prove fruitful for learning and engagement. Clearly, the minimization of boredom depends on creating meaningful and challenging learning opportunities through the appropriate calibration of instruction with learner needs and expertise. Additionally, intentional strategies can be used to offset the inevitable emotional consequences of boredom. First, learners must appraise instructional content as relevant and authentic. Ideally, when mastering content, learners should reach the conclusion that knowledge acquisition is inspiring and practical and has an applied value. Second, learners need the perception of at least some degree of control over the educational process and the associated outcomes of their cognitive effort. Enhanced learner engagement can be realized by creating an autonomy-supportive teaching environment that offers learners involvement in instructional and assessment choices (Jang, Reeve, & Deci, 2010). The calibration of instruction with learner interest and expertise can be accomplished by paying specific attention to the cognitive complexity of instructional goals and learning materials. Formative assessment strategies, such as polling learners, asking clarifying questions, promoting collaborative learning, and assessing the intentions of learners, are some well-supported instructional strategies (Black & Williams, 2009) that may eliminate or reduce boredom. Many learners, when bored, seek solace through empathy with their equally bored peers, subsequently shifting attentional resources from learning goals to interactions with other individuals. Efforts toward structuring a learning context that eliminates distractions will contribute to the self-regulation of boredom, based merely on the opportunistic physical composition of the learning environment, or as the band The Offspring declared in their song *Come out and Play*, "You gotta keep 'em separated!"

Finally, both boredom and elevated levels of anxiety promote a similar avoidance motivation, where learners seek to disengage from the source of their discontent as a means to regulate their negative affect. Thus, two approaches may be viable alternatives to promoting engagement. The MD may deliberately elect to circumvent negative cognitive appraisals and the behavioral withdrawal associated with boredom and anxiety by trying to eliminate noxious and boredom-provoking stimuli, or instead choose to create a learning environment that generates positive emotion. Although the evidence is mixed concerning the role of emotional valence and achievement (Linnenbrink, 2007), the latter strategy can effectively induce an approach motivation, the next topic of investigation.

Principle #46—Positive affect is a powerful performance determinant

> "Happiness is not achieved by the conscious pursuit of happiness; it is generally the by-product of other activities."
>
> *Aldous Huxley*

Knowing some of the familiar and enduring consequences of negative affect, it seems appropriate that the seasoned MD would focus on identifying ways to eradicate anxiety, eliminate boredom, and reduce stress perceptions. In reality, the subjective nature of emotional appraisals and the total removal of contextual and behavioral cues that prompt negativity is conceptually idealistic and logically improbable. Instead, the MD is faced with a tactical decision: If the MD wishes to defer or subdue subjective appraisals of anxiety, boredom, or stress, catalysts for negative emotion can be identified and potentially mitigated. Alternatively, a prudent and potentially more rewarding strategy is to orchestrate an environment that emboldens positivity. A deeper understanding of how individuals appraise their contextual conditions suggests that cultivating positive emotions, in contrast to simply suppressing negative affect, is a more advantageous option with resounding long-term benefits that contribute to optimal psychological functioning.

"Broaden and build" theories suggest that unlike eliminating negative emotions through primarily psychological and homeostatic reconciliation, positive experience broadens personal perceptions, thoughts, and actions (Fredrickson, 2001). The positive experience contributes to the growth of individual physical, emotional and intellectual resources, a contingency unlikely when removing avoidant, negative emotions. Pursuit of positive affect aligns with an "approach" motivation where people deliberately seek out new tasks and opportunities that expand their horizons, unlike the restrictive attentional and narrow focus exhibited when individuals fixate on dispelling toxic anxiety. Individuals motivated by positive experience tend to be more socially focused and confident. The positive motive induces frequency and receptivity for love, laughter, and having fun (Gable & Haidt, 2005). Further, unlike distracting negative affect, which is abated when a goal target is reached (e.g., you are no longer frantic and panicking after your corrupted computer document is fixed), positive affect promotes enduring memories that outlast the triggering event and continues to motivate the individual long after that loving feeling is gone (Cohn & Fredrickson, 2009).

Motivational Leader—*Alec Torelli*

On the surface, Alec Torelli seems just like any other friendly guy; he is bright, talkative, and sincere, with a cheery disposition and an affable approach to life's challenges and obstacles. In other words, in many ways he exemplifies the type of person described by the "broaden and build" view of motivation. However, Alec Torelli is no "ordinary" guy. Hailing from Orange County, California, he attended Southern Methodist University, but at the age of only 19 years, he decided to change his life and pursue his dream of financial and personal independence by becoming a professional poker player.

Alec has played over 2,000,000 hands of poker, winning tournaments around the world while cashed out at nine final tables, including twice at the World Series of Poker and twice at the World Poker Tournament. Today, he is considered a world-class poker champion, who, by age of 27 years, had collected over $3,000,000 in tournament winnings. Alec, however, is not like the slick, commercialized, and animated characters portrayed on television; instead, he is an anomaly—he does not play poker for fame or notoriety.

Alec's goals are far greater than being a top-notch player. For Alec success is not just about being a winner in poker but being a winner in life. Winning means feeling adequate, loved, healthy, and financially free to live the life he wants—a life filled with freedom, excitement, and choices. Alec craves the independence of being his own boss, free to follow his passions and dreams. At the apex of his poker career, when he was cashing in on every tournament, he had a catharsis; there is more to one's success than what happens at the poker table.

He took a hiatus from poker and started to work toward realizing some of his dreams. He gave speeches at universities, competed in an Olympic triathlon, visited 30 countries, learned Italian, trained in yoga in Bali, studied at the Gelato University, met his future wife, and began coaching other poker players. He now thrives on sharing what he has learned with others through his coaching activities, and ironically, helping others allowed Alec to increase his own motivation to play and challenge himself to reach new heights. He has been a coach for over 6 years now and is taking on bigger challenges every day, playing against the heavy hitters at Macau, China, where the best global contenders compete in the largest cash games on the planet.

When asked if he had a message for readers, Alec replied, "Don't choose a job and try to adjust it around the life you want. Choose a lifestyle and then pick the job that will allow you to make it a reality. Don't listen to what anyone else wants for you and your future. Trust yourself, and follow your dreams. Life's too short for anything else." (A. Torelli, personal communication, October 13, 2014). When not at the poker tables, Alec attains happiness through fitness, tennis, writing, reading, speaking, personal development, health, online marketing, and, of course, traveling the globe pursing his dreams with his adorable wife, Ambra.

The domains of positive psychology and subjective well-being (SWB) empirically demonstrate that individual differences in positive emotions and mood, such as happiness, relaxation, and pleasantness, contribute to consistent and enduring effects on performance in a variety of productive ways. People who report life satisfaction and positive emotions, such as Alec Torelli, have decisive advantages over those who affirm a negative and pessimistic outlook. Positive emotions provide distinct psychological and health benefits, including greater resistance to common cold viruses (Cohen, Doyle, Turner, Alper, & Skoner, 2003), using a broader repertoire of coping strategies (Fredrickson & Joiner, 2002), and earning accolades from others as an indication of being more social, creative, and likable (Lyubomirsky, King, & Diener, 2005). Individuals with higher measurable levels of SWB land more job interviews, attain better performance evaluations, and achieve higher career growth than those with lower levels (Lyubomirsky et al., 2005), including making more money (Lucas, Clark, Georgellis, & Diener, 2004). Although it is unclear if money begets well-being or if well-being leads to increased earning opportunity, meta-analytic results from over 100 studies (Pinquart & Sörensen, 2000) indicate that only 3% of the variability in SWB is explained by income level alone. These results, although correlational, imply that SWB is accounted for by many other factors beyond income.

Happiness, a major component of SWB, can not only exert a number of promising influences on optimal performance but also has a host of empirical and interpretative challenges. The primary measurement concern is the implicit and widely held subjective nature of what constitutes happiness. Individuals have extremely diverse representations of what counts as happy and are frequently unable to articulate differences between happiness and other positive emotions. In the 2014 number one hit song *Happy*, Pharrell Williams invited us to "clap along if you *know* (emphasis added) what happiness is to you." Forty-four years earlier, music icon John Lennon suggested that "Happiness is a warm gun," confounding critics who debated that the lyric had a covert sexual or drug symbolism. Perhaps the breadth of interpretations of happiness comes from the sordid story of Mark Goddard; 14 years after being in a horrendous motorcycle accident, being highly motivated by the apparent lack of suitable health care in the United Kingdom, he built a home-made guillotine and cut off his injured hand after unsuccessfully trying to slice it off with a knife. Mark still was not happy after posing with the amputated consequence of his unresolved happiness motive.

Clearly, defining happiness is exceedingly challenging, highly subjective, and culturally nuanced. Empirically, happiness is considered "a preponderance of positive emotions" (Lyubomirsky et al., 2005, p. 803) but is contingent, at least in part, on the correlation between one's successful outcomes and those valued by society. In an expansive meta-analytic study that included 293 samples and over 275,000 participants and used cross-sectional, longitudinal, and experimental methods, as well as self-reports and observations from work, school, health, and social contexts, Lyubomirsky and colleagues (2005) revealed that individuals scoring high on empirical measures of positive affect are positively perceived, sociable, likable, cooperative, healthy, and creative. Most important, for achieving optimal performance outcomes, happy people gain satisfaction from life experiences, even when things do not go according to plan. You may have noticed one common theme among all of the individuals profiled in this book. Each looked upon potentially negative experiences as opportunities to excel, not as emotional impediments. Faced with debilitating injuries (Alex Dixon, p. 53), family hardship (LaSonya Moore, p. 117), career diversions (Jessi Colter, p. 221), physical immobility (Amanda Boxtel, p. 358), and horrendous racial prejudice and discrimination (Robert Knowling, Jr., p. 317), these motivational leaders anticipated fluctuations in their happiness and used the ebbs and flows of affective life as opportunities to reverse their fortunes and restore psychological equilibrium through deliberate action.

Emerging evidence from neuropsychology supports the power of SWB and shows that biological markers substantiate the value of positive affect. Individuals with higher levels of reported SWB cognitively demonstrate greater levels of creative thinking (Amabile, Barsade, Mueller, & Staw, 2005) and enhanced problem-solving ability compared with dysphoric participants (Subramaniam & Vinogradov, 2013). Under duress, positive affect is related to using more adaptive coping behaviors (Isen, 2009), providing physiological evidence for the observed resilience described by many of our motivational leaders. Most revealing are highly targeted studies that measure heart rate variability and differences in neural signals between the brain and the pathways of the autonomic nervous system. Studies generally conclude that cardiac rhythms vary in intensity, ranging from erratic spiking oscillations when individuals are aroused and stressed, to the symmetrically smooth and wavelike oscillations observed when individuals experience harmonious and spiritual positive affect (McCraty, 2005; McCraty, Atkinson, Tomasino, & Bradley, 2005). These biological studies support the mythical affective nirvana experienced when falling in love: Heart rate variability results indicate that the heart really *does* skip a beat when the person is in love! Now, armed with the power of positive affect and the realization that, regardless of emotional valence, emotional deception is highly unlikely, we turn inward again, discussing *how* to regulate our emotions and those of others to enhance the probability of reaching desired learning and performance outcomes.

Principle #47—Individuals restructure affect to regulate their emotions

Leveraging the power of positive emotion as a prevailing influence on performance requires vigilant monitoring and regulation of emotion-provoking stimuli. Emotional regulation requires changes in the cognitive appraisal of an emotion, redirecting attentional focus, and modifying counterproductive behavioral or physiological responses to the emotion (Mauss, Bunge, & Gross, 2007). Russell (2003) contended that emotional regulation involves consciously altering the appraisal and assessment of an environmental event from one category or valence to another, effectively neutralizing the impact of the environmental "object" (p. 146). Pragmatically, regulation of emotion and the associated channeling of energy that follows emotional restructuring, serves the purpose of altering core affect from a negative to a positive state, diminishing the impact or eliminating the consequence of the event on performance. During restructuring, the individual strives to create an emotional homeostasis, allowing the regulator to be psychologically unencumbered by the potential consequences of the negative emotion. The process of regulation rations and appropriates depletable cognitive resources away from the emotion-inducing stimulus, allowing the individual to maximize cognitive focus and common-sense thinking toward achieving one's desired performance goal.

Individuals presented with emotion-restructuring opportunities have at least two choices. After being cut off in traffic, a person can metaphorically roll up the window and drive on, or succumb to anger, shouting out the window at the target of his or her contempt. An adaptive response to an emotional trigger is realized by using *problem-solving volitional strategies*, such as restructuring one's environments and removing distractions when necessary, engaging in reassuring self-talk, or consciously suppressing negativity (Corno, 2004). Concurrently, during restructuring, individuals may search for positive contingencies in a negative situation, otherwise known as finding the proverbial "silver lining in the dark cloud." Alternatively, and at the expense of positive affect, individuals may resort to *emotion-dependent coping strategies* that are motivationally maladaptive because emotion-dependent strategies impede progress toward performance goals and, instead, invest cognitive resources in battling the negative emotion. Emotion-dependent behaviors include the self-handicapping strategies described in Chapter 8, such as defensive pessimism, or displaying stereotypical emotion-consequent behaviors, such as crying or anger-induced rage (Boekaerts, 2007). These behaviors are cognitively costly and highly detrimental, doing little to help achieve one's performance goals.

Several of our motivational leaders described the use of productive volitional control strategies while consciously avoiding reliance on more maladaptive coping strategies. Alec Torelli described deliberately folding a questionable hand, thus minimizing his financial loss and avoiding the negative emotional consequences of playing a weak hand too long into the game. Alec uses the quick-fold strategy as one part of an overall emotion-regulating routine to avoid deflecting his focus from analyzing the hands of his opponents or calculating the probabilities of winning: key components for victory. Similarly, many of Bernie Madoff's transgressions demonstrated volitional strategies to regulate emotion. For instance, Madoff lacked interest in a law career but tolerated a year of law school, mostly to appease his father, while concurrently using the lessons from an unpleasant law school experience to progress toward his ultimate career goal of becoming an investment analyst. Further, Bernie demonstrated steadfast emotional regulation, as evidenced by his logical approach when he described the details of his crimes without animosity despite his projected lifetime incarceration.

Although the two examples described above involve conscious and deliberate appraisal and restructuring of emotion-provoking stimuli, in many cases, negative affective control and ensuing emotional regulation can occur implicitly and automatically. Automatic regulation involves changing "emotions without making a conscious decision to do so, without paying attention to the process of regulating one's emotions, and without engaging in deliberate control" (Mauss et al., 2007, p. 148). Automaticity of emotion is adaptive and contributes to performance because individuals can quickly and succinctly engage their preferred coping strategies without shifting attention away from the task at hand. Automaticity of emotional regulation can be observed and measured by exposing individuals to subliminal affective primes, such as a smiling face (Winkielman, Berridge, & Wilbarger, 2005) and descriptive adjectives (Bargh, 2006), and even by using olfactory primes, such as citrus fruits and coconuts (Smeets & Dijksterhuis, 2014). During priming, individuals unwittingly exhibit affective response patterns toward experimenter-determined goals without consciously recognizing that their behaviors have been manipulated and without knowing the reasons for their behaviors, sometimes even when debriefed about the purpose of the prime. Behaviors induced by affective priming are confirmed by biopsychological evidence (Li, Zinbarg, Boehm, & Paller, 2008) and have been shown to enhance motivation and activate or accelerate basic behaviors, including eating (Harris, Brownell, & Bargh, 2009) and cleaning (Holland, Hendriks, & Aarts, 2005), and the willingness to cooperate with others (Bargh, Gollwitzer, Lee-Chai, Barndollar, & Trötschel, 2001).

Recognizing the automatic nature of emotion and motivation is useful, but in all likelihood, spontaneous displays of emotion will not be within the direct control of the MD; instead, the focus will be on the deliberate regulation of emotion. However, the conscious modification of negative affect can also be particularly challenging because individuals must first detect and recognize instances of emerging negative affect. More importantly, the individual must perceive negative affective encounters as temporary obstacles that can be eradicated, rather than as impermeable or insurmountable roadblocks that might forestall goal attainment. Coping with negative affect requires a strong belief in the ability to exercise control over one's environment. In essence, an individual faced with an emotionally-charged event must have the wherewithal to recognize the need to use deliberate and intentional volitional coping strategies, understand the situational applicability and effectiveness of strategies, and know precisely when and how to use the regulatory strategies in the individual's repertoire.

Even when recognizing the need to use coping and regulatory strategies to control emotional responses, individuals are highly vulnerable to deferring to automatic patterns of affect regulation. In a series of studies, Shiv and Fedorikhin (2002) manipulated experimental conditions to investigate the degree of cognitive deliberation and type of choices individuals made when exposed to affective-laden stimuli. The researchers presented study participants with snacking decisions, offering the opportunity to indulge in high-calorie treats, such as chocolate cake or pizza, versus more innocuous and potentially healthier choices, such as fruit salad or soup. The researchers hypothesized that when individuals have time and available cognitive resources to contemplate the long-term consequences of choosing cake or fruit salad, they will make the reflective and conscientious choice of salad, knowing that cake and pizza are poor nutritional choices. The authors also speculated that when individuals were mentally preoccupied or when needing to make a quick decision, they would choose the affectively laden cake or pizza because of their preoccupation with other thoughts or the perception of pressure, disallowing a contemplative and well-reasoned cognitive choice. The researchers' hypotheses were confirmed and interpreted as meaning that when processing resources are constrained and when individuals have low levels of exposure for a decision, they will rely more on spontaneous emotion and impulse than on the deliberate and regulated emotion and cognitively-related reasoning. This unique study highlights the impulsive nature of decision making, revealing that individuals may not able to regulate emotions effectively, even when possessing the cognitive ability and available resources. This study also reveals why high-margin affectively laden snack choices, such as gum and candy, are found at grocery checkout counters, subliminally priming consumers to make impulsive choices, with little deliberation as they rush to get through the checkout line.

Many instances of emotional regulation are motivated by humans' inherent quest to experience pleasure and forestall or eliminate pain or discomfort, often described as a hedonistic motive (see Principle #20, p. 64). Although not all instances of emotional regulation are derived in the pursuit of pleasure, during the selection and pursuit of many learning and performance goals, individuals will typically engage in tasks that have sufficient challenge to maintain their interest and utilize their skills, but individuals will also seek tasks which have a strong probability of being completed successfully (Csikszentmihalyi, 1997). Successful task completion invariably contributes to a positive mood and allows individuals to exhibit pride and feel good about their accomplishments. When encountering intrusive personal thoughts or situational and task-contingent obstacles that might interfere with pleasurable outcomes, individuals undergo a series of psychological steps designed to maintain positive emotional homeostasis and regulate their emotion. The regulation process is intended to suppress, repress, reappraise, distract, project, deny, or compartmentalize sources of potential anguish and negative affect (Koole & Kuhl, 2008). In practical terms, when seeking pleasurable experience, learners use volitional strategies that enable them to maintain focus and strive toward predetermined learning and performance goals. Unfortunately, some individuals will succumb to emotional stress and be unable to meet task goals, presumably hampered by the historical legacy of learned failure during similar experiences, as more fully described earlier in this chapter by Principle #44 (p. 240).

As such, individuals exhibit a wide degree of ability differences in coping with emotional events. Research empirically links variability in affective regulation with biological predisposition, revealing that some individuals have personalities that are more prone to affective vacillation than others, hence the royal "drama" moniker ascribed to certain individuals. Extroverted individuals are more likely to display positive affect, with additional biological evidence supporting the presumption that affective regulation and associated emotionally charged behavior follows a pattern of circadian rhythms (Augustine & Larsen, 2015). Variation in affective response is also associated with neurological differences in brain localization, the extent of brain activation during emotional events, and cerebral blood flow, with personality traits, such as the degree of agreeableness or conscientiousness, being related to how an individual responds to an emotional catalyst. Structural differences in the size of brain components are also reliable predictors of how individuals will react to emotional stimuli and can be used to predict the degree of positive or negative affect individuals will display (DeYoung et al., 2010). Although neurological evidence helps confirm the behavioral consequences of emotion, it is still unknown if emotional dysregulation leads to changes in brain structure or if brain structure determines the degree of affective control.

Biological predisposition aside, cultivating adaptive affective regulation that promotes the use of the productive volitional coping strategies can be both orchestrated and taught. First, learners must believe that they have the resources, capability, and capacity to control their performance outcomes. Strong control beliefs are a necessary prerequisite to overcoming the unavoidable negative consequences that accompany some instances of learning and performance, such as subpar test performance or failing to meet one's academic goals. Control is based upon the foundational premises of control-value theory (Pekrun et al., 2002), and portends that learners correlate their effort with achieving desired results. When feeling in control, learner effort will be increased. Second, the performance outcome must be perceived as having at least some personal value, with pragmatic benefits associated with reaching learning goals. The presumption that elevated personal satisfaction will be attained by reaching academic goals leads to associating positive affect with the learning process. Information or tasks seen as inert or inconsequential for intellectual prosperity will provide little incentive for learners to persevere through the eventual learning potholes ultimately encountered during knowledge acquisition.

Specific physiological, cognitive, and behavioral strategies can help foster positive emotion. Considering that all emotional reactions have a physiological correlate, designing environments that insulate the individual from high-stakes pressure or that outwardly remove controllable stressors seems crucial for the aspiring MD. Individuals can be taught a variety of routines and rituals, such as task visualization, affirmative self-talk, or relaxation imagery, to mediate the physiological symptoms associated with emotional arousal (Hallett & Hoffman, 2014). Cognitive strategies, such as intellectual warm-ups, where learners have conversations about how to strategically overcome performance challenges, and practicing responses for likely problem-solving encounters or learning obstacles are beneficial. The use of savoring strategies (Tugade & Fredrickson, 2007) is particularly helpful and involves learners reminiscing about successful experiences in related domains. Similar to attribution training, savoring relates current performance to past success, allowing the learner to forge connections between current opportunities and past feelings of positive affect and affirmative emotions.

In academic environments, avoiding task ambiguity, giving clear directions, welcoming mistakes, and the elimination of performance pressure (e.g., time restrictions or scoring cutoffs) will aid in the cultivation of positive emotion because learners will understand performance expectations and contingencies in advance. Learners must be convinced that the assessment process is designed to measure progress toward learning goals and is not a punitive measure that leads to negative consequence and damaging self-appraisals of personal ability. Instead, assessment should be used to improve learning outcomes and be perceived as a device that aids in the identification of alternative methods of teaching and learning that will accelerate knowledge gains. If learners believe that the purpose of instruction is to support learning and that assessment is not conducted as a means to punish poor performance, negative emotions associated with testing may be reduced or eliminated.

Straightforward techniques, such as outlining performance expectations, giving learners valid reasons for the inclusion of curricular content, and integrating developing knowledge within a framework of personal learner experience, promote a learning context that is perceived as both practical and valuable. Such strategies also stimulate a learning atmosphere that does not evoke anxiety and is conducive to superior performance (Stipek, 1998). Reducing pressure requires the acceptance that affective regulation is not always possible and is a depletable resource, one that cannot be sustained indefinitely and must be replenished. Learners must realize that the perpetual transformation of negative emotions into positive experience is an unsustainable reality because of the complex and restrictive human cognitive and emotional architecture. We will ultimately encounter self-regulatory hurdles during learning and performance quests that cannot be easily overcome (Baumeister & Heatherton, 1996), hurdles that can interfere with the transitory and fleeting nature of emotional regulation.

Crafting a performance context that promotes and sustains effective regulation of emotion is one critical component contributing to the MD's overall objective of cultivating instances when the demonstration of peak or optimal performance is probable (see Principle #12, p. 37). When exhibiting peak performance, individuals show complete command of the physical, cognitive, affective, and motivational resources needed to achieve their goals (Privette, 1981). During peak performance, individuals are effectively able to block out emotional intrusions as they flawlessly execute task-contingent skills commensurate with task challenge. When peak performance occurs, emotion is rendered pragmatically inconsequential because the individual is entirely focused on the task at hand and performance is undisturbed by the distracting nature of emotion. In essence, when attaining peak performance, individuals will experience a fully automated state of emotional regulation.

Peak performance is highly idiosyncratic. Researchers studying elite performance across domains (Harmison & Casto, 2012) suggest that a single universal or precise blend of performance criterion that engenders instances of peak performance does not exist; instead, the psychological qualities of elite performance are highly personalized. However, across domains, some common themes and prototypical emotions emerge. A consensus of data from individuals in business, law enforcement, theater, and sports suggests that the antecedent qualities preceding a peak performance include feelings of competence, focus, happiness, and personal efficacy (Hays & Brown, 2004). Instances of mastery performance also are accompanied by individuals having specific and targeted goals that provide a sense of purpose, which is then reinforced by a coach or advisor that guides the peak performer to achieve his or her personal best (Hays, 2002). Surprisingly, prior to executing a memorable performance, individuals report experiencing at least some instances of anxiety and stress, with the most successful individuals using the stress as a means to energize their performance and focus ensuing effort. Despite the subjective and individualized nature of peak performance, one conclusion is indisputable: When lacking command of one's emotional self, the probability of optimal performance becomes a rare and elusive reality.

Chapter summary/conclusions

Emotion is a highly personalized and subjective response that develops when individuals interact with environmental stimuli. Interaction generates distinctive feelings (sometimes called *affect*) about an event, which are broadly influenced by personal or virtual experience, culture, and beliefs. A wide degree of response appraisal exists within and between individuals, suggesting that predicting emotional responses is tenuous at best. Two individuals can have entirely different reactions to the same event, and one individual can display the same emotion while appraising a radically different environmental stimulus.

Despite the variability in responses, three factors concerning emotions are reliable and oddly consistent. First, all emotions trigger bodily and nonverbal changes in an individual. Second, the repression of emotions is a neurological impossibility, suggesting that we are unable to mask or hide our true emotions. Third, displays of anger, disgust, fear, happiness, sadness, and surprise are fairly consistent across cultures. How we react to an emotional event is a function of what we know and how we already feel and is based, in part, upon which environmental factors we believe are salient when pursing our personal goals. Emotional displays will vary in potency or intensity, and some emotions will often be durable and demonstrated with greater frequency. Prototypical behaviors accompany many emotions, such as the glaring eyes and crimson coloration of the exasperated teacher struggling to teach uncooperative learners. However, many times, the source and reason for the emotion can be rather subtle due to the innate and automatic nature of many emotional appraisals and their ensuing responses.

The avoidance motives of anxiety and boredom are particularly relevant for educators due to their pervasive negative impact on learning and performance. Anxiety shifts attention away from learning and redirects precious cognitive resources toward anxiety resolution. Boredom prompts disengagement as well, with a disproportionate impact on low-achieving learners, and is contributory to achieving less and exerting diminished task effort. While avoidance motives are amenable to intervention through the creation of safe, robust, and authentic learning contexts, MDs may find the cultivation of positive affect preferable to mediation of negative affect. Positive affect, SWB, and happiness not only are positively related to improved health and longevity but also influence the receptivity and willingness of learners to seek intellectual challenges and develop a greater repertoire of effective emotion-coping strategies. Individuals with an optimistic outlook surpass their pessimistic peers when it comes to job performance, skill evaluation, and eventual earnings.

The negative consequences of some emotions can be influenced by emotional restructuring and by the regulation of one's emotions. Through the use of overlearned automatic responses and conscious problem-solving volitional strategies, individuals can convert obstacles into opportunities, exert control over seemingly uncontrollable events, and take deliberate action to overcome negative emotions that can inhibit peak performance. Emotional regulation can be taught through specific routines and rituals, and through the structuring of an autonomy-supportive learning and performance environment. Regulation of negative affect is one crucial step in cultivating peak performance, which results, in part, when individuals believe they have both the requisite skill and unabated control to reach their desired performance goals.

Next steps

Regulation of the self, and particularly one's emotions, is just one of the many aspects of human performance where individuals exercise control. This chapter focused almost exclusively on those strategies deemed effective in managing emotion. In addition, individuals have at least two other regulatory challenges that can enhance preferred learning and performance outcomes. Individuals can regulate both cognition and motivation through the ongoing evaluation, monitoring, and reflection upon the potency and direction of their efforts. Next, we build upon the foundation of emotional regulation and provide an in-depth discussion of why systemic self-regulation is a necessary and attainable step in meeting the ongoing goal of exhibiting and cultivating optimal learning and performance. We also meet **Senator Darren Soto**, a master regulator, who walks the fine line between allegiance to his personal beliefs, while bridging the partisan divide to honorably represent his constituents.

End of chapter motivational minute

Principles covered in this chapter:

44. **Emotional reactions are localized, subjective, and learned**—responses to emotional events are based upon individual interpretations and subjective appraisals. Prototypical behaviors are observed for the emotions of anger, disgust, fear, happiness, sadness, and surprise; however, reactions for most other emotions vary between and within persons based on the experiences, goals, and physiological profile of an individual.
45. **Anxiety and boredom are performance-restricting culprits**—academic emotions may negatively influence academic achievement. Anxiety, a subjectively interpreted perceived threat, has genetic and environmental roots that limit efficiency due to cognitive intrusions. Boredom also results in academic disengagement, as learners will actively avoid learning and performance contexts incommensurate with desired challenge or personal interest.
46. **Positive affect is a powerful performance determinant**—individuals evaluate performance contexts, making negative or positive contextual inferences. Demonstrating positive affect has broad positive implications for performance. Positive affect is related to subjective well-being and improved health. Individuals who approach performance challenges with optimism typically achieve more and feel better about themselves.
47. **Individuals restructure affect to regulate their emotions**—emotional regulation and restructuring occurs when individuals transform a negative instance to a positive one. Emotional regulation can happen automatically through learned experience and can also be orchestrated under defined circumstances by using specific strategies. When successfully regulating emotion, the probability of an elite performance is vastly enhanced, in part because individuals are able to effectively block out negative emotion.

Key terminology (in order of chapter presentation):

- **Affect**—the subjective feelings that accompany specific emotions.
- **Emotional episode**—an interaction within the person or between a person and the environment that generates subjective emotional contingencies in response to the event.
- **Somatic**—physiological and neurological bodily responses resulting from an environmental catalyst.

- **State anxiety**—the type of anxiety that is situationally specific and triggered by an identifiable environmental cue or event, such as a certification examination.
- **Trait anxiety**—a stable, nonspecific and generalized form of anxiety, similar to a personality attribute, that impacts performance across multiple performance domains.
- **Problem-solving volitional strategies**—the type of strategies that individuals use to regulate emotion, focusing on transforming negative emotional events into positive ones.
- **Emotion-dependent coping strategies**—strategies used during emotional regulation that shift the focus away from the specific problem, but instead focus on the emotion (e.g., crying).

References

Amabile, T. M., Barsade, S. G., Mueller, J. S., & Staw, B. M. (2005). Affect and creativity at work. *Administrative Science Quarterly, 50*(3), 367–403.

Arent, S. M., & Landers, D. M. (2003). Arousal, anxiety, and performance: A reexamination of the inverted-U Hypothesis. *Research Quarterly for Exercise and Sport, 74*(4), 436–444. http://dx.doi.org/10.1080/02701367.2003.10609113.

Augustine, A. A., & Larsen, R. J. (2015). Personality, affect, and affect regulation. In M. Mikulincer, P. R. Shaver, M. Cooper, & R. J. Larsen (Eds.), *APA handbook of personality and social psychology, Volume 4: Personality processes and individual differences* (pp. 147–165). Washington, DC: American Psychological Association. http://dx.doi.org/10.1037/14343-007.

Baas, M., De Dreu, C. K. W., & Nijstad, B. A. (2008). A meta-analysis of 25 years of mood-creativity research: Hedonic tone, activation, or regulatory focus? *Psychological Bulletin, 134*(6), 779–806. http://dx.doi.org/10.1037/a0012815.

Bandura, A. (1988). Self-efficacy conception of anxiety. *Anxiety Research, 1*(2), 77–98. http://dx.doi.org/10.1080/10615808808248222.

Bargh, J. A. (1997). The automaticity of everyday life. In R. S. Wyer (Ed.), Jr. *The automaticity of everyday life: Advances in social cognition* (pp. 1–61). Mahwah, NJ: Erlbaum.

Bargh, J. A. (2006). What have we been priming all these years? On the development, mechanisms, and ecology of nonconscious social behaviour. *European Journal of Social Psychology, 36*, 147–168. http://dx.doi.org/10.1002/ejsp.336.

Bargh, J. A., Gollwitzer, P. M., Lee-Chai, A., Barndollar, K., & Trötschel, R. (2001). The automated will: Nonconscious activation and pursuit of behavioral goals. *Journal of Personality and Social Psychology, 81*, 1014–1027.

Barrett, L. F. (2006). Are emotions natural kinds? *Perspectives on Psychological Science, 1*, 28–58.

Baumeister, R. F., & Heatherton, T. F. (1996). Self-regulation failure: An overview. *Psychological Inquiry, 7*(1), 1–15.

Beck, R. C. (2004). *Motivation: Theories and principles* (5th ed.). Upper Saddle River, N.J: Pearson/Prentice Hall.

Berridge, K. C., & Winkielman, P. (2003). What is an unconscious emotion? (The case for unconscious "liking"). *Cognition & Emotion, 17*(2), 181–211.

Black, P., & Wiliam, D. (2009). Developing the theory of formative assessment. *Educational Assessment, Evaluation and Accountability, 21*(1), 5–31.

Boekaerts, M. (2007). Understanding students' affective processes in the classroom. In P. A. Schutz & R. Pekrun (Eds.), *Emotion in education* (pp. 37–56). San Diego, CA: Elsevier Academic Press.

Brosch, T., Pourtois, G., & Sander, D. (2010). The perception and categorisation of emotional stimuli: A review. *Cognition & Emotion, 24*(3), 377–400. http://dx.doi.org/10.1080/02699930902975754.

Buck, R. (1980). Nonverbal behavior and the theory of emotion: The facial feedback hypothesis. *Journal of Personality and Social Psychology, 38*(5), 811–824.

Byron, K., & Khazanchi, S. (2011). A meta-analytic investigation of the relationship of state and trait anxiety to performance on figural and verbal creative tasks. *Personality & Social Psychology Bulletin, 2*, 269–283.

Carver, C. S., & Scheier, M. F. (1988). A control-process perspective on anxiety. *Anxiety Research, 1*(1), 17–22.

Chen, G., Gully, S. M., Whiteman, J., & Kilcullen, R. N. (2006). Examination of relationships among trait-like individual differences, state-like individual differences, and learning performance. *Journal of Applied Psychology, 85*, 835–847.

Cohen, S., Doyle, W. J., Turner, R. B., Alper, C. M., & Skoner, D. P. (2003). Emotional style and susceptibility to the common cold. *Psychosomatic Medicine, 65*(4), 652–657.

Cohn, M. A., & Fredrickson, B. L. (2009). Positive emotions. In S. J. Lopez & C. R. Synder (Eds.), *Oxford handbook of positive psychology* (pp. 13–24). New York, NY: Oxford University Press.

Corno, L. (2004). Work habits and work styles: The psychology of volition in education. *Teachers College Record, 106*, 1669–1694.

Covington, M. (2009). Self-worth theory: Retrospection and prospects. In K. R. Wentzel & A. Wigfield (Eds.), *Handbook of motivation at school* (pp. 141–169). New York, NY: Routledge.

Csikszentmihalyi, M. (1997). *Finding flow: The psychology of engagement with everyday life*. New York, NY: Basic Books.

Daschmann, E. C., Goetz, T., & Stupnisky, R. H. (2011). Testing the predictors of boredom at school: Development and validation of the precursors to boredom scales. *British Journal of Educational Psychology, 81*(3), 421–440. http://dx.doi.org/10.1348/000709910X526038.

DeYoung, C. G., Hirsh, J. B., Shane, M. S., Papademetris, X., Rajeevan, N., & Gray, J. R. (2010). Testing predictions from personality neuroscience: Brain structure and the big five. *Psychological Science, 21*(6), 820–828. http://doi.org/10.1177/0956797610370159.

Diener, E., Larsen, R. J., Levine, S., & Emmons, R. (1985). Intensity and frequency: Dimensions underlying positive and negative affect. *Journal of Personality & Social Psychology, 48*, 1253–1265. http://dx.doi.org/10.1037/0022-3514.48.5.1253.

Ekman, P. (1993). Facial expression and emotion. *American Psychologist, 48*, 384–392.

Eysenck, M. W., & Calvo, M. G. (1992). Anxiety and performance: The processing efficiency theory. *Cognition and Emotion, 6*, 409–434.

Fallis, R. K., & Opotow, S. (2003). Are students failing school or are schools failing students? Class cutting in high school. *Journal of Social Issues, 59*(1), 103–119.

Fredrickson, B. L. (2001). The role of positive emotions in positive psychology: The broaden-and-build theory of positive emotions. *American Psychologist, 56*(3), 218–226. http://dx.doi.org/10.1037/0003-066X.56.3.218.

Fredrickson, B. L., & Joiner, T. (2002). Positive emotions trigger upward spirals toward emotional well-being. *Psychological Science, 13*, 172–175.

Frick, P. J., & White, S. F. (2008). Research review: The importance of callous-unemotional traits for developmental models of aggressive and antisocial behavior. *Journal of Child Psychology and Psychiatry, 49*(4), 359–375. http://dx.doi.org/10.1111/j.1469-7610.2007.01862.x.

Gable, S. L., & Haidt, J. (2005). What (and why) is positive psychology? *Review of General Psychology, 9*(2), 103–110. http://dx.doi.org/10.1037/1089-2680.9.2.103.

Goetz, T., Frenzel, A. C., Pekrun, R., Hall, N. C., & Lüdtke, O. (2007). Between-and within-domain relations of students' academic emotions. *Journal of Educational Psychology*, *99*(4), 715–733.

Goldberg, Y. K., Eastwood, J. D., LaGuardia, J., & Danckert, J. (2011). Boredom: An emotional experience distinct from apathy, anhedonia, or depression. *Journal of Social and Clinical Psychology*, *30*(6), 647–666.

Graesser, A. C., & D'Mello, S. (2012). Emotions during the learning of difficult material. In B. H. Ross (Ed.), *The psychology of learning and motivation-advances in research and theory* (Vol. 57, pp. 183–226). San Diego, CA: Academic Press.

Gross, C., & Hen, R. (2004). The developmental origins of anxiety. *National Review of Neuroscience*, *5*(7), 545–552.

Gross, J. J., & Levenson, R. W. (1997). Hiding feelings: The acute effects of inhibiting negative and positive emotion. *Journal of Abnormal Psychology*, *106*(1), 95–103. http://dx.doi.org/10.1037/0021-843X.106.1.95.

Hallett, M., & Hoffman, B. (2014). Performing under pressure: Cultivating the peak performance mindset for workplace excellence. *Consulting Psychology Journal: Research and Practice*, *66*(3), 212–230.

Harmison, R. J., & Casto, K. V. (2012). Optimal performance: Elite level in the "The Zone." In S. M. Murphy (Ed.), *The Oxford handbook of sport and performance psychology* (pp. 707–725). New York, NY: Oxford University Press.

Harris, J. L., Brownell, K. D., & Bargh, J. A. (2009). The food marketing defense model: Integrating psychological research to protect youth and inform public policy. *Social Issues and Policy Review*, *3*(1), 211–271. http://dx.doi.org/10.1111/j.1751-2409.2009.01015.x.

Hays, K. F. (2002). The enhancement of performance excellence among performing artists. *Journal of Applied Sport Psychology*, *14*(4), 299–312. http://dx.doi.org/10.1080/10413200290103572.

Hays, K. F., & Brown, C. H., Jr. (2004). *You're on!: Consulting for peak performance*. Washington, DC: American Psychological Association.

Hettema, J., Neale, M., & Kendler, K. (2001). A review and meta-analysis of the genetic epidemiology of anxiety disorders. *American Journal of Psychiatry*, *158*(10), 1568–1578.

Hoffman, A., Haber, I., & Cohen, B. (1971). *Steal this book*. New York, NY: Pirate Editions.

Hoffman, B. (2010). I think I can, but I'm afraid to try: The influence of self-efficacy and anxiety on problem-solving efficiency. *Learning & Individual Differences*, *20*, 276–283.

Hoffman, B., & Schraw, G. (2009). The influence of self-efficacy and working memory capacity on problem-solving efficiency. *Learning and Individual Differences*, *19*, 91–100.

Holland, R. W., Hendriks, M., & Aarts, H. (2005). Smells like clean spirit, nonconscious effects of scent on cognition and behavior. *Psychological Science*, *16*(9), 689–693.

Isen, A. M. (2009). A role for neuropsychology in understanding the facilitating influence of positive affect on social behavior and cognitive processes. In S. J. Lopez & C. R. Synder (Eds.), *Oxford handbook of positive psychology* (pp. 503–518). New York, NY: Oxford University Press.

Izard, C. E. (1994). Innate and universal facial expressions: Evidence from developmental and cross-cultural research. *Psychological Bulletin*, *115*(2), 288–299.

Janelle, C. M., & Hatfield, B. D. (2008). Visual attention and brain processes that underlie expert performance: Implications for sport and military psychology. *Military Psychology*, *20*(Suppl. 1), S39–S69. http://dx.doi.org/10.1080/08995600701804798.

Jang, H., Reeve, J., & Deci, E. L. (2010). Engaging students in learning activities: It is not autonomy support or structure but autonomy support and structure. *Journal of Educational Psychology*, *102*(3), 588–600. http://dx.doi.org/10.1037/a0019682.

Kaspar, K., & König, P. (2012). Emotions and personality traits as high-level factors in visual attention: A review. *Frontiers in Human Neuroscience, 6.* http://dx.doi.org/10.3389/fnhum.2012.00321.

Kensinger, E. A. (2009). Remembering the details: Effects of emotion. *Emotion Review, 1*(2), 99–113. http://dx.doi.org/10.1177/1754073908100432.

Kensinger, E. A., Garoff-Eaton, R. J., & Schacter, D. L. (2007). Effects of emotion on memory specificity: Memory trade-offs elicited by negative visually arousing stimuli. *Journal of Memory and Language, 56*(4), 575–591. http://dx.doi.org/10.1016/j.jml.2006.05.004.

Koole, S. L., & Kuhl, J. (2008). Dealing with unwanted feelings: The role of affect regulation in volitional action control. In J. Y. Shah & W. L. Gardner (Eds.), *Handbook of motivation science* (pp. 295–307). New York, NY: Guilford Press.

Kounin, J. S. (1970). *Discipline and group management in classrooms.* New York, NY: Holt, Rinehart, and Winston.

Lang, P. J. (1994). The varieties of emotional experience: A meditation on James-Lange theory. *Psychological Review, 101*(2), 211–221.

Larson, R. W., & Richards, M. H. (1991). Boredom in the middle school years: Blaming schools versus blaming students. *American Journal of Education, 4,* 418–443.

Levine, J. L., & Edelstein, R. S. (2010). Emotion and memory narrowing: A review and goal-relevance approach. In J. De Houwer & D. Hermans (Eds.), *Cognition & emotion: Reviews of current research and theories* (pp. 168–210). New York, NY: Psychology Press.

Li, W., Zinbarg, R. E., Boehm, S. G., & Paller, K. A. (2008). Neural and behavioral evidence for affective priming from unconsciously perceived emotional facial expressions and the influence of trait anxiety. *Journal of Cognitive Neuroscience, 20*(1), 95–107.

Liebert, R., & Morris, L. (1967). Cognitive and emotional components of test anxiety: A distinction and some initial data. *Psychological Reports, 20,* 975–978.

Linnebrink, E. (2007). The role of affect in student learning: A multi-dimensional approach to consider the interaction of affect, motivation, and engagement. In P. A. Schutz & R. Pekrun (Eds.), *Emotion in education* (pp. 107–124). Burlingame, MA: Academic Press.

Lucas, R. E., Clark, A. E., Georgellis, Y., & Diener, E. (2004). Unemployment alters the set point for life satisfaction. *Psychological Science, 15,* 8–13.

Lyubomirsky, S., King, L., & Diener, E. (2005). The benefits of frequent positive affect: Does happiness lead to success? *Psychological Bulletin, 131*(6), 803–855. http://dx.doi.org/10.1037/0033-2909.131.6.803.

Mauss, I. B., Bunge, S. A., & Gross, J. J. (2007). Automatic emotion regulation. *Social and Personality Psychology Compass, 1*(1), 146–167. http://dx.doi.org/10.1111/j.1751-9004.2007.00005.x.

McCraty, R. (2005). Enhancing emotional, social, and academic learning with heart rhythm coherence feedback. *Biofeedback, 33*(4), 130–134.

McCraty, R., Atkinson, M., Tomasino, D., & Bradley, R. T. (2005). *The coherent heart: Heart–brain interactions, psychophysiological coherence, and the emergence of system-wide order.* Boulder Creek, CA: HeartMath Research Center, Institute of HeartMath. No. 05-022.

McKenna, F. P., & Sharma, D. (1995). Intrusive cognitions: An investigation of the emotional Stroop task. *Journal of Experimental Psychology: Learning, Memory, and Cognition, 21*(6), 1595–1607. http://dx.doi.org/10.1037/0278-7393.21.6.1595.

Moors, A. (2010). Theories of emotion causation: A review. In J. De Houwer & D. Hermans (Eds.), *Cognition & emotion: Reviews of current research and theories* (pp. 1–37). New York, NY: Psychology Press.

Nesse, R. M. (2004). Natural selection and the elusiveness of happiness. *Philosophical Transactions of the Royal Society of London Series B, Biological Sciences, 359,* 1333–1347.

Nesse, R. M., & Ellsworth, P. C. (2009). Evolution, emotions, and emotional disorders. *American Psychologist, 64*(2), 129–139.

Nett, U. E., Goetz, T., & Hall, N. C. (2011). Coping with boredom in school: An experience sampling perspective. *Contemporary Educational Psychology, 36*(1), 49–59. http://dx.doi.org/10.1016/j.cedpsych.2010.10.003.

Onwuegbuzie, A. J., & Wilson, V. A. (2003). Statistics anxiety: Nature, etiology, antecedents, effects, and treatments a comprehensive review of the literature. *Teaching in Higher Education, 8*(2), 195–209.

Parkinson, B. (1995). Emotion. In B. Parkinson & A. M. Colman (Eds.), *Emotion and motivation* (pp. 1–21). New York, NY: Longman.

Pekrun, R., Goetz, T., Daniels, L. M., Stupnisky, R. H., & Perry, R. P. (2010). Boredom in achievement settings: Exploring control-value antecedents and performance outcomes of a neglected emotion. *Journal of Emotional Psychology, 102*(3), 531–549.

Pekrun, R., Goetz, T., Titz, W., & Perry, R. P. (2002). Academic emotions in students' self-regulated learning and achievement: A Program of qualitative and quantitative research. *Educational Psychologist, 37*(2), 91–105.

Pekrun, R., Hall, N. C., Goetz, T., & Perry, R. P. (2014). Boredom and academic achievement: Testing a model of reciprocal causation. *Journal of Educational Psychology, 106*(3), 696–710. http://dx.doi.org/10.1037/a0036006.

Petrides, K. V., Pita, R., & Kokkinaki, F. (2007). The location of trait emotional intelligence in personality factor space. *British Journal of Psychology, 98*(2), 273–289. http://dx.doi.org/10.1348/000712606X120618.

Petty, R. E., Fabrigar, L. R., & Wegener, D. T. (2003). Emotional factors in attitudes and persuasion. In R. J. Davidson, K. R. Scherer, & H. Goldsmith (Eds.), *Handbook of affective sciences* (pp. 752–772). New York, NY: Oxford University Press.

Pinquart, M., & Sörensen, S. (2000). Influences of socioeconomic status, social network, and competence on subjective well-being in later life: A meta-analysis. *Psychology and Aging, 15*(2), 187–224.

Pintrich, P. R., & De Groot, E. V. (1990). Motivational and self-regulated learning components of classroom academic performance. *Journal of Educational Psychology, 82*, 33–40.

Privette, G. (1981). Dynamics of peak performance. *Journal of Humanistic Psychology, 21*(1), 57–67.

Rothermund, K., Wentura, D., & Bak, P. (2001). Automatic attention to stimuli signaling chances and dangers: Moderating effects of positive and negative goal and action contexts. *Cognition and Emotion, 15*, 231–248.

Rubio, V. J., Hernández, J. M., & Márquez, M. A. (2013). The assessment of risk preferences as an estimation of risk propensity. In J. -P. Assailly (Ed.), *The psychology of risk-taking* (pp. 53–82). New York, NY: Nova Science Publishers.

Russell, J. A. (1994). Is there universal recognition of emotion from facial expressions? A review of the cross-cultural studies. *Psychological Bulletin, 115*(1), 102–141. http://dx.doi.org/10.1037/0033-2909.115.1.102.

Russell, J. A. (2003). Core affect and the psychological construction of emotion. *Psychological Review, 110*(1), 145–172. http://dx.doi.org/10.1037/0033-295X.110.1.145.

Shiv, B., & Fedorikhin, A. (2002). Spontaneous versus controlled influences of stimulus-based affect on choice behavior. *Organizational Behavior and Human Decision Processes, 87*(2), 342–370. http://dx.doi.org/10.1006/obhd.2001.2977.

Smeets, M. A. M., & Dijksterhuis, G. B. (2014). Smelly primes when olfactory primes do or do not work. *Frontiers in Psychology, 5*. http://dx.doi.org/10.3389/fpsyg.2014.00096.

Stankowich, T., & Blumstein, D. T. (2005). Fear in animals: A meta-analysis and review of risk assessment. *Proceedings of the Royal Society B: Biological Sciences, 272*(1581), 2627–2634. http://dx.doi.org/10.1098/rspb.2005.3251.

Stipek, D. (1998). *Motivation to learn: From theory to practice*. Needham Heights, MA: Allyn and Bacon.

Subramaniam, K., & Vinogradov, S. (2013). Improving the neural mechanisms of cognition through the pursuit of happiness. *Frontiers in Human Neuroscience, 7*, 452. http://www.ncbi.nlm.nih.gov/pmc/articles/PMC3735982/.

Tamir, M., & Robinson, M. D. (2007). The happy spotlight: Positive mood and selective attention to rewarding information. *Personality and Social Psychology Bulletin, 33*(8), 1124–1136.

Tilburg, W., & Igou, E. (2012). On boredom: Lack of challenge and meaning as distinct boredom experiences. *Motivation and Emotion, 36*(2), 181–194. http://dx.doi.org/10.1007/s11031-011-9234-9.

Tugade, M. M., & Fredrickson, B. L. (2007). Regulation of positive emotions: Emotion regulation strategies that promote resilience. *Journal of Happiness Studies, 8*(3), 311–333.

van Hooff, M. L. M., & van Hooft, E. A. J. (2014). Boredom at work: Proximal and distal consequences of affective work-related boredom. *Journal of Occupational Health Psychology, 19*(3), 348–359. http://dx.doi.org/10.1037/a0036821.

Watt, J. D., & Hargis, M. B. (2010). Boredom proneness: Its relationship with subjective underemployment, perceived organizational support, and job performance. *Journal of Business and Psychology, 25*(1), 163–174. http://dx.doi.org/10.1007/s10869-009-9138-9.

Wegner, L., & Flisher, A. (2009). Leisure boredom and adolescent risk behaviour: A systematic literature review. *Journal of Child & Adolescent Mental Health, 21*(1), 1–28. http://dx.doi.org/10.2989/JCAMH.2009.21.1.4.806.

Wegner, L., Flisher, A. J., Chikobvu, P., Lombard, C., & King, G. (2008). Leisure boredom and high school dropout in Cape Town, South Africa. *Journal of Adolescence, 31*(3), 421–431.

Wigfield, A., & Eccles, J. S. (1989). Test anxiety in elementary and secondary school students. *Educational Psychologist, 24*(2), 159–183.

Wilson, M., Smith, N. C., & Holmes, P. S. (2007). The role of effort in influencing the effect of anxiety on performance: Testing the conflicting predictions of processing efficiency theory and the conscious processing hypothesis. *British Journal of Psychology, 98*(3), 411–428. http://dx.doi.org/10.1348/000712606X133047.

Wilson, M. R. (2012). Anxiety: Attention, the brain, the body and performance. In S. M. Murphy (Ed.), *The Oxford handbook of sport and performance psychology* (pp. 173–190). New York, NY: Oxford University Press.

Winkielman, P., Berridge, K. C., & Wilbarger, J. L. (2005). Unconscious affective reactions to masked happy versus angry faces influence consumption behavior and judgments of value. *Personality & Social Psychology Bulletin, 31*(1), 121–135.

Wittouck, C., Van Autreve, S., De Jaegere, E., Portzky, G., & van Heeringen, K. (2011). The prevention and treatment of complicated grief: A meta-analysis. *Clinical Psychology Review, 31*(1), 69–78. http://dx.doi.org/10.1016/j.cpr.2010.09.005.

Part III

Mediation and implementation strategies to promote optimal learning and performance

Ready, aim, fire…repeat?: Self-regulation strategies to improve adaptive motivation

Chapter outline

Principle #48—Self-regulation is personalized, transitory, and marginally predictable 274
Principle #49—Self-regulatory ability is depletable; accurate calibration is essential 281
Motivational Leader—*Darren Soto* 288
Principle #50—Optimal motivation demands monitoring, metacognition, and metamotivation 290
    Chapter summary/conclusions 294
    Next steps 295
    End of chapter motivational minute 296
References 297

Welcome to Part Three. The first two sections of the text explored fundamental components of motivational science, focusing on which factors influenced the development, perpetuation, and resolution of learning and performance challenges subsumed by issues of motivation. However, conceptual knowledge of motivation is insufficient to promote productive changes in people. Instead, optimizing motivation requires transforming conceptual knowledge into actionable strategies that contribute to attaining desired individual, subordinate, and group performance goals. Given this tactical emphasis, the remainder of the text describes specific approaches designed to instill motivational effort leading to behavior change. Motivational detectives (MDs) who are inspired to improve performance and armed with a diverse set of situational strategies will be well equipped to accelerate learning and boost performance in the self and others.

An integral protocol that supports progress toward achieving superior learning and performance goals are *self-regulation* strategies. By name, these types of strategies are proprietary, idiosyncratic, and personalized methods individuals use to exert control over their thinking, affect, and behaviors (Zimmerman, 1989). Self-regulatory strategies are used by individuals across domains and are often described as mechanisms of self-control (Baumeister & Heatherton, 1996) that help people accomplish personal goals as diverse as smoking cessation (Rothman, Hertel, Baldwin, & Bartels, 2008), physical rehabilitation from injury (Podlog, Heil, & Schulte, 2014), or refraining from promiscuity (Gailliot & Baumeister, 2007a). Self-regulatory strategies are not routine behaviors, which are designed to promote content knowledge or enhance performance, but, instead, the focus of regulatory effort is on process improvement. Regulatory strategies are evaluative, with an emphasis on determining what the individual must change to enhance the probability of reaching desired goals (Winne & Hadwin, 2008). Improvement implies the individual evaluates the current state of his or her performance in comparison with a desired state and identifies specific gaps where change will be beneficial. Performance upgrades are often associated with a re-evaluation of procedural or learning methods, a restructuring of the performance environment, or an assessment of how others (e.g., educators, peers) may contribute to an enhanced task focus. Regulatory strategies also include an introspective analysis of a person's affective reactions to environmental stress, as discussed in Chapter 9. Most importantly for educators, leaders, individuals, and the aspiring MD, self-regulation refers to monitoring, managing, evaluating, and changing motivational states as a vital component that fosters goal attainment.

In many ways, the evaluative process performers engage in during self-regulation is, by proxy, assuming the role of both the teaching master and the student apprentice. During optimal self-regulation, the individual deliberately and intentionally monitors progress toward desired goals. As learning or task attainment evolves, the person self-generates constructive feedback designed to enhance performance and improve the probability of having a rewarding and satisfying experience. For example, during homework, learners may scrutinize their task attention by reminding themselves to ignore the television playing in another room or reward themselves by checking their social media accounts, but *only* after a certain number of pages have been read, or when all work is completed. If successful, self-regulation can be the difference between mediocre performance and excellence, leading Wigfield and Eccles (2001) to conclude, "Self-regulation is one of the main ways in which individuals translate motivation into achievement" (p. 5). By using an objective and systemic regulatory approach, the individual can adapt his or her routines by taking a highly active role in determining which temperaments and which methods are best suited to achieving desired performance outcomes.

Leveraging the adaptive power of self-regulation requires that certain individual dispositions be in place, otherwise regulatory efforts may prove fruitless. First, one must be motivationally alert, open and inspired to make necessary changes. Second, even when receptive to guidance, individuals must possess strategy knowledge demonstrating awareness and knowledge of *when* to use specific strategies, in addition to anticipating the impact of strategy use on desired outcomes. The process of regulation, is at times, an enigma: possessing a vast repertoire of strategies does not guarantee enhanced performance. Individuals may take the initiative to acquire a range of strategies but must also believe that successful outcomes can be orchestrated when using the strategies. Third, performers lacking favorable competency beliefs and those who are skeptical about their capabilities to control performance outcomes may be reluctant to use the strategies they know, anticipating little value or utility of the strategy on potential outcomes. In the absence of a strong belief in strategy effectiveness, performers will find minimal justification to invest the additional time and cognitive effort needed to engage and apply otherwise productive strategies.

Motivational leader Amanda Boxtel, who is described in great detail in Chapter 12 (p. 358), is perhaps the epitome of self-regulation. When Amanda was 22 years old, working as a ski instructor in Aspen, Colorado, she suffered a severe and life-changing spinal cord injury during a freak downhill skiing accident that resulted in complete leg paralysis. Unable to walk, Amanda was devastated by her fate. For many years after the accident, she was immersed in biological and psychological struggles, focused only on regaining her mobility. Despite the numerous physical, personal, and financial obstacles she encountered through failed medical treatments and holistic therapy, Amanda did not relinquish her quest to regain mobility. Finally, after 22 years of immobility, Amanda walked, aided by the development of the world's first exoskeleton mobility system. Although mechanically assisted, Amanda regained the ability to walk, not through technology alone, but by a deliberate and structured self-designed form of psychological aerobics. Amanda persevered through obstacles and setbacks, not only because of her ability to regulate her emotions but also by using cognitive and motivational strategies to thwart the typical mental anguish associated with any radical life change.

Once Amanda realized that it was her rigid mind and not her stationary legs that impaired her growth and happiness, positive changes prevailed. She employed very specific approaches to regulate her motivation to achieve independence. Amanda recalled writing in a journal as a means to understand her thoughts and focus her motivation in a productive way. But Amanda did not write in her journal in the typical way. Instead, she used the technique of ambidextrous writing, not only as a means to ask herself questions and to reflect but also as a technique to search for answers to her own questions. She stated, "I asked myself the questions with the dominant hand and I answered with a non-dominant hand. I had all the answers within. I didn't need to ask a therapist." She added, "It (life) changed with a series of tools that I've learned throughout my life to incorporate, to pull myself out. And whether that's, um, out of the depths of challenge. Those tools have changed as I've matured. I think it's a constant evolution for any person" (A. Boxtel, personal communication, August 15, 2014). Amanda was using the self-described tools to focus her attention and effort in recovery, tools that by most descriptions were self-regulatory strategies aimed not at physical recovery but a purposeful means of psychological stamina, controlling a wandering but resolute mind that knew exactly why finding personal motivation was the key to her rejuvenation.

The story of Amanda Boxtel reveals that effective self-regulation involves interaction and dependency among cognitive, affective, motivational, and strategic components, an approach strongly supported by research across many domains (Carver & Scheier, 2000; Winne & Hadwin, 2008; Zimmerman, 2011). Indeed, many theoretical models of self-regulation emphasize how individuals exercise control over different facets and stages of the learning and performance process. Most interpretations of self-regulation involve use and control of strategies on a continuum, suggesting that contemplated tasks occur in cycles and have a preparatory phase when goals are determined, an implementation phase, when progress and performance feedback are monitored, and an evaluative phase, which provides the opportunity to reflect on observed outcomes in order to refocus subsequent task effort and emphasis.

The self-regulated learner creates an immersive cognitive environment, perpetually assessing and adjusting strategy use as work progresses. However, regulating motivation is not so simple. Even when knowing which cognitive strategies will foster desired goal-directed outcomes, learners must also maintain performance momentum and actively engage in a series of motivational strategies designed to focus attention and capitalize on effortful behavior.

The specific intent of *motivational self-regulation* is to purposefully evaluate circumstances and contextual conditions that foster optimal task progression and eventual task completeness. Some motivational strategies may be spontaneous, based upon entrenched beliefs, habits, or learned experiences (Wolters, Benzon, & Arroyo-Giner, 2011). For instance, learners can quickly evaluate the complexity of subject matter, instantly reaching a behavioral disengagement decision if the material is perceived as overwhelming or complex. Less subtle mediators of self-regulation are historical patterns of avoidance behavior that may highjack adaptive motivation based upon unsuccessful past experience. For instance, some learners operate under the belief that their subject ability is fixed (commonly observed in mathematics). The static skill perception perpetuates a belief that using alternative strategies would be useless to improve performance, subsequently discounting any need for motivational regulation. These automatic responses will prompt resolute cognitive disengagement, based upon learned patterns of failure, or result in cognitive apathy whereby the individual behaviorally participates in task completion but is psychologically detached from the activity. Optimal engagement implies active awareness of one's motivational state and involves a deliberate and intentional desire to establish, control, and mediate motivational momentum throughout the learning and performance cycle of goal selection, pursuit, and attainment (Pintrich, 2004). When actively striving to reach performance excellence, learners are more inclined seek ways to improve, which frequently means addressing motivational momentum that all too often vacillates over the course of mastering a typical learning or performance challenge.

Wolters (2003) identified at least four prominent regulatory strategies targeting motivational aspects of performance that were substantiated to promote achievement. *Self-consequating strategies* include self-derived and self-administered contingencies based upon task progress that are designed to help learners maintain focus and forestall task disengagement. Self-consequating behaviors can involve rewarding oneself with ice cream after a project milestone is reached, or engaging in a post-performance pleasurable activity when an academic goal is attained. Negative consequating occurs when individuals elect to withhold positive contingencies or defer preferred activities, such as declining participation at a desired social event, and instead choosing to advance task progress. A second contingency strategy, *self-talk*, occurs when thoughts are vocalized or when implicit cognitions reassure the individual of the purported benefits or importance of completing an activity, as opposed to fixating on the consequences of task abandonment. Self-talk provides internally-generated feedback and is used to guide the individual toward desired goals. Self-talk is especially helpful to offset the ebbs and flows of sporadic attentional focus and wavering task engagement that often occur when a learner encounters task challenges and performance obstacles. Self-talk is a method to refocus the performer to stay on task and persevere to reach the desired goals. In other words, "Stop thinking about Facebook or Pinterest; refocus and keep on reading!"

A third useful strategy to self-induce positive motivational momentum is deliberate and intentional effort devoted toward escalating interest in otherwise boring, repetitive, or obligatory tasks. Developing task interest has a long history of positive influence on task engagement, and learners who show task interest are more likely to use a variety of self-regulatory strategies when encountering interest-depleting activities (Pintrich & Zusho, 2002). Task interest can be generated by promoting intentional variety in task requirements (Staats & Gino, 2012) and can also be accomplished by incorporating novel routines or rituals into task completion, such as using games, or by seeing how quickly a mundane task can be completed (Baumeister & Heatherton, 1996; Wolters, 1998). My colleague, Morgan, quite frequently trudges through tedious reading of mountains of doctoral studies by searching for typos in published articles, taking infinite delight in any error she finds. Morgan's strategy serves as a means to focus her attention, but the approach also compensates for fluctuating material interest. Evidence from sports psychology offers related cognitively grounded strategies to induce interest, primarily through a focus on maintaining concentration. By using certain techniques, such as deliberately deciding when to concentrate, only focusing on factors within one's control, and planning for interest-reducing activities, a performer can retain concentration and focus attention while directing motivation toward reaching task-relevant goals (Moran, 1996, 2012).

Finally, *environmental restructuring* involves the direct manipulation of one's learning or performance context as a means to eliminate distractions while simultaneously scaffolding attentional focus. Environmental restructuring is accomplished in multiple ways, usually focused on either a physical modification of the learning or performance context or by renegotiation or modification of actual task requirements (Pintrich & Zusho, 2002). In organizations, restructuring is often situated as person–environment fit, described as "the discrepancy between people's ideal conditions based upon needs and values, and experienced conditions" (Johnson, Taing, Chang, & Kawamoto, 2013, p. 75). Restructuring can include simplistic contextual evaluations and cosmetic changes, such as reducing ambient noise, finding a comfortable chair, or creating personalized conditions that optimize learning or performance. Recall that Alex Dixon, during her recovery period, deliberately sought out and immersed herself in social situations that allowed her to share her experiences with others as well as show off her magnetic personality. Alex deliberately sought opportunities for socialization.

Restructuring can also offset personal vulnerabilities. An effective restructuring activity that appeases the author's compulsive personality is completing daily household chores, such as making the bed, washing the dishes, and feeding his pet iguana, before attempting any creative writing. The chore-completing routine eliminates cognitive intrusions and, at least hypothetically, permits unwavering focus on necessary work efforts. Modification of task requirements means that individuals perform qualitative assessments of what is needed to effectively complete a task under certain conditions and make modifications to task routines with the goal of cultivating optimal performance. For instance, if faced with the prospect of a challenging writing project, task restructuring could include creating a project outline or drafting charts to track progress (Graham & Harris, 1994). Further, a writing project could prosper by identifying a conceptual framework that includes a conscious focus on writing objectives, as well as anticipating how to overcome the inevitable obstacles and setbacks endemic to the writing process (Bruning & Kauffman, in press).

The strategies discussed thus far are generic and domain-general approaches used to catalyze performance, irrespective of task. The individualistic approaches described represent regulatory attempts to identify, understand, and mediate potential motivational impediments and roadblocks. However, like the Chapter 9 appraisal of emotional stimuli, regulation of motivation is a highly personalized and idiosyncratic process. A strategy that is effective and a resounding success for one individual can be a miserable failure for another. In the realm of self-regulation of motivation, one size does not fit all, and in this case, the magnitude and the type of strategy an individual chooses really does matter. As such, we turn to the highly personalized nature of motivational regulation and describe why variability within and between individuals is a formidable diagnostic and mediational challenge for the aspiring MD.

Principle #48—Self-regulation is personalized, transitory, and marginally predictable

How individuals choose to start, monitor, and complete tasks has enormous variability. Some individuals will approach a typical academic or work assignment using an orderly, deliberate, and organized methodology that demonstrates clear forethought and planning. Typically, methodical performers will first set specific outcome goals. Once goals are determined, these same individuals will intentionally think about what steps are needed for successful task completion. Perhaps you have an upcoming examination. Some individuals will make specific decisions concerning when or with whom they will be most motivated to study, how they will build necessary knowledge to do well on the examination, or if they will use comprehension aids such as highlighting text or summarizing concepts on index cards. During the study process, well-regulated individuals will evaluate the effectiveness of their study methods, assess their degree of understanding, and evaluate prospective method changes to improve learning. The regulated learner, based upon what he or she already knows and the complexity of the material, may also consciously contemplate which material requires greater effort or more study time to achieve mastery. Upon reaching study goals, the regulated learner steps back and reflects on what was learned, conducting a self-assessment to determine what, if anything, should be done differently to capitalize on the time invested in the study session or for similar future sessions. Clearly, the learner described has demonstrated regulation through self-control over the learning process by taking deliberate, conscious, and effortful steps to enhance performance (Muraven, 2012).

Other learners, however, may take an impulsive or lackadaisical approach to examination preparation by jumping in head first with little, if any, forethought about or consideration of what challenges or obstacles lie ahead. The spontaneous learner will devote minimal cognitive effort toward proactively evaluating existing knowledge or determining which domain-specific cognitive strategies are best suited to improve his or her comprehension or performance. Little consideration will be given to anticipating and avoiding potential distractions, such as knowing what to study, or developing a plan to avoid cramming, stress, or counteracting the debilitating effects of procrastination. Few, if any, contingencies will be in place for fending off the inevitable exhaustion that accompanies prolonged work or study sessions. This learner, in many ways, can be described as passive, relinquishing control of the performance process by abdicating responsibility for process improvement; instead, this learner focuses effort primarily on achieving desired outcomes. Not surprisingly, the laid-back learner frequently attributes successful outcomes to luck or rationalizes that positive results were observed because the instructor was lenient or the task was easier than expected (see Principle #36, p. 182). In the worst case, the learner may succumb to the erroneous belief that performance improvement and learning strategies are inconsequential for accelerated achievement.

Based upon the individual differences in the control strategies described, and assuming that a performer is interested in achieving success (which may not always be true), the aspiring MD may likely reach one of three logical conclusions concerning why strategy use appears to be so personalized and transitory, varying dramatically between individuals. First, some individuals may lack requisite knowledge concerning which strategies are most effective at a given time or for a given task. Second, a learner or performer may possess knowledge of regulatory strategies but may have poor timing and lack needed conditional knowledge, not understanding under which conditions particular strategies are most useful or effective (Weinstein, Acee, & Jung, 2011). Third, an individual may have extensive strategy knowledge, understanding which strategies work best at a particular time, but may be unwilling to exert the necessary cognitive effort to search a repertoire of strategies and apply existing knowledge to enhance performance. In many ways, the use of control strategies is highly idiosyncratic, applied haphazardly or inconsistently, and subject to wide variation not only within the same individual but also between individuals on similar tasks. When attempting to predict which regulatory strategies will be used by a person at a particular time at least three empirically supported interpretations are viable. The variability of self-regulatory behaviors may occur due to (1) individual attributions based upon historical response patterns; (2) implicit beliefs held by performers, including self-schemas; and (3) situational cognitive and affective factors that differ based upon task and context. Each influence is discussed separately below.

Historical response patterns influence attributions and corresponding motivational regulation because many individuals believe past experience guides future performance (Zimmerman, 2011). During task engagement, individuals frequently and subjectively appraise task progress, seeking to ascribe reasons for successful task completion or failure. Historically, when a learner experiences success, strong competency beliefs develop, but successful learners also tend to believe that they can control their own destiny. Learners who feel in control will enthusiastically put forth cognitive effort and consider a wide repertoire of motivational strategies to accomplish their learning goals because their past efforts have proven fruitful.

Conversely, learners encountering repeated obstacles develop little faith in their own abilities; instead, these learners expect learning to be a highly challenging and frustrating experience, which contributes to exceedingly skeptical beliefs about their ability to succeed. These doubtful learners find little justification to exert effort and become indifferent, reluctant to consider diverse regulatory strategies, or use the ones they have because they believe academic success is beyond their control. Instead, the dubious learner becomes passive and disengaged, believing that such factors as teacher disposition or content difficulty determine his or her performance destiny. Ultimately, the forlorn learner capitulates to the self-fulfilling prophecy of dissention, believing that there is little or no purpose in investing extra effort or using creative strategies because the strategies will not work and are considered useless to change historically poor learning outcomes.

Historical learning patterns develop early in life, with infants as young as 3 months demonstrating regulatory ability, measured by showing affect congruence with caregivers (Feldman, Greenbaum, & Yirmiya, 1999). Affect congruency is powerful, predicting enhanced self-control and delay of gratification (DOG) throughout the second year of a child's life. Children demonstrating control quickly surmise that complementary affect alleviates distress (and often gets dirty diapers changed). The emotional scaffolding from caregivers supports this rudimentary regulatory process by subliminally teaching the infant the relation between feelings and behavioral action, which prompts a belief in the personal ability to exert influence and control over the external environment. Gradually, the child internalizes the scaffolding as he or she soon realizes that differences in cognitions and emotions can influence his or her own behaviors as well as the behaviors of others (Eisenberg & Sulik, 2012). The phenomenon of control intensifies at about age 3 years, when children demonstrate an important precursor of self-regulation, inhibitory control, as evidenced by the simple game of "Simon Says" (Jones, Rothbart, & Posner, 2003), where the player deliberately refrains from acting on her own impulsive cognitions and, instead, regulates her behavior to win the game.

As the developmental milestone of theory of mind is surpassed, the nascent regulator realizes that others have different mental states than their own (Wellman, Cross, & Watson, 2001). The child learns that causality for events can be attributed either to the self, or to others. However, as any parent of a 3-year old knows, the child seeks justification for *why* things happen, frequently asking questions while cunningly experimenting with caregivers to elicit certain reactions to their litany of questions (Luebbe, Kiel, & Buss, 2011). As the child matures, attributional evaluations become increasingly more influential for future behavior, causally entwined with the use of particular strategies that produce desired results. Success breeds positive self-attributions and nurtures competency and control beliefs. Lack of accomplishment instills a sense of self-doubt while impeding task efficacy, leading to negative self-reflections that decrease adaptive motivation while cultivating the inevitable false belief that the external world is beyond one's personal control.

Perceptions of controllability are essential to jumpstart adaptive motivation. If individuals believe that attained outcomes are directly mediated by their own effort, then if a particular strategy fails, the failure will be attributed to using the wrong strategy and not to an incompetent self (Corno, 2011). Individuals operating under the perception of control will believe that using a different or more productive approach can reverse undesirable outcomes. Recall that motivational leader and NFL superstar Nick Lowery described the challenge of focusing attention and blocking out cognitive intrusions during away games in front of 60,000 screaming antagonistic fans, some shouting out obscenities about his mother and the majority wishing failure. Rarely did Nick attribute missed field goals to external causes, such as belligerent fans or wind, but instead, he expressed disappointment and personal responsibility for wayward footballs. Nick embraced the reality that his advanced skills were subject to fallibility, articulating the belief that failure was unavoidable. However, when field goals went awry, strategy changes routinely followed, based upon successful historical patterns of control.

Over time, patterns of experience generate and entrench implicit beliefs, which influence the types of goals individuals set and the strategies they will use to attain those goals. Individuals harbor implicit beliefs about knowledge development, views of how intelligence influences success, goal orientations toward a task, and competency beliefs concerning the skills and abilities necessary for success. The beliefs individuals hold in aggregate comprise *self-schemas*, or personal task-contingent self-representations that influence goals, motives, interests, fears, perceived threats, and strategies that individuals believe mediate performance outcomes (Garcia & Pintrich, 1994). Like the description on the back of a baseball card, self-schemas illuminate a profile of the individual, identifying not runs, hits, or errors but dimensions of strengths, styles, and values that contribute to self-descriptions. Self-schemas are critical to self-regulation and control because based upon the relative importance, purpose, and value we ascribe to different endeavors, diverse strategies will be used to accomplish performance objectives, some more situationally effective than others (Chatzistamatiou, Dermitzaki, Efklides, & Leondari, 2013; Sansone, Fraughton, Zachary, Butner, & Heiner, 2011).

Although self-regulation is considered to be a contextualized and domain-specific skill (Cleary, Callan, & Zimmerman, 2012), in many cases, individuals exhibit generalized academic and performance dispositions as part of their self-schemas. One critical component of self-schemas is epistemological beliefs or those beliefs concerning how knowledge is created, valued, and evaluated. Epistemological beliefs act as a road map or guide that determines how learning challenges are approached. For instance, some educators hold the belief that multiplication skill is best developed through rote learning and that using learning strategies, such as repetition and memorization, solidifies knowledge. Others may use a different approach to teaching multiplication, believing that expertise originates through application, such as when a learner is given a carpet-laying problem and must measure room dimensions and then use multiplication to calculate how much carpet to purchase in order to cover a floor. The obvious differences in these two instructional approaches would have a profound impact upon pedagogical methods but would also affect the motivation of learners, each method requiring the use of different regulatory strategies to sustain and accomplish learning goals. For some, one strategy would be motivating and accelerate performance, while the motivation of another might suffer due to a misalignment between strategy and belief. When strategies and self-schemas clash, radical and maladaptive changes in motivation may quickly follow, inhibiting the possibility of optimal performance.

Further complicating strategy and belief dissonance is the implicit nature of cognition, as many individuals will be unaware of their own epistemological influences on self-regulation (Winne, 2011). Studies that measure the specificity of epistemic beliefs indicate that individuals have personalized perspectives concerning how to navigate the learning and performance process, and these studies also reveal that individual approaches to learning influence motivational regulation. Muis and Franco (2009) empirically demonstrated that epistemic beliefs, such as the simplicity, source, and certainty of knowledge, are significant factors that influence how learners approach learning, and epistemic beliefs can predict the type of control strategies individuals will use to meet learning goals. In addition, epistemic beliefs also influence learner engagement and the willingness to invest cognitive effort to achieve learning goals. For example, if an individual believes that the creation of knowledge is a simple mechanized process, he or she may accept as undeniable truth any instructor-presented material, perhaps leading to debatable false beliefs, such as the glorification of US manifest destiny, or the denial of global climate change. This absolutist approach to knowledge defers to authority and offers little incentive to question the veracity of the information presented, forestalling critical evaluation and information scrutiny that might otherwise accompany information derived from another source.

Further, reminiscent of the self-schemas previously described, there is evidence to validate *"epistemic profiles"* that suggest consistency among the frequency and type of control strategies individuals use (Muis & Franco, 2010, p. 29). The profiles reveal that the goals individuals set and the strategies individuals prefer become situated as part of an overall approach to knowledge acquisition. Inconsistencies between epistemic beliefs and domain requirements may result in attenuated motivation and contemptuous frustration when individuals are forced to use suboptimal regulation strategies, as exhibited when the highly logical learner is forced to write a creative essay or when the visionary corporate leader is relegated to preparing boring spreadsheets and mundane reports.

Closely related to epistemology beliefs are conceptions concerning general intelligence. Polarized views suggest that individuals believe that intelligence is either subject to modification based upon the acquisition of new knowledge, representing an *incremental* view or, contrariwise, that intelligence, like flat feet or bushy eyebrows, is a reality that must be accepted, thus adopting an *entity*, or fixed belief (Dweck & Leggett, 1988). Although beliefs concerning intelligence originated through classroom research, implicit beliefs concerning the malleability of behavior and overall subjective well-being have been extended to such domains as weight management (Burnette, 2010), personal perceptions of organizational leadership ability (Hoyt, Burnette, & Innella, 2012), and even success in romantic relationships (Knee & Canevello, 2006). The commonality among these studies reveals that individuals with entity beliefs are unwilling or unlikely to use effective regulatory and control strategies because of their misconception that strategy use is unrelated to behavioral change and performance outcomes.

Conversely, individuals with incremental beliefs will embrace change and use control improvement strategies because they believe that diverse strategies result in different outcomes. Individuals with entity beliefs are far less motivated to use variable strategies to accelerate learning or performance because of invariant expectations. Entity beliefs are powerful influences on personal aspirations and are linked to underachievement, such as when a learner does not meet academic expectations despite the possession of requisite skills and knowledge (Miele, Son, & Metcalfe, 2013). Learners with an entity belief may choose less demanding academic challenges, exhibit higher school dropout rates, and elect lower status and lower paying positions (Maurer, Wrenn, Pierce, Tross, & Collins, 2003). Individuals with incremental beliefs even have emotional advantages, more frequently using coping strategies, that show lower correlations with negative emotions while engaging in fewer incidences of self-handicapping behavior (see Principle #43, p. 225) compared with individuals holding entity beliefs (Burnette, O'Boyle, VanEpps, Pollack, & Finkel, 2013). The positive affect associated with entity beliefs develops, in part, based upon the evaluation of payoffs when strategies are used. When results meet or exceed expectations, positive feelings are generated, an outcome that will rarely occur when a learner doubts that strategic effort may reap rewards.

Implicit beliefs are closely aligned with how and why individuals set goals. Burnette et al. (2013), in a meta-analysis summarizing over 30,000 observations of the relation between implicit beliefs and self-regulatory behavior, concluded that individuals with incremental views show a higher probability of adopting mastery-oriented goals and associated strategies compared with the more likely adoption of normative goals and strategies observed when individuals espouse entity beliefs. Remember, goal orientation does not focus on *what* goals learners set but, instead, represents the alleged purpose for engaging in learning or the reasons why a particular performance target is chosen. Although individuals may adopt multiple goal-orientation perspectives and at times normative orientations are preferable for academic outcomes (Senko, Hulleman, & Harackiewicz, 2011; see Principle #34, p. 154), mastery-oriented individuals typically show greater interest in the accumulation of knowledge, unlike the cosmetic intentions of relative expertise endemic to the normative-oriented learner.

Goal orientation exerts a strong influence on motivation to exercise self-control because orientation correlates with strategy choices. Since individuals with a dominant normative orientation seek to gain positive perceptions from others while avoiding negative evaluations of their competency and abilities, they are more inclined to use attention grabbing, ego-inflating regulation strategies. These strategies include setting less challenging goals, seeking easily mastered academic or athletic competitions, and focusing on the aesthetic, rather than substantive, outcomes of learning. Normative learners typical embellish the effort devoted to learning, using tactics, such as showing up to class with a pile of books or implying they spent the entire day voraciously studying in the campus library. Alternatively, learners with a dominant mastery orientation primarily set goals and engage in projects for the sake of gaining knowledge and will show a substantial inclination to use knowledge-building strategies. The mastery learner will persevere in the face of obstacles based upon the internal quest to develop expertise. Such strategies as effective time management in order to successfully meet goals, seeking help when needed while being unconcerned about the impressions of others, and demonstrating an overall greater willingness to evaluate their knowledge acquisition through vigilant monitoring are some of the hallmark regulatory strategies of mastery learner.

Ultimately, goal orientation provides valuable evidence to understand the different motives individuals have for engaging in learning and performance activities (Lichtinger & Kaplan, 2011). It is incumbent upon the MD to not only assess the engagement purpose of a learner, but also to actively determine how learner purpose influences strategy choice. By evaluating the type and frequency of strategies used, the aspiring MD can respond in kind, motivating the learner with the ultimate goal of deciding which type and degree of scaffolding is most effective to facilitate performance success despite the vast individual differences in learners and learning purpose. Simple strategies, such as providing recognition, offering extra credit, or granting time off for academic or performance accomplishments, will likely energize the normative learner. Likewise, mastery-oriented learners respond joyfully when offered book recommendations, gain pleasure when valued others listen to their ideas, and show pride and enthusiasm when nominated to be an instructional assistant or group leader. Through instructor insightfulness and perceptual calibration of what learners value, the MD can avoid the unsavory dilemma of using the right strategy with the wrong person, essentially forestalling or precluding the prospect of adaptive performance motivation.

Cognitive and affective mediators of regulation comprise such factors as goal setting, metacognitive awareness, interest, and emotions that fluctuate based upon the specific task, progress perceptions, and individual dispositions of the performer. Cognitive and emotional factors include both personal awareness of which factors and strategies mediate performance while also accounting for the willingness of individuals to use available strategies to regulate personal performance. The influence of interest upon setting and sustaining goal progress was discussed in Chapter 6 (p. 139), while affective influences and their relation to strategy activation were thoroughly reviewed in Chapter 9 (p. 253), eliminating the need for review here. Identifying which cognitive factors contribute the greatest influence to strategy choice involves sorting through a myriad of observable evidence. Prime considerations include the depth and type of background knowledge, along with resource and capacity-driven factors, such as attentional focus and memory. Evaluative aspects of cognition include techniques for effective monitoring and the consideration and integration of internal and external feedback. In total, these are crucial cognitively grounded concerns that significantly influence the frequency, type, and conditions under which known regulatory processes will be employed.

However, before examining the specific cognitive influences on strategy choice and use, a more pressing consideration must be addressed: Specifically, why do many regulatory efforts fail so often? Statistics are discouraging, as hapless regulators frequently demonstrate ineffective inhibitory control (Miller & Fillmore, 2013), failing at multiple attempts to quit smoking or gaining weight after weeks of dieting, while the recidivism rates for criminal offenses are alarming, with one study concluding that four out of five offenders will be rearrested within 4 years of an original conviction (Connecticut

Department of Corrections, 2015). In more relevant learning and performance domains, the results are less profound, yet equally disturbing. Despite the best intentions of educators and coaches, sometimes performers fail to anticipate obstacles, learners fail to act strategically, and individuals rely upon the immutable foundation of hope, committing the cardinal performance sin of repeatedly using the same strategy over and over while expecting a different outcome. The many threats to regulation and control can thwart the most studious of intentions, but these same threats can be mediated with knowledge of the fleeting and fluctuating nature of regulatory control.

Principle #49—Self-regulatory ability is depletable; accurate calibration is essential

"Turn your cell phones off." "Clear everything off of your desk." "Take out a number two pencil." "And no talking!" These words likely evoke anxiety even for the most confident learners. If you are a student, or have been one, you know these ominous test-proctor edicts foreshadow the administration of a standardized test: a measure of aptitude and ability, and a barometer of performance that evaluates mental fortitude and physical stamina. One reason that examinations, such as the SAT and GRE, are perceived as challenging is not only because of the high-stakes impact of the results, which influence college selection and placement decisions, but also because of the cognitive demands during the examination that zap energy with the test going on over 3, 4, or more hours, usually without a break. After finishing an examination, test takers frequently lament about feeling drained, exhausted, or spent, genuinely believing that they are incapable of answering one more question.

The testing scenario described mirrors, in many ways, the depletion of resources experienced when using self-regulatory strategies, which, coincidently, are strategies that significantly enhance standardized test scores (Cleary, Platten, & Nelson, 2008; Taboada, Tonks, Wigfield, & Guthrie, 2009). Depletion occurs because constant regulation of motivation and cognition is effortful. The process of regulation has both immediate and progressive effects. Similar to other conscious strategy interventions, regulation immediately usurps a component of one's limited working memory resources. Individuals are restricted from dedicating 100% of cognitive effort on learning and performance when contemplating regulatory decisions. Typical thinking functions, such as focusing attention or allocating cognitive resources to salient task aspects, become impaired when cognitive demands exceed cognitive capacity. Once the threshold of capability is exceeded, regulatory efforts will suffer (Hofmann, Schmeichel, & Baddeley, 2012).

The *strength model of regulation* suggests that individual differences in information processing (Baumeister & Heatherton, 1996) or cognitive efficiency (Hoffman & Schraw, 2009) are partially accountable for regulatory deficits, as some individuals will fare better than others due to enhanced capacity to process information. Just as some cell phones and computers work better and faster than others and may slow down or freeze when too many programs are running, regulatory efforts are hampered and subject to temporary lapses in effectiveness, until other metaphorical "operating programs" are closed and situational task demands subside. Even the most highly motivated strategy users and those with a vast repertoire of strategies cannot succeed under highly demanding task conditions that exceed existing capacity.

On a longer-term basis, the ability to effectively use regulatory skills and control strategies can suffer due to the cumulative effects of focused cognition. The *depletion model of self-regulation* suggests that prolonged cognitive effort is incrementally demanding, with behavioral control and physiological resources weakening over time, resulting in a reduction of optimal functioning. The extent of regulatory reduction is influenced by the cumulative expenditure of energy, but deficits are also contingent upon the frequency and the degree of inhibitory behavior exerted during task performance. Generally, and with some qualifications, the more an individual chooses to regulate or inhibit certain behaviors (e.g., ignoring the urge to give up on a challenging examination, attempting to abstain from unhealthy behavior, such as excessive alcohol consumption, etc.), the more likely that motivational regulation will subside and regulatory efforts will be less successful (Baumeister, Gailliot, Dewall, & Oaten, 2006). Similar to using a cell phone repeatedly, even the most efficient regulators (and batteries) eventually need recharging to operate optimally.

Biologically, the depletion of control ability is associated with decrements of blood glucose levels: when glucose is expended, control ability suffers (Benton, Parker, & Donohoe, 1996; Gailliot & Baumeister, 2007b). Glucose restoration can occur through rest, food consumption, and nutritional supplementation (Hagger, Wood, Stiff, & Chatzisarantis, 2010), quite possibly accounting for the immense popularity of glucose-restoring energy drinks among college students. However, wide discrepancies exist among individuals' baseline glucose, the rate of glucose production, and how and when glucose is allocated to the brain. Most importantly, individual differences in consumption do not follow a predictable linear pattern (Kurzban, 2009). The more aversive or complex an individual perceives a particular task to be, the greater the need to devote energy to the task, thus maximizing the need for glucose.

However, glucose allocation is inconsistent, and individual allocation differences may be the result of subjective perceptions of stress (Beedie & Lane, 2012), purported task value (Vohs, Baumeister, & Schmeichel, 2012), or implicit beliefs (Job, Dweck, & Walton, 2010). For instance, Job et al. observed that during the completion of spatial problems, similar to those folding-box problems found on intelligence quotient (IQ) tests, participants who believed (or were told) that regulatory ability was an *unlimited* resource outperformed a comparison group of individuals who believed that self-regulatory ability decreased as regulatory effort was expended. No relationship was observed between self-reported exhaustion and subsequent performance, but only for the unlimited resource group, refuting the glucose depletion hypothesis. Job et al. concluded that "exhaustion was not a sign to reduce effort" (p. 1692). Similarly, Beedie and Lane (2012) attributed individual differences in glucose allocation to individual subjective need, with greater production and allocation of glucose realized only when a task was deemed stressful or an urgent priority, corroborating the findings of Vohs et al. (2012), who concluded that depletion is moderated by beliefs, but only when depletion is "mild" (p. 946).

Another plausible, yet untested, biological explanation for diminished control is that certain activities evoke subjective impressions that invigorate individuals, simulating the impression of efficient glucose conservation. The empirical studies described indicated that at times, individuals are highly motivated to exhibit regulatory activity despite subjective energy expenditures or actual glucose depletion. The compelling motivation to regulate despite real or imagined deficits mirrors the ubiquitous "runner's high," when individuals describe euphoric mood changes subsequent to the expenditure of ample physical and cognitive resources. The reports of a perceptual "high" after running have recently been supported by evidence indicating that endogenous opioids in the frontolimbic brain area are released after vigorous and sustained exercise (Boecker et al., 2008), a phenomenon also implicated in sexual satisfaction and the anticipation of monetary reward. Replication of these subjective reactions during other tasks deemed personally rewarding or invigorating may support a conservation explanation of glucose, with promising repercussions in other learning and performance domains.

Behaviorally, the exertion of regulatory effort over time diminishes the effectiveness of self-control, a crucial aspect of motivational self-regulation (Muraven, 2012). Self-control, unlike some self-regulation strategies, always involves active and conscious inhibition. As individuals exercise coping ability and demonstrate goal persistence over time by repeatedly forgoing distractions and resisting counterproductive temptations, the ability to exercise subsequent control diminishes. Take, for example, the plight of the diligent dieter who consistently fends off ice cream impulses, but eventually succumbs to the urges and gulps down a carton of ice cream. The defeated dieter rationalizes that he has earned the right to a pleasurable experience because of his noble suppression efforts, which gradually deteriorated to a point where suppression was no longer psychologically sustainable. Broadly, diminished self-control from repeated resistance transcends personal health consequences and contributes to a greater frequency of socially undesirable behaviors. Low levels of self-control are consistently linked to lying, cheating, stealing, and social impropriety and unethical behavior in general, with disturbing frequency in the workplace (Gino, Schweitzer, Mead, & Ariely, 2011).

While understanding motives for opportunistic gain is important, the impact of depletion on the use of performance strategies is more relevant to the MD. When regulatory resources have been consumed, adaptive task-directed motivation suffers. Motivational regulation requires vigilant monitoring of task progress and yet also demands inhibition of urges to gloss over challenging problems and override negative affect, such as the boredom or frustration that typically may accompany the learning or performance process. Effective control means that individuals must muster available motivational effort to persist in solving a particular problem, fend off urges to finish quickly at the risk of compromising accuracy, and maintain an approach where a variety of functional tactics are considered to overcome task obstacles. Sadly, regulatory strategies that may be frequently and normally employed successfully may fall to the wayside when an individual experiences the common plight of unavoidable regulatory depletion.

Weathering depletion, many individuals still struggle with self-control efforts, but why? Baumeister and Heatherton (1996) suggested the liabilities of ineffectual self-regulation are a consequence of "underregulation" or "misregulation" (p. 2). Underregulation represents failed attempts to regulate due to the absence of task motivation or the unwillingness to exercise self-control, while misregulation characterizes ill-guided regulatory efforts that may fail due to lack of strategy knowledge or when applying strategies that prove counterproductive to attaining desired outcomes, including the self-handicapping strategies reviewed in Principle #43 (p. 225). Specifically, regulatory mechanisms fail when goals or standards are nebulous or vague, or during ineffective monitoring, when individuals may neglect, not recognize, or display general resistance or apathy toward addressing performance gaps. Optimally, during task engagement individuals will undergo a gap analysis that compares the current state of learning or performance with a desired state, with the objective of determining which strategy interventions will effectively close the gap between learner intention and objective reality. However, in the absence of clearly known performance standards or without taking deliberate action to override and forestall imminent failure, minding the performance gap is improbable. Clearly, the naive or recalcitrant performer cannot expect to eradicate a performance obstacle when failing to acknowledge or recognize that one exists.

Another explanation for regulatory failure is the COPES model (Winne & Hadwin, 2008). This model suggests that regulatory breakdowns can occur from lack of attentiveness to necessary performance standards and conditions, including misguided aspirations that influence goals and task definition. Ambiguity concerning ability and competency beliefs impedes progress toward goals due to a potential focus on faulty attributions and uncertain outcomes. Operational deficits, such as ineffective progress monitoring or inconsistent strategy knowledge and application, hinder performance, inhibiting the individual from reaching the product-driven outcome of his or her goals. Regulatory efforts may also fail due to insufficient evaluation of effort in comparison to requirements, precluding the ability for post hoc assessments that identify reasons for lack of goal attainment. Flawed evaluation may also occur when individuals recognize deficiencies and yet take no action, resisting efforts to study smarter or work harder.

Although optimal regulation is systemically contingent on avoiding the pitfalls described above, one key to effective regulation is accurately evaluating the difference between task requirements and the skills, abilities, and strategies individuals *believe* are needed for goal attainment. Sometimes referred to as action monitoring (Miele, Wager, Mitchell, & Metcalfe, 2011), these judgments detect the extent of divergence between observed states and expected states. Assessment of the discrepancy between expectations and outcomes can be completed proactively before attempting a task or during a postmortem evaluation after task completion. The former method is often described as the process of *calibration*, which involves measuring the degree of accuracy between individual perceptions and beliefs about what skills and abilities are needed to complete a task, compared with those actually needed (Stone, 2000). A learner believing that he can effectively master 50 pages of detailed content in 30 minutes, would likely qualify as exhibiting an exaggerated self-evaluation bias (Gramzow & Willard, 2006) and questionable calibration, based upon his irrational mastery belief.

Task calibration is often determined by self-efficacy (Schunk & Pajares, 2009). Self-efficacy beliefs have strong mediational effects on the use of regulatory skills because individuals highly confident in their domain knowledge will persevere in the face of obstacles and use a broader repertoire of strategies than individuals doubting their ability to complete a task (Bandura, 1997). Miscalibration frequently develops when individuals are overly confident but lack actual ability commensurate with task need. Inaccurate calibration is lethal, with overestimation leading to attaining quantitatively less than one expects or qualitatively inferior results, primarily due to withholding effort needed to complete a task successfully or from neglecting to override inaccurate or faulty aspects of performance (Van Loon, de Bruin, van Gog, & van Merriënboer, 2013). Underestimation of actual ability may also hinder performance when a person doubts capability despite having requisite knowledge or skill. Underestimation may result in the temporary allocation of cognitive resources to the wrong aspects of a task, not taking full advantage of existing regulatory strategies, or, in the worst case scenario, believing that information obtained during learning or applied during test performance is faulty, when, in fact, the knowledge is correct!

Additionally, throughout the regulatory cycle, individuals must make accurate, objective, and unbiased appraisals of the depth of their knowledge acquisition, including a realistic assessment of what was accomplished or learned. The process of comparing learning expectancies and outcomes is often described as making *judgments of learning* (JOLs), which are appraisals "distinguishing between what one does and does not know" (Rhodes & Tauber, 2011, p. 131). Both calibration and JOLs are contingent, in part, on exhibiting a sense of realism when evaluating one's skills and resultant performance, a process that is often flawed due to inaccurate judgment concerning task requirements (Cleary, 2009), as well as personal bias that results in inflated assessments of performance ability (Dupeyrat, Escribe, Huet, & Régner, 2011). Perhaps more important for the MD, accurate calibration and JOLs require an objective evaluation of the degree of motivational effort one is willing to expend to complete a particular task. Individuals may have the talent and abilities needed to reach task goals but may inaccurately estimate task intensity or may fail to determine precisely which motivational strategies are optimal to support task completion. Inaccurate estimates may range from something as simplistic as expecting to complete an assignment faster than possible to decisions that have dramatic impacts on life or career, such as false optimism concerning the ability to attract a mate, land a job, or generate the intellectual horsepower to earn a degree.

Motivational imprecision may result in the reality of needing to devote more time or extra effort to a task than intended, potentially disrupting the ability to reach task goals. Individuals who devote precious cognitive resources to fending off negative affect based upon lack of progress or performance frustration may simply run out of time or energy to complete the task at hand. Miscalibration of motivational effort may also occur because of miscalculated, distorted, or selective recollection of impaired motivation in the past. Positively biased memorial reconstructions of ability occur when events and performances are recalled more positively than actuality, based more on wishful thinking or the embellishment of past success, but the impressions often are objectively inconsistent (Alba & Hutchinson, 2000). Underestimation of motivation can also occur when individuals inaccurately recall the consequences of their motivated efforts, such as the psychological or behavioral sacrifices that are required to accomplish a goal or the effort needed to recover from impaired motivational judgment.

After task completion, realization of miscalibration may skew future self-perceptions. Once an individual recognizes that he or she must dedicate more time or resources to achieve desired goals, the person must also acknowledge faulty motivational assessments. Acknowledgment potentially leads to negative self-reflection, which may perpetuate task avoidance under similar conditions if individuals are unwilling to invest the effort required for task success. Luckily, not all inflated self-opinions are counterproductive. Embellished assessments of personal capability, sometimes referred to as "motivated self-enhancement" (Gramzow & Willard, 2006), or the better-than-average effect (Taylor & Gollwitzer, 1995), can lead to motivationally adaptive behavior. Individuals with inflated self-opinions typically report enhanced subjective well-being, satisfying interpersonal relationships, and better stress-coping ability (Bouffard & Narciss, 2011), suggesting that personal oblivity, at times, is psychologically useful, albeit a regulatory conundrum.

Considering the vast vulnerabilities inherent to the process of optimal regulation, a variety of generic remedies may negate the depletable and miscalibration consequences that impede self-regulation and control. Pragmatically, regulatory depletion can be forestalled by the emphasis on belief restricting described earlier. Remember, individuals who embraced implicit beliefs that regulation was an unlimited personal resource and, at least in part, a function of strong willpower, consistently outperformed a group of individuals with similar skills and experience but believed that regulatory ability was limited (Job et al., 2010). Although restructuring of belief paradigms is highly challenging because of the entrenched nature of beliefs and many changes are temporary or transitory (Dole & Sinatra, 1998; see Chapter 12, p. 346), conscious emphasis on belief restricting is fruitful to mediate regulatory issues.

Individuals skeptical about their capabilities and those with impoverished regulatory resources who are unable or reluctant to exert regulatory effort, may frequently circumvent the regulatory process, opting for immediate momentary satisfaction, succumbing to distractions and temptations at the expense of higher-order goals and long-term success (Fishbach & Trope, 2008). Possessing procrastinating philosophies, such as "I will get to it when I am ready," or "Don't do today what you can put off until tomorrow" and so on, temporally nullifies the need for motivational regulation, perpetuates counterproductive behaviors, and forestalls attainment of goals or conditions that may lead to success. Examples include putting off studying in lieu of a night out or deferring a doctor visit despite the medical necessity, time, and financial resources. Lessons from counter-active control theory (Trope & Fishbach, 2000) and DOG research (Mischel, Shoda, & Rodriguez, 1989) suggest several practical remedies to inhibit the sacrifice of long-term beneficence in favor of more gratifying short-term incentives, such as escaping academic boredom or deferring a repetitive or uninteresting work task.

Counteractive tactics (CATs) are akin to psychological aerobics individuals use to resolve conflict between meaningful long-term goals and highly tempting, often hedonistic, short-term needs. When using CATs, long-term goals are temporarily suppressed but not forgone. CATs are, at times, highly beneficial because when using CATs, individuals defer long-term goals in favor of imposing self-mandated behavioral contingencies that ultimately enhance goal striving and performance. The psychological swap, in many ways, is reflective of a personal quid pro quo arrangement ("tit for tat"), and results in the dedication of greater effort toward the superordinate goal, subsequent to satisfaction of the short-term need (Fishbach & Trope, 2008; Trope & Fishbach, 2000). Although not recommended, unabated studying for 24 hours after a night on the town would exemplify a CAT performance approach. CAT success is based on the unwavering commitment to superordinate goals, *after* the temptation is satisfied. Although CAT strategies have regulatory benefits, the approach should be approached cautiously, as goal priorities may shift as a result of the swap, resulting in a diminished value or lower interest ascribed to the long-term goal, in favor of the aggressive pursuit of more hedonistic motives.

A similar paradigm whereby a performer ascribes greater value and meaning to distal goals rather than to immediate satisfaction, is delay of gratification. The DOG interpretation of regulatory behavior involves deliberate suppression of impulse. Inhibitory control strategies are activated when demonstrating DOG because when given the option, individuals cognizant of DOG intentionally place greater value on better, frequent, or more generous longer-term payoffs than on short-term benefits or pleasures associated with proximal goals. Multi-disciplinary DOG research provides intriguing support of DOG benefits in favor of the deferral and rejection of immediately attainable satisfiers. DOG has positive consequences throughout the lifespan, as childhood DOG accurately predicts reduced body mass 30 years later (Schlam, Wilson, Shoda, Mischel, & Ayduk, 2013), implicates lower levels of adolescent drug dependency and devious behavior (Romer, Duckworth, Sznitman, & Park, 2010), and although DOG wanes during mid-adulthood, the ability to forgo immediate reward predicts overall impulse control late in life (Casey et al., 2011).

DOG is important due to the correlation with positive behavior across domains. Conscious delay is related to improved coping with stress and enhanced emotional regulation in children (Marcelo & Yates, 2014), the willingness to persevere on academic tasks (Bembenutty & Karabenick, 2004), overall job satisfaction (Mohsin & Ayub, 2014) and career growth (Peetsma, Schuitema, & Van Der Veen, 2012). Additionally, shifts from distal to proximal goals are often the precursor to regulatory failure (Baumeister & Heatherton, 1996). The particular significance of grooming DOG in individuals is the relation with other attributes that contribute to productive performance. Individuals who delay gratification have higher intrinsic motivation, more often have mastery goals for learning, and delay helps create opportunities to self regulate. DOG can be encouraged in others by providing rich descriptions of the benefits of delay along with providing visual or descriptive evidence in advance that physically exposes individuals to the better payoff (Tobin & Graziano, 2010). Emphasis on the long-term benefits of consistent and sustained performance should causally connect current efforts with more beneficial future outcomes.

Finally, closely related to delay of academic gratification is instilling a focus on the future. *Future time perspective* (FTP), or the "capacity to ascribe high value to long-term goals" (de Bilde, Vansteenkiste, & Lens, 2011, p. 333), is a dominant belief influencing the use of regulatory strategies. FTP, unlike DOG or CAT, places a heavy emphasis on predetermined goals and how current learning and performance strategies support attainment of long-term objectives. Individuals high in FTP have a mental perception that ascribes a positive valence to future events (Husman & Lens, 1999) and imagine themselves positively at a time in the future. Self-visioning primes the motivation of individuals to seek out tasks and opportunities that advance future goal-directed agendas, most notably academic achievement, which, for most individuals, means future career success. The FTP orientation contributes to positive attitudes toward school (de Bilde et al., 2011), including the development of domain-general intrinsic interest in related topics that actively support reaching the future goal (Hilpert et al., 2012).

The pragmatic aspects of regulatory control can be illustrated by examining the professional life of Senator Darren Soto. In his role as a Florida State Senator representing District #14 of Orlando, Florida, he is frequently immersed in the regulatory process, both literally and figuratively. As a minority party legislator, his efforts are often focused on mediating partisan disputes and encouraging conciliatory behavior among his peers. Darren recognizes that politics, like motivational regulation, do not always go according to plans. Frequently, his regulatory efforts are foiled when proposed bills are defeated. His political agenda and personal philosophy are both guided by the realization that there is no guarantee of success. Darren indicated, "I accept when things don't work out as planned, but I am enthusiastic in defeat. I take lemons and try to make lemonade" (D. Soto, personal communication, November 3, 2013). Commenting on the beliefs that sustain him through political challenge, he added, "Even with a firm loss I always believe there is something. There are no such things as absolute losses in life; yes, you can have a setback, but nothing bothers me in a big way" (D. Soto, personal communication, November 3, 2013). Soto perseveres by employing many of the motivational and affective regulatory techniques just described, strategies that provide him personal fortitude, even when he knows failure is imminent and he may suffer professional defeat.

Motivational Leader—*Darren Soto*

Florida State Senator Darren Soto was born and raised in Ringwood, New Jersey, to a Puerto Rican father and an Italian-American mother. From 1998 to 2001, Darren worked for the Prudential Insurance Company in finance while he attended Rutgers University, where he graduated with a Bachelor of Arts degree in Economics in 2000. He continued his education at George Washington University earning a Juris Doctor degree in 2004, opening his law practice the following year. However, unlike many politicians or lawyers, Senator Soto is measurably different from many of his political and legal peers. Evidence shows that he is truly a man of the people, devoting his professional life to improve the well-being of others.

Darren is a commercial and civil rights attorney and an ardent defender of civil rights. He is committed to rendering legal services pro bono (no charge) to benefit the underprivileged in the central Florida community. In 2006, he was named counsel in the federal class action brought on behalf of Hispanic voters against the City of Kissimmee. Soto is also a former member of the Civil Service Board for the City of Orlando and was Treasurer of the Orange County Democrats and Vice President of Communications and Co-host for the Orange County Young Democrats, all positions where he volunteered his discretionary time to help the community.

Darren's foray into politics began in 2006, when he unsuccessfully challenged incumbent Andy Gardiner for the Florida House of Representatives 40th District house seat. Undeterred by this defeat, Soto persevered, and in April 2007, he emerged victorious from a crowded Democratic primary in a special election to replace John Quinones, who had resigned. In the general election, Soto narrowly defeated former State Representative Tony Suarez, the Republican nominee, by 285 votes to win the election. Soto's election was no fluke, as he was overwhelmingly re-elected in 2008 and 2010. During his Florida House terms Soto passed legislation, to curb illegal street racing, protect families of fallen firefighters, and maintain school safety. He also protected homeowners' access to the courts in foreclosure proceedings as well as assured adequate funding for courts to deal with the unprecedented housing crisis in Florida. Soto was also a key voice in the passage of Sunrail, bringing the first commuter rail service to Central Florida. He played a critical role bridging the split of the Florida Supreme Court and preventing a highly restrictive, profiling-type immigration law from being passed in Florida.

In 2012, following redistricting, Soto opted to run for the newly created 14th District Senate seat rather than seek re-election in the House. He won his party's nomination uncontested and faced Republican Will McBride, who had previously run for the United States Senate in 2006. Although the contest was predicted to be an extremely tight race, Soto overwhelmingly defeated McBride, winning over 70% of the vote. In his first term in the Senate in 2013, Soto passed legislation expediting the time for immigrant children to acquire a driver's license, which was ultimately vetoed by Governor Rick Scott, setting off statewide protests. He also played a critical role in reducing the statute of limitations from 5 years to 1 year for banks to collect foreclosure debt, as well as helping to start Florida's Principal Reduction Program to assist struggling homeowners.

In 2014, Soto passed historic legislation giving authority to admit immigrant lawyers to the Florida Bar while being a strong advocate for successful passage of legislation giving immigrants in-state tuition. Soto secured funding to start the Poinciana Valencia Campus and the Lake Toho Restoration project, which will keep clean water flowing through Florida's Northern Everglades. Looking to the future, Soto has proposed legislation to promote economic growth in emerging businesses, including the solar, space, biotech, film, and software industries. He also is an advocate to ban fracking in Florida and has proposed a bill to boost minimum teacher pay to $50,000 per year. For Senator Soto, the fight to improve the lives of his fellow Floridians does not stop!

Darren's persona, although not explicitly articulated, exemplifies DOG orientation and FTP. He understands that short-term obstacles are part of long-term success and that setbacks should be used as stepping stones toward reaching highly coveted distal goals. He maintains motivational momentum through an unwavering commitment to his personal beliefs and the realization that "you have to quickly shift approaches if you want to respond favorably." He added, "I take an analysis of what the reality is and then I try to work within the reality as I understand it" (D. Soto, personal communication, November 3, 2013). Highly self-aware, Darren knows his strengths, and under which conditions he is most effective. He credits his success to an unwavering optimism and knowing that achieving common ground with others is within his personal control. Soto thrives on maintaining a well-balanced and moderate view in politics and in life, values that he frequently considers when interacting with others. His thoughtful and reflective style gives him the confidence and strength to persevere, even when months of hard work appear to be for naught during a resounding legislative defeat.

Principle #50—Optimal motivation demands monitoring, metacognition, and metamotivation

Avoiding motivational pitfalls underscores the importance of personal awareness and the stark realization that one's actions ultimately determine performance outcomes. By definition, a masterful performance is improbable unless the performer is eager and prepared to accurately monitor and evaluate performance conditions while demonstrating a willingness to devote necessary effort toward qualitatively improving desired outcomes. Regulatory success is contingent upon possessing crystallized knowledge of relevant task goals, embracing a sensitivity to recognize and understand when and why performance efforts are effective or misaligned. During performance assessment, individuals must conduct unbiased self-appraisals that determine which cognitive and motivational strategies work best for a particular task, in concert with a decision regarding which strategies are personally palatable. Interventions that are effective for one person in one situation may prove fruitless for a different person or in another situation. Like the conductor who carefully analyzes the complexity of a musical score, the talent of musicians and the harmonic quality of instruments, the masterful regulator monitors and activates a sophisticated and intricate network of metaknowledge about the self with keen insight about his or her own knowledge, beliefs, and values that influences motivated effort (Boekaerts, 1995). A masterful musical performance results when the conductor flawlessly harmonizes the orchestra, while the master regulator achieves success by synchronizing cognitive and motivational efforts in pursuit of one's learning or performance goal.

Monitoring and regulating cognition and motivation are conceptually related and pragmatically similar, with each performance facet having a different emphasis (Wolters, 2003). When individuals demonstrate cognitive regulation, they evaluate which aspects of a task require attention by reflecting on which skills or abilities are needed to complete the task, often described as the conscious control of thinking, or *metacognition*. Based upon the assessment and the congruence between necessary and demonstrated performance in relation to desired goals, certain strategies are activated and used by individuals to achieve their goals. During a learning task, metacognitively aware students will monitor progress and ask themselves questions, such as "Am I getting it?" "Do I understand this concept?" or "How can I apply this knowledge properly?" When demonstrating a performance skill, such as practicing a batting swing, individuals will scrutinize their progress and contemplate procedural enhancements, such as "Am I swinging the bat properly?" "Is my eye on the ball?" or "What did I do differently the last time I was victorious?" In each instance, the metacognitively aware individual analyzes the circumstances and formulates an action plan based upon domain knowledge and a determination of what skills the person believes are needed to complete the task.

Metamotivation assumes a similar style of individual scrutiny and reflection, but instead of focusing on declarative or procedural knowledge, the individual evaluates which factors influence attention and what persistence strategies are necessary to enhance the likelihood of task completion. Individuals with refined metamotivation skills anticipate and recognize declining effort or attentional abatement and use a variety of strategies to restore engagement levels. Strategies are employed for many different reasons, but deployment is always executed under the presumption that active intervention and monitoring of motivational effort contributes to goal progress. Examples include the use of volitional control strategies, such as persevering through the most complex problems as a means of attaining personal or professional growth, or the ascription of personal value to completing certain tasks (Van Beek, Qiao, Schaufeli, Taris, & Schreurs, 2012). Extrinsic goals may catalyze regulated motivation, including when individuals use instrumental incentives or when they seek materialistic gains as the substance for their accelerated effort investments. Performance lapses may be thwarted through environmental restructuring, as strategic performers will take walk breaks during study time or check social media as a means of controlling work monotony or fatigue. Motivational regulation can be socially or vicariously induced, such as when a teacher models regulatory behavior during instruction or when the educator deliberately scaffolds learners by the implementation of domain-specific self-regulation strategies (Wolters et al., 2011).

Both metacognition and metamotivation serve as self-diagnostic tools that evaluate the structural task requirements and what is needed to enthusiastically initiate and sustain a successful task performance. Metacognitive control is initiated after evaluation of the task conditions and subsequent to progress assessments. During instances of control, individuals make conscious decisions to either follow or deviate from a planned performance path with one primary objective: to enhance the quality of eventual outcomes. Regulation of motivation includes emphasis on which factors contribute to performance success; how to control and remove potential performance impediments, such as lack of focus or energy to complete a task; and how to deal with wavering engagement and distractions that may forestall reaching desired performance goals.

Recall from the chapter introduction that many instances of self-regulation follow a predictable pattern of organized behavior. Most regulatory efforts start with planning and setting task goals, continue with monitoring performance progress and conditions, and conclude with qualitative evaluation results (Winne & Hadwin, 2008; Zimmerman, 1989). Now armed with deeper knowledge of regulatory motives and specific mediational strategies, you may realize that even the most innocuous observations of human behavior can provide ample clues to help determine if, when, and how metacognition and metamotivation strategies are employed by individuals. Now, take your mind back to Chapter 1, and recall the author's own story of a fateful, lazy Saturday morning bicycle ride. Do you recall any descriptions of regulatory action? Perhaps, you noticed some of the myriad regulatory strategies listed in Table 10.1, which are extracted from the Chapter 1 narrative and summarized here:

Table 10.1 Types and examples of commonly used regulatory strategies

Statements	Page	Type of regulation	Strategy
"…taking a 50-mile bicycle ride"	3	Cognitive planning	Specific goals were set, based upon past performance and ability perceptions, before attempting the task
"I loaded my backpack with food, energy drinks, and a second shirt" and "I consciously planned my route"	3	Environmental planning	Task and control beliefs were activated to objectively assess task challenge. Environmental restructuring was used to creating conditions conducive to accelerated performance based upon the specific task conditions
"I thought about how I would motivate myself to continue cycling when swarms of insects flew into my face and mouth"	3	Motivational monitoring	Task obstacles and goal-directed interventions were evaluated for motivational impact
"I was only motivated to survive"	4	Cognitive and motivational monitoring	Goals were restructured based upon objective evaluation of conditions and available resources
"How could I continue (teaching) under the circumstances of my injuries?"	4	Cognitive and emotional monitoring and evaluation	Value-laden judgments were used to determine continued task engagement
"I thought deeply about my circumstances" and "I was committed to living up to my responsibilities"	4	Metacognitive and metamotivational monitoring and evaluation	Reflection on objective evaluation of skills, synchronized with beliefs about work and commitment, determined future behavior and engagement

Table 10.1 illustrates the prevalence of opportunities to regulate motivation during a typical task. While one example is insufficient to advocate broad and consistent adaptation of a specific strategy to enhance a particular task, studies across multiple domains and samples suggest that individual differences in motivational regulation positively influence learning and performance outcomes (Järvelä, Järvenoja, & Malmberg, 2012; Lord, Diefendorff, Schmidt, & Hall, 2010; Malmberg, Järvenoja, & Järvelä, 2010; Van Beek et al., 2012; Wolters, 1999). Given the widespread effectiveness of strategies, we might wonder why some individuals who knowingly possess meta-level knowledge of motives and cognition elect not to use the strategies they possess (Schraw & Moshman, 1995; Wolters & Benzon, 2013). Boekaerts (1999) suggested that restrictions in available time, inadequate need satisfaction achieved through strategy use, or uncertainty about the situational appropriateness of strategies in a particular performance context may account for neglected or haphazard strategy intervention. While reductions in the frequency of strategy use are logically impeded during time restrictions or when individuals ascribe minimal task value or utility, why some individuals abstain from regulatory behavior, despite the realization and verbalization that strategy use is beneficial or leads to positive outcomes, remains unexplained (Falk, Berkman, Mann, Harrison, & Lieberman, 2010)!

At least three additional explanations might account for the scarcity of regulated motivation by some individuals. First, successful regulation is based, in part, on receptivity to task feedback. Performers may elect to either act on or ignore feedback that is received from external sources or that which is self-generated during the performance process. In its most rudimentary form, self-regulation represents a response to feedback concerning progress toward task goals in relation to competency beliefs about the self and the task. Belief conceptions are so instrumental for performance that Butler and Winne (1995), in their seminal article on feedback and self-regulation, concluded that "beliefs filter and may even distort the message feedback is intended to carry" (p. 254). *How* individuals react to the feedback message depends on the correlation among these self-perception beliefs and the degree of deviation between perceived performance and the desired goal-directed state. When individuals perceive that they are able to meet task expectations, they will respond favorably to feedback and instigate positive approach behavior, while goal redirection or avoidance behavior occurs when task generated feedback and competency beliefs are incongruent with expectations. Regulatory problems also occur if the perception of the task cues is inconsistent with task goals or if a misperception of cues is realized in relation to outcomes. Discrepancies may result in the selective filtering of information that feedback provides, with feedback not permeating the monitoring process and entering into metamotivational awareness, thus providing the performer with minimal reasons to evoke self-regulated strategies (Carver & Scheier, 2000).

Second, some aspects of regulated motivation are implicit and undertaken without conscious awareness or intent (Ferguson, Hassin, & Bargh, 2008), suggesting a corresponding inhibition of the need or perceived ability to monitor motivational effort or use associated regulatory control. Dual process models of cognition, which include motivational components based upon beliefs (Evans & Stanovich, 2013), infer that two complementary and symbiotic types of thinking exist: one that is autonomous, implicit, and relatively undemanding of cognitive resources and another that is effortful, demanding, and deliberate. When thinking becomes autonomous, which usually occurs as a result of the development of experience and through habitual behavior patterns, typically conscious functions, such as goal striving and monitoring, become automatized. Previously discussed priming studies (see Principle #34, p. 154) indicated that individuals will pursue goals without conscious activation. Since priming involves taking action toward goal attainment, motivational effort may also operate independently of conscious regulation. The phenomenon of autonomous regulation is supported by the development of expertise whereby the well-organized knowledge representations of the expert learner restrict the need for metamonitoring because the process happens automatically (Kirschner, Sweller, & Clark, 2006). The diminished need for effortful processing by individuals is also affirmed by neurological evidence that indicates reduced brain activity as individuals gain expertise in deliberation and decision making, two important hallmarks of regulating motivated effort (Sanfey, Loewenstein, McClure, & Cohen, 2006). Considering humans' generally miserly approach to activating cognition (Evans & Stanovich, 2013), it seems highly plausible that individuals with expertise (or the perception of expertise) may also unconsciously conserve effort devoted toward regulating motivation.

Finally, both biopsychological (Izuma, 2013) and behavioral evidence (Wolters, 2011) reveal that individuals regulate motivation differently based upon social and contextual influences. Chapters 4 and 5 explained how individual differences, such as development and culture, influence motivational patterns. Recent evidence reveals that individual strategy use can vary at the micro-level, indicating that certain tactics, such as the use of metacognition, elaboration, and the associated effort these approaches require, vary dramatically according to country of application (Chiu, Chow, & Mcbride-Chang, 2007). Use of regulatory strategies, with specific emphasis on meta-level regulation and monitoring, is expressed far more frequently by people from individualistic cultures compared with collective cultures. Further, in some academic cultures, social influence negatively affects academic achievement (Förster, Higgins, Strack, & Bargh, 2000; Hoffman, Badgett, & Parker, 2008). Individuals interested in learning are stigmatized and chastised for their achievement intentions, inhibiting the willingness and frequency to use motivational regulation strategies. The evidence reported seems to leave little doubt that different approaches are employed across different performance cultures based upon beliefs and the cultural identity of the specific population (McInerney, 2011). As such, the next chapter is exclusively devoted to outlining domain-specific and customized strategies found best to enhance learning and performance within particular performance contexts.

Chapter summary/conclusions

Content knowledge in a particular domain is one important aspect of achievement, but generally, topic knowledge is insufficient to guarantee successful attainment of performance objectives. Optimized performance also relies upon the ability to strategically monitor, control, and regulate motivational resources during learning or task performance in order to eliminate or offset the inevitable fluctuations and misdirection of attention and motivated effort. Although regulation and control can be implemented without conscious awareness, most definitions of self-regulation focus on the active role of the performer to plan, monitor, control, and evaluate performance effort. Effective execution, at minimum, demands strategy knowledge, coupled with a devout willingness to use the tactics one possesses to enhance performance.

Which motivational regulation schemes are most effective in a particular situation depends on the cyclical regulatory process and the highly personalized and idiosyncratic nature of strategy use, operating under the key assumption that regulatory ability relies upon psychological stamina and is a depletable resource. Typical strategies used during motivational regulation include self-consequating contingencies, reflective self-talk, interest building, and environmental restructuring. Diverse methods have a singular purpose—to focus attention and direct effort to sustain optimal performance as a means to achieve learning and performance goals. Strategy use is variable and often influenced by historical attributions, control beliefs, and epistemological perspectives that supply the performer with valuable self-relevant evidence indicating the success or failure of past regulatory efforts. Regulation and control are also highly related to goal orientation with mastery-oriented learners using a broader repertoire of strategies, more frequently, compared with normative-oriented performers.

Regulation, especially inhibitory control, is limited by cumulative effort. When regulatory resources are consumed, adaptive task-directed motivation suffers. Although regulatory resources can be replenished through rest or supplements, effective use of strategies is contingent upon accurate evaluation of task requirements relative to available resources. Performers are subject to miscalibration and bias error when assessing discrepancies between what skills or abilities are actually needed for a task compared with the individual beliefs he or she realistically possesses. Practitioners can use a variety of mediational strategies to promote effective calibration and potentially enhance the probability of performers attaining quality learning and performance outcomes. By emphasizing such strategies as CAT and DOG and by embracing a FTP, performers can learn to conserve resources and judiciously apply existing regulatory knowledge.

An important regulatory competency is the ability to effectively monitor personal cognition and motivation during the course of task completion. Monitoring of cognition is often referred to as metacognition and involves the conscious awareness of gaps in declarative or conditional knowledge that must be reduced to complete a task successfully. Monitoring of motivation is equally critical as individuals with self-awareness can take deliberate steps to redirect or enhance waning motivation. Sadly, not all motivational regulatory efforts succeed, in part because of unreceptivity to internal feedback, lack of awareness of the need to regulate based on implicit and automatic regulatory efforts, and a variety of social or cultural factors indicating that regulatory fluctuation is broadly influenced by the context of application.

Next steps

The cultivation of adaptive motivational regulation, although a formidable task, is an obtainable reality under the optimal circumstances described. Many of the domain-general strategies outlined in the chapter are assumed to apply across performance contexts and should be effective regardless of the application culture or differences in the individuals involved. However, it also behooves the MD to take into strong consideration the domain of application when deciding upon strategy initiatives. We next turn to the examination of unique differences and appropriate strategies most effective for different populations of individuals, highlighting specific issues and remedies unique to academic, online, and high-pressure performance situations such as athletics and the performing arts. We also examine specific strategies to modify work motivation and behavior, featuring the approaches of **Robert Knowling, Jr.**, a prominent business leader and turnaround expert.

End of chapter motivational minute

Principles covered in this chapter:

48. **Self-regulation is personalized, transitory, and marginally predictable**—the control strategies an individual uses to sustain motivated effort are task contingent and subject to revision based on task-related beliefs, personal preferences, and the learning context. In total, beliefs about regulatory ability form self-schemas that guide the individual toward task completion.
49. **Self-regulatory ability is depletable; accurate calibration is essential**—like physical resources, self-regulatory resources are cumulatively consumed. Accurate interpretation of differences between task goals and observed results is necessary in order to harness strategies that narrow performance gaps.
50. **Optimal motivation demands monitoring, metacognition, and metamotivation**—awareness of cognitive and motivational processes is necessary to supplement performance effort. Integrative effects of context, person, and behaviors should always be evaluated before reaching conclusions concerning why motivational regulation may or may not occur.

Key terminology (in order of chapter presentation):

- **Self-regulation**—the active process used by individuals to plan, monitor, control, and evaluate cognitive, emotional, and motivational aspects of learning and performance.
- **Motivational self-regulation**—the goal-directed and specific strategies individuals actively employ to maintain attentional focus to start and improve task success.
- **Environmental restructuring**—a regulatory strategy that involves the direct manipulation of one's learning or performance context as a means to eliminate distractions while simultaneously scaffolding attentional focus.
- **Self-talk**—reassuring internally-generated feedback designed to keep a performer on task and focused toward a learning or performance goal.
- **Self-control**—a type of regulatory strategy specifically designed to inhibit behavior that may interfere with the optimal attainment of a learning or performance goal.
- **Self-schemas**—cognitive representations, self-beliefs, and personal norms that individuals have about intelligence and knowledge that influence target goals and strategies used.
- **Incremental**—a belief that exemplifies the changeable nature of a phenomenon, usually used to describe beliefs about the malleable nature of knowledge and intelligence.
- **Entity**—a belief in the fixed immutable nature of a phenomenon, and often similarly used to describe the invariant nature of knowledge and intelligence.

- **Strength model of regulation**—a regulatory model that suggests that individual differences in regulatory behavior are a result of capacity differences between individuals.
- **Depletion model of self-regulation**—a regulatory model that suggests that regulation and control cannot be sustained indefinitely, and that the availability of future strategy use is contingent upon cumulative and available effort.
- **Calibration**—the degree of accuracy between perceptions and beliefs about what skills and abilities are needed to complete a task, compared to those actually needed.
- **Judgments of learning**—self-appraisals that evaluate what knowledge a person does or does not possess.
- **Metacognition**—awareness of one's own thinking processes focusing on closing gaps in knowledge that may impede performance.
- **Metamotivation**—awareness of one's motivational deficiencies, including effort abatement and attentional lapses that may impede performance.

References

Alba, J. W., & Hutchinson, J. W. (2000). Knowledge calibration: What consumers know and what they think they know. *Journal of Consumer Research, 27*(2), 123–156.
Bandura, A. (1997). *Self-efficacy: The exercise of control.* New York, NY: Freeman.
Baumeister, R. F., Gailliot, M., Dewall, C. N., & Oaten, M. (2006). Self-regulation and personality: How interventions increase regulatory success, and how depletion moderates the effects of traits on behavior. *Journal of Personality, 74*(6), 1773–1801.
Baumeister, R. F., & Heatherton, T. F. (1996). Self-regulation failure: An overview. *Psychological Inquiry, 7*(1), 1–15.
Beedie, C. J., & Lane, A. M. (2012). The role of glucose in self-control: Another look at the evidence and an alternative conceptualization. *Personality & Social Psychology Review, 16*(2), 143–153. http://dx.doi.org/10.1177/1088868311419817.
Bembenutty, H., & Karabenick, S. A. (2004). Inherent association between academic delay of gratification, future time perspective, and self-regulated learning. *Educational Psychology Review, 16*(1), 35–57. http://dx.doi.org/10.1023/B:EDPR.0000012344.34008.5c.
Benton, D., Parker, P. Y., & Donohoe, R. T. (1996). The supply of glucose to the brain and cognitive functioning. *Journal of Biosocial Science, 28,* 463–479.
Boecker, H., Sprenger, T., Spilker, M. E., Henriksen, G., Koppenhoefer, M., Wagner, K. J., et al. (2008). The runner's high: Opioidergic mechanisms in the human brain. *Cerebral Cortex, 18*(11), 2523–2531. http://dx.doi.org/10.1093/cercor/bhn013.
Boekaerts, M. (1995). Self-regulated learning: Bridging the gap between metacognitive and metamotivation theories. *Educational Psychologist, 30*(4), 195–200. http://dx.doi.org/10.1207/s15326985ep3004_4.
Boekaerts, M. (1999). Self-regulated learning: Where we are today. *International Journal of Educational Research, 31*(6), 445–457.
Bouffard, T., & Narciss, S. (2011). Benefits and risks of positive biases in self-evaluation of academic competence: Introduction. *International Journal of Educational Research, 50*(4), 205–208. http://dx.doi.org/10.1016/j.ijer.2011.08.001.
Bruning, R.H., & Kauffman, D.F. (in press). Self-efficacy beliefs and motivation in writing development. In C. A. MacArthur, S. Graham, & J. Fitzgerald (Eds.), *Handbook of Writing Research (2e).* New York, NY: Guilford Press.

Burnette, J. L. (2010). Implicit theories of body weight: Entity beliefs can weigh you down. *Personality and Social Psychology Bulletin, 36*(3), 410–422. http://dx.doi.org/10.1177/0146167209359768.

Burnette, J. L., O'Boyle, E. H., VanEpps, E. M., Pollack, J. M., & Finkel, E. J. (2013). Mindsets matter: A meta-analytic review of implicit theories and self-regulation. *Psychological Bulletin, 139*(3), 655–701. http://dx.doi.org/10.1037/a0029531.

Butler, D. L., & Winne, P. H. (1995). Feedback and self-regulated learning: A theoretical synthesis. *Review of Educational Research, 65*(3), 245–281.

Carver, C. S., & Scheier, M. F. (2000). On the structure of behavioral self-regulation. In M. Boekaerts, P. R. Pintrich, & M. Zeidner (Eds.), *Handbook of self-regulation* (pp. 42–85). San Diego, CA: Academic Press.

Casey, B. J., Somerville, L. H., Gotlib, I. H., Ayduk, O., Franklin, N. T., Askren, M. K., et al. (2011). Behavioral and neural correlates of delay of gratification 40 years later. *Proceedings of the National Academy of Sciences, 108*(36), 14998–15003. http://dx.doi.org/10.1073/pnas.1108561108.

Chatzistamatiou, M., Dermitzaki, I., Efklides, A., & Leondari, A. (2013). Motivational and affective determinants of self-regulatory strategy use in elementary school mathematics. *Educational Psychology*, 1–16. http://dx.doi.org/10.1080/01443410.2013.822960.

Chiu, M. M., Chow, B. W.-Y., & Mcbride-Chang, C. (2007). Universals and specifics in learning strategies: Explaining adolescent mathematics, science, and reading achievement across 34 countries. *Learning and Individual Differences, 17*(4), 344–365. http://dx.doi.org/10.1016/j.lindif.2007.03.007.

Cleary, T. J. (2009). Monitoring trends and accuracy of self-efficacy beliefs during interventions: Advantages and potential applications to school-based settings. *Psychology in the Schools, 46*(2), 154–171.

Cleary, T. J., Callan, G. L., & Zimmerman, B. J. (2012). Assessing self-regulation as a cyclical, context-specific phenomenon: Overview and analysis of SRL microanalytic protocols. *Education Research International, 2012*, 1–19. http://dx.doi.org/10.1155/2012/428639.

Cleary, T. J., Platten, P., & Nelson, A. (2008). Effectiveness of the self-regulation empowerment program with urban high school students. *Journal of Advanced Academics, 20*, 70–107.

Connecticut Department of Corrections. (2015). *Recidivism*. Retrieved on April 22, 2015 from: <http://www.ct.gov/doc/cwp/view.asp?q=305970>

Corno, L. (2011). Studying self-regulation habits. In B. J. Zimmerman & D. H. Schunk (Eds.), *Handbook of self-regulation of learning and performance* (pp. 361–374). New York, NY: Routledge/Taylor & Francis Group.

de Bilde, J., Vansteenkiste, M., & Lens, W. (2011). Understanding the association between future time perspective and self-regulated learning through the lens of self-determination theory. *Learning and Instruction, 21*(3), 332–344. http://dx.doi.org/10.1016/j.learninstruc.2010.03.002.

Dole, J. A., & Sinatra, G. M. (1998). Reconceptalizing change in the cognitive construction of knowledge. *Educational Psychologist, 33*(2–3), 109–128.

Dupeyrat, C., Escribe, C., Huet, N., & Régner, I. (2011). Positive biases in self-assessment of mathematics competence, achievement goals, and mathematics performance. *International Journal of Educational Research, 50*(4), 241–250. http://dx.doi.org/10.1016/j.ijer.2011.08.005.

Dweck, C. S., & Leggett, E. L. (1988). A social-cognitive approach to motivation and personality. *Psychological Review, 95*(2), 256–273. http://dx.doi.org/10.1037/0033-295X.95.2.256.

Eisenberg, N., & Sulik, M. J. (2012). Emotion-related self-regulation in children. *Teaching of Psychology, 39*(1), 77–83. http://dx.doi.org/10.1177/0098628311430172.

Evans, J. S. B. T., & Stanovich, K. E. (2013). Dual-process theories of higher cognition: Advancing the debate. *Perspectives on Psychological Science, 8*(3), 223–241. http://dx.doi.org/10.1177/1745691612460685.

Falk, E. B., Berkman, E. T., Mann, T., Harrison, B., & Lieberman, M. D. (2010). Predicting persuasion-induced behavior change from the brain. *Journal of Neuroscience, 30*(25), 8421–8424. http://dx.doi.org/10.1523/JNEUROSCI.0063-10.2010.

Feldman, R., Greenbaum, C., & Yirmiya, N. (1999). Mother-infant affect synchrony as an antecedent of the emergence of self-control. *Developmental Psychology, 35*(1), 223–231.

Ferguson, M. J., Hassin, R., & Bargh, J. A. (2008). Implicit motivation: Past, present, and future. In J. Y. Shah & W. L. Gardner (Eds.), *Handbook of motivation science* (pp. 150–166). New York, NY: Guilford.

Fishbach, A., & Trope, Y. (2008). Implicit and explicit mechanisms of counteractive self-control. In J. Y. Shah & W. L. Gardner (Eds.), *Handbook of motivation science* (pp. 281–294). New York, NY: Guilford.

Förster, J., Higgins, E. T., Strack, F., & Bargh, J. A. (2000). When stereotype disconfirmation is a personal threat: How prejudice and prevention focus moderate incongruency effects. *Social Cognition, 18*(2), 178–197.

Gailliot, M. T., & Baumeister, R. F. (2007a). Self-regulation and sexual restraint: Dispositionally and temporarily poor self-regulatory abilities contribute to failures at restraining sexual behavior. *Personality and Social Psychology Bulletin, 33*(2), 173–186.

Gailliot, M. T., & Baumeister, R. F. (2007b). The physiology of willpower: Linking blood glucose to self-control. *Personality and Social Psychology Review, 11*(4), 303–327. http://dx.doi.org/10.1177/1088868307303030.

Garcia, T., & Pintrich, P. R. (1994). Regulating motivation and cognition in the classroom: The role of self-schemas and self-regulatory strategies. In D. H. Schunk & B. J. Zimmerman (Eds.), *Self-regulation of learning and performance: Issues and educational applications* (pp. 127–153). Hillsdale, NJ: Lawrence Erlbaum Associates.

Gino, F., Schweitzer, M. E., Mead, N. L., & Ariely, D. (2011). Unable to resist temptation: How self-control depletion promotes unethical behavior. *Organizational Behavior and Human Decision Process, 115*(2), 191–203.

Graham, S., & Harris, K. R. (1994). The role and development of self-regulation in the writing process. In D. H. Schunk & B. J. Zimmerman (Eds.), *Self-regulation of learning and performance: Issues and educational applications* (pp. 203–228). Hillsdale, NJ: Lawrence Erlbaum Associates, Inc.

Gramzow, R. H., & Willard, G. (2006). Exaggerating current and past performance: Motivated self-enhancement versus reconstructive memory. *Personality and Social Psychology Bulletin, 32*(8), 1114–1125. http://dx.doi.org/10.1177/0146167206288600.

Hagger, M. S., Wood, C., Stiff, C., & Chatzisarantis, N. L. D. (2010). Ego depletion and the strength model of self-control: A meta-analysis. *Psychological Bulletin, 136*(4), 495–525. http://dx.doi.org/10.1037/a0019486.

Hilpert, J. C., Husman, J., Stump, G. S., Kim, W., Chung, W.-T., & Duggan, M. A. (2012). Examining students' future time perspective: Pathways to knowledge building. *Japanese Psychological Research, 54*(3), 229–240. http://dx.doi.org/10.1111/j.1468-5884.2012.00525.x.

Hoffman, B., Badgett, B., & Parker, R. P. (2008). The effect of single-sex instruction in a large, urban at-risk high school. *Journal of Educational Research, 102*(1), 15–35. http://dx.doi.org/10.3200/JOER.102.1.15-36.

Hoffman, B., & Schraw, G. (2009). The influence of self-efficacy and working memory capacity on problem-solving efficiency. *Learning and Individual Differences, 19*, 91–100.

Hofmann, W., Schmeichel, B. J., & Baddeley, A. D. (2012). Executive functions and self-regulation. *Trends in Cognitive Sciences, 16*(3), 174–180. http://dx.doi.org/10.1016/j.tics.2012.01.006.

Hoyt, C. L., Burnette, J. L., & Innella, A. N. (2012). I can do that: The impact of implicit theories on leadership role model effectiveness. *Personality and Social Psychology Bulletin, 38*(2), 257–268. http://dx.doi.org/10.1177/0146167211427922.

Husman, J., & Lens, W. (1999). The role of the future in student motivation. *Educational Psychologist, 34*(2), 113.

Izuma, K. (2013). The neural basis of social influence and attitude change. *Current Opinion in Neurobiology, 23*(3), 456–462.

Järvelä, S., Järvenoja, H., & Malmberg, J. (2012). How elementary school students' motivation is connected to self-regulation. *Educational Research and Evaluation, 18*(1), 65–84. http://dx.doi.org/10.1080/13803611.2011.641269.

Job, V., Dweck, C. S., & Walton, G. M. (2010). Ego depletion—is it all in your head?: Implicit theories about willpower affect self-regulation. *Psychological Science, 21*(11), 1686–1693. http://dx.doi.org/10.1177/0956797610384745.

Johnson, R. E., Taing, M. U., Chang, C. -H., & Kawamoto, C. K. (2013). A self-regulation approach to person-environment fit. In A. L. Kristof-Brown & J. Billsberry (Eds.), *Organizational fit* (pp. 74–98). Chichester, UK: John Wiley & Sons, Ltd.

Jones, L. B., Rothbart, M. K., & Posner, M. I. (2003). Development of executive attention in preschool children. *Developmental Science, 6*(5), 498–504.

Kirschner, P. A., Sweller, J., & Clark, R. E. (2006). Why minimal guidance during instruction does not work: An analysis of the failure of constructivist, discovery, problem-based, experiential, and inquiry-based teaching. *Educational Psychologist, 41*(2), 75–86. http://dx.doi.org/10.1207/s15326985ep4102_1.

Knee, C., & Canevello, A. (2006). Implicit theories of relationships and coping in romantic relationships. In K. D. Vohs & E. J. Finkel (Eds.), *Self and relationships: Connecting intrapersonal and interpersonal processes* (pp. 160–176). New York, NY: Guilford Press.

Kurzban, R. (2009). Does the brain consume additional glucose during self-control tasks? *Evolutionary Psychology: An International Journal of Evolutionary Approaches to Psychology and Behavior, 8*(2), 244–259.

Lichtinger, E., & Kaplan, A. (2011). Purpose of engagement in academic self-regulation. *New Directions for Teaching and Learning, 126*, 9–19. http://dx.doi.org/10.1002/tl.440.

Lord, R. G., Diefendorff, J. M., Schmidt, A. M., & Hall, R. J. (2010). Self-regulation at work. *Annual Review of Psychology, 61*(1), 543–568. http://dx.doi.org/10.1146/annurev.psych.093008.100314.

Luebbe, A. M., Kiel, E. J., & Buss, K. A. (2011). Toddlers' context-varying emotions, maternal responses to emotions, and internalizing behaviors. *Emotion, 11*(3), 697–703.

Malmberg, J., Järvenoja, H., & Järvelä, S. (2010). Tracing elementary school students' study tactic use in gStudy by examining a strategic and self-regulated learning. *Computers in Human Behavior, 26*(5), 1034–1042.

Marcelo, A. K., & Yates, T. M. (2014). Prospective relations among preschoolers' play, coping, and adjustment as moderated by stressful events. *Journal of Applied Developmental Psychology, 35*(3), 223–233. http://dx.doi.org/10.1016/j.appdev.2014.01.001.

Maurer, T. J., Wrenn, K. A., Pierce, H. R., Tross, S. A., & Collins, W. C. (2003). Beliefs about improvability of career-relevant skills: Relevance to job/task analysis, competency modelling, and learning orientation. *Journal of Organizational Behavior, 24*(1), 107–131. http://dx.doi.org/10.1002/job.182.

McInerney, D. (2011). Culture and self-regulation in educational contexts. In B. J. Zimmerman & D. H. Schunk (Eds.), *Handbook of self-regulation of learning and performance* (pp. 442–464). New York, NY: Routledge/Taylor & Francis Group.

Miele, D. B., Wager, T. D., Mitchell, J. P., & Metcalfe, J. (2011). Dissociating neural correlates of action monitoring and metacognition of agency. *Journal of Cognitive Neuroscience, 23*(11), 3620–3636.

Miele, D. B., Son, L. K., & Metcalfe, J. (2013). Children's naive theories of intelligence influence their metacognitive judgments. *Child Development, 84*(6), 1879–1886. http://dx.doi.org/10.1111/cdev.12101.

Miller, M. A., & Fillmore, M. T. (2013). Poor impulse control and heightened attraction to alcohol-related imagery in repeat DUI offenders. In *International conference on alcohol, drugs and traffic safety (T2013), August 20, 2013, Brisbane, Queensland, Australia*.

Mischel, W., Shoda, Y., & Rodriguez, M. I. (1989). Delay of gratification in children. *Science, 244*, 933–938.

Mohsin, F., & Ayub, N. (2014). The relationship between procrastination, delay of gratification, and job satisfaction among high school teachers. *Japanese Psychological Research, 56*(3), 224–234. http://dx.doi.org/10.1111/jpr.12046.

Moran, A. P. (1996). *The psychology of concentration in sport performers: A cognitive analysis*. Hove, East Sussex, UK: Psychology Press.

Moran, A. P. (2012). Concentration: Attention and performance. In S. M. Murphy (Ed.), *The Oxford handbook of sport and performance psychology* (pp. 117–130). Oxford, England: Oxford University Press.

Muis, K. R., & Franco, G. M. (2009). Setting the standards for self-regulated learning. *Contemporary Educational Psychology, 34*(4), 306–318. http://dx.doi.org/10.1016/j.cedpsych.2009.06.005.

Muis, K. R., & Franco, G. M. (2010). Epistemic profiles and metacognition: Support for the consistency hypothesis. *Metacognition and Learning, 5*(1), 27–45. http://dx.doi.org/10.1007/s11409-009-9041-9.

Muraven, M. (2012). Ego depletion: Theory and evidence. In R. M. Ryan (Ed.), *The Oxford handbook of human motivation* (pp. 111–126). New York, NY: Oxford University Press.

Peetsma, T., Schuitema, J., & Van Der Veen, I. (2012). A longitudinal study on time perspectives: Relations with academic delay of gratification and learning. *Japanese Psychological Research, 54*(3), 241–252. http://dx.doi.org/10.1111/j.1468-5884.2012.00526.x.

Pintrich, P. R. (2004). A conceptual framework for assessing motivation and self-regulated learning in college students. *Educational Psychology Review, 16*(4), 385–407.

Pintrich, P. R., & Zusho, A. (2002). The development of academic self-regulation: The role of cognitive and motivational factors. In A. Wigfield & J. S. Eccles (Eds.), *Development of achievement motivation* (pp. 249–284). San Diego, CA: Academic Press.

Podlog, L., Heil, J., & Schulte, S. (2014). Psychosocial factors in sports injury rehabilitation and return to play. *Physical Medicine and Rehabilitation Clinics of North America, 25*(4), 915–930. http://dx.doi.org/10.1016/j.pmr.2014.06.011.

Rhodes, M. G., & Tauber, S. K. (2011). The influence of delaying judgments of learning on metacognitive accuracy: A meta-analytic review. *Psychological Bulletin, 137*(1), 131–148. http://dx.doi.org/10.1037/a0021705.

Romer, D., Duckworth, A. L., Sznitman, S., & Park, S. (2010). Can adolescents learn self-control? Delay of gratification in the development of control over risk taking. *Prevention Science: The Official Journal of the Society for Prevention Research, 11*(3), 319–330. http://dx.doi.org/10.1007/s11121-010-0171-8.

Rothman, A. J., Hertel, A. W., Baldwin, A. S., & Bartels, R. (2008). Integrating theory and practice: Understanding the determinants of health behavior change. In J. Y. Shah & W. L. Gardner (Eds.), *Handbook of motivation science* (pp. 494–507). New York, NY: Guilford.

Sanfey, A. G., Loewenstein, G., McClure, S. M., & Cohen, J. D. (2006). Neuroeconomics: Crosscurrents in research on decision-making. *Trends in Cognitive Science, 10*(3), 108–116.

Sansone, C., Fraughton, T., Zachary, J. L., Butner, J., & Heiner, C. (2011). Self-regulation of motivation when learning online: The importance of who, why and how. *Educational Technology Research and Development, 59*(2), 199–212. http://dx.doi.org/10.1007/s11423-011-9193-6.

Schlam, T. R., Wilson, N. L., Shoda, Y., Mischel, W., & Ayduk, O. (2013). Preschoolers' delay of gratification predicts their body mass 30 years later. *The Journal of Pediatrics, 162*(1), 90–93. http://dx.doi.org/10.1016/j.jpeds.2012.06.049.

Schraw, G., & Moshman, D. (1995). Metacognitive theories. *Educational Psychology Review, 7*(4), 351–371.

Schunk, D. H., & Pajares, F. (2009). Self-efficacy theory. In K. R. Wentzel & A. Wigfield (Eds.), *Handbook of motivation at school* (pp. 35–53). New York, NY: Routledge.

Senko, C., Hulleman, C. S., & Harackiewicz, J. M. (2011). Achievement goal theory at the crossroads: Old controversies, current challenges, and new directions. *Educational Psychologist, 46*(1), 26–47. http://dx.doi.org/10.1080/00461520.2011.538646.

Staats, B. R., & Gino, F. (2012). Specialization and variety in repetitive tasks: Evidence from a Japanese bank. *Management Science, 58*(6), 1141–1159.

Stone, N. (2000). Exploring the relationship between calibration and self-regulated learning. *Educational Psychology Review, 12*(4), 437–475.

Taboada, A., Tonks, S., Wigfield, A., & Guthrie, J. (2009). Effects of motivational and cognitive variables on reading comprehension. *Reading and Writing, 22*, 85–106.

Taylor, S. E., & Gollwitzer, P. M. (1995). Effects of mindset on positive illusions. *Journal of Personality and Social Psychology, 69*(2), 213–226. http://dx.doi.org/10.1037/0022-3514.69.2.213.

Tobin, R. M., & Graziano, W. G. (2010). Delay of gratification: A review of fifty years of regulation research. In R. H. Hoyle (Ed.), *Handbook of personality and self-regulation* (pp. 47–63). Malden, MA: Blackwell Publishers.

Trope, Y., & Fishbach, A. (2000). Counteractive self-control in overcoming temptation. *Journal of Personality and Social Psychology, 79*(4), 493–506.

Van Beek, I., Qiao, H., Schaufeli, W. B., Taris, T. W., & Schreurs, B. H. J. (2012). For fun, love, or money: What drives workaholic, engaged, and burned-out employees at work? *Journal of Applied Psychology, 61*(1), 30–55.

Van Loon, M. H., de Bruin, A. B. H., van Gog, T., & van Merriënboer, J. J. G. (2013). Activation of inaccurate prior knowledge affects primary-school students' metacognitive judgments and calibration. *Learning and Instruction, 24*, 15–25. http://dx.doi.org/10.1016/j.learninstruc.2012.08.005.

Vohs, K. D., Baumeister, R. F., & Schmeichel, B. J. (2012). Motivation, personal beliefs, and limited resources all contribute to self-control. *Journal of Experimental Social Psychology, 48*(4), 943–947. http://dx.doi.org/10.1016/j.jesp.2012.03.002.

Weinstein, C. E., Acee, T. W., & Jung, J. (2011). Self-regulation and learning strategies. *New Directions for Teaching and Learning, 126*, 45–53. http://dx.doi.org/10.1002/tl.443.

Wellman, H. M., Cross, D., & Watson, J. (2001). Meta-analysis of theory of mind development: The truth about false belief. *Child Development, 72*, 655–684.

Wigfield, A., & Eccles, J. S. (2001). Introduction. In A. Wigfield & J. S. Eccles (Eds.), *Development of achievement motivation* (pp. 1–11). San Diego, CA: Academic Press.

Winne, P. H. (2011). A cognitive and metacognitive analysis of self-regulated behavior: *Handbook of self-regulation of learning and performance*. New York, NY: Taylor & Francis. pp. 15–32.

Winne, P. H., & Hadwin, A. F. (2008). The weave of motivation and self-regulated learning. In D. H. Schunk & B. J. Zimmerman (Eds.), *Motivation and self-regulated learning: Theory, research, and applications* (pp. 297–314). Mahwah, NJ: Lawrence Erlbaum Associates Publishers.

Wolters, C. A. (1998). Self-regulated learning and college students' regulation of motivation. *Journal of Educational Psychology, 90*, 224–235.

Wolters, C. A. (1999). The relation between high school students' motivational regulation and their use of learning strategies, effort, and classroom performance. *Learning & Individual Differences, 11*(3), 281–299.

Wolters, C. A. (2003). Regulation of motivation: Evaluating an underemphasized aspect of self-regulated learning. *Educational Psychologist, 38*(4), 189–205. http://dx.doi.org/10.1207/S15326985EP3804_1.

Wolters, C. A. (2011). Regulation of motivation: Contextual and social aspects. *Teachers College Record, 113*(2), 265–283.

Wolters, C. A., & Benzon, M. B. (2013). Assessing and predicting college students' use of strategies for the self-regulation of motivation. *The Journal of Experimental Education, 81*(2), 199–221. http://dx.doi.org/10.1080/00220973.2012.699901.

Wolters, C. A., Benzon, M. B., & Arroyo-Giner, C. (2011). Assessing strategies for the self-regulation of motivation. In B. J. Zimmerman & D. H. Schunk (Eds.), *Handbook of self-regulation of learning and performance* (pp. 298–312). New York, NY: Routledge/Taylor & Francis Group.

Zimmerman, B. J. (1989). A social cognitive view of self-regulated academic learning. *Educational Psychology, 81*, 329–339.

Zimmerman, B. J. (2011). Motivational sources and outcomes of self-regulated learning and performance. In B. J. Zimmerman & D. H. Schunk (Eds.), *Handbook of self-regulation of learning and performance* (pp. 49–65). New York, NY: Routledge.

Location, location, location: Creating and implementing context-specific interventions

Chapter outline

Promoting adaptive academic motivation 307
Strategies to motivate work performance 312
Motivational Leader—*Robert Knowling, Jr.* 317
Optimizing motivation for athletic and public performances 325
Motivational strategies to enhance online learning and instructional design 329
    Chapter summary/conclusions 334
    Next steps 335
    End of chapter motivational minute 335
References 336

Chapter 10 outlined a variety of self-regulatory and self-control strategies that influenced personal performance. However, motivating the self is only one part of achieving desirable learning and performance outcomes. In many cases, the barometer of motivational detective (MD) success is the ability to intervene and implement strategies that promote personal, professional, and organizational growth for *others*. In our daily lives, teachers are accountable for motivating learners, leaders strive to create a work culture that incentivizes employees, and coaches hope to develop skills that enhance the performance of team players. Outside of traditional performance arenas, parents strive to impart motivational wisdom on their offspring, committed partners yearn to improve and motivate each other, while the mission of many teams and groups is to unify motives and consolidate the focus of team members. Pragmatically, many accounts of individual and organizational success are contingent upon a collective and concerted effort, with the degree of success frequently determined by how we harness the efforts of those around us.

    Striving to promote adaptive or success-oriented motivation in others has a unique set of applied challenges. Strategy implementation is not as simple as merely employing an inference or advancing an author's conclusion from a research study. Almost universally, the practical implications of scientific evidence are qualified by language that limits the situational applicability of the findings. Such phrases as "although the results of any single study should be viewed with some caution" (Wright, 2004, p. 73) and "our results are limited in their ability to generalize" (Sansone, Fraughton, Zachary, Butner, & Heiner, 2011, p. 209) warn practitioners to avoid making unwarranted inferences not associated with the study design. Practitioners are cautioned to apply recommendations judiciously, usually due to the specialized nature of the study population, or the unique contextual conditions under which the research was conducted.

Recalling the discussion of culture and the profound influence of individual beliefs and social factors on behavior (Chapter 5, p. 107), we must consider that in many cases, individuals possess a wide-range of beliefs concerning the self and which strategies are most instrumental in influencing motivation, learning, and performance. Normative behavior revered in one culture may be disparaged in another. For instance, many classrooms and organizations strive toward cultivating an autonomy-supportive learning environment, operating under the pretense that individuals are more motivated when they believe that their personal contributions are meaningful and valued (Moreau & Mageau, 2012; Reeve et al., 2014). Converting knowledge of autonomy into practice would imply encouraging innovation and creativity while fostering diversity of thought. While motivation for autonomy is an empirically warranted inference important for academic achievement, vocational success, and athletic performance, absolute autonomy is location based. Culturally valued innovation may be highly appropriate in some organizations, but conspicuously less desirable in others. For example, in the domain of athletic performance, strict adherence to a coach's protocol may mean the difference between ultimate success and failure, but excessive autonomy devoid of structure may lead to confusion, alienation, and strained relationships (Mageau & Vallerand, 2003), not to mention losses.

Motivational and behavioral variability within the same individual is also influenced by location. Individual behavior that is deemed desirable and appropriate in one context may be broadly stigmatized and criticized in another. To illustrate, consider your personal competency beliefs. Despite deep content knowledge and confidence in your field of study, there may be differences in *how* and *when* you communicate your knowledge to others based upon the context. By example, imagine you are a professor, would you demonstrate expertise to your students in the same manner as when communicating with your boss? Probably not; the relationship and social dynamics between the two situations are very different. In all likelihood, you would use a vastly different approach when chatting with a group of colleagues or your boss than one used when conducting a classroom lecture. As many of us have experienced, lecturing colleagues rarely promotes positive motivation and, instead, promotes defensive reactions in others and resistance to otherwise valuable ideas (see Chapter 12 (p. 345) for a discussion of implementing motivational change). An identical message embraced in some settings can clearly be a resounding failure in others, if the message is crafted without consideration of the nuances of location.

These brief examples of variable behavior between individuals in the same environment and within individuals across different settings and circumstances suggest that the success of many strategy initiatives are contextually dependent. The influence of context on the direction, scope, strength, magnitude, and consistency of motivated behavior is indisputable and necessitates a consideration of which best practices are situationally effective. As McInerney (2008) so aptly described when reflecting on the contextualization of regulatory strategies, "when motivational and learning theories are transported to new cultural and social settings to understand and manage individual and group behavior, there may be a mismatch" (p. 369). Clearly, avoiding strategy mismatches is one purpose of this chapter and should be a primary consideration when planning, executing, and evaluating mediation of motivational challenges.

For clarity, context or location refers to cultural representations and group-member perceptions regarding the knowledge, beliefs, attitudes, traditions, and values that guide normative behavior. In other words, overcoming mismatch requires knowing which motivationally adaptive strategies are aligned with the individual differences of performers in a specific learning and performance context. Three assumptions guide implementation of context-based strategies. First, different organizations emphasize different aspects of performance as reflected by group-member behavior. For instance, in classrooms, some systemic curricular efforts focus on amassing deep content knowledge in a particular domain, while the focus in other classrooms is on preparing learners for successful standardized test performance. Similarly, vocational emphasis can exhibit great variability, ranging from a corporate emphasis on quality, innovation, low cost, or productivity, with each orientation optimally correlated with particular performance improvement strategies. Second, organizational priorities are subject to significant fluctuation based upon leadership initiatives and responsiveness to sociopolitical influences. Often referred to as the "program of the month" syndrome, temporal shifts prompted by leadership changes and statutory or common law can substantially alter the emphasis of group members and corresponding strategy interventions. Third, the MD should operate under the basic premise that normative behaviors are inconsistently adapted by group members. The development of subcultures within a broader organizational culture should be expected, resulting in some individuals potentially adopting different core values, motives, and priorities of a work subculture while shunning beliefs deemed appropriate by the dominant host organization.

Promoting adaptive academic motivation

Enhancing academic motivation relies on a series of fundamental understandings. First, we must assume a degree of willingness on the part of the learner to improve academic motivation, which is not always the case. Principle #1 (p. 7) outlined the conundrum of motivational inequality, and the reality that differential motivation is a frequent teaching challenge, primarily driven by learner variation in interest, developmental trajectories, and diverse cultural beliefs. Specifically, academic motivation maybe constrained when individuals harbor a belief in the limited value of education. Second, teachers should espouse incremental beliefs and enact behaviors that support the malleable nature of academic ability and corresponding adaptive academic motivation. If teachers have lower expectations for certain learners or believe that some students will not respond favorably to teaching and strategy initiatives, they may teach some students differently by inadvertently using strategies that maintain a status quo or demotivate learners. Third, educators must hold favorable views of their own teaching capability, believing they have the skills and abilities needed to encourage positive motivational change in others. With a reasonable assurance of the three conditions mentioned, a variety of strategies are at the disposal of educators to promote academic motivation.

The breadth of achievement-enhancing motivational strategies is enormous and cannot possibly be covered in a single chapter. Many systemic approaches attempt to consolidate a variety of environmental restructuring and pedagogical strategies together to create a "program" with the intention of claiming empirically supported superiority in comparison with other similar programs. These turnkey initiatives include after-school programs, such as "My Teaching Partner-Secondary" (Gregory, Allen, Mikami, Hafen, & Pianta, 2014), or adaptations of differential program models that vary in emphasis between social and academic skills (Shernoff, 2010). Analysis at the program level is excluded from the discussion here because of the uncertain generalizability of the outcomes to other educational contexts that do not comprise a similar group of teachers, learners, or program guidelines (see Durlak, Weissberg, & Pachan, 2010, for a review). Instead, the strategies described are recommended foundational principles relevant for implementing customized strategy interventions to enhance academic motivation. The selected approaches are based upon confluent and recurring evidence observed across eclectic academic contexts and populations.

The types of initiatives sought to improve academic motivation are decisively broad. Thematically, many initiatives focus on cultivating extrinsic motivation by enhancing domain-level interest. Examples include providing financial incentives to learners for engaging in academically productive behaviors (Bettinger, 2012), using athletic activity as a motivational catalyst for academics (Vazou, Gavrilou, Mamalaki, Papanastasiou, & Sioumala, 2012), or investigating how certain activities (e.g., homework) can increase the probability of motivational regulation (Ramdass & Zimmerman, 2011). These types of studies are frequently correlational in nature and use self-report to suggest that certain extrinsic incentives foster improved motivation for academics, which, in turn, mediates academic achievement.

Another approach to foster adaptive academic motivation is to investigate how the design of different learning environments influences intrinsic motivation and achievement. Studies frequently manipulate or control for environmental factors, with the specific intention to determine whether variations in the design of instructional materials (Belland, Kim, & Hannafin, 2013), differences in teaching methods (Slavin, 2012; Wlodkowski, 2011), or the physical configuration of the learning environment influence achievement outcomes. The contextual emphasis attempts to identify components that contribute to the creation of a classroom climate conducive to the internalization of task effort or academic goals, under the expectation that a learner's intrinsic motivation is aligned with specific teaching practices and classroom-level variables that can be modified and are within control of the educator.

In essence, the studies mentioned infer that the establishment of certain types of classroom cultures are preferable for enhanced academic motivation. Classroom culture implies a proprietary and idiosyncratic set of normative teaching behaviors that guide learners toward meeting learning goals. Classroom culture, sometimes referred to as a *communities of inquiry* (Larreamendy-Joerns & Leinhardt, 2006) or *learning communities* (Greeno, 1997), suggests that when learning is approached from a group and situative perspective, a set of shared values and practices are developed among participants. Subsequently, these practices are infused into instruction and are accepted as normative and part of the learning process. For example, participants in a learning community might agree that when one person is speaking, interruption is prohibited. These socially generated practices are directly related to the type of pedagogy demonstrated by the educator, both formally through instruction, and informally through interactions and productive relationships with learners. Although the emphasis in many classroom communities is focused on teaching and learning, and frequently motivational factors that support academic excellence are neglected (Belland et al., 2013), shared practices and classroom climate dictate *how* learning takes place. Thus, any classroom climate that strives for academic excellence should also clearly recognize and define normative *motivational* behaviors as an integral component that contributes to classroom culture, structure, and, ultimately, learning.

One major climate variable that is related to optimal classroom motivation is creating an autonomy-supportive culture. Autonomy support means that educators abdicate the management of learners via autocratic edict. Instead, the autonomy-supportive educator takes deliberate and intentional steps to give learners the ability to have influence over what is done in the classroom and how learning is accomplished (Su & Reeve, 2011). By no means does modeling an autonomy-supportive approach suggest that educators relinquish classroom leadership, but it does mean educators renounce a controlling leadership style. Recalling the discussion of self-determination and internalization of motives as a key determinant of intrinsic motivation, when learners feel controlled, there is a diminished probability of integrating school or programmatic academic goals into the self. When academic integration is impeded, achievement and corresponding adaptive motivation suffer (Reeve, 2006). Creating an autonomy-supportive classroom means providing guidelines and structure about how learning is accomplished (Reeve et al., 2014), in service of the primary goal of putting learners at the forefront of classroom-level decisions through active engagement and collaboration.

Specific strategies that promote autonomous perceptions include encouraging learners, within curricular guidelines, to set their own individual or group learning goals (Slavin, 2012); affording learners the opportunity to influence classroom culture through involvement in setting classroom rules; and encouraging the expression of student dissatisfaction concerning learning tasks (Stefanou, Perencevich, DiCintio, & Turner, 2004). Additionally, by offering academic choices, including soliciting preferences concerning the type of assessments used to measure knowledge gains (Falchikov, 2013), learners tend to associate positive emotions with classroom experiences. Involvement strategies promote intrinsic motivation because learners feel their input is valued, and the controlling aspect of teaching and learning is diminished when learners are afforded choice. When learners believe they have a classroom voice, the probability of embracing curricular decisions is increased and can be measured through behavioral and cognitive engagement metrics, including attendance, participation, or time on learning tasks.

Motivating learners in the classroom goes beyond classroom structure and is decidedly based on interactions and relationships (Reyes, Brackett, Rivers, White, & Salovey, 2012). Many models of motivation emphasize the need for the educator to be perceived as much more than someone who possess advanced content knowledge but as someone who is willing and able to generate enthusiasm toward learning while making learning meaningful (Shulman, 1987). Behaviors associated with engaging learners include demonstrating humanistic qualities, such as establishing rapport, showing concern for the learner beyond academic performance, and generally having a positive relationship with the learner (Anderman, Andrzejewski, & Allen, 2011). Educators assessed as competent and effective by learners are those who establish a nurturing and developmental classroom climate exhibited through emotional support while showing respect and sensitivity toward the learner (Reyes et al., 2012). Having positive social relationships with learners does not mean forsaking control of the classroom or imply that the educator is a "friend" of the learner; instead, relationship building means promoting a sense of structure and belonging within a classroom community. Learners who feel part of a learning community will contribute more to classroom discussions, are more cooperative with their peers, and are more likely to take academic risks by choosing more challenging tasks when offered the opportunity (Rimm-Kaufman & Chiu, 2007).

Many seasoned educators may recognize that encouraging learners to set their own learning goals, providing choices, and emphasizing the socially constructed nature of knowledge building is highly reminiscent of cooperative learning. During cooperative learning and other related constructivist pedagogies, such as guided discovery, learners are at the heart of the knowledge building process, collaborating with each other, and highly influential in determining *how* learning goals are reached, compared with the generally passive role learners assume during typical direct instruction and lecture (Slavin, 2012). A myriad of evidence supports the contention that when learners are more actively involved in determining how learning occurs, motivation flourishes (Law, 2011; Skinner, Furrer, Marchand, & Kindermann, 2008; Slavin, 1996). Since cooperative learning involves group goals, learners must enlist others to help reach personal objectives. Satisfying group and individual goals engages both intrinsic and extrinsic motivational components—intrinsically by achieving personal learning gains and extrinsically in the form of praise and attention from supportive classmates. Across disciplines, when controlling for other important classroom variables, such as teacher experience and existing learner knowledge, cooperative learning is often related to motivational, learning, and social benefits in comparison with other instructional methods (Baghcheghi, Koohestani, & Rezaei, 2011; Hsiung, 2012; Rimm-Kauffman & Chiu, 2007).

A third motivational emphasis related to both classroom climate and pedagogical practice are strategies employed to generate topical interest or to capitalize on the existing interest of learners. Development of interest implies learners directing attention toward task-relevant instructional goals, which without intervention would not earn adequate learner attention to promote knowledge gains. Interest develops by outlining salient and relevant aspects of specific content, making clear connections between current learning and the learner's existing knowledge, and emphasizing the authentic value of learning content (Mayer, 2008). While interest development can be both enduring and situational as described in Chapter 6 (p. 139), many interest-generating strategies are useful regardless of the longevity of the interest because they orchestrate conditions that promote attention toward the desired or relevant topic.

Classroom interest generation begins with making a clear case to the learner as to why the particular knowledge is personally relevant. In absence of learner consensus that some applied use or authentic value exists to master the content, disengagement may follow, with the most salient knowledge potentially rejected as inconsequential to advance personal learning agendas. Perhaps the best example of the dichotomy of learner valuation of knowledge comes from the streets of Brazil. In a classic study comparing mathematics skills demonstrated in the classroom with those skills being used in practice, Carraher, Carraher, and Schliemann (1985) found that children who unsuccessfully completed simple mathematical calculations in schools were highly motivated and effective mathematical wizards while working as entrepreneurial street vendors. The setting and utility value of the mathematic knowledge, not the conceptual understanding, was the key motivating factor predicting use of mathematics knowledge. Other interest-generating strategies that motivate learners toward an academic focus include relating current knowledge acquisition to future career goals (Mikkonen, Ruohoniemi, & Lindblom-Ylänne, 2013), calibrating task challenge commensurate with existing skills as a means of enhancing competency beliefs (Sansone, Weir, Harpster, & Morgan, 1992), and by taking advantage of peer influence and the individual psychological need of belongingness, as learners working together will often experience significant task interest based merely upon group participation (Minnaert, Boekaerts, & de Brabander, 2007).

Many of the strategies described thus far are rather explicit, representing traditional scaffolding techniques upon which educators should rely to support academic excellence. Unfortunately, scaffolding efforts designed strictly for motivational purposes may not be the primary objective of many educators (Belland et al., 2013), and as outlined in Chapter 1 (p. 12), motivational engagement is frequently not within the conscious awareness of learners. Considering this dilemma, educators and the aspiring MD may be well served by overtly cuing learners to the importance of motivation as a necessary catalyst for achieving learning goals. One activating strategy is providing metacognitive support that focuses attention on the motivationally relevant aspects of a task, specifically in the form of metacognitive prompting. Prompting, whether direct or subliminal, serves as a reminder and helps guide learners toward reaching learning goals and is particularly useful in enhancing problem-solving ability (Fiorella & Mayer, 2012; Hoffman & Spatariu, 2008). Prompting is most often used during computer-based learning but can be part of an explicit teaching routine regardless of instructional modality. Prompting serves as performance feedback by using either solicited or unsolicited prompts, such as "Did you check your answers for accuracy?" or "Where should your attention be right now?" Although many prompting efforts monitor cognition, similar motivational prompts can easily be infused into both online and traditional instruction with minor adaptations in content and emphasis.

In sum, accelerating academic motivation is an obtainable reality that can be accomplished with limited instructional effort. Many of the specific strategies described here, although not all inclusive, are important steps toward convincing learners that conscious awareness of motivation is clearly related to superior learning outcomes. Perhaps more importantly, training initiatives that include motivational strategies have been found useful to improve learning across educational contexts and with a wide range of educators and learners across the academic spectrum (Zimmerman & Cleary, 2009), including children as young as 5 years of age (Dignath, Buettner, & Langfeldt, 2008). Receptivity to strategy intervention starts with educator awareness and support for training, coupled with the systemic realization that motivational training is fruitful. Intervention success is a function of establishing normative motivational standards that define the academic community. Once the obscure research finding becomes instructionally relevant, motivational focus will likely shift from a conscious effort into routine habit, providing personal growth and achievement benefits for both the educator and learner.

Strategies to motivate work performance

For some, work is a utopian dream, grounded in a system of shared values and beliefs, exemplified by empowered and creative work teams and employees, and predicated on trusting, empathetic, and democratic leadership that inspires productivity. Imagine your first day on the job at Nirvana, Inc. When you arrive you are served a gourmet, gluten-free, non–genetically modified, hot breakfast. While dining and meeting your colleagues, you mutually contemplate how your company can gain the next competitive advantage. After breakfast you rush to the company's internal social networking site, which was created to share visionary ideas and industry intelligence, and you post your idea. Immediately, the word spreads about your brilliant plan. Within an hour a senior company official is at your desk giving you feedback about your suggestion. After your conversation, you both feel invigorated yet exhausted, so you go to the snoozle room and relax in your ergonomically designed nap pod for 20 minutes to restore your depleted cognitive resources. Upon awakening you are re-energized and return to work for 6 more hours before eating your company-provided gourmet dinner. A few hours later, you hitch a ride home in the company van, which like most perks at Nirvana Inc., is provided to you at no cost. What may seem like an Orwellian fantasy, or a predawn dream, is actually a description of some of the many worker-centered policies and normative behaviors that define the culture at Google, arguably the world's premiere technology company (Frumkin, 2010).

For others, the daily office grind resembles a day in purgatory. More time and effort are devoted to dealing with bureaucracy, complaining to peers, and conjuring up reasons for your continued employment than toward work. For many, the daily routine consists of navigating political mine fields and dodging corporate power plays, avoiding confrontations with superiors, and spending endless hours deciphering hypocritical behaviors that radically deviate from the alleged corporate rhetoric. Instead of instilling a self-determined and autonomy-supportive culture, such as the one described at Google, the zeitgeist of many companies is often a series of outdated legacy policies, implemented by desensitized autocratic leaders under the auspices of consistency and control. Unfortunately, many of the archaic behaviors that are normative to beleaguered organizations are counterproductive and at the expense of employee trust, engagement, and psychological commitment to one's job, factors which ultimately influence organizational success (Crabtree, 2013).

According to the world's most comprehensive survey conducted across 150 countries on the motives of the global workforce, the Gallup organization indicated that 63%

of workers report being disengaged and lacking job motivation. Disengagement means workers are unwilling to exert effort for the corporate cause, despondent and depressed about their positions, and willing to disparage the company when given the chance (Crabtree, 2013, para 2). Worker disengagement can be devastating, both individually and organizationally, and is frequently blamed as the cause of productivity lags, lack of employee commitment, and reduced company profits (MacLeod & Clarke, 2011). Further, the degree of employee engagement has a resounding impact on critically important motivational metrics that distinguish the world's most successful and admired organizations from the laggards, such as the extent of personal innovation, the emphasis on individual development, and a focus on social responsibility (Fortune, 2014). In addition, strong correlational evidence reveals that engaged workers take fewer sick days, exhibit lower turnover, pilfer less from the company, and are involved in fewer work accidents (Macleod & Clarke, 2011), suggesting that the extent of employee engagement can be the difference between a flourishing and a failing organization.

While the idealistic conditions at Google may be considered an anomaly to some, the normative behaviors described are manifestations of a distinct and well-planned corporate strategy that dedicates fiscal resources and intellectual capital toward employee satisfaction. Unlike academic motivation that places greater emphasis on individual results, highly functioning organizations prosper through coordinated group performance, which, under optimal circumstances, suggests that individuals subrogate personal goals and dominant motivations in favor of collective efforts because individuals believe that organized and group performance is the pathway to individual gain and mutual prosperity (Chen & Kanfer, 2006).

Numerous theories that apply to academic motivation attempt to explain motivated work behavior (Grant & Shin, 2012), including several of the notable "Mount Rushmore" theorists featured in Chapter 7 (p. 179). Previously discussed theories that apply to work motivation include equity theory (Chapter 1, p. 7), self-determination (Chapter 2, p. 36), goal-orientation approaches (Chapter 6, p. 154), expectancy-value theory (Chapter 7, p. 189), and the theory of planned behavior (Chapter 8, p. 213). Each lens uses a defined framework for investigating the relative influence and integrative nature of psychological, emotional, and social factors on work performance and engagement. Some approaches stress the socially constructed nature of organizational success, suggesting that group dynamics have a dominant influence on organizational performance, while others place greater emphasis on individual development, vigorously debating the merits of intrinsic motivation and extrinsic reward as catalysts for optimal organizational success.

Regardless of theoretical orientation, in *every* case employee beliefs are at the heart of explaining organized motivated behavior, often demonstrating the reciprocal influence of individual motives on group performance (Chen & Kanfer, 2006). The primary emphasis for the MD is application of confluent findings from multiple theories as a conduit to modify behavior. As such, three major components of work motivation are advanced here. First, motivating employees is a systemic effort defined by organizational culture. Second, group cohesion and teamwork often supersede individual goals and are a primary determinant of organizational success. Third, leadership style is often the key difference between adaptive and maladaptive motivation of individuals within an organization.

Justification for a systemic view of organizational development and corresponding adaptive motivation in individuals contends that organizational growth, like human development, has a definable life cycle, including a measurable developmental trajectory, and normative behavior is a product of diverse cultural, structural, and operational influences. The most relevant empirically supported theoretical model of systemic development that explains the motives of individuals with organizations is Bronfenbrenner's (1977) Organic Ecological Systems Theory. Although postulated as an explanation of human development and change, the theory has been sporadically applied to other domains that have strong motivational underpinnings, such as mentoring (Chandler, Kram, & Yip, 2011), the development of prosocial behavior (Wentzel, 2014), and leadership style (Allen, Stelzner, & Wielkiewicz, 1999). The Bronfenbrenner model comprises a series of interdependent nested systems, each with a reciprocal and bi-directional influence. The intimate connectivity among systems in many ways parallels organizational structures because individuals rarely work in isolation, and multiple, and sometime competing, cultural systems evolve in organizations, particularly in large multi-national companies where workers have functional, staff, and regional reporting relationships.

Viewing organizational motivation as systemic suggests that a complex, intricate, and interactive network of competing forces contribute to overall employee growth and development, and evaluation of individual motivation cannot be accurately accomplished without consideration of the interconnectivity among organizational systems. At the heart of the Bronfenbrenner (1977) model is the individual, who is surrounded by variable concentric and hierarchical influences. Similar to Bronfenbrenner's original intention, application of the model to organizational motivation emphasizes the instrumentality of personal values and individual beliefs. A surrounding microsystem has a prevailing but coordinated motivational influence on individual normative behavior through such factors as the leadership style of one's supervisor, specific job responsibilities, participation in skill development programs, and compensation plans. A mesosystem provides interconnections between the various elements of the microsystem, such as the relation of performance evaluation and job skills to pay rates. Mesosystems also include the unique culture of an individual department or work units. An exosystem not only represents internal relationships with other operational departments but also includes matrixed influences, such as when regional offices are accountable to a staff function or to a larger corporate entity. Finally, the macrosystem, which represents the unique culture of the organization—including regulatory, community, and industry-related normative behaviors, such as a focus on environmental sustainability and the social responsibility goals of the organization—has a pervasive, although indirect, influence on the individual. The macrosystem influences personal motivation because organizational culture implicitly sets boundaries for normative behavior, including which behaviors will be recognized and rewarded by the organization (Figure 11.1).

Successful organizations do not follow one prescriptive formula to determine culture but, instead, emphasize particular values, beliefs, and operating principles that demarcate a corporate philosophy, or an ideology, which provides guidelines and structure for associates. A clearly communicated culture will also emphasize the preferred methods and stylistic descriptions of *how* the culture is implemented and infused within the organization by both formal and informal leaders. In ideal circumstances, corporate culture will visibly align with a strategic business plan and the

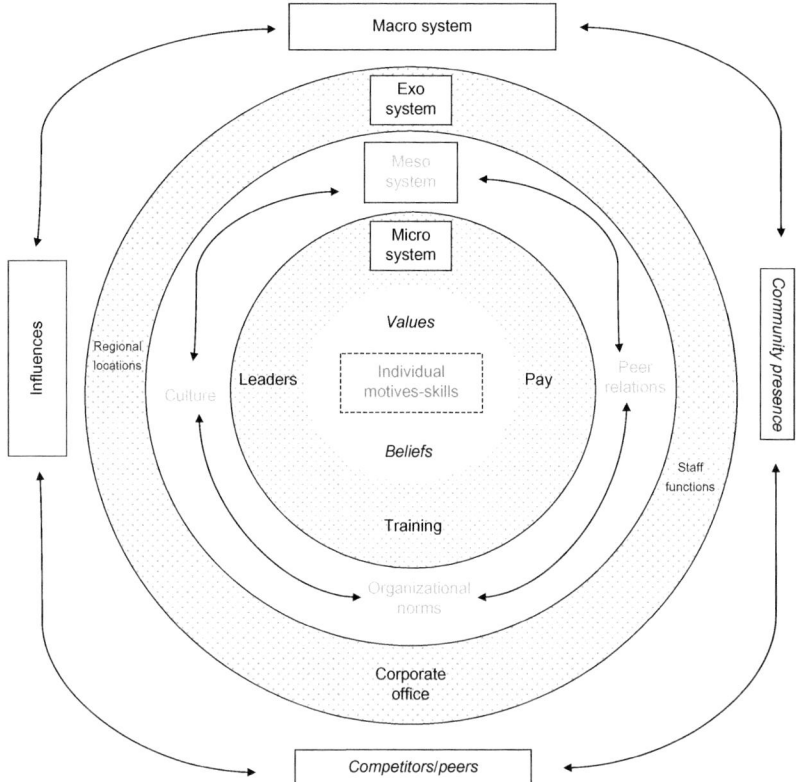

Figure 11.1 Organizational application of the Bronfenbrenner Ecosystem Model.

behaviors of the workforce will explicitly characterize a business philosophy that is consistently demonstrated to customers, competitors, and the broader community of business practice. For instance, a cursory review of the GE Capital Corporation website (www.gecapital.com), the world's most profitable non-banking global finance organization and a subsidiary of the General Electric Corporation, reveals that the corporate culture is based on five core organizational values, as listed in the table below:

External focus	Defines success through the customer's eyes, in tune with industry dynamic sees around corners
Clear thinking	Seeks simple solutions to complex problems, has a decisive focus, and communicates clear and consistent priorities
Imagination	Generates new and creative ideas, is open to change, is resourceful, and displays courage and tenacity
Inclusiveness	Teamwork—respects other's ideas and contributions, creates excitement, and drives engagement
Expertise	Has domain depth, has credibility built from experience, continuously develops self, and loves learning

Source: Reprinted with permission of GE Capital Corporation.

At least three conclusions can be inferred from the shared values of GE Capital. First, relationships with customers and employees are of the utmost importance for the organization. Company associates are valued for innovation and creativity that support customer growth and satisfaction. Next, the success of the organization is not predicated on individual performance but, instead, is based on the collective and coordinated efforts of associates. Finally, several motivational themes are prominent in the values, including employee engagement, life-long learning, and the importance of competency beliefs, measured by credibility of experience. Although the organizational focus and intentions are clearly stated, deliberate omissions also define the GE Capital corporate culture. There is no mention of being the most economical provider and being fastest to market with new products, as these factors are not core organizational strengths or normative behaviors desired from individuals. GE Capital, like many other consistently profitable companies, clearly communicates how individuals fit within the corporate exosystem and the overall macrosystem of the respective industry. The advantage of emphasizing organizational fit is a highly lucid understanding by employees as to what behaviors enhance the probability of personal growth and career advancement within the host organization.

In addition to close alignment between company culture and individual performance goals, a systemic view of motivated work behavior necessitates a positive correlation among different organizational systems. Embodied by the phrase "walk the talk," enhanced individual effort is based, in part, on clarity and consistency between stated core values and actual business practice. Regrettably, espoused corporate policy and enacted behaviors often conflict. When normative and rewarded behaviors are inconsistent with communicated organizational values, individual motivation suffers as employees perceive a behavioral mismatch. The ambiguity leads to uncertainty and conflict in relation to personal goals resulting in diminished work motivation (Wright, 2004) and to compromised perceptions of organizational trust (Läms & Pučėtait, 2006), regardless of the type of culture promoted by the organization.

Collective organizational systems are sometimes referred to as "high performance work practices" (HPWPs; Combs, Liu, Hall, & Ketchen, 2006, p. 501), and include recruiting strategies and assessment procedures used to evaluate prospective employees, the corollary between reward systems and performance, the degree of organizational emphasis on talent development, and the overall tone of human resource policies that support operations. Irrespective of the exact design of each system, HPWPs should be systemically aligned with the same operating principles that define the cultural identity of the organization. The coordination of organizational systems is highly motivating for individuals because the consistency among HPWPs empowers individuals to act without fear of scrutiny and leaves little doubt as to what it takes to be successful within the organization (Pfeffer, 1998). Not surprisingly, HPWPs, such as employee empowerment, training, and incentive compensation, are linked to greater employee retention, employee satisfaction, and higher work productivity (Combs et al., 2006).

In practical and applied terms, systems coordination at minimum means recruiting models, employee development programs, and reward systems that all have meaningful

Motivational Leader—*Robert Knowling, Jr.*

Robert E. Knowling Jr., also known as Bob, has over 30 years of experience in the telecommunications and technology sectors, leading companies through periods of high growth and organizational turnaround. Currently, Knowling is Chairman of Eagles Landing Partners (ELP). ELP specializes in helping senior management formulate strategy, lead organizational transformations, and re-engineer businesses. As such, ELP serves as an advisor to company officials across multiple industries.

Previously, Bob served as CEO of Telwares, a JP Morgan Chase/One Equity Partners Private Equity owned company from 2005 to 2009. Prior to joining Telwares, from 2001 to 2005, Knowling was CEO of the NYC Leadership Academy, an independent nonprofit corporation created by NYC Chancellor Joel I. Klein and Mayor Michael R. Bloomberg that was chartered with developing the next generation of principals in the New York City public school system.

From 2001 to 2003, Knowling was Chairman and Chief Executive Officer of SimDesk Technologies, Inc. During his time at SimDesk, he defined the company's go-to-market strategy, developed numerous strategic partnerships, and managed the successful launch of the company's software. Prior to this, Knowling was Chairman, President and Chief Executive Officer of Covad Communications; a Private Equity/Venture Capital backed startup company located in Silicon Valley. Knowling led the company through its rapid growth and Initial Public Offering to become the largest and most recognizable brand in the high-speed Internet access industry.

In 2011, Knowling published his autobiography titled *You Can Get There from Here: My Journey from Struggle to Success*. Knowling was awarded the Wall Street Project's Reginald Lewis Trailblazers Award by President Clinton and the Reverend Jesse Jackson in 1999. In presenting the award to Knowling, President Clinton commended Knowling's efforts in developing a national agenda for the spirit and mission of inclusion, opportunity, expansion, advocacy and success in the workplace for women and people of color in the high-tech industry.

Knowling received a Bachelor of Arts degree in theology from Wabash College and a Masters of Business Administration from the Kellogg School of Management at Northwestern University. Currently, Knowling serves on the board of directors for Heidrick & Struggles International, Inc. in Chicago, Illinois; Bartech in Livonia, Michigan; and Roper Industries in Sarasota, Florida. Knowling has been a YMCA volunteer for more than 20 years and served as Chair of the National Services group for the YMCA in 1993. He maintains an active nationwide corporate and public speaking schedule.

and measurable connections. For example, if instilling an organizational culture that values employee development, intentionally emphasize the developmental focus of the company during the evaluation of prospective employees. During an interview ask probing questions, such as "Can you give me an example of how you have taken responsibility for your career progression?" or "How do you influence the performance of your co-workers?" Coordination with other organizational systems would imply that the company is willing to finance and develop training programs to eliminate skill gaps, has polices in place that permit employees time-off from regular job duties to participate in training, and has a defined and transparent eligibility system to nominate employees for training. Further, system alignment infers that skill enhancement has a direct link to performance gaps identified during performance evaluation and that career advancement, additional compensation, and greater overall responsibility are all related to job competencies, and not clandestine behaviors shrouded by organizational politics. Solidifying a culture revering talent would include the elimination of bureaucratic rules and regulations that are antithetical to development, combined with a well-articulated, collective belief that skill gaps are not obstacles inhibiting career advancement but, instead, are opportunities to cultivate professional growth.

By example, if we examine some of the wisdom of motivational leader Robert Knowling, Jr., we can see several practical examples of how core values, candid communication, and organizational alignment contribute to individual work motivation. As a CEO of many companies over the course of his career, Bob conveyed that one of his most crucial roles is helping others accomplish their goals. When asked the question "How do you motivate others at work?" Bob focused almost entirely on the importance of creating a nurturing and developmental corporate culture. Bob stated, "The commitment to other people is first and foremost. I've learned that great results happen when you provide an environment where people can excel. You've got to give people a belief system that you understand their walk and that you've been in their shoes" (R. Knowling, Jr., personal communication, August 10, 2014). Bob added, "You really do need to think about what they are trying to accomplish in their jobs. If you help people reach their goals, in effect, you have created the perfect scenario for them to get a spring in their step when they leave the bed every morning. They enjoy coming to work, and they give you their best" (R. Knowling, Jr., personal communication, August 10, 2014). Knowling frequently emphasized the connections between transparent values and organizational success, mentioning the word "values" 10 different times during our 45-minute conversation. Summing up his views on accelerating teamwork, corporate culture and individual motivation, Robert concluded, "It's really about how well people embrace the values. The ability to inspire and enlist people to understand and embrace the organizational values has a direct correlation to organizational success (R. Knowling, Jr., personal communication, August 10, 2014).

When asked which specific strategies he used to motivate others, Knowling stressed the importance of setting achievable goals, but he cautioned that goal attainment should require focused effort, perseverance, and willingness to stretch one's capabilities. In addition, Knowling made it clear that goal fulfillment was a partnership and a team effort. He stressed, "People need to know that they've got full support and that we don't set lay-up targets when we set objectives. (R. Knowling, Jr., personal communication, August 10, 2014). The instrumental value of goals is a key to Bob's own success, even as a promising 13-year old entrepreneur. When he started his first venture, a landscaping business, he asked his older brother to switch beds with him and sleep on the top berth of their bunk beds. The switch allowed Bob the opportunity to constantly stare at the list of goals that he had taped to the underside of his brother's bed.

Bob added that goals alone are not the motivation to perform, stressing the role of giving people flexibility to do their jobs. Knowling, who managed the New York City Leadership Academy, worked with Jack Welch, former CEO of General Electric. Welch, who, like Knowling, has a reputation as a business turnaround expert, led a struggling General Electric Corporation in the 1980s to become one of the world's most profitable corporations during his tenure. Welch taught Knowling a valuable lesson. Reflecting on Welch's guidance Knowling stated, "He never told me what to do. I left his office always clear in my thinking, but also owning everything" (R. Knowling, Jr., personal communication, August 10, 2014). In other words, Welch convinced Knowling of the importance of instilling an autonomy-supportive work environment (see Principle #49, p. 281), a style that Knowling continues to embrace as one of the most important and enduring attributes of an effective leader.

Perhaps the most obvious conclusion from the Knowling interview is that generating motivation for work, at least in part, is based upon the quality of relationships with others, which when formalized are often accomplished through teamwork. Teamwork is relevant to business prosperity because when individuals with diverse skill sets are able to cooperate effectively, they frequently outperform a group of similar individual contributors (Clark, 2005). An important distinction when examining the motivation of teams is clarifying the difference between a group of individuals working together on independent tasks and effective team-based performance. Although definitions of teamwork moderately differ across domains of interest (e.g., sports, business, military), most teamwork descriptions accentuate the interdependence of team members in a coordinated group effort to achieve shared and common goals (Carron, Martin, & Loughead, 2012).

For example, car manufacturers rely heavily on teamwork, not based upon workers independently installing automobile parts on an assembly line (Jones, Latham, & Betta, 2013) but through coordinated, logistical and supply networks that bring desirable and functional automobiles to market. In addition to assembly, the auto production process includes marketers assessing consumer needs, design engineers creating captivating models with coveted features, suppliers contributing raw materials and making accessory parts, and a network of distributors transporting the product to consumers. Any breakdown in the interdependent network is potentially devastating, which was exactly the fate of Ford Motor Company (FMC), when the company introduced the ill-designed *Edsel* automobile, arguably the greatest consumer product failure in history.

At conception in 1956, senior management and "expert" consultants projected that the Edsel would propel FMC to become the premiere manufacturer of automobiles.

However, Edsel production was halted after only two model years. Contrary to management predictions, consumers thought that the innovative design, which was applauded by engineers and cost almost $1 billion to bring to market, was "garish and odd" (Dicke, 2010, p. 495). Total sales were less than 110,000 vehicles, contrary to a minimum sales projection of 435,000 in the first year of production alone. Teamwork at Ford was clearly not an organizational forte, as evidenced by the lack of pre-production collaboration among departments and "strategic waffling" by the senior management team (Dicke, 2010, p. 495). Poor insight into consumer needs resulted in the untimely declaration of the Edsel's demise only 7 months after release. Ironically, as predicted by the management team, the reputation of the Edsel was immortalized in manufacturing folklore, albeit for all the wrong reasons!

While the Edsel story is a vivid illustration of the difference between teamwork and a group of individuals working independently on the same project, all of the individually focused motivational strategies described in Chapter 10 are also applicable to teams. In addition, other more specific strategies apply to team motivation, based upon the overwhelming importance of group cohesion and cooperation needed for optimal team results (Hertel, 2011). Foremost, working in cohesive groups is a strong social motivator. While many organizations use team-based problem solving and group projects as a strategic business advantage, for some individuals, team participation alone is an inspiring performance incentive (Hüffmeier & Hertel, 2011). The social benefits experienced during teamwork enhance motivation for several reasons. Initially, teamwork provides the opportunity for individuals to make favorable social comparisons by modeling others who they may deem as effective leaders or mentors. Next, work, as well as personal identity, is enhanced through team affiliation as positive self-perceptions are derived from reassuring group feedback and from constructive contributions to group efforts (Gockel, Kerr, Seok, & Harris, 2008). Further, a mutual affinity of shared experiences afford team members opportunities for positive emotional encouragement, which occurs when team members display similar affective responses to work setbacks, or when celebrating collective achievements. Last, team interaction provides ways to satisfy individual altruistic motives, which are accomplished when team members benevolently mentor each other and implicitly learn skills that are of overall value to the organization (Hertel, 2011).

However, merely working on a team is insufficient to completely explain individual motivation as people desire personal accountability and the perception of task independence during teamwork to feel valued (Wageman, 1995). As such, team success is predicated upon team leaders orchestrating a work context that provides harmonic balance between internally-focused personal goals and externally-generated team goals. Goal balance starts with clarity concerning team expectations, and also requires formally defining individual roles and accountabilities that must be met to ensure team success. Little doubt should exist concerning who does what in order to avoid conditions that contribute to potential "*social loafing*," a phenomenon that occurs when some team members consciously withhold effort, under the belief that other team members will compensate for their own disproportional contributions (Clark, 2005). One strategy to forestall or eliminate social loafing is assessing that each team member possess an appropriate skill set during the recruiting and evaluation process. Accurate competency assessments are critical to team functioning, first to ensure that collectively individuals have needed team competencies and also to reassure team members that their compatriots have the ability to pull their weight, an attribute that is highly important when teams must respond favorably to pressure and impending team deadlines.

Once goals are clearly articulated, *mental models*, which are contextual and procedural guides developed to scaffold and support team efforts, are useful to outline the rules and standards that govern work processes and team behaviors (Kogler-Hill, 2007). Standards should address procedural aspects of team performance, such as team decision making and methods to resolve team conflict, when present. Next, team-based performance metrics that evaluate progress toward collective goals should be clearly identified and communicated as part of the overall team performance plan. Metrics allow for data-based team recognition and also provide an objective method for teams to assess the relative contribution of their team to the organization. Finally, qualitative performance feedback is helpful to evaluate the methods teams use to accomplish team initiatives and determine the appropriateness of behaviors in relation to normative organizational culture. Feedback can be especially motivating when the analysis is used to identify skill gaps that can be narrowed via organizational training and development initiatives.

The epitome of team performance is *self-directed work teams* (SDWTs). These formally constructed groups of empowered frontline employees assume responsibilities that are typically assigned to and expected of managers and leaders. "Frontline" means those employees who are directly responsible for producing goods or services and who will likely interface with business customers. SDWTs are differentiated from project teams because self-directed team members make tactical organizational and production decisions, without direct management intervention in day-to-day operations. Typically, the SDWT demonstrates empowerment by choosing who is hired, promoted or fired, and by determining how work is prioritized, assigned, and completed (Bedwell, Shuffler, Wildman, & Salas, 2010). Although senior management will likely determine general operational guidelines for the team and also authorizes SDWT creation and composition, the SDWT essentially operates as an independent, entrepreneurial business entity. As such, the team is fully accountable for achievements and likewise assumes primary responsibility and ownership of any setbacks or failure.

The SDWT is inherently self-managed because members are afforded ample autonomy to make leadership-level decisions (Stewart, Courtright, & Manz, 2011). An SDWT has flexibility to decide if, when, and how a team decision will be implemented and how the success of the team's action is evaluated (Kozlowski & Bell, 2003). SDWTs encourage intrinsic motivation through accountability as well as by the likelihood that organizational goals will be internalized because team participation encourages self-evaluation (Neck & Manz, 2010). When self-criticism is enacted, the individual may propose remedial action to reinforce skills through intrinsically focused skill development programs. Likewise, self-evaluation may evoke self-imposed extrinsic incentives, such as bonuses or time-off, when results warrant reward based on reaching predetermined and objective standards. While the concept of self-leadership may sound esoteric or futuristic to some, ample research suggests that self-leadership is correlated with enhanced productivity, team creativity, employee job satisfaction, personal growth and elevated organizational commitment (Stewart et al., 2011). When optimally functioning, an SDWT exemplifies the definition of a high-synergy team, which is a team "that yields a business volume per team member that is even higher than the volume the best member would achieve when working alone" (Hertel, 2011, p. 179). Perhaps, of greatest relevance to the MD is that the skills associated with synergistic work teams are contextually bound; that is, the specific cultural nuances that promote team cohesion can be influenced and controlled by managers and leaders. Control implies that optimal team behaviors are learned, and thus, synergistic behavior can be accelerated through formalized individual and team training (Carlile, 2004).

In order to sustain the high-powered motivation associated with SDWTs, at least four contextual strategies are recommended. In general, the strategies are designed to eliminate ambiguity concerning team roles and responsibilities and to counteract the potential negative consequences of SDWTs. Undesirable outcomes from SDWTs include team member stress and burnout, as well as ambivalent work attitudes from traditional supervisors who often have less control in a SDWT environment (Batt, 2004). First, definable, specific, and measurable *team* goals are indispensable. Given an inspiring charter by senior management as to team purpose, team goals provide the substance and guidance to clearly transform team responsibilities into individual roles. Second, intra-team communication is necessary in order for team members to effectively calibrate actual team progress with organizational expectations. Inconsistent or ineffective communication within teams is related to organizational distrust, which clearly undermines team performance (Kuipers, 2009). Third, sharing organizational information with the team is an important priority. Necessary information includes strategic business plans, task-focused feedback that specifically targets understanding of task requirements, and a clear understanding of standard operating procedures. Meta-analytic results reveal that task-focused feedback provided by leaders explains over 10% of the variability in team performance (Burke et al., 2006). Last, a flat organizational structure, with a clear delineation of who is leading the team is essential. Although many leadership tasks are shared across SDWT, it is highly important to eliminate leadership ambiguity. Overall, lack of leadership clarity and uncertainty as to who is responsible for team motivation is often highly detrimental to team performance (Carson, Tesluk, & Marrone, 2007).

External leadership is an absolute organizational necessity, even for the most effective high-synergy teams because SDWTs are embedded in a broader structure that determines overall organizational norms (Stewart et al., 2011). Arguably, the quality of organizational leadership contributes more variability to individual motivation than any other single factor because in the eyes of many, leadership behavior and culture are intimately entwined (Schein, 2010). Dozens of empirically substantiated leadership models and hundreds of self-proclaimed leadership experts have attempted to affirm what leadership is (Haden, 2014) and, more importantly, what behaviors individuals should exemplify to be described as successful leaders (Fleishman et al.,

1992). Definitions of leadership, like many other expansive motivational constructs vary by domain, but almost universally, leaders are defined as individuals who formally, or informally, exert influence over others with the intent to achieve common goals (Northouse, 2007).

Depending on organizational culture, leaders are determined in at least two ways: (1) Leaders may be formally appointed and anointed with specific organizational jurisdiction and job responsibilities by senior management; or (2) leadership is informally assumed during the course of business transactions, when individuals provide direction and influence, regardless of "official" job responsibilities or a designated role within the organization. Again, organizational culture will dictate the derivation as to who qualifies as a leader, as some cultures will disdain voluntary leadership as a violation of formal organizational boundaries. Northouse (2007) outlined four different perspectives on leadership that emphasize motivational components. First, the *skill* approach suggests that leaders emerge based upon the possession of talent or by demonstrating coveted organizational competencies. Leadership skills with motivational components include "human" skill (p. 37), contending that leaders inspire based upon creating trust, exhibiting empathy, and instilling cooperation in others. Another leadership orientation is the *style* approach, which is also skill based, but the emphasis is on concern for others, whereby motivation is enhanced on a relational basis. *Relational* leaders encourage positive self-worth in others by providing efficacy enhancing opportunities, seeking common ground among employees to promote harmonious intra-group relations, and leading by example through the demonstration of even-tempered emotional regulation.

Second, the *situational approach* described by Northouse (2007) is more descriptive of informal leadership as this style is predicated on assuming leadership roles under the particular circumstances encountered in one's job. Situational leadership suggests that leadership style fluctuates based upon context of application and is highly contingent upon the experience and orientation of those being led. Situational leadership operates under the premise that individual behaviors fluctuate, implying that a unitary approach to leading others may at times be a mismatch. By example, Robert Knowling, Jr. may be described as a situational leader because his style when embarking on a new leadership role is to interview all employees and understand the beliefs, values, and expectations the staff has of the organization as a prelude to determining his business strategy. Knowling described setting up regular town hall meetings, designed to give individuals a forum to express concerns. Knowling also revealed that at times he would go to the homes of employees (strategically armed with extrinsically motivating food and beverage) as a strategy to get to know colleagues so that he could effectively modify his leadership style to meet the individual needs of his constituents.

Third, related to the situational approach is the *contingency* approach to leadership, which has a greater contextual focus. Contingency leadership suggests that specific trait-based leadership qualities are more appropriate for some organizational challenges than others. For example, the previously described Edsel debacle suggests that a leader with highly refined communication and relationship skills may have averted the disaster that was based upon an erroneous assessment of consumer preferences and desires.

The style of leader needed to meet a work challenge, such as poor productivity or high operational expense, would be very different from that of a leader needed to encourage intra-team communication. The leader–challenge match, which is similar to the educator–learner zone of proximal development in classrooms, stresses compatibility as the most important criterion to illustrate the contingency leadership approach.

The more salient solution for the MD is knowing how individual differences in leaders produce positive motivation in others. Foremost, leaders enhance motivation with a prominent focus on the needs of those being led, creating conditions that offer employees the perception of progress (Amabile & Kramer, 2010). Although individual progress is highly subjective, leaders are perceived as effective based upon the belief that leader's role is to contribute to, not manage or impede, individual growth. Zhang and Bartol (2010) synthesized multiple leadership theories and advocated the concept of *psychological empowerment* as a means to inspire motivated work behavior. Unlike the process-oriented empowerment exhibited by SDWTs, psychological empowerment is based upon leaders instilling a psychological state of independence in others that inspires feelings of competency and affirms that their work has value and meaning. When individuals internalize psychological empowerment, they develop an empowered role identity (Stryker & Burke, 2000). Internalization is exemplified by a state of employee enlightenment, a condition that is empirically shown to unleash creativity and foster intrinsic motivation (Amabile, 1983; Zhang & Bartol, 2010).

Fourth, motivating inspired employees is often described as the *transformational* approach (Bass & Avolio, 1990), or the ability of leaders to first create a strategic vision and then alter the work context sufficiently by providing individuals with both the tools and motivation to reach organizational goals. The pragmatic intent of this leadership philosophy is to seemingly transform the apathetic or indifferent employee into an individual who perceives personal and organizational values and goals unified, and sufficiently congruous to change his or her own behavior for the good of the organization. Transformational leaders are unashamedly outspoken and have the ability to persuade individuals to improve skills and reach the pinnacle of their abilities. Empirically, transformative leaders are perceived by employees to be more charismatic, show a greater frequency of challenging employees intellectually, and demonstrate individualized concern for people, in comparison with those exhibiting *transactional* leadership approaches, which puts greater emphasis on improving work processes (Lowe, Kroeck, & Sivasubramaniam, 1996).

Transformative leaders use at least four strategies to motivate employees. First, the leader understands the importance of respect and trust and intentionally models behaviors grounded in ethical and moral behavior. The leader's behavior is motivating because it is predictable and forthright, facilitating feelings of safety, acceptance, and trust. Second, the transformative leader challenges the status quo and unfounded legacy beliefs. The clichéd rationalization of "we have always done it that way" is questioned, and procedures are changed when work values and strategy justify transformation. The leader models critical thinking and openly challenges prejudicial thoughts and stereotypic actions deemed unproductive and demotivating. Third, the leader is an optimistic organizational champion, fully integrating organizational values into the self while encouraging spirit and camaraderie through organized efforts and measurable events. Finally, the transformational leader is not adversarial or critical but, instead, is an inviting and dedicated partner and coach, investing time and effort into employee development as the unilateral key to personal and organizational success. In aggregate, leaders lead by example, modeling the types of behaviors they expect from others while demonstrating that organizational success is unattainable without synchronized effort that results in both the individual and the organization becoming truly co-dependent isomorphic partners harboring similar goals and a complementary vision.

Optimizing motivation for athletic and public performances

The techniques used to propel academic or work achievement are, at times, radically different from those strategies that energize athletic and public performance. Although normative comparison is often an unavoidable consequence of academic and employment success, the degree of emphasis on competitive behavior and the pervasive quest for peer-group superiority is the primary objective for most participants and team members in performance professions. Known as "performance or sport psychology," the domain examines conditions where competitive human performance is demonstrated to an audience, involving pressure and dramatic consequences for performance deficits. In addition, research examines the mental skills needed for peak performance, health-related physical activity, and high-pressure public presentations.

The primary distinction segregating performance motivation from academic or work motivation is a focus on the interaction of physiology and cognition needed for optimal performance results (Hays, 2012). Evidence from biopsychology, and specifically from neurology, indicates multiplicative and multi-dimensional interactions between how individuals psychologically prepare for episodes of performance and how the body responds (see Principle #14 (p. 50)). The symbiotic mind–body partnership of the performer implies that unlike most academic domains where biology is a subordinate influence, performance domains demand regulatory-control strategies that address both the biological and cognitive aspects of a performance challenge. Further, public performers must contend with the whims and emotions of a hostile audience, which, like many social influences, may significantly alter the quality of the performance. Unlike academics, where knowledge is often created and developed implicitly and privately, performance in public domains is rarely demonstrated in isolation and demands that the public performer maintain stout regulatory and emotional control to effectively fend off the negative contingencies when demonstrating skills in a public forum.

Competition is an absolute requirement inherent to most types of public performance. During competitions participants strive to reach certain predetermined performance standards, some of which are criterion in nature, such as bettering one's past performance, correctly reciting memorized lines, or making a desired number of basketball shots. Alternatively, and more frequently in performance domains, results are normatively evaluated in comparison with other contestants. Competitions typically reward one or more individuals who reach mutually desirable goals at the expense of other participants, designating clear "winners" and "losers." Considering the polarity of potential outcomes for performers, it is important to evaluate self-perceptions and determine whether individuals have normative or criterion goal strivings. Knowing the type of goal and the extent of social comparison will influence the choice and suitability of subsequent strategy interventions based upon the complexity of the relationship between competition and performance.

The one-size-fits-all strategy solution is unsustainable, despite the purported meta-analytic null relation between competition and performance (Murayama & Elliot, 2012), which broadly suggests that competition is neither beneficial nor detrimental to performance. Upon closer scrutiny, the nuances of competition reveal that under certain circumstances competition and the source of motives can enhance performance, while under different circumstances, competition undermines performance. When individuals believe they will compare favorably with others, which usually happens when a task is perceived as easy or is well learned, the prospect of competition will boost performance. Favorable comparisons elevate personal competency beliefs and energize the performer through associating positive affect with the process of reaching performance goals, usually as a "winner," ultimately enhancing intrinsic motivation and feelings of competency and pride. Conversely, competition will inhibit goal attainment, and interfere with reaching performance targets, when a person believes he or she compares unfavorably with others, which typically happens when tasks are perceived as overly complex, or when novice self-perceptions prevail. The dubious individual who questions personal competency may likely feel like a victim of circumstance, overmatched and faced with the precarious prospect of real or imagined impending failure. Lack of positive outcomes is attributed to personally inferior skills or to the superior ability of others, often impeding intrinsic interest and undermining the will to compete.

Individuals will go to great lengths to overcome their competitive and corresponding normative concerns. Skating historians may remember the tumultuous career of Tanya Harding, former US figure skating champion, who was implicated along with her husband and others during the 1994 US Figure Skating Championships for a clubbing attack on the knee of her top competitor, Nancy Kerrigan. The attack knocked Kerrigan out of the competition, and Harding was crowned best US female free-style skater in 1994. Although Harding denied conspirator knowledge of the dastardly plot to "squash" her competition, she pled guilty to obstructing a criminal investigation, and consequently received a lifetime ban from the skating association and had her figure-skating title stripped. Although the sensational Harding–Kerrigan fiasco was an unorthodox remedy for the trepidations of competition, the example illustrates the inescapable power of others on perceptions of individual capabilities.

More ethical and practical strategies exist to overcome the competition and develop advanced performance skill than assaulting one's rival. One prominent method specifically designed to scaffold athletic talent is the *Developmental Model of Sport Participation* (DMSP; Côté, Ericsson, & Law, 2005). The holistic model is broadly based upon cognitive models of developing expertise across domains (Ericsson & Charness, 1994; Ericsson, Krampe, & Tesch-Römer, 1993) and specifies that domain competency is achieved through deliberate practice and ardent social support. Domain mastery results from intentional, targeted, and overlearned responses initiated early in life that often take over 10,000 hours to realize. *Deliberate practice* refers to:

> ...practice activities done with the specific instrumental goal of improving performance and which (a) are performed in a daily, work-like manner; (b) require effort and attention; (c) do not lead to immediate social or financial rewards; and (d) are frequently not enjoyable to perform.
> Baker, Côté and Abernethy (2003, p. 13)

Although the DMSP is crafted as a model of skill development, many of the criteria needed for domain mastery are motivational constructs, including the role of sustained and dedicated effort, a focus on the development of intrinsic interest, and many social support contingencies. The emphasis on motivational strategies is rather implicit, and perhaps it is taken for granted that optimal performance is unattainable without resolute focus and intense drive, regardless of domain.

The DMSP model entails enlisting the support of significant others, such as parents and siblings, to create and sustain environmental conditions conducive to skill development (Côté, 1999). Social support is initially exhibited during *deliberate play*, when children gather to have fun, rather than to improve skills. Some of us may have fond childhood memories of youthful and adolescent athletic experiences guided by a loose set of context-specific rules that defy many descriptions of sport (e.g., the tree is out of bounds, and the garbage can is second base). In reality, these types of social activities were semi-organized athletics, suggested or endorsed by parents and guardians, which satisfied the need for belongingness and camaraderie among players while tacitly building interpersonal and socialization skills. By puberty, a shift occurs, and deliberate play evolves into deliberate practice targeted toward one particular domain, with the specific intention of skill development achieved through many hours of practice (Baker, & Côté, 2006). Throughout the transition from sandlot to stadium, the aspiring elite performer is emotionally supported and behaviorally encouraged, as family life often revolves around skill development and exhibitions by the dedicated performer. Emotional support includes helping the performer deal with setbacks and modulating the fluctuations in self-esteem that often accompany slumps or losing streaks; but support also includes helping the player to deal with escalating pressure as the performance stakes mount (Lauer, Gould, Roman, & Pierce, 2010).

The performance coach plays a unique role in scaffolding adaptive motivation because a coach's success is contingent solely on the effort and results of others. Expert coaching is typically determined by longevity alone, but only when the coach's experience generates quality performers who achieve winning records (Wiman, Salmoni, & Hall, 2010). Coaching exceptionalism is primarily attributed to the advanced domain knowledge of the coach. In addition, exceptionalism includes the ability to establish productive interpersonal relationships with the performer, as well as with staff, parents, and media, and by the ability to generate confidence and character in those being coached (Côté & Gilbert, 2009). Confidence means helping individuals feel competent and perceive a sense of overall positive self-worth, while character implies being a productive and caring team member. Coaches are rated as more effective when confidence is instilled by creating a mastery-orientated motivational climate whereby performers believe personal development has more value than winning or losing (Cumming, Smoll, Smith, & Grossbard, 2007). Conversely, coaches are rated poorly and deemed less effective when the coach promotes intrateam rivalries, favors the most talented players, and punishes players for making mistakes (Cumming et al., 2007). Research supporting the superiority of specific coaching motivational strategies is quite scarce (Gould & Wright, 2012), perhaps as a consequence of perceived challenges reported by coaches when teaching strategies, such as handling pressure, self-confidence, and emotional control (Gould, Medbery, Damarjhian, & Lauer, 1999). Lacking instructional confidence, many coaches may neglect to teach important motivational strategies that are critical for an athlete's overall success.

Ironically, charged with the role of developing expertise in others, a coach may unintentionally set overly aggressive performance targets by putting an inordinate emphasis on flawless performance, thus cultivating perfectionist beliefs in disciples. Empirically, perfectionism comprises two distinct components: a goal-directed adaptive *perfectionist striving* and a highly critical, self-defeating *perfectionist evaluation* (Stoeber, 2011). Perfectionist strivings are enjoyed by performers and propel the individual toward setting and attaining stretch goals while deliberately improving upon one's previous performance. Maladaptive perfectionist evaluations are grounded in an unjustified fear of mistakes and inordinate preoccupation with negative evaluations from coaches and teammates.

The quest for the impeccable is both titillating and enervating for adaptive motivation. For some, perfectionism is an obtainable reality reached through methodical and extensive practice, supported by formative coaching feedback. However, for others, the perfectionist quest is wrought with anxiety and angst and often associated with obsessive behavior and negative results because performers can never reach their own lofty expectations. Similar to the dimension of competition, perfectionism strivings have both criterion and normative roots. Adaptive perfectionism is aligned with criterion standards of self-improvement, while negative ruminations frequently develop when comparing the self with superlative others. In a meta-analytic review, Stoeber and Otto (2006) concluded that when perfectionist strivings are focused toward continuous improvement the strivings will promote elevated conscientiousness, extraversion, positive affect, and self-satisfaction. Consistent with other adaptive social influences, the focus on continuous improvement garners higher levels of social support from the performer's family, teammates, and peers. Alternatively, maladaptive perfectionist evaluations are described as neurotic and compulsive and are empirically related to higher levels of irrational behavior, forestalled social development, negative affect, and doubts about the suitability of one's actions.

A variety of other cognitive strategies are conducive to the motivational enhancement of performers. Many domain-general strategies were reviewed in Chapter 10 (p. 269), including the critical influence of goal setting, motivational monitoring, and environmental restructuring on invigorating performance. However, most premiere athletic and public performers have little flexibility negotiating unalterable team or group performance goals. In addition, athletics and public performances are highly conducive to optimal experience and perceptions of flow (see Principle #12, p. 37) because the individual perceives task challenges commensurate with skill precluding the need for skill-enhancing motivational monitoring. Additionally, the typical performer is situationally disadvantaged when contemplating environmental restructuring unless he or she can magically transport the audience to a different performance venue.

Foremost, successful performers exercise pretask mental management, including the use of strategies that moderate mental arousal, focus concentration, and block out emotional intrusions. Optimal mental arousal is accomplished by creating a state of cognitive and motivational readiness, which includes orchestrating conditions that promote a physiological homeostasis and avoiding emotional highs and lows. The self-mediated cognitive condition allows the individual to cerebrally negotiate the impending performance pressure by using a series of self-talk and relaxation techniques to reach his or her zone of optimal functioning (Hanin, 2000). Focused concentration entails envisioning a successful outcome and the ability to maintain a stalwart focus on the salient aspects of optimal performance despite distractions (Hays & Brown, 2004). Avoiding concentration lapses requires attending to factors within the performer's control and avoiding preoccupation with aspects of a task the performer is unable to influence, such as the quality of competition or the performance environment. By envisioning a performance going well, avoiding negative self-appraisals, and framing the performance as an opportunity to demonstrate practiced skill—rather than as a form for embarrassment or potential failure—a performer can control and constrain emotional intrusions. Most importantly, the most successful performers realize that motivational readiness, like every other physical skill or cognitive ability, results only through sustained and deliberate practice, reaching the point of an overlearned response (Hays & Brown, 2004). When successful the performer is in a state of anticipatory readiness, calm but not sedate, focused and attuned to relevant performance cues, significantly challenged and yet devoid of mental preoccupations, and without any inkling of being overwhelmed.

Motivational strategies to enhance online learning and instructional design

"It's more convenient," "I enjoy the anonymity," or "It's easier and takes less time," are a few of the many motives learners report as instrumental in their preference for online learning in comparison to traditional face-to-face (F2F) classroom instruction. Online learning means that 100% of the course content is delivered using computers and the Internet, while hybrid or blended courses, which are other popular instructional modalities, include both online and traditional classroom components (Tallent-Runnels et al., 2006). Online learning can be accomplished synchronously, when all learners participate at predetermined times, or asynchronously, when learners access and complete coursework at their own discretion, regardless of day or time. Distance learning, often confused with online learning, is characterized by the absence of an educator while learners engage with course material online. The appeal of online learning is massive as projections suggest by the year 2016 over 5,000,000 K-12 students will be enrolled in some type of online learning course (Picciano, Seaman, Shea, & Swan, 2012). Incidence increases in higher education, as 89% of universities offer distance education and degree programs that are fully online (Pew Research Center, 2011), with over 32% of students taking at least one course fully online (Allen & Seaman, 2013). Online and distance delivery of learning content is not limited to academia, as 41.7% of Fortune 500 companies currently use educational technology to enhance employee knowledge and skills, with greater frequency anticipated in the foreseeable future (Pappas, 2013).

Despite the ubiquitous appeal and escalating prevalence of online learning, a dichotomy exists between those learners who are motivated to engage in online learning and those who elect to disengage and abandon online education. Part of the conundrum is the debate concerning the relationship of instructional modality to achievement, which is clearly...ambiguous. Although situational use of computer technology often boosts short-term learning (Tamim, Bernard, Borokhovski, Abrami, & Schmid, 2011), direct achievement comparisons between F2F and fully online modalities often find few learning benefits attributable to learning platform alone (Clark, 1994; Ross, Morrison, & Lowther, 2010). Instead, researchers often suggest that the efficiency of instructional design, the type of pedagogy used during instruction, and specific learning strategies are more influential for learning effectiveness, regardless of the medium used to deliver learning content (Tamim et al., 2011).

Seeking to determine why more learners disengage from online courses than from F2F classes, Winiecki, Fenner, and Chyung (1999) surmised that learners found discrepancies between online course structure and personal expectations, had doubts concerning the effectiveness of their online communications, and questioned the efficacy of online learning to promote competency. Others conclusions from the same study indicated that online learning was depersonalized and lacked the necessary opportunities for social interaction needed to keep learners engaged. In a qualitative study examining learner perceptions, Mupinga, Nora, and Yaw (2006) concluded that during course participation learners expected to be intellectually challenged, have regular communication with the instructor, and get assignment feedback. Unfortunately, many learner expectations often go unfulfilled, and learners and educators lament that many online courses foster disassociation from the social learning culture that is typically encountered during traditional instruction (Larreamendy-Joerns & Leinhardt, 2006).

In addition to the learner-centered concerns outlined, course design issues can broadly influence motivation. One frequent complaint of online learners is the simplistic design of some courses. Minimalist design stymies learner interest, leading some learners to believe that course features, such as repetitive text-based discussions, impede their ability to develop and use higher-order cognitive skills, such as creative thinking (Boling, Hough, Krinsky, Saleem, & Stevens, 2012). Course complexity can also be a concern, as unsophisticated design may subject the learner to distracting and superfluous elements unessential to learning. In addition, learners tend to underestimate the initial complexity of distance and online learning and may experience significant cognitive overload attempting to learn course navigation and course protocol as they adjust to the self-regulated nature of the task (Tyler-Smith, 2006). Further, course content incommensurate with learner expertise often results in disengagement, such as when the novice learner is overwhelmed due to difficulty perceptions, or when the experienced learner becomes bored and cognitively disengages (Kalyuga, 2007). At minimum, adaptive motivation during online learning is contingent upon first understanding learner perceptions of online education, including assessing situational academic goals and intellectual needs. In addition, promoting enhanced interest, persistence, and academic engagement necessitates an examination of the best practices related to instructional design in distance education.

Evidence is limited concerning the reasons why learners choose online courses in favor of blended or F2F classes. Instead, research focuses on understanding how to retain online students, or determining reasons for dropout and disengagement. However, when reported, a frequent rationale for selecting online courses is the ability to personally control the timing and pace of learning, which allows learners to access course materials when it is convenient and suitable to individual lifestyles (Clayton, Blumberg, & Auld, 2010; Kim & Frick, 2011; Larreamendy-Joerns & Leinhardt, 2006; Paechter, Maier, & Macher, 2010). Unfortunately, motives of accessibility do not bode well for engagement and often result in superficial and questionable intrinsic motivation when learners value a course primarily for convenience purposes. Clearly, the most frequently reported reason for disengagement from an online course or program is lack of study and participation time, suggesting that learners underestimate the labor intensity needed to effectively complete an online course (Aragon & Johnson, 2008) and likely make instructional modality decisions for reasons unrelated to content mastery.

Learners often are ill-prepared to successfully master the fundamental aspects of an online course, harboring misconceptions concerning preparation and the thoroughness needed for successful completion of discussion topics, which are the primary means of communicating with instructors and fellow learners. During an analysis of asynchronous discussions, Lee (2013) determined that precourse perceptions of what was considered a thorough discussion response were predictive of academic success. Those learners with minimal advance preparation tend to produce shallow responses lacking both detail and examples of higher-order thinking. Learners accurately calibrated with discussion expectations, and those who used more deep-processing strategies, including frequent instances of critical thinking, obtained higher grades. Content relevance, and the suitability of the modality for the learner's personal needs also influences retention and engagement. When learners ascribe relevance and value to course content and also have confidence in their ability to self-regulate in a computer-based environment, motivation is consistently sustained throughout an entire course, compared with those perceiving a course as having minimal personal relevance (Kim & Frick, 2011).

Assuming that learners are informed about the realistic challenges inherent to online learning and are sufficiently aware of the structural nuances and pitfalls associated with the modality, the MD can turn to specific design strategies found to enhance learner engagement and persistence. A guiding principle to select optimal strategies is the realization that learners use different cognitive and motivational strategies to accomplish learning based on the modality of instruction (Azevedo, Johnson, Chauncey, & Burkett, 2010; Clayton et al., 2010; Kim & Frick, 2011; Shea & Bidjerano, 2010). For example, Clayton et al. (2010) investigated basic motivational differences of learners between online and traditional learning environments and found that the frequency of mastery learners and those with enhanced personal interest were more prevalently found in traditional learning environments than online. In addition, traditional learners were more willing to expend academic effort than students with an online learning preference. Those individuals who elected traditional classes believed they were more engaged based upon the spontaneous nature of F2F classes, which encourage communications with both instructors and peers, a luxury often unavailable to the online learner.

Successful online learning involves the deployment of many self-directed learning strategies, such as planning, meta-monitoring, and reflection, to mitigate the nonlinear, open-ended nature of online course design (Azevedo & Witherspoon, 2009). During online learning, the learner is given considerably more discretion, responsibility, and independence to achieve learning goals than during the traditional classroom experience. Learners must be diligent, logging in frequently to participate in discussions and effectively monitor and assess the work of peers. Sometimes, learners are overwhelmed by the required amount of participation, while at other times, learners are frustrated and dismayed at the lack of responses to their own work. The variable and unpredictable nature of participation often leads to superficial posting quality and loss of momentum by discussion participants (Dringus & Ellis, 2010). In practical terms, when online, learners must be masters of their own domains. Unlike F2F instruction, where learners rely more heavily on teacher interaction and can immediately seek instructor clarification or pose a provocative question to jumpstart a conversation, the online learner navigates content in solitude, often facing the specter of cognitive vacuity. The learner must fend off boredom, avoid distractions, and at all costs resist the alluring nature of intellectual curiosity, which during online learning can quickly propel the focused learner from targeted objectives to the farthest and almost infinite reaches of the Internet, thwarting learning goals and potentially impacting achievement.

The design of online learning environments are often based upon the principles of Keller's ARCS model of instructional design (Keller, 2008). The model is particularly useful to understand the nature of online motivation because it focuses on attention, persistence, and learner control; three recurring consequences inherent to the highly independent nature of online learning. Keller's model has four design elements (attention, relevance, confidence, and satisfaction) that are critical to engagement and learning. (1) Attention refers to arousing learner curiosity by creating an intellectual match between instructional content and learner interests. Adaptive learning technology, such as MetaTutor (Azevedo, Johnson, Chauncey, & Burkett, 2010), automatically adjusts material content and complexity based upon a pattern of learner responses and is especially useful to avoid disengagement based upon waning interest or fleeting learner curiosity. (2) Relevance refers to convincing the learner that content has utility, meaning, and value and is consistent with future learner goals (see Principle #49, p. 281). Computer-prompted directions and reminders about learning goals using language, such as "Learning this content will allow you to..." provide individual purpose and applied value for the learner. (3) Instilling confidence averts disengagement when learners believe they are ill-equipped to surmount unfamiliar technology environments or complex content. Confidence is also realized when learners feel in control of their learning destiny. Controls, such as judiciously placed hypermedia that allow recursive learning, including providing linkages to content glossaries or worked examples, provide another element of control that a learner can access when the need for elaboration or clarification is perceived. (4) Satisfaction, the last objective of Keller's model, derives from meaningful learning that promotes a sense of competence in the learner while meeting other personal learner goals, such as attaining specific learning milestones. Certain strategies, such as embedded competency-related feedback and extrinsic recognition of mastery, are useful substitutes to deliver the emotional and motivational scaffolding that is often elusive to the online instruction environment (Kim, 2012).

Besides structural design aspects of online learning, human presence is of paramount importance to motivate online learners. Considering that most instances of online learning are classified as distant, design efforts must overcompensate for the inconsistent human involvement. Presence is accomplished through active instructor interventions and by emphasizing learner-to-learner interaction (Dixson, 2010). Instructor presence is of critical importance because learners perceive instructor interaction, posting contributions, and feedback as indicative of instructor motivation and concern for the learners (Shea, Sau Li, & Pickett, 2006). Instructional approaches, such as clearly communicating discussion protocol and requiring learners to acknowledge understanding via a learning contract or a verification quiz, are easily implemented strategies to avoid misinterpretation and overcome initial unfamiliarity with course navigation (Wise, Perera, Hsiao, Speer, & Marbouti, 2012). Considering that many online learners complain about feeling isolated (Lewis & Abdul-Hamid, 2006), regular instructor interaction with learners via targeted feedback that focuses on the most salient course content (Boling et al., 2012) can serve as an important scaffold for consistent course participation and a reason for continual engagement.

Finally, advances in adaptive computer-assisted technology hold strong promise to automate many of the interactive motivational and discourse-enabling strategies described. Animated pedagogical agents (APAs), which are computer-generated tutorial scaffolds that use natural language (Baylor & Kim, 2005; Gholson et al., 2009; Moreno & Mayer, 2004) can be designed specifically to support learner motivation. APAs foster instructional advantages due to the encouragement of deep comprehension through inquiry learning and adaptive questioning based upon specific learner response patterns. Additionally, APAs can be programmed to model appropriate regulatory strategies that align with successful learning outcomes (Graesser & McNamara, 2010; Walkington, 2013). Researchers have frequently manipulated APA personality, affect, facial expressions, gestures, agent gender, and voice inflection (Baylor & Kim, 2009; Frechette & Moreno, 2010; Moreno & Mayer, 2004) to determine what type of agent is most suitable for a particular learning situation. Design variations can regulate what agents actually say to a learner, including voice inflection and emphasis.

Although specific research is rare and inconclusive concerning which type of APA best promotes adaptive motivation, studies suggest that agents that use social clues to emphasize monitoring and control of motivation, and those which provide explanatory feedback may foster enhanced motivation in learners (Heidig & Clarebout, 2011).

At least four conclusions seem warranted to promote the motivation of online and distance learners. First, learners should be informed of course expectations and clearly understand the time commitment and labor intensity of distance learning. Second, course functionality, details about course navigation, and discussion protocols should be mandatory elements of course orientation. Third, a proactive stance should be assumed to address and mitigate the probability of waning motivation over the lifespan of a course. Consistent course involvement via instructor presence and cultivation of a learning culture that emphasizes learner-to-learner interaction is essential. Fourth, the convenience motive for course selection should not be ignored. An inordinate design emphasis should be placed on creating core content with personal relevance, practical value, and future utility to mitigate course selection merely for lifestyle convenience.

Chapter summary/conclusions

The "one size fits all" approach to motivating others is often untenable. The aspiring MD would be foolhardy to expect optimal and universal applicability of strategy interventions across all domains and contexts. Although many rewarding domain-general strategy approaches were described in Chapter 10, frequently, the specific context or location of an intervention is the decisive factor to determine which interventions are situationally robust to combat maladaptive motivation. Academic contexts demand strategy flexibility; some learners are motivated by extrinsic reward, but more often motivational strategies should be directed toward the internalization of knowledge to promote intrinsic motivation. Premiere interventions leverage the social nature of learning and establish an autonomy-supportive classroom culture. Such practices as learner-determined academic goals and providing choices within curricular boundaries motivate learners because the perception of teacher control is diminished. Showing personal concern for the learner, using constructivist pedagogies, and consciously generating learner interest are also effective as these strategies are authentic and actively engage the learner.

Unlike the individual focus of academia, work environments often demand a collective emphasis on motivation. Organizational motivation benefits from a systemic effort focused on a well-articulated culture that supports a unified business strategy. Culture implicitly sets boundaries for intra-organizational normative behavior, including which behaviors are recognized and rewarded by the organization. Group cohesion and teamwork often supersede individual goals and are a primary determinant of organizational success. Working in teams is a social motivator that enhances identity by creating strong emotional connections with others while concurrently satisfying affiliation and altruistic motives. Leadership style is frequently the key difference between adaptive and maladaptive motivation within an organization. Leadership can be formally or informally assumed by individuals or created through SDWTs comprising frontline employees empowered to make critical organizational decisions. Leaders who inspire, exhume integrity, promote transparency, and who consistently model organizational values will likely cultivate enhanced motivation, loyalty, and trust among their followers.

Athletic and public performance motivation are influenced by an audience, high-stakes outcomes, and the reality of victory or defeat. Self-perceptions and knowing the performer's goals (normative or criterion) will influence strategy decisions. Favorable normative comparisons elevate personal competency beliefs and energize the performer, while negative comparisons lead to performance deficits. Social support, an experienced coach, and moderate perfectionist strivings accelerate performances because along with deliberate practice, these strategies provide emotional scaffolding that sustains the performer through inevitable obstacles. Inspiring successful athletic and public performance in others demands a focus on personal development, not performance outcomes. Individuals boost their own performance through visioning, positive self-talk, and effective emotional regulation of factors within the performer's control.

Many learners choose online learning for motives of convenience or under the belief that online courses require less effort than F2F instruction. Motivation for online instruction is contingent upon understanding learner perceptions of online education, including assessment of situational academic goals and the intellectual needs of the learner. To promote enhanced interest, persistence, and academic engagement educators should minimally communicate course expectations, explain course navigation, and stress the importance of self-regulation to thrive in an asynchronous learning environment. Learners are best motivated during online instruction when instructors have a consistent course presence, coupled with establishing a highly interactive online culture that requires frequent learner-to-learner and learner-to-educator communication.

Next steps

Devoid of the opportunity to implement change, the best strategy knowledge often becomes useless. Even when opportunities are available, inspiring change in the self and others is often extremely complex, challenging, and a potentially frustrating effort because individuals and organizations frequently resist change. In addition to comprehensive strategy knowledge, the competent MD must be adept in convincing others of the utility and benefits of motivational evolution. The final chapter focuses on why and how individuals resist change, the conditions needed to implement change, and elaboration of techniques to foster change and overcome the inevitable obstacles that can impede the overall effectiveness of the highly knowledgeable MD. The chapter reintroduces **Amada Boxtel** and describes her courageous battle to change herself after her horrendous accident. The chapter concludes with a synopsis of the motivational leaders profiled in the text, including a summary of the motivational strategies that have led to their personal and professional success.

End of chapter motivational minute

Strategies outlined in this chapter:

- **Promoting adaptive academic motivation**—these strategies are specifically designed to promote classroom learning and the mastery of curriculum.

- **Strategies to motivate work performance**—these strategies propel performance within formal organizations under the influence of leaders or work teams.
- **Optimizing motivation for athletic and public performances**—these approaches require harnessing physiological and psychological skills in audience forums.
- **Motivational strategies to enhance online learning and instructional design**—these strategies are crafted for self-paced and web-based knowledge acquisition.

Key terminology (in order of chapter presentation):

- **Deliberate play**—engaging in an activity to have fun as opposed to enhancing skill.
- **Deliberate practice**—effortful and regular practice completed in a work-like fashion to improve skill with no expectation of social or financial rewards.
- **Perfectionist striving**—adaptive performance goals that propel performers toward setting and attaining stretch goals while deliberately improving upon one's previous performance.
- **Perfectionist evaluation**—maladaptive, irrational, and unrealistic perfectionist strivings that are neurotic and compulsive because the perfectionist goal is unobtainable.
- **Psychological empowerment**—a psychological state of independence used by leaders to inspire competency in workers and show that their work has value and meaning.
- **Transformational leadership**—a leadership style that creates and communicates a strategic vision that sufficiently alters the work context and behavioral practices to encourage personal growth and organizational change.

References

Allen, I. E., & Seaman, J. (2013). *Changing course: Ten years of tracking online education in the United States.* Retrieved on November 6, 2014 from: <http://files.eric.ed.gov/fulltext/ED541571.pdf>

Allen, K. E., Stelzner, S. P., & Wielkiewicz, R. M. (1999). The ecology of leadership: Adapting to the challenges of a changing world. *Journal of Leadership & Organizational Studies, 5*(2), 62–82. http://dx.doi.org/10.1177/107179199900500207.

Amabile, T. M. (1983). The social psychology of creativity: A componential conceptualization. *Journal of Personality and Social Psychology, 45,* 357–376.

Amabile, T. M., & Kramer, S. J. (2010). What really motivates workers. *Harvard Business Review, 88*(1), 44–45.

Anderman, L. H., Andrzejewski, C. E., & Allen, J. (2011). How do teachers support students' motivation and learning in their classrooms? *Teachers College Record, 113*(5), 969–1003.

Aragon, S. R., & Johnson, E. S. (2008). Factors influencing completion and noncompletion of community college online courses. *The American Journal of Distance Education, 22*(3), 146–158.

Azevedo, R., Johnson, A., Chauncey, A., & Burkett, C. (2010). Self-regulated learning with MetaTutor: Advancing the science of learning with metacognitive tools. In M. S. Khine & I. M. Saleh (Eds.), *New science of learning* (pp. 225–247). New York, NY: Springer.

Azevedo, R., & Witherspoon, A. M. (2009). Self-regulated use of hypermedia. In D. J. Hacker, J. Dunlosky, & A. C. Graesser (Eds.), *Handbook of metacognition in education* (pp. 319–339). New York, NY: Routledge.

Baghcheghi, N., Koohestani, H. R., & Rezaei, K. (2011). A comparison of the cooperative learning and traditional learning methods in theory classes on nursing students' communication skill with patients at clinical settings. *Nurse Education Today, 31*(8), 877–882. http://dx.doi.org/10.1016/j.nedt.2011.01.006.

Baker, J., Côté, J., & Abernethy, B. (2003). Sport-specific practice and the development of expert decision-making in team ball sports. *Journal of Applied Sport Psychology*, *15*(1), 12–25. http://dx.doi.org/10.1080/10413200305400.

Baker, J., & Côté, J. (2006). Shifting training requirements during athlete development: Deliberate practice, deliberate play and other sport involvement in the acquisition of sport expertise. *Essential Processes for Attaining Peak Performance*, *1*, 92–109.

Bass, B. M., & Avolio, B. J. (1990). The implications of transactional and transformational leadership for individual, team, and organizational development. *Research in Organizational Change and Development*, *4*(1), 231–272.

Batt, R. (2004). Who benefits from teams? Comparing workers, supervisors, and managers. *Industrial Relations*, *43*, 183–212.

Baylor, A. L., & Kim, S. (2009). Designing nonverbal communication for pedagogical agents: When less is more. *Computers in Human Behavior*, *25*(2), 450–457.

Baylor, A. L., & Kim, Y. (2005). Simulating instructional roles through pedagogical agents. *International Journal of Artificial Intelligence in Education*, *15*, 95–115.

Bedwell, W. L., Shuffler, M. L., Wildman, J. L., & Salas, E. (2010). Self-directed work teams: Best practices for leadership development. In M. G. Rothstein & R. J. Burke (Eds.), *Self-management and leadership development* (pp. 251–294). Northampton, MA: Edward Elgar Publishing.

Belland, B. R., Kim, C., & Hannafin, M. J. (2013). A framework for designing scaffolds that improve motivation and cognition. *Educational Psychologist*, *48*(4), 243–270. http://dx.doi.org/10.1080/00461520.2013.838920.

Bettinger, E. P. (2012). Paying to learn: The effect of financial incentives on elementary school test scores. *Review of Economics and Statistics*, *94*(3), 686–698.

Boling, E. C., Hough, M., Krinsky, H., Saleem, H., & Stevens, M. (2012). Cutting the distance in distance education: Perspectives on what promotes positive, online learning experiences. *The Internet and Higher Education*, *15*(2), 118–126. http://dx.doi.org/10.1016/j.iheduc.2011.11.006.

Bronfenbrenner, U. (1977). Toward an experimental ecology of human development. *American Psychologist*, *32*(7), 513–531.

Burke, C. S., Stagl, K. C., Klein, C., Goodwin, G. F., Salas, E., & Halpin, S. M. (2006). What type of leadership behaviors are functional in teams? A meta-analysis. *The Leadership Quarterly*, *17*(3), 288–307. http://dx.doi.org/10.1016/j.leaqua.2006.02.007.

Carlile, P. R. (2004). Transferring, translating, and transforming: An integrative framework for managing knowledge across boundaries. *Organization Science*, *15*(5), 555–568. http://dx.doi.org/10.1287/orsc.1040.0094.

Carraher, T. N., Carraher, D. W., & Schliemann, A. D. (1985). Mathematics in the streets and in schools. *British Journal of Developmental Psychology*, *3*, 21–29.

Carron, A. V., Martin, L. J., & Loughead, T. M. (2012). Team work and performance. In S. M. Murphy (Ed.), *The Oxford handbook of sport and performance psychology* (pp. 309–327). Oxford, England: Oxford University Press.

Carson, J. B., Tesluk, P. E., & Marrone, J. A. (2007). Shared leadership in teams: An investigation of antecedent conditions and performance. *Academy of Management Journal*, *50*(5), 1217–1234.

Chandler, D. E., Kram, K. E., & Yip, J. (2011). An ecological systems perspective on mentoring at work: A review and future prospects. *Academy of Management Annals*, *5*(1), 519–570. http://dx.doi.org/10.1080/19416520.2011.576087.

Chen, G., & Kanfer, R. (2006). Toward a systems theory of motivated behavior in work teams. *Research in Organizational Behavior*, *27*, 223–267.

Clark, R. E. (1994). Media will never influence learning. *Educational Technology Research and Development*, *42*(2), 21–29. http://dx.doi.org/10.1007/BF02299088.

Clark, R. E. (2005). 5 research-tested team motivation strategies. *Performance Improvement, 44*(1), 13–16.

Clayton, K., Blumberg, F., & Auld, D. P. (2010). The relationship between motivation, learning strategies and choice of environment whether traditional or including an online component. *British Journal of Educational Technology, 41*(3), 349–364. http://dx.doi.org/10.1111/j.1467-8535.2009.00993.x.

Combs, J., Liu, Y., Hall, A., & Ketchen, D. (2006). How much do high-performance work practices matter? A meta-analysis of their effects on organizational performance. *Personnel Psychology, 13*(3), 501.

Côté, J. (1999). The influence of the family in the development of talent in sport. *The Sport Psychologist, 13,* 395–417.

Côté, J., Ericsson, K. A., & Law, M. P. (2005). Tracing the development of athletes using retrospective interview methods: A proposed interview and validation procedure for reported information. *Journal of Applied Sport Psychology, 17*(1), 1–19. http://dx.doi.org/10.1080/10413200590907531.

Côté, J., & Gilbert, W. (2009). An integrative definition of coaching effectiveness and expertise. *International Journal of Sports Science & Coaching, 4*(3), 307–323.

Crabtree, S. (2013). *Worldwide, 13% of employees are engaged at work.* Retrieved on January 26, 2015 from: <http://www.gallup.com/poll/165269/worldwide-employees-engaged-work.aspx>

Cumming, S. P., Smoll, F. L., Smith, R. E., & Grossbard, J. R. (2007). Is winning everything? The relative contributions of motivational climate and won-lost percentage in youth sports. *Journal of Applied Sport Psychology, 19*(3), 322–336. http://dx.doi.org/10.1080/10413200701342640.

Dicke, T. (2010). The Edsel: Forty years as a symbol of failure. *Journal of Popular Culture, 43*(3), 486–502. http://dx.doi.org/10.1111/j.1540-5931.2010.00754.x.

Dignath, C., Buettner, G., & Langfeldt, H. P. (2008). How can primary school students learn self-regulated learning strategies most effectively? A meta-analysis on self-regulation training programmes. *Educational Research Review, 3*(2), 101–129.

Dixson, M. D. (2010). Creating effective student engagement in online courses: What do students find engaging? *Journal of the Scholarship of Teaching and Learning, 10*(2), 1–13.

Dringus, L. P., & Ellis, T. (2010). Temporal transitions in participation flow in an asynchronous discussion forum. *Computers & Education, 54*(2), 340–349. http://dx.doi.org/10.1016/j.compedu.2009.08.011.

Durlak, J. A., Weissberg, R. P., & Pachan, M. (2010). A meta-analysis of after-school programs that seek to promote personal and social skills in children and adolescents. *American Journal of Community Psychology, 45*(3–4), 294–309.

Ericsson, K. A., & Charness, N. (1994). Expert performance: Its structure and acquisition. *American Psychologist, 49,* 725–747.

Ericsson, K. A., Krampe, R. T., & Tesch-Römer, C. (1993). The role of deliberate practice in the acquisition of expert performance. *Psychological Review, 3,* 363–406.

Falchikov, N. (2013). *Improving assessment through student involvement: Practical solutions for aiding learning in higher and further education.* New York, NY: Routledge.

Fiorella, L., & Mayer, R. E. (2012). Paper-based aids for learning with a computer-based game. *Journal of Educational Psychology, 104*(4), 1074–1082. http://dx.doi.org/10.1037/a0028088.

Fleishman, E. A., Mumford, M. D., Zaccaro, S. J., Levin, K. Y., Korotkin, A. L., & Hein, M. B. (1992). Taxonomic efforts in the description of leader behavior: A synthesis and functional interpretation. *The Leadership Quarterly, 2*(4), 245–287.

Fortune (2014). *Most admired 2014*. Retrieved on November 11, 2014 from: <http://fortune.com/worlds-most-admired-companies/>

Frechette, C., & Moreno, R. (2010). The roles of animated pedagogical agents' presence and nonverbal communication in multimedia learning environments. *Journal of Media Psychology: Theories, Methods, and Applications, 22*(2), 61–72.

Frumkin, J. J. (2010). Rewards, positive reinforcement, and incentives systems. In R. Watkins & D. Leigh (Eds.), *Handbook of improving performance in the workplace: Vol. 2. Selecting and implementing performance interventions* (pp. 465–481). San Francisco, CA: Pfeiffer.

Gholson, B., Witherspoon, A., Morgan, B., Brittingham, J. K., Coles, R., Graesser, A. C., et al. (2009). Exploring the deep-level reasoning questions effect during vicarious learning among eighth to eleventh graders in the domains of computer literacy and Newtonian physics. *Instructional Science, 37*(5), 487–493.

Gockel, C., Kerr, N. L., Seok, D. H., & Harris, D. W. (2008). Indispensability and group identification as sources of task motivation. *Journal of Experimental & Social Psychology, 44*(5), 1316–1321.

Gould, D., Medbery, R., Damarjian, N., & Lauer, L. (1999). A survey of mental skills training knowledge, opinions, and practices of junior tennis coaches. *Journal of Applied Sport Psychology, 11*(1), 28–50.

Gould, D., & Wright, E. M. (2012). The psychology of coaching. In S. M. Murphy (Ed.), *The Oxford handbook of sport and performance psychology* (pp. 349–365). Oxford, England: Oxford University Press.

Graesser, A., & McNamara, D. (2010). Self-regulated learning in learning environments with pedagogical agents that interact in natural language. *Educational Psychologist, 45*(4), 234–244. http://dx.doi.org/10.1080/00461520.2010.515933.

Grant, A. M., & Shin, J. (2012). Work motivation: Directing, energizing, and maintaining. In R. M. Ryan (Ed.), *The Oxford handbook of human motivation* (pp. 505–519). New York, NY: Oxford University Press.

Greeno, J. G. (1997). On claims that answer the wrong questions. *Educational Researcher, 26*(1), 5–17.

Gregory, A., Allen, J. P., Mikami, A. Y., Hafen, C. A., & Pianta, R. C. (2014). Effects of a professional development program on behavioral engagement of students in middle and high school. *Psychology in the Schools, 51*(2), 143–163. http://dx.doi.org/10.1002/pits.21741.

Haden, J. (2014). *Top 50 leadership and management experts*. Retrieved on November 24, 2014 from: <http://www.inc.com/jeff-haden/the-top-50-leadership-and-management-experts-mon.html>

Hanin, Y. L. (2000). *Emotions in sport*. Champagne, IL: Human Kinetics.

Hays, K., & Brown, C. (2004). *You're on! Consulting for peak performance*. Washington, DC: American Psychological Association.

Hays, K. F. (2012). The psychology of performance in sport and other domains. In S. M. Murphy (Ed.), *The Oxford handbook of sport and performance psychology* (pp. 24–45). Oxford, England: Oxford University Press.

Heidig, S., & Clarebout, G. (2011). Do pedagogical agents make a difference to student motivation and learning? *Educational Research Review, 6*(1), 27–54. http://dx.doi.org/10.1016/j.edurev.2010.07.004.

Hertel, G. (2011). Synergetic effects in working teams. *Journal of Managerial Psychology, 26*(3), 176–184. http://dx.doi.org/10.1108/02683941111112622.

Hoffman, B., & Spatariu, A. (2008). The influence of self-efficacy and metacognitive prompting on math problem-solving efficiency. *Contemporary Educational Psychology, 33*(4), 875–893.

Hsiung, C. (2012). The Effectiveness of Cooperative Learning. *Journal of Engineering Education, 101*(1), 119–137. http://dx.doi.org/10.1002/j.2168-9830.2012.tb00044.x.

Hüffmeier, J., & Hertel, G. (2011). Many cheers make light the work: How social support triggers process gains in teams. *Journal of Managerial Psychology, 26*(3), 185–204. http://dx.doi.org/10.1108/02683941111112631.

Jones, R., Latham, J., & Betta, M. (2013). Creating the illusion of employee empowerment: Lean production in the international automobile industry. *The International Journal of Human Resource Management, 24*(8), 1629–1645. http://dx.doi.org/10.1080/09585192.2012.725081.

Kalyuga, S. (2007). Expertise reversal effect and its implications for learner-tailored instruction. *Educational Psychology Review, 19*(4), 509–539.

Keller, J. M. (2008). First principles of motivation to learn and e^3-Learning. *Distance Education, 29*(2), 175–185.

Kim, C. (2012). The role of affective and motivational factors in designing personalized learning environments. *Educational Technology Research and Development, 60*(4), 563–584. http://dx.doi.org/10.1007/s11423-012-9253-6.

Kim, K. J., & Frick, T. W. (2011). Changes in student motivation during online learning. *Journal of Educational Computing Research, 44*(1), 1–23. http://dx.doi.org/10.2190/EC.44.1.a.

Kogler-Hill, S. E. (2007). Team leadership. In P. G. Northouse (Ed.), *Leadership: Theory and practice* (pp. 207–236) (4th ed.). Thousand Oaks, CA: Sage.

Kozlowski, S. W. J., & Bell, B. S. (2003). Work groups and teams in organizations. In W. C. Borman, D. R. Ilgen, & R. J. Klimoski (Eds.), *Handbook of psychology: Vol. 12. Industrial and organizational psychology* (pp. 333–375). New York, NY: Wiley-Blackwell.

Kuipers, B. S. (2009). Performability of work teams: Balancing hard and soft issues. *International Journal of Performability Engineering, 5*(2), 143.

Läms, A. M., & Pučėtait, R. (2006). Development of organizational trust among employees from a contextual perspective. *Business Ethics: A European Review, 15*(2), 130–141. http://dx.doi.org/10.1111/j.1467-8608.2006.00437.x.

Larreamendy-Joerns, J., & Leinhardt, G. (2006). Going the distance with online education. *Review of Educational Research, 76*(4), 567–605. http://dx.doi.org/10.3102/00346543076004567.

Lauer, L., Gould, D., Roman, N., & Pierce, M. (2010). Parental behaviors that affect junior tennis player development. *Psychology of Sport and Exercise, 11*(6), 487–496.

Law, Y. K. (2011). The effects of cooperative learning on enhancing Hong Kong fifth graders' achievement goals, autonomous motivation and reading proficiency. *Journal of Research in Reading, 34*, 402–425. http://dx.doi.org/10.1111/j.1467-9817.2010.01445.

Lee, S. W. Y. (2013). Investigating students' learning approaches, perceptions of online discussions, and students' online and academic performance. *Computers & Education, 68*, 345–352.

Lewis, C. C., & Abdul-Hamid, H. (2006). Implementing effective online teaching practices: Voices of exemplary faculty. *Innovative Higher Education, 31*(2), 83–98.

Lowe, K. B., Kroeck, K. G., & Sivasubramaniam, N. (1996). Effectiveness correlates of transformational and transactional leadership: A meta-analytic review of the MLQ literature. *The Leadership Quarterly, 7*(3), 385–415. http://dx.doi.org/10.1016/S1048-9843(96)90027-2.

MacLeod, D. & Clarke, N. (2011). *Engaging for success: Enhancing performance through employee engagement*. Retrieved from <http://www.engageforsuccess.org/wp-content/uploads/2012/09/file52215.pdf>.

Mageau, G. A., & Vallerand, R. J. (2003). The coach–athlete relationship: A motivational model. *Journal of Sports Sciences, 21*(11), 883–904. http://dx.doi.org/10.1080/0264041031000140374.

Mayer, R. E. (2008). Applying the science of learning: Evidence-based principles for the design of multimedia instruction. *American Psychologist, 63*(8), 760–769.

McInerney, D. M. (2008). The motivational roles of cultural differences and cultural identity in self-regulated learning. In D. H. Schunk & B. J. Zimmerman (Eds.), *Motivation and self-regulated learning: Theory, research, and applications* (pp. 369–400). New York, NY: Lawrence Erlbaum Associates.

Mikkonen, J., Ruohoniemi, M., & Lindblom-Ylänne, S. (2013). The role of individual interest and future goals during the first years of university studies. *Studies in Higher Education, 38*(1), 71–86. http://dx.doi.org/10.1080/03075079.2011.564608.

Minnaert, A., Boekaerts, M., & de Brabander, C. (2007). Autonomy, competence, and social relatedness in task interest within project-based education. *Psychological Reports, 101*(2), 574–586.

Moreau, E., & Mageau, G. A. (2012). The importance of perceived autonomy support for the psychological health and work satisfaction of health professionals: Not only supervisors count, colleagues too!. *Motivation and Emotion, 36*(3), 268–286.

Moreno, R., & Mayer, R. E. (2004). Personalized messages that promote science learning in virtual environments. *Journal of Educational Psychology, 96*, 165–173.

Mupinga, D. M., Nora, R. T., & Yaw, D. C. (2006). The learning styles, expectations, and needs of online students. *College Teaching, 54*(1), 185–189.

Murayama, K., & Elliot, A.J. (2012). The competition–performance relation: A meta-analytic review and test of the opposing processes model of competition and performance. *Psychological Bulletin, 138*(6), 1035–1070. http://doi.org/10.1037/a0028324.

Neck, C. P., & Manz, C. C. (2010). *Mastering self-leadership: Empowering yourself for personal excellence* (5th ed.). Upper Saddle River, NJ: Prentice Hall.

Northouse, P. (2007). *Leadership: Theory and practice* (4th ed.). Thousand Oaks, CA: Sage.

Paechter, M., Maier, B., & Macher, D. (2010). Students' expectations of, and experiences in e-learning: Their relation to learning achievements and course satisfaction. *Computers & Education, 54*(1), 222–229. http://dx.doi.org/10.1016/j.compedu.2009.08.005.

Pappas, C. (2013). *Top 10 e-learning statistics for 2014 you need to know*. Retrieved on November 6, 2014 from: <http://elearningindustry.com/top-10-e-learning-statistics-for-2014-you-need-to-know>

Pew Research Center. (2011). *The digital revolution and higher education*. Retrieved on November 3, 2014 from: <http://www.pewsocialtrends.org/2011/08/28/i-online-learning/>

Pfeffer, J. (1998). Seven practices of successful organizations. *California Management Review, 40*(2), 96–124.

Picciano, A. G., Seaman, J., Shea, P., & Swan, K. (2012). Examining the extent and nature of online learning in American K-12 Education: The research initiatives of the Alfred P. Sloan Foundation. *The Internet and Higher Education, 15*(2), 127–135. http://dx.doi.org/10.1016/j.iheduc.2011.07.004.

Ramdass, D., & Zimmerman, B. J. (2011). Developing self-regulation skills: The important role of homework. *Journal of Advanced Academics, 22*(2), 194–218.

Reeve, J. (2006). Teachers as facilitators: What autonomy-supportive teachers do and why their students benefit. *The Elementary School Journal, 106*(3), 225–236.

Reeve, J., Vansteenkiste, M., Assor, A., Ahmad, I., Cheon, S. H., Jang, H., et al. (2014). The beliefs that underlie autonomy-supportive and controlling teaching: A multinational investigation. *Motivation and Emotion, 38*(1), 93–110.

Reyes, M. R., Brackett, M. A., Rivers, S. E., White, M., & Salovey, P. (2012). Classroom emotional climate, student engagement, and academic achievement. *Journal of Educational Psychology, 104*(3), 700–712.

Rimm-Kaufman, S., & Chiu, Y. (2007). Promoting social and academic competence in the classroom: An intervention study examining the contribution of the Responsive Classroom approach. *Psychology in the Schools, 44*, 397–413. http://dx.doi.org/10.1002/pits.20231.

Ross, S. M., Morrison, G. R., & Lowther, D. L. (2010). Educational technology research past and present: Balancing rigor and relevance to impact school learning. *Contemporary Educational Technology, 1*, 17–35.

Sansone, C., Fraughton, T., Zachary, J. L., Butner, J., & Heiner, C. (2011). Self-regulation of motivation when learning online: The importance of who, why and how. *Educational Technology Research and Development, 59*(2), 199–212. http://dx.doi.org/10.1007/s11423-011-9193-6.

Sansone, C., Weir, C., Harpster, L., & Morgan, C. (1992). Once a boring task always a boring task? Interest as a self-regulatory mechanism. *Journal of Personality & Social Psychology, 63*(3), 379–390.

Schein, E. H. (2010). *Organizational culture and leadership* (4th ed.). San Francisco, CA: John Wiley & Sons.

Shea, P., & Bidjerano, T. (2010). Learning presence: Towards a theory of self-efficacy, self-regulation, and the development of a communities of inquiry in online and blended learning environments. *Computers & Education, 55*(4), 1721–1731. http://dx.doi.org/10.1016/j.compedu.2010.07.017.

Shea, P., Sau Li, C., & Pickett, A. (2006). A study of teaching presence and student sense of learning community in fully online and web-enhanced college courses. *The Internet and Higher Education, 9*(3), 175–190. http://dx.doi.org/10.1016/j.iheduc.2006.06.005.

Shernoff, D. J. (2010). Engagement in after-school programs as a predictor of social competence and academic performance. *American Journal of Community Psychology, 45*(3-4), 325–337.

Shulman, L. S. (1987). Knowledge and teaching: Foundations of the new reform. *Harvard Educational Review, 57*(1), 1–23.

Skinner, E., Furrer, C., Marchand, G., & Kindermann, T. (2008). Engagement and disaffection in the classroom: Part of a larger motivational dynamic? *Journal of Educational Psychology, 100*(4), 765–781.

Slavin, R. E. (1996). Research on cooperative learning and achievement: What we know, what we need to know. *Contemporary Educational Psychology, 21*(1), 43–69.

Slavin, R. E. (2012). Classroom applications of cooperative learning. In K. R. Harris, S. Graham, T. Urdan, A. G. Bus, S. Major, & H. L. Swanson (Eds.), *APA educational psychology handbook, Vol. 3: Application to learning and teaching* (pp. 359–378). Washington, DC: American Psychological Association.

Stefanou, C. R., Perencevich, K. C., DiCintio, M., & Turner, J. C. (2004). Supporting autonomy in the classroom: Ways teachers encourage student decision making and ownership. *Educational Psychologist, 39*(2), 97–110.

Stewart, G. L., Courtright, S. H., & Manz, C. C. (2011). Self-leadership: A multilevel review. *Journal of Management, 37*(1), 185–222. http://dx.doi.org/10.1177/0149206310383911.

Stoeber, J. (2011). The dual nature of perfectionism in sports: Relationships with emotion, motivation, and performance. *International Review of Sport and Exercise Psychology, 4*(2), 128–145. http://dx.doi.org/10.1080/1750984X.2011.604789.

Stoeber, J., & Otto, K. (2006). Positive conceptions of perfectionism: Approaches, evidence, challenges. *Personality and Social Psychology Review, 10*(4), 295–319. http://dx.doi.org/10.1207/s15327957pspr1004_2.

Stryker, S., & Burke, P. J. (2000). The past, present, and future of an identity theory. *Social Psychology Quarterly, 63*, 284–297.

Su, Y. -L., & Reeve, J. (2011). A meta-analysis of the effectiveness of intervention programs designed to support autonomy. *Educational Psychology Review*, *23*(1), 159–188. http://dx.doi.org/10.1007/s10648-010-9142-7.

Tallent-Runnels, M. K., Thomas, J. A., Lan, W. Y., Cooper, S., Ahern, T. C., Shaw, S. M., et al. (2006). Teaching courses online: A review of the research. *Review of Educational Research*, *76*(1), 93–135. http://dx.doi.org/10.3102/00346543076001093.

Tamim, R. M., Bernard, R. M., Borokhovski, E., Abrami, P. C., & Schmid, R. F. (2011). What forty years of research says about the impact of technology on learning: A second-order meta-analysis and validation study. *Review of Educational Research*, *81*(1), 4–28. http://dx.doi.org/10.3102/0034654310393361.

Tyler-Smith, K. (2006). Early attrition among first time e-learners: A review of factors that contribute to drop-out, withdrawal and non-completion rates of adult learners undertaking elearning programmes. *Journal of Online Learning and Teaching*, *2*(2), 73–85.

Vazou, S., Gavrilou, P., Mamalaki, E., Papanastasiou, A., & Sioumala, N. (2012). Does integrating physical activity in the elementary school classroom influence academic motivation? *International Journal of Sport and Exercise Psychology*, *10*(4), 251–263. http://dx.doi.org/10.1080/1612197X.2012.682368.

Wageman, R. (1995). Interdependence and group effectiveness. *Administrative Science Quarterly*, *40*(1), 145–180.

Walkington, C. A. (2013). Using adaptive learning technologies to personalize instruction to student interests: The impact of relevant contexts on performance and learning outcomes. *Journal of Educational Psychology*, *105*(4), 932–945. http://dx.doi.org/10.1037/a0031882.

Wentzel, K. (2014). Prosocial behavior and peer relations in adolescence. In L. M. Padilla-Walker & G. Carlo (Eds.), *Prosocial development: A multidimensional approach* (pp. 178–200). New York, NY: Oxford University Press.

Wiman, M., Salmoni, A. W., & Hall, C. R. (2010). An examination of the definition and development of expert coaching. *International Journal of Coaching Science*, *4*(2), 37–60.

Winiecki, D., Fenner, J. A., & Chyung, Y. (1999). Evaluation of effective interventions to solve the drop out problem in adult distance education. In B. Collis & R. Oliver (Eds.), *Proceedings of world conference on educational multimedia, hypermedia and telecommunications 1999* (pp. 51–55). Chesapeake, VA: AACE.

Wise, A. F., Perera, N., Hsiao, Y. T., Speer, J., & Marbouti, F. (2012). Microanalytic case studies of individual participation patterns in an asynchronous online discussion in an undergraduate blended course. *The Internet and Higher Education*, *15*(2), 108–117. http://dx.doi.org/10.1016/j.iheduc.2011.11.007.

Wlodkowski, R. J. (2011). *Enhancing adult motivation to learn: A comprehensive guide for teaching all adults*. San Francisco, CA: John Wiley & Sons.

Wright, B. E. (2004). The role of work context in work motivation: A public sector application of goal and social cognitive theories. *Journal of Public Administration Research and Theory: J-PART*(1), 59–78.

Zhang, X., & Bartol, K. M. (2010). Linking empowering leadership and employee creativity: The influence of psychological empowerment, intrinsic motivation, and creative process engagement. *Academy of Management Journal*, *53*(1), 107–128.

Zimmerman, B. J., & Cleary, T. J. (2009). Motives to self-regulate learning: A social cognitive account. In K. R. Wenzel & A. Wigfield (Eds.), *Handbook of motivation at school* (pp. 247–264). New York, NY: Routledge/Taylor & Francis Group.

The transformers: Overcoming resistance to motivational change

12

> *Whosoever desires constant success must change his conduct with the times.*
> —*Niccolo Machiavelli*

Chapter outline

Why do people resist change?   346
Which strategies will individuals use to refute change?   355
Motivational Leader—*Amanda Boxtel*   358
Overcoming change resistance in others   360
Instructional strategies supporting conceptual change   362
    Promote strategy awareness   362
    Identify plausible alternatives   363
    Provide refutational evidence   364
    Create personal relevance   364
    Scaffold strategy change   365
Learning from leaders   367
Epilogue   369
References   370

Are you a transformer? Close your eyes for 30 seconds, and imagine you are a critical care nurse specializing in oncology. Your job is keeping alive those patients diagnosed with cancer. Life in the oncology ward can be brutal, often depressing for patients and nurses alike, because many of the ill will perish. Patients not only must be stalwart and resolute battling the deadly disease but also need psychological resilience to cope with the often disturbing side effects of treatment, such as hair loss and constant nausea from chemotherapy. Your primary role as an oncology nurse is to administer medicine, but you also comfort patients emotionally by encouraging them to persevere, remain diligent, and not give up the recovery fight. Sometimes, you feel content and highly gratified by your job because you make a difference in patients' lives. You model optimism and help survivors realize that who they are, and who they can become, is not based upon superficial qualities, such as a full head of hair. Other times, you feel distraught and discouraged, such as the time when you spent 30 minutes encouraging one of your favorite patients, Aaron, to quit smoking and possibly extend his life expectancy by 5 to 10 years, only to find him puffing a cigarette in the family room, just a few minutes later.

    The story above is fictional but realistically portrays a paradigm happening in many hospitals and doctors' offices globally. Frequently, individuals patently reject highly beneficial medical advice that clashes with cultural beliefs or personal desires (Gjernes, 2010), including decisions that are physically and psychologically harmful to the self and others (Jost, Banaji, & Nosek, 2004). Unfortunately, the resistance phenomenon described transcends health decisions. Aspiring motivational detectives (MDs) should be aware and apprehensive that sometimes the most plausible, reliable, and empirically justified motivational remedies will be summarily rejected by the intended target. Metaphorically speaking, some patients will be unwilling to swallow their motivational medicine because the scientific cure conflicts with personal understanding and individual ideology. Compounding the implementation dilemma is the stark realization that "change is so rare and difficult to accomplish" (Jost, Pietrzak, Liviatan, Mandisodza, & Napier, 2008, p. 592), often resulting in motivational complacency. Instead, resistors model constancy and frequently will ardently defend the status quo, simply because it exists (Jost et al., 2004). Thus, the first step to mitigate resistance and generate change through motivational transformation is understanding why people are so reluctant to change.

Why do people resist change?

Many different reasons are advanced to explain why change is threatening, including biological and evolutionary perspectives, as well as teleological, organizational, social, and individual difference frameworks. Strictly biological or evolutionary models are often coupled and suggest that the receptivity for change has adaptive neurological, hormonal, and circadian underpinnings. Individual differences in neural networks are explained in three ways: (1) by how people evaluate environmental stimuli, (2) by how they categorize phenomena, and (3) upon the temporal conditions that produce energy and stimulate arousal. Evaluation means individuals make subjective assessments of environmental events that lead to either approach or avoid behaviors—behaviors that consequently determine the extent of neuronal development. When an environmental target is approached, exceedingly complex neural hierarchies are formed. Without appropriate environmental opportunity, neuronal development is forestalled, inhibiting the creation of more elaborate neural networks that are highly conducive to the probability of cognitive change (Berntson, Norman, & Cacioppo, 2009). In behavioral terms, the evaluative approach is similar to Piaget's model of biological determinism (Wadsworth, 1996), which suggests individuals adapt cognitive structures based upon interaction with the environment by either integrating or adapting existing thought patterns to reach a state of cognitive equilibrium. Lacking opportunities for disequilibration, cognitive growth is stymied, just as cognitive change is less probable when neuronal structures lack the opportunity for complex and elaborate development.

The second biological interpretation of change resistance, the categorization model, suggests individuals must possess the ability and willingness to recognize structural differences in objects and ideas in order to modify mental representations. Cognitive categorization is broadly influenced by particular viewpoints abstracted from personal beliefs and can be measured through biological responses, such as inferotemporal neurons in the eye, retinal position, and brain localization that indicate discrepant classifications are learned and can be modified by experience (Mack, Richler, Palmeri, & Gauthier, 2009). For example, if you observe my pet iguana, your mental representation may categorize Luigi as either a pet or a predator, or possibly both, but regardless, conceptions of an iguana can vary, evoking different mental representations in individuals. Inaccurate categorization among individuals stimulates misconceptions about reptiles, which may have drastic consequences when encountering unfriendly lizards. The categorization view, which is similar to ontological perspectives in educational psychology, contends that shifts in abstractions and proper categorization are necessary to overcome cognitive misrepresentations, which are a prerequisite for enduring conceptual change (CC) (Chi, 2005; Murphy & Mason, 2006).

The third biological perspective, the temporal arousal view, contends that dispositions and motivation, in general, are a function of physiological regulation that is influenced by the time of day, nutrition, and activity. Together, these exogenous catalysts result in the creation of idiosyncratic circadian rhythms, which can radically alter personal motivations because cyclical changes in energy influence mood. Individuals have greater arousal proclivity and are more biologically receptive to intervention and motivated for action during periods of energetic arousal than during tense or depleted periods when feeling tired, hungry, or exceedingly grumpy (Thayer, 2012). Clearly, analogous to approach and avoidant behavior, the bipolar moods modulated by energy and tension suggest that during periods of eating, exercise, or sleep deprivation, change initiatives should be avoided until the necessary resources are replenished. In practical terms, the biological interpretations of change readiness collectively suggest that adaptive motivational change is a function of opportunity driven by past experience, conceptual familiarity with the reasons for a change, and a function of natural physiological cycles, which may enhance or inhibit change receptivity.

Teleological-based views of resistance, which are frequently used to explain science literacy (Sinatra & Chinn, 2012), rely upon the assumption that objects and occurrences observed in the natural world have a fundamental purpose and were designed with a specific intentionality in mind (Kampourakis, Pavlidi, Papadopoulou, & Palaiokrassa, 2012). Often conflated with dogmatic explanations of evolution, teleological perspectives defy scientific explanations, resulting in conceptual misunderstandings. For instance, a teleological and scientifically unwarranted explanation for the reason bears living in the North Pole are white is as follows: Bears hibernate in the winter, and during the artic summer, they are outside in the 24-hour sunshine and their fur is bleached white by exposure to the sun. In actuality, polar bears do not hibernate, and the hair of a polar bear is not white at all, but colorless! However, the teleological cause-and-effect relationship described is held by many individuals. Although teleological perspectives are often associated with the development of higher-order thinking in children, adults also espouse teleological views, a phenomenon that is exacerbated under the perception of performance pressure (Kelemen & Rosset, 2009).

Motivation is also a seemingly naturally occurring phenomenon. A teleological perspective would suggest that exhibited behaviors are the consequence of certain preconceived needs or notions about the fulfillment of personal motives. For example, the statement "Jobs exist so people can fill idle time" would be a teleological-based explanation of work motivation. Despite the flawed logic of the statement, some individuals with anomalous beliefs may attribute work causality and similar motivations to unwarranted teleological causes. The rationalization is so prevalent that Lombrozo and Carey (2006) suggested that a "promiscuous teleology is intimately related to goal-directed action" (p. 199) because individuals frequently misinterpret the causality of their own behaviors. Individuals defaulting to teleological explanations for motives and behavior would be highly resistant to alternative conceptions because flawed teleological thinking reflects "deep underlying commitments about the causal structure of the world" (Lombrozo & Carey, 2006, p. 197). Empirically, teleological thinking is related to the reinforcement of intuitive cognitive biases (Sinatra, Brem, & Evans, 2008), suggesting that prior to any motivational intervention, teleological beliefs should be examined to determine receptivity to contradictory evidence that might discount a teleological belief.

Organizational perspectives of change resistance differ from individual viewpoints because the culture of organizations is inherently socially based, with change largely determined by social influence (Battilana & Casciaro, 2012; Marsden & Friedkin, 1993). Compounding the resistance lacuna is the intimate connectivity between organizational culture and normative behaviors, as discussed in Chapter 11 (p. 312), which indicated that behavior and corresponding motivations vary dramatically across different groups. Behavior encouraged and deemed normative in one company or context may be openly chastised and stigmatized in another. Organizational variability aside, the socialized nature of groups implies that at the individual level, employees are vulnerable to persuasion and highly motivated to demonstrate conformist behavior (Coyne & Coyne, 2007). Conformity, exemplified by adhering to organizational norms, is both personally and professionally valuable because conformity frequently leads to enhanced social identity with colleagues and is often linked to career development. Social conformity also operates at the organizational level through mimetic behavior, equivalent of the colloquial "keeping up with the (organizational) Joneses," which occurs when successful organizations emulate each other (Barreto & Baden-Fuller, 2006).

However, individualistic and organizational conformity is often a double-edged motivational sword. When social conformity occurs, it is often driven by the need for organizational survival and demonstrated by individuals enacting the desired behaviors expected by autocratic leaders. Perceptions of being controlled forestall internalization of organizational goals because the goals are pursued primarily to gain external contingencies (Gagne & Deci, 2005), such as staying in the good graces of a supervisor, keeping one's job, or to earn a promotion. Ultimately, change merely for incentive gratification impedes intrinsic motivation, especially when employees perceive the organizational change to be a unilateral leadership mandate, which is frequently the case during change initiatives (Senge, 2014).

A key reason for individual resistance to organizational efforts is skepticism concerning the sincerity of leadership's commitment to a proposed change. Many times employees will assess prospective changes in strategic focus or operational policies as temporary, faddish, and noncommittal, implemented to appease senior management or stockholders. The programs are perceived as historically temporary, disdained and labeled as the metaphorical "flavor of the month." Employees become disenchanted because leadership commitment often vacillates and is frequently coupled with a revisionist philosophy that lacks clarity and results in employees questioning organizational integrity with uncertainty as to what qualifies as an appropriate and expected behavior. Renowned leadership expert and Harvard professor John Kotter, when listing his eight reasons why organizational transformations fail, solemnly warned readers that "without motivation people won't help and the [organizational] effort goes nowhere" (Kotter, 1995, p. 60). The probability of garnering employee support is naturally compromised when individuals lack confidence in the longevity of the change initiative. Shallow change assessments induce skepticism in those affected by changes, and the programs frequently suffer the same ill fate as Nehru jackets, phrenology, and pet rocks—burgeoning popularity at first, followed by a quick and linear demise when individuals realize the futility of the endeavor.

The failure list (Kotter, 1995) emphasizes numerous other organizational blunders related to motivated behavior and change receptivity in general. Kotter stresses paying attention to personal needs of employees first, promoting an autonomous culture by empowering employees and ensuring that leaders are not perceived as showing favoritism and by providing sufficient resources that allow individuals to meet organizational goals. The liabilities of organizational change suggest numerous opportunities to use employee-centered motivational strategies that include setting attainable proximal goals, accomplished through balanced participation, and by providing individuals with the emotional support to conquer the psychological turbulence that often accompanies significant change. Overall resistance to organizational change is frequently the byproduct of misaligned organizational culture and interpretation of the "nouveau norm," as discussed at length in Chapter 10. In other words, leaders must "walk the talk," or those individuals subjected to the change initiative and expected to follow leadership demands will quickly detect inconsistencies between rhetoric and action, breeding employee contempt, lack of organizational trust, and, in all likelihood, resistance to change.

Evidence from social psychology is useful to explain resistant behavior because the discipline seeks to understand how beliefs, thoughts, and feelings of individuals are influenced by others. Research is targeted toward understanding how humans form attitudes, succumb to persuasion, and make decisions. How individuals respond to mind-changing efforts can reveal valuable information to predict why individuals buy certain products but reject others, support ideological social and political causes, and are useful to determine the basis of prejudice toward specific individuals or bias against certain ideas. The primary emphasis of social psychology research is on cognitive processing, with many research conclusions suggesting that observed behavioral differences are related to a continuum of motivational and affective factors previously discussed. The instrumental change factors include the degree of effort a person is willing to invest in a decision, what factors distinguish the strength of beliefs, and exactly how the presence or absence of others can modify individual or group behavior.

An important social psychology behavioral model that includes numerous motivational components is the Elaboration Likelihood Model (ELM). The model is based on the principles of attitude formation and persuasion and is a useful to explain resistant behavior because the focus of the model is on the strength of judgments, which broadly influence individual motivation for a cause (Petty & Briñol, 2012; Petty & Cacioppo, 1986). Individuals with deeply entrenched beliefs are considered more resistant to persuasion and change than those with superficial commitments. The ELM addresses factors that are closely related to the receptivity of new ideas, and emphasizes the relation between cognitive processing and motivated action, which suggests when individuals perceive a strategy as unfamiliar or undesirable, the strategy will be summarily rejected. Strategy endorsement requires that strategies be both understandable and personally palatable in order for the individual to put forth sufficient effort to implement the strategy. Not surprisingly, if an individual does not believe a change is helpful, little cognitive effort follows.

The degree of engagement with a proposition operates along a continuum according to the ELM, influenced by the clarity of the recommendation, a qualitative evaluation of the message source, the situational relevance of the message, and the self-determined utility of the strategy to meet the individual's learning or performance needs. The ELM indicates that the degree of effort invested in the process of evaluating the idea and the associated depth of engagement the person exhibits when contemplating motivated action, will determine the likelihood and longevity of behavior change. Shallow engagement leads to temporary or only situational change, such as agreeing to avoid profanity, but only refraining from cussing when one's mother is present, while deep engagement would imply a durable and unwavering commitment to appropriate vernacular, regardless of maternal presence. According to the ELM, "the more a judgment is based on thinking about the merits of an issue, the more it tends to persist over time, resist change attempts, and has consequences for other judgments and behavior" (Petty & Briñol, 2012, p. 226). Deep thinking often promotes change receptivity, but not always.

The ELM portends that effort investments are influenced by different types of thinking; some types of thinking are effortful, cognitively complex, and energy depleting, while other types of cognitive challenges are less cerebral, with understanding occurring with minimally effort or automatically, sometimes outside of the direct stream of consciousness. By example, one would expect automatic and greater resistance to the suggestion to divorce one's spouse when engaged in a harmonious relationship, in comparison with the willingness to switch seats with a stranger on an airplane flight. Contemplating divorce would likely be an elaboration of substantial proportions for the satisfied partner, with considerably more ramifications than an aerial seat swap. Of course, situational relevance and the extent of affective engagement are also critical ELM factors that influence the likelihood and sustainability of change. As you may surmise, some individuals would be highly committed, affectively primed, and motivated to consider a marriage dissolution strategy, after a major argument, than after a romantic anniversary celebration. Thus, based upon the features of the ELM, when an individual understands a strategy recommendation and perceives the message originating from a credible and reliable source, the proclivity to change one's beliefs and corresponding behavior in the direction of influence is more likely, provided the recommendation is deemed personally relevant and available effort is commensurate with the strategy demands.

Still unraveled is why individuals who deploy sufficient effort, have a clear conceptual understanding, and demonstrate deep engagement may elect to rebuke an otherwise effective motivational intervention. CC models in psychology and education address the dilemma of mistaken application and wavering commitments that occur when individuals have adequate background knowledge and personal awareness, but still resist change (Chi, 2013; Dole & Sinatra, 1998; Gregoire, 2003). Although the ability to describe each CC model in full detail is limited here, CC has a specific premise. CC refers only to knowledge revision necessary to mediate prior faulty or misconceived representations that are often based upon personal or cultural interpretations of the world but excludes the generation of new knowledge needed for understanding (Vosniadou, 2013). Most CC interventions focus on restructuring misconceptions of scientific knowledge; however, the approach is a useful lens to examine motivational strategies because of the highly idiosyncratic and personalized nature of strategy conceptions, which often may be antithetical to evidence-based strategy recommendations. For example, some individuals believe that procrastination is a fruitful motivational remedy to attain high-quality academic outcomes and use the strategy to bolster performance, but there is little, if any, empirical evidence to support this contention (Schraw, Wadkins, & Olafson, 2007). A learner embracing false beliefs concerning the benefits of procrastination would likely be highly disadvantaged, resistant, and unmotivated to use more warranted and effective strategies to achieve academic excellence, even when provided with disconfirming evidence that contradicts the effectiveness of a familiar and comfortable approach.

Collectively, CC models include important motivational constructs, which, unilaterally or in combination, mediate the receptivity, sustainability, and durability of alternative conceptions. Such factors as the extent of dissatisfaction with existing conceptions, many emotional, social, or cultural influences, and basic beliefs individuals harbor concerning motivation and cognition provide important clues to determine why individuals may accept or reject a strategy recommendation. Dissatisfaction with current approaches is often vital to CC because when satisfied with ideas, individuals are not motivated to change those ideas (Dole & Sinatra, 1998). Several factors influence dissatisfaction. First, the individual must be uncomfortable with current conceptions and conscious of dissatisfaction, which is not always the case. To illustrate, when examining how individuals go about solving personal motivational issues and problems in general, we may observe an exceedingly rigid approach. In academic problem-solving realms, such as mathematics, individuals often exhibit a cognitive paralysis and resort to tried and true solutions that may work for one problem but are fruitless with other dissimilar problems (Walczyk & Griffith-Ross, 2006). In addition, individuals are prone to execute complex solution methods when simpler solutions are in their grasp (Hambrick & Engle, 2003). Unfortunately, a rigid problem-solving stance and comfort using familiar and predictable approaches decreases receptivity to new, more efficient, or effective remedies.

Receptivity to approaches considered novel will increase when individuals are aware of their dissatisfaction with existing methods. When dissatisfied, revision usually occurs during the trial-and-error testing of different strategies until one approach is deemed sufficiently superior to replace existing methods. In the absence of dissatisfaction and lacking a compelling reason to change or having a perceived conflict with existing methods, the likelihood of strategy revision is reduced. Complicating acceptance of revisionist recommendations is the distinct possibility that even when deeply conflicted and when acknowledging the futility of an existing strategy, some individuals will be reluctant to consider change because of unique situational, social, or normative influences. For example, strong evidence reveals that protecting your head with a helmet when cycling may save your life in the event of an accident or fall. However, motorcyclists securing their helmets to the back of their seats and not to the head is a clear example of the "cool dude" social mystic whereby cultural norms trump reliable knowledge and endorsement of a seemingly common sense helmet-wearing strategy. In addition, flawed thinking may preclude individuals from reaching logical and honest conclusions when presented with disconfirming strategy evidence. A recurring and pervasive thinking flaw arises when individuals demonstrate myside bias believing in the ultimate superiority of personal perspectives, which happens when individuals test hypotheses and evaluate outcomes in favor of existing opinions, not upon the actual results observed (Stanovich & West, 2008). Anyone who is a sports fan or has a favorite recipe knows that individuals will adamantly defend their allegiance to particular teams or methods despite objective disconfirming evidence.

Dissatisfied with current conceptions or not, social and emotional factors, such as variation in classroom culture, the impact of change on self-views, and emotional evaluations linked to change outcomes, can all derail change receptivity, ultimately determining the acceptance or rejection of a recommendation. Classrooms, as communities of practice, have particular group standards and normative behaviors that are socially constructed by the members of the community (Hickey, 2003). The routines and rituals inherent to a classroom are a reflection of contextually-based world views that manifest in practices such as language or beliefs, similar to the individualist orientation described in Chapter 5, p. 118. For strategy recommendations to be considered viable, the suggestions must align with in-group norms and mores that individuals consider part of their identity and culture. Suggestions inconsistent with normative values are prone to rejection. For instance, some performance cultures encourage help seeking when individuals encounter obstacles, while other cultures stigmatize help seeking and support a philosophy of independent problem solving. Advocating help seeking within a normative culture that values in-group independence creates a cultural clash and ignores the situative view of motivation that contends individual motives are contextually dependent and collectively derived (Greeno & the Middle School Mathematics through Application Project, 1998). When cultures clash, change receptivity is doubtful.

Change receptivity can also be a reflection of individual self-assessments. When faced with evaluative opportunities, people often compare their competencies and ideals with those valued by in-groups as part of an overall referent sociocultural framework. Aligned competencies are embraced while those inconsistent with group values and expectations are often rejected. Gregoire (2003), in her CC model contended that when individuals encounter a prospective reform message, they evaluate the message based upon the implications of the message to the self, by evaluating the message to determine a path of conceptual acceptance or resistance. When the individual perceives an idea or recommendation as a threat to personal values and beliefs, the message is likely discounted because self-threats lead to discomfort and anxiety, inhibiting change motivation. Conversely, when an individual assesses a message as supportive to self-appraisal, receptivity to the reform message is not compromised, enhancing the probability of adaptation and accommodation of alternative conceptions.

Gregoire's (2003) model further posits that self-appraisals generate affect and the valence of the subsequent emotion is instrumental in change receptivity. This "hot" model of CC suggests that affective assessments are inescapable when contemplating change. Again, recall previous discussions of academic emotions (Chapter 9, p. 245), indicating that individuals exhibit approach or avoid behaviors contingent upon a subjective emotional evaluation of a task. Applying Gregoire's model to strategy evaluation, similar affectively laden assessments would likely occur, broadly influencing consideration and adaptation of the suggested strategy contingent on the derived affective valence ascribed to the recommendation. A confluence of evidence indicates when learners and performers are faced with conflicting evidence they evaluate the emotional consequences of the decision, and the restructuring of knowledge is often dominated by emotion alone (Sinatra, Broughton, & Lombardi, 2014).

Motivational beliefs related to change willingness include a variety of individual difference factors, such as goal orientation, personal epistemologies, and self-efficacy. These select motivational variables exert influence independently and collectively to determine when and why an individual will consider change. Research that considers goal orientation as a change mediator is relatively rare (Sinatra & Mason, 2013), with the limited findings leading to the conclusion that a mastery goal orientation is preferable for CC because mastery learners are deeply engaged in learning and generally seek more elaborative approaches to knowledge building, two prerequisites for CC. As a result, mastery learners gain a more refined conceptual understanding of revisionist knowledge and concurrently avoid generating negative affect that often occurs during the restructuring process (Linnenbrink & Pintrich, 2002). For the mastery learner, receptivity to new knowledge is often perceived as rewarding, hence the generation of positive affect and the greater willingness by mastery learners to consider revised conceptions.

Epistemic beliefs are conceptions individuals harbor about the nature of knowledge. Some individuals hold naive views and perceive knowledge as absolute, easily acquired, relatively stable, derived from defined sources (e.g., teachers, books), and accumulated with minimal effort. Conversely, other people have sophisticated knowledge views and perceive knowledge acquisition as complex and challenging, operating under the belief that knowledge is transient and evolves through scientific inquiry, resulting in frequent revision. When holding a simplistic knowledge view, the probability of receptivity to change is reduced in comparison with a person who believes that is knowledge is complex (Sinatra, Kienhues, & Hofer, 2014). Epistemic beliefs influence receptivity to motivational interventions because thinking is related to strategy choice during the learning and performance process. Individuals who harbor sophisticated epistemic views show greater receptivity to variable motivational and learning strategies, based on a revisionist theory of knowledge. When presented with contrasting opinions, or evidence disconfirming existing conceptions, epistemically sophisticated individuals will employee critical thinking and evaluation tools more so than their naive epistemic peers (Greene, Muis, & Pieschl, 2010), which results in a deeper evaluation of strategy choices.

Finally, self-efficacy, or the belief in one's ability to achieve desired learning outcomes (Bandura, 1997), can influence change receptivity. Intuitively, elevated self-efficacy beliefs are thought to be detrimental to CC because individuals who are overly confident are typically more resistant to CC, as they harbor little doubt in the veracity of their knowledge and are committed to what they know (Pintrich, Marx, & Boyle, 1993). Evidence implicating the role of self-efficacy on CC is extremely sparse, and the few studies that directly control for self-efficacy reveal an ambiguous and complex relationship among background knowledge, interest, and strength of commitment to one's prior knowledge. Recently, Cordova, Sinatra, Jones, Taasoobshirazi, and Lombardi (2014) shed some light on the intricacies of the self-efficacy or change readiness dilemma. Their study measured content interest, confidence in learning new material, existing misconceptions, and background knowledge about seasonal change. They observed that learners with a profile of high confidence in prior knowledge, elevated self-efficacy beliefs, and greater interest in learning were more likely to experience CC. Although no research has been conducted specifically concerning self-efficacy and the receptivity for motivational interventions, the aforementioned results suggest moderate levels of self-efficacy, coupled with interest in change, may potentially transfer to the consideration of alternative motivational strategies. Similar to sophisticated epistemic beliefs, it seems that if individuals believe knowledge evolves, critical thinking and receptivity to improvement should logically follow. More research in this area is surely needed for conclusive inferences.

Despite taking preemptive steps to mitigate the resistance efforts described thus far, the practitioner may still encounter numerous obstacles when attempting to initiate change, but why? Jost (2011), Jost et al. (2004) offer "Systems Justification Theory" (2004, p. 882), a systemic and sociological explanation of psychological resistance. Viewing change resistance as systemic suggests that individuals, especially those who are socially or economically disadvantaged, are highly motivated to maintain the status quo, based upon how they perceive themselves integrating within an overall culture or social hierarchy. Satisfaction of three different motives reveals why people adhere to a systems justification dogma that often limits personal growth and is self-deprecating. First, individuals seek *ego justification* (2004, p. 887), the functional equivalent of maintaining positive self-worth, as discussed in Chapter 8 (p. 207); that is, individuals are broadly motivated and strive to attain positive self-assessments. Second, individuals seek *group justification* (2004, p. 887), by forging positive alliances and affiliations with in-group members, which occurs when individuals validate their identity and closely align personal values with particular group ideologies. Third, a *system justification*, (2004, p. 887) exists, which contends that individuals legitimatize and internalize perceptions of group inequality by placing more value on within-group identification than on individual self-assessments. Whenever perceptions of ego justification or group justification falter, system justification views prevail. System justification satisfies individual psychological and social needs by supporting the belief that the global social order is inevitable and immutable, thereby reducing cognitive distress and personal insecurity over the seemingly uncontrollable factors that limit personal growth and foster group injustice.

When individuals defend systems legitimacy, the defense reduces the negative affect resulting from personal attacks. Individuals embrace the totality of disadvantage as not personally based, controllable, or malleable. Depersonalization supports the need for stability and provides an emotional safe haven, deflecting focus from the individual to the "justified" system. While this view may appear rather illogical and esoteric on face value, Jost (2011), Jost et al. (2004) assert that disadvantaged individuals are often fraught with anxiety when trying to circumvent the realities of their perceptual world. Reduction of dissonance is more easily achieved when supporting an unjust system than when constantly battling sociological inequities. The authors advocated that societal inequality and exogenous-induced inferiority is internalized creating a sense of false consciousness that leads people to "endorse system-serving beliefs that are contrary to their own social and political interests" (Jost, 2011, p. 225). The prevalence of encountering individuals with the stereotypical disadvantage described may be limited, but clearly recognition of the justification ideology can be a valuable perspective to explain the resistance and amotivation when some individuals are faced with prospective change.

Which strategies will individuals use to refute change?

Armed with an understanding of the sources and etiology of misconceived beliefs that impede motivational interventions, it is critical to anticipate and identify which strategies individuals will use to challenge the arguably brilliant suggestions the sage MD has worked so hard to advance. Refutation is often preceded by the words, "I don't like," "I don't want," or "I don't believe," and "No." As such, individuals will offer a litany of reasons why their own thinking and personal methods for addressing motivational lapses are far superior to the suggestions and recommendations from learned others, including respected scholars, teachers, parents, or friends. The ardent resistance is grounded in myside bias and deeply entrenched worldviews. The refutation scenario is often exacerbated when personal development suggestions are offered, as this type of feedback may be perceived as a threat to positive self-evaluations and lead to lower perception of self-esteem (Campbell, Hoyle, & Bradfield, 2011).

A broad continuum of responses will be encountered when offering advice or proposing strategy solutions to help others meet personal and organizational goals. Individuals may embrace the idea, mull it over, and get back to you, or they may blatantly reject or ignore the suggestion. Paradoxically, sometimes an individual will give the impression of enthusiastic endorsement of recommendations via verbal feedback and encouraging, but obligatory, behavior. However, in actuality, you may be duped! Frequently, individuals will demonstrate motivational engagement, while, in reality, the person is ideologically distant and conceptually disengaged from the strategy intervention (Fredricks, Blumenfeld, & Paris, 2004). Devoid of psychological commitment to strategy suggestions, the MD is vulnerable to reaching false conclusions of intervention success based upon only cursory behavior and superficial change.

In all likelihood, within the past 24 hours, you were the object of a persuasion effort, which occurs every time you watch or listen to an advertisement. Perhaps at this very moment, you are being persuaded as I attempt to convince you that your best change efforts may be refuted by many individuals. Are you convinced the strategies suggested thus far are effective, unbiased, and useful? Possibly, but more likely than not, you have a degree of skepticism, potentially doubting the credibility of the source or the utility of the advice. Now, consider that I want to persuade you and change your mind about the type of car you drive. Assume for the moment that you are not dissatisfied with your current vehicle, remembering that dissatisfaction may be a catalyst for CC (see pp. 351–352). Instead, imagine that your current vehicle is your most prized possession, and there is little anyone could say or do to persuade you to purchase the latest innovation in automobile technology, the "potato car."

One look at the sleek potato car and you will realize that you need this vehicle. The potato car accelerates from 0 to 60 miles per hour in under 6 seconds, the vehicle has a five-star safety rating, and is the latest rage in Germany, arguably the leader in automotive design. Yes, the potato car actually runs on potatoes. When the potatoes are heated, an enzyme is produced, which, when combined with methane gas, becomes a noncombustible fossil fuel with no carbon footprint, emitting no air pollution, and getting 40 miles per gallon (mpg) on average. Oh yes, there is one more thing, the potato car costs less than $10,000! Skeptical? Perhaps you believe that a $10,000 car is impossible to manufacture or that it probably uses shoddy materials and will quickly break down. Maybe you do not believe me, or you think that as an owner of the potato car, I am biased and giving you misleading or faulty information. Maybe you do believe me, but are you convinced? Will you purchase a new potato car?

Chinn and Brewer (1993) explained how students respond to contradictory scientific data that conflicts with personal understandings of the physical world. The seven-step seminal framework details reactions and responses to data considered anomalous, otherwise known as information or persuasive arguments that are inconsistent with one's core beliefs. The framework is highly relevant for motivational interventions because in all likelihood, individuals will use a similar system of evaluation and rationalization to refute strategy interventions. Strategies inconsistent with beliefs will be challenged or blatantly rejected. The seven responses to anomalous data include ignoring the data, rejecting the data, excluding the data from a personal theory about a domain, holding the data in abeyance, reinterpreting the data while maintaining one's existing theory, reinterpreting the data by making marginal changes to one's theory on a topic, or accepting the information as instrumental in changing one's theory. Table 12.1 outlines the continuum of possible responses to my persuasive effort to get you to buy the potato car according to the Chinn and Brewer (1993) taxonomy.

Ignoring data usually occurs when individuals are highly committed to their own impressions and beliefs. This type of response is frequently observed when learners completely discount recommendations, such as starting a project the day before a due date, despite the instructor's guidance. Rejecting data means individuals consider the

Table 12.1 Reactions to persuasive information about the potato car

Responses to persuasion (per Chinn & Brewer, 1993)	Cognitive representation (basis of response)
Ignore	This idea is silly and not worthy of my time.
Reject	Potato cars could not possibly work. I am suspicious you are trying to extort my money.
Exclude	Cars made out of vegetables are scientifically impossible and likely unsafe.
Abeyance	The potato car has merits, but I need more information and maybe a test drive.
Reinterpret and maintain existing theory	I think developing a potato car is scientifically possible, but I will stay with my current ride.
Reinterpret and revise existing theory	Potato cars are feasible and interesting; take me for a test drive to convince me.
Accept alternative theory and change	Eureka! Potato cars are awesome. I want one.

merits of the information but neglect to change their theory or behaviors related to the topic. Holding data in abeyance is a deferral strategy, suggesting neither acceptance nor rejection of an alternative theory or approach, and, instead, signifies the intention to revisit the information at another time. Reinterpreting anomalous data and maintaining existing theory involves conceptual consideration of the ideas advanced. During reinterpretation, the information is closely scrutinized, but the individual concludes after evaluation that the information provided was flawed, unclear, or irrelevant, leaving existing conceptions intact. Reinterpretation and revision, also known as "peripheral change," implies partial modification of one's thinking based upon the information provided.

Partial revision occurs when the change message is believable and credible but lacks strength or explanatory power to promote complete CC. Partial revision is also known as "compartmentalization," or the process that occurs when individuals experience disequilibrium with current thoughts, recognize and accept the anomalous information, and incorporate the new information as part of a peaceful coexistence with current thinking. Partial revision of automotive theory could be realized by accepting the viability of a potato car but not succumbing to the persuasion effort with a purchase. Finally, when an individual is convinced that new information is accurate and reputable, enduring change results. Acceptance of an alternative theory means the information provided was deemed credible and merited an alteration of one's mental representation to replace existing conceptions with a new theory.

While the potato car example is obviously contrived, the viability of Chinn and Brewer's (1993) taxonomy is well substantiated. The model has been used as evidence to explain conceptual shifts in domain knowledge in topics as diverse as how video games promote scientific inquiry (Zimmerman, 2014) to increasing the effectiveness of pediatric medical diagnoses (Balslev, de Grave, Muijtjens, & Scherpbier, 2010). The paradigm supports motivational interventions in several ways. First, knowing why an idea or possible strategy is rejected will assist in the selection of targeted refutational strategies. For example, one would use a highly different approach to refute data veracity (e.g., potato cars cannot get 40 mpg) in comparison with objecting to the source of flawed data. Second, objections to anomalous data can assist in the identification of the core beliefs that underlie change resistance. Knowing core beliefs, such as epistemologies or cultural norms, permits an informed response addressing the motive source, as opposed to concentrating on symptomatic behaviors, which are unlikely to mediate fundamental misconceptions. However, perhaps you are skeptical of the utility of Chinn and Brewer's (1993) taxonomy to explain motivated behavior. Before outlining specific strategies to overcome cognitive resistance, we examine an authentic application of the Chinn and Brewer model, which evaluates the veracity of one's *own* deeply entrenched beliefs.

Motivational Leader—*Amanda Boxtel*

A measurable transformation of mind, body, and motivation is Amanda Boxtel. At age 24, Amanda felt invincible. Her unstoppable and charismatic personality not only brought her often to the ski slopes as way to relax but also to display her exceptional talent. In 1992, a skiing accident shattered four of her vertebrae, along with her dreams of immortality. Amanda sustained a permanent spinal cord injury, immobilizing her from the pelvis down, but a broken back did not break her spirit. Her indomitable will and positive attitude have contributed to her reputation today as an internationally renowned and inspiring motivational speaker.

After her injury, through sheer will and determination, she pursued her love of skiing by teaching skiing *while sitting down*! "But on the inside I still ached to walk," she remembers (A. Boxtel, personal communication, December 3, 2014). While adaptive sports equipment helped her to live a rich and adventurous lifestyle, nothing enabled her to walk again until the invention of a bionic exoskeleton suit. The wearable technology provides a means to advance human mobility beyond wheelchairs and unpowered orthotics and mobilizes those unable to walk unassisted. As the world's first exoskeleton recipient, Amanda serves as the founding Executive Director for Bridging Bionics Foundation, demonstrating how bionic technology changes lives. In November 2013, she displayed the first partially 3D-printed exoskeleton in the world for Singularity University's European Summit in Budapest, Hungary, and then again in July 2014 at the Aspen Ideas Festival in Colorado. She continues to appear at venues globally, displaying her robotic suit, remarkable abilities, and competitive spirit.

Amanda's achievements include serving for 10 years as a professional ski instructor for Aspen Skiing Company; being named the Colorado Ski Country

USA Adaptive Athlete of the Year in 1999; carrying the Olympic Torch in 2002 on her mono-ski; orchestrating the first disability whitewater rafting trip down the Grand Canyon, and co-founding the Challenge Aspen, which has grown into a successful nonprofit organization.

What is her greatest life lesson? "It's taken 22 years of paralysis for me to understand that acceptance and hope must coexist. I accept who I am this moment, which frees me to be hopeful for what the next moment might bring" (A. Boxtel, personal communication, December 3, 2014). As a dynamic, passionate speaker she has shared the stage with high-profile figures, such as Deepak Chopra, Les Brown, President Jimmy Carter, Ali Velshi, Michael York, and Florence Griffith-Joyner. Amanda has been featured as a speaker at numerous conferences and venues around the world, including TEDCity2.0 Salon in Chengdu, China, TED (2011), TEDx San Antonio, TEDxDU, TEDxSF, *The Wall Street Journal*'s NewFronts 2014, and the USA Science and Engineering Festival 2014.

Amanda lives near Aspen, Colorado, in the quaint town of Basalt with her loveable golden retriever Benson (pictured above). Everyone in town knows Amanda, as she is involved in many community and outreach projects that aim to improve the lives of individuals with disabilities. In her spare time, and when she's not walking in her wearable robot suit, Amanda enjoys writing, painting and drawing.

The story of Amanda Boxtel is a perfect example to show the applied value of the Chinn and Brewer (1993) taxonomy and understand the evolution of personal behavior that occurs through belief change. Amanda's motivational journey evolved from a physiological and psychological rejection of her paralysis to eventual acceptance of her condition prompted by dramatic change of her self-beliefs. Immediately following the accident, Amanda was unwilling to accept her medical diagnosis of paralysis. Her initial reactions were one of complete disbelief, ignoring the medical data and rejecting the permanency of her physical reality. Her transformation began as she reinterpreted the medical data and accepted the diagnosis that changed her life. Amanda revealed how the change began:

> *I was paralyzed when I was 22 years old from a freak somersault while downhill skiing. And that was a pivotal moment in my life, yes. But the greater pivotal moment was five years later. I lived with nothing but hope and I took acceptance out of my vocabulary. I was not going to accept paralysis. And so I did everything I could to walk out of those hospital doors. You know, to prove the doctor wrong. It's like no. I'm going do this. I tried every type of holistic healing method, um, and dammit, you know, five years later I was still paralyzed.*
>
> A. Boxtel, personal communication, August 15, 2014

Amanda further explained why it took 5 years for her to realize the permanence of her paralysis. She described the moment as an "awakening" and an "epiphany" when she accepted the reality of her injuries. What Amanda experienced created a personal transformation of her beliefs from resistance to acceptance. She explained:

> At some point acceptance and hope must coexist. There's a dance. They must interplay and I've learned and it's still an ongoing life lesson that I had to accept my paralysis. It's like Amanda, paralysis can be for life. And so is arriving at a place, I accept that is the lesson to be able to reach a place of acceptance of my reality whatever it is. And that acceptance is right here, right now.
> A. Boxtel, personal communication, August 15, 2014

Amanda's revelations parallel what Chinn and Brewer (1993) described as a *theory change*. The catharsis Amanda experienced ended with eventual acceptance of the medical diagnosis that she initially ignored and rejected. Acceptance occurred without compartmentalization or selective exclusions of anomalous data. Amanda did not hold "theory-preserving responses" (p. 14), which occur when individuals remain attached to epistemological commitments, despite contrary evidence. Amanda's theory revision occurred through a 5-year process of deep introspection and close scrutiny of her self-beliefs, consummated by psychological liberation when she accepted the reality that her indomitable will and relentless passion were insufficient to overcome physical limitations. Eventually, Amanda accepted the permanency of limited mobility, but she learned that disability, psychological growth, and personal contentment were neither mutually exclusive nor dependent on physiological factors alone. Similar to the ontological shift and categorization of revised conceptions described earlier (Chi, 2005; Murphy & Mason, 2006), Amanda's beliefs were permanently changed when she finally realized that disability was both an obstacle and a rewarding opportunity conducive to personal growth that could also impact the lives of others.

Amanda Boxtel's transformation illustrates some of the circumstances and contingencies associated with conceptual evolution when applied to *personal* motivation. The Boxtel example demonstrates how conceptual understanding and motives are closely entwined and work together to promoting cognitive revision and subsequent motivational change (Pintrich et al., 1993; Weiner, 2014). As Amanda's beliefs evolved, her motives and corresponding behaviors also evolved, eventually leading to the launch of a successful career as a writer and speaker. Amanda's personal change was achieved, in part, by using deep-processing strategies, one of many pragmatic tools that are also useful when attempting to modify naive or alternative conceptions held by others, which, in all likelihood, will be the primary focus of the aspiring MD.

Overcoming change resistance in others

Modifying the flawed or inefficient motivational strategies of others requires consideration of at least three factors that influence change receptivity. First, individuals will hold beliefs and use corresponding motivational strategies that are both *incorrect* and *inappropriate* when striving to achieve learning and performance goals. "Incorrect" means using a strategy based upon misconceived knowledge (Chi, 2013). A learner who quits school as a motivational remedy after earning a poor course grade would be described as using the incorrect and maladaptive strategy of goal abandonment. "Inappropriate" means using a less than optimal approach to achieve a desired outcome (Chi, 2013). A basketball player motivated to practice foul shots until muscle exhaustion would illustrate the use of a potentially adaptive strategy (i.e., automating a procedural skill) in a counterproductive and inappropriate way. Distinguishing inaccurate from inappropriate strategies is crucial as inaccuracy is driven by misconceived beliefs and highly resistant to change, while inappropriate beliefs imply that a misconception may merely be a product of misguided learning and likely more amenable to revision. Ultimately, misconception type determines the optimal instructional or strategic intervention needed for change (Chi, 2013).

Second, individuals will harbor both discrete false beliefs as well as broader flawed mental models concerning the merits of particular conceptions or motivational strategies. Flawed individual beliefs are based upon singular ideas or, as Chi (2013) indicates, are examined at a "small grain size" (p. 51). A learner who typically demonstrates a mastery goal orientation but believes a normative orientation is best suited for Algebra learning would be categorized as harboring a misconception at the individual belief level. Alternatively, mental models are a more organized and numerous collection of related beliefs that are influential in directing behavior (Chi, 2013). Flawed mental models also include misconceptions, but with broader impact. For example, a learner with a mental model that vocational success is predicated upon solidifying relationships with others may be highly motivated to make socially driven decisions that transcend career plans. The pervasive mental model based on affiliation may be a domain-general strategy guiding important decisions, such as choosing a college major, picking specific courses, or extracurricular activities. Again, the distinction is important because different mediation approaches would be used contingent upon the breadth and grain size of an individual's misconception.

Third, some beliefs are more entrenched and resilient than others. Entrenched beliefs are enduring, highly resistant to change, and likely nested in a foundation of hierarchical, cultural, and social beliefs. From the individual's perspective, entrenched beliefs make intuitive sense that helps them navigate their perceptual world. The beliefs are substantiated by accumulated evidence garnered through experience and hold broad explanatory power for the individual (Chinn & Brewer, 1993). Consider the parent who quit school before graduation and perceives little benefit in continuing education, harboring unfavorable views about schools and teaching in general. From a strategy perspective, the doubting parent would likely show little receptivity to help a struggling child with homework because of negative superordinate beliefs about education, which would have hierarchical influence over subordinate beliefs concerning schools and homework. Extent of entrenchment, like type of belief and grain size, is a powerful determinant to assess which type of strategy is best suited to overcome resistance. Having outlined some important change moderators, I now summarize five empirically supported strategies designed to promote conceptual revision, under the pretense that when enduring CC is achieved, different motives will be aroused resulting in behavioral modifications that would not occur in the absence of CC (Weiner, 2014).

Instructional strategies supporting conceptual change

Empirically supported instructional strategies to overcome naive thinking, false beliefs, and misconceptions are pervasive and primarily focus on stimulating knowledge revision in science domains on topics, such as gravity, climate change, and evolution. However, researchers infrequently study the motivational strategy implications that accompany evolving mental representations beyond identifying motivational beliefs that contribute to CC (Dole & Sinatra, 1998; Gregoire, 2003; Johnson & Sinatra, 2014; Linnenbrink & Pintrich, 2002). The dearth of empirical research outlining how motivational strategies change as cognitive misconceptions are revised is surprising, considering the ubiquitous influence of motivation beliefs on learning and performance. Learners also hold many misconceptions in regard to motivation (McAfee, Xu, & Hoffman, 2015; Murphy & Alexander, 2008), and specific motivational beliefs and regulation strategies are associated with optimal learning and performance (Wolters, 2003). Thus, the following recommendations are warranted by the consensus of evidence shown to be effective in overcoming resistance to cognitive change, suggestions which are similarly hypothesized to activate strategy revision based on the restructuring of motivational false beliefs and misconceptions.

Promote strategy awareness

Considering that many motives are implicit (Greenwald, 1992; Thrash, Maruskin, & Martin, 2012), and individuals are commonly unaware of their own motives, lack of motivational strategy awareness should be expected. Although learners can and do revise knowledge conceptions automatically below an active level of consciousness, intentionality and awareness of one's beliefs and emotions often enhance the probability of CC. Intentionality assumes individuals have awareness of both the goals they intend to reach and the strategies they will employ to reach their goals (Sinatra & Pintrich, 2002). Thus, a first step toward creating revision of a maladaptive strategy is developing a process that explicitly brings goal-directed targets and corresponding strategies to the forefront of individual awareness.

One beneficial approach used to foster awareness is to create cognitive conflict or disequilibrium about current motivational approaches used to reach goals. For example, a learner who sets lofty goals may not realize that often setting outlandish performance targets is a failure-avoiding strategy, designed to protect self-worth (De Castella, Byrne, & Covington, 2013). Although stimulating cognitive conflict by no means guarantees strategy revision, conflict minimally will promote awareness of motivational misconceptions and the flawed strategy implications of those conceptions. Post awareness, individuals can also be probed to assess the degree of satisfaction with existing strategies while concurrently prompting the individual to consider why the preferred strategy might fail. Employing these learner-centered approaches fosters the needed awareness that is often lacking when individuals use motivational strategies that are automatic and have become part of habitual behavior.

Identify plausible alternatives

After arousing attention concerning the type and usage of strategies, the next step is persuading the individual that plausible strategy alternatives exist. Plausibility means that, at a minimum, the individual is willing to consider an alternative strategy because the recommendation is understood, coherent, and relatively simple and because the proposal is deemed a viable and logical alternative to solve the specific challenge at hand (Strike & Posner, 1992). Plausibility has little direct bearing on valence of the evaluation, or if the individual will adopt the strategy recommendation but, instead, means that the suggestion is appraised as sensible and is under consideration. Recommendations evaluated as plausible by some will be patently rejected by others based on individual differences in background knowledge and perceived cultural suitability. Suggestions inconsistent with norms may promote anxiety and negative affect (Broughton, Sinatra, & Nussbaum, 2013), while those incommensurate with degree of expertise result in excessive processing demands on the individual (Kirschner, Sweller, & Clark, 2006), two factors that will promote resistance and inhibit strategy change.

Further, plausibility does not imply belief acceptance as an individual may completely understand a recommendation but reject the idea because it does not fit within one's theory or domain beliefs (Chinn, Duncan, Dianovsky, & Rinehart, 2013). Even if a strategy is belief consistent, enacted behavior may not parallel the belief. For example, many students know that note-taking is an effective learning strategy to help remember lecture content and an approach that often leads to higher grades (Boyle & Forchelli, 2014). Despite a belief in the effectiveness of note-taking, many learners deliberately avoid note-taking, because the strategy is perceived as effortful and potentially promotes anxiety when lecture notes are spelled wrong or written incorrectly (Igo, Riccomini, Bruning, & Pope, 2006). Ironically, a strategy known to be effective is consciously avoided, as individuals prefer to risk academic failure in favor of insulating themselves from the negative self-beliefs which may accompany poor note-taking.

Plausibility assessments should also consider the hierarchical and nested nature of personal theories (Vosniadou, 1994). "Nested" not only means consideration of superordinate influences on strategy recommendations but also suggests that strategy approaches deemed inconsistent with epistemology will likely lack personal plausibility. For instance, teachers, in stark contrast to research findings, consistently heavily rely on extrinsic reward as a motivational strategy to accelerate student achievement. Teachers with an absolutist view of motivation and rewards would be unlikely to consider strategies cultivating intrinsic motivation as plausible, even when they understand the concept because the alternative is perceived as an epistemological clash. Further, plausibility is a function of normative cultural behavior, with strong resistance to be expected if a strategy recommendation is inconsistent with culture norms, as would be the case when recommending collaborative group work to learners that hold strong individualistic beliefs.

Provide refutational evidence

Having addressed the awareness and plausibility hurdles, the next step to overcome conceptual resistance is providing refutational evidence that promotes the formation of alternative knowledge frameworks. Refutational evidence seeks to persuade individuals to believe that existing representations are flawed in light of inconsistencies with scientific evidence. By instigating doubt, the goal of refutation strategies is to encourage the nonbeliever to relinquish an existing belief in favor of another (Hynd, 2001). Refutation can be accomplished through written text, dialogue, or via presenting visual evidence, with each method designed to reduce commitments to current perspectives.

Refutational arguments can be delivered textually through written passages using a one-sided persuasive approach or by presenting counterarguments on a singular topic. Two-sided refutational texts prompt the reader to make comparisons between existing conceptions and empirically supported data. The two-sided approach and texts that discuss the causality that undermines available evidence are generally more effective at inducing belief change than texts that present one-sided arguments or disconfirming data alone (Murphy & Alexander, 2013). The two-sided model is preferable because alternative perspectives inspire psychological conflict, which individuals are motivated to resolve (Lee & Byun, 2012). Verbal strategies conceptually mirror the written refutational process but are most effective when misconceptions are refuted by disconfirming data. By presenting anomalous data verbally, the persuader can augment weak oppositional and conceptual arguments that are based on intuitive theory alone.

The overall key to successful refutation is using tangible high-quality evidence that prompts the misbeliever to think deeply about their current beliefs in light of evidence. A strong positive relationship exists between the degree of elaboration and contemplation on a topic and the probability of lasting, not transitory, or peripheral belief change (Petty & Briñol, 2012; Petty & Cacioppo, 1986). At a minimum, refutation promotes cognitive dissonance with regard to existing ideas (Guzzetti, Snyder, Glass, & Gamas, 1993). Dissonance frequently generates an affectively laden response to the presented evidence. Subsequently, the response is assigned a valence by the recipient, contingent upon his or her subjective evaluation of the message, source, and the context of the belief. Negative affect motivates cognitive withdrawal as the individual holds onto existing beliefs avoiding CC, while positive affective assessments support cognitive engagement with the refutational concept, enhancing change probability (Johnson & Sinatra, 2014). Reactions to refutational evidence also provide important clues concerning the strength of existing beliefs, especially when evaluating a person's emotional response. In sum, refutation is a valuable tool that reveals the specific counterevidence most salient to dispel misconceptions held by the desired reform target (Sinatra & Mason, 2013).

Create personal relevance

Another essential requirement to foster CC is a reasonable assurance that the persuasive message and concomitant evidence is appraised as fruitful by the targeted recipient (Posner, Strike, Hewson, & Gertzog, 1982). "Fruitful" implies that the individual believes there is value and tangible application of the proposed alternative conception. When individuals doubt prospective benefits from a strategy recommendation, they will often filter out the message even before evaluating the merits of what is suggested, failing to incorporate the strategy into one's mental model of the concept (Jones, Ross, Lynam, Perez, & Leitch, 2011). When individuals believe tangible benefits are possible from adapting an alternative perspective, existing conceptions will evolve to accommodate the new belief. In essence, perception of usefulness is an individual difference variable that changes based upon the degree of importance and utility the individual assigns to the proposed recommendation. Individuals will have a higher probability of CC and be more motivated to consider alternative conceptions when the change effort satisfies their personal goals (Dole & Sinatra, 1998).

A particular helpful strategy to enhance personal relevance and meet the fruitful test is making a meaningful connection with the learner's existing knowledge, cultural background, or current motivational challenges. Personal relevance will be assessed based upon situational needs. As an individual becomes more dissatisfied with existing conceptions, openness to alternative perspectives will be enhanced and relevance will be increased (Hewson, 1992). Information that is highly valued by one individual may seem superfluous and inconsequential to another because relevance is highly personalized. By example, presenting a motivational engagement strategy, such as metamonitoring, to an individual who perceives limited interest in a topical domain would likely be pointless. Recommendations perceived to hold limited value will be rejected, even when based on sound empirical data, when individual relevance is lacking.

Scaffold strategy change

From a revisionist perspective, change requires at least some intentionality that is activated by personal volition and accomplished by focused effort toward reaching change goals (Limón, 2002). However, change does not happen spontaneously, and many times, individuals will be motivated to change but may lack knowledge concerning how to capitalize on their desires. Considering the vast variability of change motivation, and the litany of resistance factors that impede change momentum, it is prudent to encourage, scaffold, and support individually desired change objectives. Assuming the aforementioned factors of awareness, plausibility, refutational evidence, and personal relevance have been met, the individual will likely exhibit motivation to adapt new approaches. The final hurdle is providing the person with specific instructional and metacognitive tools enabling him or her to cultivate adaptive motivational strategies that are practical, useful, and enduring.

To scaffold change, individuals must master how to evaluate persuasive efforts and reason effectively. Appropriate reasoning means repression of personal bias and the evaluation of persuasive arguments based upon the merits of available evidence presented, not upon historical outcomes, personal experience, or hearsay findings. As Sinatra and Chinn (2012) revealed, "one cannot think and reason without some raw material" (p. 258). What raw material is provided for evaluation and assessment is clearly within the jurisdiction and grasp of the savvy MD. Foremost, good reasoning starts with explanations regarding why a strategy change is beneficial. When motivational strategies are introduced, individuals should be shown how adaptation of particular strategies directly leads to personal goals and growth. For example, if advocating the benefits of self-regulatory control strategies, as mentioned in Chapter 10 (p. 274), individual learners should also be shown evidence that reveals how self-regulatory ability influences performance and alternatively what consequences result in the absence of using a particular strategy.

Once given sufficient evidence to support a persuasive argument, explicit instruction on evaluating counterarguments should be provided as well as the use of educator prompts and hints to help channel the learner toward their desired outcomes (Sinatra and Chinn, 2012). One assistive approach to scaffolding change initiatives is via the use of targeted questioning and inquiry methods (Chinn et al., 2013). Starting with relating resolution of motivational challenges to students' background knowledge (e.g., Can you think of a time when you overcame a physical or psychological obstacle? What did you do?) and making connections between problems and solutions, the MD can then develop strategies based upon the outcome of the reasoning process just described.

Hatano and Inagaki (2003) proposed a particular classroom questioning procedure that leverages the active engagement inherent to most inquiry methods. The process is particular well suited and generalizable to motivational strategies because of the individualistic nature of strategy use, where a strategy suitable for one individual may be situationally inappropriate for another based upon background knowledge or cultural fit. The process is focused on presenting "perplexing" (p. 416) statements or ideas to a group of learners and involves scaffolding learners toward arriving at the correct solution when several viable answers to the problem are feasible. For example, if attempting to induce CC in preservice teachers concerning learning strategies, the following type of question would likely be evaluated as perplexing:

Q. What strategy is best suited to promote knowledge gains when learners lack interest in a topic?
   a. Setting proximal goals
   b. Providing extrinsic rewards
   c. Giving learners topic options
   d. Instituting collaborative learning

While strong arguments could be provided to support each answer alternative, each answer (a, b, c, or d) is assigned to groups of learners to allow the opportunity to defend an answer choice using evidence-based data. The strategy of providing multiple plausible response facilitates inquiry, discussion, and evaluation as the educator guides learners toward reaching the correct answer (for this question, choice "c" is best supported by research), while simultaneously considering the merits of the alternative conceptions. Eventually, learners realize why the research-based solution is correct, with the hopes of concurrently dispelling any prior misconceptions.

Using inquiry methods also provides an ideal context to leverage sociocultural influences that are conducive to CC because during inquiry people work together solving educational and performance challenges. If learning and corresponding CC is a situative process as advocated by many CC scholars (Hatano & Inagaki, 2003; Mason, 2007; Murphy, 2007); clearly socially constructed knowledge can also be generalized to accumulating a diverse repertoire of motivational strategies. When individuals work together, diverse opinions are generated and knowledge is contextually developed, leading Mason (2007) to conclude, "Learning is essentially a social phenomenon and thus should occur in very rich social and physical environments in which learners deal with problems of everyday life" (p. 3).

Mason (2007) further advocated, "It is a teacher's responsibility to arrange sociocultural factors to stimulate and support knowledge restructuring" (p. 4). Thus, inspiring motivational knowledge reconstruction through the social exchange of ideas is an additional method to potentially mitigate resistance to new ideas. Through discourse, individuals can evaluate the merits and drawbacks of strategies collectively, resulting in normative values that determine approved patterns of behavior. Murphy (2007) described a variation of the collaborative process where educators lead change efforts through "pedagogical persuasion" (p. 50). This strategy involves both educators and learners evaluating existing beliefs through reasoning activities and collectively justifying knowledge based upon sound evidence and cultural artifacts. Persuasive pedagogical is particularly useful to examine motivational strategies because studies reveal that not only is knowledge gained from the process, but underlying beliefs that support the knowledge also change (Alexander, Fives, Buehl, & Mulhern, 2002). Also, recall from Chapter 8 (p. 212) that collaboration supports modeling of positive behavior through upward social comparisons. Educators who demonstrate unbiased reasoning and objective assessment of data and who reach logical evidentiary conclusions serve as a respected and likely emulated behavioral models for CC.

Finally, a number of very specific cognitive strategies can be used to scaffold revision of existing knowledge. These remedies leverage the intimate linkage between motivation and cognition, dictating clear conceptual understanding, a foundation for agentic motivational effort (Weiner, 2014). Kahneman (2011) while explaining reasons why individuals often demonstrate basic, but illogical, flaws in the thinking process, revealed multiple, high-impact strategies. He suggested that approaches as simplistic as repetition of false information, waging persuasive arguments when individuals are tired, and using simple and rhyming terminology promote greater retention of wrong information, leading to deeply entrenched and resistant false beliefs. The flawed beliefs lead to cognitive bias (and performance errors) when solving basic conceptual problems because the retrieval of the information, although wrong, is easily accessible for the "lazy" thinker. Further, familiarity often replaces accuracy as individuals perpetuate false but recognizable information because individuals are suspicious of novelty. Last, Kahneman reveals a secret that the seasoned MDs should already know; good moods enhance receptivity to disparate personal beliefs. When a person is happy, he or she is far more likely to be gullible, accommodating, and intuitive, showing receptivity to new ideas. According to Kahneman, if you want to promote change, take the frown away, and make your best suggestions on a metaphorically sunny day.

Learning from leaders

Throughout the book, you have figuratively met a diverse group of individuals describing motivated behavior. All the comments and examples provided are true and were revealed through actual interviews with the author. Each person disclosed highly personal information and sometimes intimate stories and strategies that define their beliefs, motives, and behaviors. Each explained their unique approach to life and the methods he or she used to set goals, achieve targets, and rebound from setbacks. The personalities were selected for inclusion in the book, not based on how they navigated life's challenges but, instead, based upon their chosen professions or because their personal circumstances were relevant examples of how motivation drives agentic behavior.

Bernie Madoff volunteered his story to show how consummate will and passionate motivation clouded his judgment and led to making decisions he knew were wrong, while Alex Dixon, LaSonya Moore, and Amanda Boxtel revealed how the power of motivation helped overcome many cultural and physiological obstacles. Jessi Colter, Darren Soto, and Robert Knowling, Jr. shared their relationship and leadership strategies, revealing how perseverance, faith, and affiliation satisfied their own motives and also fostered goal attainment in others. Nick Holes and the Hines sisters provided us with a glimpse into how mastery-oriented performers think and why what the world believes about you does not really matter. Finally, Alec Torelli, Nick Lowery, and Bill Gramática shared how different forms of self-regulation and control contributed to goal attainment and adaptive motivation, regardless of task success or failure.

Despite the diversity of personalities, cultural backgrounds, and professions, there were several common themes pervasive among the interviewees. The themes that emerged during the course of interviews and the subsequent inferences were discerned by listening to each person's story and analyzing interview transcripts. First, each person set predetermined goals that guided his or her behavior, as each exhibited an intrinsic locus of control. Nothing was left to happenstance by these leaders, as all told similar stories revealing that they almost always felt in control of their own destiny, attributing both success and failure to factors within personal influence. Perhaps a surprise to some, each individual experienced setbacks, and even defeat. Cheryl Hines was rejected three times for the same role, Darren Soto frequently supported legislation that was eventually defeated, and the NFL stars often suffered humiliation and fan ridicule when game-changing field goals were missed. Despite setbacks, each person communicated elevated self-efficacy beliefs, resilience, and perseverance, all within the boundaries of accurate calibration of his or her personal skills and abilities.

Although all these persons are bona fide leaders in their respective fields, few overestimated their talents and abilities to a point where it affected their motivation or performance. Perhaps most importantly, each person has made mistakes, experienced dejection, and encountered obstacles, but universally all of the leaders explained that mistakes contributed to their growth and what defines them today. Table 12.2 provides a snapshot of preferred strategies used by the leaders, as well as page references to document how the described behaviors are supported by a confluence of empirical data.

The strategies summarized in Table 12.2 reveal a collection of behaviors; normative behaviors for the motivational leaders profiled in the book. On face value, the combined strategies appear to support a model of optimal motivation. Arguably, each leader is successful in his or her domain of interest and expertise. Each person clearly expressed happiness and contentment, but not complacency with his or her lives. While there is no aggregate empirical data to collectively portray the strategies listed above as a validated motivational model, each strand of evidence is supported by a

Table 12.2 Examples of strategies used by the author and the motivation leaders

Who (in order presentation)	Strategy	Example/page
Author	Forethought and motivational self-regulation	3
Bernard Madoff	Normative orientation and extrinsic motivation	24
Alexis Dixon	Goal setting and control beliefs	52
Rebecca/Cheryl Hines	Self-efficacy and resilience	84
LaSonya Moore	Conscious rejection of stereotype	116
Nick Holes	Discounting normative behavior	148
Nick Lowery	Mastery orientation and self-regulation	187
Jessi Colter	Spiritual beliefs and positive channeling of affect	221
Alec Torelli	Emotional regulation using volitional coping strategies	251
Darren Soto	Building affiliation and gaining consensus	288
Robert Knowling, Jr.	Empowering others by creating an autonomous culture	317
Amanda Boxtel	Intentional conceptual change	358

confluence of multi-disciplinary findings linking the strategy to adaptive motivation, which contributes to accelerated achievement and enhanced performance. The qualities exemplified by the leaders in aggregate by no means imply that the listed factors are responsible for or a cause of their success as determined by North American cultural standards. However, there is little doubt that the factors listed in the Table have contributed to the personal growth, satisfaction, and psychological well-being of the individuals, based upon their own admission and as a result of the interpretation of interview remarks within the shadow of reliable empirical data. I only hope that you consider each person as a respected model and possibly emulate one or more, so that you, too, can be a motivational leader in your academic career or chosen profession.

Epilogue

The idea for this text was originally conceived by students who, like many renowned educational psychologists (Anderman, 2011; Berliner, 2006; Patrick, Anderman, Bruening, & Duffin, 2011), have lamented the lack of applied and practical emphasis found in scholarly publications that address teaching, learning, and motivation. As the text blossomed from a nascent idea into a contractual reality, it became clear that the students were right. The need for a multi-disciplinary, evidence-based, authentic approach to motivation for learning and performance was apparent. The ensuing challenge became devising a format that students would enjoy reading, while concurrently crafting an informative text based upon the latest scientific evidence in the field of motivation.

Four main intentions guided the writing of the text. First, instilling self-awareness was paramount, as knowing one's own motives is often a conceptual gateway to increase the understanding of others. As revealed through the vignettes in Chapter 1 (p. 5) and the motivational profiles found throughout the book, mediation of motivational challenges is not haphazard and is often accomplished by objective, intentional assessment of personal beliefs, intended objectives, and strategy choices. Second, interpretative myopia, which occurs when staunch inferences and conclusions are based upon findings from a single or unitary source, was avoided by offering multi-disciplinary evidence from the fields of neuroscience, athletics, social psychology, and organizational development in addition to describing confluent outcomes from research in education and general psychology. Third, relevant strategy suggestions and practical recommendations to instill optimal motivation in the self and others were advanced by describing, analyzing, and evaluating authentic and realistic examples of motivational challenges and accompanying behaviors. Last, through the voices of contemporary motivational leaders from diverse fields and occupations, the reader was afforded an intimate glimpse into the minds of successful others, revealing how motivational momentum can be sustained despite encountering formidable obstacles, judgmental errors, or naive mistakes.

Finally, the success of the aspiring MD is not achieved exclusively by modeling others or through the mere accumulation of motivational knowledge. Cultivating adaptive motivation in the self and others requires an integrative and introspective approach that suppresses personal desires and beliefs in favor of scientific evidence while concurrently evaluating the situational, contextual, and cultural applicability of a particular solution. If devoid of objectivity and lacking in empirical conviction, the egocentric MD is destined to fail, fooled by misguided hope and mired in false optimism. Ultimately, the MD's success will not be judged by how much is known but by how much his or her knowledge can energize the focus and productivity of others.

References

Alexander, P. A., Fives, H., Buehl, M. M., & Mulhern, J. (2002). Persuasive pedagogy. *Teaching and Teacher Education, 18*, 795–813.

Anderman, E. M. (2011). Educational psychology in the twenty-first century: Challenges for our community. *Educational Psychologist, 46*(3), 185–196. http://dx.doi.org/10.1080/00461520.2011.587724.

Balslev, T., de Grave, W. S., Muijtjens, A. M., & Scherpbier, A. J. (2010). Enhancing diagnostic accuracy among non-experts through use of video cases. *Pediatrics, 125*(3), e570–e576.

Bandura, A. (1997). *Self-efficacy: The exercise of control*. New York, NY: Freeman.

Barreto, I., & Baden-Fuller, C. (2006). To conform or to perform? Mimetic behaviour, legitimacy-based groups and performance consequences. *Journal of Management Studies, 43*(7), 1559–1581. http://dx.doi.org/10.1111/j.1467-6486.2006.00620.x.

Battilana, J., & Casciaro, T. (2012). Change agents, networks, and institutions: A contingency theory of organizational change. *Academy of Management Journal, 55*(2), 381–398.

Berliner, D. C. (2006). Educational psychology: Searching for essence throughout a century of influence. In P. A. Alexander & P. H. Winne (Eds.), *Handbook of educational psychology* (pp. 3–27) (2nd ed.). Mahwah, NJ: Lawrence Erlbaum Associates.

Berntson, G. G., Norman, G. J., & Cacioppo, J. T. (2009). Evaluative processes. In G. G. Berntson & J. T. Cacioppo (Eds.), *Handbook of neuroscience for the behavioral sciences* (pp. 617–634). Hoboken, NJ: J. Wiley.

Boyle, J. R., & Forchelli, G. A. (2014). Differences in the note-taking skills of students with high achievement, average achievement, and learning disabilities. *Learning and Individual Differences, 35*, 9–14. http://dx.doi.org/10.1016/j.lindif.2014.06.002.

Broughton, S. H., Sinatra, G. M., & Nussbaum, E. M. (2013). "Pluto has been a planet my whole life!" Emotions, attitudes, and conceptual change in elementary students' learning about Pluto's reclassification. *Research in Science Education, 43*(2), 529–550.

Campbell, W. K., Hoyle, R. H., & Bradfield, E. K. (2011). Compensating, resisting, and breaking: A meta-analytic examination of reactions to self-esteem threat. *Personality and Social Psychology Review, 15*(1), 51–74.

Chi, M. T. H. (2005). Commonsense conceptions of emergent processes: Why some misconceptions are robust. *The Journal of the Learning Sciences, 2*, 161–199.

Chi, M. T. H. (2013). Two kinds and four sub-types of misconceived knowledge, ways to change it, and the learning outcomes. In S. Vosniadou (Ed.), *International handbook of research on conceptual change* (pp. 49–70) (2nd ed.). New York, NY: Routledge.

Chinn, C. A., & Brewer, W. F. (1993). The role of anomalous data in knowledge acquisition: A theoretical framework and implications for science instruction. *Review of Educational Research, 63*, 1–49.

Chinn, C. A., Duncan, R. G., Dianovsky, M., & Rinehart, R. (2013). Promoting conceptual change through inquiry. In S. Vosniadou (Ed.), *International handbook of research on conceptual change* (pp. 539–559) (2nd ed.). New York, NY: Routledge.

Cordova, J. R., Sinatra, G. M., Jones, S. H., Taasoobshirazi, G., & Lombardi, D. (2014). Confidence in prior knowledge, self-efficacy, interest and prior knowledge: Influences on conceptual change. *Contemporary Educational Psychology, 39*(2), 164–174. http://dx.doi.org/10.1016/j.cedpsych.2014.03.006.

Coyne, K. P., & Coyne, S. E. J. (2007). Surviving your new CEO. *Harvard Business Review, 85*(5), 62–69.

De Castella, K., Byrne, D., & Covington, M. (2013). Unmotivated or motivated to fail? A cross-cultural study of achievement motivation, fear of failure, and student disengagement. *Journal of Educational Psychology, 105*(3), 861–880. http://dx.doi.org/10.1037/a0032464.

Dole, J. A., & Sinatra, G. M. (1998). Reconceptualizing change in the cognitive construction of knowledge. *Educational Psychologist, 33*, 109–128.

Fredricks, J. A., Blumenfeld, P. C., & Paris, A. H. (2004). School engagement: Potential of the concept, state of the evidence. *Review of Educational Research, 59*, 117–142.

Gagne, M., & Deci, E. L. (2005). Self-determination theory and work motivation. *Journal of Organizational Behavior, 26*(4), 331–362. http://dx.doi.org/10.1002/job.322.

Gjernes, T. (2010). Facing resistance to health advice. *Health, Risk & Society, 12*(5), 471–489. http://dx.doi.org/10.1080/13698575.2010.509492.

Greene, J. A., Muis, K. R., & Pieschl, S. (2010). The role of epistemic beliefs in students' self-regulated learning with computer-based learning environments: Conceptual and methodological issues. *Educational Psychologist, 45*(4), 245–257. http://dx.doi.org/10.1080/00461520.2010.515932.

Greeno, J. G., & the Middle School Mathematics through Application Project Group (1998). The situativity of knowing, learning, and research. *American Psychologist, 53*, 5–26.

Greenwald, A. G. (1992). New Look 3: Reclaiming unconscious cognition. *American Psychologist, 47*, 766–779. http://dx.doi.org/10.1037//0003-066X.47.7.6.766.

Gregoire, M. (2003). Is it a challenge or a threat? A dual-process model of teachers' cognition and appraisal process during conceptual change. *Educational Psychology Review, 15*(2), 147–179.

Guzzetti, B. J., Snyder, T. E., Glass, G. V., & Gamas, W. S. (1993). Promoting conceptual change in science: A comparative meta-analysis of instructional interventions from reading education and science education. *Reading Research Quarterly, 28*, 117–159.

Hambrick, D., & Engle, R. (2003). The role of working memory in problem solving. In J. Davidson & R. Sternberg (Eds.), *The psychology of problem solving* (pp. 176–206). New York, NY: Cambridge University Press.

Hatano, G., & Inagaki, K. (2003). When is conceptual change intended? A cognitive-sociocultural view. In G. M. Sinatra & P. R. Pintrich (Eds.), *Intentional conceptual change* (pp. 407–428). Mahwah, NJ: Lawrence Erlbaum.

Hewson, P. W. (1992). Conceptual change in science teaching and teacher education. In a meeting on *Research and Curriculum Development in Science Teaching* under the auspices of the National Center for Educational Research, Documentation, and Assessment, Ministry for Education and Science, Madrid, Spain.

Hickey, D. T. (2003). Engaged participation versus marginal nonparticipation: A stridently sociocultural approach to achievement motivation. *The Elementary School Journal, 4*, 401–429.

Hynd, C. R. (2001). Refutational texts and the change process. *International Journal of Educational Research, 35*, 699–714. http://dx.doi.org/10.1016/S0883-0355(02)00010-1.

Igo, L. B., Riccomini, P. J., Bruning, R. H., & Pope, G. G. (2006). How should middle-school students with LD approach online note taking? A mixed-methods study. *Learning Disability Quarterly, 2*, 89–100.

Johnson, M. L., & Sinatra, G. M. (2014). The influence of approach and avoidance goals on conceptual change. *The Journal of Educational Research, 107*(4), 312–325. http://dx.doi.org/10.1080/00220671.2013.807492.

Jones, N., Ross, H., Lynam, T., Perez, P., & Leitch, A. (2011). Mental models: An interdisciplinary synthesis of theory and methods. *Ecology and Society, 16*(1), 46.

Jost, J. T. (2011). Systems justification theory as compliment, complement, and corrective to theories of social identification and social dominance. In D. Dunning (Ed.), *Social motivation* (pp. 223–263). New York, NY: Psychology Press.

Jost, J. T., Banaji, M. R., & Nosek, B. A. (2004). A decade of system justification theory: Accumulated evidence of conscious and unconscious bolstering of the status quo. *Political Psychology, 25*(6), 881–919.

Jost, J. T., Pietrzak, J., Liviatan, I., Mandisodza, A. N., & Napier, J. L. (2008). System justification as conscious and nonconscious goal pursuit. In J. Y. Shah & W. L. Gardner (Eds.), *Handbook of motivation science* (pp. 591–605). New York, NY: Guilford Press.

Kahneman, D. (2011). *Thinking fast, and slow*. New York, NY: Farrar, Straus, & Giroux.

Kampourakis, K., Pavlidi, V., Papadopoulou, M., & Palaiokrassa, E. (2012). Children's teleological intuitions: What kind of explanations do 7–8 year olds give for the features of organisms, artifacts and natural objects? *Research in Science Education, 42*(4), 651–671.

Kelemen, D., & Rosset, E. (2009). The human function compunction: Teleological explanation in adults. *Cognition, 111*(1), 138–143.

Kirschner, P. A., Sweller, J., & Clark, R. E. (2006). Why minimal guidance during instruction does not work: An analysis of the failure of constructivist, discovery, problem-based, experiential, and inquiry-based teaching. *Educational Psychologist, 41*(2), 75–86. http://dx.doi.org/10.1207/s15326985ep4102_1.

Kotter, J. P. (1995). Leading change: Why transformation efforts fail. *Harvard Business Review, 73*(2), 59–67.

Lee, G., & Byun, T. (2012). An explanation for the difficulty of leading conceptual change using a counterintuitive demonstration: The relationship between cognitive conflict and responses. *Research in Science Education, 42*(5), 943–965.

Limón, M. (2002). Conceptual change in history. In M. Limón & L. Mason (Eds.), *Reconsidering conceptual change: Issues in theory and practice* (pp. 301–336). Dordrecht, Netherlands: Kluwer Academic Publishers.

Linnenbrink, E. A., & Pintrich, P. R. (2002). The role of motivational beliefs in conceptual change. In M. Limón & L. Mason (Eds.), *Reconsidering conceptual change: Issues in theory and practice* (pp. 115–135). Dordrecht, Netherlands: Kluwer Academic Publishers.

Lombrozo, T., & Carey, S. (2006). Functional explanation and the function of explanation. *Cognition, 99*(2), 167–204.

Mack, M. L., Richler, J. J., Palmeri, T. J., & Gauthier, I. (2009). Categorization. In J. Y. Shah & W. L. Gardner (Eds.), *Handbook of motivation science* (pp. 395–418). New York, NY: Guilford Press.

Marsden, P. V., & Friedkin, N. E. (1993). Network studies of social influence. *Sociological Methods & Research, 22*(1), 127–151.

Mason, L. (2007). Introduction: Bridging the cognitive and sociocultural approaches in research on conceptual change: Is it feasible? *Educational Psychologist, 42*, 1–7.

McAfee, M. A., Xu, L., & Hoffman, B. (2015). *Identifying the educational psychology misconceptions among pre-service teachers.* Paper presented at the annual meeting of the American Psychological Association, Toronto, CA, August 2015.

Murphy, P. K. (2007). The eye of the beholder: The interplay of social and cognitive components in change. *Educational Psychologist, 42*(1), 41–53.

Murphy, P. K., & Alexander, P. A. (2008). The role of knowledge, beliefs, and interest in the conceptual change process: A synthesis and meta-analysis of the research. In S. Vosniadou (Ed.), *International handbook of research on conceptual change* (pp. 538–616). Netherlands: Springer.

Murphy, P. K., & Alexander, P. A. (2013). Situating text, talk, and transfer in conceptual change: Concluding thoughts. In S. Vosniadou (Ed.), *International handbook of research on conceptual change* (pp. 603–621) (2nd ed.). New York, NY: Routledge.

Murphy, P. K., & Mason, L. (2006). Changing knowledge and beliefs. In P. A. Alexander & P. H. Winne (Eds.), *Handbook of educational psychology* (pp. 305–324) (2nd ed.). Mahwah, NJ: Erlbaum.

Patrick, H., Anderman, L. H., Bruening, P. S., & Duffin, L. C. (2011). The role of educational psychology in teacher education: Three challenges for educational psychologists. *Educational Psychologist, 46*(2), 71–83. http://dx.doi.org/10.1080/00461520.2011.538648.

Petty, R. E., & Briñol, P. (2012). The elaboration likelihood model. In P. M. Van Lange, A. W. Kruglanski, & E. Higgins (Eds.), *Handbook of theories of social psychology* (Vol. 1, pp. 224–245). Thousand Oaks, CA: Sage Publications Ltd.

Petty, R. E., & Cacioppo, J. T. (1986). The elaboration likelihood model of persuasion. *Advances in Experimental Social Psychology, 19*, 123–205.

Pintrich, P. R., Marx, R. W., & Boyle, R. A. (1993). Beyond cold conceptual change: The role of motivational beliefs and classroom contextual factors in the process of conceptual change. *Review of Educational Research, 63*(2), 167–199.

Posner, G. J., Strike, K. A., Hewson, P. W., & Gertzog, W. A. (1982). Accommodation of a scientific conception: Toward a theory of conceptual change. *Science Education, 66*, 211–227.

Schraw, G., Wadkins, T., & Olafson, L. (2007). Doing the things we do: A grounded theory of academic procrastination. *Journal of Educational Psychology, 99*(1), 12–25. http://dx.doi.org/10.1037/0022-0663.99.1.12.

Senge, P. M. (2014). *The dance of change: The challenges to sustaining momentum in a learning organization.* New York, NY: Random House LLC.

Sinatra, G. M., Brem, S. K., & Evans, E. M. (2008). Changing minds? Implications of conceptual change for teaching and learning about biological evolution. *Evolution: Education and Outreach, 1*(2), 189–195. http://dx.doi.org/10.1007/s12052-008-0037-8.

Sinatra, G. M., Broughton, S. H., & Lombardi, D. (2014). Emotions in science education. In R. Pekrun & L. Linnenbrink-Garcia (Eds.), *Handbook of emotions and education* (pp. 415–436). New York, NY: Routledge.

Sinatra, G. M., & Chinn, C. A. (2012). Thinking and reasoning in science: Promoting epistemic conceptual change. In K. R. Harris, S. Graham, T. Urdan, A. G. Bus, S. Major, & H. L. Swanson (Eds.), *APA educational psychology handbook, Vol 3: Application to learning and teaching* (pp. 257–282). Washington, DC: American Psychological Association.

Sinatra, G. M., Kienhues, D., & Hofer, B. K. (2014). Addressing challenges to public understanding of science: Epistemic cognition, motivated reasoning, and conceptual change. *Educational Psychologist, 49*(2), 123–138. http://dx.doi.org/10.1080/00461520.2014.916216.

Sinatra, G. M., & Mason, L. (2013). Beyond knowledge: Learner characteristics influencing conceptual change. In S. Vosniadou (Ed.), *International handbook of research on conceptual change* (pp. 377–394) (2nd ed.). New York, NY: Routledge.

Sinatra, G. M., & Pintrich, P. R. (2002). The role of intentions in conceptual change learning. In G. M. Sinatra & P. R. Pintrich (Eds.), *Intentional conceptual change* (pp. 1–18). Mahwah, NJ: Lawrence Erlbaum.

Stanovich, K. E., & West, R. F. (2008). On the relative independence of thinking biases and cognitive ability. *Journal of Personality & Social Psychology, 94*(4), 672–695.

Strike, K. A., & Posner, G. J. (1992). A revisionist theory of conceptual change. In R. A. Duschl & R. J. Hamilton (Eds.), *Philosophy of science, cognitive psychology, and educational theory and practice* (pp. 147–176). Albany, NY: State University of New York Press.

Thayer, R. E. (2012). Moods and energy and tension that motivate. In R. M. Ryan (Ed.), *The Oxford handbook of human motivation* (pp. 408–419). New York, NY: Oxford University Press.

Thrash, T. M., Maruskin, L. A., & Martin, C. C. (2012). Implicit–explicit motive congruence. In R. M. Ryan (Ed.), *The Oxford handbook of human motivation* (pp. 141–156). Oxford, England: Oxford University Press.

Vosniadou, S. (1994). Capturing and modeling the process of conceptual change. *Learning and Instruction, 4*(1), 45–69.

Vosniadou, S. (2013). Framework theory approach. In S. Vosniadou (Ed.), *International handbook of research on conceptual change* (pp. 11–30) (2nd ed.). New York, NY: Routledge.

Wadsworth, B. J. (1996). *Piaget's theory of cognitive and affective development: Foundations of constructivism*. White Plains, NY: Longman Publishing.

Walczyk, J. J., & Griffith-Ross, D. A. (2006). Time restriction and the linkage between subcomponent efficiency and algebraic inequality success. *Journal of Educational Psychology, 98*, 617–627.

Weiner, B. (2014). Motivation from the cognitive perspective. In W. K. Estes (Ed.), *Handbook of learning and cognitive processes* (Vol. 3, pp. 283–308). New York, NY: Taylor & Francis.

Wolters, C. A. (2003). Regulation of motivation: Evaluating an underemphasized aspect of self-regulated learning. *Educational Psychologist, 38*(4), 189–205. http://dx.doi.org/10.1207/S15326985EP3804_1.

Zimmerman, C. (2014). Developing scientific thinking in the context of video games: Where to next? In F. Blumberg (Ed.), *Learning by playing: Frontiers of video gaming in education* (pp. 54–68). New York, NY: Oxford University Press.

Appendix: Measuring motivation

Accurate measurement of motivational constructs provides important evidence to justify, evaluate, and reflect upon the effectiveness of motivational interventions. Through measurement the researcher or MD may examine belief, motive, or behavior change over time when using the strategies described in Chapters 10–12. The probability of reaching warranted conclusions from measurement evidence, however, is precarious unless rigorous controls and structured design protocols are followed. A review of every motivational measure and the associated methodological procedures related to each approach is beyond the scope of the current work. The listings here are provided to give the reader a starting point and to suggest which measures are validated and used to measure specific motivational constructs in education and psychology literature.

Assessment of motivated behavior is a formidable challenge for three fundamental reasons: First, most of the motivation measures listed are self-report, primarily questionnaires and verbal reports. As described in Principle #5 (p. 12), frequently individuals are unaware of their own motivations, and even when aware respondents are notoriously inaccurate when describing the source and expression of their motives. Second, self-report measures have multiple analytical liabilities due to response bias, especially because participants frequently report themselves through favorable self-images (Hoffman & Seidel, 2015). In addition, self-report measures are prone to deliberate fabrications from participants and answers may be skewed based on social desirability or perceptions of researcher expectation. During administration, responses are sometimes randomly selected because individuals are unmotivated to complete instruments based on boredom or tedious procedures. Third, many motivational measures are designed and used for descriptive or correlational purposes, which, if interpreted inaccurately, may result in unjustified causal inferences as outlined by Principle #8 (p. 29).

The measures listed below are not endorsed nor suggested to be used in particular circumstances because the nature of personal research inquiries may differ based on the intentions of the instrument developer or researcher. The assessments below are reliable measures that have been validated for use with certain populations of participants. Reliable measures show measurement consistency over multiple administrations, or when using alternate and parallel forms of the same instrument. Valid measures are those suitable for making theoretical inferences or evaluative interpretations of numerical scores (AERA, APA, & NCME, 1999). Measures were selected based on the identical criteria advocated by Hoffman and Seidel (2015).

A measure was considered reliable if tests of stability, equivalence, or internal consistency yielded reliability coefficients > .70. Qualitative measures were considered reliable if adequate inter-rater reliability was reported. Sources of validity evidence were evaluated through examination of instrument content, reported internal structure of test items, and indices of convergent, discriminate, or covariance evidence (p. 107).

Measures are listed alphabetically according to the construct(s) assessed, followed by the instrument name and type. Empirical examples signify either an empirical study using the measurement method or the source of instrument design and validation. Psychometric information indicates the procedures to determine reliability and validity. Potential usage indicates the specific sample used to validate the measure and/or how the measure has been used in practice.

Constructs measured	Name/Type of measure	Empirical examples	Psychometric evidence	Sample/Focus
Academic engagement	Student Engagement Inventory (SEI)/ Questionnaire	Lovelace, M. D., Reschly, A. L., Appleton, J. J., & Lutz, M. E. (2014). Concurrent and predictive validity of the Student Engagement Instrument. *Journal of Psychoeducational Assessment, 32*(6), 509–520. http://dx.doi.org/10.1177/0734282914527548.	Factor analysis, internal consistency, graduation predictive validity	Enormous middle-school sample used to measure cognitive and affective engagement
Academic motivation	Academic Motivation Scale (AMS)/ Questionnaire	Vallerand, R. J., Pelletier, L. G., Blais, M. R., Briere, N. M., Senecal, C., & Vallieres, E. F. (1992). The academic motivation scale: A measure of intrinsic, extrinsic, and amotivation in education. *Educational and Psychological Measurement, 52*(4), 1003–1017.	Confirmatory factor analysis, test–retest correlation with other versions of the measure	With many international samples the scale measures self-regulation, intrinsic motivation, and amotivation
Academic resilience	5-C Model of Academic Resilience (unnamed)/ Questionnaire	Martin, A. J., & Marsh, H. W. (2006). Academic resilience and its psychological and educational correlates: A construct validity approach. *Psychology in the Schools, 43*(3), 267–281.	Confirmatory factor analysis, cluster analysis	Australian high-school students used to identify five factors associated with academic resilience, self-efficacy, control, planning, low anxiety, and persistence

(*Continued*)

Constructs measured	Name/Type of measure	Empirical examples	Psychometric evidence	Sample/Focus
Academic self-handicapping	Academic Self-Handicapping Scale (ASHS)/ Questionnaire	Urdan, T., Midgley, C., & Anderman, E. M. (1998). The role of classroom goal structure in students' use of self-handicapping strategies. *American Educational Research Journal*, 35(1), 101–122.	Factor analysis, internal consistency, HLM for group differences	Using fifth-grade students tested differences in effort withdrawal, self-handicapping strategies, perceived competence and learning goals
Academic self-handicapping	Self-Handicapping Scale (SHS)/ Questionnaire	Strube, M. J. (1986). An analysis of the self-handicapping scale. *Basic and Applied Social Psychology*, 7(3), 211–224.	Factor analysis, internal consistency, divergent validity	Undergraduate students used to assess self-consciousness, social anxiety, extroversion, and self-esteem
Achievement emotions	Achievement Emotions Questionnaire (AEQ)/ Questionnaire	Pekrun, R., Goetz, T., Frenzel, A. C., Barchfeld, P., & Perry, R. P. (2011). Measuring emotions in students' learning and performance: The Achievement Emotions Questionnaire (AEQ). *Contemporary Educational Psychology*, 36(1), 36–48. http://dx.doi.org/10.1016/j.cedpsych.2010.10.002	Confirmatory factor analysis, correlational analysis	Addressed activity emotions of enjoyment, boredom, and anger and prospective emotions of hope, anxiety, and helplessness along with retrospective emotions of pride relief and shame
Anxiety-state vs. trait	State-Trait Anxiety Inventory (STAI)/ Questionnaire	Spielberger, C. D. (1983). *Manual for the State-Trait Anxiety Inventory STAI (form Y)* ("*Self-Evaluation Questionnaire*"). Palo Alto, CA: Consulting Psychology Press.	Factor analysis, construct validity	Classic instrument that assessed apprehension, nervousness, and worry
Arousal, physical and cognitive	Activation–Deactivation Adjective Check List (AD ACL), Checklist	Thayer, R. E. (1986). Activation-deactivation adjective check list: Current overview and structural analysis. *Psychological Reports*, 58(2), 607–614.	Factor analysis	Rapid bipolar assessment of core arousal highlighting the curvilinear relationship between energetic and tense arousal

Aspirations	Aspirations Index/Questionnaire	Kasser, T., & Ryan, R. M. (1996). Further examining the American dream: Differential correlates of intrinsic and extrinsic goals. *Personality and Social Psychology Bulletin, 22,* 280–287.	Factor analysis, regression analysis, convergent validity	Measured extrinsic aspirations of wealth, fame, and image, the intrinsic aspirations of meaningful relationships, personal growth, and community contributions, and aspirations of good health
Athletic self-efficacy	Physical Self-Efficacy Scale (PSE)/Questionnaire	Ryckman, R. M., Robbins, M. A., Thornton, B., & Cantrell, P. (1982). Development and validation of a physical self-efficacy scale. *Journal of Personality and Social Psychology, 42*(5), 891–900. http://dx.doi.org/10.1037/0022-3514.42.5.891	Test–retest reliability, concurrent validity with other scales	Classic scale to assess perceived physical ability and physical self-presentation confidence of undergraduates
Avoidance behavior	Acceptance and Action Questionnaire-II (AAQ-II)/Questionnaire	Bond, F. W., Hayes, S. C., Baer, R. A., Carpenter, K. M., Guenole, N., Orcutt, H. K., et al. (2011). Preliminary psychometric properties of the Acceptance and Action Questionnaire–II: A revised measure of psychological inflexibility and experiential avoidance. *Behavior Therapy, 42*(4), 676–688.	Factor analysis, face validity, convergent and discriminant validity, test–retest reliability	Primarily used in clinical applications, the instrument measures intent to alter thoughts and feelings, including psychological inflexibility

(*Continued*)

Constructs measured	Name/Type of measure	Empirical examples	Psychometric evidence	Sample/Focus
Boredom	English Precursors to Boredom Scales (E-PBS)/Questionnaire	Tze, V. C., Daniels, L. M., & Klassen, R. M. (2014). Examining the factor structure and validity of the English Precursors to Boredom Scales. *Learning And Individual Differences, 32*, 254–260. http://dx.doi.org/10.1016/j.lindif.2014.03.018	Factor analysis, internal consistency	A Canadian university sample revealed negative associations between self-regulated learning and boredom especially in learners over-challenged
Collective teacher self-efficacy	Collective Teacher Efficacy Scale (CTES)/Questionnaire	Goddard, R. D., Hoy, W. K., & Hoy, A. W. (2000). Collective teacher efficacy: Its meaning, measure, and impact on student achievement. *American Educational Research Journal, 37*(2), 479–507.	Factor analysis, concurrent validity	School-level efficacy including trust in colleagues and institutional integrity
Collectivism vs. individualism	Individualism and Collectivism Scale (aka, Culture Orientation Scale)/Questionnaire	Triandis, H. C., & Gelfand, M. J. (1998). Converging measurement of horizontal and vertical individualism and collectivism. *Journal of Personality and Social Psychology, 74*, 118–128.	Factor analysis, multi-trait, multi-method concurrent validity	Measured collective and individualistic vertical and horizontal self with Korean/US university students
Control orientation, motivating others at work	Problems at Work/Vignettes	Deci, E. L., Connell, J. P., & Ryan, R. M. (1989). Self-determination in a work organization. *Journal of Applied Psychology, 74*, 580–590.	Empirical study, convergent validity	Work technicians and field managers assessed manager work orientation through responding to verbal case problems to measure degree of support, autonomy, and control

Control orientation, motivating others in school	Problems in Schools Questionnaire (PIS)/Vignettes	Deci, E. L., Sheinman, L., Schwartz, A. J., & Ryan, R. M. (1981). An instrument to assess adults' orientations toward control versus autonomy with children: Reflections on intrinsic motivation and perceived competence. *Journal of Educational Psychology, 73*, 642–650.	Internal consistency and convergent validity with behavioral measures	Evaluated the degree of control vs. autonomous orientation when addressing classroom challenges
Cultural competence	Cultural Competence Self-Assessment Questionnaire (CCSAQ)	Mason, J. L. (1995). Cultural competence self-assessment questionnaire: A manual for users. Portland, OR: Research and Training Center on Family Support and Children's Mental Health. Retrieved http://files.eric.ed.gov/fulltext/ED399684.pdf	Content validity, internal consistency	Cultural competency in the form of attitudes/ practice, policy/structure with administrative and service personnel
Egoism	Egoism Scale/Questionnaire	Weigel, R. H., Hessing, D. J., & Elffers, H. (1999). Egoism: Concept, measurement and implications for deviance. *Psychology, Crime and Law, 5*(4), 349–378.	Test–retest reliability, factor analysis, internal consistency	Measured excessive concern with one's own interests, self-centeredness and narcissism using Dutch sample
Epistemological beliefs[a]	Epistemological Beliefs Questionnaire (EBQ)—Questionnaire	Chai, C. S., Khine, M. S., & Teo, T. (2006). Epistemological beliefs on teaching and learning: A survey among pre-service teachers in Singapore. *Educational Media International, 43*(4), 285–298. http://dx.doi.org/10.1080/09523980600926242	Factor analysis, internal consistency	Evaluated effect of demographics on personal epistemology among pre-service teachers in Singapore

(*Continued*)

Constructs measured	Name/Type of measure	Empirical examples	Psychometric evidence	Sample/Focus
Ethnic identity development	Multi-group Ethnic Identity Measure (MEIM)/Questionnaire	Ponterotto, J., Gretchen, D., Utsey, S., Stracuzzi, T., & Saya, R. (2003). The multigroup ethnic identity measure (MEIM): Psychometric review and further validity testing. *Educational and Psychological Measurement*, 63(3), 502–515.	Confirmatory factor analysis	Measured affirmation and belonging, ethnic identity, and other group orientation in adults and adolescents
Extrinsic and intrinsic motivation at work	Work Extrinsic and Intrinsic Motivation Scale (WEIMS)/Questionnaire	Tremblay, M. A., Blanchard, C. M., Taylor, S., Pelletier, L. G., & Villeneuve, M. (2009). Work Extrinsic and Intrinsic Motivation Scale: Its value for organizational psychology research. *Canadian Journal of Behavioural Science*, 41(4), 213–226.	Construct validity, internal consistency, regression analysis	Military and civilian workers were used to evaluate the extent of workplace self-determination and work internalization
Fear of failure	Performance Failure Appraisal Inventory (PFAI)/Questionnaire	Conroy, D. E., Willow, J. P., Metzler, J. N. (2002). Multidimensional fear of failure measurement: The Performance Failure Appraisal Inventory. *Journal of Applied Sport Psychology*, 14(2), 76–90. http://dx.doi.org/10.1080/10413200252907752	Factor analysis	Used undergraduate students to measures fear of athletic failure

Global life satisfaction	Satisfaction With Life Scale (SWLS)	Diener, E., Inglehart, R., & Tay, L. (2013). Theory and validity of life satisfaction scales. *Social Indicators Research, 112*(3), 497–527.	Factor analysis, Convergent and discriminant validity	Enduring instrument used to measure subjective well-being and affect. Scale correlates with positive moods, life conditions (i.e., income), free choice, and quality of life
Goal orientation	Patterns of Adaptive Learning Scales (PALS)/Questionnaire	Midgley, C., Maehr, M. L., Hruda, L. Z., Anderman, E., Anderman, L., Freeman, K. E., & Urdan, T. (2000). *Manual for the patterns of adaptive learning scales.* Ann Arbor, MI: University of Michigan.	Confirmatory factor analysis	Separate student and teacher scales measure goal orientations and achievement beliefs
Goal orientation	Goal Orientation Scales (unnamed)/ Questionnaire	Midgley, C., Kaplan, A., Middleton, M., Maehr, M. L., Urdan, T., Anderman, L. H., et al. (1998). The development and validation of scales assessing students' achievement goal orientations. *Contemporary Educational Psychology, 23*(2), 113–131.	Confirmatory factor analysis, convergent and discriminant validity	Assesses student task, approach and avoid goal orientations included as part of the PALS
Goal orientation/ academic engagement	Attitude Toward Mathematics Survey/ Questionnaire	Miller, R. B., Greene, B. A., Montalvo, G. P., Ravindran, B., & Nichols, J. D. (1996). Engagement in academic work: The role of learning goals, future consequences, pleasing others, and perceived ability. *Contemporary Educational Psychology, 21*(4), 388–422.	Factor analysis, multiple regression	Measured future consequences, intent to please others, goal orientation, and strategy use as instrumental in engagement

(*Continued*)

Constructs measured	Name/Type of measure	Empirical examples	Psychometric evidence	Sample/Focus
Hope	Integrative Hope Scale (IHS)/Questionnaire	Schrank, B., Woppmann, A., Sibitz, I., & Lauber, C. (2011). Development and validation of an integrative scale to assess hope. *Health Expectations: An International Journal of Public Participation in Health Care and Health Policy, 14*(4), 417–428. http://dx.doi.org/10.1111/j.1369-625.2010.00645.x	Factor analysis, discriminant validity	Used a general population sample to measure constructs of time, goals, control, and personality
Hope	State Hope Scale/Questionnaire	Snyder, C. R., Sympson, S. C., Ybasco, F. C., Borders, T. F., Babyak, M. A., & Higgins, R. L. (1996). Development and validation of the State Hope Scale. *Journal of Personality and Social Psychology, 70*(2), 321.	Factor analysis, discriminant validity	Psychology students indicated goal-directed thinking is influenced by the belief in one's ability to initiate and sustain actions and via generating pathways
Identification with academics	Unnamed composite scale based on expectancies, interest and attainment value/Questionnaire	Jones, B. D., Paretti, M. C., Hein, S. F., & Knott, T. W. (2010). An analysis of motivation constructs with first-year engineering students: Relationships among expectancies, values, achievement, and career plans. *Journal of Engineering Education, 99*(4), 319–336.	Empirical study	Expectancy and value-related beliefs decrease over an academic year. Expectancies predicted achievement, values predicted career plans
Implicit bias and implicit cognition	The Implicit Association Test (IAT)	Greenwald, A. G., McGhee, D. E., & Schwartz, J. L. (1998). Measuring individual differences in implicit cognition: The Implicit Association Test. *Journal of Personality and Social Psychology, 74*(6), 1464.	Convergent, discriminate, and covariance validity	Measured attitudes and beliefs that people may be unwilling or unable to report including stereotyping and prejudice

Instrumentality, task value	Perception of Instrumentality—Endogenous, Exogenous/Questionnaire	Husman, J., Derryberry, W. P., Crowson, H., and Lomax, R. (2004). Instrumentality, task value, and intrinsic motivation: Making sense of their independent interdependence. *Contemporary Educational Psychology, 29*(1), 63–76.	Empirical study, structural equation modeling	Undergraduates revealed that intrinsic orientation, endogenous instrumentality, and task value make unique contributions to study time
Interest	Intrinsic Motivation Inventory (IMI)/Questionnaire	Deci, E. L., Eghrari, H., Patrick. B. C., & Leone, D. (1994). Facilitating internalization: The self-determination theory perspective. *Journal of Personality, 62*, 119–142.	Confirmatory factor analysis, internal consistency	Interest/enjoyment, perceived competence, effort, perceived choice, value/usefulness and felt pressure and tension choice
Intrinsic and extrinsic motivation	The Work Preference Inventory (WPI)/Questionnaire	Amabile, T. M., Hill, K. G., Hennessey, B. A., & Tighe, E. M. (1994). The Work Preference Inventory: Assessing intrinsic and extrinsic motivational orientations. *Journal of Personality and Social Psychology, 66*(5), 950–967.	Factor analysis, internal consistency, test-retest reliability	Separate student and work versions measured self-determination, competence, task involvement curiosity, and enjoyment along with concerns for competition, recognition, and other incentives
Locus of control and self-concept	Unnamed instrument/Questionnaire	Wang, Z., & Su, I. (2013). Longitudinal factor structure of general self-concept and locus of control among high school students. *Journal of Psychoeducational Assessment, 31*(6), 554–565.	Confirmatory factor analysis and latent growth modeling	Using the NELS-88 data set measured control beliefs and self-worth beliefs

(*Continued*)

Constructs measured	Name/Type of measure	Empirical examples	Psychometric evidence	Sample/Focus
Metacognition and heuristics[a]	Videotaping and interviews, Metacognitive model analysis	Depaepe, F., De Corte, E., & Verschaffel, L. (2010). Teachers' metacognitive and heuristic approaches to word problem solving: Analysis and impact on students' beliefs and performance. *ZDM-The International Journal on Mathematics Education, 42*(2), 205–218. http://dx.doi.org/10.1007/s11858-009-0221-5	Inter-rater reliability, member checking, content analysis	Qualitatively compared teachers to determine what beliefs influence the use of metacognitive and heuristics related to word problem solving
Mindfulness	Kentucky Inventory of Mindfulness Skills (KIMS)/Questionnaire	Baer, R. A., Smith, G. T., & Allen, K. B. (2004). Assessment of mindfulness by self-report: The Kentucky Inventory of Mindfulness Skills. *Assessment, 11*(3), 191–206. http://dx.doi.org/10.1177/1073191104268029	Confirmatory factor analysis, test–retest reliability, content validity	Examined the latent structure of mindfulness with openness, attention to feelings and external thinking, emotional intelligence most often reported by students
Mood	Positive and Negative Affect Schedule (PANAS)/Questionnaire	Watson, D., Clark, L. A., & Tellegen, A. (1988). Development and validation of brief measures of positive and negative affect: The PANAS scales. *Journal of Personality and Social Psychology, 54*(6), 1063–1070.	Test–retest reliability, internal consistency, factor analysis	Popular instrument with strong psychometric properties to measure mood
Moral reasoning	Revised Moral Authority Scale (MAS-R)/Questionnaire	White, F. A. (1997). Measuring the content of moral judgment development: The revised Moral Authority Scale (MAS-R). *Social Behavior and Personality, 25*(4), 321–334. http://dx.doi.org/10.2224/sbp.1997.25.4.321	Test–retest reliability, discriminate validity	University students and parents investigated the source of moral authority

Moral reasoning	Visions of Morality Scale (VMS)/ Questionnaire	Shelton, C. M., & McAdams, D. P. (1990). In search of everyday morality: The development of a measure. *Adolescence, 25*(100), 923–944.	Multiple regression (no validity evidence indicated)	Composite scale used with secondary students to assesses empathy and pro-social inclinations of moral behavior
Motivation to exercise	Subjective Exercise Experiences Scale (SEES)	McAuley, E., & Courneya, K. S. (1994). The subjective exercise experiences scale (SEES): Development and preliminary validation. *Journal of Sport and Exercise Psychology, 16*, 163–163.	Factor analysis, convergent and divergent validity	Measured student affective responses to exercise including psychological distress, positive well-being, and fatigue
Motivational climate in Sports	Perceived Motivational Climate in Sport Questionnaire-2 (PMCSQ-2)/ Questionnaire	Newton, M., Duda, J. L., & Yin, Z. (2000). Examination of the psychometric properties of the Perceived Motivational Climate in Sport Questionnaire-2 in a sample of female athletes. *Journal of Sports Sciences, 18*(4), 275–290.	Confirmatory factor analysis, convergent validity	Task involving and ego involving scales used with female athletes showing cooperative learning, team satisfaction, and effort. Greater ego involvement is related to greater pressure perception
Motivational climate in Sports	Motivational Climate Scale for Youth Sports (MCSYS)/ Questionnaire	Smith, R. E., Cumming, S. P., & Smoll, F. L. (2008). Development and validation of the motivational climate scale for youth sports. *Journal of Applied Sport Psychology, 20*(1), 116–136.	Confirmatory factor analysis	Indicated what behaviors children (9–16 years) perceive as valuable in coaching, distinguishes mastery- and ego initiating behavior in coaches

(*Continued*)

Constructs measured	Name/Type of measure	Empirical examples	Psychometric evidence	Sample/Focus
Motivational regulation	Self-Regulation Strategy Inventory—Self-Report (SRSI-SR)/Questionnaire	Cleary, T. J. (2006). The development and validation of the self-regulation strategy inventory—self-report. *Journal of School Psychology, 44*(4), 307–322.	Factor analysis, convergent, discriminant, and differential validity estimates	Used ninth- and tenth-grade students to assess seeking and learning information, environmental restructuring, and maladaptive regulatory behaviors
Occupational self-efficacy	Occupational Self-Efficacy Scale (OCCSEFF)/Questionnaire	Schyns, B., & von Collani, G. (2002). A new occupational self-efficacy scale and its relation to personality constructs and organizational variables. *European Journal of Work and Organizational Psychology, 11*(2), 219–241.	Exploratory and confirmatory factor analysis, internal consistency	Occupational self-efficacy predicted job satisfaction and is influenced by job experiences
Optimism and hope	Life Orientation Test (LOT)/Questionnaire and The Hope Scale (HS)/Questionnaire	Steed, L. G. (2002). A psychometric comparison of four measures of hope and optimism. *Educational and Psychological Measurement, 62*(3), 466–482.	Factor analysis, convergent validity, test-retest reliability	Used undergraduate psychology students to compare four related scales: Generalized Expectancy for Success Scale, the Life Orientation Test, the Hope Scale, and the Hunter Opinions and Personal Expectations Scale
Optimism	Questionnaire for the Assessment of Personal Optimism and Social Optimism-Extended (POSO-E)/Questionnaire	Schweizer, K., & Koch, W. (2001). The assessment of components of optimism by POSO-E. *Personality and Individual Differences, 31*(4), 563–574.	Internal consistency, correlation with other scales	Measured the expectation of positive outcomes by German university students via personal, social, and self-efficacy optimism

Organizational learning	Dimensions of the Learning Organization Questionnaire (DLOQ)	Yang, B. (2003). Identifying valid and reliable measures for dimensions of a learning culture. *Advances in Developing Human Resources*, 5(2), 152–162.	Exploratory and confirmatory factor analysis	Seven-factor solution with organizational participants to determine which factors contributed to a learning culture
Perceptions of online discussions	Perceptions of Asynchronous Online Discussion (PAOD)/ Questionnaire	Lee, S. W. Y. (2013). Investigating students' learning approaches, perceptions of online discussions, and students' online and academic performance. *Computers and Education*, 68, 345–352. http://dx.doi.org/10.1016/j.compedu.2013.05.019	Factor and cluster analysis	Measured factors that influence student perceptions of online learning revealing that elaborated responses and intrinsic motivation are most important
Procrastination	Flinders Decision Making Questionnaire (DMQ)	Burnett, P. C., Mann, L., & Beswick, G. (1989). Validation of the Flinders Decision Making Questionnaire on course decision making by students. *Australian Psychologist*, 24(2), 285–292. http://dx.doi.org/10.1080/00050068908259567	Concurrent validity	Measured vigilance, defensive avoidance, hypervigilance, and decision self-esteem of Australian students
Procrastination	Unnamed scale/Questionnaire	Choi, J. M., & Moran, S. (2009). Why not procrastinate? Development and validation of a new active procrastination scale. *The Journal of Social Psychology*, 149(2), 195–211.	Exploratory and confirmatory factor analysis, internal consistency	Used Canadian university students to develop measure of outcome satisfaction, preference for pressure, intentional decision, and ability to meet deadlines

(Continued)

Constructs measured	Name/Type of measure	Empirical examples	Psychometric evidence	Sample/Focus
Pro-social behavior	Prosocial Tendencies Measure (PTM)/Questionnaire	Carlo, G., & Randall, B. A. (2002). The development of a measure of prosocial behaviors for late adolescents. *Journal of Youth and Adolescence, 31*(1), 31–44.	Test–retest reliability, concurrent validity, and factor analysis	Assessed altruistic, compliant, emotional, public, and anonymous pro-social behavior in college students
Readiness for online learning	Tertiary Students' Readiness for Online Learning Survey (TSROL)/Questionnaire	Pillay, H., Irving, K., & Tones, M. (2007). Validation of the diagnostic tool for assessing tertiary students' readiness for online learning. *Higher Education Research and Development, 26*(2), 217–234.	Factor analysis, internal consistency	Technical skills, computer self-efficacy, learner preferences, and attitudes toward computers influenced online learning motivation in Australian students
Reading motivation, sense of efficacy to teach reading[a]	Teachers' Beliefs About Students' Motivation For Reading/Questionnaire (based on the Motivation to Read Inventory; Wigfield, Guthrie, & McGough, 1996)	Quirk, M., Unrau, N., Ragusa, G., Rueda, R., Lim, H., Velasco, A., & Loera, G. (2010). Teacher beliefs about reading motivation and their enactment in classrooms: The development of a survey questionnaire. *Reading Psychology, 31*(2), 93–120. http://dx.doi.org/10.1080/02702710902754051	Internal consistency, content validation, concurrent validity	Confirmed a strong positive relationship between beliefs about student motivation to read and teaching sense of self-efficacy
Relational self-esteem	Relational Self-Esteem Scale/Questionnaire	Du, H., King, R. B., & Chi, P. (2012). The development and validation of the Relational Self-Esteem Scale. *Scandinavian Journal of Psychology, 53*(3), 258–264. http://dx.doi.org/10.1111/j.1467-9450.2012.00946.x	Confirmatory factor analysis, internal consistency	Chinese university students used to validate measure of personal, relational, and collective self-worth and self-esteem

Self-determination	General Causality Orientations Scale (GCOS)/Vignettes and Questions	Deci, E. L., & Ryan, R. M. (1985). The general causality orientations scale: Self-determination in personality. *Journal of Research in Personality, 19*(2), 109–134.	Temporal stability, correlation between subscales	Measured the impact of hostility, shame, fear, and guilt on autonomy, control, and impersonal factors to predict behavior
Self-determination	The Self-Determination Scale (SDS)/Questionnaire	Sheldon, K. M., Ryan, R. M., & Reis, H. T. (1996). What makes for a good day? Competence and autonomy in the day and in the person. *Personality and Social Psychology Bulletin, 22*(12), 1270–1279.	Empirical study, internal consistency, test–retest reliability	Designed to assess individual differences in self-contact and choice indicating the extent to which people function in a self-determined way
Self-determination (need for autonomy)	Learning Self-regulation Questionnaire (LSRQ)	Williams, G. C., & Deci, E. L. (1996). Internalization of biopsychosocial values by medical students: A test of self-determination theory. *Journal of Personality and Social Psychology, 70*(4), 767–779.	Empirical study	Adapted from the GCOS (see above) measures reasons for course participation, control, and autonomy
Self-efficacy for self-regulated learning	Self-Efficacy for Self-Regulated Learning Scale (SESRL)/Questionnaire	Usher, E. L., & Pajares, F. (2008). Self-efficacy for self-regulated learning a validation study. *Educational and Psychological Measurement, 68*(3), 443–463.	Factor analysis	Invariant structure for gender/age differences in academic self-concept of grade 3–12 students

(*Continued*)

Constructs measured	Name/Type of measure	Empirical examples	Psychometric evidence	Sample/Focus
Self-efficacy to teach mathematics	Self-Efficacy for Teaching Mathematics Instrument (SETMI)/ Questionnaire	McGee, J. R., & Wang, C. (2014). Validity-supporting evidence of the self-efficacy for teaching mathematics instrument. *Journal of Psychoeducational Assessment, 32*(5), 390–403. http://dx.doi.org/10.1177/ 0734282913516280	Confirmatory factor analysis, internal consistency, expert validation	Highly reliable instrument used with in-service teachers to assess domain-specific efficacy
Self-efficacy to teach science to diverse learners[a]	Self-Efficacy Beliefs about Equitable Science Teaching (SEBEST)/ Questionnaire	Ritter, J. M., Boone, W. J., & Rubba, P. A. (2001). Development of an instrument to assess prospective elementary teacher self-efficacy beliefs about equitable science teaching and learning (SEBEST). *Journal of Science Teacher Education, 12*(3), 175–198.	Content analysis, factor analysis	Added an additional dimension to similar instruments by using a diverse sample of learners
Self-esteem	Rosenberg Self-Esteem Scale/Single-item Self Esteem Scale/ Questionnaire	Robins, R. W., Hendin, H. M., & Trzesniewski, K. H. (2001). Measuring global self-esteem: Construct validation of a single-item measure and the Rosenberg Self-Esteem Scale. *Personality and Social Psychology Bulletin, 27*(2), 151–161.	Test–retest reliability, construct and convergent validity	Measured the well-being and global self-esteem of college students across ethnic groups and occupations
Self-regulated learning	Motivated Strategies for Learning Questionnaire (MSLQ)	Pintrich, P. R., Smith, D. A., García, T., & McKeachie, W. J. (1993). Reliability and predictive validity of the Motivated Strategies for Learning Questionnaire (MSLQ). *Educational and Psychological Measurement, 53*(3), 801–813.	Confirmatory factor analysis, internal consistency	Highly popular measure to assess college students' goal orientation and control beliefs, in addition to the use of learning strategies and metacognition

Self-regulation	Self-Control and Self-Management Scale (SCSM)/Questionnaire	Mezo, P. G., & Short, M. M. (2012). Construct validity and confirmatory factor analysis of the Self-Control and Self-Management Scale. *Canadian Journal of Behavioural Science, 44*(1), 1–8. http://dx.doi.org/10.1037/a0024414	Confirmatory factor analysis, test–retest reliability, convergent validity	Canadian students assessed general self-monitoring, self-evaluation and self-management
Self-regulation perceptions	Student Perceptions of Classroom Knowledge Building (SPOCK)/Questionnaire	Shell. D. F., & Husman, J. E. (2008). Control, motivation, affect, and strategic self-regulation in the college classroom: A multidimensional phenomenon. *Journal of Educational Psychology, 100*(2), 443–459.	Factor analysis, internal consistency	Measured four aspects of students' perceptions of self-regulation: self-regulated strategy use, knowledge building, high- and low-level question asking, and a lack of regulation
Self-worth	Contingencies of Self-Worth Scale (CSWS)/Questionnaire	Crocker, J., Luhtanen, R. K., Cooper, M. L., & Bouvrette, A. (2003). Contingencies of self-worth in college students: Theory and measurement. *Journal of Personality and Social Psychology, 85*(5), 894–908.	Test–retest reliability, discriminant validity	College students were used to measure self-esteem for academics, appearance, approval from others, competition, and family support
Self-worth	Academic Contingencies of Self-worth/Questionnaire	Griffin, T. M., Chavous, T., Cogburn, C., Branch, L., & Sellers, R. (2012). Dimensions of academic contingencies among African American college students. *Journal of Black Psychology, 38*(2), 201–227.	Exploratory and confirmatory factor analyses	Used a sample of African-American college freshmen to assess the relationship between self-worth and positive achievement

(*Continued*)

Constructs measured	Name/Type of measure	Empirical examples	Psychometric evidence	Sample/Focus
Social characteristics[a]	Vignettes; Revised Cheek & Buss Shyness Scale (RCBS)/ Questionnaire	Coplan, R. J., Hughes, K., Bosacki, S., & Rose-Krasnor, L. (2011). Is silence golden? Elementary school teachers' strategies and beliefs regarding hypothetical shy/quiet and exuberant/talkative children. *Journal of Educational Psychology, 103*(4), 939–951. http://dx.doi.org/10.1037/a0024551	Factor analysis	Found a correlation among teachers' beliefs toward social characteristics (i.e., shyness, exuberance) and student learning outcomes
Social comparison	Social Comparison Scale/Questionnaire	Allan, S., & Gilbert, P. (1995). A social comparison scale: Psychometric properties and relationship to psychopathology. *Personality and Individual Differences, 19*(3), 293–299.	Factor analysis, test–retest reliability	Although used to affirm student connections with psychopathology, this instrument measures aspects of social comparison and relationship behavior
Social comparison	Iowa-Netherlands Comparison Orientation Measure (INCOM)/ Questionnaire	Gibbons, F. X., & Buunk, B. P. (1999). Individual differences in social comparison: Development of a scale of social comparison orientation. *Journal of Personality and Social Psychology, 76*(1), 129–142.	Factor analysis, construct validity, discriminant validity	Adolescents and college students used to measure upward and downward comparisons, performance and ability

Social desirability	Marlowe-Crowne Social Desirability Scale (MCSDS)/ Questionnaire	Ventimiglia, M. & MacDonald, D. (2012). An examination of the factorial dimensionality of the Marlowe Crowne Social Desirability Scale. *Personality and Individual Differences, 52*(4), 487–491.	Confirmatory factor analysis, test–retest reliability, convergent validity	Identification of non-pathological, socially desirable test performance and impression management in undergrads
Study strategies and academic orientations	Learning and Study Strategies Inventory (LASSI)/Questionnaire	Cano, F. (2006). An in-depth analysis of the learning and study strategies inventory (LASSI). *Educational and Psychological Measurement, 66*(6), 1023–1038.	Factor analysis, latent structure analysis	Measured time management, motivation, concentration, and attitude
Success in online learning	Test of Online Learning Success (TOOLS)/Questionnaire	Kerr, M. S., Rynearson, K., & Kerr, M. C. (2006). Student characteristics for online learning success. *The Internet and Higher Education, 9*(2), 91–105.	Factor analysis, construct validity, criterion validity, test–retest reliability	Computer skills, independent learning (i.e., self-regulated), need, dependent learning, and academic skills motivate online learning success
Teacher self-efficacy	Teachers' Sense of Efficacy Scale (TSES)/Questionnaire	Tschannen-Moran, M., & Woolfolk Hoy, A. (2001). Teacher efficacy: Capturing an elusive construct. *Teaching and Teacher Education, 17*, 783–805.	Factor analysis, concurrent validity	Gold standard to measure efficacy for student engagement, instructional strategies, and classroom management of pre- and in-service teachers

(*Continued*)

Constructs measured	Name/Type of measure	Empirical examples	Psychometric evidence	Sample/Focus
Test anxiety	The Test Anxiety Measure for Adolescents (TAMA)/ Questionnaire	Lowe, P. A. (2014). The Test Anxiety Measure for Adolescents (TAMA): Examination of the reliability and validity of the scores of a new multidimensional measure of test anxiety for middle and high school students. *Journal of Psychoeducational Assessment, 32*(5), 404–416. http://dx.doi.org/10.1177/0734282913520595	Confirmatory factor analysis, internal consistency, concurrent validity	Designed for students in grades 6–12, this measure revealed test anxiety is influenced by cognitive interference, physiological hyperarousal, social concerns, task irrelevant behavior, and worry
Test emotions	Test Emotions/ Questionnaire	Pekrun, R., Goetz, T., Perry, R. P., Kramer, K., Hochstadt, M., & Molfenter, S. (2004). Beyond test anxiety: Development and validation of the Test Emotions Questionnaire (TEQ). *Anxiety, Stress & Coping, 17*(3), 287–316. http://dx.doi.org/10.1080/10615800412331303847	Confirmatory factor analysis, internal and divergent validity	Measured which emotions are most prevalent when university students take tests, concluding that hope, pride, relief, angry, anxiety, shame, and hopelessness

[a]Previously reported in Hoffman and Seidel, 2015.

References

AERA, APA, & NCME (1999). *Standards for educational and psychological testing*. Washington, DC: American Educational Research Association.

Hoffman, B., & Seidel, K. (2015). Measuring teacher beliefs: For what purpose? In H. Fives & M. G. Gill (Eds.), *The international handbook of research on teachers' beliefs* (pp. 106–127). New York, NY: Routledge.

For more information on measurement and a complete list of motivation resources for educators, students, researchers and practitioners access the book website at: www.findingmo.com

Index

Note: Page numbers followed by "*b*," "*f*," and "*t*" refer to boxes, figures, and tables, respectively.

A

Ability attributions, 184
Academic disengagement, 116–118
Academic motivation, 307–308
  accelerating, 311–312
  achievement-enhancing motivational strategies, 308
  classroom culture, 308–309
  classroom motivation, 309
  cooperative learning, 310
  interest-generating strategies, 311
Acceleration hypothesis, 23–24
Acetylcholine, 56
Achievement-goal approach. *See also* Organizational promotion or prevention
  avoidance-approach, 159
  mastery-approach orientation, 159–160
  mastery-avoid learners, 160
  mastery-oriented learners, 157
  multiple goals perspective, 161
  normative-approach orientation, 160
  normative-oriented learners, 157–159
  performance-avoid learners, 160
Adaptive motivation, 153, 161
  negative self-reflections effect, 276
  perceptions of controllability, 276–277
"Affect", 239
  activation, 241–242
  core, 243
Affective mind reading, 61–62
Affiliation mimic parasympathetic nervous system activation displays, 59
  affective mind reading, 61–62
  higher basal OT levels, 62
  motive of affiliation, 59–60
  OT
    production, 61–62
    transmission, 60–61
  PNS, 60
Agency motives, 97

Agreeableness (A), 32, 33*t*
Alpha-numeric document identifier, 146–147
Altruism, 220, 222–223, 229
Altruistic behavior, 224
Altruistic motives, 223
Ambiguous temporal precedence, 52
Andragogy, 89
Animated pedagogical agents (APA), 333–334
Anophoric pronoun drop, 122
ANS. *See* Autonomic nerve system
Anxiety, 245
  "clutch performances", 246–247
  performance accuracy, 247
  primary consequence of, 246
  state anxiety, 245–246
Applied motivation, bedrock theories of
  difficulty in resisting motives, 189–192
  grand theories, 179–180
  mini-theories, 179–180
  motivational theory, 197–203
  past performance, 182–189
  self-efficacy, 192–197
  summary, utility, application, and comparison, 199*t*–200*t*
"Approach and avoid" models, 189
Athletic performance, motivation optimization for. *See also* Work performance
  competition, 325–326
  DMSP, 326–327
  one-size-fits-all strategy solution, 326
  optimal mental arousal, 329
  perfectionism, 328
  and public performance, 325
Attributions, 183–184
  behavioral implications, 185
  causal, 186*t*
  and emotions, 185
  motivational leader, 187–189, 188*b*–189*b*
  social nature, 187

Autonomic nerve system (ANS), 56
Autonomy, 36
Avoidance-approach, 159

B

Basic behaviors, 108–109
Behavioral universals, 108
Beliefs, 8–10, 12–13. *See also* Motivational beliefs
  control, 88–89
  evolution of academic, 86
  false, 22
  gendered, 96
  self-efficacy, 89
  stereotypical gendered, 98–99
Bias, 13, 26
  cognitive, 347–348
  confirmation, 198
  cultural, 110
  emotional, 244
  myside, 351–352, 355
  personal, 7, 24
  self-serving, 185–187
  self-evaluation, 284
"Big Five" model, 32
Biobehavioral synchrony, 60
Biological change, 81
  cognitive and psychosocial development, 81
  cognitive processing, 82–83
  cognitively oriented dimensions, 81–82
  critical periods, 83
  individuals, 82
  motivational leaders, 84b–86b
  point of developmental stagnation, 83
Biopsychological evidence, 48–49
Biopsychology of motivation. *See also* Motivation
  achievement and incentive reward, 62
    achievement motivation control, 63
    assumptions, 62–63
    constancy in biological response patterns, 64
    fMRI measures, 63–64
    localization, 63
  affiliation mimic parasympathetic nervous system activation displays, 59
    affective mind reading, 61–62
    higher basal OT levels, 62
    motive of affiliation, 59–60
    OT production, 61–62
    OT transmission, 60–61
    PNS, 60
  brain's perceptual filter, 54
    implications, 55
    qualia, 54–55
    sensory stimuli, 55
    suggestibility, 55–56
  conundrums, 65
  hedonic motivation, 66
  individuals, 68
  motivated behavior, 68–69
    heritable estimates, 69t
    innate predispositions, 70
    multiple diagnostic approaches, 71
    neuronal plasticity, 70–71
    niche picking, 69–70
  neurological evidence, 48–49
    functional utility of physiological evidence, 49
    interpretations, 49f
    outcomes, 49
  neurological inferences, 50
    case study, 52–54
    interpretive errors, 51
    motivational leader, 53b–54b
    neurological system, 51–52
    neuropsychology studies, 51t
    psychological construct, 52
    spurious interpretations of data, 50–51
  neurological studies, 68
  neurological system organization, 56
    divisions of ANS, 56
    lessons in neuroanatomy, 56–57
    primary neurotransmitter, 56
  pleasure and pain, 65–67
  positive and negative evidence, 68
  power and social dominance, 57
    biological markers of SNS, 58
    cortisol, 58–59
    display of power, 57
    laboratory studies, 59
    testosterone, 58
  psychological hedonism, 64–65
  striatum, 67–68
  ultimate and instrumental goals, 65
Boredom, 247
  and anxiety, 249–250

disengagement and, 249
eliminating circumstantial factors, 249
sampling approach, 248
Boxtel, Amanda, 271, 358*b*–359*b*, 359–360, 368, 369*t*
Bronfenbrenner Ecosystem Model, 314
  organizational application, 315*f*
Bystander effect, 212–213

C

Calibration process, 284
Catharsis, 113–114
CATs. *See* Counteractive tactics
Causal locus, 183–184
Central nervous system (CNS), 53, 56
Change resistance, 345–346, 354–355
  categorization model, 346–347
  organizational perspectives, 348
  overcoming, 360–361
    entrenched beliefs, 361
    mental models, 361
Character, 31, 41
Classroom culture, 308–309
"Clutch performances", 246–247
CNS. *See* Central nervous system
Cognition, 27
Cognitive development, 81
Cognitive interpretations, 94
Collective efficacy, 194
Collectivism, 119, 121
Collectivist–individualist dichotomy, 125
Colter, Jessi, 221*b*–222*b*, 223, 368, 369*t*
Common sense, 8–9
Communal motives, 97
Communication and language patterns, 121, 125–126
  collectivist–individualist dichotomy, 125
  cultural modifications in technology, 124
  culture of attention, 124
  etymological considerations, 122
  lexical analysis, 122
  motives, 123
  online interference, 124–125
  process of attention, 124
  rate of speech, 122–123
  social media, 125
  impact of technology, 123
"Communities of inquiry". *See* Classroom culture

Compartmentalization. *See* Partial revision
Competence, 36
Competition, 325–326
Conceptual change, instructional strategies supporting, 362–367
Confederates, 212
Confirmation bias, 198
Conscientiousness (C), 32, 33*t*
Contentious issues
  motivated behavior, 35
    adaptive model, 35–36
    incremental and regulatory nature, 36–37
    mind-centered orientation, 36
    paradigms, 37
    SDT, 36
  motivational beliefs, 22
    acceleration hypothesis, 23–24
    federal investigation, 24
    influence, 22
    knowledge-or-belief dilemma, 24–26
    MD, 23
    misconceptions, 22
    motivational leader, 24, 25*b*
    self-beliefs, 26
    self-righteous beliefs, 23
  motivational evidence, 26
    cognition, 27
    components, 26–27
    foundational premises, 28
    MD, 27–28
    motivational science questions, 29*t*
    premise of fallibility, 28
  optimal motivation, 37
    beliefs, 40–41
    deviation method, 40
    efficiency theory, 39–40
    "experience sampling" method, 39
    flow experience, 39
    optimal experience, 38–39
    optimal performance, 37–38
    phenomenon of peak performance, 38
Context-specific interventions
  academic motivation, 307–312
  implementing change, 335
  MD, 305
  motivation optimization, 325–329
  motivational and behavioral variability, 306

Context-specific interventions (*Continued*)
  motivational strategies, 329–336
  "one size fits all" approach, 334
  organizational motivation, 334–335
  strategies to motivating work performance, 312–325
  success-oriented motivation, 305–306
Contingencies, 141
  approach, 323–324
Control beliefs, 88–89
Controllability, 184–185
COPES model, 284
"Core affect", 243
Cortisol, 58–59
Cost–benefit analysis, 224
Counteractive tactics (CATs), 286–287
Critical periods, 83
Cross-cultural behavior, 107–108
Culture/cultural/culturally, 112–113
  communication and language patterns, 121–126
  diversity, 109–110
  ethnic identity, 113–118
  labels, 112–113
  leadership, 126–132
  measuring, 113
  motivational differences, 118–121
  norms, 108–109
  nuanced behaviors, 108
  orientation, 120–121
  relevant pedagogy, 109–110
  responsive education, 109–110
  sensitivity and awareness, 110
  specific practices, 108

D

Decision-making process, 181
Delay of gratification (DOG), 276
Deliberate play, 327
Deliberate practice, 326–327
Depletion model of self-regulation, 282
Developmental change, 82
Developmental Model of Sport Participation (DMSP), 326–327
Developmental trajectory of motivation, 79.
  See also Motivation
  academic and competency motives, 86
  andragogy, 89
  control beliefs, 88–89
  evidence, 86*f*
  evolution of academic beliefs, 86
  formal learning, 86–87
  performance variability, 88
  progression, 87
  self-awareness, 87–88
  self-efficacy beliefs, 89
  trajectory of motivation, 90
biological change, 81
  cognitive and psychosocial development, 81
  cognitive processing, 82–83
  cognitively oriented dimensions, 81–82
  critical periods, 83
  developmental change and structure of development, 82
  individuals, 82
  motivational leaders, 84*b*–86*b*
  point of developmental stagnation, 83
evolution of values and morality, 93
  cognitive interpretations, 94
  MD, 94
  moral exemplars, 95
  moral motivation on behavior, 95
  morally determined decisions, 94
  theory of mind, 94–95
excellence judgments, 90
  downward social comparisons, 92–93
  interpersonal comparisons, 91–92
  motivated behavior examples, 90
  negative self-evaluations, 91
  physical competencies, 92
  social comparison motives, 92
  social comparison view, 90–91
gender congruity evaluations, 95–96
  agency or communal motives, 97
  gender perceptions, 96
  gender stereotypes, 98
  gender-related competence differences, 97–98
  gendered beliefs, 96
  psychological or physiological consequences, 97
  self-assessments, 99
  socialization patterns, 98
  stereotypical gendered beliefs, 98–99
MD, 79–80
motivational inequality, 80–81
nature–nurture debate, 80

Disparate motives, 107–108
Display of power, 57
Dispositions, 34
Dixon, Alexis, 53b–54b, 159t, 214–215, 273, 368, 369t
DMSP. *See* Developmental Model of Sport Participation
DOG. *See* Delay of gratification
"Dominance", 58
Dominant culture, 115
Downward social comparisons, 92–93
Dualism, 48

E

Efficiency theory, 39–40
Effort attributions, 184, 187–189
Egoism, 217
Elaboration Likelihood Model (ELM), 349–350
Emotion/emotional, 120, 239–240
　"affect", 239
　anxiety and boredom, 259
　emotion-dependent coping strategies, 254
　episode, 237–238
　intentional action, 239
　negative consequences, 259
　personalized and subjective response, 259
　reactions, 240
　　automatic responses, 244
　　categorical consistency of, 242
　　categorization, 241
　　"core affect", 243
　　"gist" ideas, 244
　　naturally occurring emotions and behavioral implications, 242t
　regulation, 256
　signs and symptoms, 240
Environmental restructuring, 273
Equifinality, 11
Ethnic identity, 114
　academic disengagement, 116–118
　acceptance or rejection, 116
　belief affirmation, 118
　influence of culture, 115
　motivational leader, 117b
　three-stage model, 115–116
Expectancy-value theory, 189–190
　value and usefulness, 190–191
"Experience sampling" method, 39

External leadership, 322–323
Extraversion (E), 32, 33t
Extrinsic motivation, 142
Extrinsically motivated individuals, 141–142

F

Face-to-face classroom instruction (F2F classroom instruction), 329–330
False beliefs, 22
False enlightenment, 22
Flow experience, 39
Flow theory, 38–39
"Folk wisdom", 8–9
Ford Motor Company (FMC), 319
Former method, 284
Free-rider effect, 228
functional magnetic resonance imaging (fMRI), 49
Future time perspective (FTP), 287–288

G

Gender congruity evaluations, 95–96
　agency or communal motives, 97
　gender perceptions, 96
　gender stereotypes, 98
　gender-related competence differences, 97–98
　gendered beliefs, 96
　psychological or physiological consequences, 97
　self-assessments, 99
　socialization patterns, 98
　stereotypical gendered beliefs, 98–99
GLOBE research project, 126
Goal emphasis and strategy choice, 144
　confluence of evidence, 149
　internalization, 146–149
　introjected task orientation, 147
　motivational leader, 148b–149b
　OIT, 145–146
　setting lofty goals, 144–145
Goal orientation, 155. *See also* Incentives, individual reaction to; Interest
　academic, 158t
　　behavioral and motivational examples, 159t
　　achievement-goal approach, 157–161
　　achievement-goal orientation, 157

Goal orientation (*Continued*)
  differences between goals and goal orientations, 155
  individual, 156–157
  optimal, 156
  organizational promotion or prevention, 161–163
  overlapping terminology, 157
  priming studies, 156
  specificity and transience, 156
Grand theories, 179–180

H

Habitual behavior, 13
Happiness, 252–253
"Having NO motivation", 9
Hedonic motivation, 66
Heterogeneity, 49
Heterogeneous behaviors, 49
High performance work practice (HPWP), 316
High self-esteem (HSE), 215
High-synergy team, 321–322
Hines, Cheryl, 84*b*–86*b*, 87–88, 192–193, 195, 368, 369*t*
Hines, Rebecca, 84*b*–86*b*, 195, 368, 369*t*
Holes, Nick, 148*b*–149*b*, 157, 192–193, 368, 369*t*
Homogeneous behaviors, 49
Hormone arginine vasopressin, 63
Human behavior, 180
Humanity, 64
  conundrums, 65
  hedonic motivation, 66
  individuals, 68
  neurological studies, 68
  pleasure and pain, 65–67
  positive and negative evidence, 68
  psychological hedonism, 64–65
  striatum, 67–68
  ultimate and instrumental goals, 65

I

Impression management, 213
Incentives, individual reaction to, 149–150
  adaptive motivation, 153
  benefits of incentives, 150
  contingences, 150–152
  using incentives to promote learning and performance, 154
  intrinsic motivation, 153
  MDs, 152–153
  performance-contingent rewards, 153–154
  psychological conflict, 151
  reward programs, 152
Individualism, 10, 119, 121
Individuals restructure, 253–254. *See also* Emotions
  Alec Torelli, 254
  cognitive strategies, 257
  emotion and motivation, 255
  with emotion-restructuring opportunities, 254
  emotional regulation, 256
  outlining performance expectations, 258
  peak performance, 258
Intentional behaviors, 13
Interest. *See also* Goal orientation
  contextual conditions, 166–167
  disparate conceptualizations, 164
  key points, 165
  multi-media science learning, 167
  on performance motivation, 164
  personal, 164–166
  situational, 164–166
  use of seductive details, 167
Internalization, 146–149
Interpretive errors, 51
Intrinsic motivation, 140–141
Intrinsically motivated individuals, 141
Introjected task orientation, 147

J

Judgments of learning (JOL), 285
Justified true belief, 26–27

K

Knowledge, 35–36
Knowling, Robert E., Jr., 317*b*, 318–319, 323, 368, 369*t*

L

Language, 81. *See also* Communication and language patterns
Leader–challenge match, 323–324
Leadership, 126

choices for leaders, 127–128
external, 322–323
GLOBE research project, 126
individual's motivations, 130
managerial *vs.* leadership traits, 129*t*
organizational culture, 128
PWM, 128–129
reconciliation of internal conflict, 129–130
universal dimensions, 127
variability of leadership behaviors, 128
Learning, 82–84, 86
"Learning communities". *See* Classroom culture
Localization, 63
Locus of control, 141, 154–155
Long-term learning contingencies, 141
Low self-esteem (LSE), 215
Lowery, Nick, 187–189, 188*b*–189*b*, 214–215, 228–229, 276–277, 368, 369*t*

M

Macrosystem, 314
Madoff, Bernard, 24–26, 25*b*, 254, 368, 369*t*
Mastery-approach orientation, 159–160
Mastery-avoid learners, 160
Mastery-oriented learners, 157
Matthew effect, 69–70
MDs. *See* Motivational detectives
Mental models, 321
Mesosystem, 314
Metacognition, 290–291
Metacognition monitoring. *See also* Self-regulation strategies
cognitive and motivational strategies, 290
performance process, 293
regulatory strategies, 292*t*
self-diagnostic tools, 291
Metamotivation, 291
Metamotivational monitoring. *See also* Self-regulation strategies
cognitive and motivational strategies, 290
performance process, 293
regulatory strategies, 292*t*
self-diagnostic tools, 291
Mind-centered orientation, 36
Mini-theories, 179–180
Misconceptions, 22

Moore, LaSonya, 116, 117*b*, 146*t*, 162–163, 208–209, 368, 369*t*
Morality, 94
exemplars, 95
morally determined decisions, 94
motivation, 94
reasoning, 93–95
Motivated behavior, 10, 10*t*, 35, 68–69
adaptive model, 35–36
heritable estimates, 69*t*
incremental and regulatory nature, 36–37
innate predispositions, 70
mind-centered orientation, 36
multiple diagnostic approaches, 71
niche picking, 69–70
paradigms, 37
plasticity, 70–71
SDT, 36
Motivated self-enhancement, 286
Motivation, 8, 239–240, 347–348. *See also* Contentious issues; Emotion; Optimal motivation
conceptions, 140–141
"folk wisdom", 8–9
interpretations, 8
learning and performance, 29
causality and correlation, 30
individual motivation and strategy differences, 30–31
MD, 29–30
measurement of, 375–376
motivational metaphors and subliminal messages, 9
optimization
athletic and public performance, 325
competition, 325–326
DMSP, 326–327
one-size-fits-all strategy solution, 326
optimal mental arousal, 329
perfectionism, 328
responsibility of leaders, 34
changing beliefs, 34–35
dispositions, 34
teaching motivation process, 34
subordinate to character and personality, 31
Big Five, 32
prediction business, 31–32

Motivational beliefs, 22
  acceleration hypothesis, 23–24
  federal investigation, 24
  influence, 22
  knowledge-or-belief dilemma, 24–26
  MD, 23
  misconceptions, 22
  motivational leader, 24, 25b
  self-beliefs, 26
  self-righteous beliefs, 23
Motivational change
  individuals using to refute change
      strategies
    motivational leader, 358b–359b, 359
    partial revision, 357
    personal motivation, 360
    persuasive arguments, 356
    reactions to persuasive information,
        357t
    refutation, 355
  instructional strategies, 362–367
  learning from leaders, 367–368
    epilogue, 369–370
    strategies using by author and
        motivation leaders, 369t
  overcoming change resistance in others,
      360–361
    entrenched beliefs, 361
    mental models, 361
  people resisting change, 346
    conceptual change models, 351
    Elaboration Likelihood Model, 349–350
    epistemic beliefs, 353–354
    individuals defend systems, 355
    organizational blunders, 349
    organizational perspectives, 348
    self-efficacy, 354
    social and emotional factors, 352
    teleological-based views of resistance, 347
    temporal arousal view, 347
  personal relevance creation, 364–365
  plausible alternatives identification, 363
  refutational evidence, 364
  strategy awareness promoting, 362
  strategy change scaffolding, 365–367
Motivational detectives (MDs), 4, 107–108,
    140, 207–208, 269, 345–346
  acceptance or rejection of ethnic identity,
      116

  adjustment, 110–111
  biobehavioral evidence use, 48–49
  cultural diversity, 109–110
  cultural sensitivity and awareness,
      110
  detecting elements, 181–182
  development, 79–80
  enhancing personal awareness, 110
  misconceptions, 23
  success, 305
Motivational differences, 118–119
  collectivism, 119, 121
  cultural orientation, 120–121
  emotion, 120
  individualism, 119, 121
  self-evaluations, 120
Motivational inequality, 6–7
  embodiment, 7
  implications, 7
  organizations, 7
  utility of equity theory, 7–8
Motivational science, foundational doctrines
    of
  analysis techniques, 12
  case studies, 5b, 6b
  diagnostic tools, 12
  equifinality, 11
  explicit and implicit ways, 13
  habitual behavior, 13
  "having NO motivation", 9
  individualism, 10
  intentional behaviors, 13
  motivated behavior, 10, 10t
  motivation, 8–9
  motivational inequality, 6–8
  motives, 11
  observed behaviors, 11
  self-report, 12–13
  source of misinformation for practitioners,
      14
Motivational science questions, 29t
Motivational self-regulation, 272
Motivational strategies
  APAs, 333–334
  deployment of self-directed learning
      strategies, 332
  F2F classes, 331
  learners, 331
  online learning, 329–330

Motivational theory, 197–198. *See also* Past
   performance; Self-efficacy
 avoiding theoretical bias, 198
 contextual factors, 198
Motives, 11
Motives, difficulty in resisting
 "approach and avoid" models, 189
 compendium of evidence, 192
 expectancy-value theory, 189–190
  value and usefulness, 190–191
  stability of assessments, 191
  task valuations, 191–192
  variation, 191
Motives, individual differences in
 extrinsically motivated individuals,
  141–142
 goal emphasis and strategy choice, 144
  confluence of evidence, 149
  internalization, 146–149
  introjected task orientation, 147
  motivational leader, 148b–149b
  OIT, 145–146
  setting lofty goals, 144–145
 goal orientation, 154–155
  academic, 158t
  achievement-goal approach, 157–161
  achievement-goal orientation, 157
  differences between goals and goal
   orientations, 155
  individual, 156–157
  optimal, 156
  organizational promotion or prevention,
   161–163
  overlapping terminology, 157
  priming studies, 156
 individual reaction to incentives, 149–150
  adaptive motivation, 153
  benefits of incentives, 150
  contingences, 150–152
  using incentives to promote learning
   and performance, 154
  intrinsic motivation, 153
  MDs, 152–153
  performance-contingent rewards,
   153–154
  psychological conflict, 151
  reward programs, 152
 interest
  contextual conditions, 166–167
 disparate conceptualizations, 164
 key points, 165
 multi-media science learning, 167
 on performance motivation, 164
 personal, 164–166
 situational, 164–166
 use of seductive details, 167
 intrinsic and extrinsic orientations,
  141–142
 intrinsic motivation, 140–141
 intrinsically motivated individuals, 141
 SDT, 143–144
Multiple diagnostic approaches, 71
Myers-Briggs Type Indicator, 198

N

National Football League (NFL), 180
Negative self-evaluations, 91
Neural networks, 346
Neuroanatomy, 47–48, 56–57
Neurological evidence, 48–49
 interpretations, 49f
 outcomes, 49
 physiological evidence, functional utility
  of, 49
Neurological inferences, 50
 case study, 52–54
 interpretive errors, 51
 motivational leader, 53b–54b
 neurological system, 51–52
 neuropsychology studies, 51t
 psychological construct, 52
 spurious interpretations of data, 50–51
Neurological system, 51–52
Neurological system organization, 56
 divisions of ANS, 56
 lessons in neuroanatomy, 56–57
 primary neurotransmitter, 56
Neuropsychology studies, 51t
Neuroticism (N), 32, 33t
NFL. *See* National Football League
Niche picking, 69–70
"Noise", 71
Normative-approach orientation, 160
Normative-oriented learners, 157–159

O

Observed behaviors, 11
OIT. *See* Organismic Integration Theory

Online learning, 329–330
  motivational strategies, 329–336
Openness (O), 32, 33t
Optimal experience, 38–39
Optimal motivation, 36–37
  beliefs, 40–41
  deviation method, 40
  efficiency theory, 39–40
  "experience sampling" method, 39
  flow experience, 39
  optimal experience, 38–39
  optimal performance, 37–38
  phenomenon of peak performance, 38
Organismic Integration Theory (OIT), 35, 145
Organizational change, 348–349
Organizational motivation, 314
Organizational promotion or prevention, 161–163. *See also* Achievement-goal approach
  emotional consequences and performance implications, 163
  prevention-and promotion-oriented individuals, 162–163
  regulatory focus, 162–163
Oxytocin (OT), 56
  production, 61
  transmission, 60–61

P

Pain, 65–67
Parasympathetic nervous system, 56–57, 59–62
Partial revision, 357
Past performance, 182. *See also* Motivational theory; Self-efficacy
  assessments, 183
    of stability, 184
  attributional musings, 183
  attributions, 183–184
    behavioral implications, 185
    causal, 186t
    and emotions, 185
    motivational leader, 187–189, 188b–189b
    social nature, 187
  controllability, 184–185
  "self-serving" bias, 185–187
PBS. *See* Positive Behavior Support

Peak performance, 38, 258, 325. *See also* Athletic performance, motivation optimization for
Pedagogical persuasion, 367
Perfectionism, 328
Perfectionist
  evaluation, 328
  striving, 328
Performance. *See also* Work performance
  improvement, 307
  inhibiting strategies augmenting self-worth, 225–226
    deliberate handicapping, 226
    liabilities of academic self-handicapping, 227t
    SHS, 225–227
    social loafing, 228
  performance-restricting culprits, 245–250
  psychology, 325
  variability, 88
Performance-avoid learners, 160
"Peripheral change", 356–357
Peripheral nervous system (PNS), 56
Personal belief, 26–27
Personal interest, 164–166
Personal relevance creation, 364–365
Personality, 31–32
Physiological evidence, functional utility of, 49
Plasticity, 70–71, 80
Plausibility, 363
  plausible alternatives identification, 363
Pleasure, 65–67
PNS. *See* Peripheral nervous system
Positive affect, 250
  "broaden and build" theories, 250–252
  evidence from neuropsychology, 253
  happiness, 252–253
  motivational leader, 251b
  positive psychology domains, 252
Positive Behavior Support (PBS), 117
Potency, 241–242
Prevention orientation, 161–163
Primary neurotransmitter, 56
Priming, 156
Principle of reciprocity, 217–218
Problem-solving volitional strategies, 254
"Program of month" syndrome, 307
Promotion orientation, 161–163

Proposition. *See* Personal belief
Prosocial behaviors, 216
   benefits, 216–217
   goal attainment process, 217
   human consciousness, 217–218
   practical aspects, 220
   self-focus, 219
   social hierarchies, 218–219
Prosocial motives, 220
   altruistic behavior, 224
   altruistic motives, 223
   cost–benefit analysis, 224
   motivational leader, 221*b*–222*b*
   self-protection strategies, 225
Prototype Willingness Model (PWM), 128–129
Psychological construct, 52
Psychological empowerment, 323–324
Psychological hedonism, 64–65
Psychosocial development, 81

Q
Qualia, 54–55

R
Reality television, 92–93
Reciprocal determination, 180
Reciprocity, 217–218
Refutation, 355
Refutational evidence, 364
Relatedness, 36
Research methods, 28
Resistance
   to organizational change, 349
   teleological-based views, 347
Response to Intervention (RTI), 117

S
Scripted behaviors, 108
SDT. *See* Self-determination theory
SDWTs. *See* Self-directed work teams
SEC. *See* US Securities and Exchange Commission
Self-awareness, 14, 87–88, 208–210
Self-belief influence on motivated behavior, 208
   downward comparisons, 210
   performance inhibiting strategies
      augmenting self-worth, 225–226
      deliberate handicapping, 226
      liabilities of academic self-handicapping, 227*t*
      SHS, 225–227
      social loafing, 228
   prosocial behaviors, 216
      benefits of, 216–217
      goal attainment process, 217
      human consciousness, 217–218
      practical aspects of, 220
      self-focus, 219
      social hierarchies, 218–219
   prosocial motives, 220
      altruistic behavior, 224
      altruistic motives, 223
      cost–benefit analysis, 224
      motivational leader, 221*b*–222*b*
      self-protection strategies, 225
   psychological or physical presence of others, 212
      HSE individual, 216
      HSE–LSE distinction, 215
      impression management, 213
      self-evaluations, 214–215
      sociocultural norms on exhibited behavior, 214*t*
      TPB, 213
   psychological vulnerability, 209
   self-definition, 211–212
   self-portrayal, 208–209
   upward comparisons, 210
Self-consequating strategies, 272–273
Self-control, 283
Self-determination theory (SDT), 36, 118–119, 143–144
   spectrum of internalized motivation, 146*t*
Self-directed work teams (SDWTs), 321
Self-efficacy, 192–193. *See also* Motivational theory; Past performance
   beliefs, 89, 193, 196
   collective efficacy, 194
   conceptions of performance, 193
   elevated levels, 194–195
   interdependency, 197
   physiological and emotional predispositions, 196
   plausible assessments of prospective ability, 196–197
   power, 193–194
   self-reported beliefs, 196
   verbal encouragement, 195

Self-evaluations, 120
Self-focus, 219
Self-handicapping strategies (SHS), 225–226
Self-regulation, 269–270. *See also* Adaptive motivation
  Boxtel, Amanda, 271–272
  metacognition, 295
  motivational regulation strategies, 295
  motivational self-regulation, 272
  performance objectives, 294–295
  personalized, transitory, and marginally predictable, 274
    cognitive and emotional factors, 280
    DOG, 276
    epistemology beliefs, 278
    goal orientation, 279–280
    motivational regulation, 275
    self-schemas, 277–278
  restructuring, 273–274
  self-consequating strategies, 272–273
  self-induced positive motivational momentum, 273
  self-regulatory ability, 281
    CATs, 286–287
    COPES model, 284
    depletion model of self-regulation, 282
    FTP, 287–288
    glucose allocation, 282
    JOLs, 285
    "motivated self-enhancement", 286
    motivational leader, 288b–289b, 290
    multi-disciplinary DOG research, 287
    self-control, 283
    strength model of regulation, 281–282
    task calibration, 285
Self-report, 12–13
Self-righteous beliefs, 23
Self-schemas, 277–278
"Self-serving" bias, 185–187
Self-talk, 272–273
Self-views, 215
Sensory stimuli, 55
SHS. *See* Self-handicapping strategies
Situational approach, 323
Situational interest, 164–166
SNS. *See* Sympathetic nervous system
Social comparison
  motives, 92
  view, 90–91
Social loafing, 228, 320–321
Social media, 125
Social psychology, 349–350
Soto, Darren, 288b–289b, 290, 368, 369t
Spillover effect, 217–218
Sport psychology. *See* Performance—psychology
Spurious interpretations of data, 30, 50–51
State anxiety, 245–246
Stereotyping, 115
Strategy awareness promoting, 362
Strategy change scaffolding, 365
  cognitive strategies, 367
  using inquiry methods, 366–367
  "pedagogical persuasion", 367
  persuasive argument, 366
Strength model of regulation, 281–282
Striatum, 67–68
Style approach, 323
Subjective well-being (SWB), 252
Suggestibility, 55–56
Sympathetic nervous system (SNS), 56, 59, 243
  biological markers, 58
"Systems Justification Theory", 354–355

T

Task feedback, 38–39
Temporal transformation, 107
Testosterone, 58
Theories of planned behavior (TPB), 213
Theory of Knowledge Acquisition, 35
Theory of mind, 94–95
Three-stage model, 115–116
Torelli, Alec, 143–144, 151–152, 159t, 192–193, 251b, 254, 368, 369t
Traits, 32
  anxiety, 245–246
Transformational approach, 324
Transformers, 345

U

University of Central Florida (UCF), 84–85
Unjustified belief, 26–27
US Securities and Exchange Commission (SEC), 25

W

Work performance. *See also* Performance
   academic motivation, 313
   Bronfenbrenner Ecosystem Model
       organizational application, 315*f*
   contingency approach, 323–324
   external leadership, 322–323
   high-synergy team, 321–322
   HPWPs, 316
   individual motivation, 320–321
   Knowling interview, 319
   mental models, 321
   motivational leader, 317*b*, 318
   organizational
      culture, 323
      development, 314
      motivation, 314
   primary emphasis for MD, 313
   strategies to motivating, 312
   transformational approach, 324
   transformative leaders, 324–325
Working memory capacity, 27
Worldviews, 90

9780128007792